Cross-Platform Development in C++

Building Mac OS X, Linux, and Windows Applications

Syd Logan

♦♦ Addison-Wesley

Upper Saddle River, NJ • Boston • Indianapolis • San Francisco
New York • Toronto • Montreal • London • Munich • Paris • Madrid
Cape Town • Sydney • Tokyo • Singapore • Mexico City

Many of the designations used by manufacturers and sellers to distinguish their products are claimed as trademarks. Where those designations appear in this book, and the publisher was aware of a trademark claim, the designations have been printed with initial capital letters or in all capitals.

The author and publisher have taken care in the preparation of this book, but make no expressed or implied warranty of any kind and assume no responsibility for errors or omissions. No liability is assumed for incidental or consequential damages in connection with or arising out of the use of the information or programs contained herein.

The publisher offers excellent discounts on this book when ordered in quantity for bulk purchases or special sales, which may include electronic versions and/or custom covers and content particular to your business, training goals, marketing focus, and branding interests. For more information, please contact:

U.S. Corporate and Government Sales
(800) 382-3419
corpsales@pearsontechgroup.com

For sales outside the United States please contact:

International Sales
international@pearsoned.com

 This Book Is Safari Enabled

The Safari® Enabled icon on the cover of your favorite technology book means the book is available through Safari Bookshelf. When you buy this book, you get free access to the online edition for 45 days.

Safari Bookshelf is an electronic reference library that lets you easily search thousands of technical books, find code samples, download chapters, and access technical information whenever and wherever you need it.

To gain 45-day Safari Enabled access to this book:

- Go to http://www.awprofessional.com/safarienabled
- Complete the brief registration form
- Enter the coupon code H1L7-ZRUN-SXI9-R1NT-HQBH

If you have difficulty registering on Safari Bookshelf or accessing the online edition, please e-mail customer-service@safaribooksonline.com.

Visit us on the Web: www.informit.com/title/9780321246424 and www.crossplatformbook.com

Library of Congress Cataloging-in-Publication Data:

Logan, Syd.
  Cross-platform development in C++ : building Mac OS X, Linux, and Windows applications / Syd Logan.
     p. cm.
  ISBN 0-321-24642-X (pbk. : alk. paper) 1. Cross-platform software development.
2. C++ (Computer program language) I. Title.
  QA76.76.D47L65 2007
  005.13'3--dc22

                                                                    2007036292

ISBN-13: 978-0-321-24642-4
ISBN-10: 0-321-24642-X
Text printed in the United States on recycled paper at RR Donnelly in Crawfordsville, Indiana.
First printing December 2007

Editor-in-Chief
Mark Taub

Acquisitions Editor
Greg Doench

Development Editor
Michael Thurston

Managing Editor
Gina Kanouse

Project Editor
Anne Goebel

Copy Editor
Keith Cline

Indexer
Erika Millen

Proofreader
Kathy Ruiz

Technical Reviewers
Jim Dunn
Amy Fong
Hang Lau
Stephen Morse
Lew Pitcher
Sean Su
Namachivayam
  Thirumazshusai
Doug Turner
Roy Yokohama

Publishing Coordinator
Andrea Bledsoe

Cover Designer
Gary Adair

Composition
Nonie Ratcliff

This book is dedicated to all of the members of Netscape CPD and Mozilla, from whom I have learned so much. It was truly an honor to be a part of the team.

Contents

Foreword . . . . **xiii**

Preface . . . . **xv**

Acknowledgments . . . . **xxiii**

About the Author . . . . **xxv**

Introduction **1**
Areas That Can Affect Software Portability 3
The Role of Abstraction 10

1   Policy and Management **17**
Item 1: Make All of Your Platforms a Priority 17
Item 2: Code from a Common Codebase 22
   Platform Factory Implementations *29*
   Implementation Classes *31*
   Platform-Specific ProcessesImpl Classes *32*
   Creating the Instance Hierarchy *42*
   Organizing the Project in CVS or SVN *45*
   Makefiles and Building the Code *49*
Item 3: Require Developers to Compile Their Code
   with Different Compilers 52
Item 4: Require Developers to Build Their Code on
   Multiple Platforms 56
Item 5: Test Builds on Each Supported Platform 60
Item 6: Pay Attention to Compiler Warnings 61
   GNU Flags *62*
   Microsoft Visual C++ *63*

2   Build System/Toolchain **65**

Item 7: Use Whatever Compiler Makes the Most Sense
   for a Platform 66
Item 8: Use Native IDEs When Appropriate 67
Item 9: Install and Use Cygwin on Windows 71
Item 10: Use a Cross-Platform Make System 76
   Make 77
   Building on Windows 81
   Autoconf/Automake 87
   Imake 91
   Installing on Mac OS X 91
   Installing on Windows 91
   Using Imake, an Example 93
   Imakefiles 94
   Building a Complete Program from Multiple Sources .. 95
   Overriding Defaults with site.def 99
   Eliminating #ifdefs in Code 101
   Files Used by Imake 107
   Building Projects with Subdirectories 108
   Building Debug 130

3   Software Configuration Management **131**

Item 11: Use a Cross-Platform Bug Reporting and
   Tracking System 132
   Accessibility 133
   Ability to Track Platform-Specific Bugs 133
   Bugzilla 133
Item 12: Set Up a Tinderbox 140
Item 13: Use CVS or Subversion to Manage Source Code 147
   Setting Up and Using CVS 152
Item 14: Use Patch 157
   An Example 158
   Patch Options 161
   Dealing with Rejects 162
   Patch and Cross-Platform Development 163

4 Installation and Deployment **165**

  Item 15: Provide Support for Native Installers 165
    XPInstall *166*
    Platform Installs *170*

5 Operating System Interfaces and Libraries **221**

  Item 16: Use Standards-Based APIs (For Example, POSIX) 222
    POSIX *222*
    Support for POSIX, SVID, XPG, and BSD *226*
    Using Standards Support in GCC *227*
    Microsoft Runtime Library Support for POSIX *231*
    Using GCC on Microsoft Windows *234*
    Deciding Which Standards to Support *240*
  Item 17: Consider Using a Platform Abstraction Library
    Such as NSPR 242
    Why NSPR? *242*
    NSPR Basics *245*
    Threads *249*
    Additional NSPR Functionality *260*

6 Miscellaneous Portability Topics **273**

  Item 18: Take Care When Using Floating Point 274
    Don't Serialize Floating-Point Values as Binary *276*
    Equality *277*
  Item 19: Be Explicit Regarding the Sign of Char Types 278
  Item 20: Avoid the Serialization of Binary Data 280
  Item 21: Avoid Problems Related to the Size and
    Organization of Types 293
    Size of Integer Types *293*
    NSPR and Types *296*
    Sizes and Efficiency *297*
    Integer Conversions *298*
    Struct Alignment and Ordering *299*

7 User Interfaces **303**

  Item 22: Separate the User Interface from the Model 304
    *Separating the User Interface and Application Logic
      with Model/View* *305*

Using Publish/Subscribe to Communicate between
   the View and the Model *318*
Summary *322*
Item 23: Develop a Cross-Platform User Interface Strategy 323
Issues Affecting Portable Cross-Platform GUI
   Development *323*
Choosing a GUI Strategy *325*

8   wxWidgets **329**

wxWidgets 331
Licensing *332*
Installing wxWidgets *332*
A Simple Example: Hello wxWidgets *335*
Creating the Application User Interface *337*
Building wxWidgets Applications *345*
Controls and Events *349*
Container Widgets *363*
Dialogs *392*
Composite Widgets *404*
Internationalization and Localization *410*

9   Developing a Cross-Platform GUI Toolkit in C++ **427**

What is XUL? 428
DHTML 429
HTML *429*
Scripting Language *433*
The Document Object Model *434*
Style Systems *437*
XUL 438
Windows and Dialogs *439*
Boxes *439*
Toolbars *440*
Menus *441*
Controls *441*
Other Widgets *442*
Programming with XUL *442*
Adding Logic to the UI with JavaScript *443*

*Interfacing JavaScript and C/C++ Code with XPCOM
and XPConnect* *444*
Trixul *446*
  Widget Support in Trixul *447*
  Basic Operation of Trixul *448*
  Widgets *449*
  Implementation Classes *452*
  Creating Widget Implementation Objects *459*
  Widget Factories *463*
  Application Main Loop *466*
  Steps Taken by Trixul to Create a User Interface *471*
  Documents, Elements, and the DOM *472*
  Widget Creation *475*
  Layout *477*
  Scrolled Windows and Layout *484*
  Integration with JavaScript *485*
  Integrating with C++ Components *496*

Index **519**

Foreword

As the Hypertext Markup Language / Extensible Markup Language / Cascading Style Sheets (HTML/XML/CSS) parsing and rendering engine for the Firefox, Mozilla, and Netscape browsers, Gecko is one of the most widely deployed cross-platform rendering engines in the world.

As both a Netscape engineer and later as the development manager of the Mozilla Gecko team, I had the privilege to work on the Gecko engine from its inception.

Gecko was born out of the desire to create a cross-platform, small-footprint, fast, state-of-the-art, embeddable Web browsing engine that would leapfrog our competition in the "browser wars." It had become painfully apparent that it was too difficult to add full CSS2, CSS3, and XML Web standards support to the lumbering Netscape 4.x engine. The idea was to start from scratch using only a few libraries from the original engine. Early in the Gecko project, there were discussions about using Java rather than C++ to leverage Java's cross-platform capabilities. It was ultimately decided that C++, along with special development processes, tools, and design techniques, would yield the best solution. Many of those processes, tools, and design techniques are described as best practices throughout this book.

Before coming to Netscape, I worked at several companies that produce cross-platform software. However, the Mozilla project took it to a whole other level. We utilized and developed software architectures, tools, and processes that enabled cross-platform development on a wide scale.

My first task was to port Gecko from Microsoft Windows to Motif/Xlib. As anyone who has written cross-platform software knows, the early ports are the most challenging. That's where you discover just how portable your software really is. Even though Gecko was designed from the beginning to be portable, small differences between platforms and compilers came back to bite us. This is why it's so important to have a continuous build system such as the Mozilla Tinderbox that verifies every source code check-in for portability and a software development process that requires engineers to verify their new code on at least two platforms before they check into the source code repository.

As the Gecko engine development gained momentum, the decision was made to re-create the Netscape Communicator user interface experience on top of it. This would require a cross-platform user interface solution because Netscape Communicator worked on multiple platforms with diverse graphical user interface environments. I was given the opportunity to develop a strategy to solve the thorny cross-platform user interface problem. I authored a document that described how to achieve a cross-platform user interface by combining an XML meta description of the user interface elements and JavaScript as control/event logic within the Gecko rendering engine. This document was the seed document for what later became the XUL (XML User Interface Language) language. Later, the Firefox developers took advantage of XUL and the Gecko engine to build a small, fast, cross-platform, Web browser that has become wildly popular. Chapter 9 describes how you can also build on top of XUL to create your own cross-platform user interfaces.

As an original member of the W3C SVG (Scalable Vector Graphics) working group, I am particularly excited to see that Gecko continues to evolve and solve additional cross-platform challenges. The recent addition of SVG native support marks yet another chapter in Gecko's portability success.

The information Syd Logan is presenting here is the collective insight of the myriad engineers who ironed out the special problems associated with creating cross-platform production software. Although it is written with C++ in mind, many of the techniques can be adapted to non-C++ software projects, too. I hope you will be able to use some of the tools, techniques, and processes described in these pages to avoid some of the pitfalls of cross-platform development and make your project a huge success.

—*Kevin McCluskey*

Preface

During the ten or so years of my career prior to joining Netscape in 1998, I had the good fortune to work on a wide variety of projects, on an equally diverse set of platforms. I worked on an embedded kernel of my own design for a somewhat obscure CPU (the TMS34020). I obtained experience in Windows kernel development, writing file systems drivers for the Windows NT and Windows 98 kernels, to support the development of a Network File System (NFS) client. In user space, I mostly specialized in user interface development, initially developing Motif (Z-Mail) and OpenWindows applications for UNIX, eventually getting exposure to Win32 and the Microsoft Foundation Classes (MFC) toolkit on the Windows platform. I even had the chance to write code for the Classic Mac OS to support a project that would be shipped by Apple, using the Mac Toolbox application programming interface (API). All of this code was written in the C language, and all of it was highly nonportable, written only with a concern for the job, and platform, at hand.

But then I joined Netscape, as a UNIX expert of sorts. Initially, I was assigned the task of working on bugs in the 4.x Netscape browser, specifically handling defects filed against a port of the browser to IBM's Advanced Interactive eXecutive (AIX) platform. Netscape had a contract with IBM to ensure that bugs filed against the AIX version of the Netscape browser, or bugs that IBM considered important, were fixed in a timely fashion, and this contract funded my hiring. Similar deals were cut with SGI, Hewlett-Packard, and Sun, and perhaps others, and these deals funded additional Netscape staff. Two or three of us were assigned to deal with AIX, specifically.

During this time, portability had not yet been perfected at Netscape. Although much of the codebase of Netscape was portable, the project did not have a unified build system, and the user interface code was completely platform specific. Many bugs had a decidedly platform-specific nature to them (hence the need to have separate teams to support individual platforms). Code that worked flawlessly on the Windows version of Netscape ran horribly on less well-supported platforms. Not all platforms had the same set of features, and features varied from platform to platform.

Within a year of joining Netscape and fixing AIX bugs, I somehow earned my way onto the Netscape Instant Messenger team, and worked on the new codebase based on the open source Mozilla platform. This team, which consisted of three engineers, was tasked with porting the AOL Instant Messenger client to the Netscape browser. The Netscape IM team was hastily formed right after AOL acquired Netscape, to try to bring AOL-based functionality into the application. (The other major AOL property integrated into Netscape was support for AOL Mail.)

The new Netscape client, in development at that time, was, as mentioned previously, based on the open source codebase named Mozilla. This codebase, at the time, was largely the product of Netscape engineers located in offices located in San Diego, and Mountain View, but contributions from the open source community were on the rise. (I refer to the project as Netscape/Mozilla in the remainder of this Preface.)

Netscape was in fierce competition with Microsoft for the browser market at this time, which meant the browser of course had to work well, and ship on time on the Windows platform. Netscape also generated significant advertising revenue through the Netscape portal, and clicks there were highest when a new version of the browser was released, and tens of millions of users visited the portal to download a fresh copy of Netscape. Supporting Netscape not only on Windows but also on Mac OS and Linux helped keep the number of visits high and generate revenue. So, Linux and Mac OS were treated as equals with Windows within the Netscape culture, not only because it was the morally right thing to do (as many of us believed), but also because every visit to the Netscape portal was important to the bottom line of the company.

Netscape/Mozilla was a complete departure from anything that I had ever seen or worked on before. First of all, this new version of Netscape was not just a browser, it was a platform, capable of hosting applications. (The primary examples shipped with Netscape were AIM, the Mail/News client, a WYSIWYG HTML editor named Composer, the Chatzilla IRC client, and the browser itself. Extensions, such as those available for Firefox today, are closely related.) Instead of building the graphical user interface (GUI) for these applications in C or C++, using APIs provided by a native platform

GUI toolkit such as MFC or Gtk+, Netscape/Mozilla-developed technologies were used instead. Static Extensible Markup Language (XML) files were used to describe the layout of the user interface, much like HTML is used to describe the layout of a Web page. The XML dialect developed for this purpose was called XML User Interface Language (XUL). JavaScript code, linked to the XML elements via attributes much like JavaScript is linked to HTML elements in a Web page, was used to respond to menu item selections and button clicks. To build an application for Netscape/Mozilla, all one needed was this combination of XML and JavaScript; and because both JavaScript and XML are intrinsically portable, so were the user interfaces that were designed using these technologies. When JavaScript wasn't enough to do the job (as was the case for any real applications, like those shipped with Netscape and Mozilla), JavaScript code could call C++ functions that provided the guts of the application, housed in shared libraries. These shared libraries, or components, were directly supported in the Netscape/Mozilla architecture via two technologies: XPConnect and XPCOM. These technologies allowed component developers to define platform-agnostic interfaces using an Interface Description Language (IDL). Using XPCOM and XPConnect, JavaScript code could query for the existence of a component, and from there, query for a specific interface. If all was good, the JavaScript code was handed an object that it could call just like any other object, except the object was written in C++, and was capable of doing things that JavaScript programmers could only dream of. The interfaces, by their nature, were highly platform agnostic.

The impact of the work done to support portability in the Netscape/Mozilla architecture was not, quite frankly, immediately apparent to me. But, over time, I came to appreciate the power of such an approach. The positive effects of the decisions of those who came up with the architecture are indisputable; during its heyday, Netscape was shipping tens of millions of browsers to users, not just for Windows, Mac, and Linux, but for SunOS, AIX, HP-UX, SGI Irix, and a host of other UNIX-based platforms. The "tier-1" platforms (Mac OS, Linux, and Windows) literally shipped at the same time. Each of these ports had, for the most part, the same feature set, and mostly shared the same set of bugs and quirks. To achieve portability at such a grand scale required a very special architecture, and it is one of the goals of this book to give you a good understanding (if not an appreciation) for how the Netscape/Mozilla architecture directly impacted the portability of the codebase.

However, it was not just the architecture of Netscape/Mozilla that made the browser and related applications (AIM, Mail, Composer) portable. To pull this sort of thing off, one needs not only a solid architecture, but also a culture of policies and procedures that put cross-platform development high on their lists of priorities—as well as large doses of discipline to ensure these best practices were followed. Tools, such as Tinderbox and Bugzilla, both of which are described in this book, were invested in heavily by Netscape and Mozilla, and the investment paid off in spades. Engineers were forced to consider other platforms, not just their own, and a regression found during daily testing on just one platform could halt development on all platforms, not just the one affected, because Netscape and Mozilla realized that the only true way to achieve portability was to deal with the issues in the here and now. A good chunk of this book steps away from the code, and describes these best practices, because no matter how good your architecture is in supporting cross-platform, you have to work all the platforms you plan to support with the level of care and devotion to detail if they are going to make it to the finish line with the same levels of quality.

Similar to the way that the programs we write are made up of data structures and algorithms, portability, in my opinion, consists largely of architecture and process, and this conviction is at the foundation of the book that you now hold in your hands.

How This Book Is Organized

This book is organized as a series of themed chapters. Most of these chapters consist of a set of items, with each item covering a specific topic supporting the chapter's overall theme. Early in the book, you will find sections that contain items presenting best practices that must be communicated to the entire development organization, including management, development, and testing. Later chapters cover software-engineering topics that management should be aware of, but these chapters have been written primarily for readers who will be implementing the code. In all, there are 23 items presented in these initial chapters.

The implementation of a user interface is a major concern in the development of cross-platform desktop applications. Item 23 serves to introduce the topic. The final two chapters of the book are therefore devoted to cross-platform GUI-related topics. The first of these chapters provides a comprehensive introduction and tutorial to the wxWidgets cross-platform GUI toolkit. After reading my introduction to wxWidgets, you may want to check out Prentice Hall's detailed treatment on the subject, *Cross-Platform GUI Programming with wxWidgets,* by Julian Smart, et al. wxWidgets is not the only cross-platform GUI toolkit available for use in your projects. Another capable, and very popular cross-platform GUI toolkit, Qt, is not covered in this book. However, if you are interested in Qt, a few books are currently available that cover the subject in great detail, perhaps most notably *C++ GUI Programming with Qt 4,* by Jasmin Blanchette and Mark Summerfield, also published by Prentice Hall (see also their Qt 3-specific book).

The last chapter of this book, Chapter 9, "Developing a Cross-Platform GUI Toolkit in C++," starts with an introduction to the cross-platform GUI toolkit, XPToolkit, which is a major component of Netscape and Mozilla's cross-platform browser suite. It then goes on to detail the implementation of a toolkit I created especially for this book, Trixul. Trixul has many of the same attributes that made up the Netscape/Mozilla XPToolkit we used at Netscape to construct cross-platform GUIs. Both XPToolkit and Trixul, for example, allow you to describe the user interface of an application in XML and JavaScript, both support a component-based model that allows the user interface to call into shared libraries written in C or C++, and both are highly portable. However, there are two major differences between Trixul and the Mozilla offering. First, Trixul is a desktop GUI toolkit, whereas XPToolkit applications execute within the context of a Web browser only. Second, the overall design of Trixul is (I think) much simpler than XPToolkit, which (I am certain) allowed me to do a much better job of describing both the architecture of the toolkit, and the concepts behind its design, than I otherwise would have been able to do. Although I don't really expect that you will want to design a custom cross-platform GUI toolkit for your project, there is much to be learned from taking a look at how Trixul was designed and implemented.

The chapters, for the most part, have been written such that they can be read in any order. If you are in technical management, I recommend that you read the following chapters carefully:

- Chapter 1, "Policy and Management"
- Chapter 2, "Build System/Toolchain"
- Chapter 3, "Software Configuration Management"

Technical managers who are so inclined should consider at least scanning through the following sections:

- Chapter 4, "Installation and Deployment"
- Chapter 5, "Operating System Interfaces and Libraries"
- Chapter 6, "Miscellaneous Portability Topics"
- Chapter 7, "User Interface"

Developers should plan to read the entire book, although you might want to invert the recommendations made here for technical managers, and skim what they are supposed to read carefully, and read carefully what they are supposed to skim. If your focus is user interface development, I recommend reading Items 22 and 23, and Chapter 8, "wxWidgets." If you are interested in GUI toolkit internals, or plan to help out with the development of Trixul (described in the following section), you will definitely want to read Chapter 9, "Developing a Cross-Platform GUI Toolkit in C++."

A Word about Trixul

Trixul is an open source project that I put together specifically to aid me in the writing of this book. In part, I had the same intentions of the original authors of the Gtk+, to learn by doing. However, the more relevant goal behind Trixul was to develop a simple, cross-platform toolkit, the architecture and design of which could be easily described in fewer than 100 pages, and understood by mere mortals without the need to read huge globs of code. The design is heavily inspired by Netscape/Mozilla (the Document Object Model [DOM], the Gecko layout engine, XUL, XPConnect, and XPCOM are all Netscape/Mozilla technologies that have analogs in Trixul); and although the details differ, I am certain that much of what you learn about Trixul's architecture will help you to understand Netscape/Mozilla. Not everyone will want, or need, to write his own GUI toolkit, but Netscape did, and so did America Online (a not-so-portable effort named Boxely was developed in the years following Netscape's demise), and perhaps it makes sense for your company, too. The story of Mozilla/Netscape's portability is not at all complete without a discussion of the way in which the user interface problem was solved, and Trixul is, in my opinion, the best way to get the idea across in a reasonable number of pages.

However, Trixul isn't just for learning. It is my sincere hope that Trixul will take on a life of its own as a viable, next-generation desktop GUI toolkit. The project, at the time of writing this book, is in its infancy. If you like what you read about Trixul and are interested in contributing to its development, or work on a port, I certainly want to hear from you. You can learn more by visiting www.trixul.com or the project page at http://sourceforge.net/projects/trixul.

References

The following is a short list of books that are either mentioned directly in the text, or have influenced in some way the content of this book:

Andrei Alexandrescu, *Modern C++ Design: Generic Programming and Design Patterns Applied* (Reading, MA: Addison-Wesley, 2001).

Jasmine Blanchette and Mark Summerfield, *C++ GUI Programming with Qt 3* (Upper Saddle River, NJ: Prentice Hall, 2004).

Randal E. Bryant and David O'Hallaron, *Computer Systems A Programmer's Perspective* (Upper Saddle River, NJ: Prentice Hall, 2003).

David R. Butenhof, *Programming with POSIX Threads* (Upper Saddle River, NJ: Prentice Hall, 1997).

Paul Dubois, *Software Portability with imake* (Sebastopol, CA: O'Reilly Media, Inc., 1996).

Erich Gamma, et al., *Design Patterns* (Reading, MA: Addison-Wesley, 1995).

Simson Garfinkel and Michael K. Mahoney, *Building Cocoa Applications: A Step-by-Step Guide* (Sebastopol, CA: O'Reilly Media, Inc., 2002).

Ian Griffiths, et al., *.NET Windows Forms in a Nutshell* (Sebastopol, CA: O'Reilly Media, Inc., 2003).

Greg Lehey, *Porting UNIX Software* (Sebastopol, CA: O'Reilly Media, Inc., 1995).

Syd Logan, *Developing Gtk+ Applications in C* (Upper Saddle River, NJ: Prentice Hall, 2001).

Scott Meyers, *Effective C++* (Reading, MA: Addison-Wesley, 2005).

Andrew Oram and Steve Talbot, *Managing Projects with make* (Sebastopol, CA: O'Reilly Media, Inc., 1993).

Eric S. Raymond, *The Art of UNIX Programming* (Reading, MA: Addison-Wesley, 2003).

Julian Smart, et al., *Cross-Platform GUI Programming with wxWidgets* (Upper Saddle River, NJ: Prentice Hall, 2006).

Bjarne Stroustrup, *The C++ Programming Language* (Reading, MA: Addison-Wesley, 2000).

Acknowledgments

Writing a book is, as you might imagine, very much a solitary effort. However, producing a book is, in reality, anything but a solo effort—it takes the talent, the time, and the dedication of a great many people to get a book from concept to completion. In that spirit, I would like to thank the following people for their role in helping me to get this book out the door.

First of all, thanks to Greg Doench of Prentice Hall for believing in me, and for giving me the chance to once again put my thoughts down on paper. Michelle Housley, his assistant, provided much-needed support along the way. I'd also like to thank the team at Pearson Education who helped turn my manuscript into its final form, including Keith Kline who did much of the copyediting, Anne Goebel, and Gina Kanouse. I am particularly grateful to Anne for her willingness to work with me through numerous "minor" changes I requested during the final review process. There is no doubt in my mind that these requests caused her much extra work (not to mention pain upon receiving each new e-mail from me with the "latest corrections"). Regardless, she carefully considered and applied each of my requests, flawlessly, and without complaint. For this, she deserves an extra dose of "thank yous." As is standard practice, all errors not caught by them remain my responsibility alone. (On that note, please visit www.crossplatformbook.com for errata related to this edition of the book.)

Next, I'd like to thank the reviewers of this book, many of whom worked with me at Netscape. Specifically, thanks to Sean Su, formerly of Netscape and now at AOL, who took the time to read an early draft of Item 15 and give me his feedback. Jim Dunn, my first manager at Netscape, helped me get my facts straight regarding the development of the Netscape 4.x browser. Doug Turner, also from Netscape, and now at Mozilla, provided plenty of constructive feedback, leading to the addition of several pages to the manuscript. Roy Yokohama, who was a senior internationalization engineer at Netscape, took the time to provide many useful comments related to my coverage of internationalization and localization in wxWidgets. Others who provided helpful feedback include Netscapers Stephen Morse and Namachivayam Thirumazshusai (Shiva). Thanks also go to Kevin McCluskey, who wrote the book's Foreword, and who taught me so much back when we worked together at Netscape's San Diego office.

Thanks to all of my friends, who helped me to keep a proper perspective on life during the long process of getting this book done; and to Mei, for giving me the time, space, and encouragement needed for me to see this project to its completion during its final stages.

About the Author

Syd Logan is a software developer living and working in Southern California. A graduate of San Diego State University with BS and MS degrees in computer science, Syd was a member of the Netscape Client Product Development (CPD) team where he held both engineering and management positions during the development of Netscape 6 and 7. After Netscape, Syd remained at AOL where he implemented VOIP and peer-to-peer video features as a member of the AOL Instant Messenger team. Syd's previous publications include *Developing Imaging Applications with XIELib* and *Gtk+ Programming in C*, both published by Prentice Hall. His technical interests include machine learning, operating systems design, algorithms, and just about anything that has to do with C, C++, and Unix.

Introduction

The typical definition of portability goes something like this:

Portability is a measure of how easily software can be made to execute successfully on more than one operating system or platform.

This definition, however, is only a starting point. To truly define the term *portability,* one must consider more than the mere fact that the software can be made to execute on another operating system. Consider the following C++ code:

```
#include <iostream>

using namespace std;

int
main( int argc, char *argv[])
{
    cout << "Hello\nWorld";
}
```

Most readers will agree that the preceding code will compile and execute on just about any platform that supports a decent C++ compiler.

However, potential problems lurk, even in code as simple as this. Let's run this program from a shell prompt on a Windows machine (assume the Windows executable that results from building the preceding source has the name foo.exe), and redirect the output to a text file:

```
c:\ > foo > foo.txt
```

We can use wc(1) to see how many characters are in the resulting file:

```
c:\ > wc -c foo.txt
12 foo.txt
```

Now let's do the same thing on Mac OS X:

```
% foo > foo.txt
% wc -c foo.txt
11 foo.txt
```

Notice on Windows that wc reports that the file contains 12 characters, whereas on Mac OS X, it reports that it contains 11 characters. Surprised? Let's use od(1) to figure out what happened. First, let's run od(1) on Windows:

```
C:\> od -c foo.txt
0000   H   e   l   l   o  \r  \n   W   o   r   l   d
0014
```

And, then do the same on Mac OS X:

```
% od -c foo.txt
0000   H   e   l   l   o  \n   W   o   r   l   d
0013
```

What has happened here is that on Windows, the \n in our string was converted to DOS line endings, which are always \r\n. On Mac OS X, the \n was left alone.

In most cases, this difference is of no consequence. After all, running the application on either platform gives the same basic output when viewed in a console. If console output were the only criteria, you would be perfectly correct to consider the code as being portable, and leave it at that. But what if the size of the resulting file did matter, somehow? For example, what if the code snippet is part of a system that uses the content of the file to determine a size, which is then used by some process on another system to allocate a buffer? In one case (Windows computes the size, and Mac OS performs the allocation), we'd end up wasting a byte of data, because we would be writing an 11-byte value into a 12-byte buffer. Computing the size on Mac OS X and writing the result on Windows might, however, result in overflow of the buffer by a byte, which could lead to undefined behavior.

So, even the venerable "Hello World" can be the source of portability issues depending on how that code is actually used. Let's look at some of the major factors that can impact your ability to write portable software.

Areas That Can Affect Software Portability

Language

As the title implies, this book covers C++, but because of their close relationship, the C language is also covered, if only indirectly. The C language has been considered a portable one ever since the late 1970s when it was first described in K&R, and it's well known that one of the major reasons the UNIX operating system has found itself on so many different hardware platforms is because a majority of the operating systems have been written in the C language. Standardization efforts (notably ANSI and the more recent C99) have led C to become an even more portable programming language. Programming against the ANSI standard, and avoiding language extensions introduced by compiler vendors, is an important step toward eliminating portability issues in C. You can increase your odds of writing portable C by instructing your compiler (via its command-line flags or settings) to only accept standards-based language constructs, and to reject any and all language extensions provided by the compiler manufacturer. This advice also holds true for C++.

Compilers

Closely tied to the portability of both the C and C++ languages are, of course, the compilers that are used to turn source code into an executable form. I mentioned previously that the compiler can be used to control standards adherence, but there is more to say about the contribution a compiler makes to overall portability. Several compilers are available for the platforms that we care about in this book, the most popular being, by far, Microsoft Visual C++ 6.0 and Visual C++ 7.0 .NET, which are available for Microsoft Windows; and GNU's GCC, an open source compiler that is available on numerous platforms, including Mac OS X, Linux, and via the Cygwin project, Windows, too.

The C and C++ languages, as they are defined, leave the details regarding the implementation of several language features in the hands of compiler vendors. Subsequently, the use of these features can be inherently nonportable. Things to avoid, or be aware of, include the following:

- **Sizes of the short, int, and long built-in types**
  The size of these types is, by definition, compiler dependent. The C standard says that shorts must be at least 16 bits in size. It also says that ints have to be at least as large as shorts. Finally, it says the longs have to be at least as big as ints. However, this means a 32-bit machine can either implement shorts as 16-bit, ints as 32-bit, and longs as 32-bit, or it can implement shorts and ints as 32-bit, and longs as 64-bit. There are obviously other ways to adhere to the standard. Typically, 32-bit machines will support a 32-bit int, and a 64-bit int would be expected on 64-bit systems, because int is typically defined in terms of the native word size. But, even that is not guaranteed. In this book, I introduce the Netscape Portable Runtime Library (NSPR), which provides a solution to this particular problem.

- **Bitwise operators**
  Errors can be introduced by assuming the sizes of the short, int, and long types being manipulated. These sizes are, once again, determined by the compiler. Right-shifting a value can result in either propagation of the sign bit, or zero filling the leftmost bits, and this is also compiler dependent.

- **Signed versus unsigned char types**
  C and C++ do not specify whether the char data type is signed or unsigned; this is left to the discretion of the compiler writer. This can be a problem when mixing char and int types in code—the classic example is reading characters from stdin in C into a unsigned char using the getchar() function, which returns an int and typically uses −1 to indicate end of file. If you are in a loop comparing −1 to an unsigned char, your loop will never end, regardless of whether getchar() has encountered EOF or not. You can avoid the problem by explicitly declaring the signed attribute of a character variable as follows:

```
signed char foo;   // signed, range -128 to 127;
unsigned char fee; // unsigned, range 0 to 255;
```

Assigning and comparing only like types (assigning only chars to chars, for example), using C++-style casts whenever conversions are necessary, adhering to function prototypes (for instance, don't assign the return value of getchar() to anything other than an int), and fixing each and every warning that your compiler generates—all are ways to overcome portability issues such as this.

Binary Data

In addition to endian issues (the order in which bits and bytes are arranged in memory), binary data can also suffer from how the compiler chooses to lay out structs in memory, which is entirely compiler dependent, and impacted by the architecture being targeted. Structs written as binary (to memory or disk) by code generated by one compiler may be a completely different size, or be organized in memory in a completely different way, by another compiler, even on the same platform. The best way to avoid this problem is to avoid writing or interchanging binary data, and use text instead. This might not always be practical, however, and so I discuss strategies for dealing with binary data in Item 20.

Standard Libraries

The standard libraries (and headers) extend the capabilities provided by the core C and C++ languages. Portability is a central motivation for having a standard library. C standard library headers include the familiar `<stdio.h>`, `<ctype.h>`, and `<string.h>`, among several others. Functions and macros declared in these headers, including `strncmp()`, `getchar()`, `printf()`, `malloc()`, `fopen()`, and countless others, have been used by nearly every C program that has ever been written. Because the standard library provides so much value to the average programmer, and because it is supported by every C implementation, using the functions, constants, and macros provided by these libraries and headers increases the chances that C code that you write will port successfully from one compiler (or platform) to another.

   In the C++ world, there is the STL, the Standard Template Library, which is formally defined as a part of the standard C++ language. The STL preserves what the C standard library provides (but renames the headers by adding the character `c` as a prefix, and dropping the `.h` suffix (for example, `<cstdio>`, `<cctype>`, and `<cstring>`), and extends it with additional functionality that plays rather nicely with the C++ language in several critical ways. The STL provides not only I/O support, but also a well-designed set of container classes that the standard makes promises about in terms of performance. In general, I recommend that you always use the STL in favor of using similar functionality that might be provided elsewhere (including custom code that you have written). It makes no sense to beat your head against the wall trying to come up with an efficient linked list implementation, when someone before you has gone to the effort to supply you with an optimal implementation in the STL. Using the STL is one more way to increase the chances that your code will port. The same holds true for the rest of the standard library; learn it, and use it whenever possible.

Related to the STL is the open source Boost project (www.boost.org), an effort to fill gaps in what the STL provides, with the premise that some of the work that results will eventually find its way into the STL.

Operating System Interfaces

Operating system interfaces (also referred to as system calls) add to what the core language and standard library provide, enabling applications to perform system-dependent tasks. Many of the functions that one finds in the standard library are implemented in terms of the functions provided in this category. Functionality includes such things as process creation, interprocess communication (IPC), low-level input and output, interfacing to device drivers, and network I/O, to name a few. As you might guess, much of the functionality provided in this category is highly system dependent.

A look at the process creation functions on UNIX and Win32 provides an illustration of just how differently system calls can be implemented. To create a process in Win32, you use the **CreateProcess()** function:

```
BOOL CreateProcess(
  LPCTSTR lpApplicationName,
  LPTSTR lpCommandLine,
  LPSECURITY_ATTRIBUTES lpProcessAttributes,
  LPSECURITY_ATTRIBUTES lpThreadAttributes,
  BOOL bInheritHandles,
  DWORD dwCreationFlags,
  LPVOID lpEnvironment,
  LPCTSTR lpCurrentDirectory,
  LPSTARTUPINFO lpStartupInfo,
  LPPROCESS_INFORMATION lpProcessInformation
);
```

For example, to launch the Notepad.exe application, you might write and execute the following code under Windows:

```
#include <windows.h>

STARTUPINFO si;
PROCESS_INFORMATION pi;

ZeroMemory( &si, sizeof(si) );
si.cb = sizeof(si);
```

```
ZeroMemory( &pi, sizeof(pi) );

// Start the child process.
if(!CreateProcess(NULL, "notepad", NULL, NULL,
    FALSE, 0, NULL, NULL, &si,  &pi))
            return E_FAIL;
else
    return S_OK;
```

On UNIX, we would use fork(2) and the exec(3) family of functions to create and execute a process. The prototype for fork(2), which creates a process, is this:

```
#include <sys/types.h>
#include <unistd.h>

pid_t fork(void);
```

The prototype for exec1(3), which instructs a process to load and execute a specified program, is this:

```
#include <unistd.h>

extern char **environ;
int execl(const char *path, const char *arg, ...);
```

The following program illustrates how you would use fork and exec to launch the UNIX date(1) program. In the following, the return value from fork(2) determines which process was created (the child) and which process called fork(2) to begin with (the parent). Here, the child process will execute the date program by calling exec1(3), while the parent process simply exits:

```
#include <sys/types.h>
#include <unistd.h>

int
main(int argc, char *argv[])
{
    pid_t pid;

    pid = fork();
    if (pid == 0) {
```

```
    /* child process */

    execl("/bin/date", "date", NULL);
  }
  return(0);
}
```

It should be obvious from this source code that process creation is anything but portable. However, all is not lost. In Items 16 and 17, I discuss ways in which nonportable native system functionality can be made portable by using standard interfaces and portability libraries such as NSPR. The standard interfaces covered in these items also includes POSIX, the IEEE 1003 standard interface for operating systems, the System V Interface Description (SVID), and finally XPG, The X/Open Portability Guide, which is required of all operating systems that call themselves "UNIX." The GCC compiler family supports all three of these standards on the platforms that this book addresses. If you decide to go with Cygwin and GCC on Microsoft Windows, most of the battle is won. If not, and you choose to use Microsoft or some other vendor to provide your compiler and supporting libraries, other strategies will need to be considered to obtain pure source code compatibility. NSPR (described in Item 17) and Boost can help here. Building your own abstraction layer above the corresponding Win32 interfaces is another way to deal with this problem, and I discuss how abstraction layers can be developed in Item 22.

User Interface

The user interface is perhaps the least portable aspect of modern desktop platforms (at the application level), and we will spend a great deal of time in this book discussing how to overcome this limitation to writing highly portable software.

Each platform provides its own user interface toolkit to support native graphical user interface (GUI) development. On the Windows platform, one finds Win32, Microsoft Foundation Classes (MFC), and the evolving .NET application programming interfaces (APIs) that will eventually replace both. On Mac OS X, one finds the Objective-C based Cocoa framework, and the Carbon API, which was designed to be similar to the legacy Mac OS Toolbox, and to ease the portability of legacy programs from Classic Mac OS 7/8/9 to Mac OS X. And on Linux, you have a wide variety of choices, ranging from Gtk+ (GNOME), Qt (KDE), and in some applications, Xt/Motif (CDE), all of which are based on the X Window System.

None of these toolkits is source code compatible. Nor do any of these toolkits have the same look and feel. Two of the toolkits that were mentioned previously, Qt and Gtk+, are available for Microsoft Windows, but they are not commonly used there, mainly because of the overwhelming dominance that Microsoft-supplied toolkits enjoy on that Windows platform.

A lot can be said for programming to the native GUI toolkits and their APIs. Your application will integrate nicely with the environment when native APIs are used. The users of your application will likely find your user interfaces easy to learn and use, and the ability of your application to interact seamlessly with other applications on the desktop can arguably be expected to be better when you program against a natively supplied toolkit. If portability is not an issue, then using native APIs is usually the way to go. But, because you are reading this book, portability is in all likelihood *the* issue, so we need to find ways to maximize code portability while minimizing the negatives that might be associated with not using native toolkits. We explore ways to solve this problem in Chapters 7, 8, and 9 of this book.

Build System

A build system can vary from a simple script that executes the compiler and linker command line, to a full-blown system based on automake or Imake. The key reason for using a standard and shared build system is so that developers can easily move between machines while in development. For example, if you are a Win32 developer, you can easily move over to OS X and kick off a build with your changes, because the tools you are interfacing with are largely the same. In this book, I describe Imake, focusing on how it supports code portability. Automake and autoconf, popular in the open source community, supply another strategy for dealing with cross-platform Makefile generation, and are well documented elsewhere. Integrated development environments (IDEs) such as those provide with Microsoft Visual Studio .NET, or Apple's Interface Builder and Project Builder, inhibit the development of portable build systems, not to mention portable code. Item 8 discusses the place of IDEs in cross-platform development.

Configuration Management

Imagine you are the only developer on a project, consisting of no more than a couple of dozen source files, all located in a directory somewhere on your hard drive. You edit the files, compile them, and test. Occasionally, you take the source directory, compress it using zip or gzip, and then you save it somewhere in case a catastrophe occurs (such as accidentally deleting the source, or a hardware failure). For the sake of this discussion, let's assume these backups are made weekly.

Now, let's suppose you make a first release of your software, get feedback from others, and spend a few weeks working on bugs and adding several requested features. And then you release a new version to testers, and get the unwelcome news that a feature that was once working is now broken. It is obvious that the feature once worked, and that something you changed since your first release and now is what led to the bug. How do you figure out what you changed in source code that led to the problem? One strategy is to build from your weekly backups, and isolate the bug to the work done on a particular week. Comparing the changes in that build's source code with the source code corresponding to the release that failed will identify what changes were made, and from there you can start making educated guesses as to what went wrong.

However, there is a better solution, one that solves even more problems than the one just outlined. The solution is configuration management. Even if you are the only developer on a project, a configuration management system is highly beneficial; but on projects with multiple developers, configuration management becomes critical, because the problems become magnified, and new problems are introduced, when more than one developer is contributing to a single codebase. Perhaps the most notable of these is how to effectively merge changes made by multiple developers into a single codebase without introducing errors in the process.

There are numerous configuration solutions out there, many which are platform specific, but the best by far are open source, including the Concurrent Version System (CVS) and Subversion. Besides being open source, both are available in command-line and GUI form on almost every platform worth considering. CVS is the standard source control system for the open source community, and it is extremely popular in industry, too. In Item 13, I introduce CVS, giving you all you need to know to use it effectively. A related tool, `patch(1)`, which increases the usefulness of a configuration system, especially when multiple developers are involved in a project, is covered in Item 14.

The Role of Abstraction

Abstraction is a theme central to several of the tips and techniques presented in this book. The importance of abstraction to engineering, if not to the world that we live in, cannot be understated. To *abstract* something means to deal with it *without concern to its concrete details.* Without abstraction, something that was once simple risks becoming overly complicated, its true essence lost in the minutiae. Take, for example, the following PowerPC binary code:

```
0011540 0000 0000 7c3a 0b78 3821 fffc 5421 0034
0011560 3800 0000 9001 0000 9421 ffc0 807a 0000
0011600 389a 0004 3b63 0001 577b 103a 7ca4 da14
```

Do you have any idea what sort of program this code (snippet) corresponds to? (If you do, perhaps you need to get out more often!) Although it is hard to imagine, at one time people actually wrote code at this primitive level, typing in numbers that corresponded directly to machine-level instructions. It's amazing that programming in this way ever resulted in getting computers to do anything useful. (Of course, back in the days of machine language programming, not much was asked of computers, compared to what is asked of them today).

Even today, with all the hardware advances that have occurred, programmers would be rare, and the programs they would write would be fairly lacking in functionality, if they were forced still to program at such a low level of abstraction. Such programming would be error prone; it would be impossible for anyone trying to maintain such code to glean any meaning from a bunch of binary values, such as those illustrated here.

The difficulties that are inherent in working with programs at the binary level were overcome by introducing an abstraction: assembly language.

The following code, written in PowerPC assembler, represents an abstraction over the binary code that was presented previously:

```
_F:
    mflr r0
    stmw r29,-12(r1)
    stw r0,8(r1)
    stwu r1,-80(r1)
    mr r30,r1
    stw r3,104(r30)
    lwz r0,104(r30)
    cmpwi cr7,r0,0
    bne cr7,L8
    li r0,0
    stw r0,56(r30)
    b L10
L8:
    lwz r0,104(r30)
```

```
    cmpwi cr7,r0,1
    bne cr7,L11
    li r0,1
    stw r0,56(r30)
    b L10
L11:
    lwz r2,104(r30)
    addi r0,r2,-1
    mr r3,r0
    bl _F
    mr r29,r3
    lwz r2,104(r30)
    addi r0,r2,-2
    mr r3,r0
    bl _F
    mr r0,r3
    add r29,r29,r0
    stw r29,56(r30)
L10:
    lwz r0,56(r30)
    mr r3,r0
    lwz r1,0(r1)
    lwz r0,8(r1)
    mtlr r0
    lmw r29,-12(r1)
    blr
```

However, this level of abstraction is far from ideal. Spend a few minutes looking at the code, and see whether you can determine which well-known mathematical sequence the preceding code is generating. Not so easy, is it? I wrote the code (actually, the GNU C compiler generated the assembly code for me from C code I supplied), and even I have a hard time knowing what this assembly language actually represents, or mapping it back to the C source from which it was generated.

The truth is that although assembly language is a big improvement over machine code, it is not abstract enough to make much of a difference. To most of us, it might as well be in machine code; programming applications at this level is inappropriate, at best. Yet, when introduced, assembly language did lead to the creation of more meaningful applications, and it did make debugging and maintaining code easier to deal with. But, it was only an incremental improvement.

As you no doubt know, assembly language was not the end of the story. Let's take a look at a further abstraction of the above, this one provided courtesy of the C programming language:

```c
int F(const int n)
{
    if (!n || n == 1)
        return n;
    return (F(n - 1) + F(n - 2));
}
```

The C programming language provides our first hope of understandable, maintainable code. We can see that the function F() is a recursive function that generates an integer result. The result is a Fibonacci number, which is based on the recurrence relation shown in Figure Intro-1.

$$f(x) := \begin{cases} 0 & \text{if } x = 0; \\ 1 & \text{if } x = 1; \\ f(x-1) + f(x-2) & \text{if } x > 1. \end{cases}$$

Figure Intro-1 Fibonacci sequence

Of course, in the end, the code written in C ends up being generated by the compiler to a form less abstract than C itself, and then ultimately, the object code is a series of 1s and 0s. But we don't need to concern ourselves with this level of detail. Programming languages like C make large-scale software development possible, because the abstractions that they provide make the act of writing, debugging, and maintaining programs much easier than it would be done in assembly language.

We can go even further in our quest for abstraction. We can place the preceding code in a library, place the function prototype in a header file, and allow programmers to call F() from their applications, without needing to know a thing about how it is implemented. Related techniques might involve using Component Object Model (COM) or Common Object Request Broker Architecture (CORBA), where interactive data language (IDL) is used to define the interface of functions abstractly; but, effectively, the level of abstraction achieved is the same. Once hidden, we can vary the implementation of a function without affecting the code that calls it. (Depending on who is using the function, we can vary its interface, too; but ideally, the interface is a contract between the producer of F() and the consumer that does not vary.) We can take advantage of optimizations present on one platform that might not be available on others (for example, hardware support for computing Fibonacci sequences). We can make F() available in whatever way a particular platform requires, and no one need be the wiser to what is actually going on.

Let's return for a moment to the C programming language. Although C wasn't the first programming language to provide a suitable level of abstraction, it was perhaps the first language to demonstrate the impact that abstraction could have on code portability on a large scale. Early versions of the UNIX operating system were written completely in assembly language, making it hard (if not impossible) to port from one architecture to another. When faced with the daunting task of porting UNIX to other architectures, the designers of UNIX faced a choice: reimplement the miles of PDP-7 assembly language code, or come up with an abstraction. One choice would have been to come up with an abstract machine and correspondingly abstract assembly language, but by then, procedural languages were coming into existence, and the designers of UNIX made a better choice. They invented the C language explicitly to ease the porting of UNIX to other architectures, and the decision to implement the majority of the UNIX operating system in C, a novel idea back in the 1970s, was essential to the eventual widespread adoption of both C and the UNIX operating system.

Writing code in the C programming language often doesn't make it portable enough, however. We must use, or invent, additional layers of abstraction to make the software we write truly portable. This is especially true for userland application software that is intended to run on Linux, Windows, and Mac OS X. Just like assembly language varies among processor architectures, APIs vary from operating system to operating system, and this is especially true when it comes to the APIs associated with GUIs. To gain portability in our code, we must abstract these APIs. For example, where we might call open() on Linux or Mac OS X to open a file, we are forced to call _open() under Win32, and so we might abstract this by creating a wrapper function, like this:

```
int PortableOpen(const char *path, int flags, mode_t mode)
```

The function PortableOpen() is designed to hide the platform-specific details of opening a file. Programmers use this function, rather than the platform-specific function, allowing them to ignore the details of the platform implementation. In this book, you will see techniques for implementing such abstractions, both in C and C++. Some of these abstractions are simple, like those shown here. Item 17, in particular, introduces NSPR, a C-based API that is an abstraction layer above commonly used native operating system APIs such as open().

The book deals with GUI abstractions in several items. In Chapter 9, I describe XPToolkit and XUL, Netscape's and Mozilla's approach to solving the cross-platform GUI problem, and the design of Trixul, a related GUI toolkit of my own design. Both of these abstract the native GUI APIs found on Mac OS X, Linux, and Windows. They make use of abstractions that are more complex, and considerably more powerful, than the ones used by NSPR, and are based on design patterns such as factory, observer, and model/view. Combined, these abstractions are critical to designing portable software in the fashion that was employed by Netscape, and in the fashion used by Mozilla and Firefox to this day.

The concept of abstraction is mentioned explicitly, or otherwise implied, in numerous items presented in this book. Chapter 8, which covers wxWidgets, and Chapter 9, which covers the design of cross-platform GUI toolkits, both discuss technologies that are based on architectures involving high levels of abstraction.

1 Policy and Management

This book starts with a series of items best categorized in the domain of policy and management. The items presented here describe the essential best practices of a culture that was adopted companywide within Netscape, and embraced by Mozilla, which was critical in enabling Netscape and Mozilla to ship product with approximately the same level of quality across a wide spectrum of platforms to tens of millions of users.

As is the case with writing secure code, one must develop cross-platform software from the ground up to get a good result. You simply can't graft on cross-platform support as an afterthought and expect your project to be successful. Because of this, it is important to make all of your platforms a priority from the beginning, a concept that I believe is so critical to success that I made it the first item of this book. The remaining items in this chapter all support, and to some degree enforce, this concept.

Item 1: Make All of Your Platforms a Priority

It's a familiar problem. The roadmap for a product includes cross-platform support, but because the market (and revenue stream) is stronger on one of the three platforms you plan to support, the decision is made to devote all the engineering resources to that one platform, and port to the others after that first platform has shipped and a revenue stream has been generated.

Don't do it. I am not ignoring the fact that most of your users and income may very well come from one platform. And I'm not saying that it is ever wrong to have a favorite operating system. (Mac OS X happens to be mine, with Linux closely behind.) Nor am I saying that individuals on a project can't use the platform(s) and toolchain(s) of their choice to do the bulk of their development and debugging. However, what I *am* saying is that it is not in the best interest of your project, or your users, to treat Mac OS X, Linux, or any of the other platforms that you plan to support as second citizens—that is, if you are truly committed to successfully developing a cross-platform product, one that looks and behaves the same on each of the platforms you want to support.

To do cross-platform software well, parity, both in terms of functionality and quality, must be fully met on all the supported platforms, at all phases of the product's development and release. What I mean by *parity* is that, by and large, each platform has (generally) the same set of features, documentation, and even bugs in the bug tracking system. Whatever the platform mix, treating each of the supported platforms with equal priority, as early as possible in the project, will result in much better software, a much smoother project, and in the end, much happier end users (and developers, too).

Early in the project, you (or product management) should make a list of the tier-1 platforms that the organization plans to support. At Netscape, Mac OS X, Linux, and Windows were the tier-1 platforms on that list, with other UNIX-like operating systems (BSD, Solaris, AIX, and HP/UX) following closely behind. Netscape defined a tier-1 platform as a platform for which Netscape had to implement all the required product features, and those features had to be stable and pass all the internal testing required before release. No release of Netscape was possible until all the tier-1 platforms met this criteria. All other platforms (those not labeled as tier-1) were made available for download from Mozilla, did not have the Netscape branding, and achieved, at any given point of time, varying levels of quality and feature parity.

To support each platform in your tier-1 list correctly, it is imperative that you have at least one platform expert on your team. Ideally, each tier-1 platform will have at least a few experienced developers on the project to support it. Inside of Netscape, the bulk of developers (out of a team of approximately 300) specialized in the Microsoft Windows platform. Of the remaining developers, perhaps one or two dozen were Mac OS experts, and a smaller group of developers specialized in development under UNIX and Linux.

Furthermore, for each tier-1 platform, at least one developer who is considered a true expert in developing for his or her platform should be made available to the project at the earliest stages of product/project planning. An experienced platform developer can help those who are making the initial decisions about the project to better understand all the issues related to a given platform by doing the following:

- Identifying the hardware and software (particularly toolchains) best suited for development on the platform
- Interviewing candidates to ensure that the needed technical skills for the platform are in fact present
- Identifying platform-specific aspects of the software and proposing solutions during the requirements and design phases of the project

It is perhaps adherence to this last point that is most critical for overall success. For a cross-platform project to be successful, you must ensure that it is designed in such a way that each platform is supported equally in terms of feature parity. Basically, only those features that can truly be implemented in a cross-platform fashion should be allowed into a product's feature set. For example, an image manipulation program that is designed to import images from a USB scanner should support this functionality on all the tier-1 platforms, or not at all. There are a couple of reasons for such a policy.

First of all, parity differences make it more difficult to manage a project schedule. Projects with different parity requirements make it difficult to schedule releases, for example, because in all likelihood, the time that is needed to complete work on each platform will differ. Of course, there is no guarantee that, even with feature parity, all platforms will be completed at the same time, but proper engineering and planning of cross-platform features will tend to minimize the differences.

Even if features are completed at the same time, features lacking parity almost certainly will impact the rest of the product from an engineering perspective. Subtle bugs can be introduced into software due to the interaction of a nonparity feature with the rest of the system. And, the architecture of the software itself can be vastly impacted by the inclusion of platform-specific features. To cite a simple example, the design and implementation of menus and dialogs in a graphical user interface (GUI) application will be more difficult if the menus and dialogs are impacted by a platform-specific feature.

Furthermore, implementing platform-specific features makes QA/test more difficult, because it requires test plans to be developed in a platform- and feature-specific fashion. Documentation and marketing are impacted, because they need to produce materials that vary across platforms. Finally, users are impacted—what worked on one of the tier-1 platforms may not be supported when the user switches to another tier-1 platform, causing confusion and often dissatisfaction.

That said, there are times when parity cannot be achieved exactly in some area critical to the structure of an application. For example, MS Windows, Mac OS X, and Linux/Gtk+ all have different standards for the content, placement, and layout of their menu bars. Dealing with these differences is unavoidable—you simply can't remove menu bars from your application because of platform differences. In the case of menu bars, a toolkit such as XUL or Trixul is capable of taking a cross-platform specification (the Extensible Markup Language [XML] used to describe the menus) and mapping it into an implementation that is conformant to the requirements of the platform.

In some cases, a platform will provide a unique feature that is so compelling as to justify a violation of the parity rule. For example, Mac OS X supports application integration with a feature named Spotlight. Spotlight is a search technology that is integrated tightly with Apple's HFS+ file system. Spotlight enables users to find files stored in a file system based on metadata that is written to the file by applications. Many digital cameras embed metadata along with image files to describe the camera settings at the time the image was captured (for example, shutter speed, aperture, ISO setting, and whether a flash was used). Spotlight knows how to find this metadata in an image file because it is written to the file according to a standard (for example, the Exchangeable image file format). However, your application may write data to files in a format that is completely proprietary, adhering to no standard whatsoever. Spotlight provides a software development kit (SDK) that enables developers to develop a plug-in that supports Spotlight. This plug-in implements a function that Spotlight will call to obtain metadata from the application about an instance of a file that the application has created. Integrating a plug-in of this kind does not affect the user interface of the application, because the plug-in requires no user interaction, and performs its work behind the scenes.

Regardless of whether the change in parity is forced upon you, as in the case of menu bars, or it is a choice that you have made, as in the case of Spotlight integration, abstraction is the key to managing its impact.

As discussed in Item 14, each Netscape developer had the hardware, toolchains, and skills needed to build the source code, and smoke test it, on all three platforms. No developer was allowed to check in software that crippled any of the tier-1 platforms. If the developer did check in code that caused a problem, it was caught in one of two ways. First, Tinderbox (see Item 12) was there to catch any compile-time failures, and to sanity check the state of the resulting executable should a successful build occur. If there was a problem with the build that caused Tinderbox to "go red," the developer was contacted and given a chance to fix the problem. If the problem could not be immediately fixed, the code that was checked in was pulled from the repository, effectively forcing the developer to correct the problem and try again. The second line of defense was the smoke test. Every morning, the build team would deliver to QA the latest nightly build. QA would then run a comprehensive set of tests designed to determine the overall health of the tree on each platform. If there was a problem, all of Netscape's developers were asked to try to help find and fix the problem. Usually, the problem could be isolated to a single component (browser, mail news, composer, instant messenger, for example), and that team took on the bulk of the responsibility for identifying and fixing the problem. However, the tree would be closed to check-ins, so all developers were impacted and in practice worked together to try to find the problem.

The idea behind all this activity was to keep the project moving forward on all platforms, with all features appearing at about the same time, all with the same level of quality. Perhaps the scariest situation one can face in cross-platform development is this question: "Now that we have it working on platform x, what about getting it to work on platform y?" By answering that question each day, we avoided that issue for the most part. Perhaps more important, we were able to do the following:

- Take advantage of compiling source code with three different compilers, on three different platforms. This helped developers to identify a number of coding errors that might have otherwise gone undetected.
- Ensure that the architecture used to solve a problem would allow for portability. There was no better time than the present to ask that question, or to obtain the answer (one way or the other).

Too many cross-platform projects put Windows at the top of the tier-1 list, and then delay dealing with the inevitable port to Mac OS X / Linux. In the end, quality suffers, and users deal with different behavior and feature sets on different platforms. Identifying your tier-1 platforms at the start, and by enforcing some simple rules to ensure that every platform moves forward at the same clip with the same set of features, and with the same level of quality, is the only sure way to combat cross-platform parity problems.

Item 2: Code from a Common Codebase

The success of any cross-platform project can be enhanced by writing code so that it is shared across as many of the product's supported platforms as possible. Functionality common to all platforms should be factored so that it is not duplicated within platform-specific sources, and it should be built, tested, and deployed on all platforms throughout the lifetime of the product. When code cannot be shared, it should be hidden behind abstractions that provide a unified application programming interface (API). Applications using the abstract API should do so ignorant that the API is abstracting platform-specific functionality.

The primary benefit associated with sharing code across all supported platforms is that it forces developers (and, in turn, those who define the product requirements) to consider each of the platforms early in the design and implementation process, which in turn helps to raise portability issues as early as possible. During the design, prototype, and implementation stages of a feature or product, much can be learned by attempting to design and implement features with each supported platform in mind, as opposed to constraining the process to a subset of the target platforms. What might be possible, for example, on Windows XP, might not be easily implemented on Linux or Mac OS X. In some cases, a feature might not be portable at all, and this lack of portability may render the inclusion of that feature on any platform to be undesirable. Even if a feature is portable, it may require platform-specific code, and the design of an abstraction layer to isolate platform implementations from one another. Whatever the situation, the truth about portability will often not become apparent until some effort has been made to design and implement on all affected platforms.

It is the use of an abstraction layer that often makes code sharing across platforms possible. Various design patterns can be applied to implement an abstraction layer; the factory design pattern is perhaps the most useful of these. With a factory, you code an interface class that abstracts the functionality that you want to expose, and then provide concrete implementations that implement the functionality for each of the supported platforms. At compile time, or at runtime, you then decide which concrete implementation is applicable, based on the platform, you instantiate that concrete implementation, and then you glue it somehow to the interface class. When the application calls the interface class, it delegates platform-specific functionality to the concrete implementation. Any functionality that is portable should be factored up into, and implemented by, the interface class, and not duplicated in the concrete implementations.

Suppose you want to implement a function that lists the names and IDs of all processes currently running on the system. Of course, this program must run the same on Mac OS X, Linux, and Windows. A possible interface class for such functionality might contain the following, platform-independent functions:

```
class ProcessList {
public:
    int Scan(); // read the current list of processes
    int GetCount(); // get the number of processes \
in the last scan
    const char *GetName(const int i); // the name of \
the ith process found
    int GetPID(const int i); // get the process ID of \
the ith process found
    ...
};
```

A `main` program illustrates how the preceding class might be used:

```
#include <stdio.h>
#include "processes.h"

int
main(int argc, char *argv[])
{
    ProcessList processList;

    processList.Scan();

    for (int i = 0; i < processList.GetCount(); i++) {
        printf("%d %s\n",
            processList.GetPID(i),
            processList.GetName(i));
    }
}
```

In general, you should always strive to design APIs like those shown here, so that they are completely platform agnostic. Obviously, however, platform-specific code must exist somewhere, because each of the supported platforms, in this case, has its own distinct way of retrieving the list of process name / process ID (PID) pairs. This functionality, it turns out in our implementation, is encapsulated within the `Scan()` function. `Scan()` does the work of getting the process names and PIDs, and places the results in a platform-agnostic data structure, so that we can implement the functions

GetCount(), GetName(), and GetPID() in a platform-independent manner.
The fact that names are strings, and PIDs are integers, makes this trivial to
implement. One way to implement the platform-specific scanning would be
to implement, at the API level, platform-specific functions, for example:

```
class ProcessList {
public:
#if defined(WIN32)
int ScanWindows();   // read the current list of \
processes
#endif
#if defined(DARWIN)
int ScanMacOSX();   // read the current list of \
processes
#endif
#if defined(LINUX)
int ScanLinux();   // read the current list of \
processes
#endif
int GetCount(); // get the number of processes in \
the last scan
const char *GetName(const int i); // the name of the \
ith process found
int GetPID(const int i); // get the process ID of the \
ith process found
...
};
```

The main program that uses the above class would then be:

```
#include <stdio.h>
#include "processes.h"

int
main(int argc, char *argv[])
{
    ProcessList processList;

#if defined(WIN32)
    processList.ScanWindows();
#endif
#if defined(DARWIN)
    processList.ScanMacOSX();
```

```
#endif
#if defined(LINUX)
    processList.ScanLinux();
#endif

    for (int i = 0; i < processList.GetCount(); i++)
    {
        printf("%d %s\n", processList.GetPID(i),
            processList.GetName(i));
    }
}
```

Obviously, the preceding code is ugly. Even in this simple example, one has a hard time reading through the class definition. It's also a bit of a maintenance headache; adding (or subtracting) platforms requires a change to the class, and to the `main` program. In addition, it breaks the guideline that interfaces not expose which platforms are supported by the API.

More subtly, because the implementation of the scanning operation provides no abstraction whatsoever, developers must continually inspect and maintain each of the platform-specific implementations, to factor out shared code as it creeps in. Without a place to locate commonalities, it is easy for redundancies to creep in. It is much better to factor as much code as possible into a single `Scan` function, which then can call on platform-specific code as needed, and maintain the abstractions and factorizations that evolve as requirements and design changes occur. This relationship between an abstract class and platform-specific classes is key to good cross-platform design. And factories allow it to happen, as you will see.

Let's return to the original definition of the `ProcessList` class:

```
class ProcessList {
public:
    int Scan();   // read the current list of processes
    int GetCount();// get the number of processes in \
the last scan
    const char *GetName(const int i); // the name of the\
 ith process found
    int GetPID(const int i);       // get the process ID of the\
 ith process found
...
};
```

As you can see, the interfaces are platform neutral. Calling Scan(), of course, ultimately executes platform-specific code to do its job. So, we can push down the #ifdefs a level, and implement Scan like this:

```
int
ProcessList::Scan()
{
#if defined(WIN32)
    return ScanWindows();
#endif
#if defined(DARWIN)
    return ScanMacOSX();
#endif
#if defined(LINUX)
    return ScanLinux();
#endif
    return -1;
}
```

A return of –1 at the bottom of the function catches calls made to Scan() that do not have a platform implementation.

This is an almost ideal situation. No longer do we need to place #ifdefs in main, or in any other place of the code that is using an instance of ProcessList in this way. And even better, we now have a suitable place to put common code. To give a simple example of this, assume that we need to write into some log the fact that Scan() was called. We clearly don't want to require the caller to do this, because it is liable not to get done. But, we can rewrite Scan() as follows (assume LOG is a macro that knows how to do the right things regarding logging [for example, adding timestamps]):

```
int
ProcessList::Scan()
{
    LOG("Scan was called!");
#if defined(WIN32)
    return ScanWindows();
#endif
#if defined(DARWIN)
    return ScanMacOSX();
#endif
#if defined(LINUX)
    return ScanLinux();
#endif
    return -1;
}
```

However, there is a bit of a problem. Suppose we add a new, platform-specific function to the `ProcessList` class. For example, let's add a function to change the priority of a process. In UNIX, you do this by calling `nice()`, which takes as an argument an integer priority. In Windows, you can open a process and then call a function named `SetPriorityClass()`. (You can find more information about the `SetPriorityClass()` function at http://msdn. microsoft.com.) The UNIX implementations are different in the value returned; on Linux, the return value will be 0 to indicate success, and –1 to indicate failure. On BSD systems such as Darwin, the return value is the process priority (which one cannot reliably use to indicate failure or success).

To implement this new functionality, we can do the same trick. We can add an abstract API to `ProcessList`—let's call it `SetPriority()`—and then use `#ifdefs` to isolate calls to platform-specific helper functions within its body. However, you can see where this leads. As more and more platform-specific functionality is added, the number of `#ifdefs` will grow. To better manage this, and to be more object oriented about the whole thing, we can use a factory. In at least one implementation of the factory, `#ifdefs` are not entirely eliminated, but they are reduced to a single location, making code much more readable.

In essence, what a factory does is allow us, within the body of the function `Scan()` (or other abstract API function defined in `ProcessList`), to request and obtain an object that can provide the needed platform-specific implementation. This object derives from a base class that defines an API to the platform-specific implementation; this API generally mirrors the one we seek to support. Our class, `ProcessList`, maintains a pointer to the class, and the factory is the object that will provide us this pointer. With a pointer to this object, the structure of `Scan()` becomes this:

```
int
ProcessList::Scan()
{
    if (m_processesImpl)
        return m_processesImpl->Scan();
    return -1;
}
```

Here, `m_processesImpl` is a pointer to the object that was provided by the factory. We can obtain this object from the factory either on demand, within the body of `Scan()`, or we can grab it in the constructor of `ProcessList`, like this:

```
#include "processesfactory.h"

ProcessList::ProcessList(): m_processesImpl(NULL)
{
    ProcessesFactory *factory =
ProcessesFactory::GetProcessesFactory();

    if (factory)
        m_processesImpl = factory->MakeProcesses();
}
```

ProcessesFactory is a singleton object, a pointer to which is obtained by calling a function named GetProcessesFactory(), which is implemented by the platform-agnostic code. It is within the source file that implements GetProcessesFactory() that we see our only #ifdefs:

```
class ProcessesFactory;

#if defined(HAVE_WIN32)
#include "windows\windowsfactory.h"
#endif
#if defined(HAVE_MACOS)
#include "cocoa/cocoafactory.h"
#endif
#if defined(HAVE_LINUX)
#include "linux/linuxfactory.h"
#endif

ProcessesFactory *
ProcessesFactory::GetProcessesFactory()
{
    static ProcessesFactory *processesFactory = 0;

    if (!processesFactory)
#if defined(HAVE_WIN32)
        processesFactory =
            WindowsFactory::GetFactoryInstance();
#endif
#if defined(HAVE_MACOS)
        processesFactory =
            CocoaFactory::GetFactoryInstance();
#endif
#if defined(HAVE_LINUX)
        processesFactory =
```

```
            LinuxFactory::GetFactoryInstance();
#endif
    return processesFactory;
}
```

The preceding code is conditionally compiled, and the build system guarantees that only one of the defines (for example, HAVE_WIN32) will be set. Generally, you will want to do this in your Makefile so that it is passed as a compiler argument (for example, g++ -DHAVE_WIN32) when GetProcessesFactory() is compiled. (We'll assume that HAVE_WIN32 was defined from here on out.)

Platform Factory Implementations

Each platform provides a class that can create and return a pointer to a platform-specific factory implementation (for example, WindowsFactory). This class is compiled into a platform-specific library that is linked to the application. There is one instance of this library for each platform supported. After the platform-agnostic code has obtained this pointer, it can use it to create objects that provide platform-specific functionality.

WindowsFactory

WindowsFactory implements a single static function, GetFactoryInstance(), which creates and returns the platform-specific implementation singleton:

```
#if !defined(__WINDOWS_FACTORY_H__)
#define __WINDOWS_FACTORY_H__

#include "../processesfactory.h"
#include "../processesimpl.h"

class WindowsFactory : public ProcessesFactory
{
public:
    static WindowsFactory *GetFactoryInstance()
    {
        static WindowsFactory *factory = 0;
        if (!factory)
            factory = new WindowsFactory;
        return factory;
```

```
    }
    virtual ~WindowsFactory();
    virtual ProcessesImpl *MakeProcesses();
private:
    WindowsFactory();
};
```

```
#endif
```

Two things are happening here. First, we have a static
`GetFactoryInstance()` function that allows us to create and obtain the
singleton instance of `WindowsFactory`. We've seen above how that is used.
The other critical thing to notice is that the factory implements a function
named `MakeProcesses()`, which returns the pointer to the `ProcessesImpl`
object that we desire. `WindowsFactory` is not restricted to creating objects
that support processes; in general, a factory can (and should be used to)
create a wide variety of objects, each object providing platform-specific
functionality related to a specific area. Here, we see that `WindowsFactory` is
able to create an object that can provide support for dealing with processes,
but let's say we need to provide platform-independent code that can handle
the reading and writing of files. To do this, we can create a new abstract factory class, perhaps named `FilesFactory`, and extend `WindowsFactory` as
follows (changes in bold):

```
#if !defined(__WINDOWS_FACTORY_H__)
#define __WINDOWS_FACTORY_H__

#include "../processesfactory.h"
#include "../processesimpl.h"
#include "../filesfactory.h"
#include "../filesimpl.h"

class WindowsFactory : public ProcessesFactory,
    public FilesFactory
{
public:
    static WindowsFactory *GetFactoryInstance()
    {
        static WindowsFactory *factory = 0;
        if (!factory)
            factory = new WindowsFactory;
        return factory;
    }
```

```
    virtual ~WindowsFactory();
    virtual ProcessesImpl *MakeProcesses();
    virtual FilesImpl *MakeFiles();
private:
    WindowsFactory();
};
```

```
#endif
```

Note that `GetFactoryInstance()` should really be made thread-safe. See Chapter 6 of *Modern C++ Design: Generic Programming and Design Patterns Applied* (Addison-Wesley, 2001), by Andrei Alexandrescu, for more details on making singletons thread-safe.

Before we go on, let's summarize where we are now, because a lot of information has been provided in the past few pages. We have platform-agnostic code, within `ProcessList`, that implements an abstraction, `Scan()`. From the perspective of the application, `Scan()` can be used to obtain a list of process names and IDs. `Scan()`, not knowing how exactly to do the platform-specific work, needs help. To get this help, `Scan()` obtains a pointer to a factory object, which itself is platform-agnostic. This factory object can create further objects that provide interfaces, themselves abstract, to the functionality we seek. These objects created by the factory encapsulate similar functionality; for example, one kind of object that the factory can create supports processes, another supports file system access, and so forth. When the factory is obtained by the application, it calls on one of these functions (for example, `MakeProcesses()`) to obtain a pointer to an object that implements the desired functionality.

Implementation Classes

Now let's see how the platform-specific code is implemented. We can see that `MakeProcesses()` returns a pointer to an object of type `ProcessesImpl`. `ProcessesImpl` is a base class with pure virtual functions that we must provide platform-specific implementations for. (A pure virtual function is C++'s way of forcing classes deriving from a base class to implement the function in the derived class. The base class does not provide any implementation for the function.) It can also contain platform-agnostic code that all platforms can share. Here is the definition of `ProcessesImpl`:

```
#if !defined(__PROCESSES_IMPL_H__)
#define __PROCESSES_IMPL_H__
```

```
#include "processes.h"
#include <vector>

class ProcessesImpl
{
public:
    ProcessesImpl() {};
    virtual ~ProcessesImpl() {};
    virtual int Scan() = 0;
    int GetCount();
    const char *GetName(const int which);
    int GetPID(const int which);
protected:
    std::vector <Process> m_processList;
};


#endif
```

Most of this class happens to implement code that is shared by all platforms. The list of process names and IDs is managed in a Standard Template Library (STL) vector, which is highly portable. Functions such as GetCount(), GetName(), and GetPID() interact with, and rely only upon, this vector, and thus are naturally implemented in the base class, too.

Platform-Specific `ProcessesImpl` Classes

The function Scan(), on the other hand, is platform specific, and must be implemented in a deriving class, which, on Windows, is WindowsProcessesImpl:

```
#if !defined(__WINDOWSPROCESSESIMPL_H__)
#define __WINDOWSPROCESSESIMPL_H__

#include "../processesimpl.h"

#include <windows.h>
#include <stdio.h>
#include <tchar.h>
#include "psapi.h"

class WindowsProcessesImpl : public ProcessesImpl
{
public:
    WindowsProcessesImpl();
    virtual ~WindowsProcessesImpl();
```

```
    virtual int Scan();
private:
    void ScanProcesses();
    void PrintProcessNameAndID(DWORD processID);
};
#endif
```

Note the inclusion of Windows-specific headers (for example, windows.h). Because this code is only ever compiled on Windows, it is okay to include this, or any other platform-specific code here in the header. The function Scan() makes use of two helper functions that are private to WindowsProcessesImpl: ScanProcesses() and PrintProcessNameAndID(). As long as Scan() is declared as required by the base class, anything goes. The following code shows the bulk of the WindowsProcessesImpl class implementation:

```
#include "windowsprocessesimpl.h"

int
WindowsProcessesImpl::Scan()
{
    m_processList.clear();

    ScanProcesses();

    return m_processList.size();
}

void
WindowsProcessesImpl::PrintProcessNameAndID(
    DWORD processID)
{
    TCHAR szProcessName[MAX_PATH] =
        TEXT("<unknown>");

    // Get a handle to the process.

    HANDLE hProcess = OpenProcess(
        PROCESS_QUERY_INFORMATION | PROCESS_VM_READ,
        FALSE, processID );

    // Get the process name.

    if (NULL != hProcess )
    {
```

```
        HMODULE hMod;
        DWORD cbNeeded;

        if ( EnumProcessModules( hProcess, &hMod,
            sizeof(hMod), &cbNeeded) )
        {
            GetModuleBaseName(hProcess, hMod,
                szProcessName,
                sizeof(szProcessName)/sizeof(TCHAR));
        }
    }

    // Print the process name and identifier.

    Process proc;
    proc.SetPID(processID);
    proc.SetName(szProcessName);
    m_processList.push_back(proc);

    CloseHandle( hProcess );
}

void WindowsProcessesImpl::ScanProcesses()
{
    // Get the list of process identifiers.

    DWORD aProcesses[1024], cbNeeded, cProcesses;
    unsigned int i;

    if (!EnumProcesses(aProcesses, sizeof(aProcesses),
        &cbNeeded))
        return;

    // Calculate how many process identifiers were
    // returned.

    cProcesses = cbNeeded / sizeof(DWORD);

    // Print the name and process identifier for each
    // process.

    for ( i = 0; i < cProcesses; i++ )
        if (aProcesses[i] != 0)
            PrintProcessNameAndID( aProcesses[i]);
}
```

The code in bold is code that I wrote; the rest is code that was sample code produced by Microsoft and found at http://msdn.microsoft.com using Win32 APIs. My code simply needed to provide the implementation of the Scan() interface. (This is enforced because Scan() is pure virtual in the base class.) And, each process scanned needed to be pushed onto the end of the vector that is being maintained in the base class. But that was it.

Linux

If you look at the Linux and BSD/Darwin implementations, you will see that they follow the same basic approach. Here is the Linux implementation, which uses the proc file system to obtain process information.

First, the header:

```
#if !defined(__LINUXPROCESSESIMPL_H__)
#define __LINUXPROCESSESIMPL_H__

#include "../processesimpl.h"
#include <dirent.h>

class LinuxProcessesImpl : public ProcessesImpl
{
public:
    LinuxProcessesImpl();
    virtual ~LinuxProcessesImpl();
    virtual int Scan();
};
#endif
```

And then, the implementation:

```
#include "linuxprocessesimpl.h"

#include <unistd.h>
#include <sys/stat.h>
#include <fcntl.h>
#include <ctype.h>

int
LinuxProcessesImpl::Scan()
{
    DIR *dir;
```

```
m_processList.clear();

dir = opendir("/proc");
if (dir == NULL)
    return 0;

// Read all proc contents, and record all that 1)
// are numeric in name, 2) are themselves
// directories, and 3) contain a file named
// cmdline. The directory name is the PID, and
// the contents of cmdline is the command. This
// has to be slower than using sysctl(3) in BSD,
// and a bit more clunky, but it is the Linux way
// of getting process info.

std::string name;
struct dirent *dirEnt;
struct stat statBuf;

while ((dirEnt = readdir(dir))) {
    name = "/proc/";
    name += dirEnt->d_name;
    if (!stat(name.c_str(), &statBuf)) {
        if (statBuf.st_mode & S_IFDIR) {
            char *p;
            p = dirEnt->d_name;
            bool allDigits = true;
            while (*p) {
                if (!isdigit(*p)) {
                    allDigits = false;
                    break;
                }
                p++;
            }
            if (allDigits) {
                // Okay, it's a directory with all
                // digits. Open it, and see if it
                // has a file named cmdline
                // as a child.

                Process proc;

                proc.SetPID(atoi(dirEnt->d_name));
                std::string path = name +
```

```
                std::string("/cmdline");
    int fd = open(path.c_str(),
        O_RDONLY);
    if (fd != -1) {
        char buf[1024];
        memset(buf,'\0',sizeof(buf));
        int n;
        if ((n = read(fd, buf,
            sizeof(buf)-1)) > 0) {
            proc.SetName(buf);
            m_processList. \
                push_back(proc);
        } else if (n == 0) {
            path = name +
                std::string("/status");
            int fd2 = open(
                path.c_str(),O_RDONLY);
            if (fd2 != -1) {
                memset(buf, '\0',
                    sizeof(buf));
                if ((n =
                    read(fd2, buf,
                    sizeof(buf)-1))>0)
                {
                    char *p = buf;
                    while (*p) {
                        if (*p == '\n')
                        {
                            *p = '\0';
                            break;
                        }
                        p++;
                    }
                    if ((p = strstr(buf,
                       "Name:"))) {
                      p +=
                      strlen("Name:");
                      while (*p &&
                          isspace(*p))
                              p++;
                    }
                    else
                        p = buf;
                    proc.SetName(p);
```

```
                            m_processList.\
                              push_back(proc);
                  }
                close(fd2);
            }
          }
        close(fd);
      }
    }
   }
  }
 }
 closedir(dir);
 return m_processList.size();
}
```

The preceding code was inspired by an inspection of the sources for the `top` command, which confirmed that the Linux way to do this chore was to read through the proc file system.

Mac OS X

Now, finally, we turn to the Darwin implementation, which uses BSD's marvelous `sysctl()` function to obtain process information.

First, the header:

```
#if !defined(__COCOAPROCESSESIMPL_H__)
#define __COCOAPROCESSESIMPL_H__

#include "../processesimpl.h"

#include <assert.h>
#include <errno.h>
#include <stdbool.h>
#include <stdlib.h>
#include <stdio.h>
#include <sys/sysctl.h>

typedef struct kinfo_proc kinfo_proc;

class CocoaProcessesImpl : public ProcessesImpl
{
public:
    CocoaProcessesImpl();
    virtual ~CocoaProcessesImpl();
    virtual int Scan();
```

```
private:
    int GetBSDProcessList(kinfo_proc **procList,
        size_t *procCount);
};
#endif
```

And then, the implementation:

```
int
CocoaProcessesImpl::Scan()
{
    kinfo_proc *procList = NULL;
    size_t procCount = 0;

    m_processList.clear();

    if (!GetBSDProcessList(&procList, &procCount)) {
        if (procList) {
            for (int i = 0; i < procCount; i++) {
                Process proc;
                proc.SetPID(
                    procList[i].kp_proc.p_pid);
                proc.SetName(
                    procList[i].kp_proc.p_comm);
                m_processList.push_back(proc);
            }
            free(procList);
        }
    }
    return m_processList.size();
}


int
CocoaProcessesImpl::GetBSDProcessList(
    kinfo_proc **procList, size_t *procCount)

    // Returns a list of all BSD processes on the
    // system. This routine allocates the list and
    // puts it in *procList and a count of the
    // number of entries in *procCount.  You are
    // responsible for freeing this list (use "free"
    // from System framework).
    // On success, the function returns 0.
    // On error, the function returns a BSD errno
    // value.
{
```

```
int                err;
kinfo_proc *       result;
bool               done;
static const int   name[] = {
    CTL_KERN, KERN_PROC, KERN_PROC_ALL, 0 };

// Declaring name as const requires us to cast it
// when passing it to sysctl because the prototype
// doesn't include the const modifier.

size_t length;

assert(procList != NULL);
assert(*procList == NULL);
assert(procCount != NULL);

*procCount = 0;

// We start by calling sysctl with result == NULL
// and length == 0. That will succeed, and set
// length to the appropriate length. We then
// allocate a buffer of that size and call sysctl
// again with that buffer. If that succeeds, we're
// done. If that fails with ENOMEM, we have to
// throw away our buffer and loop. Note that the
// loop causes use to call sysctl with NULL again;
// this is necessary because the ENOMEM failure
// case sets length to the amount of data returned,
// not the amount of data that could have been
// returned.

result = NULL;
done = false;
do {
    assert(result == NULL);

    // Call sysctl with a NULL buffer.

    length = 0;
    err = sysctl( (int *) name, (sizeof(name) /
        sizeof(*name)) - 1,
        NULL, &length,
        NULL, 0);
    if (err == -1) {
        err = errno;
    }
```

```
        // Allocate an appropriately sized buffer based
        // on the results from the previous call.

        if (err == 0) {
            result = (kinfo_proc *) malloc(length);
            if (result == NULL) {
                err = ENOMEM;
            }
        }


        // Call sysctl again with the new buffer. If we
        // get an ENOMEM error, toss away our buffer and
        // start again.

        if (err == 0) {
            err = sysctl( (int *) name, (sizeof(name) /
                sizeof(*name)) - 1, result, &length,
                    NULL, 0);
            if (err == -1) {
                err = errno;
            }
            if (err == 0) {
                done = true;
            } else if (err == ENOMEM) {
                assert(result != NULL);
                free(result);
                result = NULL;
                err = 0;
            }
        }
    } while (err == 0 && ! done);

    // Clean up and establish post conditions.

    if (err != 0 && result != NULL) {
        free(result);
        result = NULL;
    }
    *procList = result;
    if (err == 0) {
        *procCount = leng1th / sizeof(kinfo_proc);
    }

    assert( (err == 0) == (*procList != NULL) );

    return err;
}
```

Once again, the bulk of the implementation is borrowed, this time from sample code embedded in documentation found on the Apple Computer developer site (http://developer.apple.com). And, like the Linux and Windows implementations, all that I needed to do was integrate this sample code into the implementation class so that it could be invoked by calling `Scan()`, and make sure that it stored its results in data structures defined and maintained in the `ProcessesImpl` base class.

Each of these platform implementations is built only on the platform it is designed for. In general, I like to compile these down into a shared library, which includes not only the functional implementation (for example, scan), but also the platform-specific portion of the factory. But that is just a personal preference. All that matters is that this code is somehow linked to the final executable, and that it only be built for the platform it supports.

Creating the Instance Hierarchy

To see how the classes interact, it helps to look at sequence diagrams illustrating the creation of the various classes previously described, and the calls that are made to `ProcessList::Scan()`, `ProcessList::GetCount()`, `ProcessList::GetPID()`, and `ProcessList::GetName()`. (The following figures were created using the open source program Umbrello, which is available at http://uml.sourceforge.net.) First, let's take a look at what happens when an instance of `ProcessList` is created (see Figure 1-1).

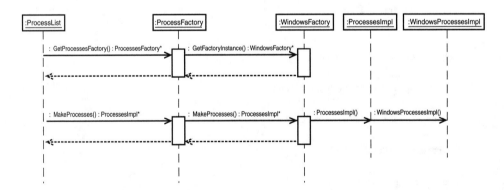

Figure 1-1 Creating an instance of `ProcessList`

The `ProcessList` constructor's job is to obtain a pointer to a class that derives from `ProcessesImpl`, which is the base class that defines the interfaces `Scan()`, `GetSize()`, `GetID()`, and `GetName()`. When the application calls `ProcessList::Scan()`, for example, `ProcessList` will invoke the platform-specific version of `Scan()` via this pointer. To get this pointer, `ProcessList` calls `ProcessesFactory::GetProcessesFactory()`, which in turn will call `WindowsFactory::GetFactoryInstance()`, because `ProcessesFactory::GetProcessesFactory()` was conditionally compiled to do so. Here is the code:

```
ProcessList::ProcessList(): m_processesImpl(NULL)
{
    ProcessesFactory *factory =
ProcessesFactory::GetProcessesFactory();

    if (factory)
        m_processesImpl = factory->MakeProcesses();
}


ProcessesFactory *
ProcessesFactory::GetProcessesFactory()
{
    static ProcessesFactory *processesFactory = 0;

    if (!processesFactory)
#if defined(HAVE_WIN32)
        processesFactory =
            WindowsFactory::GetFactoryInstance();
#endif
...
    return processesFactory;
}
```

`WindowsFactory::GetFactoryInstance` will instantiate `WindowsProcessesImpl`, which derives from `ProcessesImpl`, and the pointer to this object will be returned back to the `ProcessList` constructor.

The sequence diagram in Figure 1-2 illustrates what happens when the application calls `Scan()`. (Similar sequence diagrams can be made for the other public interfaces defined by `ProcessList`.)

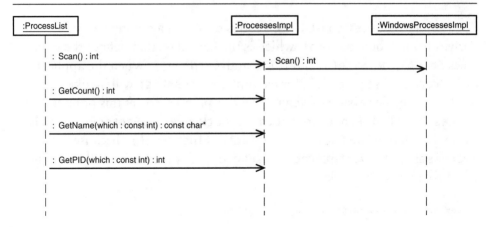

Figure 1-2 Scan( ) sequence diagram

Each of these functions is coded similarly in `ProcessList`; a check is made to see whether the `ProcessesImpl` pointer returned by the factory is NULL or not, and if it is non-NULL, the corresponding method implemented by the `ProcessesImpl` instance is called. Here is the code:

```
int
ProcessList::Scan()
{
    if (m_processesImpl)
        return m_processesImpl->Scan();
    return -1;
}


int
ProcessList::GetCount()
{
    if (m_processesImpl)
        return m_processesImpl->GetCount();
    return -1;
}


int
ProcessList::GetPID(const int i)
{
    if (m_processesImpl)
        return m_processesImpl->GetPID(i);
    return -1;
}
```

```
const char *
ProcessList::GetName(const int i)
{
    if (m_processesImpl)
        return m_processesImpl->GetName(i);
    return NULL;
}
```

In the case of `Scan()`, `WindowsProcessesImpl`'s implementation is invoked. (Recall it was defined pure virtual in `ProcessesImpl`.) The other functions (`GetCount()`, `GetPID()`, and `GetName()`) are all implemented by the `ProcessesImpl` base class, as indicated in the preceding sequence diagram.

Organizing the Project in CVS or SVN

Now that you know about factories and how they can be used to effectively isolate the platform-specific code in your project, let's talk about how you might organize your project in a Concurrent Version System (CVS) or Subversion (SVN) repository, and design Makefiles, both in an effort to support a factory-based architecture. There are many ways to do this, but the method I generally prefer, which is inspired by my experiences with Mozilla and Netscape, is a good starting point. Here is a template for the repository layout of a generic project:

```
lib
   lib1
         mac
                include
                debug
                release
         win
                include
                debug
                release
         linux
                include
                debug
                release
   lib2
         mac
                include
                debug
                release
         win
```

```
                include
                debug
                release
        linux
                include
                debug
                release
src
    component1
        src
                mac
                win
                linux
        inc
                mac
                win
                linux
    component2
        src
                mac
                win
                linux
        inc
                mac
                win
                linux
    component3
        src
        inc
    main
```

Basically, the project, at the highest level, is broken down into two sections. The first of these, lib, stores debug and release versions of prebuilt libraries (obtained from commercial vendors, or compiled from open source), and their associated header files. The second, src, contains the source files that you and your developers will create for the project.

Let's look first at the structure below lib, and then we will go on to look at src. Below lib is a directory for each precompiled library that is stored in the repository. Here, I gave these libraries the names lib1 and lib2, but you should give these directories names that identify the library and the version number (for example, libpng-1.2.13). Below this directory, you find a directory for each platform supported (here, named mac for Mac OS X, win for Windows, and linux for Linux). Within each of these directories are the prebuilt library or libraries for that particular platform, further separated by whether it was compiled debug or release, and an `include` directory that contains the include files (organized by whatever means they were distributed by the library supplier).

Depending on the situation, you might need to store source code below `lib`, rather than prebuilt binaries. Sometimes, source will be needed, to fix bugs in the library, or to address the specific needs of your application. But, generally, if you can get away with treating libraries below `lib` as the black boxes that they should be treated as, my feeling is that it is much more efficient just to have developers pull binaries directly from the repository and to link them, instead of incorporating them into the build. If you do need to put source below the `lib` directory, strive to organize it in a way that is similar to how the application and component source is organized below `src`, as I explain now.

The organization below `src` is similar to that which is found below `lib`. Each component, or related set of components, that the project builds (component being a library, usually shared) is given its own directory. The name of the directory reflects the functionality that is provided by the component. And usually, the name of the shared library created within that directory has a direct correlation with the name of the directory, too. For example, the source for a shared library that is named `libwidget.so` would be found within the directory named `widget`. And one would assume that `libwidget.so` provides support for, well, widgets.

Below each component directory (for example, `widget`), one finds two directories; one named `src`; the other named `inc`. The directory named `src` contains platform-neutral sources; the directory named `inc` contains platform-neutral header files. These sources and headers are built and linked by all platforms. One typically finds abstract or base classes here, not concrete classes. In the processes example given in this item, the source code and headers for the `ProcessList`, `ProcessesFactory`, and `ProcessesImpl` classes would be found in `src` and `inc`, respectively.

Diving deeper, the platform-specific sources and headers for the component are found in directories that are located below `src` and `inc`. The names of these directories explicitly reflect the platform to which the code applies (for instance, `mac`, `win`, `linux`). Code and headers in these directories are most definitely not cross-platform, but is, instead, built only for the platform implied by the name of the directory within which it is located. That is, the code found below the directory named `mac` is destined to be built only on Mac OS X, and not on Linux or Windows. Concrete classes are the norm here, in contrast to the abstract classes that one finds in the directory above. In the processes example presented in this item, you would find the source code for the `WindowsFactory` and `WindowsProcessesImpl` classes located in the `win` directory below `src` and `inc`.

The final directory where one finds source code is named `main` (or, if you prefer, it can be given the name of the application; for example, `processes`). Here is located code containing the `main` application (for instance, the body of `main()`), and related sources that are platform neutral, but do not belong in a component.

Once again, treat these suggestions as a guideline, not an absolute requirement. In fact, the layout of the processes project in my home CVS repository is a variation of what I just described:

```
cocoa/
    cocoa/cocoafactory.cpp
    cocoa/cocoafactory.h
    cocoa/cocoaprocessesimpl.cpp
    cocoa/cocoaprocessesimpl.h
    cocoa/Makefile.macosx
linux
    linux/linuxfactory.cpp
    linux/linuxfactory.h
    linux/linuxprocessesimpl.cpp
    linux/linuxprocessesimpl.h
    linux/Makefile.linux
windows
    windows/Makefile.windows
    windows/windowsfactory.cpp
    windows/windowsfactory.h
    windows/windowsprocessesimpl.cpp
    windows/windowsprocessesimpl.h
main
    main/main.cpp
    main/Makefile.linux
    main/Makefile.macosx
    main/Makefile.windows
Makefile.linux
Makefile.macosx
Makefile.windows
processes.cpp
processes.h
processesfactory.cpp
```

```
processesfactory.h
processesimpl.cpp
processesimpl.h
```

The differences here are numerous, but the similarities are evident:

- There is no `lib` directory because the application does not require the use of external libraries.
- There is no `src` directory. I omitted this because of the lack of a need for a `lib` directory, and because everything is source, I just moved the contents of what would have been the `src` directory up one level.
- The directory that holds Mac OS X sources is named `cocoa`. (Cocoa is the Objective-C API used for Mac OS X GUI programming, and although this code does not call upon Cocoa, I often use `cocoa`, `mac`, and `macosx` to mean the same thing in CVS.)
- Below `linux`, `cocoa`, and `windows` there are no `src` and `inc` directories. Given the small number of files, I omitted these directories and opted for locating both the headers and source files one level higher.

Makefiles and Building the Code

The next, and final, issue to tackle is how to deal with Makefiles, and the build in general. I have adopted a strategy that is fairly simple, and does not require anything other than a basic understanding of make and some modest shell scripting skills. Use the following as a starting point. Surely, some of you will want to come up with something more elaborate, but I have found that simplicity goes a long way toward solving headaches down the road, and what I am about to share has worked quite well for me over the years.

The key problem in executing a cross-platform build is ensuring that all the following happens:

- Only platform-specific components/libraries are built.
- The proper Makefiles (or Makefile rules) are invoked during the build.
- The proper `#defines` are enabled on the command line (for example, `–DHAS_LINUX`).
- The resulting components and application are copied to a suitable location for testing and distribution.

Here, in a nutshell, are the steps I generally follow to set up and execute a build. Again, this is all done with shell scripts and simple Makefiles:

1. The shell script creates a top-level directory named `dist` that will hold the results of the build. The structure of this directory depends on the platform. It contains both a `debug` and a `release` directory, to hold debug and release versions of the build, respectively.
2. It then creates a directory named `inc`, to which copies of the headers corresponding to the prebuilt libraries and components located below `lib` are copied before the build kicks off.
3. A copy of the debug and release versions of prebuilt libraries and components is made to the `debug` and `release` subdirectories below `dist`, respectively. This location is predefined as the linker search path in all the Makefiles.
4. Now that `dist` has been created and populated with header files and components, the script iterates through the `src` directory, copying the platform-specific Makefile located therein (for instance, Makefile.macosx) to a file named Makefile in the same directory.
5. The script then runs through the source directories, in dependency order, and issues a make `-f` Makefile to build the components and application.

The script that creates the `dist` directory structure uses the `uname` command to determine what operating system we are executing on. It then does simple calls to `mkdir` to create the needed structure. Here, I show how this is done, and how the debug portion of the `dist` directory is created:

```
#!/bin/sh

platform=`uname`;
echo "Configure begin";
if [ ! -d dist ]
then
    mkdir dist
fi
if [ `echo $platform | grep -i "Linux"` ]
then
platform="linux"
fi
if [ `echo $platform | grep -i "Darwin"` ]
then
platform="macosx"
fi
if [ `echo $platform | grep -i "NT"` ]
then
```

```
platform="windows"
fi
echo "Configuring for $platform."
if [ ! -d dist/$platform ]
then
    echo "Creating dist/$platform..."
    mkdir dist/$platform
fi
if [ ! -d dist/$platform/debug ]
then
    echo "Creating dist/$platform/debug..."
    mkdir dist/$platform/debug
fi
```

On Mac OS X, a more elaborate directory structure is required for applications (see Item 15). The following portions of the script handle this chore:

```
if [ $platform = "macosx" ]
then
echo "Creating debug structure..."
if [ ! -d dist/$platform/debug/processes.app ]
then
    mkdir dist/$platform/debug/processes.app
fi
if [ ! -d dist/$platform/debug/processes.app/Contents ]
then
    mkdir dist/$platform/debug/processes.app/Contents
fi
if [ ! -d dist/$platform/debug/processes.\
    app/Contents/MacOS ]
then
    mkdir dist/$platform/debug/processes.app/Contents/\
        MacOS
fi
if [ ! -d dist/$platform/debug/processes.app/Contents/\
    Resources ]
then
    mkdir dist/$platform/debug/processes.app/Contents/\
        Resources
fi
echo "Generating PkgInfo file..."
echo "APPL????" > dist/$platform/debug/processes.app/\
    Contents/PkgInfo
```

```
echo "Copying Info.plist file..."
sed -e 's/LAYOUT_VERSION/$version/' install/macosx/\
    Info.plist > dist/$platform/debug/processes.app/\
        Contents/Info.plist
echo "Copying desktop icon file..."
cp install/macosx/processes.icns
dist/$platform/debug/processes.app/Contents/Resources
```

Obviously, for these scripts to work on Windows, Cygwin needs to be installed. See Item 9 for more details.

With regard to Makefiles, you have several options. (Item 10 discusses these options in detail.) However, all you need to ensure, in the end, is that the correct compiler and linker is invoked (in my world, this means g++ on Linux and Mac OS X, and Visual C++ on Windows), that the correct flags are passed as arguments to the compiler, and that the results of the build are copied to the correct locations below `dist`. This can be done in a variety of ways. A brute-force way to manage Makefiles is to have a copy for each platform; the problem with this is one of maintenance—when new files are added to the project, three Makefiles will need to be updated. Closely related to this strategy is to have a single Makefile that sets variables (CC, CFLAGS, and so on) based on the platform. It's really up to you how this is best done in your organization, depending on the skill set of your team and the amount of time you want to put into it.

Item 3: Require Developers to Compile Their Code with Different Compilers

Building your software on all platforms (see Item 4) helps to ensure that each of the platforms you support moves forward at the same pace during the project timeline, helps to identify portability problems in the codebase, and ensures that developers who chose to (or must) work on a platform other than your primary platform are not blocked by a codebase that does not build and execute cleanly everywhere.

Related to this is building your source code with multiple compilers. This can be done on a single platform (building with Microsoft Visual C++ and Borland C++, for example), or by building using different compilers available on other platforms. By building on multiple platforms, Netscape exposed the browser codebase to three completely different compilers: GCC on Linux (and later, on Mac OS X); Microsoft Visual C++ on Windows; and

Metrowerks CodeWarrior on Classic Mac OS. In truth, even more compilers were involved in the project; Netscape had relationships with IBM (AIX) and Sun (Solaris) that required compiling the codebase with their native compilers. Beyond that, the Mozilla project had its "ports" effort, which exposed the codebase to even more platforms/compilers (mostly UNIX-based operating systems, such as FreeBSD). A good number of the ports systems were GCC based, although not all were using the same version of GCC. As of this writing, BeOS and OS/2, both historical operating systems, have documented (although not tier-1, obviously) support for building the Mozilla codebase at mozilla.org, using various versions of GCC.

So, why is building with different compilers so important? Here are the main reasons:

- It helps you to avoid the use of compiler-specific features, flags, and macros.
- It minimizes the impact of various interpretations of C/C++ standards, and helps you avoid using unproven language features.
- Each compiler will produce different sets of warnings and errors, which makes development easier, and strengthens the code that you write.
- Different compilers generate different code, which can illuminate problems you might otherwise not detect.

Let's start with compiler-specific features. Certainly, there will be times when developers are going to find the use of some compiler-specific feature or language extension to be necessary. (If that were not the case, there would have been little motivation for the compiler vendor to provide support for the feature in the first place.) However, doing so is inherently non-portable, and should be avoided if you are writing cross-platform code.

To avoid such features, compiler flags to restrict the dialect of C and C++ accepted by the compiler to a specific standard should be used whenever possible. Doing so may help ensure that compiler-specific features are also flagged as warnings or errors. When you are using GCC, the `-ansi` or `-std=c99` flags (`-std=c++98` in the case of C++) can be used to ensure that your code conforms to a specific standard, and that any GCC extensions that conflict with that standard are disabled. The `-pedantic-errors` argument should also be specified with GCC because it causes compiler errors, not warnings, whenever standard violations are detected, forcing programmers to deal with the issue immediately. (Dealing with warnings is a good idea, always, but sometimes warnings are not addressed by programmers as rapidly as they should be. See Item 6.)

Programming languages, especially popular ones such as C and C++, will change over time. New features will be dreamed up, old features will evolve, and standards bodies will work through the details and produce new standards. Compiler vendors will then implement these new features and finally, programmers will learn about them and make use of them in their projects. In the process, lots of things can go wrong. Standards can be ill conceived. Compiler vendors can make mistakes when implementing new features or supply only partial implementations. Developers can misunderstand, or misuse, new features. Any of these potential failures can, in the end, conspire against you, affecting the stability and correctness of the code you write. Passing your code through multiple compilers, and testing the results rigorously, can help to identify these problems. If a particular compiler vendor is having problems implementing a language feature reliably, or the resulting code exhibits problems during execution, this might imply that the implementation is flawed, or that the standard itself is not really ready for prime-time usage. A subtle misunderstanding in how a particular language feature is to be used by the programmer (or implemented by the compiler vendor) can sometimes result in code that executes flawlessly when passed through one compiler, and a spectacular crash or runtime error when passed through another. Until all the compilers that you use in your project support a feature reliably, as required by the standard, and until the programs that are generated by these compilers using the new feature are fully tested and are known to execute correctly, it might be a good idea to avoid using any new language feature altogether. Doing so will help to ensure that you are working with something that has withstood the test of time, and won't come back to bite you, or your end users. After all, you were able to write great programs before the new language feature was introduced, right? I know I was!

Another important ramification of putting your code through different compilers is that, inevitably, different compilers generate different sets of warnings and errors, and this may lead to the discovery of problems in your code that might otherwise have gone unnoticed. This is particularly true when it comes to compiling code that uses complicated language features, features that are perhaps ill defined or, as discussed previously, features that are relatively new to the language. But, even compiling routine code lead to surprises. Take for example, the following code:

```
#include <stdio.h>

int
main(int argc, char *argv[])
{
    int i;

    printf("i is %d\n", i);
}
```

GCC, when compiled with no flags, doesn't mind at all that an uninitialized variable is being de-referenced; compiling the preceding code does not result in any warnings, or errors. Adding –Wall results in the same situation, no warnings. When given –Wextra, I get the following:

```
% gcc -o initialize –std=c99 –pedantic-errors -Wall -Wextra
initialize.c
initialize.c:4: warning: unused parameter 'argc'
initialize.c:4: warning: unused parameter 'argv'
```

Although this code caught unused variables `argc` and `argv` (arguably the compiler is complaining a bit much here, because `argc` and `argv` are often not used in simple C programs), it still did not catch the fact that I am using an uninitialized variable as an argument to `printf`. Referring to the man pages, I noticed that GCC has a –Wuninitialized flag. Trying this gets one the same result:

```
% gcc -o initialize –std=c99 –pedantic-errors -Wall \
    -Wextra -Wuninitialized initialize.c
ccl: warning: -Wuninitialized is not supported \
    without -O
initialize.c:4: warning: unused parameter 'argc'
initialize.c:4: warning: unused parameter 'argv'
```

Adding –O to the compile line, however, finally got me what I wanted:

```
% gcc -o initialize –std=c99 –pedantic-errors \
    -Wall -Wextra -Wuninitialized initialize.c -O
initialize.c: In function 'main':
initialize.c:8: warning: 'i' is used uninitialized \
    in this function
```

```
initialize.c: At top level:
initialize.c:4: warning: unused parameter 'argc'
initialize.c:4: warning: unused parameter 'argv'
```

As it turns out, the key arguments needed to see this warning with GCC are
–O and –Wall. But, it took a bit of playtime with the man page and compiler
flags to figure this out. Worse, I almost never do development with the opti-
mizer enabled, favoring debug builds, so it would have been a very long
time before I ran into this particular warning, if ever at all.

One final point about dealing with compiler errors and warnings: Even
if each and every compiler that you put your code through catches the same
problem/issue and reports it, the compiler warnings or errors that are generated by one compiler might be more easily understood than those generated
by the other compilers. If a compiler generates some warning or error that is
hard to decipher, running the offending code through another compiler may
help you to better understand, and deal with, the problem being reported,
and is certainly worth the effort.

Finally, different compilers generate different code and execute under
different runtimes. This is obvious when the compilers are targeting different CPUs (for instance, your product is designed to run on Windows XP and
PowerPC-based Mac OS X), but it is also true even with code that is being
generated for the same hardware platform. When languages are standardized, compiler vendors need to look for other ways to stand out in the mar-
ketplace, and runtime performance and code size are key ways for compiler
vendors to differentiate themselves from one another. Even if the goals are
the same, different compiler engineers are going to create different back
ends for their compilers.

Item 4: Require Developers to Build Their Code on Multiple Platforms

At Netscape, each developer who was working on the Netscape browser
(post version 4.x) or on the Mozilla codebase was supplied with a
Macintosh and a PC (which usually only ran Windows XP, but in some
cases dual-booted Linux; more on that below).

As you might guess, just like you, each developer at Netscape had a
development platform that he or she preferred to use for writing and debugging code. For most, the platform of choice was Windows XP, but there
were also sizable groups of developers within Netscape who called Mac OS

or Linux home. Much of the code could be written on whatever platform the developer preferred. (The cross-platform GUI code, written in XUL and JavaScript is an obvious example, but a lot of the C++ code in Mozilla is platform agnostic, too.) In some cases, however, the code in Mozilla/Netscape was highly platform specific, and developers were forced to write and debug their code using a specific operating system and toolchain.

Regardless of the platform a developer might prefer to use in his or her daily work, Netscape required all developers to build their code on all three platforms before checking in, even if the code was located in platform-specific areas of the source tree. Often, code reviewers would ask whether a developer had built the code being reviewed on all three platforms before giving it a successful code review, to help ensure that this policy was enforced. Why was this requirement put in place, and what were the ramifications?

As it turns out, all sorts of architectural dragons can rise up and bite you if you don't actually try to compile your work on each of the supported platforms before landing it in the repository. For example, consider an abstract interface that requires platform-specific, concrete implementations. How easy would it be to forget to provide a stub implementation of a concrete implementation for the other two platforms, resulting in a linker error? Or, how easy would it be to introduce a typo into the code that causes one of the platforms that you did not build for to fail at compile time? If that wasn't enough, it is easy to forget to add new files that you created for the project to the Makefiles for the other platforms, or make other Makefile-related changes, resulting once again in compile-time or link-time errors. These are all problems that I saw occur time and time again while at Netscape, causing developers, and those who policed the state of Tinderbox, all sorts of grief. (It also affected families of developers who caused the breakage to Tinderbox; sheriffs had the right to call developers who busted a tree at home if the problem could not be resolved without their help.)

I wasn't immune to this, and I recall causing trouble back then on at least one occasion by assuming, falsely, that some change I made on Linux would have no effect on either Windows or Mac OS, only then to see the Tinderboxes for those platforms burning brightly after I had committed to CVS. Had I simply pulled fresh trees on those platforms, applied my patch, and recompiled, I would have run into the problem and fixed it, avoiding the embarrassment of causing Tinderbox to burn, but more important, I would have saved other developers a lot of wasted time as they dealt with the problems that I had caused. Other developers are affected because when a tree becomes red in Tinderbox, developers who pull and build at about the same time as Tinderbox will also run into the same build (or runtime) errors.

A few more points related to this item are worth mentioning. First off, building and smoke testing on all platforms isn't just about keeping the tree in a happy state. It is also important to exercise the code (smoke test) and see whether it actually performs correctly on all the supported platforms. Although Tinderbox and QA/test are going to get around to it eventually, it really is a developer's job to at least make an attempt at ensuring that what he or she is submitting to the repository doesn't regress the product. This can only be done by building on the supported platforms and exercising the code.

Second, not all developers will want to, or be able to, abide by the rule to build code on all platforms before check-in. At Netscape, Mac OS was perhaps the platform that was least adopted by developers, especially pre-Mac OS X versions of the operating system, where the toolchain, Metrowerks CodeWarrior, was unfamiliar to many. (The other platforms, and later Mac OS X, are all built using gmake from the command line, whereas CodeWarrior was GUI based.) The way around this sort of situation is for developers who need assistance to find what we called at Netscape a "build buddy." A build buddy is a person who is willing to take a patch file, apply it to a local copy of the trunk, build it, and smoke test it. Usually, the developer who wrote the code will need to work with the build buddy, to help the build buddy through any issues with patching and testing. A build buddy is also useful in helping a developer navigate areas that are not familiar based on his or her knowledge of the platform involved. For example, the Mac OS build buddies at Netscape were often the ones who made the changes to the CodeWarrior project files, to absorb needed changes to how a project was built, to add new files to the project, or to create new project files for any new components that were being added.

However it is done (by the developer, or with the assistance of a build buddy), requiring developers to build and smoke test on all platforms before landing changes will go a long way toward ensuring a stable tree, and eliminating bottlenecks that may cause other developers on the project to be blocked from doing their work and meeting their deadlines.

Building on different platforms usually (but does not always) implies building code with different compilers. Item 3 explores the ramifications of this in more detail.

There are some real benefits to building on multiple platforms. Linux, for example, has some wonderful tools, such as valgrind, that can help you to isolate memory problems, even if they first manifest themselves as bugs on Windows or Mac OS X, and they are available at no cost. If you are developing for Mac OS X and Windows, chances are Windows is going to have better tools for use in analyzing such errors than Mac OS X. Crashes or other bugs that are hard to debug on Linux might be easier to isolate by using Microsoft's debugger; although I'm very comfortable using the GNU debugger (gdb), sometimes I do prefer using Microsoft's debugger to analyze the state of a program, and I can only do that if my code is building everywhere (not just on Linux).

Finally, forcing developers to build and test on all three platforms before checking code into the repository helps to enforce the goal (see Item 1) of making sure all platforms are developed at the same time, greatly improving your chances of a successful cross-platform deployment.

In writing this, I am reminded of another major piece of software that must have benefited greatly from being built on multiple platforms concurrently: Apple's Mac OS X. In June 2005, Apple Computer announced that they would be migrating their entire line of Macintosh computers from PowerPC over to Intel-based processors. This switch was done mainly because the PowerPC architecture was not keeping pace with the performance gains seen by Intel's line of CPUs, and perhaps more important, the G5 (the last, and fastest of the PowerPC chips used by Apple) ran too hot to be used in laptop computers. (Laptops were, and are, a very important product for Apple.) Apple made the entire transition to the Intel-based hardware in a short period of time, by August 2006, and the software ported included not only the Mac OS X operating system, but also all the applications that Apple normally bundles with Mac OS X. The major reason for this remarkable achievement was that Apple had been secretly maintaining Intel-based versions of the Mac OS X operating system since its introduction in the late 1990s. There is no doubt in my mind that not only did this help accelerate the release of Intel-based Macintosh computers, but it also helped to make Mac OS X for PowerPC a much more robust operating system, because building software for multiple platforms invariably leads to better written software. Microsoft Windows NT, for a time, was available for the DEC Alpha processor, but Microsoft abandoned it, presumably because the market for Alpha-based machines was so minimal. In defense of Microsoft, Windows is a beast of an ecosystem, with a much greater legacy than Mac OS X and a lot of nonportable applications to support, perhaps making support of anything other than Intel-based processors highly impractical. One can only wonder how much Microsoft Windows (and end users) would have benefited from Windows being maintained on Alpha (or some other processor); surely some nasty bugs and security exploits would have been uncovered if cross-CPU portability had been attempted.

Item 5: Test Builds on Each Supported Platform

If you want (or need) to ship all platforms concurrently (Item 1), it is best to ensure that all platforms move forward at the same pace during development. To do this requires a lot of coordination, not the least of which, testing. At Netscape, each of the three tier-1 platforms (Mac OS, Linux, Windows) were subjected to testing each and every morning in an attempt to catch bugs that might have crept into the product during the previous day's (and night's) round of check-ins to the CVS repository. It was particularly important that this be done because, as I mention in Item 4, not every developer who is checking into a source code repository will be as complete as he or she should be in terms of cross-platform testing; unit testing of platforms other than the one the developer created and debugged the code on (usually Windows XP) did not always occur as it should have at Netscape. Even then, unit testing has its limits, so even if developers did their due diligence and unit tested on each platform, they were unlikely to be as complete in their smoke testing of the overall product as would be the test engineers assigned to the project.

To perform the smoke testing, early each morning, Tinderbox builds were collected and sent to QA. At this time, all check-ins to the tree were halted until smoke testing was completed. QA teams inside of Netscape were organized around features in the Netscape application suite. There was a QA team, for example, that specialized in testing the mail component; another team was dedicated to testing the browser, and so on. These teams, like developers, all had physical access to each of the tier-1 platforms and ran smoke tests on each.

Usually, smoke testing would take a few hours to complete. If testing of any of the platform builds generated a new problem, both Tinderbox and bonsai would be used to try to isolate the issue to a particular check-in that had been made from the day before. All developers who checked in during the past 24 hours (or 72 hours, if it was a Monday morning) needed to be available during this time, in one way or another, to respond to a plea for help should any problems arise with a check-in that they had made. If the developer was not available for some reason, the person(s) who did the code review would be called upon to help. (Each check-in to CVS required notation in the check-in log as to who performed the code review, making it possible to identify the code reviewers.) If the problem was trivial to fix, a check-in to CVS was made to resolve the issue. In more severe cases, the developer was asked to back out the change entirely from CVS. When all the problems, if any, were cleared up, the tree would reopen for check-ins. And the process would continue.

It was amazing to see how well this worked, and the amount of support from the developers that the policy enjoyed. To cause Tinderbox to go red was bad, but to cause a regression in smoke testing was even worse. I know that I, for one, made certain that I did all I could to try to catch problems on all the platforms before I landed anything into CVS. When I was a code reviewer, I made sure that the developer at least told me that he or she had tried to test on all platforms, or had asked for help in doing so. I don't think I was alone, and I think this culture we embraced at Netscape (and at Mozilla) was a major contributor to the consistent level of quality seen on Mac, Linux, and Windows whenever the browser suite was released.

In truth, there is not much else to say. The key idea is this: It is not enough to just claim you want to support a cross-platform product. One must enforce it, and that can only be done by frequent testing, and engaging oneself in a development process that does not allow problems to go undetected, nor when detected, allowed to persist.

Item 6: Pay Attention to Compiler Warnings

No doubt you have seen them scroll by during a build: compiler warnings. Uninitialized variables, nonvoid functions that don't return a value, comparisons involving a conversion from one type to another, among other conditions that are flagged by the compiler as being questionable. Many of us simply ignore these warnings and move on; after all, they are just warnings, not errors, and by stopping to fix these warnings, we would consume precious time that is otherwise needed for other development tasks.

However, warnings are a compiler's way of telling you about uncertainty: that the code it is generating on your behalf may lead to undefined or incorrect behavior at runtime. When other platforms are added to the mix, this uncertainty takes on another dimension because each platform may deal with the warned issue in different ways at runtime, which leads to a near certainty that the code causing the compiler warning will not be portable.

At Netscape, fixing compiler warnings was not universally mandated at first. Eventually, however, it became clear to developers and management that fixing warnings had a major upside in terms of stability and portability. At that point, two changes to the culture occurred. First, Netscape allocated a period of time during which developers, in addition to their normal duties, carefully looked for warnings in compiler output and checked in patches to address the warnings found. The overall goal was to rid the source of any code that resulted in a warning being generated. Second, Tinderbox (see Item 12) was modified so that it displayed a count of warnings generated during a build. Those monitoring Tinderbox (sheriffs) could close a tree for check-ins if the warning situation was showing signs of regressing.

Probably the most important compiler options affecting portability are those designed to enforce standards compliance and generate errors and warnings when such compliance is not met. In general, the code that you and your teammates write is more likely to be portable if it follows a standards-based definition of the language. This is based on the assumption that a compiler vendor that adheres to a given standard will generate the same result for a given input that some other compiler vendor, following the exact same standard, would generate given the same input. Compiler vendors have a distinct advantage when following a standard, in that the standard determines what syntax is allowed (and the semantics behind it). Compiler vendors are left to differentiate product based on user interface, speed of compilation, and code optimization.

The following describes compiler flags that I recommend using. These flags will cause your code to conform to language standards, and will cause the compiler to generate warnings when the conditions of such standards are not met, as well as complain when otherwise standard-conformant code is of a questionable nature (for example, it involves the use of uninitialized variables).

GNU Flags

The following GNU compiler flags, primarily applicable to Mac OS X and Linux platforms (but also supported on Windows if you use g++ to compile Windows sources for your project), are, in my opinion, the most effective when it comes to generating warnings and ensuring that your code adheres to standard C++.

-Wall

-Wall will enable most of the warning flags that g++ is capable of generating, with some exceptions; for example, the "Effective C++" warnings enabled by -Weffc++ (yes, there is such a flag; see *Effective C++* [Addison-Wesley, 2005], by Scott Myers) are not enabled by -Wall; see the man page for details.

-Werror

The -Werror flag will cause the discovery of warnings to fail the build (that is, it turns the warnings into errors), requiring you to fix them, instead of ignoring them.

-std=c++98

Using this argument to g++ causes the compiler to follow the 1998 ISO C++ language standard.

-pedantic-errors

The -pedantic-errors flag can be used to ensure that only strictly ISO-standard-conformant C++ code is ever allowed to compile successfully. A compile of code that is not strictly conformant will fail to complete; what might be warnings with -std become errors when -pedantic-errors is used, because it will not let you ignore any standards violations in your code or allow any GNU extensions to be used. The use of GNU extensions would certainly be a deal killer when trying to port your code to another compiler, for example, Microsoft Visual C++.

Microsoft Visual C++

The following compiler flags, specific to Visual C++ on Windows, are roughly analogous to those listed above for GNU g++ on Linux and Mac OS X. Some of you might be thinking that if you build your code using g++, along with the compiler flags listed in the previous section, then you don't need to enable the following flags for Visual C++ since g++ already has you covered, so to speak. However, it is possible, perhaps it is even likely, that code that would lead to the issuance of warnings by one compiler will be missed by another compiler (see Item 3). Therefore, to maximize your chances of identifying and correcting code that might be questionable, I feel it is best to enable high warning levels in all compilers used by your cross-platform project.

/Wn

The /Wn flag is used to define the warning level to n, which can be 1, 2, 3, or 4. By default, level 2 warnings are automatically generated by Visual C++. For new code, it is recommended by Microsoft that you set the warning level to 4 to generate the maximum amount of noise possible.

/Wall

/Wall is analogous to g++'s –Wall, enabling all warnings, including those that are normally disabled by default.

/WX

The /WX flag is like g++'s –Werror flag, because when specified, it causes all warnings to be treated as errors. Thus, when enabled, your project will fail to build should the compiler encounter any conditions that lead to the issuance of a warning, forcing you to deal with the warning, instead of ignoring it.

/Za

Specifying /Za on the command line is roughly analogous to the –std=c++98 flag in g++. (At the time of writing, Microsoft states that Visual C++ conforms to the following language standards: ISO C 95, ISO C++ 98, and Ecma C++/CLI 05.) When /Za is specified, language constructs that are not compatible with ANSI C++ will result in errors. Without it, language extensions specific to Microsoft will be enabled. These extensions can be viewed by searching for "Microsoft Extensions to C and C++" at www.msdn.com.

2 Build System/Toolchain

A *toolchain* is software that is used by developers to write, compile, and debug code. The major components of a toolchain are the editor, the compiler, and the debugger. Ask an experienced developer to name his or her preferred set of tools, and you are certain to get a quick, and likely passionate, response. To be sure, preferences vary and certainly, one cannot expect a developer's favorite setup to be available on all the other platforms your project must support. (It's going to be a very long time before Visual C++ is ported to Linux, I can promise you, although there was a [short] time that it was actually available for Solaris.) And if available, they may not be the best possible choice.

Beyond developer comfort and preference, one must also consider the following:

- Quality of the end result. Does the tool generate the best code, and does it provide the best support possible for catching errors and debugging them before the code gets installed by the end user?
- Does the tool support features that result in a program that integrates properly with the target platform? If the product supports a user interface, are the application programming interfaces (APIs) for the user interface toolkit of choice supported?
- Does the use of a given tool foster ease of administration or make administration more difficult?

As mentioned in this book's Introduction, abstraction is a key enabler of success in any cross-platform project. As you may well know, the use of platform-specific toolkits and libraries often requires the use of platform-specific toolchains. For example, Cocoa on Mac OS X requires the use of the Objective-C language, which is only supported by GCC, Microsoft tools are needed to create a .NET GUI, and so on. To support this, Netscape and Mozilla used abstraction and relevant design patterns such as a compile-time factory to provide a platform-neutral API that sits above the platform-specific APIs of graphical user interface (GUI) toolkits such as Gtk+, Mac OS toolkit, Cocoa, and Win32. In this chapter, we focus on elements of the toolchain. See Items 22, 23, and Chapter 9, "Developing a Cross-Platform GUI Toolkit in C++," for more information about the GUI software supported by the toolchain strategy described here.

Item 7: Use Whatever Compiler Makes the Most Sense for a Platform

This may at first seem like a contradiction, but when it comes to choosing a compiler for a cross-platform project, it is usually best to select whatever compiler and linker has the best *native* support for the given platform. On Windows, this typically means using Visual C++, and GNU g++ on Mac OS X and Linux. In order to produce cross-platform code, you need not standardize all your platforms upon a single toolchain.

Besides the potential for better support and performance, there are some perhaps less-than-obvious advantages to *not* choosing a cross-platform compiler. By introducing a different compiler into the project, you will be less likely to write compiler-specific code (code that depends on compiler-specific flags and extensions is inherently nonportable) because code compiled against a compiler that makes use of a compiler-specific feature will cause the code to fail when compiled using a compiler that does not provide support for the feature. By using a different compiler, you will also be exposing yourself to different sets of compiler warnings and errors (see Item 6).

When it comes to developing GUI applications that make calls to native GUI toolkit APIs, one often has little choice in terms of which compiler must be used. Mac OS X GUI applications are implemented using Cocoa, for example. Cocoa is Objective-C/C++ based and the only compiler available for Mac OS X that supports Objective C/C++ is GCC. (The freely available Apple compiler, Xcode, is really just an IDE implemented above GCC.) On Windows, development of .NET GUI applications requires a compiler that can compile code written for the .NET Common Language

Runtime (CLR), and this pretty much restricts you to using Visual Studio .NET or some third-party compiler other than GCC. The point is, when it comes to compilers, you can make a choice that is best for your product in terms of platform support and performance. As long as you ensure that code common to all platforms adheres to C and C++ standards and these standards are supported by all the compilers you choose, and as long as you hide any platform-specific code behind suitable abstractions, you should feel free to use whatever compiler performs the best for a given platform, and is most comfortable for developers on that platform to work with.

Item 8: Use Native IDEs When Appropriate

Item 10 describes GNU make (gmake), autoconf/automake, and Imake, which are cross-platform tools that can be used in the design and implementation of a build system for your cross-platform project. In this item, I briefly mention the role of IDEs (such as Visual Studio .NET and others) in the context of a cross-platform development project that is based on gmake.

Early on, the Mozilla project source was built using nmake on Windows, Metrowerks CodeWarrior IDE on Mac OS System 7/8/9 (the start of the Mozilla project predated Apple's introduction of Mac OS X), and gmake on UNIX-like platforms. On Mac OS, the CodeWarrior IDE was not run directly, but was launched and controlled through a combination of Perl and AppleScript scripts; this automation was needed to support building Mozilla for Mac OS via Tinderbox (see Item 12), and it definitely made life easier on developers as well. Windows programmers used the Visual Studio IDE to edit source files and to debug applications. (In my opinion, Visual Studio's debugger is the best available for the platform.) Likewise, Mac OS developers relied on CodeWarrior's excellent debugger to debug code.

When the switch to autoconf/automake and gmake builds occurred, the use of IDEs for source code editing and debugging did not go away.

While developers were free to use IDEs to edit and debug code, there were some guidelines that were followed. Regarding editors, the major concern was with tabs and line endings. It is important to standardize a project on the use of tabs and line endings so that the formatting the programmer intended is reproduced faithfully, regardless of the editor one uses. To do this, I recommend the following:

■ Configure the editor to expand tabs into spaces, with three or four spaces per tab. For the vi editor, you can do this by adding the following lines to a file named .vimrc in your home directory:

```
set expandtab
set tabstop=4
```

Both Visual Studio's editor and the Xcode editor can be configured using their settings GUIs to convert tabs into a specified number of spaces.

■ Ensure that lines of text end with newlines. On Linux and Mac OS X, this is the default. Visual Studio also uses this as a default, but not all editors do. When installing Cygwin (see Item 9), make sure to choose the UNIX line endings option when prompted.

As far as debugging goes, on Mac OS X, you can use the Xcode IDE to debug applications that were compiled with gmake by launching the application and then attaching the debugger to the running process. The same is true for Windows and Linux, too, using Visual Studio's debugger and gdb, respectively.

Let's see how you can attach an IDE debugger to a running process on both Windows and Mac OS X. (I'll assume that under Linux, you are using gdb. There is a graphical debugger under Linux named DDD, but I don't cover its use here.)

To debug a process on Windows, you just press Ctrl-Alt-Delete to bring up the Windows Task Manager, select the Processes tab, and locate the process that is to be debugged in the list. After you have located the process, select the process with the mouse, right-click to bring up a context menu (see Figure 2-1), and then choose Debug. This process launches the Visual Studio debugger. There is no need to create a Visual Studio project beforehand to debug; just locate a file in the source tree, open it, and set breakpoints; that's all that is needed.

In Mac OS X, when using the Xcode debugger, things are a bit more difficult. You must create an Xcode project to debug a binary, and then open that project in the Xcode environment. Here is a summary of the steps provided by Apple. Search for "Debugging Arbitrary Applications with Xcode" at http://developer.apple.com for this and other details regarding using the Xcode debugger:

1. In Xcode, create a new, empty project to manage the executable environment for the application. Choose File, New Project, and then select Empty Project and follow the instructions in the dialog that appears.

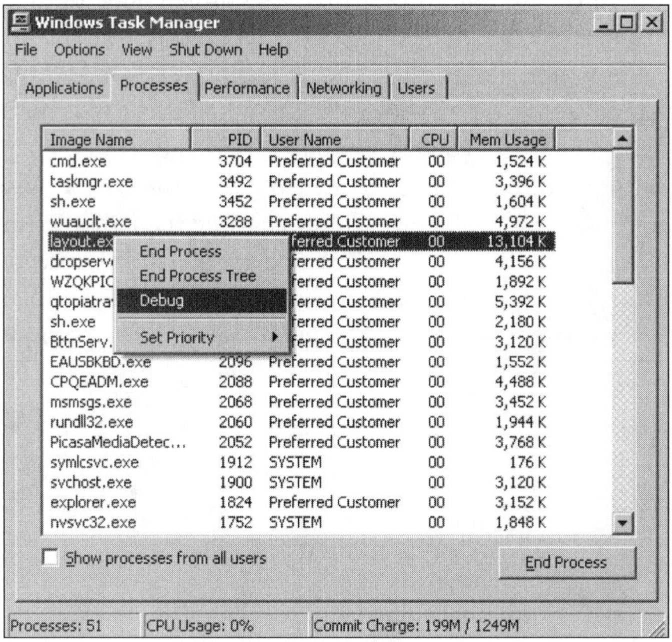

Figure 2-1 Attaching Visual Studio debugger to a process

2. Create a new custom executable environment for the application. To do this, choose Project, New Custom Executable. When done, click Finish.
3. After you have done this, you can open up a terminal window, launch the application, launch Xcode, open the project, and then attach the debugger to the application using the Attach menu item in Xcode's Debug menu. You'll probably need to click the Continue button in the debugger to cause the application to continue.

Another option for debugging under Mac OS X visually is to install X11 and the DDD debugger. You can search Google for "DDD Mac OS X" to get a download for DDD; X11 is available for install directly from the Mac OS X installation DVD provided by Apple.

Of course, the GNU debugger (gdb) is always an option for Mac OS X. Both Xcode and DDD debuggers are actually graphical front ends to gdb.

Before I leave the topic of debugging, I want to share one trick with you, and that is how to cause your application to go into the Visual Studio debugger on Windows without actually attaching to a process. (This technique is required if your application, as assumed here, does not have a project file from which it can be launched.) To do this, you just make a call at the point you would like to enter the debugger at to an API available in Windows that causes it, effectively, to fault. When this call is made, you will be given a dialog that tells you the application has generated an exception, and that gives you an opportunity to attach the process to the Visual Studio debugger to debug the "problem." This technique really comes in handy if your application is not based on an IDE project file and you need to get into the debugger very early in the life of the application (for example, in main()). The call, itself, is simple (__debugbreak() , for example):

```
int
main(int argc, char *argv[])
{
    __debugbreak();

...

    return 0;
}
```

In Mac OS X, you can simply use gdb to launch the program and set a breakpoint before issuing the gdb "run" command. For Xcode debugging, you have a debugger window via the project file, so opening the project, launching the debugger, and setting a breakpoint before launching the application from within the debugger is all you need to do.

Returning to the topic of IDEs, we can summarize the situation by saying that it is always okay to use an IDE for editing and debugging, but you really should avoid using an IDE in place of gmake (or some other command-line-based build system) when it comes to architecting a solution to your build system. Consider a hypothetical project that starts out as Windows only, with the intent of porting everything later to Mac OS X. (This should be a red flag already because it violates the suggestions made in Item 1.) Besides all the problems caused by not making Mac OS X equal in priority to Windows at the start of the project, assume that the lead developer makes the poor decision to base the implementation of the build system on Visual Studio-based project files. (It is common for Windows developers to create projects through the IDE and let the IDE manage the builds.) Making the build system IDE based makes it very difficult later in the project when it becomes time to port to Mac OS X; the IDE-based projects will have to be replaced with Makefiles. Doing so would be disruptive; it would have been much better for the project, in addition to coding for Mac OS X from the start, to use Makefiles from the beginning when the project was small and there was enough time to get a solution together without causing disruption at a later stage of the project.

Item 9: Install and Use Cygwin on Windows

This item is mainly for those UNIX developers who might be forced from time to time while working on a cross-platform development project to build or debug on a Windows system, and for build-system architects who need to come up with a build system that scales across Windows, Linux, and Mac OS X platforms.

UNIX-based operating systems are well known (well, at least to UNIX-based developers) for being a command-line tool paradise. If you are developing an application for Windows, Mac OS X, and Linux, Windows is somewhat of an oddball platform because, of the three, Windows is the only platform that is not UNIX-like. (Technically speaking, Linux is not UNIX, but is UNIX-like, and Mac OS X is based on Darwin, which is based on the BSD variant of UNIX, which is not UNIX, either. But I digress.) Because it is not UNIX-like, Windows is missing the rich arsenal of command-line tools available under Linux and Mac OS X.

This poses a problem; the Linux and Mac OS X developers on a cross-platform project may need, from time to time, to write or (more likely) debug code on Windows systems. If and when they do need to spend time on a Windows-based system, the tools that they rely on will be missing. Tools such as `grep`, which they might want to use to find content in files, or the `find` command, which is used to locate files in a file system, or `od`, which is used to dump the contents of a file in various formats, will not be available to them. There are literally dozens of command-line tools that UNIX developers may find useful in solving engineering problems, and the lack of access to these tools on a Windows system will be frustrating to most UNIX developers.

I acknowledge that debugging code on a Windows system is going to be the exception for Mac OS X and Linux developers, not the norm. And I acknowledge that a skilled UNIX developer can be taught the basics of attaching a process to the Visual Studio debugger and setting breakpoints to investigate a crash. Still, a UNIX developer is going to be less productive, depending on the context, without access to the tools he or she is used to.

To level the playing field, UNIX developers can install Cygwin on their Windows system. Cygwin is "a Linux-like environment for Windows." It consists of three parts:

- A dynamic link library (DLL) that implements much of the core (that is, POSIX) APIs that programmers on UNIX-like systems are familiar with
- Ports of open source UNIX libraries that require the above DLL to execute
- A rich set of UNIX command-line tools and languages, distributed in binary form

The Cygwin DLL and the library ports are intended to aid developers in recompiling UNIX command-line applications for Windows, and are not of interest to us in this item. What *is* of interest to us here are the command-line tools that the Cygwin environment provides. From my experience, pretty much anything you would want in terms of UNIX command-line tools is available in Cygwin. In particular, let's turn our attention to the build system. Although a Mac OS X (or Linux) developer might never have to sit down on a Windows machine, the architect of the build system is not so lucky. The job of the build-system architect is to come up with a portable cross-platform build solution. If you are supporting Linux, Mac OS X, and Windows, UNIX-based command-line tools are available to help you with your job natively on both Linux and Mac OS X; and with Cygwin, they can be available on all three. Contrast this to Windows shell commands, which are only available on Windows. The Mozilla project's build system is based on the following UNIX command-line tools, all available in Cygwin:

- bash (sh)
- make
- perl
- grep
- awk
- cvs
- autoconf

Item 10 suggests that you consider using GNU make (gmake) as the basis of your build system, and Cygwin is the place to go for a Windows port of gmake. Shell scripts, often a needed part of a build system, can be written in sh, a far more powerful shell than the DOS shell. The Bourne Again Shell (also known as bash or sh) is also a part of Cygwin, and scripts written against bash should port effortlessly to Mac OS X and, of course,

Linux. In the Trixul build system, I use sh scripts to kick off the build, and to perform initialization tasks needed at the start of the build. I use Cygwin's uname command to determine the operating system building built, and then, based on the operating system, use other commands (such as mkdir and cp) to set up a directory structure to hold the results of the build. Then, platform-specific builds of libraries used by the application are copied into the directory structure. (The Makefiles set the library search patch to point into dist so that collisions with system versions of the libraries are avoided. The application ships with the libraries that are used to create the build.)

The following is a subset of the sh script that does the above work. The first line executes uname to get the platform name ("Linux", "Darwin", or "NT"). It then looks at the result and rewrites the platform variable, which is used in commands later in the script:

```
platform=`uname`;
echo "Configure begin";
if [ `echo $platform | grep -i "Linux"` ]
then
platform="linux"
fi
if [ `echo $platform | grep -i "Darwin"` ]
then
platform="macosx"
fi
if [ `echo $platform | grep -i "NT"` ]
then
platform="windows"
fi
```

Now that the platform variable is set, we can create the dist directory, where the results of the build will be copied. For example, if the platform variable is set to "linux", the directory dist/linux will be created:

```
if [ ! -d dist ]
then
    mkdir dist
fi
if [ ! -d dist/$platform ]
then
    echo "Creating dist/$platform..."
    mkdir dist/$platform
fi
```

What follows in the script are blocks of code that perform platform-specific duties. One of the major tasks performed by the script is setting up a directory structure into which the results of the build are copied. The `dist` directory, created in this step, contains all the files needed for application execution; I usually keep a terminal window open that has the `dist` directory for the platform being built as its current directory, and from there, run the application after each successful build. As it turns out, a specific directory structure layout is mandated by Mac OS X for applications, so in the script, if the platform variable was set to `"macosx"`, a block of code is executed that creates, below `dist`, the required directory structure, and also creates two files, PkgInfo and Info.plist, which are also required by Mac OS X. The other major task performed by the script is to copy prebuilt libraries taken from the Concurrent Version System (CVS) repository (for example, the open source library expat) into the `dist` directory, where they are needed.

Here is the code that performs the platform-specific setup of the `dist` directory:

```
echo "Configuring for $platform."
if [ $platform = "macosx" ]
then
echo "Creating release structure..."
if [ ! -d dist/$platform/debug/layout.app ]
then
    mkdir dist/$platform/debug/layout.app
fi
if [ ! -d dist/$platform/release/layout.app ]
then
    mkdir dist/$platform/release/layout.app
fi
...
echo "Generating PkgInfo file..."
echo "APPL????" > \
    dist/$platform/release/layout.app/Contents/PkgInfo
echo "Copying Info.plist file..."
sed -e 's/LAYOUT_VERSION/$version/' \
    install/macosx/Info.plist > dist/$platform/release/layout.app/Contents/Info.plist
...
else
if [ $platform = "linux" ]
then
echo "Copying debug libs...";
cp -r libs/nspr4-3/linux/lib/debug/*.* \
    dist/linux/debug/
```

```
cp -r libs/expat-1.95.6/linux/lib/debug/*.* \
    dist/linux/debug/
echo "Copying release libs...";
cp -r libs/nspr4-3/linux/lib/release/*.* \
    dist/linux/release/
cp -r libs/expat-1.95.6/linux/lib/release/*.* \
    dist/linux/release/
...
else
if [ $platform = "windows" ]
then
echo "Copying debug libs...";
cp -r libs/nspr4-3/windows/lib/debug/*.* \
    dist/windows/debug/
cp dist/windows/debug/libnspr4.dll \
    dist/windows/debug/nspr4.dll
cp -r libs/expat-1.95.6/windows/lib/debug/*.* \
    dist/windows/debug/
echo "Copying release libs...";
cp -r libs/nspr4-3/windows/lib/release/*.* \
    dist/windows/release/
cp dist/windows/release/libnspr4.dll \
    dist/windows/release/nspr4.dll
cp -r libs/expat-1.95.6/windows/lib/release/*.* \
    dist/windows/release/
echo "Copying includes...";
...
fi
fi
fi

echo "Configure done"
```

In the preceding script, a number of UNIX commands were used:

- **cp**—Copy a file from one location to another
- **echo**—Display a message to stdout (the screen)
- **mkdir**—Create a directory
- **sed**—A stream editor that can be used to modify the contents of a file directly from a script

These commands are all provided by Cygwin, making the script highly portable. The above script, named setup, is run from a DOS command window like this:

```
C:/> sh setup
```

Installing Cygwin is fairly simple. Visit www.cygwin.com, download the installer from one of the mirrors, and run it. If you have the room, install all of it. Otherwise, the installer allows you to select packages for installation in terms of categories. (You can view the list of packages at http://cygwin.com/packages/.) Categories that you will want to include in your install are the Base category and the Devel category. Once installed, you can launch a shell by opening up a DOS command window and typing `sh` (or `bash`) at the prompt. However, as mentioned previously, you can execute bash shell scripts from a DOS command line (or a DOS bat file) by running the `sh` command and specifying the path of the script as an argument.

It's not always going to be the case that a solution like Cygwin presents itself; you might be required to support a platform that does not have support for UNIX-like commands. If you are limiting your platform support to UNIX-like systems and Windows, however, using Cygwin just makes things easier.

Item 16 also describes Cygwin, and its use in developing portable applications based on the POSIX standards.

Item 10: Use a Cross-Platform Make System

This item covers the important topic of managing and building source code in a portable manner. Even the simplest cross-platform project can become chaotic if attention is not given to how to build and maintain source portably, and it gets even more chaotic when large numbers of people become involved.

It's probably fair to guess that most of you have, at one time or another, made use of some tool to automate the building of software. An IDE like Microsoft's Visual Studio or Apple's Project Builder certainly makes things simple; you supply a list of source files, and by clicking a button or two in the user interface of the IDE, your software is built. Some of you, because you live in an IDE most of the time, probably are not able to list, with any certainty, half of the flags that are passed to your compiler during a build, or perhaps you don't even know how to invoke the compiler from a command line. All of this is fine and well, to an extent. However, using a proprietary IDEs usually flies in the face of portability. To be truly portable, you need to walk away from using IDEs and instead use a cross-platform solution.

There are several ways to manage builds in a cross-platform way, and at the heart of each of these is a program named make, which I describe in the follow section.

Make

The make utility has long been a part of the UNIX and Windows toolset. Ignoring IDEs for the moment, it is impossible to conceive of building anything other than the simplest of projects without use of a tool like make. To understand why make is as valuable as I claim, let's start at the bottom of the food chain and work our way up.

Assume you have a program named bar that consists of two C++ source files bar.cpp and main.cpp, and a header file named bar.h, as shown in the following listings.

main.cpp

```
#include "bar.h"

int
main(int argc, char *argv[])
{
    Bar bar;

    bar.SetBar(17);
    bar.PutBar();
}
```

bar.h

```
#ifndef __BAR_00__
#define __BAR_00__

class Bar
{
public:
    void SetBar(int bar);
    void PutBar();
private:
    int m_bar;
};
```

bar.cpp

```
#include <stdlib.h>
#include <stdio.h>
#include "bar.h"

void Bar::SetBar(int bar)
{
    m_bar = bar;
}

void Bar::PutBar()
{
    char buf[16];
    snprintf(buf, , sizeof(buf) - 1, "%d", m_bar);
    setenv("BAR", buf, 1);
}
```

There is nothing special about this code. All that a Bar object does is maintain an integer, m_bar. The value of m_bar can be set by making a call to SetBar(), and the function PutBar() does nothing more than cause the value of m_bar to be stored in an environment variable named BAR. Totally useless as far as applications go, but perfect for illustration purposes.

Let's start simple by creating a shell script named build.sh that compiles and links these sources into an debug application named bar:

```
#!/bin/sh
g++ -g -o bar bar.cpp main.cpp
```

And which we can execute as follows:

```
$ sh build.sh
$ .
```

For building such a simple program, a shell script isn't that bad of a solution, at least at first blush. Type a short command, wait perhaps 500 milliseconds, and then out pops an executable. Clearly, this is much better than typing the command by hand each time you want to build something. However, there are definitely problems with this approach, including the following:

- Try executing the preceding script on Windows. Unless Cygwin (see Item 9), or some package that provides an implementation of sh(1), has been installed on the Windows system, the preceding shell script is not going to execute.

- The C++ compiler might not be g++, but some other compiler (for example Visual C++).
- The compiler, because of the platform the code is being built on, may require different arguments than those that are being passed by the preceding script.
- Each time the script executes, the developer is forced to build all the sources from scratch. Although this might not be a big problem for a small set of source files, such as those in the preceding example, building larger projects from scratch each time a change is made to the sources is usually not practical.

The make utility strives to overcome these problems. In essence, make enables you to execute a set of commands to obtain a target, or a result, from a set of known dependencies. In the preceding example, the target is an executable named bar, the dependencies are the source files bar.cpp and main.cpp, and the command that generates the executable for the sources is g++ -o bar bar.cpp main.cpp. Make requires you to specify the targets, dependencies, and commands in a file, typically named Makefile. The following Makefile can be used to build our example program:

```
bar: bar.cpp main.cpp
    g++ -g -o bar bar.cpp main.cpp
```

Given this Makefile, we can type the following command:

```
$ make
```

And make will generate a program named bar.

Let's take a look at the list of the four issues raised against using shell scripts and see how using make addresses each of them:

- Make doesn't shield us from the tools portability issue. On Windows, make is not a native application as it is on Linux and Mac OS X. Microsoft Visual C++ provides a make utility named nmake, but nmake and GNU make are not compatible, so you will want to install either Cygwin or MinGW and use GNU make on Windows, Mac OS X, and Linux. From here on out, when I mention make, I am referring to GNU make.

- The preceding Makefile still does not address the problem of specifying a different compiler to build the project.
- Similarly, the command-line arguments remain hard-coded.
- Overcoming the dependencies problem is perhaps the most dramatic advantage we have gained by moving to the simple Makefile above. Make will execute the command to rebuild bar if and only if the modification time of the source code is later in time than the modification time of the executable (or if the execute does not exist yet).

Can we improve upon the preceding Makefile? Absolutely.

In the preceding Makefile, we build both bar.cpp and main.cpp, even if only one of bar.cpp or main.cpp is modified. It would be better to build only those files that had changed. We haven't specified the dependency that both main.cpp and bar.cpp have on the bar.h include file. Whenever bar.h changes, we want make to rebuild both main.cpp and bar.cpp.

To solve these problems, we can once again rewrite the Makefile, as follows:

```
bar: bar.o main.o
        g++ -g -o bar main.o bar.o

bar.o: bar.cpp bar.h
        g++ -g -c bar.cpp

main.o: main.cpp bar.h
        g++ -g -c main.cpp
```

The preceding Makefile addresses the dependency issues by introducing two new targets, bar.o and main.o. The dependencies are now specific to the target, so bar.o should be rebuilt if bar.cpp and bar.h change, for example. The dependencies for bar itself have been changed; bar is dependent on the object files, not the sources. By touching main.cpp and then reissuing the make command, we will get the following result:

```
$ touch main.cpp
$ make
g++ -g -c main.cpp
g++ -g -o bar bar.o main.o
$
```

Notice that make only rebuilt the main.o and bar targets, which is the expected result because these are the only targets affected by a change to main.cpp. There are still two issues that remain, however: The compiler and the command-line arguments are still hard-coded. These issues can be solved by using macros, as in the following example:

```
OBJS = bar.o main.o
CXXFLAGS = -g

bar: $(OBJS)
    $(CXX) $(CXXFLAGS) -o $@ $(OBJS)

bar.o: bar.cpp bar.h
    $(CXX) $(CXXFLAGS) -c bar.cpp

main.o: main.cpp bar.h
    $(CXX) $(CXXFLAGS) -c main.cpp
```

We can improve this file even more by noticing that the only dependency each .o file has is on its corresponding .cpp file, and bar.h, and by using additional make facilities such as pattern rules, we can further simplify our Makefile:

```
OBJS = bar.o main.o
CXXFLAGS = -g

bar: $(OBJS)
        $(CXX) $(CXXFLAGS) -o $@ $(OBJS)

%.o : %.cpp
        $(CXX) $(CXXFLAGS) -c $<

$(OBJS) : bar.h
```

We have improved things, but we still have some issues. Factoring the -g out of the commands and placing it in a macro named CXXFLAGS is a big improvement, but it is still hard-coded into the Makefile, and, even worse, it is decoupled from the compiler: If CXX were set to something other than g++ by make, the -g flag might mean something entirely different than it does when passed to g++, or it might mean nothing at all.

Building on Windows

Let's see what happens when we move the Makefile and sources to Windows and then try to build the program. For the purposes of this

discussion, we assume that we do not have Cygwin installed on the
Windows system.

First, let's try typing make and see what happens:

```
C:\>make
'make' is not recognized as an internal or external command.
```

This tells us, obviously, that make is not available, which is not surprising,
given make is not native on Windows and Cygwin has been installed. We
can do two things at this point to get around this hurdle. Installing Cygwin
will provide us with a copy of GNU make, and with GNU make we will get
the same results as would be seen on Mac OS X or Linux. However, let's try
the second option, and invoke Microsoft's nmake utility to see what
happens:

```
C:\>nmake -f Makefile

Microsoft (R) Program Maintenance Utility   \
    Version 6.00.8168.0
Copyright (C) Microsoft Corp 1988-1998. \
    All rights reserved.


        cl -g -o bar bar.o main.o
Microsoft (R) 32-bit C/C++ Optimizing Compiler \
    Version 12.00.8804 for 80x86
Copyright (C) Microsoft Corp 1984-1998. \
    All rights reserved.

Command line warning D4002 : \
    ignoring unknown option '-g'
Command line warning D4024 : \
    unrecognized source file type 'bar.o', object file
assumed
Command line warning D4024 : unrecognized source \
    file type 'main.o', object file
 assumed
Microsoft (R) Incremental Linker Version 6.00.8447
Copyright (C) Microsoft Corp 1992-1998. \
    All rights reserved.

/out:bar.exe
/out:bar.exe
bar.o
main.o
```

```
LINK : fatal error LNK1181: \
    cannot open input file "bar.o"
NMAKE : fatal error U1077: 'cl' : return code '0x2'
Stop.
```

As you can see, Microsoft make doesn't recognize .o files, nor does it recognize the –g flag. However, it did supply a reasonable value for the CXX macro (cl). Let's rewrite the Makefile to be more accommodating to nmake and the Windows platform:

```
OBJS = bar.obj main.obj
CXXFLAGS = /Zi

bar: $(OBJS)
    $(CXX) $(CXXFLAGS) $(OBJS)

%.obj : %.cpp
    $(CXX) $(CXXFLAGS) -c $<

$(OBJS) : bar.h
```

Here, I have changed the values of the OBJS macro to reflect the different object file suffixes used by Microsoft C++, and changed the CXXFLAGS macro to /Zi, which is Microsoft C++'s version of the –g flag. Typing nmake now gets us the following output:

```
C:\bookdev\makefiles>nmake -f Makefile.win

Microsoft (R) Program Maintenance Utility   \
    Version 6.00.8168.0
Copyright (C) Microsoft Corp 1988-1998. \
    All rights reserved.

        cl  /c bar.cpp
Microsoft (R) 32-bit C/C++ Optimizing Compiler \
    Version 12.00.8804 for 80x86
Copyright (C) Microsoft Corp 1984-1998. \
    All rights reserved.

bar.cpp
bar.cpp(22) : error C2065: 'setenv' : \
    undeclared identifier
NMAKE : fatal error U1077: 'cl' : return code '0x2'
Stop.
```

As you can see from the preceding output, bar.cpp failed to compile. The problem we ran into is that Microsoft C++ does not support setenv() in its runtime library (RTL). However, it does support a function named _putenv() (notice the leading underscore), which is similar to the POSIX function putenv(), except for the leading underscore, of course. With this knowledge, we could convert the source to use putenv() and _putenv(), but we would still run into a build issue because of the leading underscore. Ultimately, my recommendation is to use neither of these functions, and instead use the Netscape Portable Runtime Library (NSPR, see Item 17) function PR_SetEnv(), which provides a portable implementation of setenv() and putenv(). But let's assume for the moment that NSPR does not exist, and we have to deal with this in some other way. There are two solutions to the problem that come to mind. These aren't the only solutions, but they are ones that fit the current discussion about make:

- Use conditional compilation (that is, #ifdef).
- Provide two implementations of base.cpp, one for systems that support the POSIX name of the function, and one for use with the Microsoft RTL.

I take a look at each of these solutions in the following subsections.

Conditional Compilation

Conditional compilation is the vintage way to deal with platform dependencies. It is also widely considered to be one of the worst possible methods for dealing with problems of this type. To illustrate how it works, we can modify the source code of bar.cpp as follows to support both putenv() and _putenv():

```
int Bar::PutBar()
{
    char buf[16];
    sprintf(buf, "BAR=%d", m_bar);
#if defined(XP_WIN)
    return _putenv(buf);
#else
    return putenv(buf);
#endif
}
```

And modify the Makefile to define XP_WIN for Windows:

```
CXXFLAGS = /Zi /DXP_WIN=1
```

Now, with these changes in place, nmake successfully compiles and links our sources, resulting in an application named bar.exe.

Separate Source Files

The other way around the problem is to place the platform-specific code of the application into a separate source file, and modify the Makefile so that one source file is built on Windows and the other source file is built on Mac OS X and Linux. Let's name the Windows version of the source barwin.cpp. It is then a simple matter of replacing the bar.cpp and bar.o references in the Makefile to barwin.cpp and barwin.obj.

There is a related way of solving this problem that comes to mind: You can create a macro in the Makefile that is used in place of putenv() or _putenv() in the sources. In the Mac OS X and Linux Makefile we might use the following:

```
CXXFLAGS=-g -DXP_PUTENV=putenv
```

Whereas in the Windows Makefile, we might use this:

```
CXXFLAGS=/Zi /DXP_PUTENV=_putenv
```

And change the source for PutBar() to be this:

```
int Bar::PutBar()
{
    char buf[16];
    sprintf(buf, "BAR=%d", m_bar);
    return XP_PUTENV(buf);
}
```

The other solution applies when using a common make system such as GNU make. We might factor out the portions of the Makefile that are platform independent into separate files (for example, Windows.mk and Unix.mk), and then include the appropriate file using make's `include` statement:

```
include Windows.mk

bar: $(OBJS)
    $(CXX) $(CXXFLAGS) $(LINKFLAGS)$(OBJS)

%.obj : %.cpp
    $(CXX) $(CXXFLAGS) -c $<

$(OBJS) : bar.h
```

Where Windows.mk contains the following:

```
OBJS = bar.obj main.obj
CXXFLAGS = /Zi
LINKFLAGS =
```

And Unix.mk contains this:

```
OBJS = bar.o main.o
CXXFLAGS = -g
LINKFLAGS = -o $@
```

I needed to introduce the LINKFLAGS macro above to deal with the fact that no equivalent to −o $@ is usable in the nmake version of the Makefile.

In the end, none of the solutions that I have described here is completely satisfactory from a portability standpoint, although solutions such as these are commonly encountered. Although using a common make system goes a long way toward a more portable build system, it does not isolate you completely from dealing with platform differences. Historically (and perhaps surprisingly to those of you who are only vaguely familiar with UNIX and its history), writing code for UNIX-like systems has been a portability nightmare. With so many variants out there (BSD, AT&T System V, SunOS/Solaris, HP/UX, AIX, and many others), it was difficult for programmers to come up with source code that would port to all variants of UNIX, unchanged. APIs that existed on one UNIX-like system might not be available on others. (Even if two systems were POSIX-based [see Item 16], they might implement different versions of the standard.) The problem continues today—with BSD-derived operating systems (FreeBSD, Darwin), Solaris, and Linux representing the major UNIX-like operating systems in use today. (There are others, but they are not as widely deployed as these.)

Fortunately, some tools exist that extend make and reduce some of the difficulty that is inherent in writing and building UNIX software in a portable manner. Best of all, both of these tools are available for Microsoft Windows, making them candidates for use (in the context of platforms covered by this book). These tools are GNU's autoconf/automake and X11's Imake.

Autoconf/Automake

Autoconf/automake is very popular and commonly used in both open source and industry. (The build system for Mozilla, for example, is based on autoconf/automake.) The idea behind autoconf/automake is to supply a configure script and Makefile templates along with the source code to a program. Using the configure script and Makefile templates, autoconf/ automake investigates the platform hosting the build, testing for the presence of features, and then generates Makefiles that are tailored to the features that were discovered. Assuming that nothing changes in terms of configuration options or the makeup of the project (for example, no new source files are added to the project, and no Makefile changes are made), this step has to be done only once; from then on, all that needs to be done to build the project is to type make.

When the configure script is run (here I am illustrating the configure script from the open source gaim project, run on a stock Fedora Core 4 system), you can see some of the analysis that is performed:

```
[syd@fc3 gaim-2.0.0beta3]$ ./configure
checking build system type... i686-redhat-linux-gnu
checking host system type... i686-redhat-linux-gnu
checking target system type... i686-redhat-linux-gnu
checking for a BSD-compatible install... \
    /usr/bin/install -c
checking whether build environment is sane... yes
checking for gawk... gawk
checking whether make sets $(MAKE)... yes
checking for sed... /bin/sed
checking for gcc... gcc
checking for C compiler default output file name... \
    a.out
checking whether the C compiler works... yes
checking whether we are cross compiling... no
checking for suffix of executables...
checking for suffix of object files... o
```

```
checking whether we are using the GNU C compiler... \
    yes
checking whether gcc accepts -g... yes

...

checking for the %z format string in strftime()... \
    yes

...
```

As you can see, configure announces a series of tests that it is performing on the build environment, and the result of those tests. This is just a subset of what is displayed (for gaim); the actual output would take up a few pages. Each test is specified in the configure script using autoconf macros. Here is the portion of the configure script that performs the "checking for the %z format string in strftime() ..." test, shown above:

```
AC_MSG_CHECKING(for the %z format string in \
    strftime())
AC_TRY_RUN([
#ifdef HAVE_SYS_TIME_H
#include <sys/time.h>
#endif
#include <time.h>
#include <stdio.h>

int main()
{
    char buf[6];
    time_t t = time(NULL);

    if (strftime(buf, sizeof(buf), "%z", \
        localtime(&t)) != 5)
        return 1;

    fprintf(stderr, "strftime(\"%%z\") yields: \
        \"%s\"\n", buf);

    return !((buf[0] == '-' || buf[0] == '+') &&
             (buf[1] >= '0' && buf[1] <= '9') &&
             (buf[2] >= '0' && buf[2] <= '9') &&
             (buf[3] >= '0' && buf[3] <= '9') &&
             (buf[4] >= '0' && buf[4] <= '9')
            );
```

```
    }
  ],
  [
      AC_MSG_RESULT(yes)
      AC_DEFINE([HAVE_STRFTIME_Z_FORMAT], [1],
          [Define to 1 if you have a strftime() \
          that supports the %z format string.])
  ],
  [
      AC_MSG_RESULT(no)
  ],
  )
```

The AC_MSG_CHECKING macro causes the message "checking for the %z format string in strftime() ..." to be displayed on stdout when the test is begun. The AC_TRY_RUN macro constitutes the body of the test, and consists here of three blocks, each of which is bounded by [and] characters. The first block contains a complete C program that will be compiled by the configure script. The result of the compilation will determine whether the test passes or fails. If the test passes, the second block, beginning with AC_MSG_RESULT(yes), will be invoked. This block causes a #define to be made available to the compiled source, via an include file named config.h that is generated by the configure script. The #define in this case is HAVE_STRFTIME_Z_FORMAT. Finally, if the test fails, the block beginning with AC_MSG_RESULT(no) will be invoked, and as you can see, no such #define is enabled.

Code in the gaim source makes use of the result of this step to provide an implementation of strftime that supports the %z format on platforms that don't provide it, or to simply call strftime directly if %z is supported. The code is organized something like this:

```
#ifndef HAVE_STRFTIME_Z_FORMAT
static const char *get_tmoff(const struct tm *tm)
{
...
}
#endif

#if !defined(HAVE_STRFTIME_Z_FORMAT) || \
    defined(_WIN32)
static size_t gaim_internal_strftime(char *s, \
    size_t max, const char *format, const struct tm *tm)
{
```

```
        const char *start;
        const char *c;
        char *fmt = NULL;
...


    for (c = start = format; *c ; c++)
    {
...


#ifndef HAVE_STRFTIME_Z_FORMAT
            if (*c == 'z')
            {
                char *tmp =
                    g_strdup_printf("%s%.*s%s",
                        fmt ? fmt : "",
                        c - start - 1,
                        start,
                        get_tmoff(tm));
                g_free(fmt);
                fmt = tmp;
                start = c + 1;
            }
#endif


...


    }


...


    return strftime(s, max, format, tm);
}
#else /* HAVE_STRFTIME_Z_FORMAT && !_WIN32 */
#define gaim_internal_strftime strftime
#endif
```

This is about all I have to say about autoconf and automake; if you need more information about how to set up a project based on autoconf/automake, there are books and online documentation through the GNU project that cover the topic well, not to mention plenty of open source projects that can be used as examples.

Imake

Using make is not a terribly difficult task when the project is simple and we are required to support only a single platform or compiler. However, things can become more complicated as the complexity of the project grows, or the number of platforms we must support increases. Library differences complicate the creation and maintenance of cross-platform Makefiles and software. Compiler and linker flags often differ, even among compilers and linkers that are hosted on the same platform.

Perhaps the first project that I encountered (way back in 1990) that demanded a better solution than what make provides was the X Window System. The solution that the MIT X Consortium came up with for dealing with the complexity of building for multiple platforms was Imake. An early version of Imake was introduced with X11R1 back in 1987, and as of X11R6.6, which was released in 2001, the number of platforms for which Imake configuration files are supplied stands at 41.

Imake is present on Linux distributions natively, but needs to be installed on Mac OS X and Windows. There are a few places to get Imake, notably from Xfree86.org and X.org. Because both Mac OS X and Linux are Xfree86.org based, I advocate using this version on all platforms, with one exception that will be described when I talk about getting Imake set up on Windows.

Installing on Mac OS X

To get Imake on Mac OS X, you must install X11, which can be installed at any time from the installation CD (Tiger and greater). You can find instructions at Apple's Web site at http://developer.apple.com/opensource/tools/runningx11.html.

Installing on Windows

Before installing on Windows, you need to decide whether you are going to be using GCC as your compiler or using Microsoft Visual C++.

Installing Imake for GCC with Cygwin

If you are using GCC, X11R6 for Windows can be downloaded and installed using Cygwin's Setup.exe program. If Cygwin has already been installed on your machine, just rerun Setup.exe and install the Xfree86 package. You must install the Cygwin shell, and because the Imake client links to the Cygwin DLL, you must install it, too. My recommendation is if you have the space required (1.4GB), go ahead and install all of Cygwin. For more information about the Cygwin/X project, see Item 9.

Assuming that you installed to c:\Cygwin, you need to add c:\Cygwin\usr\X11R6\bin to your PATH variable, and c:\Cygwin\usr\X11R6\lib to your LIB variable. On Windows XP, you can set or modify these variables by clicking the Environment Variables button in the System control panel's Advanced tab. Make sure to restart any DOS command windows after changing any environment variables in this manner; environment variable changes do not affect current DOS windows.

In a DOS command window, type the following:

```
c:\> Imake
Imake: No such file or directory
Imake: No description file.
      Stop.
c:\>
```

The preceding indicates the system was able to find Imake. If you get messages about the Imake command not being found, or you are unable to start Imake because of missing libraries, make sure that you installed X11R6 correctly, and check your PATH and LIB variables to make sure that they are set to the correct values.

Installing Imake for Visual C++

I am going to assume for the rest of this section that you will be using Imake with Visual C++ tools. To get Imake binaries installed on the system, we are going to download and build them from X.org, because the binaries provided by Cygwin assume a Cygwin environment, which is an assumption I am not going to make about your environment. The configuration files that will be used by Imake will come from modified XFree86.org versions from either Linux or Mac OS X.

Follow these steps to create an Imake binary on Windows that is compatible with Microsoft Visual C++ and does not depend on Cygwin:

1. Visit ftp://ftp.x.org/pub/R6.6/tars.
2. Create a directory on your C: drive named X11R6.
3. Download and unpack xorg-1.tar.gz, xorg-2.tar.gz, xorg-3.tar.gz, and xorg-4.tar.gz into C:\X11R6.
4. Change to the xc\config\cf directory.

5. Type the following:

```
c:\> copy site.sample site.def
```

6. If compiling with Visual C++ 7.0, open the file Win32.cf and locate the line containing the following:

```
#define MkdirHierCmd $(CONFIGSRC:/=\)\util\mkdirhier
```

Because of what appears to be a bug in Microsoft C++ 7.0's universal character support, this macro will not compile. (It complains about the \u in \util\mkdirhier being malformed.) As it turns out, Windows mkdir is enough to get by with, so replace the preceding line with the following:

```
#define MkdirHierCmd mkdir
```

7. Regardless of which version of Visual C++ you are using, locate the following two lines in Win32.cf:

```
#define CppCmd CcCmd -nologo -batch -E
```

and

```
#define CppCmd CcCmd -nologo -E
```

and remove the -E from the end of both.

8. Now it is time to build X11R6. Change to the xc directory, and type the following:

```
c:\> nmake World.Win32
```

On a 2GHz or faster machine, X11R6 should build after five or ten minutes.

Using Imake, an Example

A good way to appreciate what Imake does is to give it a try. If you are on Linux or after installing Imake on Mac OS X or Windows, create a new directory, and inside this directory create three files named hello.h, hello.cpp, and Imakefile, with the following contents.

hello.h

```
const char *msg = "Hello World!\n";
```

hello.cpp

```
#include <stdio.h>
#include "hello.h"

int
main(int argc, char *argv[])
```

```
{
    printf(msg);
}
```

Imakefile

```
NormalProgramTarget(hello, hello.o, NullParameter,
NullParameter, NullParameter)
```

Creating the Imakefile

In the same directory where these files exist, type xmkmf -a:

```
$ xmkmf -a
Imake -DUseInstalled -I/usr/X11R6/lib/X11/config
make Makefiles
make: Nothing to be done for `Makefiles'.
make includes
make: Nothing to be done for `includes'.
make depend
make: Nothing to be done for `depend'.
```

xmkmf is a Bourne shell script that executes Imake and creates a Makefile from the result.

Now, type make hello to build the program:

```
$ make hello
/usr/bin/c++ -Os     -I/usr/X11R6/include   \
-D__powerpc__ -D__DARWIN__   -DNO_ALLOCA -DX_LOCALE \
-DCSRG_BASED -c -o hello.o hello.cpp
rm -f hello
/usr/bin/cc -o hello -Os -Wall -Wpointer-arith \
-no-cpp-precomp     -L/usr/X11R6/lib     hello.o
```

The preceding output was generated on Mac OS X, and will differ on Linux and Windows. Now all that is left is to test the application:

```
$ ./hello
Hello World!
```

Imakefiles

The Makefile that was generated by Imake contains all the platform-specific knowledge needed for you to compile your application on the platform for which Imake was run. The Makefile is actually quite a bit larger than the Imakefile used to generate it:

```
$ wc -l Makefile
    979 Makefile
```

In addition to the Imakefile, Imake uses configuration files that are supplied with X11R6, and cpp macros named rules. The configuration files contain all the platform-specific information that ultimately makes its way into the Makefile that Imake creates. On Mac OS X, the configuration file is /usr/X11R6/lib/config/darwin.cf. (Darwin is the name given to the BSD-based operating system underlying all of Mac OS X.) Rules are macros that expand to constructs that make can parse and execute against. Many of these rule macros take arguments that are specified in the Imakefile. For example, the LinkRule rule is defined as follows:

```
#ifndef LinkRule
#define LinkRule(program,options,objects,libraries) \
$(CCLINK) -o program options objects libraries \
$(EXTRA_LOAD_FLAGS)
#endif /* LinkRule */
```

The platform-specific portions of LinkRule, CCLINK and EXTRA_LOAD_FLAGS, are #defines that come either from vendor- or site-specific configuration files (for example, darwin.cf), or they take on default values. On Darwin, EXTRA_LOAD_FLAGS ends up evaluating to the empty string; for Cygwin builds on Windows, it evaluates to -Wl,--enable-auto-import.

Rule macros are defined in a file named Imake.rules, and there are somewhere in the neighborhood of 100 of these rule macros provided. The following sections describe some of the most important rules macros and give examples of their use.

Building a Complete Program from Multiple Sources

Let's return to the example used earlier to illustrate make, the bar program. As you might recall, bar consisted of two source files, bar.cpp and main.cpp, and an include file named bar.h. The Makefile we created, in its final form, is repeated here:

```
OBJS = bar.o main.o
CXXFLAGS = -g

bar: $(OBJS)
```

```
        $(CXX) $(CXXFLAGS) -o $@ $(OBJS)

%.o : %.cpp
        $(CXX) $(CXXFLAGS) -c $<

$(OBJS) : bar.h
```

The three major problems with this Makefile, as noted earlier, are as follows:

- The .o suffix is specific to UNIX.
- The –g flag is specific to GNU, and might not be correct for other compilers like Microsoft Visual C++.
- The –o flag is also compiler specific.

Still, this Makefile will work on two of the platforms we care about in this book, Mac OS X and Linux, so it isn't all that bad. However, modifications would be needed if we moved it over to Windows and tried using it with a compiler other than GCC. The whole point of looking at Imake is to overcome platform dependencies such as this.

The following Imakefile supports the same functionality as the Makefile above:

```
SRCS = main.cpp bar.cpp
OBJS = main.o bar.o
ComplexProgramTarget(bar)
```

Typing xmkmf –a (on Mac OS X), we get the following:

```
$ xmkmf -a
mv -f Makefile Makefile.bak
Imake -DUseInstalled -I/usr/X11R6/lib/X11/config
make Makefiles
make: Nothing to be done for `Makefiles'.
make includes
make: Nothing to be done for `includes'.
make depend
make: Nothing to be done for `depend'.
```

What happens if we move the code and Imakefile over to Windows XP and try to build? The intent of the following is to show you some of the things that you might run into on Windows, and I don't suggest you actually try any of this yourself. First, let's try executing xmkmf:

```
c:/> xmfmf -a
'xmkmf' is not recognized as an internal or external \
command, operable program or batch file.
c:/>
```

Oops! xmkmf is a Bourne shell script, and does not run natively in Windows, because it requires a shell like the one provided by Cygwin. However, if we fire up the Cygwin shell, and run xmkmf from there, we will get the XFree86 version of the configuration files. Instead, it would be better to create a simple DOS batch file that performs that same basic tasks that xmkmf -a performs, and use that instead. Here is just such a batch file (xmkmf.bat), which executes Imake directly from a compiled X11R6 source tree:

```
copy Makefile Makefile.bat
c:\X11R6\xc\config\Imake\Imake.exe -DUseInstalled \
-I/X11R6/xc/config/cf
nmake Makefiles
nmake includes
nmake depend
```

With the xmkmf.bat file in my path, we now get the following:

```
c:\ >xmkmf
c:\ >Copy Makefile Makefile.bak
        1 file(s) copied.

c:\ >C:\X11R6\xc\config\Imake\Imake -DUseInstalled \
-I/X11R6/xc/config/cf
Imakefile.c

c:\ >nmake Makefiles

Microsoft (R) Program Maintenance Utility \
Version 7.10.3077
Copyright (C) Microsoft Corporation.  All rights \
reserved.

c:\ >nmake includes

Microsoft (R) Program Maintenance Utility \
Version 7.10.3077
Copyright (C) Microsoft Corporation.  All rights \
reserved.
```

```
c:\ >nmake depend
```

```
Microsoft (R) Program Maintenance Utility \
Version 7.10.3077
Copyright (C) Microsoft Corporation.  All rights \
reserved.
```

```
c:\ >
```

Notice that Imake executes Microsoft nmake. Now let's try using nmake to build the project:

```
c:\>nmake
```

```
Microsoft (R) Program Maintenance Utility \
Version 7.10.3077
Copyright (C) Microsoft Corporation.  \
All rights reserved.
```

```
        cl -nologo -DWIN32 -DWIN32_LEAN_AND_MEAN \
-D_DLL -D_MT -D__STDC__ -D_X86_
   /c bar.cpp
bar.cpp
bar.cpp(22) : error C3861: 'putenv': identifier not \
found, even with argument-dependent lookup
NMAKE : fatal error U1077: 'cl' : return code '0x2'
Stop.
```

Now we are back to a familiar problem, described earlier in the chapter: Because our code is being built by Microsoft C++, and we are linking to the Microsoft RTL, putenv() is not available.

As it turns out, the configuration file used on Windows, Win32.cf, has the following entry:

```
#define HasPutenv          YES
```

Imake.tmpl defines the constants YES as 1, and NO as 0. These two constants are used in numerous macros, such as HasPutenv. The intent is for Imake files to incorporate these macros to control conditional compilation. These constants can be used in Imakefile constructs like the following:

```
#if !HasPutenv
put Imakefile content here on platforms for which \
HasPutenv is NO
#endif
```

Or

```
#if HasPutenv
put Imakefile content here on platforms for which \
HasPutenv is YES
#endif
```

Overriding Defaults with site.def

Clearly, we don't have a putenv( ), for if we did, there would be no compiler error. We could modify Win32.cf and change the HasPutenv define to NO, but it is best to leave the platform configuration files alone. Imake provides a file named site.def that can be used to override the settings made in the platform configuration files. Open the site.def, and add the following immediately after the line #ifdef AfterVendorCF:

```
#if defined(Win32Architecture)
#if defined(HasPutenv)
#undef HasPutenv
#endif
#define HasPutenv NO
#endif
```

With that change in place, we can modify the Imakefile as follows:

```
SRCS = main.cpp bar.cpp
OBJS = main.o bar.o
#if !HasPutenv
DEFINES = -DNOPUTENV
#endif
ComplextProgramTarget(bar)
```

DEFINES is an Imake variable that can be used to augment the #defines passed to the compiler. It is documented as being the way that Imakefile should modify compiler flags; using CFLAGS is explicitly recommended against. The following changes to bar.cpp are all that remain:

```
int Bar::PutBar()
{
    char buf[16];
    sprintf(buf, "BAR=%d", m_bar);
#if defined NOPUTENV
#if defined(WIN32)
    return _putenv(buf);
#else
    error putenv() is not defined
#endif
#else
    return putenv(buf);
#endif
}
```

After running xmkmf and nmake clean, type in nmake bar.exe to see the
result:

```
c:\>nmake bar.exe

Microsoft (R) Program Maintenance Utility \
Version 7.10.3077
Copyright (C) Microsoft Corporation.  All rights \
reserved.

        cl -nologo -DWIN32 -DWIN32_LEAN_AND_MEAN \
-D_DLL -D_MT -D__STDC__ -D_X86_
   /c main.cpp
main.cpp
        cl -nologo -DWIN32 -DWIN32_LEAN_AND_MEAN \
-D_DLL -D_MT -D__STDC__ -D_X86_
   /c bar.cpp
bar.cpp
bar.cpp(29) : error C3861: 'putenv': identifier not \
found, even with argument-dependent lookup
NMAKE : fatal error U1077: 'cl' : return code '0x2'
Stop.
```

It looks like the changes that were made did not take effect. (Notice the lack
of a NOPUTENV define.) After we debug the problem, it turns out that the
DEFINES variable is not being used as documented. Another change to
site.def takes care of this problem:

```
#ifdef AfterVendorCF

#if defined(Win32Architecture)
#define StandardDefines $(DEFINES) -DWIN32 \
-DWIN32_LEAN_AND_MEAN -D_DLL -D_MT -D__STDC__ \
CpuDefines
#if defined(HasPutenv)
#undef HasPutenv
#endif
#define HasPutenv NO
#endif
```

Here I have replaced the StandardDefines macro that was specified in
Win32.cf with a new version that incorporates the value of the DEFINES
variable. With this change, reissuing the xmkmf, nmake clean, and nmake
commands yields the desired results:

```
c:\> nmake

Microsoft (R) Program Maintenance Utility \
Version 7.10.3077
Copyright (C) Microsoft Corporation.  All rights \
reserved.

        cl -nologo -DNOPUTENV -DWIN32 \
-DWIN32_LEAN_AND_MEAN -D_DLL -D_MT -D__STDC__  -D_X86_ \
/c main.cpp
main.cpp
        cl -nologo -DNOPUTENV -DWIN32 \
-DWIN32_LEAN_AND_MEAN -D_DLL -D_MT -D__STD
C__ -D_X86_   /c bar.cpp
bar.cpp
        if exist bar.exe del bar.exe
        cl -Febar.exe -O -nologo -G4 -W2        \
main.obj bar.obj msvcrt.lib kernel32.lib wsock32.lib \
-link -nodefaultlib:libc
```

Finally, success!

Eliminating #ifdefs in Code

As you know, #ifdefs often make code hard, if not impossible, to read. Just
this simple change added to the complexity of the source considerably. In
the Microsoft RTL, there are 40 or so functions that are like _putenv()

(POSIX functions that are named with a leading underscore). On top of this, numerous POSIX functions are missing altogether. But, for now, let's assume that putenv() is the only one we have to deal with, and continue looking at how we can use Imake to overcome the problem, this time without using #ifdefs.

A First Attempt

The first non-#ifdef solution involves using a macro to define the name of the function, either _putenv or putenv. The following Imakefile and changes to bar.cpp illustrate how this can be done. First the Imakefile, in its entirety:

```
SRCS = main.cpp bar.cpp
OBJS = main.o bar.o
#if !HasPutenv
#if defined(Win32Architecture)
DEFINES = -DXP_PUTENV=_putenv
#else
DEFINES = -DXP_PUTENV=error putenv not defined for \
this platform
#endif
#else
DEFINES = -DXP_PUTENV=putenv
#endif
ComplexProgramTarget(bar)
```

Here, we use the DEFINES variable once again, but this time to define a constant named XP_PUTENV. If HasPutenv is defined as NO in the configuration files, we define XP_PUTENV to be _putenv on Windows, or we define it to be a string that will lead to a compiler error. If HasPutenv is defined as YES, we define XP_PUTENV to be putenv.

Next, we modify the C++ code to use the XP_PUTENV define, as follows:

```
int Bar::PutBar()
{
    char buf[16];
    sprintf(buf, "BAR=%d", m_bar);
    return XP_PUTENV(buf);
}
```

With these changes, we get the following after rerunning xmkmf, nmake clean, and nmake bar.exe:

```
c:\>nmake bar

Microsoft (R) Program Maintenance Utility \
Version 7.10.3077
Copyright (C) Microsoft Corporation.  All rights \
reserved.

        cl -nologo -DXP_PUTENV=_putenv -DWIN32 \
-DWIN32_LEAN_AND_MEAN -D_DLL -D_MT -D__STDC__ \
-D_X86_   /c main.cpp
main.cpp
        cl -nologo -DXP_PUTENV=_putenv -DWIN32 \
-DWIN32_LEAN_AND_MEAN -D_DLL -D_MT -D__STDC__ -D_X86_\
  /c bar.cpp
bar.cpp
        if exist bar.exe del bar.exe
        cl -Febar.exe -O -nologo -G4 -W2 main.obj \
bar.obj    msvcrt.lib kernel32.lib wsock32.lib -link \
-nodefaultlib:libc
```

All the complexity for dealing with the different forms of putenv() is now in the Imakefile, and all that needs to be done is to document the fact that XP_PUTENV should be used in place of putenv() in code.

Using a Platform-Specific Implementation of putenv()

Another way to manage this in the Imakefile without #ifdefs is to create a source file that contains platform-specific implementations of putenv(), and add this source file to the build if we are on a platform that needs it. Here's the source for just such a file, compatibility.cpp, which contains the Win32 definition of putenv() that we desire:

```
#if defined(WIN32)
#include <stdlib.h>

int putenv( const char *envstring )
{
  return _putenv(envstring);
}
#endif
```

To use `putenv()` in bar.cpp, we also need an include file, which I've named compatability.h:

```
#if defined(WIN32)
int putenv(const char *envstring);
#endif
```

The Imakefile changes are similar to the ones made immediately above. This time, instead of setting the `DEFINES` variable if `HasPutenv` is `NO` and `Win32Architecture` is defined, we instead add compatibility.cpp to the `SRCS` variable, and compatibility.o to the `OBJS` variable, causing it to be added to the build:

```
SRCS = main.cpp bar.cpp
OBJS = main.o bar.o
#if !HasPutenv
#if defined(Win32Architecture)
SRCS = $(SRCS) compatibility.cpp
OBJS = $(OBJS) compatibility.o
#endif
#endif
ComplexProgramTarget(bar)
```

Finally, we include compatibility.h in bar.cpp, which has been recoded to call `putenv()`:

```
#include <stdlib.h>
#include <stdio.h>
#include "bar.h"
#include "compatibility.h"

Bar::Bar() : m_bar(0)
{
}

Bar::~Bar()
{
}

void Bar::SetBar(int bar)
{
    m_bar = bar;
}
```

```
int Bar::PutBar()
{
    char buf[16];
    sprintf(buf, "BAR=%d", m_bar);
    return putenv(buf);
}
```

Executing xmkmf, nmake clean, and nmake bar.exe one final time, we see that compatibility.cpp has been added to the build, and that we link without any errors:

```
c:\>nmake bar.exe

Microsoft (R) Program Maintenance Utility \
Version 7.10.3077
Copyright (C) Microsoft Corporation.  All rights \
reserved.

        cl -nologo  -DWIN32 -DWIN32_LEAN_AND_MEAN \
-D_DLL -D_MT -D__STDC__ -D_X86_   /c main.cpp
main.cpp
        cl -nologo  -DWIN32 -DWIN32_LEAN_AND_MEAN \
-D_DLL -D_MT -D__STDC__ -D_X86_   /c bar.cpp
bar.cpp
        cl -nologo  -DWIN32 -DWIN32_LEAN_AND_MEAN \
-D_DLL -D_MT -D__STDC__ -D_X86_   /c compatibility.cpp
compatibility.cpp
        if exist bar.exe del bar.exe
        cl -Febar.exe -O -nologo -G4 -W2 main.obj \
bar.obj compatibility.obj msvcrt.lib kernel32.lib \
wsock32.lib -link -nodefaultlib:libc
```

A More General Solution

Let's take one final look at the Imakefile in search of a more general solution to the problem:

```
SRCS = main.cpp bar.cpp
OBJS = main.o bar.o
#if !HasPutenv
#if defined(Win32Architecture)
SRCS = $(SRCS) compatibility.cpp
```

```
OBJS = $(OBJS) compatibility.o
#endif
#endif
ComplexProgramTarget(bar)
```

An alternative, but closely related approach, is to provide per-platform compatibility files (for example, WinCompatibility.cpp, OSXCompatibility.cpp, and LinuxCompatibility.cpp). In doing so, we only provide implementations of the functions that are missing, we eliminate (or significantly reduce) the need for #ifdefs of any kind in the sources, and best of all, there is, generally speaking, no longer a need to test for HasPutenv or other Imake #defines. Here's an Imakefile that adopts this approach:

```
SRCS = main.cpp bar.cpp
OBJS = main.o bar.o
#if defined(Win32Architecture)
SRCS = $(SRCS) WinCompatibility.cpp
OBJS = $(OBJS) WinCompatibility.o
#endif
#if defined(LinuxArchitecture)
SRCS = $(SRCS) LinuxCompatibility.cpp
OBJS = $(OBJS) LinuxCompatibility.o
#endif
#if defined(DarwinArchitecture)
SRCS = $(SRCS) OSXCompatibility.cpp
OBJS = $(OBJS) OSXCompatibility.o
#endif
ComplexProgramTarget(bar)
```

Both OSXCompatibility.cpp and LinuxCompatibility.cpp contain nothing at this point, because both of these platforms provide a POSIX putenv(). There is no longer a need for #ifdefs in WinCompatibility.cpp:

```
#include <stdlib.h>

int putenv(const char *envstring)
{
  return _putenv(envstring);
}
```

Files Used by Imake

Now that you have a flavor for Imake, let's list the Imake files that we've discussed so far (and some we haven't):

- **Imake.tmpl.** This file, which should not be modified, defines default values for Imake. For example:

  ```
  #ifndef HasPutenv
  #define HasPutenv        NO  /* assume not */
  #endif
  ```

- **Imake.rules.** This file, which should not be modified, contains most of the rule macros, such as ComplexProgramTarget, that you will use in your Imakefiles.

- **Win32.cf, linux.cf, darwin.cf.** These files contain platform-specific defines, overriding those specified in Imake.tmpl. As with Imake.tmpl, you should not modify these files. Using `grep(1)`, we can see that many of the platform-specific configuration files override the `HasPutenv` define specified in Imake.tmpl:

  ```
  $ grep HasPutenv *
  Amoeba.cf:#define HasPutenv             YES
  DGUX.cf:#define HasPutenv               YES
  FreeBSD.cf:#define HasPutenv            YES
  NetBSD.cf:#define HasPutenv            YES
  Oki.cf:#define HasPutenv               YES
  Win32.cf:#define HasPutenv              YES
  bsdi.cf:#define HasPutenv               YES
  hp.cf:#define HasPutenv                 YES
  ibm.cf:#define HasPutenv                YES
  linux.cf:#define HasPutenv              YES
  lynx.cf:#define HasPutenv               YES
  mach.cf:#define HasPutenv               YES
  minix.cf:#define HasPutenv              YES /* xsm */
  os2.cf:#define HasPutenv                YES
  osf1.cf:#define HasPutenv               YES
  sgi.cf:#define HasPutenv                YES
  sony.cf:#define HasPutenv               YES
  sun.cf:#define HasPutenv                YES
  ultrix.cf:#define HasPutenv             YES
  ```

- **Win32.rules, darwin.rules.** Just as Win.cf overrides values specified in Imake.tmpl, platform-specific rule files override macros defined in

Imake.rules. Win.cf, for example, overrides the ComplexProgramTarget rule with a version of its own. The platform-specific rule files, like the others we have seen so far, should not be modified.

- **Site.def.** This file is, unlike the others, modifiable, and contains overrides of macros and defines specified in the previous files. In this file, you might correct errors in defines or rules, or even specify new rules that are specific to the projects that you support. It was in site.def that we overrode the Win32 setting for HasPutenv earlier in this chapter.

- **Imakefile.** This file is the equivalent of a Makefile in traditional environments (ones that are not Imake based). It is in the Imakefile where you place the platform independent description of how to build your program's sources. There is usually one Imakefile for each directory in your source tree. (I talk more about this in the next section when I describe how to build subdirectories.)

- **Makefile.** This file is generated by Imake based on the contents of an Imakefile and the various Imake configuration and rules files that are provided by your Imake installation. Because this file is generated, you should not modify it.

Building Projects with Subdirectories

In this section, we are going to get serious about setting up an environment for Imake that works on all three platforms, and we will design a strategy for organizing a project that is based on the use of Imake. If you haven't done so already, find a Windows machine and follow the instructions for building X11R6.6 Imake from X.org. Also, find a Mac OS X machine or a Linux machine, and ensure that it has an XFree86 Imake installation. (Instructions for installing XFree86 on Mac OS X were provided earlier in this chapter. On Linux, XFree86 is undoubtedly already present.)

Typically, the source code of anything other than a trivial project will be organized in a tree-like hierarchy of some sort on disk. Directories in the source tree may correspond to a component or a library, or to some logical partitioning of the architecture. For example, user interface (UI) code might be located in one directory and core (non-UI) code in another. The source code for the X Window System is organized in this fashion, and as a result, Imake has built-in support for building projects that are organized in this fashion.

Without Imake support, building a source tree can be done in a relatively straightforward manner by writing a script (or a set of scripts) that traverses the source tree and executes make in each directory. But, here we find portability issues, such as the language that the script is to be written in, and whether the script should execute make or nmake. The availability of Cygwin minimizes the first of these issue to a certain degree, because it provides both perl and sh, and you can easily construct a script using either of these languages to walk a source tree and to build the software contained therein. And we could solve the make versus nmake issue simply by providing a top-level script for each tool. Each script could simply set an environment variable to the appropriate tool, make or nmake, and this environment variable could then be read by the remainder of the build scripts in the tree.

However, with Imake, we don't need to go to all this trouble. Imake provides a cross-platform, shell-independent, make-independent way of building a source tree.

To illustrate how this works, let's take our `putenv()` sample from earlier in this chapter and make some modifications so that the source code is located in a directory structure that is suitable for our current discussion. Here is a copy of the Imakefile that we ended up with:

```
SRCS = main.cpp bar.cpp
OBJS = main.o bar.o
#if defined(Win32Architecture)
SRCS = $(SRCS) WinCompatibility.cpp
OBJS = $(OBJS) WinCompatibility.o
#endif
#if defined(LinuxArchitecture)
SRCS = $(SRCS) LinuxCompatibility.cpp
OBJS = $(OBJS) LinuxCompatibility.o
#endif
#if defined(DarwinArchitecture)
SRCS = $(SRCS) OSXCompatibility.cpp
OBJS = $(OBJS) OSXCompatibility.o
#endif
ComplexProgramTarget(bar)
```

The work performed by this Imakefile can be broken down into the following steps:

1. Build cross-platform sources bar.cpp and main.cpp.
2. Build platform-dependent sources: WinCompatibility.cpp, Linux-Compatibility.cpp, or OSXCompatibility.cpp, depending on which platform we are building for.
3. Link the results from above into an executable program named bar.

An obvious organization for a project like this would be to place the platform-dependent and platform-independent sources into separate directories. We can also view the source as being either a part of the application (bar.cpp and main.cpp) or part of a supporting library (the compatibility sources; for example, LinuxCompatbility.cpp). Let's create a directory structure that attempts to exploit a library-based organizational view. Within such a structure, platform-dependent subdirectories can be added if needed.

Create a directory named `src`, and below that, create two subdirectories, one named `app`, and the other named `lib`. The `app` directory will contain one subdirectory for each application created by the project, and `lib` will contain one directory for each library that is part of the project. Because our application is named bar, create a directory named `bar` beneath app; this is where the application sources bar.cpp and app.cpp will be located. Similarly, a subdirectory of `lib` named `compat` will hold the sources that are used to create the `compat` library:

```
src/
    app/
    bar/
        bar.cpp
        main.cpp
lib/
    compat/
        WinCompatibility.cpp
        LinuxCompatibility.cpp
        OSXCompatibility.cpp
include/
    config/

locale/
    en/
    en_IE/
    es/
    ru/
```

We will need to create an Imakefile for both the `bar` and the `compat` directories. In the `compat` directory, the Imakefile will create a shared library that contains the compatibility routines needed by the application. The Imakefile located in `bar`, on the other hand, is responsible for creating the bar executable, and will link to the shared compatibility library to resolve compatibility routines such as `putenv()`. The `include` directory contains include files needed for the build—in our case, a file named compatibility.h, which contains declarations for the functions defined in the compatibility library. Note that bar.h is not located in this directory because it is not a general-purpose include. Imakefiles in `src`, `app`, and `lib` will be used to tell Imake how to navigate and build the source code in the tree.

Two additional directories, `dist\lib` and `dist\bin`, will be created during the build, as you will see later. Both the shared library and the executable will be installed in the `dist\bin` directory, and on Windows, `dist\lib` will contain the .lib file that is also generated by the build.

As you can see, there is also a directory named `config` in our source tree. Into the `config` directory, we will move all of the configuration files from the XFree86 distribution, along with the Windows executables for tools like Imake. This will allow us to distribute a known set of configuration files, a modified site.def, and precompiled Windows tools along with our source code. It will also save developers on our project from having to download and build X11R6, or go through the hassle of modifying configuration files.

Implementing on Windows

Let's set this all up on Windows, because it is the platform that is going to require the most work. After we have everything building there, we can move the tree over to Mac OS X and Linux.

Earlier in this chapter, you were told how to download X11R6 and build it from scratch on Windows. The reason we need to do this is to get Windows versions of Imake.exe, and other tools, ones that are not dependent on Cygwin. If you haven't yet done this, follow the instructions for downloading and building X11R6.6 located in the section "Installing Imake for Visual C++," earlier in this chapter. You also need to obtain a copy of the XFree86 `config` directory; this can be copied directly from a Linux or a Mac OS X system, or you can get it by downloading it directly onto your Windows system from XFree86.org from www.xfree86.org/4.3.0/ Install.html. You only need to download the file named Xprog.tgz from the binary distribution to obtain the config files; you are not required to build XFree86.org.

Assuming that you have unpacked the Xprog.tgz file in into c:\XF86, c:\X11R6 is where you downloaded the X11R6.6 sources and have a built copy of X11R6.6, and c:\src is where your project is going to be located, execute the following commands to create the source tree and copy the necessary Imake configuration files and binaries:

```
c:\> mkdir src
c:\> mkdir app
c:\> cd app
c:\> mkdir bar
c:\> cd ..
c:\> mkdir lib
c:\> cd lib
c:\> cd ..
c:\> mkdir include
c:\> mkdir config
c:\> cd config
c:\> mkdir cf
c:\> cd cf
c:\> copy c:\XF86\lib\X11\config\* .
c:\> cd ..
c:\> mkdir Imake
c:\> mkdir makedepend
c:\> copy c:\X11R6\xc\config\Imake\Imake.exe Imake
c:\> copy c:\X11R6\xc\config\makedepend\makedepend.exe\
 makedepend
c:\> copy c:\X11R6\xc\config\util\mkdirhier.exe .
```

In `src\app\bar`, create the following source files: bar.h and bar.cpp.

bar.h

```
#ifndef __BAR_00
#define __BAR_00

class Bar
{
public:
    Bar();
    ~Bar();
    void SetBar(int bar);
    int PutBar();
private:
    int m_bar;
};

#endif
```

bar.cpp

```
#include <stdlib.h>
#include <stdio.h>
#include "bar.h"
#include "compatibility.h"

Bar::Bar() : m_bar(0)
{
}

Bar::~Bar()
{
}

void Bar::SetBar(int bar)
{
    m_bar = bar;
}

int Bar::PutBar()
{
    char buf[16];
    sprintf(buf, "BAR=%d", m_bar);
    return putenv(buf);
}
```

In src\lib\compat, create a file named WinCompatibility.cpp with the following contents:

```
#if defined(WIN32)
#include <stdlib.h>

int putenv( const char *envstring )
{
    return _putenv(envstring);
}

#endif
```

That does it for the source code. In the `src`, `app`, and `lib` directories, we must provide Imakefiles, in addition to those needed in directories with source code. These Imakefiles are different from the Imakefiles that we have seen so far. Let's take a look at the one in the `src` directory, which is the more complicated of the bunch:

```
#define IHaveSubdirs

SUBDIRS=lib app

MakeSubdirs($(SUBDIRS))
DependSubdirs($(SUBDIRS))

World.lib:
    (cd lib && $(MAKE));

World.app:
    (cd app && $(MAKE));
```

This simple Imakefile contains everything that is needed for Imake to
descend into the lib and app subdirectories and to process the Imakefiles
located therein. The IHaveSubdirs define is required, and should be located
at the top of the file. The SUBDIRS variable contains a list of directories
immediately below the current directory that are a part of your project. The
MakeSubdirs and DependSubdirs rules expand into the platform-specific
statements that are required for the subdirectories to be processed, both by
Imake, and at build time. For now, ignore the World.lib and World.app
rules; they will be described later.

Here are the remainder of the Imakefiles. The next two are nearly
identical to the one in the src directory, and are designed to tell Imake to
navigate into subdirectories to process Imakefiles and build the sources that
are contained therein:

```
app\Imakefile:

#define IHaveSubdirs

SUBDIRS=bar

MakeSubdirs($(SUBDIRS))
DependSubdirs($(SUBDIRS))

lib\Imakefile:

#define IHaveSubdirs

SUBDIRS=compat

MakeSubdirs($(SUBDIRS))
DependSubdirs($(SUBDIRS))
```

In the bar directory, the Imakefile describes how to create the bar application. Let's look at this Imakefile in detail. (The line numbers to the left of the listing are not a part of the actual Imakefile.)

app\bar\Imakefile:

```
01 SRCS = main.cpp bar.cpp
02 OBJS = main.o bar.o
03 INCLUDES = -I$(TOP)/include
04 #if defined(DarwinArchitecture)
05 LIBS = $(TOP)/dist/lib/libCOMPAT.dylib
06 #endif
07 #if defined(Win32Architecture)
08 LIBS = $(TOP)/dist/lib/compat.lib
09 #endif
10 #if defined(LinuxArchitecture)
11 LIBS = $(TOP)/dist/lib/libcompat.so
12 #endif
13 BINDIR = $(TOP)/dist/bin
14 LOCAL_LIBRARIES = $(LIBS)
15 DEPLIBS =
16 SYS_LIBRARIES =
17 DEFINES =
18
19 #if defined(DarwinArchitecture)
20 ComplexProgramTargetNoMan(bar)
21 #else
22 ComplexProgramTarget(bar)
23 #endif
```

Lines 01 through 03 are, as previously described, required by `ComplexProgramTarget`, and define the sources, object files, and include files processed during the build. On lines 04 through 12, we define a variable named `LIBS` that will be used later in the Imakefile to describe the local (versus system) shared libraries that need to be linked to the application, which, in our case, is the single compatibility library. The names of these libraries vary depending on the platform; on Mac OS X systems, for example, the filename has a .dylib suffix; on Linux, the suffix is .so; and on Win32, it is .lib. Whatever the filename, the value of the `LIB` variable is later used on line 14 to set the `LOCAL_LIBRARIES` make variable. The `BINDIR` variable, set on line 13, specifies the final location of the bar application once it builds and links correctly. `DEPLIB`, `SYS_LIBRARIES`, and `DEFINES` are required but set to empty values. Finally, on lines 19 through 23, the

`ComplexProgramTarget` rule macro embodies the bulk of the processing performed by the Makefile generated by Imake from this Imakefile. Notice we have to special-case the rule macro for Darwin/Mac OS X. This is because the `ComplexProgramTarget` rule on Mac OS X tries to generate a man page for each program it creates. Because we do not supply a man page with our program, we use the `ComplexProgramTargetNoMan` rule that, thankfully, the developer of the Darwin configuration file thought fit to supply. This is an illustration of one of the weaknesses with Imake: Rules can be different (or even inconsistent) among platforms. However, we can, as I have illustrated here, do things in the Imakefile to compensate for these differences, or we can make changes in the site.def file, as I illustrate later. If things go terribly wrong, and neither Imakefile or site.def changes can be made, there is always the option of modifying the configuration and rule files directly. Because we are storing these files in our source tree, we have a certain amount of freedom to hack their contents, because the changes will only affect the project that these files are supporting.

Creating the Compatibility Library Imakefile

The final Imakefile we need to look at is the one that creates the compatibility library. As previously mentioned, this Imakefile needs to generate a shared library. Although there are rules for creating both static and shared libraries, I am going to take the advice found in the X11 Imake documentation and copy an Imakefile from the X source tree and modify it for our needs. For a starting point, I've chosen the Imakefile found in xc\lib\XIE, which is listed here:

```
XCOMM $Xorg: Imakefile,v 1.3 2000/08/17 19:45:25 cpqbld Exp $

#define DoNormalLib NormalLibXie
#define DoSharedLib SharedLibXie
#define DoDebugLib DebugLibXie
#define DoProfileLib ProfileLibXie
#define LibName XIE
#define SoRev SOXIEREV
#define IncSubdir X11
#define IncSubSubdir extensions

#include <Threads.tmpl>

#ifdef SharedXieReqs
REQUIREDLIBS = SharedXieReqs
#endif
```

```
#if Malloc0ReturnsNull
ALLOC_DEFINES = -DMALLOC_0_RETURNS_NULL
#endif

DEFINES = $(ALLOC_DEFINES)

HEADERS = XIElib.h

SRCS = abort.c \
       await.c \
       clientdata.c \
       colorlist.c \
       conven.c \
       elements.c \
       free.c \
       errors.c \
       events.c \
       ieee.c \
       init.c \
       lut.c \
       photoflo.c \
       photomap.c \
       photospace.c \
       roi.c \
       technique.c \
       utils.c

OBJS = abort.o \
       await.o \
       clientdata.o \
       colorlist.o \
       conven.o \
       elements.o \
       errors.o \
       events.o \
       free.o \
       ieee.o \
       init.o \
       lut.o \
       photoflo.o \
       photomap.o \
       photospace.o \
       roi.o \
       technique.o \
       utils.o
```

```
#include <Library.tmpl>

#ifdef NativeFPFormat
NATIVE_FP_FORMAT = NativeFPFormat
FP_DEFINES = -DNATIVE_FP_FORMAT=$(NATIVE_FP_FORMAT)
SpecialCLibObjectRule(ieee,$(ICONFIGFILES),\
$(FP_DEFINES))
#endif


DependTarget()
```

After a small amount of surgery, we are left with something that is more appropriate for our intent, which is stored as lib\compat\Imakefile:

```
01 LIBRARY_VERSION= 1.0
02 #define DoNormalLib NO
03 #define DoSharedLib YES
04 #define DoDebugLib NO
05 #define DoProfileLib NO
06 #define LibName COMPAT
07 #define SoRev LIBRARY_VERSION
08 #define IncSubdir
09 #define IncSubSubdir
10
11 USRLIBDIR = $(TOP)/dist/lib
12 BINDIR = $(TOP)/dist/bin
13
14 #if defined(Win32Architecture)
15 SRCS = WinCompatibility.cpp
16 OBJS = WinCompatibility.o
17 #endif
18 #if defined(DarwinArchitecture)
19 SRCS = OSCompatibility.cpp
20 OBJS = OSCompatibility.o
21 #endif
22 #if defined(LinuxArchitecture)
23 SRCS = LinuxCompatibility.cpp
24 OBJS = LinuxCompatibility.o
25 #endif
26
27 #include <Library.tmpl>
28
29 DependTarget()
```

The following defines (lines 02 through 05) control how Imake will generate the library:

```
#define DoNormalLib NO
#define DoSharedLib YES
#define DoDebugLib NO
#define DoProfileLib NO
```

In the XIE version of the Imakefile, you'll notice that symbolic constants were used; but in the end, these `#defines` either resolve to NO or YES, and these are the values I have chosen to use. Here, we have set `DoNormalLib` to NO, and `DoSharedLib` to YES to generate a shared library. The `LibName` `#define` (line 06) specifies the name of the generated library; on Win32, this will result in a file named COMPAT.dll. The `IncSubdir` and `IncSubSubdir` `#defines` (lines 08 and 09) are set to nothing because they do not apply to us, but they are referenced by rules in Library.tmpl so we need to define them. The purpose of the `SRCS` and `OBJS` variables should be obvious to you by now; these variables are referenced by rules in Library.tmpl and need to be supplied. The variables `USRLIBDIR` and `BINDIR` (lines 11 and 12) control where the .lib and .dll files, respectively, are copied during an install.

On line 27 we see the following:

```
#include <Library.tmpl>
```

This line is required for all Imakefiles that generate libraries, be they static or shared. Its purpose is to redefine rules that are needed for libraries to be built. Line 29, `DependTarget()`, does all the work related to building the sources and linking them into the shared library, and is somewhat analogous to the `ComplexProgramTarget` rule used to build executables.

Creating the Makefiles

Now that we have our source tree created and I have described the structure of the Imakefiles, let's go ahead and run Imake on the result. First, a quick reminder of the content of xmkmf.bat on Windows:

```
C: \src\config\Imake\Imake -I/ src/config/cf \
-DTOPDIR=. -DCURDIR=.
```

Type the following command:

```
C:\bookdev\src>xmkmf
```

That command results in the following output:

```
C: \src>c:\ src\config\Imake\Imake -I/src/config/cf \
-DTOPDIR=. -DCURDIR=.
Imakefile.c
\src\config\cf\Win32.cf(72) : warning C4129: 'u' : \
unrecognized character escape sequence
\src\config\cf\Win32.cf(72) : error C3847: wrong \
symbol in universal character; must use hex digits
c:\src\config\Imake\Imake: Exit code 2.
  Stop.
```

This is the problem that was discussed earlier, where Visual Studio 7.0 interprets \u as the start of a Unicode character sequence: Because we copied mkdirhier into the config directory, we can simply drop the \util prefix in Win32.cf, by changing

```
#define MkdirHierCmd $(CONFIGSRC:/=\)\util\mkdirhier
```

to

```
#define MkdirHierCmd $(CONFIGSRC:/=\)\mkdirhier
```

Now, assuming c:\src\config is in our path, when we issue xmkmf, we should get this:

```
C: \src>c:\src\config\Imake\Imake -I/src/config/cf \
-DTOPDIR=. -DCURDIR=.
Imakefile.c
```

The next step is to make the Makefiles, but before we do this, the site.def file needs to be modified. Open site.def and replace its contents with the following, which is a modified version of the site.sample file located in the same directory:

```
COMM site:  $Xorg: site.sample,v 1.3 2000/08/17 \
19:41:48 cpqbld Exp $

/* if you want host-specific customization, this is \
one way to do it. */
/*
#ifndef SiteIConfigFiles
#define SiteIConfigFiles $(IRULESRC)/host.def
#define LocalConfigFiles host.def
```

```
#endif
*/

#ifdef BeforeVendorCF

/* #include <host.def> */

/*
On systems where cpp doesn't expand correctly macros in
include directives the two following macros need to be
defined directly (where "X11" is really whatever the
TopLevelProject macro is defined to be).
*/
# if defined(AIXArchitecture) || \
     defined(SVR4Architecture) || \
     defined(SCOArchitecture) || \
     defined(Win32Architecture) || \
     defined(UXPArchitecture) || \
     defined(SunArchitecture)
#  ifndef ProjectRulesFile
#    define ProjectRulesFile <X11.rules>
#  endif
#  ifndef ProjectTmplFile
#    define ProjectTmplFile  <X11.tmpl>
#  endif
# endif

#endif /* BeforeVendorCF */

#ifdef AfterVendorCF

#define ProjectRoot $(TOP)/..

#if defined(Win32Architecture)
#ifdef CppCmd
#undef CppCmd
#endif
#define CppCmd   CcCmd -nologo

#ifdef StandardDefines
#undef StandardDefines
#endif
#define StandardDefines $(INCLUDES) $(DEFINES) \
$(CDEBUGFLAGS) -DWIN32 -DWIN32_LE
AN_AND_MEAN CpuDefines
```

```
#ifdef ExtraLibraries
#undef ExtraLibraries
#endif
#define ExtraLibraries msvcrt.lib kernel32.lib \
wsock32.lib -link -nodefaultlib:libc

#if defined(ProgramTargetHelper)
#undef ProgramTargetHelper
#endif
#define ProgramTargetHelper(program,srcs,objs,deplib,\
locallib,syslib)    @@\
ProgramTargetName(program): $(objs:.o=.obj) $(deplib)\
        @@\
    RemoveTargetProgram($@)                          @@\
    LinkRule($@,$(LDOPTIONS),$(objs:.o=.obj),locallib\
$(LDLIBS) syslib) @@\
                                        @@\
InstallProgram(program,$(BINDIR))

#endif /* Win32Architecture */

#if defined (DarwinArchitecture)
#ifdef InstallFlags
#undef InstallFlags
#endif
#define InstallFlags -c

#ifdef InstLibFlags
#undef InstLibFlags
#endif
#define InstLibFlags
#endif /* DarwinArchitecture */

#ifdef BuildBinDir
#undef BuildBinDir
#endif
#define BuildBinDir $(TOP)/dist/bin
#ifdef BuildBinTop
#undef BuildBinTop
#endif
#define BuildBinTop ../.. /* relative to BuildBinDir */
#ifdef BuildLibDir
#undef BuildLibDir
#endif
#define BuildLibDir $(TOP)/dist/lib
#ifdef BuildLibTop
```

```
#undef BuildLibTop
#endif
#define BuildLibTop ../.. /* relative to BuildLibDir */
#ifdef LibDir
#undef LibDir
#endif
#define LibDir $(TOP)/dist/lib

#endif /* AfterVendorCF */
```

The major changes made to the site.sample file are as follows:

- `ProjectRoot` was set to `$(TOP)/...`
- All commented-out entries were removed from the file.
- On Win32 systems, `CppCmd` was redefined without the `-E` flag, and `StandardDefines` was modified to include `$(INCLUDES) $(DEFINES)`, so builds will pick up any settings that are made to `INCLUDES` or `DEFINES` made in the Imakefiles.
- Also on Win32, added definition for `ProgramTargetHelper` to site.def for Win32. This was done for two reasons. First, `ComplexProgramTargetNoMan` does not have a definition in Win32.rules, so it tries linking without the .exe, and tries building .o files, using stock rules in Imake.rules. To get the correct behavior without man page building, I replaced `ProgramTargetHelper`, which does the right Win32 things, while removing the macro that builds man pages.
- On Mac OS X, `InstallFlags` and `InstLibFlags` were modified to eliminate calls to `chown`, `chgrp`, and `chmod`, which would require root capabilities and are needless when installing binaries and libraries to a local directory.
- Finally, for all platforms, several defines picked up from X11.tmpl (`BuildBinDir`, `BuildBinTop`, `BuildLibDir`, and `BuildLibTop`) were replaced with values that make sense for our situation and the organization of our source tree. These defines control where the lib, dll, and executable files are written during the build and install phases, and are used by both the bar and compat Imakefiles, as described earlier.

Finally, some changes to host.def are needed for Mac OS X. Modify host.def so that it looks like the following:

```
#ifdef BeforeVendorCF
#if defined (DarwinArchitecture)
# undef CcCmd
# define CcCmd cc -arch ppc

# undef CplusplusCmd
# define CplusplusCmd c++ -arch ppc

# define DarwinArchEnv RC_ARCHS='ppc '  RC_ppc='YES' \
RC_i386='NO' RC_m68k='NO' RC_hppa='NO' RC_sparc='NO'
#endif  /* DarwinArchitecture */
#endif
```

If you happen to get your host.def build from an Apple distribution of
XFree86, it might already contain most of the above. What you need to do,
if so, is add the #if defined(DarwinArchitecture) and the matching
#endif so that the contents of the file have no impact on Linux and
Windows.

Having made these changes, we can now try creating some Makefiles
back on Windows; but because we've changed the site.def and host.def files,
we will need to rerun xmkmf:

```
c:\src> xmkmf
C:\src>c:\src\config\Imake\Imake -I/src/config/cf \
-DTOPDIR=. -DCURDIR=.
Imakefile.c
```

Now to build the Makefiles:

```
C:\src>nmake Makefiles

Microsoft (R) Program Maintenance Utility \
Version 7.10.3077
Copyright (C) Microsoft Corporation.  All rights \
reserved.
        cd lib
        if exist Makefile.bak del Makefile.bak
        ..\.\config\Imake\Imake -I..\.\config/cf \
-DTOPDIR=..\. -DCURDIR=./lib
Imakefile.c
        nmake -nologo -                  Makefiles
        cd compat
        if exist Makefile.bak del Makefile.bak
        ..\..\.\config\Imake\Imake \
```

```
-I../../config/cf  -DTOPDIR=../../. -DCURDIR=\
./lib/compat
Imakefile.c
        nmake -nologo -L              Makefiles
        cd ..
        cd ..
        cd app
        if exist Makefile.bak del Makefile.bak
        ..\.\config\Imake\Imake -I../config/cf \
-DTOPDIR=../. -DCURDIR=./app
Imakefile.c
        nmake -nologo -              Makefiles
        cd bar
        if exist Makefile.bak del Makefile.bak
        ..\..\.\config\Imake\Imake -I../../config/cf\
  -DTOPDIR=../../. -DCURDIR=./app/bar
Imakefile.c
        nmake -nologo -L              Makefiles
        cd ..
        cd ..


C:\src>nmake


Microsoft (R) Program Maintenance Utility \
Version 7.10.3077
Copyright (C) Microsoft Corporation.  All rights \
reserved.


        cd lib
"making" all in ./lib...
        nmake -nologo - CDEBUGFLAGS="-O" all
        cd compat
"making" all in ./lib/compat...
        nmake -nologo -L CDEBUGFLAGS="-O" all
        cl -nologo    -O -DWIN32 -DWIN32_LEAN_AND_MEAN \
-D_X86_    /c WinCompatibility.cpp
WinCompatibility.cpp
NMAKE : fatal error U1073: don't know how to make \
'COMPAT-def.cpp'
Stop.
NMAKE : fatal error U1077: \
'"c:\Program Files\Microsoft Visual Studio .NET 2003\
VC7\BIN\nmake.exe"' : return code '0x2'
Stop.
NMAKE : fatal error U1077: \
'"c:\Program Files\Microsoft Visual Studio .NET 2003\
```

```
VC7\BIN\nmake.exe"' : return code '0x2'
Stop.
NMAKE : fatal error U1077: \
'"c:\Program Files\Microsoft Visual Studio .NET 2003\
VC7\BIN\nmake.exe"' : return code '0x2'
Stop.
NMAKE : fatal error U1077: \
'"c:\Program Files\Microsoft Visual Studio .NET 2003\
VC7\BIN\nmake.exe"' : return code '0x2'
Stop.
```

The last several lines of the preceding output indicate that an error was encountered. To understand this error, let's take a look at a portion of the rule used to create shared libraries in Win32.rules:

```
#define SharedLibraryTarget(libname,rev,solist,down,up)\
@@\
AllTarget(libname.dll) @@\
@@\
CppFileTarget(libname.def,libname-def.cpp,\
-DLIBRARY_VERSION=rev,$(ICONFIGFILES)) @@\
@@\
XVARdef0 = solist@@\
@@\
LibraryTargetName(libname): $(XVARuse0:.o=.obj) \
libname.def $(EXTRALIBRARYDEPS) @@\
RemoveFile($@) @@\
MakeLibrary($@,-def:libname.def $(XVARuse0:.o=.obj)) @@\
LinkBuildLibrary($@) @@\
```

As you can see, the CppFileTarget rule adds a target, the name of which is formed by concatenating the name of the library (COMPAT, specified in the Imakefile with the LibName #define), and the suffix .def. This is a standard Windows def file, which provides information about the library and its exports, and is needed to create a shared library. The name of dependency for this target is of the form libname-def.cpp, which in this case is COMPAT-def.cpp. Because we do not have a source file named COMPAT-def.cpp, the build fails. To get around this problem, we need to supply a COMPAT-def.cpp file in the compat directory, with the following contents:

```
LIBRARY COMPAT
VERSION 1.0
EXPORTS
  putenv
```

The structure of this file is simple. The first line supplies the name of the library, and the second line the version of the library. Following the EXPORTS line is a list, on separate lines, of the names of functions that are exported by the shared library. After this file has been created, we can issue nmake one final time:

```
C:\src>nmake

Microsoft (R) Program Maintenance Utility \
Version 7.10.3077
Copyright (C) Microsoft Corporation.  All rights \
reserved.


        cd lib
"making" all in ./lib...
        nmake -nologo - CDEBUGFLAGS="-O" all
        cd compat
"making" all in ./lib/compat...
        nmake -nologo -L CDEBUGFLAGS="-O" all
        cl -nologo    -O -DWIN32 -DWIN32_LEAN_AND_MEAN\
 -D_X86_   /c WinCompatibility.cpp
WinCompatibility.cpp
        if exist COMPAT.def del COMPAT.def
        cl -nologo -EP    -O -DWIN32 \
-DWIN32_LEAN_AND_MEAN -D_X86_  -I. CppTmpFile.c
@C:\DOCUME~1\PREFER~1\LOCALS~1\Temp\nm4299.tmp \
>COMPAT.def
CppTmpFile.c
        if exist COMPAT.lib del COMPAT.lib
        lib @C:\DOCUME~1\PREFER~1\LOCALS~1\Temp\\
nm429A.tmp
Microsoft (R) Library Manager \
Version 7.10.3077
Copyright (C) Microsoft Corporation.  All rights \
reserved.

-out:COMPAT.lib -def:COMPAT.def WinCompatibility.obj
   Creating library COMPAT.lib and object COMPAT.exp
        ..\..\.\config\mkdirhier ..\..\.\dist\lib
        if exist ..\..\.\dist\lib\COMPAT.lib del
..\..\.\dist\lib\COMPAT.lib
        cd ..\..\.\dist\lib && \
copy ..\..\.\lib\compat\COMPAT.lib .
        1 file(s) copied.
```

```
        if exist COMPAT.dll del COMPAT.dll
        link @C:\DOCUME~1\PREFER~1\LOCALS~1\Temp\\
nm429C.tmp
Microsoft (R) Incremental Linker \
Version 7.10.3077
Copyright (C) Microsoft Corporation.  All rights \
reserved.

-dll -out:COMPAT.dll COMPAT.exp WinCompatibility.obj \
msvcrt.lib kernel32.lib wsock32.lib -link \
-nodefaultlib:libc
LINK : warning LNK4044: unrecognized option '/link'; \
ignored
        ..\..\.\config\mkdirhier ..\..\.\dist\bin
        if exist ..\..\.\dist\bin\COMPAT.dll del
..\..\.\dist\bin\COMPAT.dll
        cd ..\..\.\dist\bin && copy ..\..\.\lib\\
compat\COMPAT.dll .
        1 file(s) copied.
        cd ..
        cd ..
        cd app
"making" all in ./app...
        nmake -nologo - CDEBUGFLAGS="-O" all
        cd bar
"making" all in ./app/bar...
        nmake -nologo -L CDEBUGFLAGS="-O" all
        cl -nologo -I../../././include  -O -DWIN32 \
-DWIN32_LEAN_AND_MEAN -D_X86_ /c main.cpp
main.cpp
        cl -nologo -I../../././include  -O -DWIN32 \
-DWIN32_LEAN_AND_MEAN -D_X86_ /c bar.cpp
bar.cpp
        if exist bar.exe del bar.exe
        cl -Febar.exe -O -nologo -G4 -W2 main.obj \
bar.obj ../../././dist/lib/compat.lib msvcrt.lib \
kernel32.lib wsock32.lib -link -nodefaultlib:libc
        cd ..
        cd ..
```

So far, everything looks good. We descended into compat, built a library called COMPAT.dll, which was copied to the dist\bin directory in our project root, and then we descended into app and built the application, linking it to the compatibility library. Now all that remains is to install the

bar application into the dist\bin directory. This can be done by typing
nmake install:

```
C:\src>nmake install

Microsoft (R) Program Maintenance Utility \
Version 7.10.3077
Copyright (C) Microsoft Corporation.  All rights \
reserved.

        cd lib
"installing" in ./lib...
        nmake -nologo - DESTDIR= install
        cd compat
"installing" in ./lib/compat...
        nmake -nologo -L  DESTDIR= install
        ..\..\.\config\mkdirhier ..\..\.\dist\lib
        copy   COMPAT.lib ..\..\.\dist\lib\\
COMPAT.lib
        1 file(s) copied.
        ..\..\.\config\mkdirhier ..\..\.\dist\bin
        copy   COMPAT.dll ..\..\.\dist\bin\\
COMPAT.dll
        1 file(s) copied.
"install in ./lib/compat done"
        cd ..
        cd ..
        cd app
"installing" in ./app...
        nmake -nologo - DESTDIR= install
        cd bar
"installing" in ./app/bar...
        nmake -nologo -L DESTDIR= install
        ..\..\.\config\mkdirhier ..\..\.\dist\bin
        copy   bar.exe ..\..\.\dist\bin\\bar.exe
        1 file(s) copied.
"install in ./app/bar done"
        cd ..
        cd ..
```

As you can see, Imake visits both lib\compat and app\bar, running nmake
install in each of these directories. The make done in compat is superfluous,
because the dll and lib files were installed earlier when they were built. The

important work performed during the install phase happens when app\bar
is visited, where nmake install causes the bar.exe file to be copied to dist.
If you visit dist and type dir, this is what you should see:

```
C:\src>cd dist\bin
C:\src\dist\bin>dir
 Volume in drive C is PRESARIO
 Volume Serial Number is ECA4-3E20

 Directory of C:\src\dist\bin

01/17/2004  09:36 PM    <DIR>          .
01/17/2004  09:36 PM    <DIR>          ..
01/17/2004  09:36 PM             3,584 bar.exe
01/17/2004  09:36 PM            11,776 COMPAT.dll
               2 File(s)         15,360 bytes
               2 Dir(s)  86,027,026,432 bytes free
```

Building Debug

To build debug, you need to make one modification to the top-level
Imakefile (located in the src directory), as well as to the ones in app
and lib. Add the following line immediately after the line #define
IHaveSubdirs:

```
#define PassCDebugFlags CDEBUGFLAGS="$(CDEBUGFLAGS)"
```

Now, to build debug, issue the following command (on Windows):

```
C:\src>xmkmf
C:\src>nmake Makefiles
C:\src>nmake "CDEBUGFLAGS=/Zi"
```

This will cause the CDEBUGFLAGS macro to be passed to all builds. On Linux
and Mac OS X, use the following line to build debug:

```
$ make "CDEBUGFLAGS=-g"
```

3 Software Configuration Management

A software configuration management (SCM) system consists of tools and processes used to manage the source code of a project and to assess its state. With these tools, management and developers can do the following:

- Peruse the source code managed by the SCM system
- Obtain a local copy of the source code
- Submit modifications made to the source code by developers
- Understand which changes have been made to the source code by developers
- Determine the state of the source code (for example, whether it compiles)
- Log and track defects associated with binaries created from the source code

In a cross-platform project, certain aspects of an SCM system take on added importance. In this chapter, I describe the tools that were most important to Netscape and Mozilla in this regard:

- CVS, the Concurrent Version System, which was used to maintain and manage a central copy of the Netscape/Mozilla source code
- Bugzilla, used to track defects in programs generated from the source code stored in CVS
- Tinderbox, used to determine the state of the source code as changes were made to the copy stored in CVS
- Patch, a tool that fosters the distribution and communication of changes among developers (in particular, between a developer and code reviewers) prior to it being permanently stored in CVS

These tools, combined with some best practices for using them that I describe in this chapter, helped greatly in ensuring that Netscape shipped cross-platform products that were similar in features and overall quality, and did so on the same schedule.

Item 11: Use a Cross-Platform Bug Reporting and Tracking System

A major component of a cross-platform toolset is the bug reporting and tracking system (which I refer to as a "bug system" here for brevity). A bug system is used by developers and testers to report defects and issues encountered during the software development and testing phases of a project. In general, a bug system should allow the reporter to specify the problem encountered, identify the context or state of the system at the time the bug was discovered, and list the steps required to reproduce the bug. The bug system also must allow for the tracking of any issues it contains. In terms of tracking, bugs generally go through the following states:

- **New.** A bug that has been discovered, but has not been investigated by a developer.
- **Assigned.** The developer acknowledges the bug and is investigating.
- **Resolved.** The developer has fixed the bug, or has some other resolution (for example, unable to reproduce the problem, or the feature is working as designed).
- **Verified.** QA/test has acknowledged the resolution of the developer, and has verified it to be correct.

In addition, a bug can be in the reopened state, an indication that a once-verified bug has resurfaced in testing after originally being verified by QA.

Finally, a bug system should allow someone to specify the relative priority of bugs filed against a product. Initially, this will be the person filing the bug, but ideally, it is done in a "triage" session, with participation of the following teams: development, QA/test, and product management. Tracking priorities is not easy, it takes discipline for people to sit down for an hour or two and grind through a list of bugs, but doing so allows developers to prioritize their work, and allows those who are making ship/no-ship decisions the opportunity to objectively decide what state the project is in.

When it comes to cross-platform development, you should always look for a couple of attributes and features when selecting a bug system for use in your project.

Accessibility

Perhaps the most important cross-platform attribute you should look for when selecting a bug system is accessibility. In a cross-platform development project, everyone will have his or her preferred development platform (see Item 1). For some developers, it will be Mac OS X, and for many it will be Windows. If the bug system is not accessible to everyone on the team via their native platforms, it risks not being used by those who would rather not boot into one of the operating systems that the bug system does support. Therefore, the bug system itself needs to be cross-platform. And, it must support all of your tier-1 platforms.

These days, by and large, the accessibility requirement is best met by using a Web-based bug system. Web browsers are available for every platform, including PDAs and mobile phones. Bug reporting/tracking systems based on LAMP (Linux, Apache, MySQL, PHP) or Java/JSP are available.

Ability to Track Platform-Specific Bugs

In some cases, a bug will be reproducible on all platforms, and in other cases, only a subset of the supported platforms will exhibit the given problem. It is critical that the platforms affected by the problem be tracked. The bug system should allow the person filing the bug, or even someone updating the bug at a later time, to specify the platform(s) affected by any given bug. Doing so will allow someone searching the bug database to specify a subset of the supported platforms as search criteria (for example, "find all assigned Linux bugs"). By specifying the platforms as part of the search criteria, platform specialists will be able to quickly identify bugs that affect their platform, and management will be able determine the number of open (and resolved) issues on a per-platform basis.

Bugzilla

Most of my experience with bug reporting systems has been with a bug tracking system named Bugzilla—yet another result of the Netscape/Mozilla project. Bugzilla is implemented as a Web application, allowing the database to be viewed from any platform that supports a Web browser. Bugzilla has been in active development for years, and is used by hundreds of organizations. Because Bugzilla originated during the development of the cross-platform Netscape/Mozilla system (it replaced a Netscape-internal bug system in use during the development of the 4.x browser called bugsplat), it has always supported cross-platform development directly.

Installing Bugzilla is pretty straightforward, and is well documented. A basic installation of Bugzilla can be done in about an hour, depending on your setup. (That was my experience on a stock Red Hat Fedora Core 4 system, and your results may vary.)

The following instructions are based on a Fedora Core 4 setup, using Apache and MySQL. (The default versions of Apache, Perl, and MySQL that come with FC4 are suitable for use with Bugzilla 2.22.)

Visit www.bugzilla.org, and download the latest stable release (2.22 as of this writing) onto the Linux machine that you will use to host the Bugzilla server. Then:

```
$ su
# tar -zxvf bugzilla-2.22.tar.gz
# mkdir /var/www/html/bugzilla
# cd bugzilla-2.22
# cp -r * /var/www/html/bugzilla
# cd /var/www/html/
# chown -R apache bugzilla
# chgrp -R apache bugzilla
```

The next step is to install required Perl modules. To do this, enter the following:

```
# perl -MCPAN -e 'install "Bundle::Bugzilla"'
```

You may be prompted for inputs. If so, just take whatever default responses are offered. To validate that the required modules are installed, issue the following (as root):

```
# cd /var/www/html/bugzilla
# perl checksetup -check-modules
```

When that completes, you need to rerun checksetup once again:

```
# perl checksetup.pl
```

This will create a file named localconfig. To configure Bugzilla to work with MySQL, follow the instructions at www.bugzilla.org/docs/2.22/html/configuration.html#mysql. Finally, rerun checksetup.pl one last time. The checksetup.pl script will create the Bugzilla database and prompt you for information needed to set up an administrator account in the Bugzilla database. Following this, you should be able to use the following URL to access bugzilla from your local Web browser:

http://localhost/bugzilla

If you have any problems with these instructions (or have a setup that differs from mine), refer to file://var/www/html/bugzilla/docs/index.html for help.

After you have installed Bugzilla, you need to add products to the bug database, and modify the list of platforms (hardware and operating systems) that can be specified when bugs are filed in the database. To do this, log in as the administrator; you should see a screen similar to the one shown in Figure 3-1.

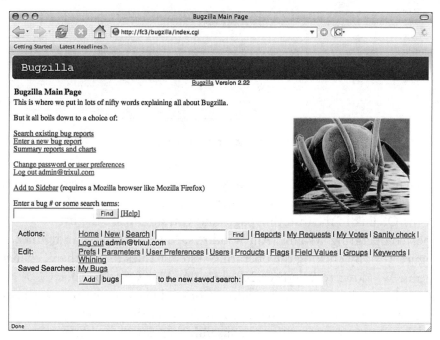

Figure 3-1 Bugzilla main screen

In the bottom half of Figure 3-1, there is a link labeled Products. Clicking that link takes you to a screen on which you can enter the name and attributes of a product. Enter the product name and a description, accept defaults for the remaining fields, and click the Add button. You should get something like Figure 3-2.

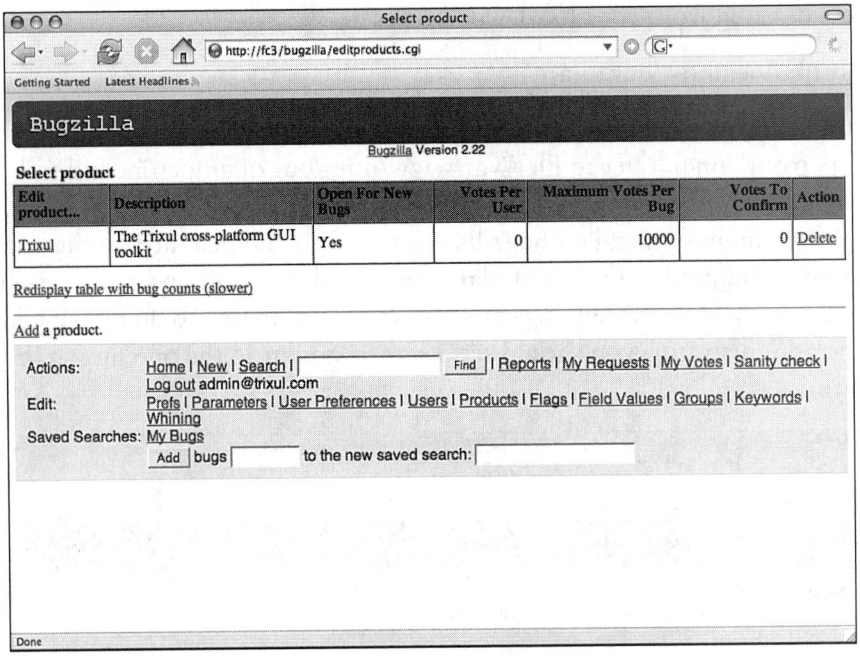

Figure 3-2 Products screen

The next step manages the list of supported operating systems. To view the list, click the Field Values link (visible in Figures 3-1 and 3-2). Then, click the OS link in the resulting page, and you should see the list of supported operating systems (All, Windows, Mac OS, Linux, and Other, as in Figure 3-3). By clicking the operating system names to edit them, change the value Windows to Windows XP, the value Mac OS to be Mac OS X 10.4, and the value Linux to be Fedora Core 4. I personally think it is better to be fine-grained when it comes to the list of operating systems; Linux, for example, is far too vague to be truly useful. You can also add or remove operating systems using the provided controls.

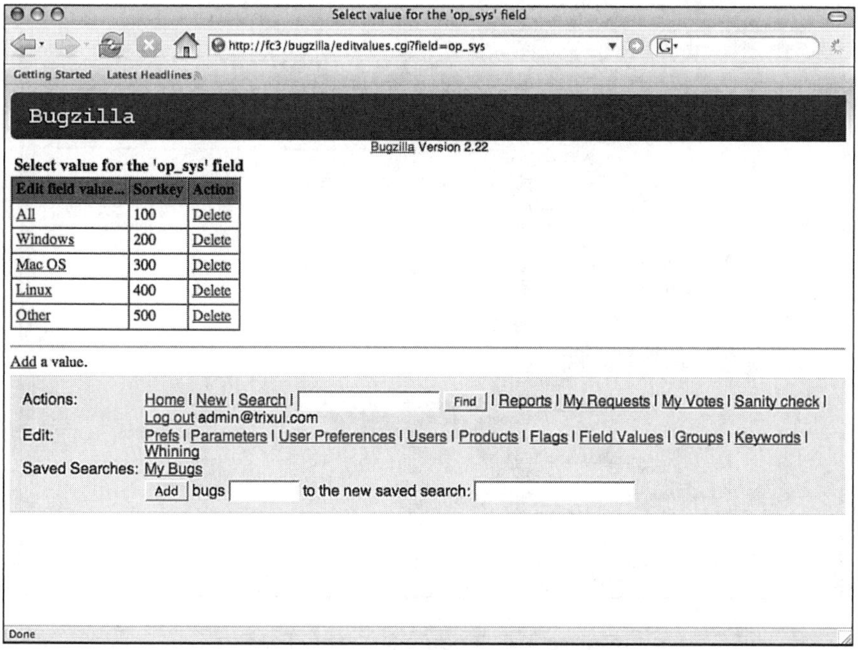

```
Select value for the 'op_sys' field

http://fc3/bugzilla/editvalues.cgi?field=op_sys

Getting Started    Latest Headlines

Bugzilla
                                   Bugzilla Version 2.22
Select value for the 'op_sys' field

Edit field value...  Sortkey  Action
All                  100      Delete
Windows              200      Delete
Mac OS               300      Delete
Linux                400      Delete
Other                500      Delete

Add a value.

Actions:      Home I New I Search I [          ]  Find | I Reports I My Requests I My Votes I Sanity check I
              Log out admin@trixul.com
Edit:         Prefs I Parameters I User Preferences I Users I Products I Flags I Field Values I Groups I Keywords I
              Whining
Saved Searches: My Bugs
              Add | bugs [        ]  to the new saved search: [          ]

Done
```

Figure 3-3 Platforms screen

To modify the list of supported hardware, click the Field Values link again, click the Hardware link on the resulting page, and then modify the list of supported hardware types so that it is consistent with your supported hardware platforms. Again, being fine-grained can help in diagnosing problems. For example, instead of Macintosh, you might add choices based on type and CPU (for example, PowerBook and MacBook).

Before any bug can be filed against a product, components and version numbers need to be added for the product. This can be done by clicking the Product link, clicking the product name in the resulting table, and then clicking the Edit Components and Edit Versions links, respectively. Components are specific areas of a product. For Trixul, I defined three components: JavaScript Integration, Layout engine, and liblayout. Additional components can be added by the administrator as needed. Version numbers can be any text string that helps to identify the versions of the product; I specified 0.1.0 and 1.0. Figure 3-4 illustrates the resulting product summary page displayed by Bugzilla. As soon as at least one component and one version number has been specified, users should be able to add new bugs to the database.

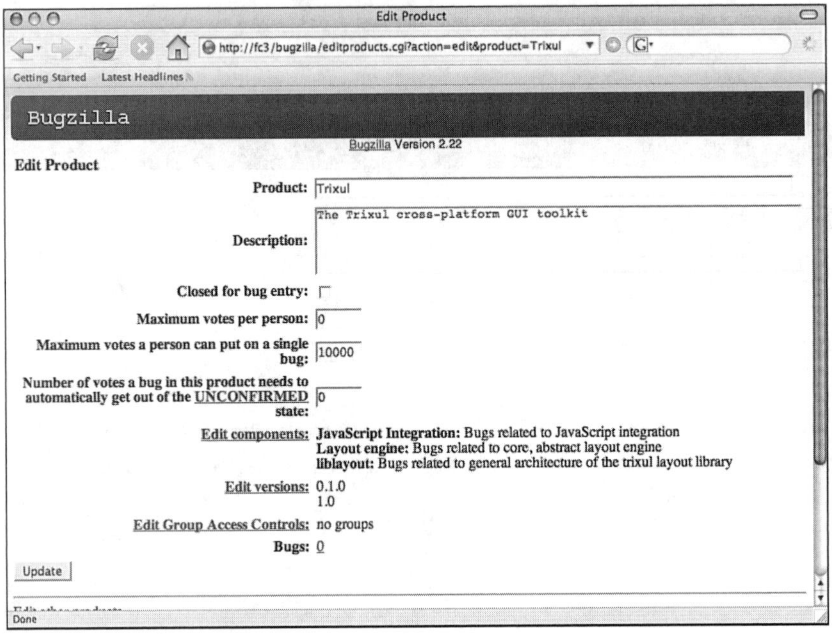

Figure 3-4 Product Summary Page

Returning to the cross-platform issues of platform and hardware, let's see how they are specified by filing a bug against Trixul. One problem with Trixul is that under Microsoft Windows XP, the layout engine is built as an executable, whereas on all other platforms, the layout engine is built as a shared library that is then linked to a small executable. The reason for this bug (I believe) is a difficulty with linking a mixed (native and Common Language Infrastructure [CLI]) .NET application to a shared library using Visual Studio .NET 2003.

To file this bug, I logged on to Bugzilla, clicked the Enter a New Bug Report link, filled out the form as shown in Figure 3-5, and then clicked Commit.

Notice how I selected Windows XP in the OS field, and PC (Intel Pentium 4) in the Platform field.

Platform-specific bugs can be easily located using the search feature of Bugzilla. To do so, visit the main Bugzilla page and click the Search Existing Bug Reports link. The resulting page allows you to specify a wide variety of search criteria, including the OS and Platform fields. Figure 3-6 illustrates a search of all open bugs filed against both Fedora Core 4 and Windows XP on the Pentium 4 platform.

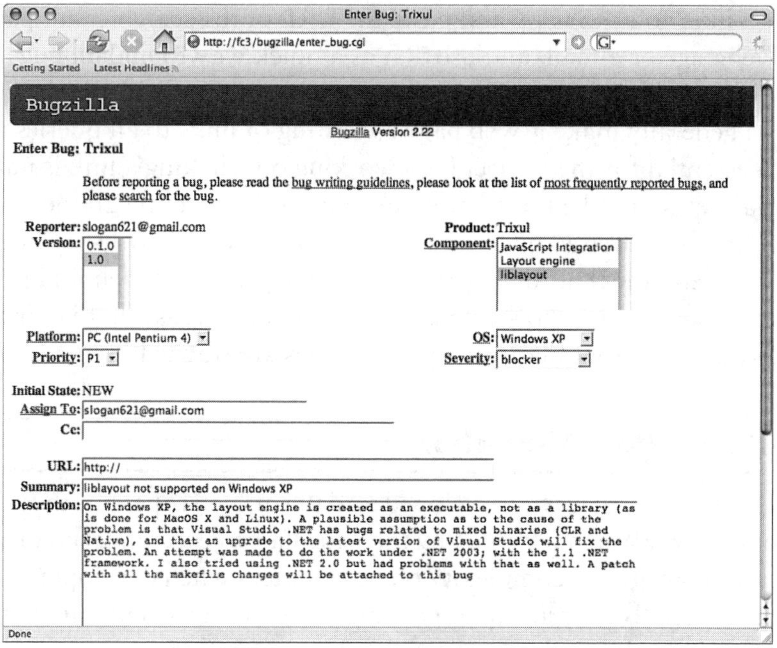

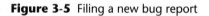

Figure 3-5 Filing a new bug report

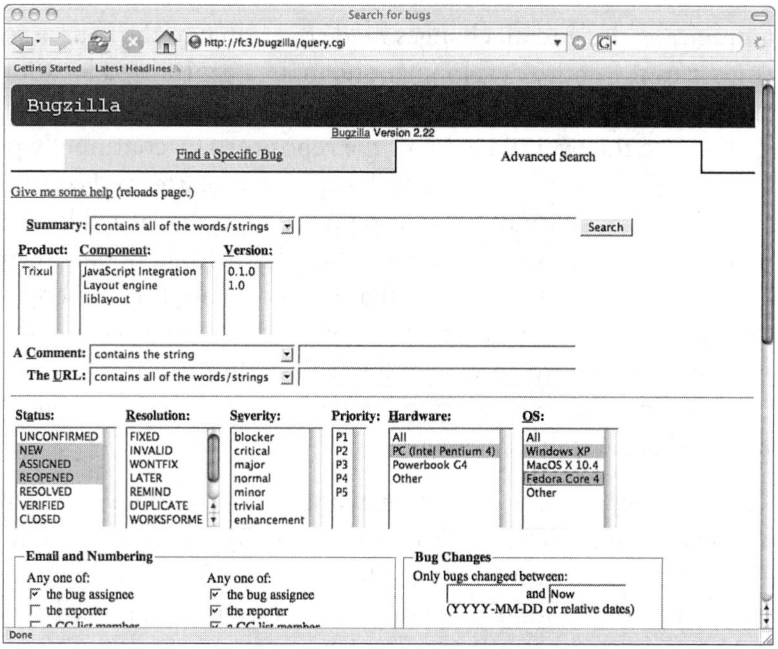

Figure 3-6 Searching for bugs

If you like, you can copy and paste the URL of the search result page into a Web page or e-mail, and use that as a quick way to find all bugs related to a specific platform/operating system combination. When using Bugzilla I generally make a Web page consisting of links to all queries that I consider essential for the project I am working on; clicking a link is much easier than revisiting the Bugzilla search page and reentering all the parameters of the desired query each time I go to look at my list of bugs.

That's pretty much it for Bugzilla. Using the general guidelines I just provided, it is fairly easy to set up and maintain a database that is capable of helping you ensure that platform-specific issues are tracked accurately.

Item 12: Set Up a Tinderbox

Tinderbox is a tool that was developed initially at Netscape, but that is now open source software maintained by the Mozilla project. Tinderbox is designed to manage the complexity one encounters when developing software, especially in terms of large-scale cross-platform software that involves a widely distributed team of developers. Tinderbox is particularly useful in cross-platform projects, as you will see. Coupled with a system known as bonsai, the goals of Tinderbox are fairly simple:

- Communicate any and all changes made over time to the source code repository to the entire development team, in a centralized location, as soon as the changes have been made.
- Communicate the overall health of the repository by continually pulling and building the source code on each supported platform. For each pull and build cycle, a pass/fail status is reported to a centralized location. This allows developers to determine when they should update their local trees to avoid pulling source code that will not build (or run) correctly.
- Combining the above, Tinderbox can be used to assign accountability of the health of the tree to specific individuals and/or changes to the repository. Knowing this information helps get problems solved as quickly and accurately as possible.

Basically, Tinderbox is a group of machines that continually pull and build the contents of a CVS repository (see Item 13), and a server that retrieves and reports the status of these builds on a Web server that everyone in the organization can monitor. Tinderbox is currently supported as three versions. Version 1, perhaps the most widely used, was developed by Netscape/Mozilla, and is still in use by mozilla.org. Tinderbox 2.0 is a rewrite of version 1, providing essentially the same feature set. The goal of Tinderbox 2.0 was to essentially clean up the implementation of version 1. Both Tinderbox 1 and Tinderbox 2 are available from mozilla.org. Tinderbox 3 is a more recent version, available as a tarball from John Keiser, an ex-Netscape developer. Tinderbox 3 adds a number of desirable features, and strives to make Tinderbox easier to set up and administer.

Figure 3-7 illustrates the Web page displayed by a Tinderbox server. (You can access a large number of live Tinderboxen by visiting http://Tinderbox.mozilla.org.)

creating a profile called default, covering up the fact that -CreateProfile doesn't actually work. revision 1.311 doesn't have this bug, so the tinderbox is now orange.

The tree is **open**

Build Time	Guilty	Linux balsa Dep (gcc 3.4)	Linux balsa Dep (static) %	Linux/x86_64 blackdeath Clbr	MacOSX Darwin 7.9.0 binus Dep Debug	SunOS/i386 5.10 nba Clbr	SunOS/sparc 5.10 putt Clbr
Click time to see changes since then	Click name to see what they did						
07/04 13:16:00					L/ C		
13:13:05				L/ C			
13:13:00		L/ C					
13:12:09							L/ C
13:12:00							
13:09:41	sspitzer		L/ C			L/ C	
13:07:00							
07/04 12:58:44				L			
12:46:31							
12:45:59							
12:42:51							
12:42:00					L C		
12:41:46							
12:37:00							
12:27:46							
12:20:59				L C			
12:10:33		L C Lk:4.61MB NH:9.39MB A:257K					
12:10:00							
12:04:00					L		
12:03:37							L
12:00:00	mozilla.mano						
07/04 11:58:00			L	L			
11:42:34							

Figure 3-7 Tinderbox

The Tinderbox in Figure 3-7 illustrates the state of Mozilla's Seamonkey reporting the health of some of the "port" platforms that are defined by the Mozilla project. (Seamonkey was the code name used by Netscape/Mozilla during the development of the Mozilla browser suite. A port is a platform that is not considered to be tier-1 by Mozilla.)

The use of Tinderbox is pervasive in the software development community. Not only is it used by mozilla.org, but by other open source projects (for example, OSDL) and in commercial development (AOL, for example). Tinderbox is particularly well-suited to cross-platform development, as we discuss later.

The Tinderbox Web page consists of a table viewed as a series of mutually exclusive columns that are organized from left to right. In the first column (Build Time), each row contains a timestamp that can be used to identify the time associated with events that are represented in the remaining columns of the table. The second column identifies each check-in made by developers; the time of these check-ins can easily be determined by looking at the corresponding row in the Build Time column. The remaining columns each represent a specific platform that is being reported on by the Tinderbox. (An organization may have several Tinderboxen, each reporting a specific group of builds. You can see an example of this by visiting http://tinderbox.mozilla.org/showbuilds.cgi.)

Any given column represents a build machine, and a platform, and contains a series of colored boxes. Green boxes indicate a successful build of the repository for that platform on that machine. Conversely, a red box indicates a failed build, and a yellow box indicates a build that is currently in the process of being produced. Furthermore, the lower edge of any of these boxes represents the start of a pull and build cycle, and the upper edge represents the time of completion. The time corresponding to both of these events, for a particular colored box, can be determined by looking at the timestamp at the same row in column one as the upper or lower edge of that box. For example, the uppermost failed build in Figure 3-7 (Linux balsa Dep (static), represented by column four of the table) was started at about 13:07, and failed about five minutes later, at about 13:12.

Let's take a closer look at this failed build, and see what we can infer about it. It is clear that the check-in by sspitzer at 13:09:41 did not result in the failure of the build for two reasons. First of all, the Linux balsa Dep build was already burning prior to sspitzer's check-in. (See the red box in the same column that completed around 12:00, and also notice how the lower edge of the uppermost red box is lower than the entry for sspitzer's check-in.) Another piece of evidence that sspitzer is not the cause of the problem is that each of the other Linux platform builds are green. (Generally, one finds that Linux builds of Mozilla are generally are either all red at the same time, or all green.) Finally, and perhaps most important, we can see that the build was previously red at noon (12:00), and had not gone through a green cycle since then. (Gray portions of the Tinderbox indicate no build was in progress, or the progress of a build was not reported to the Tinderbox server.)

For largely the same reasons cited previously for sspitzer, we can also infer that mozilla.mano is not to blame for the redness of the build, either.

The tree was already red prior to his or her check-in, and the other Linux builds were not affected.

Let's say I am not entirely sure that sspitzer is not to blame, and want to take a closer look at what the exact cause of the broken build might be. There are several other facilities provided by Tinderbox that you can use to drill down for further information. The L (or L1) link inside of the red box can be used to obtain a log of the build; this log contains compiler and perhaps linker output that should identify what caused the build to break. Clicking the L1 link gives the result shown in Figure 3-8.

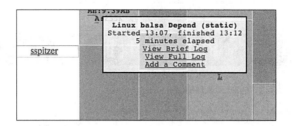

Figure 3-8 L1 link output

Clicking View Brief Log results in Figure 3-9, which indicates a problem building libmozjs.so, the shared library that contains the implementation of the Mozilla Spidermonkey JavaScript engine (which is used in Trixul; see Chapter 9, "Developing a Cross-Platform GUI Toolkit in C++").

```
Build Error Summary

gmake[5]: *** [libmozjs.so] Error 1
gmake[5]: Leaving directory `/builds/tinderbox/SeaMonkey/Linux_2.4.7-10_Depend/mozilla/js/src'
gmake[4]: *** [libs] Error 2
gmake[4]: Leaving directory `/builds/tinderbox/SeaMonkey/Linux_2.4.7-10_Depend/mozilla/js'
gmake[3]: *** [libs_tier_2] Error 2
gmake[3]: Leaving directory `/builds/tinderbox/SeaMonkey/Linux_2.4.7-10_Depend/mozilla'
gmake[2]: *** [tier_2] Error 2
gmake[2]: Leaving directory `/builds/tinderbox/SeaMonkey/Linux_2.4.7-10_Depend/mozilla'
gmake[1]: *** [alldep] Error 2
gmake[1]: Leaving directory `/builds/tinderbox/SeaMonkey/Linux_2.4.7-10_Depend/mozilla'
gmake: *** [alldep] Error 2

Build Error Log

 Skipping 705 Lines...

/lib/libc.so.6: undefined reference to `_dl_lookup_symbol@GLIBC_2.0'
/lib/libc.so.6: undefined reference to `__libc_stack_end@GLIBC_2.1'
/lib/libc.so.6: undefined reference to `_dl_argv@GLIBC_2.2'
/usr/lib/gcc-lib/i386-redhat-linux/2.96/../../../libpthread.so: undefined reference to `_dl_cpuclock_offset
/lib/libc.so.6: undefined reference to `_dl_loaded@GLIBC_2.1'
/lib/libc.so.6: undefined reference to `_dl_origin_path@GLIBC_2.1.1'
/lib/libc.so.6: undefined reference to `_dl_check_map_versions@GLIBC_2.2'
/lib/libc.so.6: undefined reference to `_dl_map_object@GLIBC_2.0'
/lib/libc.so.6: undefined reference to `_dl_main_searchlist@GLIBC_2.1'
```

Figure 3-9 View brief log output

The other major source of input that I would want to consider is an understanding of what portion of the tree was impacted by sspitzer. If the check-in he made does not correlate to the error messages displayed in the log (Figure 3-9), I can eliminate him from the "blame" list and focus my search elsewhere. I can do this in two ways. First, by clicking the C link in the red box; this will display a list of checkins that were made prior to the start of the build. It is these checkins that likely would be the cause of any state change in the build (that is, going from red to green, or from green to red, which is not the case here since the tree was already red at the 12:00 hour). Figure 3-10 shows the result of clicking the C link.

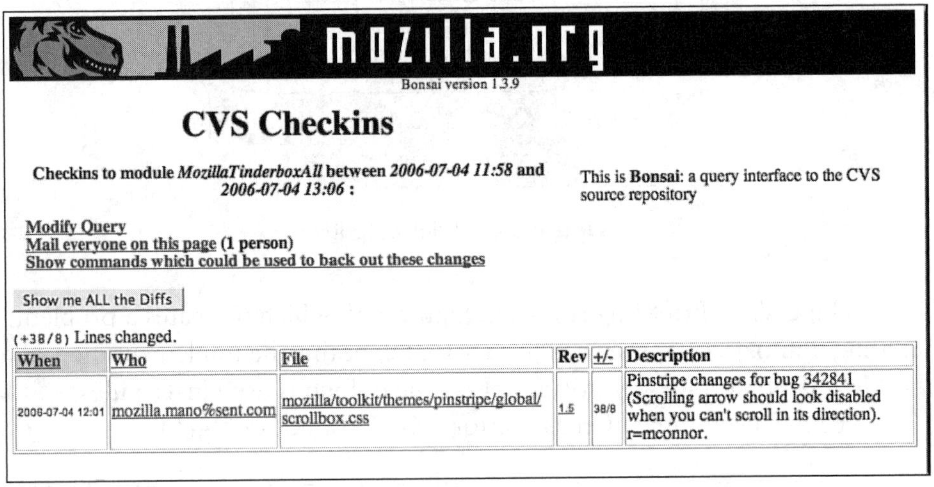

Figure 3-10 List of checkins

This result clearly confirms that sspitzer is not on the blame list—and it also shows that the problem is not related to a check-in by mozilla.mano, because this change was made to a Cascading Style Sheets (CSS) source file that would have no impact on the JavaScript engine.

The final technique to eliminate sspitzer from the blame list (short of sending him an e-mail and asking him whether his check-in caused the build failure) would be to click the sspitzer link in column one and see what changes he made. Doing so gives us Figure 3-11.

Once again, these are changes to Extensible Markup Language (XML) markup and JavaScript sources that have no bearing whatsoever on the stability of the JavaScript engine, the failure of which was clearly the cause of the red tree.

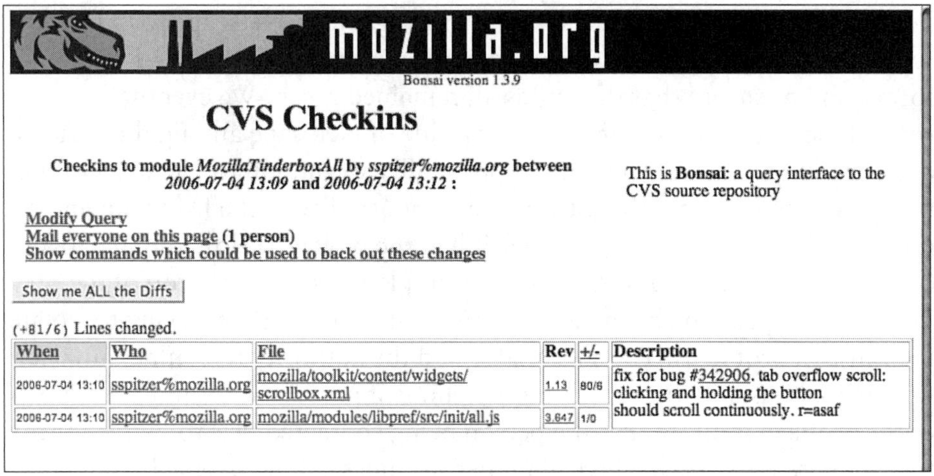

Figure 3-11 List of checkins made by sspitzer

In terms of cross-platform development, it is best not to rely on a Tinderbox to find all of your portability problems. At Netscape, developers were required to ensure that any changes they were considering for checkin built and executed cleanly on each tier-1 platform, before submitting the changes to the repository (see Item 4). However, you can never be sure that all developers will follow this rule all the time, without exception. Because of this, having a Tinderbox monitor the health of the repository is an especially good idea. It isolates the problems in terms of change made, time of the change, and developer who made the change, focusing the area of investigation to a small fraction of the overall possibilities.

At Netscape, Tinderbox was a way of life (as it remains for Mozilla and many other development projects). The state of the tree was closely monitored, and acted as the focal point of development. If the tree was red, you could not checkin to the tree until it turned green. After you checked in your changes, you were added to a group called "the hook," and as a member of the hook, you were required to watch the Tinderbox and ensure that the your changes built cleanly (that is, were green) for each platform affected. (Obviously, if the change was only made to, say, Mac-specific code, you were only obligated to see the Mac builds go green.) If the tree affected by your changes was green when you checked in, and then it went red in the first build that followed, then, as a member of the hook, you were required to help identify and fix the problem.

In addition to the hook, a *sheriff* was assigned by Netscape (or Mozilla) to monitor the overall state of the Tinderbox monitoring the tier-1 platforms, and to ensure that the builds all remained green. We eventually rotated the responsibility of sheriffing inside of Netscape among the various development teams, one day the responsibility would fall to members of the mail-news team, on another, it was the responsibility of the IM team, and so on. Should a problem arise, the sheriff had the power to close the tree to all check-ins (this was communicated by a simple message at the top of the Tinderbox page), which was done in an attempt to aid those trying to isolate the cause of problems. The sheriff also had the authority to contact anyone on the hook, usually by e-mail, but by phone if necessary, should a diagnosis of the problem indicate that the person being contacted was to blame for the tree going red. As sheriff, I recall numerous times calling people by phone who had left the tree burning and had gone home for the night. Not everyone was happy about the policy, but it did cause people to be more careful about their work.

In a nutshell, Tinderbox plays an important role in cross-platform development because it forces developers to confront issues that affect the portability of code being committed to the repository. Although a responsible developer will try to determine the impact of changes on other platforms before landing code in the tree, this is not always done. Tinderbox acts as a backstop, ensuring that nothing slips through the cracks. And when problems are detected, either because of a red tree or a failed QA test the next day, Tinderbox can be used as an aid in determining which changes had been made that might be the cause of the problem.

Getting a green build on all the platforms is, of course, not the end of the story. A green build does not ensure that cross-platform feature parity is met for the platform, for example. A developer could implement a cross-platform feature and check in a full implementation for, say, Mac OS X and only stub implementations for Linux and Windows, and Tinderbox will not make this fact evident. What Tinderbox does do a good job of is ensuring that code shared among platforms builds everywhere, and that no one platform can hijack the stability of the tree (that is, leave the repository in a state such that it builds cleanly for only a subset of the supported platforms). As such, Tinderbox helps ensure that when platforms are worked on at the same time, the cross-platform train is moving ahead at the same pace for all platforms involved. This in turn helps ensure that the organization will be able to release a product to the market for all the supported platforms at about the same point in time, which is something that we strived for at Netscape. Remember, however, that Tinderbox is just an aid—only by testing the resulting builds carefully can you confirm that a product or feature has achieved cross-platform parity.

Item 13: Use CVS or Subversion to Manage Source Code

An SCM system does exactly what the name implies; it helps you manage source code and related resources. To appreciate why SCM is important, consider for a moment what life without it might be like. Assume that you are a developer working on a new project that will consist of C++ sources files, a Makefile, and perhaps some resources such as icons or images. Obviously, these items must live somewhere, and so on day one of the project, you create a directory on your local desktop system where these files will live, and write a few hundred lines of code, storing the results in that directory. After a few weeks of hacking, you come up with version 0.1 of your creation, and after some light testing, you decide that your creation is ready to be pushed out onto the Web, with the hope of generating some user feedback from a small community of users.

After a few weeks, your e-mail inbox has accumulated several feature requests from users, and perhaps a dozen or so bug reports (in addition to a ton of spam because you gave out your e-mail address to the public). You get busy implementing some of these features and fixing the worst of the bugs, and after a few more weeks, you are ready to post version 0.2. This process repeats itself for a few months, and before you know it, you are shipping version 1.0 to an even wider audience.

The 1.0 release is a success, but isn't without its share of problems. First off, users are beginning to report a nasty bug in a feature that was first introduced in version 0.8, and was working flawlessly until version 1.0 was released to the public. You are able to duplicate the bug in a release version of the 1.0 binary, but can't duplicate it in a debugger. In an attempt to understand the problem, you pour over the code in search of clues; but after numerous hours of looking, you realize that you have no idea what might have caused this bug to surface. About the only way you can think of identifying the cause of the problem is to determine what specific changes you made to the codebase that might have led to the bug's manifestation. However, all you have to work with is the 1.0 source code, and you have no way of identifying the changes you made between 0.9 and 1.0.

The second problem before you is a request. It turns out that you removed a feature that was present in version 1.0, and removing the feature has angered a lot of your users, who are clamoring for it to be reinstated in version 1.1. However, the code for this feature no longer exists, having been deleted from the source code long ago.

It is these two situations that, in my experience, make the use of a source code management system a necessity, cross-platform or not, no matter how large the project is or how many developers are involved. A good source code management system will allow you to re-create, in an instance, a snapshot of the source tree at some point in the past, either in terms of a specific date and time, or in terms of a specific release version. It will also help you to keep track of where and when changes to the source code have been made, so that you can go back and isolate specific changes related to a feature or a bug fix.

Had the developer used a source control management system, he or she could have retrieved versions of the source code starting at 0.9 and used this to isolate exactly what change(s) to the source caused the bug to first surface. And, to retrieve the source code for the feature that was removed in 1.0, the developer could have used the source code management system to retrieve the code associated with the feature, and undo its removal (or reengineer it back into the current version of the source code).

The benefits of a source code management system increase significantly as soon as multiple developers are assigned to a project. The main benefits from the point of view of a multideveloper project are accountability and consistency. To see how these benefits are realized, I need to describe in more detail how a source code management system works. Earlier, I described how a developer will typically manage a body of source code, in the absence of a source code management system, in a directory, which is usually created somewhere on the developer's system where a single copy of the source is stored and edited. The use of a source code management system changes things dramatically, however. When using a source code management system, the source code for a project is maintained in something called a repository, which you can think of as being a database that stores the master copy of a project's source code and related files. To work with the project source code, a developer retrieves a copy of the source code from the repository. Changes made to the local copy of the source code do not affect the repository. When the developer is done making changes to his or her copy of the source, he or she submits the changes to the source code management system, which will update the master copy maintained in the repository. It is important to realize that the repository records only the changes made to the file, instead of a complete copy of the latest version.

By storing only changes, you can easily retrieve earlier versions of files stored in the repository. The date of the change, the name or the ID of the developer who made the change, and any comments provided by the developer along with the change are all stored in the repository along with the change itself. The implications for developer accountability should be obvious; at any time, you can query the source code management system for a log of changes, when they were made, and by whom. This is a great help in locating the source of bugs and who may have caused them.

The ability to attribute a change in the repository to a developer, bug, or feature is directly affected by the granularity of check-ins made by developers on the project. Frequent, small changes to the repository will increase the ability of a developer to use the source control management system to identify and isolate change, and will also help ensure that other developers on the project gain access to the latest changes in a timely manner. A good rule of thumb is to limit the number of bugs fixed by a check-in to the repository to one (unless there are multiple, related bugs fixed by the same change).

So, now that you know the basic ideas being using an SCM, let's talk briefly about the implications to portability. First off, using an SCM is not a magic pill that makes your project portable. Portability requires attention to a lot more than just a source code management system to happen. (If that were not the case, this book would not need to be written.) But, using a source code management system that is available on each of the platforms that your organization is supporting (or plans to support) is, in my view, a critical part of any successful cross-platform project. It does no one any good if only Windows developers are able to pull source code, but Linux and Macintosh developers are left without a solution, after all. Not only should the SCM software be available everywhere, it at least should support a "lowest common denominator" user interface that behaves the same on all platforms, and to me, that means that the user interface needs to be command line based (both CVS and Subversion [SVN] support a command-line interface).

Because cross-platform availability and a common user interface are requirements, there are only two choices for an SCM system that I can see at the time of writing this book: CVS and SVN. At Netscape, and at countless other places (open source or not), CVS is the SCM of choice. It has stood the test of time, and is capable. It has been ported nearly everywhere, and its user interface is command line based. A very close cousin of CVS is SVN. After using SVN in a professional project, I have come to the conclusion that for the programmers using it, SVN is quite similar to CVS in terms of how one approaches it and the commands that it offers, so either would be a good choice. (It is not without its quirks, however.) In this book, when I refer to an SCM, I am referring to CVS, but I could have easily said the same thing about SVN.

Besides providing a location from which Tinderbox can pull sources (see Item 12) and its support for Windows, Mac OS X, and Linux, perhaps the most important contribution of CVS to cross-platform development is its ability to create diff (or patch) files. The implications to cross-platform development of patch files are detailed in Item 14; in the following paragraphs, I describe what a patch file is and how CVS can be used to create a patch file.

A diff file, or a patch, is created by executing the `cvs diff` command. For example, assume I have added a method called `GetAlignment()` to a file named nsLabel.h in the Mozilla source tree. By typing `cvs diff`, I can easily identify the lines containing changes that I made:

```
$ cvs diff
cvs server: Diffing .
Index: nsLabel.h
===================================================================
RCS file: /cvsroot/mozilla/widget/src/gtk/nsLabel.h,v
retrieving revision 1.21
diff -r1.21 nsLabel.h
61a62
>    NS_IMETHOD GetAlignment(nsLabelAlignment *aAlignment);
71d71
<    GtkJustification GetNativeAlignment();
```

The preceding output tells us that a line was added around line 61 of the file nsLabel.h, and one was removed around line 71 of the file. I can take this output, mail it to others on my team, and ask them to review it for errors or comments before checking in the changes. I can also look at this patch and make sure that it contains only those changes that I intended to land in the repository. I can't stress how important `cvs diff` is as a tool for identifying inadvertent check-ins before they are made.

With a lot of changes, the default output format that is shown here can be difficult to understand. A better output would show context lines, and make it more obvious which lines were added to the source, and which lines were deleted. The –u argument to `cvs diff` causes it to generate a "unified" diff, as follows:

```
$ cvs diff -u
cvs server: Diffing .
Index: nsLabel.h
======================================================================
RCS file: /cvsroot/mozilla/widget/src/gtk/nsLabel.h,v
retrieving revision 1.21
diff -u -r1.21 nsLabel.h
--- nsLabel.h    28 Sep 2001 20:11:17 -0000        1.21
+++ nsLabel.h    1 Feb 2004 02:47:21 -0000
@@ -59,6 +59,7 @@
   NS_IMETHOD SetLabel(const nsString &aText);
   NS_IMETHOD GetLabel(nsString &aBuffer);
   NS_IMETHOD SetAlignment(nsLabelAlignment aAlignment);
+  NS_IMETHOD GetAlignment(nsLabelAlignment *aAlignment);

   NS_IMETHOD PreCreateWidget(nsWidgetInitData *aInitData);

@@ -68,7 +69,6 @@

 protected:
   NS_METHOD CreateNative(GtkObject *parentWindow);
-  GtkJustification GetNativeAlignment();

   nsLabelAlignment mAlignment;
```

The differences in the output are the inclusion of context lines before and after the affected lines, and the use of + and – to indicate lines that have been added, or removed, respectively, from the source. This format is generally much easier on everyone who must read the patch, and it is the format that I recommend you use. You can change the number of lines of context generated by `cvs diff` by appending a count after the –u argument. For example, to generate only one line of context, issue the following command:

```
$ cvs diff -u1
cvs server: Diffing .
Index: nsLabel.h
======================================================================
RCS file: /cvsroot/mozilla/widget/src/gtk/nsLabel.h,v
retrieving revision 1.21
diff -u -1 -r1.21 nsLabel.h
--- nsLabel.h    28 Sep 2001 20:11:17 -0000        1.21
+++ nsLabel.h    1 Feb 2004 02:50:45 -0000
@@ -61,2 +61,3 @@
```

```
   NS_IMETHOD SetAlignment(nsLabelAlignment aAlignment);
+  NS_IMETHOD GetAlignment(nsLabelAlignment *aAlignment);

@@ -70,3 +71,2 @@
   NS_METHOD CreateNative(GtkObject *parentWindow);
-  GtkJustification GetNativeAlignment();
```

Generally, you'll want to generate somewhere between three or five lines of context for patches of moderate complexity. I use –u3 almost religiously, and it is the default number of lines for svn diff (which does context diffs by default, too). However, don't be surprised if developers working with your patch files ask for more lines of context.

Setting Up and Using CVS

For those of you who are interested, I describe the steps it takes to set up a CVS server on a Red Hat-based system. The steps I provide here are almost certainly going to be the same when executed on non-Red Hat systems, and may differ in certain ways on other UNIX-based systems, including Mac OS X. The work involved in getting a CVS server up and running is not terribly difficult, and can be done in a relatively short amount of time. You will need root access to the system upon which you are installing the server, and it will help to have a second system with a CVS client so that you can test the result.

That said, if doing system administration makes you nervous, or site policy disallows it, or you do not have root access, check with a local guru or your system administrator for help.

To start the process of getting a CVS server running, you need to download the source for CVS from the Internet, build it, and install it. I retrieved a nonstable version of CVS by downloading the file cvs-1.11.22.tar.gz from http://ftp.gnu.org/non-gnu/cvs/source/stable/1.1.22. You are probably best, however, grabbing the latest stable version you can find.

After you have unpacked the file, cd into the top-level directory (in my case, cvs-1.11.22), and enter the following to build and install the source:

```
$ ./configure
$ make
$ su
$ make install
```

Next, while still logged in as root, you need to do some work so that the CVS server daemon executes each time the system is rebooted. The first step is to check to see whether entries like the following are located in /etc/services:

```
cvspserver 2401/tcp     # CVS client/server operations
cvspserver 2401/udp     # CVS client/server operations
```

If these lines don't exist, add them to /etc/services as shown. Next, you need to create a file named cvspserver in /etc/xinetd.d that contains the following:

```
service cvspserver
{
    socket_type = stream
    protocol    = tcp
    wait        = no
    user        = root
    passenv     = PATH
    server      = /usr/bin/cvs
    server_args = -f --allow-root=/usr/cvsroot pserver
}
```

Make sure the permissions of this file are -rw-r--r--, and that its group and owner are **root**. This is probably the default, but it doesn't hurt to check.

If you are not yet running the desktop graphical user interface (GUI), fire it up, and from the Red Hat Start menu, select System Settings, Users and Groups to launch the Red Hat User Manager.

In the dialog that is displayed, click the Add Group button and add a group named cvsadmin. Next, click the Add User button, and add a user named cvsuser. You will be asked to provide a password; enter in something you can remember, and when you are done, exit the Red Hat User Manager.

Back in a terminal, and still as root, enter the following:

```
# cd /usr
# mkdir cvsroot
# chmod 775 cvsroot
# chown cvsuser cvsroot
# chgrp cvsadmin cvsroot
```

The preceding commands create the root directory for the CVS server. The
path /usr/cvsroot corresponds to the value used in the server_args field of the
service aggregate that was created earlier in /etc/xinetd.d. The following
commands create a locks directory below cvsroot:

```
# cd cvsroot
# mkdir locks
# chown cvsuser locks
# chgrp cvsadmin locks
```

Now that the directory exists for the repository, it is time to create the
repository. You can do this by executing the cvs init command, as
follows:

```
# cvs -d /usr/cvsroot init
```

The –d argument specifies the location of the repository.

Now that the repository has been created, change to your home
directory (for example, /home/syd), and execute the following command,
which will check out the CVSROOT module from the repository that was just
created:

```
# cvs -d /usr/cvsroot checkout CVSROOT
cvs checkout: Updating CVSROOT
U CVSROOT/checkoutlist
U CVSROOT/commitinfo
U CVSROOT/config
U CVSROOT/cvswrappers
U CVSROOT/editinfo
U CVSROOT/loginfo
U CVSROOT/modules
U CVSROOT/notify
U CVSROOT/rcsinfo
U CVSROOT/taginfo
U CVSROOT/verifymsg
```

Next, cd into the CVSROOT directory that was created by the preceding
command, and open up the file named config using your favorite editor.
Make the contents of this file consistent with the following:

```
# Set this to "no" if pserver shouldn't check system
# users/passwords.
SystemAuth=no
```

```
# Put CVS lock files in this directory rather than
# directly in the repository.
#LockDir=/var/lock/cvs


# Set 'TopLevelAdmin' to 'yes' to create a CVS
# directory at the top level of the new working
# directory when using the 'cvs checkout' command.
TopLevelAdmin=yes


# Set 'LogHistory' to 'all' or 'TOFEWGCMAR' to log all
# transactions to the history file, or a subset as
# needed (ie 'TMAR' logs all write operations)
#LogHistory=TOFEWGCMAR


# Set 'RereadLogAfterVerify' to 'always' (the default)
# to allow the verifymsg script to change the log
# message. Set it to 'stat' to force CVS to verify
# that the file has changed before reading it. This can
# take up to an extra second per directory being
# committed, so it is not recommended for large
# repositories. Set it to 'never' (the previous CVS
# behavior) to prevent verifymsg scripts from changing
# the log message.
#RereadLogAfterVerify=always
```

After you have made changes to the config file, check it into CVS as follows:

```
# cvs commit
cvs commit: Examining .
Checking in config;
/usr/cvsroot/CVSROOT/config,v  <--  config
new revision: 1.2; previous revision: 1.1
done
cvs commit: Rebuilding administrative file database
```

In the same directory, run the following command to create a password for each user for whom you want to grant access to the repository. Every time you add a new developer to the project, you need to update the passwd file as I am about to describe, and check the changes into the repository:

```
# htpasswd passwd syd
New password:
Re-type new password:
Adding password for user syd
```

Now, open the file passwd (which was just created). At the end of the password, append :cvsuser. The result should look something like this:

```
syd:B9TyxNZ11EKb6:cvsuser
```

Next, you must add the password file to the repository, and commit the result:

```
# cvs -d /usr/cvsroot add passwd
cvs add: scheduling file 'passwd' for addition
cvs add: use 'cvs commit' to add this file permanently
# cvs -d /usr/cvsroot commit
RCS file: /usr/cvsroot//CVSROOT/passwd,v
done
Checking in passwd;
/usr/cvsroot//CVSROOT/passwd,v  <--  passwd
initial revision: 1.1
done
cvs commit: Rebuilding administrative file database
```

This should result in two files in /usr/cvsroot/CVSROOT, one named passwd,v and the other named passwd. If there is not a file named passwd in /usr/cvsroot/CVSROOT (this could happen because of a bug in CVS), return to the checked-out version of CVSROOT (for example, the one in your home directory), edit the file named checkoutlist, and add a line to the end of the file that contains the text passwd. Then, doing a cvs commit on the checkoutlist file will cause the passwd file in /usr/cvsroot/CVSROOT to appear.

Now all that is left is to make the modules. Each directory you create under /usr/cvsroot is, logically, a project that is maintained in the repository. You can organize the hierarchy as you see fit. Here, I create a project named client:

```
# cd /usr/cvsroot
# mkdir client
# chown cvsuser client
# chgrp cvsadmin client
```

Now that we have created the repository, added a project, and set up some users, we can start the CVS server daemon by kicking xinetd:

```
# /etc/init.d/xinetd restart
Stopping xinetd:                         [  OK  ]
Starting xinetd:                         [  OK  ]
```

To ensure that the CVS server is running, run the following command:

```
# netstat -a | grep cvs
```

If you see output like the following, everything is in order, and you can use the repository:

```
tcp       0       0 *:cvspserver    *:*        LISTEN
```

To test out the new server and repository, find another machine, open up a shell (or a GUI CVS client if you prefer), and then check out the project named client. In the following example, I am using a command-line CVS client, and the server is located on my local network at the IP address 192.168.1.102:

```
$ cvs -d :pserver:syd@192.168.1.102:/usr/cvsroot login
(Logging in to syd@192.168.1.102)
CVS password:
$ cvs -d :pserver:syd@192.168.1.102:/usr/cvsroot co \
client
cvs server: Updating client
```

There now should be a directory named client in the current directory. If you cd into the client directory, you should see the following contents:

```
$ cd client
$ ls
CVS
```

At this point, you can add files and directories to the project with cvs add, and commit them to the repository using cvs commit.

Item 14: Use Patch

The patch program is considered by some to be the prime enabler behind the success of open source software. To quote Eric Raymond, "The patch program did more than any other single tool to enable collaborative development over the Internet—a method that would revitalize UNIX after 1990" (*The Art of UNIX Programming,* Addison-Wesley, 2003). Of course, it is hard to imagine patch taking all the credit; after all, what would development be without vi(1)? But still, there is a ring of truth in what he says.

In the open source community, at any given moment, on any given project, there are dozens, if not hundreds of developers, all working on some derivation of what is in currently on the tip (or branch) of some source code repository. All of them are working relatively blind to the changes that their counterparts are making to the same body of source code.

An Example

Integrating (and evaluating) the changes made to a shared body of source code in such an environment can be difficult and error prone without a tool like patch. To see how, consider a team of three developers (A, B, and C) all working from the tip of the repository. Developer B is the team lead, and his job is to perform code reviews for Developer A and C, and integrate their changes into the source tree once an acceptable code review has been obtained. He also does development on the same body of source code, because he owns the overall architecture.

Let's say that Developer A finishes his work and is in need of a code review. To obtain the code review, Developer B needs to communicate his changes to Developer B. I've seen this done a few different ways over the years:

■ Developer A copies and pastes the changes made to the source file(s) into a text file, and sends the result to Developer B. In addition, Developer A adds comments to the text file to describe what the changes are, and where in the original source file the changes were made (or Developer A e-mails this information separately to Developer B). This is perhaps the worst method of all for conducting a code review, for two reasons:

1. Developer A may make a mistake and not copy and paste all the changes that were made, or miss entire source files that have modification. The omission of a single line of change can greatly affect the ability of a code reviewer to accurately perform his task. Worse yet, if the code reviewer is responsible for integrating the changes into the repository and changes were missed, the process will surely lead to bugs.

2. Even if all changes are copied and pasted by Developer A, there is a chance that context will be lost or incorrectly communicated. One way to counter this problem would be for Developer A to include extra lines above and below the code that actually changed, but this is a better job for a tool like `cvs diff`, which can generate a patch file that contains the needed lines of context.

■ Developer A sends to Developer B copies of all the source files that were changed. This is better than sending a series of hand-constructed diffs, because Developer B can now take the source files and create a patch that correctly captures the changes made by Developer A, along with the context of those changes. If Developer A sends source files that are not being modified by Developer B, Developer B can simply use the diff program (not `cvs diff` or `svn diff`) to generate a patch file relative to his current working tree. If Developer A, however, sends changes that do affect files modified by Developer B, Developer B can either diff against his working tree to see the changes in the context of work he is performing, or Developer B can pull a new tree somewhere and generate a patch file from it. The actual method used is usually best determined by the code reviewer. The downsides of this method are as follows:

1. It is error prone. (Developer A might forget to include source files that contain change.)
2. It places a burden on the code reviewer to generate a patch file. The last thing you want to do on a large project is make more work for the code reviewer. Usually, a code reviewer is generally always struggling to keep up with not only his own development task, but with all the code review requests that are pouring in. Anything you can do to make his job easier will generally be appreciative (and may result in the code reviewer giving your requests a higher priority).

■ Developer A generates a patch file using `cvn` or `svn diff`, and sends it to the code reviewer. This is the best method because

1. The changes are relative to Developer A's source tree.
2. `cvs diff` won't miss any changes that were made, assuming that `cvs diff` is run at a high-enough level of the source tree. (There is one exception: new source files that have not been added to the repository, along with forgetting to pass the –N argument to `cvs diff` when creating a patch file [this is not a problem with `svn diff`, which automatically includes new source files in its diff output.])

After the code reviewer (Developer B) receives the patch from Developer A, he or she has a few options:

- Simply look at the patch file, performing the code review based on its contents alone. Most of the time, this is what I do, especially if the patch file is a unified diff (as it should always be), and if the changes do not intersect any that I am making.
- Apply the patch file to his local tree, build the result, and then perhaps test it. This can be helpful if Developer B would like to step through an execution of the code in a debugger, or to see that the patch builds correctly and without warnings. If Developer A has made changes to some of the source files that were modified by Developer B, Developer B can either
    1. Pull a new tree and apply the patch to it so that his or her changes are not affected.
    2. Use `cvs diff` to generate a patch file that contains his own changes, and then attempt to apply the changes from Developer A into his source tree. This allows Developer B not only to see the changes made by Developer A, but also to see them in the context of the changes that he is making. When the code review has been completed, Developer B can continue working on his changes, and check both his and Developer B's changes in at a later time, or Developer B can have Developer A check in the changes, and then do a `cvs` or `svn update` to get in sync.

The patch program is the tool used by a code reviewer to apply changes specified in a patch file to a local copy of the repository. In essence, if both you and I have a copy of the same source tree, you can use `cvs diff` to generate a patch file containing changes you have made to your copy of the sources, and then I can use the patch program, along with your patch file, to apply those changes to my copy of the sources. The patch program tries very hard to do its job accurately, even if the copy of the sources the patch is being applied to have been changed in some unrelated way. The type of diff contained in the patch file affects the accuracy attained by the patch program; patch is generally more successful if it is fed a set of context diffs rather than normal diffs. The `cvs diff -u3` syntax (unified diff with three lines of context) is enough to generate a patch file that gives a good result. (SVN by default generates unified diffs with three lines of context.)

Patch Options

The patch program has a number of options. (You can refer to the patch man page for more details.) However, in practice, the only option that matters much is the -p argument, which is used to align the absolute paths used in the patch file with the local directory structure containing the sources that the patch is being applied to. When you run cvs diff to create a patch file, it is best to do it from within the source tree, at the highest level in the directory hierarchy necessary to include all the files that have changes. The resulting patch file will, for each file that has changes, identify the file with a relative path, and patch uses this relative path to figure out what file in the target directory to apply changes to. For example:

```
Index: layout/layout.cpp
===================================================================
RCS file: /usr/cvsroot/crossplatform/layout/layout.cpp,v
retrieving revision 1.33
diff -u -3 -r1.33 layout.cpp
--- layout/layout.cpp    27 May 2006 09:31:47 -0000   1.33
+++ layout/layout.cpp     7 Jun 2006 10:43:22 -0000
@@ -327,7 +327,7 @@
    return document;
 }


-int main(int argc, char *argv[])
+int LayoutMain(int argc, char *argv[])
 {
    int run, parse;
    char *src = NULL;
```

The first line in the preceding patch (the line prefixed with Index:) specifies the pathname of the file to be patched. Assuming that the patch is contained in a file named patch.txt, then, if the preceding patch file were copied to the same relative location in the target tree, then issuing the following command is sufficient for patch to locate the files that are specified in the patch file:

```
$ patch -p0 < patch.txt
```

The -p argument will remove the smallest prefix containing the specified number of leading slashes from each filename in the patch file, using the result to locate the file in the local source tree. Because the patch file was copied to the same relative location of the target tree that was used to generate the patch file in the source tree, we must use -p0 because we do not want patch to remove any portion of the path names when searching for files. If -p1 were used (with the same patch file, located in the same place in the target tree), the pathname layout/layout.cpp would be reduced to layout.cpp, and as a result, patch would not be able to locate the file, because the file would not be located in the current directory. Copying the patch file down into the layout directory would fix this, but this could only be done if, and only if, the patch file affected only sources that were located in the layout directory, because the -p0 is applied by patch to all sources represented in the patch file.

Dealing with Rejects

So much for identifying which files to patch. The second difficulty you may run into is rejects. If patch is unable to perform the patch operation, it will announce this fact, and do one of two things. Either it will generate a reject file, which is a filename in the same directory as the file being patched, but with a .rej suffix (for example, bar.cpp.rej), or it will place text inside of the patched file to identify the lines that it was unable to resolve. (The –dry-run option can be used to preview the work performed by patch. As the name implies, it will cause patch to do a "dry run" of the patch operation, to let you know if it will succeed, without actually changing any of the target files.)

If either of these situations happens, there are a few ways to deal with it. The first thing I would do is remove the original source file, re-pull it from the repository using cvs update, and try to reapply the patch, in case I was applying the patch to a file that was not up-to-date with the tip. If this didn't work, I would contact the person who generated the patch and ask that person to verify that his or her source tree was up-to-date at the time the patch file was generated. If it was not, I would ask that person to run cvs update on the file or files and generate a new patch file.

If neither of these strategies works, what happens next depends on the type of output generated by patch. If patch created a .rej file, I would open it and the source file being patched in an editor, and manually copy and paste the contents of the .rej file into the source, consulting with the author of the patch file in case there are situations that are not clear. If, on the other hand, patch inlined the errors instead of generating a .rej file, open the source that was patched and search for lines containing <<<. These lines (and ones containing >>>) delimit the original and new source changes that were in conflict. By careful inspection of the patch output, and perhaps some consultation with the author of the patch, you should be able to identify which portions of the resulting output should stay, and which portions of the result need to go, and perform the appropriate editing in the file to come up with the desired final result.

Thankfully, problems like this happen only rarely. The two most common causes of conflict occur when a developer is accepting a patch that affects code that he or she has also modified, or the patch files are created against a different baseline. There is little to do to avoid the first case, other than better communication among developers to ensure that they are not modifying the same code at the same time. The second case is usually are avoided when developers are conscientious about ensuring that their source trees (and patches) are consistent with the contents of the CVS repository. When this is done, problems are relatively rare, and if they do occur, usually are slight and easy to deal with.

Patch and Cross-Platform Development

Now that you have an idea of why patch is so important to open source software, and how to use it, I need to describe how patch can make developing cross-platform software easier. At Netscape, each developer had a Mac, PC, and Linux system in his or her cubicle, or was at least encouraged to have one of each platform. (Not all did, in reality.) Each developer, like most of us, tended to specialize in one platform. (There were many Windows developers, a group of Mac developers, and a small handful of Linux developers.) As a result, it would only be natural that each developer did the majority of his or her work on the platform of his or her choice.

At Netscape, to overcome the tendency for the Windows developers to ignore the Linux and Macintosh platforms (I'm not picking on just Windows developers; Macintosh and Linux developers at Netscape were just as likely to avoid the other platforms, too), it was required that each developer ensure that all changes made to the repository correctly built and executed on each of the primary supported platforms, not just the developer's primary platform. To do this, some developers installed Network File System (NFS) clients on their Macintosh and Windows machines, and then pulled sources from the repository only on the Linux machine, to which both Mac and Windows machines had mounts. Effectively, Linux was a file server for the source, and the other platforms simply built off that source remotely. (The build system for Netscape/Mozilla allowed for this by isolating the output of builds; see Item 12.) This allowed, for example, the Windows developers to do all of their work on Windows, walk over to the

Mac and Linux boxes, and do the required builds on those platforms, using the same source tree.

But what if NFS (or, Samba these days) was not available? Or, more likely, developers did not have all three platforms to build on (or if they did, have the skills needed to make use of them)? In these cases, the patch program would come to the rescue. Developers could create a patch file, for example, on their Windows machine, and then either copy it to the other machines (where a clean source tree awaited for it to be applied to), or they could mail it to a "build buddy" who would build the source for those platforms that the developer was not equipped to build for. (Macintosh build buddies were highly sought after at Netscape because most developers at Netscape did not have the desire, or the necessary skills, to set up a Macintosh development system; it was much easier to ask one of the Macintosh helpers to be a build buddy.)

Netscape's policy was a good one, and patch was an important part of its implementation. The policy was a good one because, by forcing all check-ins to build and run on all three platforms at the same time, it made sure that the feature set of each of the three platforms moved forward at the about the same pace (see Item 1). Mozilla, Netscape, and today, Firefox, pretty much work the same on Mac, Windows, and Linux, at the time of release. The combination of `cvs diff`, which accurately captured changes made to a local tree, and patch, which accurately merged these changes into a second copy of the tree, played a big role in enabling this sort of policy to be carried out, and allows projects such as Mozilla Firefox to continue to achieve cross-platform parity.

4 Installation and Deployment

In this chapter, we turn to the topic of software installation and runtime environment. Although much of this book is oriented toward the writing of code, installation is such an important part of a cross-platform project that I felt obliged to devote considerable space to the topic. First, I describe XPInstall, the technology that was developed by Netscape and Mozilla to support cross-platform installation of the browser, plug-ins, and extensions. XPInstall uses a recurring theme in this book—abstraction—to achieve its goals.

Unfortunately, XPInstall is tightly coupled to Mozilla, so much so that it is not appropriate for use by non-Mozilla projects. Therefore, I go on to describe three platform-specific install techniques: shell scripts for Linux, drag-and-drop installs for Mac OS X, and Nullsoft Scriptable Install System (NSIS), an open source GUI installer for Windows. These installers are, from my point of view, important because they provide the basic needs of installation, are low in cost, and they are all fairly simple to develop and deploy. In describing these installation techniques, I spend some time describing the basics of the runtime environments associated with each platform, to give you a perspective on what areas need to be addressed.

Item 15: Provide Support for Native Installers

Netscape/Mozilla did a lot of great things when it came to cross-platform development. The overriding policy at Netscape and Mozilla was that all tier-1 platforms (Mac OS, Windows, and Linux) would be given equal priority, and would ship at the same time, with, as much as possible, the same level of quality. The software was highly object oriented, and used design patterns to build abstractions above the platform implementations to achieve this. The user interface was implemented in XML User Interface Language (XUL) and JavaScript, hiding, for the most part, platform issues from the developers of extensions and components.

Netscape even went as far as implementing a cross-platform installer technology named XPInstall. (I became the manager of the XPInstaller team during the development of the Netscape 6.1 browser.) XPInstall is the mechanism by which the browser is initially installed on the system, which of course is the traditional use of an installer. Beyond that, XPInstall supports the installation of plug-ins and extensions to an existing browser installation.

XPInstall

Although I don't want to get into all the details related to XPInstall (for that, you can visit www.mozilla.org and search on XPInstall), it is instructive to know how XPInstall performs its work. An XPInstall of the browser requires the following items: a stub installer, the XPInstall engine, and packages. Let's start with the installer engine. The installer engine is C++ code that is highly Mozilla specific in that it relies on several core Mozilla technologies. Perhaps the most important of these technologies are XPCOM and the JavaScript engine. The JavaScript engine is needed because the install scripts that one writes for use with XPInstall are all written in JavaScript. XPCOM is the Mozilla cross-platform COM engine, and it is needed because it provides the means by which JavaScript code can call C++. The C++ that is being called from JavaScript is the XPInstall engine, which exposes interfaces that are useful to the JavaScript-based XPInstall script.

The stub installer is a native C++ application that has the following responsibilities:

- Provide a user interface for the installation. This user interface allows the user to select from the available components to install, to initiate or cancel the install, and to monitor the progress of the install.
- Initialize the XPInstall engine.
- Download (via FTP or HTTP, depending on the choice of the user) the XPI files that correspond to the packages that were selected for installation by the user.
- Install each XPI file that was downloaded, in the order required by package dependencies.

Each XPI package contains a component or application. The browser, mail, and instant messenger applications are among several component-based applications that were distributed as XPI packages in the Netscape installation. Each XPI basically consists of platform-specific component binaries, resources, and an XPInstall script that describes the logic and steps of the installation. An XPI file itself is nothing more than a zip file that contains a directory hierarchy specific to XPInstall, along with the install script. Here is the content of an example XPI file. (The example we will use here and in the remaining discussion is based on the installer for the JavaScript debugger, Venkman.)

```
chrome/
    chrome/venkman.jar
components/
    components/venkman-service.js
install.js
install.rdf
```

The file install.js, which is included in each XPI file, is a script that is used to perform the install. This script, written in JavaScript, makes calls directly into application programming interfaces (APIs) provided by the XPInstall engine. The directories correspond to locations within the Mozilla installation on the user's system, and after installation, contain binaries and resources placed within these locations by the installer. The following JavaScript code represents a basic template for the install.js file. Many of the install.js files found in the Mozilla LXR (http://lxr.mozilla.org) are structured in a manner similar to this. (The following example is based on the install.js script used by Venkman.)

```
// This function verifies disk space in kilobytes.
function verifyDiskSpace(dirPath, spaceRequired)
{
  var spaceAvailable;

  // Get the available disk space on the given path.
  spaceAvailable = fileGetDiskSpaceAvailable(dirPath);

  // Convert the available disk space into kilobytes.
  spaceAvailable = parseInt(spaceAvailable / 1024);
```

```
  // Do the verification.
  if(spaceAvailable < spaceRequired)
  {
    logComment("Insufficient disk space: " + \
        dirPath);
    logComment("  required : " + \
        spaceRequired + " K");
    logComment("  available: " + \
        spaceAvailable + " K");
    return(false);
  }


  return(true);
}


var srDest = 1;

var err = initInstall("JavaScript Debugger", \
    "venkman", "0.9.87");


logComment("initInstall: " + err);

if (verifyDiskSpace(getFolder("Program"), srDest))
{
    addFile("JavaScript Debugger", \
        "chrome/venkman.jar",
        getFolder("Chrome"), "");

    addFile("JavaScript Debugger Service",
        "components/venkman-service.js",
        getFolder("Components"), "");

    registerChrome(CONTENT | DELAYED_CHROME,
        getFolder("Chrome","venkman.jar"),
        "content/venkman/");
    registerChrome(CONTENT | DELAYED_CHROME,
        getFolder("Chrome","venkman.jar"),
        "content/venkman/sm/");
    registerChrome(LOCALE | DELAYED_CHROME,
        getFolder("Chrome", "venkman.jar"),
        "locale/en-US/venkman/");
    registerChrome(SKIN | DELAYED_CHROME,
        getFolder("Chrome", "venkman.jar"),
        "skin/modern/venkman/");
```

```
    if (err==SUCCESS)
        performInstall();
    else
        cancelInstall(err);
}
else
    cancelInstall(INSUFFICIENT_DISK_SPACE);
```

An install script initializes the install by calling `initInstall()`, which takes as arguments the name of the package being installed, the name of a registry key where information about the package is installed (Mozilla maintains a registry of all installed components), and a version number. The install script then optionally determines whether there is enough space on the system needed to perform the install, adds directories and files to the install (using calls to `addDirectory()` and `addFile()`, respectively to tell the installer which files in the XPI to install), registers chrome (more on this later), and then launches the install by making a call to `performInstall()`. If any errors are encountered during the install, the install can be canceled by the script with a call to `cancelInstall()`, which will leave the system unmodified.

The JavaScript API defined by XPInstall is much more extensive than the above implies; functions for modifying the file system (creating directories, copying files around, and so forth) all exist, and have platform-specific implementations in the XPInstall engine. Some of the functionality provided at the API level is not so platform independent, but is necessary nonetheless; a prime example is the XPInstall API that supports writing to, and reading from, the Windows registry file.

File registration is performed in the preceding install.js script by making calls to the XPInstall interface `registerChrome()`. In Mozilla, *chrome* is a term that refers to the XML files that make up the XUL user interface (UI), and related resources. *PACKAGE* refers to the actual XUL and JavaScript that make up the UI, *SKIN* refers to Cascading Style Sheet (CSS) that defines the style associated with the UI, and, finally, *LOCALE* corresponds to XML Document Type Definition (DTD) files that contain entities that provide localization support for the UI.

I am omitting a lot of details here. You can find further information about XPInstall, and its API, by searching for "XPInstall" at mozilla.org.

The question before us now is this: Is it strictly necessary to use a cross-platform installer such as XPInstall to successfully deploy a cross-platform project? I don't believe so. In the case of Mozilla-based software, XPInstall is currently necessary; although it is conceivable to use a platform installer to install some portions of Firefox, Mozilla, or Netscape, it is not possible to do a complete install of Mozilla software without it. (Chrome and component registration, for example, would not be possible.) However, I imagine those portions of XPInstall that deal with chrome and component registration could be factored out of XPInstall, and executed outside of the context of the installer (perhaps as a program executed after all the bits have been downloaded to the system, before the application is first launched). The cost of developing the stub installers was high, and the quality was not at all comparable to other options that existed on Mac OS, Linux, and Windows at the time. Another problem was portability; going to a new platform required development of a new stub installer, and modifications to the XPInstall engine, work that would have not been necessary had platform-native solutions been used.

Platform Installs

When it comes to installers, you have a lot of choices out there, from the simple (tar files and shell scripts) to full-blown, cross-platform graphical user interface (GUI) installer applications. In the remainder of this item, I focus on the basics: tar.gz and bash script-based installs for Linux, drag-and-drop installation on Mac OS X, and an installer solution for Windows that is based on the powerful open source NSIS installer. Attention will be given to the topic of desktop integration; if your users cannot find the application on the desktop or via the platform's preferred launching mechanisms, it will be of little use. The degree to which you integrate your application with a particular desktop is dictated largely by the needs of your users. For example, the requirements imposed on a developer creating a command-line tool to be used by a small group of researchers will be much less than those imposed upon the developer of a full-blown, mass-market GUI application. These requirements are cumulative, fortunately; whatever needs to be done to support a simple command-line executable will also need to be supported in a GUI application.

Linux

On Linux, files have a set of permissions that dictate the specific operations that a user can perform on a file (and directories) in the file system. Users on

UNIX systems are identified by a unique user ID and belong to a group, both of which are represented by the system by a small integer ID. The IDs in both cases are mapped to a symbolic name. (For example, my username on a Linux system might be syd, which is assigned user ID 500, and I might belong to the group users, which is assigned group ID 100.) The mapping between the symbolic name and the user and group IDs is maintained, on Linux, in the /etc/passwd and /etc/group files, respectively. In /etc/password, I might be represented by the following line:

```
syd:x:500:100:Syd Logan:/home/syd:/bin/bash
```

The above line is broken down into several fields. Relevant to our discussion are fields 1, 3, and 4.

Field 1 is the username, which is syd. Field 3 is the user ID, 500, and field 4 is the group ID, 100. In the file /etc/group, group 100 is represented by the following line:

```
users:x:100:
```

Here, field 1 is the name of the group (users), and field 2 is the group ID, 100. Combined, this information tells us the user named syd belongs to the group named users. Files that I create will show this user and group when a full listing is done. For example:

```
$ ls -l ~/
total 1448
drwxrwxr-x  3 syd   users    4096 Oct 18 22:44 book
drwx------  3 syd   users    4096 Oct  7 17:04 Desktop
-rw-rw-r--  1 syd   users  324229 Sep 24 12:06 posix.html
```

Linux and other UNIX-based systems implement a special user and group, both with the name root, and both assigned the unique ID value of 0. Logging in to a UNIX system as root allows you to create, modify, execute, or delete any file on the system, which is a good reason to avoid using Linux as the root user unless absolutely necessary, because running as root makes it more likely that a careless mistake will cause damage to your system that cannot be undone.

Each file and directory in the system has an owner, identified by a user ID, and a group, identified by a group ID. In addition, each file and directory has a permissions mask that defines the operations that can be performed on the file by the owner, members of the group, and for users belonging to other groups. Three permissions are defined for both the owner and the group of a file or directory: read (r), write (w), and execute (x). The ls -l command shows the permissions that apply to the owner of the file, the group of the file, and all others (users other than the owner who do not belong to the group of the file). In the preceding listing, the permissions for posix.html are -rw-rw-r--. Ignoring the first - in the mask, the initial rw- indicates that the owner of the file, syd, can read and write the file. The second rw- indicates that users belonging to the group users can also read and write the file. Finally, all other users and groups (except of course the root user, who can do anything regardless of the permissions mask) can read the file; this is shown by the remainder of the mask, which is r--.

The first character or position in the mask defines the type of file. If it is -, the file is a normal file (for example, a text, binary, or executable file). If d, the file is a directory, and the execute bit (x) in the permissions mask controls whether the owner, group, or other users are allowed to navigate into that directory and inspect its contents. In UNIX-based systems, a user cannot access or execute a file unless the execute bits are appropriately set for all directories in the path to the file. For example, the ls command is executable for me when I am logged in as syd, even though ls, and every directory in its path, is owned by root, and belongs to the root group:

```
$ which ls
/bin/ls
$ ls -l / | grep bin
drwxr-xr-x  2  root    root    4096 Jun  4 17:55 bin
drwxr-xr-x  2  root    root    8192 Sep 13 16:57 sbin
$ ls -l /bin/ls
-rwxr-xr-x  1  root    root   67668 Feb 18  2003 /bin/ls
```

I can execute /bin/ls because the other portion of the mask associated with each component in the path (/ and /bin) has the execute bit set, and so even though I am not root, nor do I belong to the root group, the other portion of the permissions mask being set to x in both / and /bin allows me (or any other user) to execute the /bin/ls command without restriction.

When you execute a program on Linux, in most cases, the executable takes on your user and group identity. For example, if I were to log in to a system as syd and run the find command, find runs with the user ID syd as its effective user ID, and the group ID users as its effective group ID. This can be seen by running the top or ps commands. (The output has been edited to fit nicely on the page.)

```
$ top

...

  PID USER  %CPU %MEM   TIME CPU COMMAND
 1211 root   7.5  2.6   1:13   0 X
 1808 root   4.9  0.1   0:05   0 updatedb
 1816 syd    3.3  0.0   0:01   0 find
 1316 syd    2.7  2.0   0:08   0 gnome-terminal
    4 root   0.5  0.0   0:00   0 kswapd
```

Here, we see syd is the user associated with both the find and gnome-terminal processes, whereas the other processes have an effective ID of root.

So, what is the point of all this? First, consideration needs to be given when installing software onto a Linux system as to what owner, group, and permissions mask should to be assigned to each file that is installed. In addition, you must be concerned with where on the system files are installed so that users are given execute access to each directory in the file's path. (Remember, the user must have execute permission, via user, group, or other, for each component of the path that defines where the file being accessed is located.)

Generally, users will either install applications as root or as the user they are logged in as at the time the program is installed. An installer program is just like any other executable, so if I were to run an installer as syd, for example, the installer would only be allowed to write files in directories that the user syd has access to. Meaning, as syd, I would be unable to install programs in places such as /bin, or /usr/local, and I would likely be restricted to installing somewhere below my home directory. The implication here is that, depending on the permissions of the files being installed and the groups to which other users on the system belong, I (syd) will be the only user able to execute the software that I just installed, which is not what is always desired. Generally speaking, you should arrange for software to be installed as root, unless there is a specific need to restrict access to the program to the person doing the installation.

Execution Environment

In addition to the permissions issues described previously, you also need to be concerned with the execution environment. Applications are not self-contained, but link dynamically to libraries that are already present on the system, or are installed by you along with the application. To locate these libraries, a special environment variable named LD_LIBRARY_PATH must be

set, or the libraries need to be installed in locations that are searched by the
loader by default. If the installer is run without root permissions, these
standard locations are off limits, requiring the use of environment variables
to assist the loader in finding the libraries you have installed or required.
Even if the user runs the installer as root, from a installation management
point of view it makes good sense not to install in standard places, instead
creating a sandbox of sorts where your application and the libraries it loads
can be installed without worry that some other application installer (or
uninstaller) will clobber them. It's such a good idea that UNIX-like
operating systems provide a sandbox named /usr/local, where binaries,
libraries, and related files that are not part of the standard distribution are
located:

```
$ cd /usr/local
$ ls
bin  etc  games  include  lib  libexec  man  sbin\
   share  src
```

Mozilla's Linux installer provides an example of an application that uses
the sandbox approach, and we will spend the rest of this section discussing
it in detail. The mozilla binary, which on Red Hat 9 is located in /usr/bin,
is actually a script. This script is installed in /usr/bin by default, and the
sandbox I referred to previously, where the actual binaries and libraries are
located, is the directory /usr/lib/mozilla-1.2.1. (This is true for Mozilla
version 1.2.1, which is what Red Hat 9.0 distributed; other versions will
have a different name, obviously.)

The /usr/bin/mozilla script is designed to bootstrap the execution
environment required by mozilla; the main tasks that it performs are to set
and export LD_LIBRARY_PATH to /usr/lib/mozilla-1.2.1 (the sandbox), and
then run the actual Mozilla binary located in /usr/lib/mozilla-1.2.1. I
encourage you to take a look at the latest version of the Mozilla script to get
a feel for the kind of work it does; but in the end, setting the library search
path and kicking off the executable are the big ticket functions that are
performed by the script.

If you download an installer from mozilla.org, it will sandbox Mozilla
within /usr/local/mozilla. If you are running as root, this is all fine and well,
but installing as nonroot requires you to install to a location that you have
permission to install to. In either case, neither /usr/local/mozilla nor the
location you install to is likely to be in your PATH, so the Mozilla script will
not be executable without manually editing your PATH variable. I think in

this respect the Mozilla Linux installer needs some overhaul; it would be better for the installer to do as Red Hat has done and place the Mozilla script in a location that is in the default PATH (for example, /usr/bin) if it has the ability to. (It surely can check the effective user ID of the installer and realize it has permissions to install there.) It might even prompt the user for the root password, if only to install the Mozilla script in a well-known place (including replacing the Mozilla script placed in /usr/bin by Red Hat). Other problems exist with how the Mozilla installer integrates with the GNOME and KDE desktops, and I will discuss these in the next section.

Why not just have the installer tweak the user's PATH and LD_LIBRARY_PATH variables (for example, by appending a command or two to the user's .cshrc or .bashrc file, or equivalent?). Unlike installing to a standard directory, an installer has sufficient permissions and ability to modify the user's environment in this way; but in the end, doing so is ill advised. Let's start with PATH, the lesser of two evils. Generally speaking, tweaking someone's PATH variable is a dangerous thing because doing so may inadvertently cause the user to execute a different set of executables than prior to the change. For example, we might install to /usr/local/bin and change the PATH so that /usr/local/bin is placed at the front of the search path. Now, assume /usr/bin/foo is an application also in /usr/local/bin, but /usr/bin/foo and /usr/local/bin/foo are different versions (also assume that prior to the PATH change, when the user typed foo at a shell prompt, it was /usr/bin/foo that executed). Now, when the user types foo at a shell prompt, a completely different program with potentially different, and unwanted, behavior and consequences will be executed. Even if /usr/local/bin is placed at the end of the PATH variable, we may be inducing different and unexpected behavior on the user. For example, what if foo was previously not found in the search path, and some other program the user executes takes this into account, executing a different program rather than foo, one that produces a different result? By making foo available all of a sudden, we might cause the user headaches that are best avoided. As unlikely as it seems, the possibility is there, so I really don't advocate tweaking PATH variables on the user's behalf. Likewise, changing LD_LIBRARY_PATH may result in similar issues, but the damage may be worse: global changes to LD_LIBRARY_PATH potentially affect a much larger set of executables, because the loader will use this variable for all programs it loads, not just the one we installed. Thus, many programs may be dynamically linked to libraries that are different from what were linked to before the change to LD_LIBRARY_PATH.

Enough with the problem, what about the solution? You can see the solution by looking at (simplified) portions of the /usr/bin/mozilla script:

```
if [ "$LD_LIBRARY_PATH" ]
then
  LD_LIBRARY_PATH=/usr/lib/mozilla-1.2.1:\
/usr/lib/mozilla-1.2.1/plugins:$LD_LIBRARY_PATH
else
  LD_LIBRARY_PATH=/usr/lib/mozilla-1.2.1:\
/usr/lib/mozilla-1.2.1/plugins
fi
export LD_LIBRARY_PATH
MOZ_PROGRAM="/usr/lib/mozilla-1.2.1/mozilla-bin"
exec $MOZ_PROGRAM 2>/dev/null >/dev/null
```

As you can see, this script sets the LD_LIBRARY_PATH and exports it, and then executes the actual Mozilla binary, replacing the shell script (see man 1 exec for details on exec). The setting (or modification) of LD_LIBRARY_PATH is restricted in scope to the script, and so we do not affect the execution of other commands issued by the user as might happen if LD_LIBRARY_PATH were modified at a greater scope. Because we are able to encode the actual path of Mozilla and related files directly in the script, there is no need to modify the user's PATH environment variable.

I mentioned previously that an installer can be made to execute as root. To do this, the installer needs to prompt the user for a root password, and then it needs to change the effective ID of the process to 0. (In UNIX, the root is assigned the ID 0.) A commonly used way to do this is to launch the installer from a script like the following:

```
#!/bin/sh

# check to see if we are root already. if so, \
just run the installer
id=`id --user`
if [ $id -eq 0 ]
then
    ./mozilla-installer
else

# Ask the user if he or she wants to install as root.
# If the user wants to run as root, run via su, which
# prompts for a password, otherwise just execute it
# with effective ID of the user executing this script.
```

```
echo ""
echo "Welcome to the mozilla installer. To install"
echo "in a standard location, such as /usr/local, "
echo "you must run as root."
echo ""
while true
do
    echo "Would you like to install as root (Y/N/Q)?"
    read input
    if [ $input = 'Y' -o $input = 'y' ]
    then
        # run as root
        su -c ./mozilla-installer
        break
    else
    if [ $input = 'N' -o $input = 'n' ]
    then
        # run with same perms as the script
        ./mozilla-installer
        break
    else
    if [ $input = 'Q' -o $input = 'q' ]
    then
        # bail, user doesn't want to install
        break
    fi
    fi
    fi
done
fi
```

With such a script, and by changing the installer so that, if the effective ID of the installer is root it replaces the default Red Hat install of Mozilla, we can solve a big problem with the current installer by making the newly installed version of Mozilla available to all users on the system, and without requiring users to change their search paths to locate the Mozilla binary just installed.

Integrating with the GNOME and KDE Desktop

I mentioned earlier that the current Mozilla installer does a rather poor job of integrating with GNOME and KDE desktops. On KDE and GNOME, desktop integration involves the following areas:

- Making an application available to users in the desktop Start menu.
- Associating MIME types (and filenames) with an application. In the case of Mozilla, we want Mozilla to launch (or open a new browser window) to display any HTML files that the user double-clicks, or tries to open from the desktop or from an application such as Nautilus.
- Defining desktop icons for both the application and related files. We want Mozilla to display a distinctive icon on the desktop and in the Start menu, and we also want HTML files to display with an icon that makes it clear to the user that Mozilla will be launched should the user double-click or open the file from a program such as Nautilus.

Obviously, GNOME and KDE are two different desktop environments, each created and maintained by different organizations in a competition with each other for ownership of the Linux desktop. Worse case, this competition would result in vastly different ways for applications to provide the desktop integration points listed above. Fortunately, both GNOME and KDE adhere to a desktop integration standard defined by freedesktop.org, which organizes and promotes standards for desktop integration. (For more information, visit www.freedesktop.org.)

The desktop integration of an application is achieved by the installer. In the next several subsections, I describe how this is done.

Adding an Application to the Start Menu

Let's start with adding the application to the Start menu. To do this, the standard requires the installer to create and install a "desktop" file. This file describes where in the Start menu the menu item corresponding to the application will be placed, the label and icon that will be displayed by the menu item, and the application that will be executed when the menu item is selected by the user. The directory into which the desktop file is installed on Red Hat 9.0 is /usr/share/applications; the name of the desktop file can be anything as long as it ends with .desktop and is unique in that directory. (The standard provides conventions for the construction of the filename.)

Here is a condensed version of the desktop file for Mozilla as preinstalled by Red Hat 9.0. (Translations other than English and Spanish were removed; otherwise this is the complete file as shipped with Red Hat 9.0.)

```
01 [Desktop Entry]
02 Name=Mozilla Web Browser
03 Name[es]=Navegador de Web Mozilla
04 Comment=Browse the Internet
05 Comment[es]=Navegar por Internet
```

```
06 Exec=mozilla %u
07 Icon=redhat-web-browser.png
08 Terminal=0
09 Type=Application
10 Encoding=UTF-8
11 Categories=Application;Network;X-Red-Hat-Base;\
     X-Red-Hat-Base-Only;
12 StartupWMClass=Mozilla
```

In the preceding listing, I added line numbers at the beginning of each line to facilitate the following discussion. Line 01 identifies the file as a desktop file. The remaining lines in the file are of the form key=value, with the allowable set of keys defined in the standard. On line 02, the Name key is defined to be the string Mozilla Web Browser. This is the label that will be displayed in the menu item. Line 03 is the Spanish (es) translation. Additional lines in the actual desktop file define translations for several additional languages. The Comment key and translations (lines 04 and 05) define text that is shown in a tooltip when the user hovers the cursor over the menu item. Again, translations for additional languages are present in the actual desktop file; here I only show the Spanish translation.

Line 06 defines the command that is executed when the user selects the menu item. In this case, it is assumed that Mozilla will be in the user's search path, which is undeniably the case in the default environment for Red Hat 9. If an explicit path is needed, it can be specified, too. The %u argument is one of several parameters defined by the standard. In this case, %u is taken to be a single URL. About a dozen parameters are defined by the standard.

Line 07 defines an icon that is displayed in the Start menu as a part of the menu item being defined, as well as in other locations such as file managers. An implementation-dependent search algorithm is used to locate the icon if a relative path (as in this example) is used. On my Red Hat 9.0 system, this icon is located in the following places:

```
# cd /usr/share
# find . -print | \
     grep redhat-web-browser.png
./pixmaps/redhat-web-browser.png
./icons/Bluecurve/48x48/apps/redhat-web-browser.png
./icons/gnome/48x48/apps/redhat-web-browser.png
```

As is implied from the above (but not stated in the standard anywhere), the icon described is 48 x 48 pixels in size, and is encoded as PNG. As it turns

out, the icon below Bluecurve/48x48/apps is simply a symlink to /usr/share/
pixmaps/redhat-web-browser.png. Therefore, installing a 48 x 48 PNG icon
to /usr/share/pixmaps, and symlinking a file of the same name below
/usr/share/icons/Bluecurve/48x48/apps to the one installed in /usr/share/
pixmaps should be all you need to do to integrate with Red Hat 9.0's
Bluecurve environment. Notice that the icon located in /usr/share/icons/
gnome/48x48/apps/ actually links to a different file, namely /usr/share/
pixmaps/mozilla-icon.png. The Mozilla icon is the standard icon that is
supplied by mozilla.org, and shown in Figure 4-1. The Bluecurve icon is one
designed by Red Hat, and styled with their Bluecurve environment in mind.

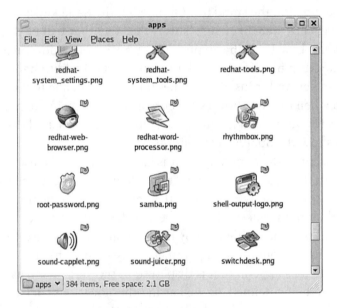

Figure 4-1 Application icons

Let's continue looking at the desktop file. The following line specifies
whether the application should be run from a terminal:

```
08 Terminal=0
```

Console and Curses-based applications should set the value of this key to 1.
The Type key (in this case, set to Application) can be one of the following:
Application, Link, FSDevice, or Directory. You should use Application
for all desktop files that you create. Line 10, Encoding, should be set to
UTF-8 in all cases.

The `Categories` key (line 11) is a set of semicolon-separated strings used to classify the application being installed. The Desktop Menu Specification published by freedesktop.org supplies a large list of valid, case-sensitive strings that can be used in the `Categories` key. Categories not defined in the spec must be prefixed with X- to indicate they are extensions. What you should do is start by adding applications, and then scan the categories that are defined in the spec, adding categories to the key that strongly correlate to the use of your application. The standard advises not going overboard with this, however, at the risk of your application being added to the Start menu in more places than is reasonable.

Restricting an Application for Use with GNOME or KDE

Two keys, `OnlyShowIn` and `NotShowIn`, can be used to specify the desktop environments for which the desktop file is applicable. Only one of these keys can be used within the desktop file. Valid values for these keys include `GNOME`, `KDE`, `ROX`, `XFCE`, and `Old`. For example, adding the line

```
OnlyShowIn=KDE
```

would cause the desktop file to be processed only if the user is currently executing within the KDE environment.

Setting the MIME Types of an Application

Many applications will find the need to create content using a file format that is unique to that application. Microsoft Word, for example, uses "doc" files to store the content of documents on disk. Backprop, an application I wrote for simulating neural networks, supports its own file types—.net, .wgt, and .exm—each encoded in XML, but designed to work with, and only with, the Backprop application. Users of desktop environments expect that these files will be displayed by a file manager application (such as Nautilus) in a way that unambiguously identifies the purpose and content of the file, and they also expect that the environment will launch the correct program if the file is opened or double-clicked. To achieve these goals, the user must provide the desktop environment with a way to formally identify the type of the file, and it must map this type to the icon that will be displayed by the desktop environment, and the program that the desktop environment will launch to handle it. In the following section, I describe how the system determines the type of a file, and in the section after that, I describe how to map this type to a desktop icon, and to the application that will be launched to handle it.

Determining File Types

As mentioned previously, Backprop creates three different file types, one to hold the architecture of a network (.net files), one to store weights after a training session (.wgt files), and one to store training exemplars (.exm files). These file extensions (.net, .wgt, and .exm) provide the first mechanism by which to identify application-specific file types to the system.

By installing a file containing the following in /usr/share/mime-info, all files that have net, exm, or wgt suffixes (either all lowercase or all upper-case) will be mapped to the MIME type application/x-backprop:

```
# mime types for backprop ...
application/x-backprop
    ext: net NET exm EXM wgt WGT
```

The name of the file that stores these associations must have an extension of .mime, and must be unique in the /usr/share/mime-info directory. (Backprop.mime would be a good choice for this example.) In some cases, it is more appropriate to use regular expressions to identify a file. To support this, you can use a `regex:` field. For example, the following associates all files ending in .wgt, .net, and so forth with the MIME type application/x-backprop, and is equivalent to the earlier backprop.mime file that used the `ext:` field:

```
application/x-backprop
    regex: *.wgt
    regex: *.net
    regex: *.exm
    regex: *.WGT
    regex: *.NET
    regex: *.EXM
```

As another example, the following associates all files with names that start with README. to the MIME type text/x-readme:

```
text/x-readme
    regex: README.*
```

You can refer to the file /usr/share/mime-info/gnome.mime for additional examples.

As it turns out (and as you may have observed), identifying file content based on the name of a file can be risky business. Nothing prohibits a user from renaming an Microsoft Word file to myimage.jpg, or an image file to foo.txt, resulting in an inaccurate identification of the file content. For that reason, the system, before using the MIME type associations just described, will attempt to inspect the content of the file to determine the content type. Only if this fails to identify the file will the filename be used.

The GIF file format provides a well-known example of the use of "magic numbers" to aid in the identification of a file. Every GIF file stores, at offset 0, the ASCII string GIF8. PNG files are similar, storing PNG at offset 0. Image processing programs, such as the GIMP and Photoshop, look for these strings when trying to determine the encoding of an image file that is being opened by a user.

The magic number mappings are made in one of two files: /etc/gnome-vfs-mime-magic or /etc/mime-magic. New applications such as Backprop do not, as of this writing, have a mechanism by which to specify a magic number mapping. However, for the time being, you should at least inspect these two files to determine whether content that you are writing matches any of the mappings defined in these files. (A simple way to check for conflicts would be to view one of the files generated by your program in a file manager such as Nautilus to see whether it maps the file to an application other than yours.)

The following illustrates the line in /etc/mime-magic that identifies a file as being application/gif if the string GIF8 is found at offset 0 in the file:

```
0       string          GIF8            image/gif
```

As you can see, the first item on the line specifies the offset in the file of the string. The second item identifies the type of data to be located (in this case, a string of ASCII characters). The third item, GIF8, is the string to search for; and final item, image/gif, is the MIME type to be associated with the file if the string GIF8 is found at offset 0. For more information on the format of this file, refer to instructions provided at the beginning of /etc/gnome-vfs-mime-magic.

Associating Icons with Files

After the MIME type mapping just described has been made, the next step is to associate the MIME type with an icon and the application that handles it. To do this, a file with a .keys extension must be created in the same directory as the .mime file (/usr/share/mime-info).

Let's take a look at the gnumeric keys file, gnumeric.keys:

```
application/x-gnumeric:
    open=gnumeric %f
    view=gnumeric %f
    icon-filename=/usr/share/pixmaps/ \
        gnome-application-x-gnumeric.png

application/vnd.ms-excel:
    open=gnumeric %f
    view=gnumeric %f
    icon-filename=/usr/share/pixmaps/\
        gnome-application-x-xls.png

application/vnd.lotus-1-2-3:
    open=gnumeric %f
    view=gnumeric %f
    icon-filename=/usr/share/pixmaps/ \
        gnome-application-vnd.lotus-1-2-3.png

application/x-applix-spreadsheet
    open=gnumeric %f
    view=gnumeric %f
    icon-filename=/usr/share/pixmaps/ \
        gnome-application-x-applix-spreadsheet.png

application/x-oleo
    open=gnumeric %f
    view=gnumeric %f
    icon-filename=/usr/share/pixmaps/ \
        gnome-application-x-generic-spreadsheet.png

application/x-xbase
    open=gnumeric %f
    view=gnumeric %f
    icon-filename=/usr/share/pixmaps/ \
        gnome-application-x-generic-spreadsheet.png
```

As you can see, the keys file for gnumeric contains several sections formatted as follows:

```
mime type
    open=command
    view=command
    icon-filename=path
```

Simply put, each section specifies a MIME type that is handled by gnumeric, the commands that should be issued to open and view content of that MIME type, and the icon to display in the file manager for files identified as being of that MIME type. (The MIME type of the file is determined as described earlier, in the section "Determining File Types.") Let's take a look at the section defined for applix spreadsheets:

```
application/x-applix-spreadsheet
    open=gnumeric %f
    view=gnumeric %f
    icon-filename=/usr/share/pixmaps/ \
        gnome-application-x-applix-spreadsheet.png
```

We see that the open and view commands for files matching this type are both the same: gnumeric %f. The %f represents the name of the file. Other valid parameters are defined in the previously mentioned Desktop Entry Specification. The icon-filename field is set to /usr/share/pixmaps/ gnome-application-x-applix-spreadsheet.png. Notice that all images defined in the gnumeric keys file are located in /usr/share/pixmaps. This is the directory that you should install your icons to, as well. Gnumeric provides icons for each MIME type supported, which is helpful to users because the icon both identifies the application that will process the file (gnumeric) and the application that generated the file originally (in this case, applix).

For Backprop, we will learn from this and create new MIME types for each file we support (.net, .wgt, and .exm), and then specify icons for each. First, let's modify backprop.mime as follows:

```
# mime types for backprop ...

application/x-backprop-network
    ext: net NET

application/x-backprop-weights
    ext: wgt WGT

application/x-backprop-exemplar
    ext: exm EXM
```

The preceding file defines three MIME types for each file type Backprop supports. Now, all that is left to do is create and install a keys file for Backprop:

```
application/x-backprop-network:
    open=backprop -n %f
    view=backprop -n %f
    icon-filename=/usr/share/pixmaps/ \
      backprop-application-x-network.png

application/x-backprop-weights:
    open=backprop -w %f
    view=backprop -w %f
    icon-filename=/usr/share/pixmaps/ \
      backprop-application-x-weights.png

application/x-backprop-exemplar:
    open=backprop -e %f
    view=backprop -e %f
    icon-filename=/usr/share/pixmaps/ \
      backprop-application-x-exemplar.png
```

The content of this file should be self-explanatory at this point. The image files should be 48 x 48 in size.

Man Pages

The man program dates back to the early days of UNIX. The man command, which is issued from a command line, is used to generate basic information about a command, file, or programming interface. The UNIX manual is divided into several sections, including (but not limited to) section 1 for commands (for example, cat), section 2 for system call APIs (for example, open()), section 3 for library APIs (for example, fopen()), and section 5 for files (for example, /etc/passwd). The command lines for accessing the man pages associated with each of the above examples are as follows:

```
$ man 1 cat
$ man 2 open
$ man 3 fopen
$ man 5 passwd
```

When the man page section is not ambiguous (as is the case with all but passwd), the manual number argument can be omitted. For example:

```
$ man cat
```

If you are not sure about a command's name, or what manual it is in, you can specify the -k argument, which will cause man to report all man pages that contain the text you supply. For example, suppose I want to find a system call for reading the contents of a directory from a C language program. I might issue the following command:

```
$ man -k directory
<many lines of output cut here>
pawd   (1)  - print automounter working directory
pax    (1)  - read and write file archives and \
   copy directory hierarchies
pwd    (1)  - print name of current/working directory
pwd    (n)  - Return the current working directory
readdir  (2)  - read directory entry
readdir  (3)  - read a directory
<many lines of output cut here>
```

From this, I can see that both readdir(2) and readdir(3) describe APIs that are capable of reading the contents of a directory. Assuming I want to look at the system call interface in section 2, I can then issue the following command:

```
$ man 2 readdir
READDIR(2)                    Linux Programmer's Manual                    READDIR(2)

NAME
       readdir - read directory entry

SYNOPSIS
       #include <unistd.h>
       #include <linux/dirent.h>
       #include <linux/unistd.h>

       _syscall3(int, readdir, uint, fd, \
           struct dirent *, dirp, uint, count);

       int readdir(unsigned int fd, \
           struct dirent *dirp, unsigned int count);

DESCRIPTION
       This is not the function you are interested in. \
       Look at readdir(3) for
```

```
        the POSIX conforming C library interface.  This \
        page documents the bare
        kernel system call interface, which can change, \
        and which is superseded
        by getdents(2).

<additional lines omitted>
$
```

There are several reasons why you might consider providing a man page with your application, some of them implied by the previous examples:

- Man pages are easily viewable from a command line, meaning the user is not dependent upon a particular desktop environment or help system to locate information.
- Man pages provide basic information needed by users to launch a program. If the help system for a program is embedded inside the program, and the user cannot launch the program to begin with, the help system is effectively useless. Man pages provide this necessary kick-start information, and the –k argument to man effectively makes man a search engine for commands and APIs available to users and programmers.
- Man pages provide pointers to related commands and information that may be useful to the user.
- Finally, there is the tradition aspect to consider: On UNIX-based systems, it's just the right thing to do.

Here's an example of how man can be used to find applications that provide image or image processing-related functionality. As you noticed earlier, the man command we used to locate APIs that can be used to read the content of a directory displayed man section numbers in the output:

```
$ man -k directory
pwd     (1)  - print name of current/working directory
pwd     (n)  - Return the current working directory
readdir (2)  - read directory entry
readdir (3)  - read a directory
```

As you can see, the manual number is provided in parentheses in the preceding output. I can use grep on the output from man –k to isolate all commands; by issuing a man –k image | grep \(1\), I can identify all programs and commands (with man pages) that have something to do with imaging:

```
$ man -k image | grep \(1\)
411toppm          (1)  - convert Sony Mavica .\
    411 image to PPM
GQview [gqview]  (1)  - GTK based multiformat \
    image viewer
ImageMagick       (1)  - commandline utilities \
    to create, edit, or convert images
Magick-config     (1)  - get information about \
    the installed version of ImageMagick
animate           (1)  - animate a sequence of images
anytopnm          (1)  - convert an arbitrary \
    type of image file to PBM, PGM, or PPM
cjpeg             (1)  - compress an image file \
    to a JPEG file
composite         (1)  - composite images together
convert           (1)  - convert an image or \
    sequence of images
display           (1)  - display an image on any \
    workstation running X
djpeg             (1)  - decompress a JPEG file \
    to an image file
eqn2graph         (1)  - convert an EQN equation \
    into a cropped image
fiascotopnm       (1)  - Convert compressed FIASCO \
    image to PGM, or PPM
<additional output omitted here>
$
```

Creating a Man Page

Now that you understand the benefits of creating a man page, let's create a simple man page for a neural network simulator named Backprop. Suppose I issue the following command:

```
$ man 1 backprop
```

The user should see the following output:

```
BACKPROP(1)                                              BACKPROP(1)


NAME
       backprop - train and execute backpropagation neural networks
```

SYNOPSIS

    backprop [-w weights][-n network] -x exemplars]

DESCRIPTION

    Backprop is a stand-alone multilayer neural network simulator that is based on
the popular backpropagation learning algorithm. The goal of this simulator is to
provide users with a friendly and easy-to-use environment for experimenting with
backpropagation networks. To achieve this, I put a lot of effort into making the user
interface give as much visual feedback as possible, especially during network
training, as well as giving the user easy to use interfaces for changing the
attributes of the network, such as learning rates, momentum, and so forth. You
can zoom in on the network graphically to see weight values in more detail, or zoom
out to make visible larger, more complicated network architectures. You can speed
up, or slow down, the rate at which error graphics and network state are updated
during training.

    Backprop displays activation and weights during training as they change,
and allows the user to enable/disable/configure the use of momentum and learning
rate during training. You can also enable or disable a bias term to see what effect
it has on convergence during training. Finally, Backprop allows you to specify the
use of sigmoid or htan activation functions.

    Please refer to the release notes for more information and instructions.

OPTIONS

    -w weights

        An XML weights file. This file is usually generated by Backprop as the
result of a training session, however, it can be generated from other sources. The
topology of the weight file must exactly match that of the network file.

    -n network

        An XML architecture file. This file describes the topology of the
neural network. The following is an example of a three layer network that contains
two input nodes, three hidden layer nodes, and an output node. Such a network
topology can be used to solve the classic XOR problem.

```
<network>
  <layer size="2"/>
  <layer size="3"/>
  <layer size="1"/>
</network>
```

    -x exemplars

        An XML exemplars file. Exemplars are used during training, supplying
both the training input and expected output. The exemplar

file is generated outside of Backprop using either a text editor or a script of some sort that generates the file using data supplied from some external source. The following example exemplars file can be used to train a three layer network with two inputs and one output to solve the XOR problem:

```
<exemplars>
    <exemplar>
        <input value="0"/>
        <input value="0"/>
        <output value="0"/>
    </exemplar>
    <exemplar>
        <input value="1"/>
        <input value="0"/>
        <output value="1"/>
    </exemplar>
    <exemplar>
        <input value="0"/>
        <input value="1"/>
        <output value="1"/>
    </exemplar>
    <exemplar>
        <input value="1"/>
        <input value="1"/>
        <output value="0"/>
    </exemplar>
</exemplars>
```

AUTHOR

backprop was originally written by Syd Logan

REPORTING BUGS

Report bugs to <sydlogan at backprop dot net>.

COPYRIGHT

Copyright ¬© 2004, 2005 Syd Logan

SEE ALSO

While the README file contains background information, backpropagation neural networks require some study to be used effectively. There are numerous references to backpropagation networks on the internet should you need a more detailed overview.

BACKPROP(1)

Man pages are processed by the `nroff` command, which is supported on just about every UNIX system that has ever been created. New roff (nroff) is a markup language, like HTML, but is primitive and rather limited in scope. The `man` command uses nroff to format the man page source file, as can be seen with `ps` as I execute the command `man who`:

```
syd  1841  1783  0 20:45 pts/2     00:00:00 man who
syd  1844  1841  0 20:45 pts/2     00:00:00 sh -c (cd \
 /usr/share/man && (echo ".pl 1100i"; /usr/bin/gunzip \
-c '/usr/share/man/man1/who.1.gz'; echo; echo \
".pl\n(nlu+10") | /usr/bin/gtbl | /usr/bin/nroff -c \
-mandoc | /usr/bin/less -isr)
```

The source for the man page contains nroff macros, analogous to elements or tags in HTML. The first line of the man page identifies the name of the command and the section of the man page to which it belongs, using the `.TH` macro:

```
.TH BACKPROP 1
```

Each of the major sections of the man page (for example, `NAME`, `SYNOPSIS`, `DESCRIPTION`) is specified with a line of text with the following format:

```
.SH <section name>
```

which, as you can see, uses the `.SH` macro. Lines below the `.SH` line provide the content for that section. Other macros include `.B`, for making a line of text bold, and `.TP`, which is particularly suited to listing and describing program or argument options.

What I suggest you do is use the backpropagation man page, listed below, as a template for your own man pages. By looking at the source, you should have all the information that you need to come up with a man page of your own. Man pages, having been around several decades, have rather firmly established conventions, so it is best to work from templates and avoid inventing formats of your own. Finally, if you want to test out a man page without installing it, use the `nroff` command with the `-man` page, as in the following example:

```
$ nroff -man backprop.man
```

You can find a complete list of the man-supported nroff macros, and much more detailed documentation, by issuing the following command:

```
$ man groff_man
```

Immediately following the source code listed here, I describe where to install man pages on Linux and Mac OS X systems:

```
.TH BACKPROP 1
.SH NAME
backprop \- train and execute backpropagation neural \
networks
.SH SYNOPSIS
.B backprop [\-w weights][\-n network] [\-x exemplars]
.SH DESCRIPTION
Backprop is a stand-alone multilayer neural network
simulator that is based upon the popular
backpropagation learning algorithm. The goal of this
simulator is to provide users with a friendly and
easy to use environment for experimenting with
backpropagation networks. To achieve this, I put a lot
of effort into making the user interface give as much
visual feedback as possible, especially during network
training, as well as giving the user easy to use
interfaces for changing the attributes of the network,
such as learning rates, momentum, and so forth. You
can zoom in on the network graphically to see weight
values in more detail, or zoom out to make
visible larger, more complicated network architectures.
You can speed up, or slow down, the rate at which error
graphics and network state are updated during training.

Backprop displays activation and weights during
training as they change, and allows the user to
enable/disable/configure the use of momentum and
learning rate during training. You can also enable or
disable a bias term to see what effect it has on
convergence during training. Finally, Backprop allows
you to specify the use of sigmoid or htan activation
functions.

Please refer to the release notes for more information
and instructions.
.SH OPTIONS
.TP
```

```
.B \-w weights
```
An XML weights file. This file is usually generated by
Backprop as the result of a training session, however,
it can be generated from other
sources. The topology of the weight file must exactly
match that of the network file.
```
.TP
.B \-n network
```
An XML architecture file. This file describes the
topology of the neural network. The following is an
example of a three layer network that contains
two input nodes, three hidden layer nodes, and an
output node. Such a network topology can be used to
solve the classic XOR problem.

```
<network>
  <layer size="2"/>
  <layer size="3"/>
  <layer size="1"/>
</network>
.TP
.B \-x exemplars
```
An XML exemplars file. Exemplars are used during
training, supplying both the training input and
expected output. The exemplar file is generated outside
of Backprop using either a text editor or a script of
some sort that generates the file using data supplied
from some external source. The following example
exemplars file can be used to train a three layer
network with two inputs and one output to solve the
XOR problem:

```
<exemplars>
    <exemplar>
        <input value="0"/>
        <input value="0"/>
        <output value="0"/>
    </exemplar>
    <exemplar>
        <input value="1"/>
        <input value="0"/>
        <output value="1"/>
    </exemplar>
```

```
    <exemplar>
        <input value="0"/>
        <input value="1"/>
        <output value="1"/>
    </exemplar>
    <exemplar>
        <input value="1"/>
        <input value="1"/>
        <output value="0"/>
    </exemplar>
</exemplars>
.SH AUTHOR
backprop was originally written by Syd Logan
.SH REPORTING BUGS
Report bugs to <sydlogan at sydlogan dot com>.
.SH COPYRIGHT
Copyright ¬© 2004, 2005 Syd Logan
.SH SEE ALSO
While the README file contains background information,
backpropagation neural networks require some study to
be used effectively. There are numerous references to
backpropagation networks on the internet should you
need a more detailed overview.
```

Distributing Man Pages

In this section, I describe how to install man pages on both Red Hat Linux and Mac OS X. On Red Hat Linux, your installer must be running as root to install under /usr/local/man. Below this directory are subdirectories, one for each section of the man page (for example, man1, man2). Simply copying the man page file to the appropriate subdirectory is all that is needed for the man command to locate your man page. (Your installer might need to create subdirectories for sections not already represented in /usr/local/man.) Once again, commands (such as backprop) are in section 1 of the man page and therefore need to be installed in /usr/local/man/man1. However, you are not limited to section 1 of the man page; a more complete set of man pages for Backprop might include a man page in section 5 of the manual to describe the XML formatting that is behind the network, exemplar, and weights files. If I were to create an entry in section 5 for Backprop, I would also want to mention it in the SEE ALSO section of the section 1 man page for Backprop.

The following example shows how cross-references to other commands and sections typically appear in a man page (in this case, the `passwd` command):

```
SEE ALSO
     pam(8), and pam_chauthok(2).
```

To obtain the man pages for pam and pam_chauthok using this information, I would issue the following commands, respectively:

```
$ man 8 pam
$ man 2 pam_chauthok
```

For Mac OS X, the situation is exactly the same, except for the name of the man page file, which should have as its suffix the man page section rather than "man." For Backprop, which is in man section 1, the appropriate path to use is /usr/local/man/man1/backprop.1.

Mac OS X

Mac OS X is a UNIX (BSD) system under the hood, but installation of software, as well as the execution environment, is dramatically different when compared to Linux. There are basically two ways to get software onto a Mac OS X system: via an installer and via a disk image. Disk images are the easiest to construct, and are the recommended method of installation according to Apple. For many applications and users, this installation method represents the ideal method: The user downloads the disk image, and drags the application to the Applications folder to install the application. Installers are preferable, however, if the application is complex (if the installation requires prompting the user for information, or system files need to be modified during installation). Both installer and disk image methods are supported directly by Apple. A final option is to go with a third-party installer, something that I don't cover in this book.

Application Layout

Before we start, it helps to look at the layout of an application. To see how an application exists on disk, open a shell using Terminal (Terminal is located in /Applications/Utilities). We might as well use Terminal as the example application, so from the shell, change to /Applications/Utilities and issue an `ls` command, like this:

```
$ cd /Application/Utilities
$ ls -l | grep Terminal
drwxrwxr-x 3 root admin  102 Jun 3 15:13 Terminal.app
```

As you can see, the Terminal application is actually a directory named Terminal.app. Located inside this directory is the binary executable and support files needed for the binary to execute and integrate with the Mac OS X desktop. Users navigating to the parent folder see this directory (known in Mac OS X as a bundle) as an icon (more on how this icon is specified later) named Terminal (the .app suffix is hidden). Double-clicking the Terminal bundle causes Mac OS X to load and execute the Terminal application. Storing the application and its resources together in a single file system location is an elegant solution, reminiscent of the way Mac OS Classic (System 7/8/9) used resource forks to store application resources such as string tables, icons, and so forth. In the Mac OS X world, XML files are now used to store most of the additional information that is associated with the application, with specialized editors provided by Apple's development toolchain to aid in the manipulation of these files. Of course, vi(1) works just as well for viewing and making changes to these files. Later we look at some of these files in detail; you will need to know how to construct them as a part of the build process.

Descending down into Terminal.app, we see the following:

```
$ cd  Terminal.app
$ ls -l
total 0
drwxrwxr-x  7 root  admin  238 Jun  3 15:13 Contents
```

and in Contents, we find the following:

```
$ cd  Contents
$ ls -l
total 24
-rw-rw-r--  1 root admin 2597 Jun  1 18:16 Info.plist
drwxrwxr-x  3 root admin  102 Sep 19 09:29 MacOS
-rw-rw-r--  1 root admin    8 Nov 12  2002 PkgInfo
drwxrwxr-x 26 root admin  884 Aug 11  2003 Resources
-rw-rw-r--  1 root admin  456 Jun  3 15:13 version.plist
```

Let's take a look at each of these files, starting with perhaps the simplest, version.plist, and then work our way down into the Mac OS and Resources subdirectories. If you were to open version.plist in an editor, you would see something like this:

```
<?xml version="1.0" encoding="UTF-8"?>
<!DOCTYPE plist PUBLIC "-//Apple Computer//DTD PLIST \
1.0//EN" "http://www.apple.com/DTDs/PropertyList- \
```

```
1.0.dtd">
<plist version="1.0">
<dict>
    <key>BuildVersion</key>
    <string>3</string>
    <key>CFBundleShortVersionString</key>
    <string>1.3.3</string>
    <key>CFBundleVersion</key>
    <string>82</string>
    <key>ProjectName</key>
    <string>Terminal</string>
    <key>SourceVersion</key>
    <string>820103</string>
</dict>
</plist>
```

As you can tell, this file is XML based. The DTD, PLIST, is used by all the files that we will be looking at. The general organization of this file, and of the others, is a series of key/value pairs. The keys are specified using <key> elements, and the values are wrapped in elements that identify the type (usually <string> to denote UTF-8 string data, but other types, such as arrays, are also used).

Of the remaining keys, the following are important:

- **BuildVersion**—Version of the build
- **CFBundleShortVersionString**—Version of the application, displayed to the user by Finder in Get Info
- **SourceVersion**—Source code version

To create a version from a version.plist file, the Apple Installer computes a 5-tuple from three keys in the version.plist file: the CFBundleShortVersionString key, the SourceVersion key, and the BuildVersion key. For a 5-tuple of the form a.b.c.d.e, a.b.c is obtained from the value of CFBundleShortVersionString, d is obtained from the value of SourceVersion, and e is obtained from the value of BuildVersion. If any of these keys is missing, the corresponding element is replaced with the value 0.

The next file in the Contents subdirectory, PkgInfo, is used to express the type and creator codes for an application. For Terminal, this file contains the single line:

```
APPLtrmx
```

The first four characters of this string, AAPL, specify the creator code. The remaining characters specify the type code, which in this case is trmx. The PkgInfo file is not a required file; the information is duplicated in the next file we will look at, Info.plist.

Info.plist is the only required file in this directory. As with version.plist, the file is XML and contains a series of key/value pairs. Keys in the Info.plist cover many desktop integration points, including desktop icons, supported MIME types and file extensions, help system integration, and copyright and version information. Here is the bulk of the content found in Terminal's Info.plist file, followed by a summary of the key/value pairs it contains.

```
<?xml version="1.0" encoding="UTF-8"?>
<!DOCTYPE plist PUBLIC "-//Apple Computer//DTD \
PLIST 1.0//EN" "http://www.apple.com/DTDs/ \
PropertyList-1.0.dtd">
<plist version="1.0">
<dict>
    <key>CFAppleHelpAnchor</key>
    <string>trmnl001</string>
    <key>CFBundleDevelopmentRegion</key>
    <string>English</string>
    <key>CFBundleDocumentTypes</key>
    <array>
        <dict>
            <key>CFBundleTypeExtensions</key>
            <array>
                <string>term</string>
            </array>
            <key>CFBundleTypeIconFile</key>
            <array>
                <string>TermDoc.icns</string>
            </array>
            <key>CFBundleTypeName</key>
            <string>Terminal</string>
            <key>CFBundleTypeRole</key>
            <string>Editor</string>
        </dict>
    </array>
    <key>CFBundleExecutable</key>
    <string>Terminal</string>
    <key>CFBundleGetInfoString</key>
    <string>Terminal v 1.3.3</string>
    <key>CFBundleIconFile</key>
    <string>icon.icns</string>
```

```
<key>CFBundleIdentifier</key>
<string>com.apple.Terminal</string>
<key>CFBundleInfoDictionaryVersion</key>
<string>6.0</string>
<key>CFBundleName</key>
<string>Terminal</string>
<key>CFBundlePackageType</key>
<string>APPL</string>
<key>CFBundleShortVersionString</key>
<string>1.3.3</string>
<key>CFBundleSignature</key>
<string>trmx</string>
<key>CFBundleURLTypes</key>
<array>
    <dict>
        <key>CFBundleURLName</key>
        <string>telnet URL</string>
        <key>CFBundleURLSchemes</key>
        <array>
            <string>telnet</string>
        </array>
    </dict>
</array>
<key>CFBundleVersion</key>
<string>82</string>
<key>LSHasLocalizedDisplayName</key>
<true/>
<key>NSAppleScriptEnabled</key>
<true/>
<key>NSHumanReadableCopyright</key>
<string>Copyright © 1995-2001, Apple Computer, \
    Inc.</string>
<key>NSMainNibFile</key>
<string>Terminal</string>
<key>NSPrincipalClass</key>
<string>TerminalApp</string>
</dict>
</plist>
```

The following list summarizes most of the key/value pairs found in the Terminal Info.plist file. You can find more detailed information at http://developer.apple.com.

- **CFAppleHelpAnchor**—The name of the application's HTML help file (without the .html or .htm extension).

- **CFBundleDevelopmentRegion**—The default language that will be used if resources for the locale are not found in the application bundle.
- **CFBundleDocumentTypes**—This key contains an array of dictionaries, each associating a document type with the application. Each contains keys used to define the document type supported by the application. In the preceding listing, one such dictionary is shown. (More are present in the actual Info.plist file distributed with Terminal.) The keys for that dictionary, CFBundleTypeExtensions, CFBundleTypeIconFile, CFBundleTypeName, and CFBundleTypeRole define, respectively, the filename extension associated with the type (term), icon file (TermDoc.icns), abstract name for the document type (Terminal), and role (Editor). Possible values for role can include Editor, Viewer, Shell, or None.
- **CFBundleExecutable**—The name of the main executable file (in this case, Terminal).
- **CFBundleGetInfoString**—A human-readable plain text string that will be displayed in the Info window of the bundle. This string can be localized by storing it in the InfoPlist.strings file that is located in each .lproj directory supported.
- **CFBundleIconFile**—This key identifies the file containing the icon that will be displayed by the finder for the application. The Finder looks for this file in the Resources directory. See the section "Creating the Bundle Icon File," later in this chapter, for details on how to create this icon.
- **CFBundleIdentifier**—A unique identifier string in the form of a Java-style package name (in this case, com.apple.Terminal). This string is used to locate the application at runtime, and by the preference system to identify applications uniquely.
- **CFBundleInfoDictionaryVersion**—This key identifies the current version of the property list structure. More information about this key can be found at developer.apple.com.
- **CFBundleName**—This key identifies the short name of the bundle and must be fewer than 16 characters long and be suitable for displaying in the menu and the About box. It can be localized by placing it in the InfoPlist.strings file located in the .lproj subdirectory.
- **CFBundlePackageType**—This key is analogous to the Mac OS 9 file type code and consists of a four-letter code. Applications should always set the value of this key to APPL.
- **CFBundleShortVersionString**—This key defines the marketing version of the application, which consists of a major number, and two minor

version numbers of the form a.b.c, where a is the major number, and b and c are minor numbers. This number differs from the `CFBundleVersion` key, which is the build number.

- **`CFBundleSignature`**—This key is analogous to the MacOS 9 file creator code, and consists of a four-letter code that is specific to the application.
- **`CFBundleURLTypes`**—This key contains dictionaries that enumerate the URL schemes supported by the application. It is similar in structure to `CFBundleDocumentTypes`, described previously, but it describes URL schemes rather than document types. For a description of this key and the related keys (`CFBundleTypeRole`, `CFBundleURLIconFile`, `CFBundleURLName`, and `CFBundleURLSchemes`), visit developer.apple.com.
- **`LSHasLocalizedDisplayName`**—If set to 1 or true, the Finder displays the name of the application as a localized string. Use of this key requires localized versions of the key `CFBundleDisplayName` in the language-specific InfoPList.strings files.
- **`NSHumanReadableCopyright`**—This key contains a string with copyright information which the application can load and display in an About dialog box, or other places where copyright information needs to be displayed. You can localize this key by placing it in InfoPlist.strings files.

The MacOS Folder

Let's continue our investigation of Terminal.app by looking in the Mac OS folder, where we find the application binary:

```
$ cd  MacOS
$ ls
Terminal
$ file Terminal
Terminal: Mach-O executable ppc
```

The Mac OS folder is also the place for locating any shared library files that you want to distribute exclusively with the application. In the case of Weather Manager, a cross-platform application that I wrote (see www. sydlogan.com/weathermanager.html), copies of the platform independent core, along with expat, the GUI libraries (for example, wxWidgets), and nspr are all copied into the Mac OS folder and distributed with the application. Doing so simplifies installation, enabling the drag-and-drop install recommended by Apple, described later.

It is critical that any shared libraries that are located within the bundle be built so that they can be found by the loader at application startup. Expat is an example of a open source library that gets it wrong by default for those who want to distribute it in an application bundle. (At least, they did as of the version 1.95.6, which was used to develop the applications for this book.) Taking a look at the problem with expat in detail will illustrate how you can identify and fix the problem in libraries that you use and create. Here are the steps. Download the expat-1.95.6 tar.gz from sourceforge.net, unpack it, and then build it as follows:

```
$ cd expat-1.95.6
$ ./configure
$ make
```

After the build is done, `cd` into .libs (a hidden directory that contains the results of the build), and then use the Mac OS X otool utility as follows:

```
$ cd .libs
$ otool -l libexpat.dylib | grep name | grep expat
      name /usr/local/lib/libexpat.0.dylib (offset 24)
```

The problem here is that the name of the library is set to /usr/local/lib/libexpat.0.dylib. As a result, any applications linking to this instance of the expat shared library during a build will expect the library to be installed on the end user's system at that location. However, the library will not be located there because we are distributing the application as a bundle. To change this situation, we need to change the way expat is built. The library name is set by a linker argument named `-install_name`. Grepping around in the expat source tree, we can see where this is set:

```
sh-2.05a$ find . -print | xargs grep install_name
./configure: archive_cmds='$nonopt $(test "x$module"
 = xyes && echo -bundle || echo -dynamiclib)
$allow_undefined_flag -o $lib $libobjs
$deplibs$linker_flags
-install_name $rpath/$soname $verstring'
./conftools/libtool.m4:    archive_cmds='$nonopt
$(test "x$module" = xyes && echo -bundle ||
echo -dynamiclib) $allow_undefined_flag -o $lib
$libobjs $deplibs$linker_flags
-install_name $rpath/$soname $verstring'
./libtool:archive_cmds="\$nonopt \$(test
\\\"x\$module\\\" = xyes && echo -bundle ||
```

```
echo -dynamiclib) \$allow_undefined_flag -o \$lib
\$libobjs \$deplibs\$linker_flags -install_name
\$rpath/\$soname \$verstring"
```

To fix the problem, change the `install_name` argument to
`@executable_path/$soname` in the configure script, and rebuild as above.
(Generating a new configure script is not possible without checking expat
out from CVS.) Then, once again using otool, we see the following:

```
$ cd .libs
$ otool -1 libexpat.dylib  | grep name | grep expat
     name @executable_path/libexpat.0.dylib (offset 24)
```

In the above, `@executable_path` represents the location of the executable
within the bundle, regardless of what that location actually is. For Terminal,
that would be most likely /Applications/Utilities/Terminal.app/Contents/
MacOS. Regardless of where the application is installed, the loader will be
able to determine the correct value of `executable_path`, and as a result, be
able to find all libraries named with the `@executable_path` prefix.

The Resources Folder
Now we come to the last major subdirectory, `Resources`:

```
$ cd ../Resources
$ ls -1
total 192
drwxrwxr-x 10 root admin   340 Nov 13 2002 Dutch.lproj
drwxrwxr-x 10 root admin   340 Aug 11 2003 \
English.lproj
drwxrwxr-x 10 root admin   340 Nov 13 2002 French.lproj
drwxrwxr-x 10 root admin   340 Nov 13 2002 German.lproj
drwxrwxr-x 10 root admin   340 Nov 13 2002 \
Italian.lproj
drwxrwxr-x 10 root admin   340 Nov 13 2002 \
Japanese.lproj
drwxrwxr-x 10 root admin   340 Nov 13 2002 \
Spanish.lproj
-rw-rw-r-- 1 root admin   282 Nov 12 2002 TIbeam.tiff
-rw-rw-r-- 1 root admin  2878 Nov 12 2002 \
TermDoc.icns
-rw-rw-r-- 1 root admin  3849 Nov 12 2002 \
Terminal.rsrc
-rw-rw-r-- 1 root admin  5948 Nov 12 2002 \
Terminal.scriptSuite
```

```
-rw-rw-r-- 1 root admin  5610 Nov 12 2002 \
Terminal.scriptTerminology
drwxrwxr-x 10 root admin   340 Nov 13 2002 da.lproj
drwxrwxr-x 10 root admin   340 Nov 13 2002 fi.lproj
-rw-rw-r-- 1 root admin 54052 Nov 12 2002 icon.icns
drwxrwxr-x 10 root admin   340 Nov 13 2002 ko.lproj
drwxrwxr-x 10 root admin   340 Nov 13 2002 no.lproj
drwxrwxr-x 10 root admin   340 Nov 13 2002 pt.lproj
-rw-rw-r-- 1 root admin   248 Nov 12 2002 \
split-close.tiff
-rw-rw-r-- 1 root admin   255 Nov 12 2002 \
split-open.tiff
-rw-rw-r-- 1 root admin   865 Nov 12 2002 split.gif
drwxrwxr-x 10 root admin   340 Nov 13 2002 sv.lproj
drwxrwxr-x 10 root admin   340 Nov 13 2002 zh_CN.lproj
drwxrwxr-x 10 root admin   340 Nov 13 2002 zh_TW.lproj

$ cd  Spanish.lproj
ls -l
total 64
drwxrwxr-x 3 root admin   102 Nov 13 2002 \
CommandPanel.nib
drwxrwxr-x 3 root admin   102 Nov 13 2002 Find.nib
-rw-rw-r-- 1 root admin    58 Nov 13 2002 \
InfoPlist.strings
drwxrwxr-x 3 root admin   102 Nov 13 2002 \
InspectorX.nib
-rw-rw-r-- 1 root admin 26944 Nov 13 2002 \
Localizable.strings
drwxrwxr-x 3 root admin   102 Nov 13 2002 \
Preferences.nib
drwxrwxr-x 3 root admin   102 Nov 13 2002 Term.nib
drwxrwxr-x 3 root admin   102 Nov 13 2002 Terminal.nib
```

Each of the .lproj directories contains the same data, localized to the language that is designated by the name of the directory (in this case, Spanish). Because nib files are not used in wxWidgets or Qt applications, I'm going to ignore these. Let's start by looking at Localizable.strings, where most of the action occurs. The following is a snippet of the English language version of the file:

```
/* Attention panel title */
"Inappropriate Font";

"OK";
```

```
/* Attn panel title */
"Nonexistent Font";

"The font '%@' does not exist." = "The font '%@' \
does not exist.";

/* Appears in find panel. */
"Not Found";

/* Attn panel title */
"Font Too Large";

"That font is too large to use in a Terminal window. \
Choose a font smaller than %d point.";
```

In the Spanish.lproj directory, the same lines of the\
file look like this:

```
/* Attention panel title */
"Inappropriate Font" = "Tipo incorrecto";


"OK" = "OK";

/* Attn panel title */
"Nonexistent Font" = "Tipo no existente";

"The font '%@' does not exist." = \
"El tipo '%@' no existe.";

/* Appears in find panel. */
"Not Found" = "No encontrado";

/* Attn panel title */
"Font Too Large" = "Tipo demasiado grande";

"That font is too large to use in a Terminal window.  \
Choose a font smaller than %d point." = "Ese tipo es \
demasiado grande para usarse en una ventana de \
Terminal. Elija un tipo de menos de %d puntos.";
```

As you can see, the files are the same except in the Spanish language
version of the file, each string is accompanied on the same line with a
Spanish language translation, separated by an = character and spaces.

Creating the Bundle Icon File

The `CFBundleIconFile` key in the application's Info.plist file specifies the artwork that will be displayed by the finder to represent the application in various situations. Creating an icns file is straightforward:

1. Draw a 48 x 48 icon using a tool such as GIMP or Photoshop. If possible, include an alpha channel.
2. Use the Mac OS X utility IconComposer to import your icon and create an icns file.
3. Copy the icns file to the Contents/Resources folder of the application bundle.

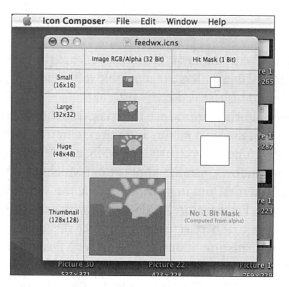

Figure 4-2 IconComposer UI

The icns file actually maintains icons and masks for the following sizes: 16 x 16, 32 x 32, 48 x 48, and 128 x 128. Figure 4-2 illustrates the IconComposer initial screen after the Weather Manager icon has been inserted into the 48 x 48 region of the editor. To specify an icon, double-click the Image RGB/Alpha (32 Bit) region and a file chooser will display allowing you to select an image source. IconComposer will scale your images as needed after prompting for confirmation. If the results are not to your liking, you can always draw icons for each of the required sizes, and

use them instead. After you've added the icons and Hit Masks (recommended), save the file with a .icns extension and copy it to the application
bundle.

Drag-and-Drop Installation

Creating a drag-and-drop installer for Mac OS X is even easier than creating
the icns resource:

1. Launch the Disk Copy application.
2. Locate your application bundle in the Finder.
3. Drag the application bundle onto Disk Copy.
4. Save and distribute the result.

Windows XP

In the Windows XP environment, GUI installers are the generally expected
norm. Numerous GUI installers are available to developers, from open
source implementations to third-party offerings.

In this section, I briefly introduce the basic desktop integration points
such as the desktop, the Start menu, and the system tray. After that has been
done, I describe the open source installer NSIS, and illustrate how it can be
used to create a Windows installer application. Much information is
available on the Internet, and in print, regarding the Windows runtime, as
you might imagine. Furthermore, NSIS comes with excellent documentation. Therefore, my goal here is just to introduce the main points behind
each. For more information about the Windows XP runtime, visit
http://msdn.microsoft.com. Documentation for the NSIS installer is
available on the Internet at http://nsis.sourceforge.net/Docs/.

Documents and Settings

Windows XP, like Linux and Mac OS X, supports the concept of user
logins. And, like on UNIX-based systems, there is the concept of a home
directory. To understand how to integrate an application into the Windows
XP desktop, you need to have a basic understanding of how Windows XP
implements home directories. Below C:\ on every Windows XP system, one
finds a directory named Documents and Settings. Within this directory there
are two directories, one named All Users, and the other named Default User.
Finally, for each user configured to sign on to the system, there is a directory
with the user's login name. On my main XP system, the name of this

directory is syd. I can determine the location of this directory by running regedit and searching for the following key:

```
HKEY_CURRENT_USER\Software\Microsoft\Windows\CurrentVersion\Explorer\Shell Folders
```

This key maintains a large set of values, a few of which are of interest to us. The first, AppData, is set to the following value on my system:

```
C:\Documents and Settings\syd\Application Data
```

AppData is where applications store data specific to the application and the user. Each application should create a directory below AppData that will be used by the application to store application-specific data and preferences at runtime. The name of this directory should be unique to the application; usually it is the application name, but this is not a hard requirement. In Weather Manager, XML feed data downloaded from the National Oceanic and Atmospheric Administration (NOAA) during updates is stored in files located in a folder named weatherxml. (When the UI needs refreshing, the application will read weather data from there, instead of from the Internet.) For those of you familiar with UNIX, think of the directories inside of Application Data as being analogous to application-specific hidden directories that would be located below $HOME (for example, ~/.weatherxml). Weather Manager maintains the list of feed URLs in a file named wxsites.xml, which is located in the same directory.

The next registry value of interest, Desktop, contains files, usually shortcuts, that are located on the user's desktop. Installers can place shortcuts to application binaries in this folder to cause shortcut icons to appear on the desktop; double-clicking these icons will cause the application to start.

The final key/value that we will consider here, StartMenu\Programs, also contains shortcuts to application binaries. The contents of this directory define what displays in the Windows Start menu for the application. If your application consists of more than one binary (Weather Manager includes an uninstaller in addition to the main application binary), a directory immediately below StartMenu\Programs (in this case, named Weather Manager) can be used to contain these binaries, and in the Start menu, the result will be a pull-right menu with the same name as the directory. You can nest subdirectories to whatever level you need below StartMenu\Programs, although more than two or three levels of menus is probably too complex for most users to navigate easily.

Program Installation

NSIS is a powerful, open source installer system that can be used to implement Windows installers of varying degrees of complexity. The fundamental task of NSIS (or any Windows installer) is to install the application binary in its proper location below c:\Program Files or some user-specified location, provide a mechanism for program uninstall, (optionally) integrate the application into the desktop and Start menu, and (optionally) place configuration data below HKEY_CURRENT_USER\Software\Microsoft\Windows\CurrentVersion\Explorer\Shell Folders\AppData.

Using NSIS

To create NSIS installers, follow these steps:

1. Define the installer (and uninstaller) in a text file, using NSIS commands and syntax.
2. Compile the text file using the NSIS script compiler, generating an installer executable.
3. Test and debug the installer, repeating the preceding steps until you are satisfied with the results.
4. Distribute the debugged installer executable to end users.

Defining the Installer

An NSIS installer is defined in a text file, using whatever editor you have available. The contents of this file consist of variables, sections, and functions, all written in the NSIS scripting language. The NSIS scripting language is very general, much like awk or Perl, but it has features designed to support installers directly. For example, assignment of a pathname to the variable InstallDir will define the default install location of your program to the NSIS installer. Although the NSIS scripting language supports general constructs such as while loops and if statements, an effective installer can be written without the use of any flow of control whatsoever.

The minimal usable installer script for NSIS specifies four things: a variable that holds the path of the default location of the install, a variable that specifies the name of the generated install executable, a section that defines what pages are displayed to the user by the install wizard, and a section that defines the files (executable, DLLs) that are to be installed. The following example illustrates a minimal installer script for a NSIS installation:

```
; the name of the installer

Name "My App"
OutFile "wminstall.exe"

; The default installation directory
InstallDir $PROGRAMFILES\MyApp

; Pages

Page components
Page directory
Page instfiles

; what to install
Section "MyApp"

SectionIn RO
SetOutPath $INSTDIR

; Put file there
File /r "..\..\dist\windows\release\*.dll"
"..\..\dist\windows\release\myapp.exe"

SectionEnd
```

Let's look at the preceding script in more detail. The line

```
Name "My App"
```

defines the name of the installer, as it is displayed in the installer GUI. It has no other purpose. The line

```
InstallDir $PROGRAMFILES\MyApp
```

defines the default installation location for the application. $PROGRAMFILES is one of the many built-in variables defined by NSIS. On Windows XP, $PROGRAMFILES evaluates to c:\Program Files, so InstallDir will contain the value c:\Program Files\WeatherManager after the preceding line is executed. Note that this assignment in the script is done at runtime, not compile time, because $PROGRAMFILES is not the same for all versions of Windows.

The next few lines define the pages that will be displayed to the user by the install wizard at runtime. The following pages are possible:

- **License.** Displays the text of a license (text or RTF) that you supply, and optionally requires the user to agree to the terms before the rest of the installation is performed.
- **Components.** A list of the basic components installed by the application. Check boxes are displayed to allow the user to opt out of optional components (for example, documentation, source, examples).
- **Directory.** Displays the installation directory (as specified by the $InstallDir variable) and provides a browse function that allows the user to modify it.
- **Instfiles.** Provides the UI that is used to commence the installation and display progress.

Finally, the installer script above defines a section named MyApp that defines the application that is to be installed, and defines attributes that control how the installer will perform the installation task:

```
; what to install
Section "MyApp"

        SectionIn RO
        SetOutPath $INSTDIR

        ; Put file there
        File /r "..\..\dist\windows\release\*.dll"
"..\..\dist\windows\release\myapp.exe"

SectionEnd
```

Sections are defined between the keywords Section and SectionEnd. The text following the Section keyword defines the name of the section. The text within the keywords define commands and attributes associated with a section. The first of these, SectionIn RO, tells the installer that this section is required, and cannot be opted out by the user. (The section will display on the Components page, but it will be dimmed and the check box to its left will be selected, and disabled.) The NSIS installer supports an arbitrary set of installation types (for example, Full, Typical, Custom). If not otherwise specified, there will be one type of installation performed, and the user will not be prompted to select the installation type as a result. However, the `InstallType` command can be specified before the sections are specified to define multiple installation types. For example:

```
InstType "Full"
InstType "Minimal"
```

where `"Full"` and `"Minimal"` are arbitrary labels that will be displayed to the user in a pop-up menu from which the install type can be chosen. The first `InstType` command encountered in the script will be assigned the value 1, the second will be assigned the value 2, and so on. These values then can be used as arguments to `SectionIn`. For example:

```
SectionIn 1
```

would add the section to install type 1 (Full), meaning the section would be included in a Full install, and

```
SectionIn 1 2
```

would add the section to both 1 (Full) and 2 (Minimal) install types. Finally,

```
SectionIn 1 2 RO
```

causes the section to be in both the Full and Minimal install types, and the user will not be able to opt out in either case. Next, the line

```
SetOutPath $INSTDIR
```

tells NSIS to install the content defined by the section at the path defined by $INSTDIR. $INSTDIR is another built-in NSIS variable, which, in this case, defines the installation directory that was selected by the user (in contrast to $InstallDir, which defines the default installation directory that was displayed to the user in the directory page of the install wizard).

The remaining lines in the section

```
File /r "..\..\dist\windows\release\*.dll"
"..\..\dist\windows\release\myapp.exe"
```

are used to tell the NSIS install what files are to be installed for this section. The pathnames are relative to where the NSIS script compiler is run. The /r argument tells NSIS to recursively add the contents of any subdirectories found in the specified location. It's not strictly necessary in this case; *.dll and myapp.exe will not match any directory names in my development tree. File also supports an -x command that allows you to specify a mask as an argument; files matching that mask will be excluded (not copied) by the installer compiler when creating the installer executable.

Now that we have specified a minimal installer, let's compile it and generate the installer executable.

Compiling the NSIS Install Script and Generating an Installer Executable
To compile the NSIS script into an installer executable, follow these steps:

1. Build your application and make sure the binary files, DLLs, examples, documentation, README files, and so on that are specified in the NSIS script are in their proper locations.
2. Execute the makensis command as follows:

```
c:\> makensis scriptname
```

The makensis command will generate output to the console describing what is happening as the installer script is parsed. Should makensis encounter syntax or logical errors, it will report these and, depending on the severity, abort. It is very important to scan the output from makensis to determine whether any errors occurred. If all goes well, the installer binary specified by the $OutFile variable will be created.

Testing the Installer
Testing the installer amounts to running through all the possible use cases (install types, user selections), and ensuring that the installer works as intended. This is done by using the Windows Explorer to determine whether files are where they should be, and using regedit to inspect registry keys that your installer modifies. Of course, being able to launch the program and execute it successfully should also be a part of the installer testing. Should the installer misbehave, you can debug the installer by going back into the script and adding debug statements to display variables during the execution of the installer. The MessageBox command essentially wraps the Win32 MessageBox function (for details, see the aforementioned NSIS documentation) and can be used for this purpose.

Distributing the Installer
All that remains is uploading the installer binary to the network, or copying it to distribution media. The installer is self-contained, and will maintain

compressed versions of your application and any other files that the installer is responsible for, so there is no need to compress the installer further.

Adding an Uninstaller

Adding support for application uninstalls in NSIS is fairly straightforward, and can be basically accomplished by adding a new section to the NSIS script containing commands to execute at uninstall time, and by adding commands in the install section we created earlier to store information in the Windows registry that can be used by the uninstaller to locate files and other resources. (Recall that the user is allowed to select the install location at runtime, so we can't encode this information into the installer script—the only fixed location we can rely on for storing this information until uninstall time is the Windows registry.) Below is the code added to `Section "MyApp"` above that does the required work of storing registry information at install time and creates the uninstaller. The following code is mostly boilerplate; changing `MyApp` (in bold) to the name of your application is the only change that a simple installer will require:

```
; Write the installation path into the registry
WriteRegStr HKLM SOFTWARE\MyApp "Install_Dir" \
"$INSTDIR"

; Write the uninstall keys for Windows
WriteRegStr HKLM
"Software\Microsoft\Windows\CurrentVersion\Uninstall\\
MyApp" "DisplayName" \ "MyApp"
WriteRegStr HKLM
"Software\Microsoft\Windows\CurrentVersion\Uninstall\\
MyApp" "UninstallString" \ '"$INSTDIR\uninstall.exe"'
WriteRegDWORD HKLM
"Software\Microsoft\Windows\CurrentVersion\Uninstall\\
MyApp" "NoModify" 1
WriteRegDWORD HKLM
"Software\Microsoft\Windows\CurrentVersion\Uninstall\\
MyApp" "NoRepair" 1
WriteUninstaller "uninstall.exe"
```

The uninstall section looks like the following, consisting mainly of `Delete` and `RMDir` commands to remove any files or directories created by the installer and removal-of-registry keys:

```
Section "Uninstall"

; Remove registry keys
 DeleteRegKey HKLM
"Software\Microsoft\Windows\CurrentVersion\Uninstall\\
MyApp"
DeleteRegKey HKLM SOFTWARE\MyApp

; Remove files and uninstaller
Delete $INSTDIR\*.*
Delete $INSTDIR\uninstall.exe

; Remove shortcuts, if any
Delete "$SMPROGRAMS\MyApp\*.*"

; Remove directories used
RMDir "$SMPROGRAMS\MyApp"
RMDir "$INSTDIR"

SectionEnd
```

With the preceding changes, all we need to do is specify which pages are displayed by the uninstaller. Two instances of the `UninstPage` command (located next to the `Page` commands in the script, at global scope) are all that is needed:

```
UninstPage uninstConfirm
UninstPage instfiles
```

Integrating into the Start Menu and Desktop

It is fairly easy to incorporate support for both a desktop shortcut and Start menu entries into both the NSIS installer and uninstaller. As mentioned earlier, placing items into the Start menu on Windows XP is simply a matter of creating a shortcut to the application binary in a directory; the same holds true for placing a shortcut on the desktop. NSIS scripts define the $SMPROGRAMS variable, which specifies the directory into which a shortcut can be placed, causing a program to be displayed in the All Programs area of the Start menu. This is just one of a large number of variables that contain the locations of various special directories found on a Windows system. The following section contains code that, if the option is selected by the user, will create a pull-right menu in Start, All Programs named MyApp that contains menu items that represent links to the MyApp application and its uninstaller:

```
Section "Start Menu Shortcuts"

; create the pullright menu by creating a directory
; named MyApp below $SMPROGRAMS
CreateDirectory "$SMPROGRAMS\MyApp"

; create shortcuts inside of $SMPROGRAMS\MyApp for the
; uninstaller and the application binary
CreateShortCut "$SMPROGRAMS\MyApp\Uninstall.lnk"
"$INSTDIR\uninstall.exe" "" \
"$INSTDIR\uninstall.exe" 0
CreateShortCut "$SMPROGRAMS\MyApp\MyApp.lnk" \
"$INSTDIR\MyApp.exe" "" "$INSTDIR\MyApp.exe" 0

SectionEnd
```

The third argument to `CreateShortCut`, in both cases `""`, defines command arguments to pass to the application on execution. (`""` means there are no command-line arguments.) The reason it is being specified is so that the fourth and fifth arguments can be included. The fourth argument specifies the name of a binary from which to obtain the icon that will be displayed in the Start menu, and the fifth argument (`0`) is the index of the icon resource in that executable. Omitting these arguments will cause defaults to be used, which is fine for most applications. However, if you want to provide a custom icon for the uninstaller in particular, adding the icon to the *application (not the installer) executable* and then referencing it in the `CreateShortCut` command above will allow you to customize the icon that is displayed in the Start menu for the uninstaller.

Application Data

Finally, let's discuss how the installer can create and populate application data in the Application Data folder for the user installing the application. Recall that HKEY_CURRENT_USER\Software\Microsoft\Windows\ CurrentVersion\Explorer\Shell Folders contains a key named `AppData`, which on my system is set to C:\Documents and Settings\syd\Application Data. For the Weather Manager application, I would like to create a directory there named `weatherxml`, where I will store at install time an XML file containing some sample weather feed URLs, and at runtime where

I will store data downloaded from the NOAA via HTTP. To do this, I can add the following new section to the NSIS installer script:

```
Section "XML Feeds File"

; Set output path to weatherxml below the appdata
; directory.
SetOutPath $APPDATA\weatherxml

; Put file there
File /r "..\wxsites.xml"

SectionEnd
```

The variable $APPDATA is a NSIS variable that points to my AppData directory. SetOutPath defines the location to which the file specified in the File command will be installed. Executing this section in the installer will create the weatherxml directory, if it does not exist, and copy wxsites.xml into it.

Complete Sample for Weather Manager
The following is the complete NSIS installer script for Weather Manager:

```
;-------------------------------

; The name of the installer
Name "Weather Manager"

; The file to write
OutFile "wminstall.exe"

; The default installation directory
InstallDir $PROGRAMFILES\WeatherManager

; Registry key to check for directory (so if you
; install again, it will overwrite the old one
; automatically)
InstallDirRegKey HKLM "Software\WeatherManager" \
"Install_Dir"


;-------------------------------

; Pages

Page components
Page directory
```

```
Page instfiles

UninstPage uninstConfirm
UninstPage instfiles


;--------------------------------


; The stuff to install
Section "WeatherManager"

SectionIn RO

; Set output path to the installation directory.
SetOutPath $INSTDIR

; Put file there
File /r "..\..\dist\windows\release\*.dll"
"..\..\dist\windows\release\feedwx.exe"

; Write the installation path into the registry
WriteRegStr HKLM SOFTWARE\WeatherManager "Install_Dir" \
"$INSTDIR"

; Write the uninstall keys for Windows
WriteRegStr HKLM
"Software\Microsoft\Windows\CurrentVersion\Uninstall\\
WeatherManager" "DisplayName" "Weather Manager"
WriteRegStr HKLM
"Software\Microsoft\Windows\CurrentVersion\Uninstall\\
WeatherManager" "UninstallString" \
'"$INSTDIR\uninstall.exe"'
WriteRegDWORD HKLM
"Software\Microsoft\Windows\CurrentVersion\Uninstall\\
WeatherManager" "NoModify" 1
WriteRegDWORD HKLM
"Software\Microsoft\Windows\CurrentVersion\Uninstall\\
WeatherManager" "NoRepair" 1
WriteUninstaller "uninstall.exe"

SectionEnd

; Optional section (can be disabled by the user)
Section "Start Menu Shortcuts"

CreateDirectory "$SMPROGRAMS\WeatherManager"
CreateShortCut "$SMPROGRAMS\WeatherManager\\
Uninstall.lnk" "$INSTDIR\uninstall.exe" "" \
"$INSTDIR\uninstall.exe" 0
```

```
CreateShortCut "$SMPROGRAMS\WeatherManager\\
WeatherManager.lnk" "$INSTDIR\feedwx.exe" "" \
"$INSTDIR\feedwx.exe" 0


SectionEnd

; Optional section (can be disabled by the user)
Section "XML Feeds File"

; Set output path to the weatherxml directory
; below AppData.
SetOutPath $APPDATA\weatherxml

; Put file there
File /r "..\wxsites.xml"

SectionEnd

;-------------------------------

; Uninstaller

Section "Uninstall"

; Remove registry keys
DeleteRegKey HKLM
"Software\Microsoft\Windows\CurrentVersion\Uninstall\\
WeatherManager"
DeleteRegKey HKLM SOFTWARE\WeatherManager

; Remove files and uninstaller
Delete $INSTDIR\*.*
Delete $INSTDIR\uninstall.exe

; Remove shortcuts, if any
Delete "$SMPROGRAMS\WeatherManager\*.*"

; Remove directories used
RMDir "$SMPROGRAMS\WeatherManager"
RMDir "$INSTDIR"

Delete $APPDATA\weatherxml\wxsites.xml
Delete "$APPDATA\weatherxml\*.*"
RMDir "$APPDATA\weatherxml"

SectionEnd
```

5   Operating System Interfaces and Libraries

In this chapter, we turn our attention to code, which will remain our focus for the rest of this book. As stated earlier, abstraction is a common theme in this book. Without the proper application of abstraction, it is difficult to build portable software. This idea is not new. A well-known example of the power of abstraction can be found by looking back over three decades ago, to when the UNIX operating system was ported to the C programming language. (C was invented just for this task.) Prior to C, UNIX was coded in assembly language, making it anything but portable, and this inhibited its migration to architectures beyond its original incarnation, the PDP/11. The use of C, and its libraries, provided an abstraction layer hiding large portions of the Unix source code from the details of the architecture to which Unix was being ported. To port the C programming language and its libraries to a new architecture was a much simpler (although by no means trivial) task than what would have been faced by developers trying to rewrite, and debug, all the source code for UNIX had it been written in assembly language. (The fact that a C compiler and its libraries can be bootstrapped from a small instance of the language helped to make this possible.)

The legacy of the early days of portable UNIX is with us today in the form of a vast array of libraries and application programming interfaces (APIs). POSIX is a standardization of APIs that originated back when UNIX was first rewritten in C, and is available, with some differences, as an API for programmers on both Mac OS X and Linux. Even the Microsoft C++ library is influenced by some of these APIs. (See www.crossplatformbook.com/posix.html for a survey I did of POSIX-like interfaces on these three platforms.)

Abstractions are prevalent in C++, too; the C++ Standard Template Library (STL) and Boost are two familiar examples.

In some cases, these standards are not enough. In the worst case, POSIX or other standard APIs may not be available on a platform that you want to support. To that end, Netscape came up with NSPR, the Netscape Portable Runtime Library. The use of a library like NSPR can greatly improve the portability of your source code by providing an even higher level of abstraction above the APIs that are otherwise available. Item 16 covers POSIX and other C/C++ related standard APIs, and Item 17 provides a very detailed tutorial of NSPR, illustrating how it made the non-GUI (graphical user interface) portions of the Netscape and Mozilla source code portable to a wide variety of dissimilar platforms. Items 22 and 23, in Chapter 7, "User Interfaces," cover abstractions that exist above the native GUI environment, the other major piece of the portability puzzle that had to be solved by Netscape and Mozilla.

Item 16: Use Standards-Based APIs (For Example, POSIX)

This item describes standards-based APIs and their role in the writing of portable source code. I briefly introduce each of the following standard APIs: POSIX, BSD, SVID, and the X/Open XPG. Each of these APIs is based on libraries that have been used for many years in UNIX-based operating systems. Following this, I describe support for these APIs on Mac OS X, Linux, and Windows, and then make recommendations regarding their use in writing portable software.

POSIX

The Portable Operating System Interface for Computer Environments, more commonly known as POSIX, is arguably the most fundamental of the standards-based APIs discussed in this item. POSIX is actually a family of standards, the first of which was released back in the early 1980s. In this book, I focus on POSIX.1, which is the popular name for ISO/IEC 9945-1, a standard that defines the APIs that can be used portably in application development. POSIX has a rich UNIX legacy, and it is based largely on UNIX implementations of the interfaces that it defines. The GNU library (part of the GCC product family) is compatible with POSIX.1, with support provided by Cygwin on Windows. POSIX.1 is also supported as a sub-system on Windows NT, which exists at roughly the same level as the

Win32 subsystem that most Windows programmers program against. I describe the POSIX.1 API and the Windows NT POSIX subsystem in more detail later in this item.

POSIX.1 is deep; there are numerous functions defined by the POSIX.1 API, in several areas of functionality. These interfaces are now published as a part of the Single UNIX Specification, which is described in detail here. A couple of books—Richard Stevens' and Stephen Rago's *Advanced Programming in the Unix Environment* (Addison-Wesley, 2005) and Marc Rochkind's *Advanced Unix Programming* (Addison-Wesley, 2004)—provide plenty of details and examples illustrating how to write applications that make use of the POSIX APIs.

System V Interface Definition

The System V Interface Description (SVID) is a document describing the AT&T UNIX System V operating system. It is also conformant to POSIX.1, making it somewhat of a superset. SVID is defined in terms of a base system and extensions. Like POSIX.1, no user-level commands are defined, only C programming APIs. The base system is further refined into several categories, which I summarize here.

Base OS Service Routines

The first category, Base OS Service Routines, consists of three subgroups:

- **Group 1.** This group contains approximately 150 functions that represent the core functionality of the Base OS Service Routines category. Functions such as `mkdir`, `malloc`, `popen`, `sigaction`, `fopen`, `fread`, `fwrite`, `fclose`, `getcwd`, `getpid`, `ioctl`, `kill`, `access`, `alarm`, `chmod`, `opendir`, `readdir`, and `closedir` are found in this group.
- **Group 2.** This group contains the following lower-level operating system functions: `close`, `creat`, `dlclose`, `dlerror`, `dlopen`, `dlsym`, `execl`, `execle`, `execlp`, `execv`, `execve`, `execvp`, `fork`, `lseek`, `mount`, `open`, `read`, `readv`, `umount`, `write`, and `writev`.
- **Group 3.** Group 3 contains only the functions `_exit` and `sync`.

Mathematical Functions

This category contains approximately 40 functions that support math-related operations, such as `abs`, `floor`, `ceil`, `sin`, `cos`, `tan`, `log`, `log10`, `pow`, and `sqrt`.

String and Character Handling

This category contains more than 150 functions, including the `str` functions (`strtok`, `strncat`, `strncpy`, and so on); `ctype` functionality such as `toascii`, `tolower`, `isupper`, and `isdigit`; conversion functions such as `asctime`, `atof`, `atol`, and `atoi`; multibyte and wide character functions such as `mblen`, `mbrtowc`, `wcsncpy`, `wcsstr`, and `wcsncpy`; and the `mem` functions, including `memchr`, `memcpy`, `memset`, and `memmove`.

Networking Functions

Most developers are aware of the role that the Berkeley sockets API plays in networking applications. However, functions such as `socket`, `bind`, `listen`, `accept`, `connect`, and so forth are not a part of the SVID. In place of Berkeley sockets, the SVID standardizes on XTI as its network API. XTI (X/Open Transport Interface) is an extension to and refinement of TLI developed by X/Open. TLI (Transport Layer Interface) is an API that was developed by AT&T. Mac OS X developers who wrote networking code for legacy versions of Mac OS will likely be familiar with the functions in this group, because TLI/XTI was the basis for the network APIs used in OpenTransport. One of the nice features of TLI/XTI is that it is transport independent. Richard Stevens' *Network Programming, Volume 1* (Addison-Wesley, 2003) describes TLI/XTI in detail. However, its use is rare; the use of Berkeley sockets is ubiquitous at this point.

General Library Functions

This category contains more than 100 functions that you would otherwise find in the ISO Standard C Library, including `glob`, `drand48`, `nrand48`, `bsearch`, `catgets`, `gets`, `puts`, `fgets`, `fputs`, `getopt`, `printf`, `putchar`, `getc`, `sprintf`, `sscanf`, and many others.

XPG, X/Open, and the Single UNIX Specification

The Open Group Base Specifications Issue 6, IEEE Std 1003.1, 2003 Edition, or The Single UNIX Specification, is a relatively recent event in the world of UNIX standards. In essence, it consists of a merging of the X/Open Portability Guide (or XPG), which was developed by X/Open, and POSIX, which was developed by IEEE and described previously. The Single UNIX Specification was jointly developed by the IEEE and the Open Group, and as such, it is considered both an IEEE Standard and an Open Group Technical Standard. X/Open, as of this writing, owns the trademark for UNIX and specifies the requirements for operating systems that want to call themselves UNIX, and licenses the use of the UNIX trademark to the vendors of these systems.

You can view the specification online at no cost; a link is available on the home page of www.unix-systems.org, or you can search for it at www.opengroup.org.

There are four major components (volumes) of the specification, three of which we are concerned with. The first, the Base Definitions volume (XBD), contains general terms, concepts, and interfaces common to all volumes of the standard. This includes utility conventions, standards conformance, and the relationship of the standard to POSIX. The second component, the System Interfaces volume, or XSH, provides definitions for system service functions and subroutines, and language-specific system services for the C programming language. The XSH is where you would find, essentially, man pages for all the functions defined by the standard, grouped together in a single document. The third component, XRAT, defines the rationale for the various portions of the standard. XRAT also defines what it means to be portable, specifying several general requirements that must be met before applications can be considered portable.

A handy table (in PDF format) which cross-references the APIs defined in the Single UNIX Specification with other standards, including UNIX 98, UNIX 95, the ISO POSIX-1 standard, the ISO POSIX-2 standard, the ISO C standard, SVID3 and 4.3BSD, can (after a simple registration process is completed) be downloaded directly from the Open Group at www.unix-systems.org/version3/apis.html.

XPG

XPG refers to a set of standards, developed by X/Open, that predate the Single UNIX Specification. These standards are now essentially deprecated in favor of the Single UNIX Specification.

BSD

BSD (Berkeley Standard Distribution) versions of UNIX, such as BSD 4.x, add to the original AT&T versions of UNIX and to System V in various important ways. As mentioned earlier, sockets and related APIs (`listen`, `bind`, `connect`, `accept`, `htons`, `recv`, `send`, and so forth) are a significant part of the BSD offering.

Support for POSIX, SVID, XPG, and BSD

Support for the POSIX, SVID, XPG, and BSD standards that were introduced previously mainly comes by way of the GNU C library (www.gnu.org/software/libc/). Because the following is based on online documentation for the GNU C library; I encourage you to refer to the online documentation for updates that may become available. In this section, we take a look at what support is provided for each of the standards, and then I describe how to go about enabling this support in your code.

POSIX

The GNU C library implements all the functions specified in ISO/IEC 9945-1:1996, the POSIX System API, commonly referred to as POSIX.1.

Some facilities from ISO/IEC 9945-2:1993, the POSIX Shell and Utilities standard (POSIX.2), are also implemented in the GNU library. These include utilities for dealing with regular expressions and other pattern-matching facilities.

SVID

The GNU C library defines most of the facilities required by the SVID that are not also required by the ISO C or POSIX standards, for compatibility with System V UNIX and other UNIX systems (such as SunOS) that include these facilities. However, many of the more obscure and less generally useful facilities required by the SVID are not included.

The supported facilities from System V include the methods for interprocess communication and shared memory, the `hsearch` and `drand48` families of functions, `fmtmsg`, and several of the mathematical functions.

XPG

The GNU C library complies with the X/Open Portability Guide, Issue 4.2, with all extensions common to XSI (X/Open System Interface)-compliant systems and all X/Open UNIX extensions.

BSD

The GNU C library defines facilities from some versions of UNIX that are not formally standardized, specifically from the 4.2 BSD, 4.3 BSD, and 4.4 BSD UNIX systems (also known as Berkeley UNIX) and from SunOS (a popular 4.2 BSD derivative that includes some UNIX System V functionality).

Using Standards Support in GCC

It is important to realize that you have a choice to make when it comes to which standards you want to support in your code. GCC supports this choice by providing compiler flags and macros that can be used to select the standards you want your code to adhere to. Using these flags and macros can help to make your code more portable. Header files are provided to ensure that your code properly calls the functions as intended by the standard. The next several sections provide more details on how to enable and use standards-based library code in your applications.

Compiler Flags

Perhaps the first thing you will want to do is to add -ansi and -pendantic as arguments to the command line of GCC. The -ansi argument tells GCC to strictly adhere to the ANSI/ISO C language standard, and it removes GNU extensions that are not a part of the language. The -pedantic argument tells GCC to reject any code that does not adhere to the standard. The omission of this argument does not preclude you from calling functions defined in the C library that pertain to the standards, but it helps you to avoid misusing the APIs by, for example, passing arguments of the wrong type to functions defined in the library.

    You should also add -Wall as an argument to the compiler command line. Writing correct code is an important step to writing portable code, and you should let the compiler help you to enforce this. See Item 6 for a discussion of compiler warnings.

Headers

The next thing you should do is include header files that define the functions that you will be calling. This will be all but required if you enable -ansi and -pedantic as I recommend. You can determine which header file to include by referring to man(1) pages, either in a console window, or online via a search engine such as Google. The header file you should include is generally found in the Synopsis section of the man(1) page, as it is in this example taken from the man(1) page on Mac OS X for atof():

```
ATOF(3)                    System Library Functions Manual                    ATOF(3)

NAME
     atof - convert ASCII string to double

LIBRARY
```

```
Standard C Library (libc, -lc)
```

SYNOPSIS
```
#include <stdlib.h>

double
atof(const char *nptr);
```

To use `atof()`, we need to include `<stdlib.h>` in our code, as follows. For C source code, use the following form:

```
#include <stdlib.h>
```

The preceding syntax works for C++ code, too, but the preferable usage for C++ is to prefix the include filename with `c`, and remove the `.h` suffix, as follows:

```
#include <cstdlib>
```

The headers provided with GCC are written so that it doesn't matter whether one is included more than once, and including a header file a second time has no effect. Also, the order in which they are included doesn't matter.

Macros

Compiling with the `-ansi` command-line argument enables only ISO/ANSI features. To gain access to interfaces supported by POSIX.1, or SVID, you need to enable certain macros that are defined by GCC. These macros should be defined at the top of each source file, before any headers are specified. Doing so makes the macros available to the C preprocessor, which affects which function, constant, and macro declarations and definitions will be allowed in your source code from the GNU-supplied headers. You can also define these macros in your Makefile using –D command-line options, but the GNU documentation recommends that the macros be included in source code directly so that their affects on source code can be more deterministic.

The following code snippet, taken from `<dirent.h>`, illustrates the use of the `_POSIX_SOURCE` macro. If your code defined `_POSIX_SOURCE` ahead of the inclusion of the `dirent.h` header—for example:

```
...
#define _POSIX_SOURCE 1
....
#include <dirent.h>
```

. . . .

—the DIR type would be defined by the statement:

```
typedef void *DIR;
```

Otherwise, the definition of DIR that is supplied in the **#else** clause of the include file would be used:

```
#include <sys/dirent.h>

#ifdef _POSIX_SOURCE
typedef void *  DIR;
#else

#define d_ino d_fileno /* backward compatibility */

/* definitions for library routines operating on
   directories. */

#define DIRBLKSIZ   1024

/* structure describing an open directory. */
typedef struct _dirdesc {
    int     dd_fd;       /* file descriptor associated
                            with directory */
    long    dd_loc;      /* offset in current buffer */
    long    dd_size;     /* amount of data returned by
                            getdirentries */
    char    *dd_buf;     /* data buffer */
    int     dd_len;      /* size of data buffer */
    long    dd_seek;     /* magic cookie returned by
                            getdirentries */
    long    dd_rewind;   /* magic cookie for rewinding */
    int     dd_flags;    /* flags for readdir */
} DIR;

#define dirfd(dirp) ((dirp)->dd_fd)

/* flags for opendir2 */
#define DTF_HIDEW 0x0001    /* hide whiteout entries */
#define DTF_NODUP 0x0002    /* don't return duplicate
                               names */
#define DTF_REWIND 0x0004   /* rewind after reading
                               union stack */
```

```
#define __DTF_READALL 0x0008   /* everything has been
                                  read */

#ifndef NULL
#define NULL     0
#endif


#endif /* _POSIX_SOURCE */
```

Here is a list of macros supported by GCC that correspond to the previously discussed standards:

- **_POSIX_SOURCE**—Defining this enables POSIX.1 standard (IEEE Standard 1003.1) and all the ISO C facilities.
  _POSIX_SOURCE is ignored if _POSIX_C_SOURCE is defined to be to a positive integer.
- **_POSIX_C_SOURCE**—Define _POSIX_C_SOURCE to be greater than or equal to 1 to include functionality from the 1990 edition of the POSIX.1 standard (IEEE Standard 1003.1-1990).
  Define _POSIX_C_SOURCE to be greater than or equal to 2 to include functionality from the 1992 edition of the POSIX.2 standard (IEEE Standard 1003.2-1992).
  Define _POSIX_C_SOURCE to be greater than or equal to 199309L, and then the functionality from the 1993 edition of the POSIX.1b standard (IEEE Standard 1003.1b-1993) is made available.
- **_BSD_SOURCE**—When defined, you have access to 4.3 BSD UNIX, ISO C, POSIX.1, and POSIX.2 functionality.
  4.3 BSD definitions that conflict with POSIX.1 or POSIX.2 take precedence when this macro is defined. You must also link your application with -lbsd-compat so that the linker will resolve BSD-defined functions before searching for them in the normal C library.
- **_SVID_SOURCE**—If defined, SVID-derived functionality is included, as well as that provided by ISO C, POSIX.1, POSIX.2, and X/Open standards.
- **_XOPEN_SOURCE**—Defining _XOPEN_SOURCE enables functions that are defined by the X/Open Portability Guide, in addition to those functions that are enabled by the _POSIX_SOURCE and _POSIX_C_SOURCE macros.
  Defining _XOPEN_SOURCE as 500 includes _XOPEN_SOURCE functionality, and new functionality from the Single UNIX Specification, version 2.
- **_ISOC99_SOURCE**—GNU libc is tracking the implementation of the new C99 standard, and by enabling the _ISOC99_SOURCE macro, you can

make use of the features of this standard that have been implemented so far. Some of the features supported include C++ style comments and local variable declarations within conditional expressions (which appear within `for, if, while,` and `switch` statements). Furthermore, it prohibits explicit declarations of functions and variables that would default to int, and allows declarations of variables to occur anywhere within a block, as opposed to requiring the declarations before the first statement occurring in the block. This flag has no bearing on C++ code, as you might have guessed.

■ **_GNU_SOURCE**—Defining this macro brings in everything described previously: ISO C89, ISO C99, POSIX.1, POSIX.2, BSD, SVID, and X/Open, and GNU-defined extensions. Should there be any conflicts with POSIX.1 and BSD, POSIX definitions take precedence over the BSD ones. You should avoid using this macro because the use of GNU extensions is inherently nonportable.

Microsoft Runtime Library Support for POSIX

Because Mac OS X and Linux both based their development on GCC and other GNU tools, there isn't really much that needs to be made in terms of decisions regarding choice of compilers and library support. On Microsoft Windows, it's an entirely different story.

It's interesting to look at what Microsoft adds to the standards picture. When Windows NT 3.51 came out back in the early 1990s, Microsoft made a public commitment to support both POSIX and Win32 APIs on a more or less equal basis. Figure 5-1 shows how Win32 and POSIX relate to each other and to the overall Windows NT architecture. As you can see, there are two subsystems, one for POSIX 1003.1 (POSIX.1) and another for Win32. Both subsystems provide a client-level API that acts as a wrapper above the native Windows NT API, which in turn provides the actual implementation of the functions that the APIs support. Client applications are free to call either or both of these APIs from the same process.

Windows NT 2000, Windows XP, and Vista are essentially Windows NT-based systems, meaning that the architecture just described applies to these operating systems, too. Versions of Windows that are not NT based include Windows 95, Windows 98, and Windows Me, which are operating systems that Microsoft no longer supports, and application developers really should no longer be supporting, either.

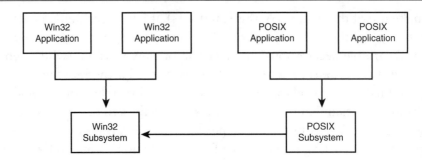

Figure 5-1 Win32 and POSIX subsystems

The APIs for creating a file illustrate how Win32, POSIX, and Windows NT-based systems work together. In Win32, creating a file is performed by calling the `CreateFile()` function. In the POSIX API, `creat()` provides this functionality. Both of these functions end up doing the same thing. They take their arguments, massage them as needed, and then pass them as arguments to the Windows NT function `NtCreateFile()`:

```
void NtCreateFile(
    PHANDLE FileHandle,
    ACCESS_MASK DesiredAccess,
    POBJECT_ATTRIBUTES ObjectAttributes,
    PIO_STATUS_BLOCK IoStatusBlock,
    PLARGE_INTEGER AllocationSize,
    ULONG FileAttributes,
    ULONG ShareAccess,
    ULONG CreateDisposition,
    ULONG CreateOptions,
    PVOID EaBuffer,
    ULONG EaLength
);
```

However, there is a glitch in the preceding code. The POSIX `creat()` function does not exist in the Microsoft Runtime Library (RTL), but a function named `_creat()` does. (Notice the leading underscore.) There are several POSIX-like functions in the Microsoft RTL that are named using this convention: `_dup()`, `_fdopen()`, `_exec()`, `_open()`, `_read()`, `_write()`, and `_close()`, among them. What is the effect of the leading underscore? At best, it means that it is not possible to use these functions portably (in either their POSIX or Microsoft RTL form) without some sort of macro or wrapper to map from one version of the function name to the other.

Naming is not the only issue that you need to contend with. In some cases, the arguments to the Microsoft RTL functions differ from the POSIX definitions, if only slightly. For example, the documentation for open() that one gets from the man pages on Mac OS X lists the possible values in Table 5-1 for the second argument to open(), flags:

Table 5-1 open() Flags and Their Meanings

Flag	Meaning
O_RDONLY	Open for reading only
O_WRONLY	Open for writing only
O_RDWR	Open for reading and writing
O_NONBLOCK	Do not block on open or for data to become available
O_APPEND	Append on each write
O_CREAT	Create file if it does not exist
O_TRUNC	Truncate size to 0
O_EXCL	Error if create and file exists
O_SHLOCK	Atomically obtain a shared lock
O_EXLOCK	Atomically obtain an exclusive lock

The documentation for open() in the Microsoft RTL adds O_BINARY, O_TEXT, O_RANDOM, and a few other flags that are not defined by POSIX, and does not mention support for the O_SHLOCK and O_EXLOCK flags. Besides this, all the flags are prefixed with an underscore—for example, _O_BINARY—making the syntax even more incompatible. Even greater differences exist between POSIX and the Microsoft RTL for the third argument to open(), mode. Finally, the errno settings on failure may be different, because the Microsoft version of the function supports only a subset of the values that are supported by the Mac OS X version of open().

In the end, it turns out that some of the POSIX code that you will write for Mac OS X and Linux can be ported directly to Microsoft Windows without modification. Although there is no "penalty" for using the POSIX APIs rather than Win32 APIs for similar functionality, you should take care to write your code to the absolute least common denominator, and to test your work to ensure runtime compatibility.

Using GCC on Microsoft Windows

For those of you who do not have access to a commercial compiler such as
Microsoft Visual C++, you might consider using GCC to compile your code
on Windows. There are two options that I am familiar with. The first,
MinGW (www.mingw.org), provides GCC and related tools, and supports
linking directly to the Microsoft RTL, which is bundled with Microsoft
Windows. The other, Cygwin (www.Cygwin.com), is also GCC based, but is
much more comprehensive. The following sections briefly describe these
two projects and what they have to offer.

MinGW

The MinGW project (www.mingw.org) is, in the words of the maintainers,
"a collection of freely available and freely distributable Windows specific
header files and import libraries combined with GNU toolsets that allow
one to produce native Windows programs that do not rely on any third-
party C runtime DLLs."

Installing and using MinGW is fairly straightforward. There are two
major components, MSYS and MinGW, but you only need to install
MinGW to get the functionality that we are after. (We will use Cygwin to
get the functionality that MSYS provides, and more.)

Downloading MinGW

To download and install MinGW, follow these steps:

1. Create a directory named `mingw` on your system (for example,
   c:\mingw).
2. Point your Web browser at www.mingw.org and click the Download
   link.
3. Select a mirror and click it.
4. Click MinGW-3.1.0-1.exe (or a later version) to download the
   MinGW installer, saving it in c:\mingw.
5. Back in Windows, double-click the MinGW-3.1.0-1.exe icon to run
   the installer, selecting c:\mingw as the installation directory when
   prompted.
6. Add the following to your path environment variable, preferably at
   the beginning (before any Cygwin components, should they exist):

```
c:\mingw\bin;c:\mingw\lib
```

Testing MinGW

A simple test program can be used to verify that everything is in working order after MinGW has been installed. Type the following into a file named mingwtest.cpp using your favorite text editor or integrated development environment (IDE):

```cpp
#include <iostream>
#include <dirent.h>

using namespace std;

int
main(int argc, char *argv[])
{
    DIR *dir;

    dir = opendir(".");
    if (dir != (DIR *) NULL) {
      cout << "Directory opened successfully!";
      closedir(dir);
    } else
      cout << "Couldn't open directory\n";
}
```

This program illustrates a MinGW program based on STL (`iostream`) and POSIX functionality (`dirent.h`). `opendir(2)` accepts a path name as an argument. In this case, we pass ".", which represents the current directory of the executable. The returned value, a pointer to a variable of type `DIR`, can be passed to another POSIX function named `readdir()` to iterate the contents of the directory. Type `man opendir` in a terminal window on Linux or Mac OS X for more details on these functions.

To compile, just open a MS-DOS command window, and type the following:

```
c:\> g++ -o mingwtest mingwtest.cpp
```

If everything goes right (and it should), type the following:

```
c:\> .\mingwtest
Directory opened successfully!
c:\>
```

   If you are unable to compile or execute the sample program, make sure that your path variable is set as instructed earlier.

Verifying the Libraries That MinGW Uses

The MinGW license agreement states that applications you create with MinGW can be distributed without restriction, for commercial uses or otherwise. This is because the MinGW runtime libraries are in the public domain. On systems that include Cygwin as well as MinGW, it is important to verify that your binary does not link to the Cygwin.dll library (described in the next section). To verify this, you can use a freely available tool named ListDLLs to check the dynamic link libraries (DLLs) that your application has loaded. (A tool supplied with Cygwin and MinGW called objdump can also be used.) The listdlls application is available for download from Microsoft; visit www.microsoft.com and search for ListDLLS. After you download this tool, start your application, and then run listdlls from a command line, redirecting the output to a file as follows:

```
c:\> listdlls > out.txt
```

   When listdlls has completed, open the file (out.txt in this case) and search for your application by name. Here is the output from listdlls when executed while mingwtest was loaded and running. (I added a `while(1);` to the end of the source code and rebuilt so that mingwtest would stay in memory.)

```
mingwtest.exe pid: 2476
Command line: .\ mingwtest

Base              Size           Version          Path
0x00400000        0x5000
       C:\mingw\ mingwtest.exe
0x77f50000        0xa7000        5.01.2600.1217
       C:\WINDOWS\System32\ntdll.dll
0x77e60000        0xe6000        5.01.2600.1106
       C:\WINDOWS\system32\kernel32.dll
0x77c10000        0x53000        7.00.2600.1106
       C:\WINDOWS\system32\msvcrt.dll
```

   Notice that mingwtest has loaded the Microsoft RTL (msvcrt.dll), which is distributed with all Windows systems. This is the same DLL that provides support for Microsoft RTL functionality in Visual C++. However, `opendir()` is not a part of the Microsoft RTL, which raises the question:

From where does support for opendir() and related functions come? The answer is that MinGW comes with public domain libraries that are statically linked to the application. In this case, opendir() and related functions come from a library named libmingwex.a. There is no need to explicitly link this library, because MinGW's GCC takes care of the details automatically.

The other thing to notice is that the output from listdlls does not list the Cygwin DLL, meaning that on my system, which has Cygwin installed, my path was correctly set so that the MinGW tools were found before the Cygwin directories were searched. Had Cygwin been ahead of MinGW in the search path, Cygwin.dll would have invariably been displayed in the output generated for the executable by listdlls (and I would have used Cygwin tools rather than MinGW tools to build the application). This is important because the MinGW runtime libraries, being in the public domain, do not have the same licensing requirements that Cygwin's runtime library has.

MinGW does ship with tools and libraries that are licensed under the General Public License (GPL) and the Lesser GPL (LGPL). As with any commercial application, you may distribute LGPL libraries without need of disclosing your source code. Included with version 3.1.0 of MinGW is documentation that identifies a library, libiberty.a as GPL, and warns that linking to this library, or distributing it with your application binary, requires that you adhere to the GPL and distribute your source code along with your application binary. libiberty is a library that provides implementations for a number of the functions defined in POSIX.1. The license for this file is complicated by the fact that it is a conglomeration of source code from various points of origin, some of it coming from BSD, some of it from the public domain, and some of it from GPL'd origins. Because the most restrictive of the licenses involved appears to be the GPL, MinGW identifies it as such, and provides the aforementioned warning. libiberty.a is not linked to your application by default, so this is not a problem in general. To verify this, add the –v argument to GCC or g++; this will generate a complete listing of the libraries that are linked to your application when you build, and you will see that libiberty is nowhere to be found.

Of course, if the software you are writing is GPL, and you plan to distribute your sources, there is even less to worry about. If you are planning to distribute your application under the GPL, however, you are likely going to want to use Cygwin rather than MinGW. The following section introduces Cygwin.

Cygwin

Cygwin is a project hosted by Red Hat that aims to promote the portability of open source applications to the Windows platform. Its goals are much more ambitious than those of MinGW. Its main contribution to the world, besides a rather complete offering of Linux/GNU tools (an informal count of executables found in the distribution I have installed on my Windows systems shows better than 450, compared to perhaps 650 on my Mac OS X system), is a library named Cygwin.dll, which acts as an emulation layer providing Linux/POSIX APIs to applications. Use of the Cygwin.dll is free for noncommercial uses of the library. However, developers of commercial software must pay a licensing fee to Red Hat to link the Cygwin DLL to their applications and distribute it with their software. Detailed instructions for downloading and installing Cygwin, and linking to the Cygwin DLL, can be found at www.cygwin.com/. The following instructions, however, should be enough to get you up and running with Cygwin.

Downloading and Installing Cygwin

To download and install Cygwin, follow these steps:

1. Point your Web browser at www.cygwin.com.
2. On the home page, there are a number of "Install Cygwin Now" icons. Click one of them to download the Cygwin installation program setup.exe.
3. Double-click the setup.exe program after you have downloaded it.
4. Follow the instructions and prompts provided by setup.exe and install Cygwin on your system. When prompted, select UNIX as the default text file type, and c:\cygwin as the installation directory.
5. Add the following entry to your path environment variable:

```
c:\cygwin\bin;c:\cygwin\usr\bin;c:\cygwin\lib
```

If you have installed MinGW on your system, I recommend doing the following.

1. Remove any and all MinGW components from your path variable.
2. Create a batch file (.bat extension) named mingenv.bat that contains the following:

```
set PATH=c:\mingw\bin;c:\mingw\lib;%PATH%;
```

You can execute this batch file from a command window when using MinGW to ensure that your build uses the GCC toolchain distributed with MinGW and your application links to the MinGW runtime.

Testing Cygwin

We can test Cygwin in the same way we tested MinGW. Type the following into a file named cygwintest.cpp using your favorite text editor (or make a copy of mingwtest.cpp from above if you have it handy):

```
#include <iostream>
#include <dirent.h>

using namespace std;

int
main(int argc, char *argv[])
{
    DIR *dir;

    dir = opendir(".");
    if (dir != (DIR *) NULL) {
      cout << "Directory opened successfully!";
      closedir(dir);
    } else
      cout << "Couldn't open directory\n";
}
```

Before compiling, run the following to ensure that your path is pointing to the Cygwin toolchain:

```
c:\> which g++
/usr/bin/g++
```

If you get output that indicates that which is not a recognized command, you probably don't have Cygwin installed, or your path variable does not point to the Cygwin tools. If you get output that says g++ is not found, however, try the following:

```
c:\> which g++-2
/usr/bin/g++-2
```

If you get the preceding result, g++-2 is your C++ compiler for Cygwin.
(This might happen if you install Cygwin after having installed MinGW.) As
long as your path variable is correct, is no reason not to rename g++-2 to
g++, or create a g++ simlink that points to it.

To compile, just open an MS-DOS command window and type the
following:

```
c:\> g++ -o cygwintest cygwintest.cpp
```

If everything goes right (and it should), type the following:

```
c:\> .\cygwinwtest
Directory opened successfully!
c:\>
```

Deciding Which Standards to Support

Standards support is dependent on the compiler that you use and its runtime
library. Assuming that your choice of compiler on Linux and Mac OS X is
GCC, the only choice left to make is a compiler for Windows. A majority of
commercial vendors have standardized development on Microsoft C++, but
other compilers, from vendors such as Borland, also exist. According to the
documentation shipped with the free version of Borland C++ (5.5), the
Borland runtime library is compatible with the Microsoft RTL, at least as
far as the POSIX functions are concerned. So, with the presumption that
compatibility with Microsoft C++ at the source code level is a market
requirement for any compiler that wants to compete with Microsoft C++,
coding to the Microsoft RTL is a relatively safe move.

If you are using Microsoft C++, restrict your use of functions to those
that are supported in the Microsoft RTL, and avoid direct calls to any
functions that are prefixed with an underscore character (for example,
_access()). Try to use the least common denominator of functionality
provided by the various implementations of the POSIX APIs involved,
referring to the man pages on Linux and Mac OS X and the online
documentation for the Microsoft RTL (located at http://msdn.microsoft.
com) to ensure that the use of these functions is consistent across platforms.
Although some errors caused by using other than the least common
denominator will be detected by the compiler, other errors won't; errno
values and function return value differences, for example, which may exist,
but won't be detected by the compiler and can lead to runtime errors. For

example, the documentation for `rename()` on Mac OS X and for the Microsoft RTL implies differences that could lead to errors at runtime: `rename()` on Mac OS X returns 0 on success, and –1 on failure, whereas the Microsoft RTL version of `rename()` returns 0 on success and a nonzero value on failure. The following code, based on the published documentation, behaves differently in the case of failure on these two platforms, because it checks for failure based on –1 as defined by the Mac OS X documentation:

```
int retval;

retval = rename("foo.txt", "bar.txt");
if (retval == -1)
      // handle failure
else
      // handle success
```

The common denominator one gets from reading the documentation is that successful execution of `rename()` yields a return value of 0, leading to a more correct version of the code:

```
int retval;

retval = rename("foo.txt", "bar.txt");
if (retval == 0)
      // handle success
else
      // handle failure
```

ANSI/ISO C89, Standard C++, and POSIX.1 are your best bets if you must work with a mixed set of compilers, which I assume here are Microsoft C++ on Windows and the GCC compiler on Mac OS X and Linux.

At www.crossplatformbook.com/posix.html, I have compiled a list of the POSIX.1 APIs found in the Open Group Base Specifications (Issue 6 IEEE Std 1003.1, 2003 Edition), and for each function listed there, I have indicated support for the following compilers/libraries: GCC 3.3 on Mac OS X, GCC 3.2.2 on Red Hat Linux, and Microsoft Visual C++ 7.0 .NET runtime library. In addition to these, I have indicated which functions are supported in Cygwin and have listed equivalent functionality that is found in NSPR 4.3. (See Item 17 for a discussion of NSPR.)

Item 17: Consider Using a Platform Abstraction Library Such as NSPR

This item takes a look at the Netscape Portable Runtime Library (NSPR). Originally developed by engineers at Netscape and now a part of the Mozilla open source codebase, NSPR provides solutions to several commonly encountered portability problems. The item starts by discussing some of the motivations for a portability library such as NSPR. We then take a look at types in NSPR and a simple "Hello World" style program. Then we get deeper into NSPR, looking at its thread and dynamic library support.

At the end of the item, we take a look at C/C++, the C Standard Library, POSIX, Boost, STL, and NSPR as a whole, focusing on the thought process to go through to effectively choose a solution best suited for the job at hand.

Why NSPR?

Before we talk about NSPR in detail, it helps to look at some of the problems that it solves. What it all boils down to is these two concepts:

- Compilers can differ in certain ways, even compilers that are designed to generate code for the same platform.
- APIs designed to do a conceptually similar task, or to provide a conceptually similar service, are often different in terms of their implementation, their behavior, or both.

Compilers Are Different

Most of you would expect, with good reason, that on 16-bit systems, the C/C++ int type is 16 bits in size, on 32-bit systems, 32 bits in size, and so forth. But what about the size of a short? Or a long? What about pointers?

K&R will tell you that in the ANSI C language, the size of the integer types (int, short, long) is compiler dependent, subject to the following simple rules: Shorts must be at least 16 bits in size, longs must be at least 32 bits in size, and shorts cannot be longer than ints, which in turn cannot be longer than longs. A compiler that implements a 16-bit short, a 32-bit int, and a 64-bit long will satisfy this criteria, as will a compiler that implements short, int, and long all as 32-bit types. The situation is the same for C++.

In many cases, the size of an int will have little or no impact at all on code portability. A for loop, for example, will yield the same results (in most cases, independent of the size of its loop variable). Typically, a programmer chooses the size of integer that he or she expects will cover the range of values that the loop variable will take on. For example, a loop that needs to iterate 5,000 times can safely be coded using a loop variable declared as short because the value 5000 is a value that can be safely stored in 16 bits (which shorts must be, at a minimum, according to the C/C++ language definition).

Problems creep up, however, when assumptions are made about the size of the integer data type. To illustrate a simple case, assume that we have the following code:

```
#include <limits.h>

...

int bar;
bar = INT_MAX;
```

On machine A where an int is 64 bits in size, the variable bar is going to be assigned the value 0xffffffffffffffff, whereas on a machine where ints are the more typical 32 bits in size, the value assigned will be 0xffffffff. Although the code will compile and execute on both machines, the result is different and therefore, the code may or may not be correct and should be considered nonportable. The following code that uses bar.

```
for (int i=0; i<bar; i++)
    cout << i << "\n";
```

is going to generate quite a bit more output on the console of the 64-bit machine, which may or may not be a correct result, depending on what the application is intending to do. However, indexing an array that only has a 32-bit range of elements in it will generate an exception on the 64-bit machine (because the loop variable will go far beyond that value), a much more serious situation indeed.

NSPR provides facilities that help programmers write code that is more portable in terms of the sizes of C/C++ data type sizes, not only for ints, but for the other intrinsic types, too.

APIs Differ in Terms of Implementation and Behavior

A major contribution of NSPR is its platform-agnostic API. The intent of this API is to provide abstractions of functionality present on each platform but for which a portable API does not exist. The creation and management of threads is an example of functionality for which NSPR provides an abstraction. Every modern operating system provides APIs that can be used by a process to create, execute, and manage independent threads of execution. The act of creating and executing a thread generally involves operating system-specific semantics, and the APIs for thread creation and management that one finds on the various platforms are, as a result, usually very different. For example, the function that is used to create a thread on a POSIX system is `pthread_create()`, whereas on Windows it is `CreateThread()`. However, many qualities intrinsic to thread creation and execution are shared among the various operating system implementations, including the following:

- All threads have an entry point.
- All threads can be killed.
- All threads can be waited on.

To capitalize on the similarities that exist among the various platform-specific threading models and implementations, and to insulate developers from their differences, NSPR provides portable abstract data types such as `PRThread`, and functions such as `PR_CreateThread()`, that can be used in place of the natively supplied types and APIs. Later in this item, I will describe how NSPR supports threading in detail.

Another example in this category has to do with case insensitive string comparisons. On Windows, you can achieve this by making a call to `stricmp()`, but it turns out `stricmp()` is not available on Linux or on Mac OS X, both of which provide the standard `lib` function `strcasecmp()`. NSPR provides its own version of `strcasecmp()` named `PL_strcasecmp()` which is available on all platforms to which NSPR has been ported.

Threads and string comparison functions are not the only areas touched upon by NSPR. System IPC (for example, pipes and shared memory), I/O (similar to sockets), memory management (for example, `malloc()`), system timers and calendaring functions, and even dynamic linking (shared library loading and symbol lookup) are all covered by NSPR.

Certain trade-offs had to be made by the designers of NSPR to provide abstract APIs, but in general these trade-offs are usually ones that are not going to have an effect on the majority of programs. One of the design goals of NSPR is not to provide "common denominator" implementations of features, but to try to exploit the strengths of each platform in a highly portable fashion.

NSPR Basics

Let's begin by taking a look at what NSPR provides us in greater detail. My intent here is not to provide exhaustive documentation for every aspect of NSPR; for the latest, detailed information, I refer you to the NSPR documentation maintained at www.mozilla.org/projects/nspr. What I do here is survey the major areas of functionality covered by NSPR, and drill down into one or two of the areas that I consider to be particularly important to a successful cross-platform deployment, The first of these areas, the way the NSPR represents C/C++ intrinsic types, is covered in the next section.

NSPR Types

Earlier in this item, I mentioned the C/C++ integer data types (short, int, long), and pointed out some ways in which their (mis)use can affect code portability; NSPR deals with this by providing replacement integer types that unambiguously specify the number of bits in their representation. For signed integer values, use PRInt8, PRInt16, PRInt32, PRInt64, which NSPR guarantees to provide signed 8-bit, 16-bit, 32-bit, and 64-bit integers on all platforms to which NSPR has been ported. The types PRUint8, PRUint16, PRUint32, and PRUint64 provide the same guarantees for their unsigned counterparts.

In addition to these types, several macros/defines are provided that can be used regardless of platform when dealing with variables declared using these types. For example, the PR_INT16_MIN and PR_INT16_MAX defines can be used to specify the minimum and maximum values, respectively, that can be stored in a variable of type PRInt16. Similar defines exist for the other types, both signed and unsigned. (There are no unsigned min defines—for example, PR_UINT16_MIN—because 0 is always the minimum value that can be stored in an unsigned variable.)

Our example from the start of this item can be rewritten using the NSPR integer types. All we need to do is decide how big of an integer we want to use (in this case, 32 bits), and recode using NSPR integer types:

```
PRInt32 bar;
bar = PR_INT32_MAX;
for (PRInt32 i=0; i<bar; i++)
    cout << i << "\n";
```

The preceding code will execute the same regardless of the platform, 32-bit or 64-bit. Let's see what happens if we change the type of bar to PRInt64:

```
PRInt32 bar;
bar = PR_INT64_MAX;
for (PRInt64 i=0; i<bar; i++)
    cout << i << "\n";
```

and recompile:

```
$ cc -I/usr/local/nsprpub/include/nspr/ -g -Wall -c ints.c
ints.c: In function `main':
ints.c:10: error: `PR_INT64_MAX' undeclared (first use\
    in this function)
```

The reason there is no PR_INT64_MAX macro is because unlike 8-, 16-, and 32-bit sizes, support for 64-bit platforms is inconsistent. With compilers that define a long long type, it is possible to declare a constant to reflect the maximum size of a 64-bit int, but on some platforms PRInt64 has no intrinsic support and must be defined as a struct:

```
typedef struct {
#ifdef IS_LITTLE_ENDIAN
    PRUint32 lo, hi;
#else
    PRUint32 hi, lo;
#endif
} PRInt64;
```

Although you can declare a variable of type PRInt64 simply by including prtypes.h, you need to include prlong.h to make use of the 64-bit macros that NSPR provides. One of the macros in prlong.h, LL_MAXINT, can be used to replace PR_INT64_MAX in the 64-bit version of this code. The LL stands for "long long," which is how the 64-bit type is defined by NSPR on non-64-bit machines when the compiler being used supports a long long type. The macros defined in prlong.h fall into the following major categories.

Relational Operators

You can use macros defined in prlong.h to compare the value of one PRInt64 value to another. For example, LL_EQ(a, b) compares two PRInt64 values and evaluates to true if they are equal.

Logical Operators

NSPR provides macros for doing bitwise and (LL_AND), or (LL_OR), xor (LL_XOR), and one's complement negation (LL_NOT) operations on PRInt64 typed variables. Left- and right-shift operators, such as LL_SHL for left-shifting a PRInt32 value some number of bits, are also provided.

Mathematical Operators

Two's complement negation, addition, subtraction, multiplication, division, and modulus operations are provided for. The macros for these operations are, respectively, LL_NEG, LL_ADD, LL_SUB, LL_MUL, LL_DIV, and LL_MOD.

Conversion Operators

Finally, prlong.h defines macros that can be used to convert PRInt64 values from one type to another. For example, you can convert (subject to range restrictions) a PRInt64 value to a signed 32-bit value using LL_L2I, or convert a floating-point value to PRInt64 with LL_F2L.

The following listing corrects the port of our sample to PRInt64:

```c
#include <stdio.h>

#include "prtypes.h
#include "prlong.h"

int
main(int argc, char *argv[])
{
    PRInt64 i, bar;
    PRFloat64 s;

    bar = LL_MAXINT;
    i = 0;
    while (LL_NE(i, bar)) {
        LL_L2F(s, i);
        printf("%.0f\n", s);
        LL_ADD(i, i, 1);
    }
    return 0;
}
```

Binary Data and NSPR

NSPR's types allow you to write type-portable code. Issues related to the cross-platform sharing of binary data are not as easily solved, however, but can be overcome to a certain degree if you are careful. The goal is to ensure that all platforms are dealing with a canonical representation of the data being shared. The following explains what I mean by *canonical* data and describes how NSPR can be used to achieve the goal.

Consider the following type:

```
typedef struct _item {
    short id;
    char name[64];
} Item;
```

The preceding code may not be binary portable to another platform (or compiler) for the following reasons:

- The id field may be 16 or 32 bits in size, depending on the platform and the compiler.
- Even if the id field sizes were the same, there may be alignment issues introduced by the compiler.
- The size of the item type may vary, based on compiler alignment of the struct or the size of the id field.
- Finally, there may be endian issues with the id field.

We can get past the first issue by using the PRInt16 type rather than short to define the id field. This will also ensure, only if there are no alignment issues, that the struct size is constant.

The more difficult problem lies in the area of structure alignment. By converting the id field to a 16-bit quantity, we may find the compiler inserting 2 extra bytes between the id field and the name field so that the name field starts on a 4-byte boundary. Because of this, we can't be sure if the size of the struct is going to be 66 bytes or 68 bytes.

Most compilers support pragmas and/or compiler flags that can be used to control the alignment of fields in a structure. If you are staying within a compiler family, such as GCC, using compiler-supported flags may be appropriate; in general, however, the solution is not strictly portable. Perhaps the best way overall to deal with binary data is just to avoid using it. Serializing your binary data to ASCII is, I believe, a much better way to deal with the issue. In Item 20, I describe some ways that the serialization of binary data to ASCII (and vice versa) can be achieved.

Now we turn our attention to the endian issue, one that is no doubt familiar to many of you. On Intel machines, one encounters little endian storage. On a little endian machine, the first byte in memory of a 16-bit value is the low-order byte, and the second byte in memory stores the high-order byte. On big endian machines, you encounter exactly the opposite; the high-order byte comes first, followed by the low-order byte. Figure 5-2 shows how the 16-bit value 0x48 is stored both on little endian and big endian architectures as a16-bit value. PowerPC (Mac OS X) is big endian, and Intel/AMD/x86 (Windows and the majority of Linux installations) is little endian. (Apple has switched to Intel as its supplier of CPUs, so new Macintoshes sold are little endian, too.)

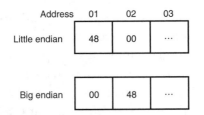

Figure 5-2 Little endian versus big endian

Assuming that we still are planning to interchange binary data, we can then make use of functionality provided by NSPR to convert our data to a canonical format known as network byte order. The process of converting data to network byte order requires overhead, but less than would be required to serialize binary data to ASCII. The functions that can be used to convert to and from network byte order are PR_ntohs(), PR_ntohl(), PR_htons(), and PR_htonl(). PR_htons() and PR_htonl() convert 16-bit and 32-bit integers, respectively, to 16-bit network byte order values of the same size. Network byte order is, by definition, big endian, so on big endian systems such as the PowerPC, these functions do nothing, The companion functions PR_ntohs() and PR_ntohl() convert network byte order values to the values appropriate for the system they are executing on. On a little endian machine, these functions take a network byte order value and return a little endian result.

Threads

In the next few sections, I describe NSPR threads. By taking a close look at NSPR's threading implementation, we will learn, by example, how NSPR supports a fairly coarse-grained feature that has different implementations, and in some cases, semantics across distinct platforms.

Introduction to Threads

A thread is a body of code that executes in its own context. A thread is similar to a process, but processes carry additional baggage to support general application execution, such as an address space, file descriptors, and all the other things that make a process what it is. A thread, on the other hand, executes within the context of a process and shares the address space, file descriptors, and so forth that the enveloping process provides, which is why threads are sometimes referred to as lightweight processes. Threads do need to maintain their own context, usually an instruction pointer, a stack, and a copy of the CPU register values. Thread-local storage, when supported, allows threads to maintain their own private storage.

A Web browser is a good example of an application that benefits in measurable ways from the use of threads. Consider a browser loading a page that contains images stored on a few different Web servers. The most *inefficient* way to load this Web page would be for the browser to iterate the URLs on the page in series, and for each image, to open an HTTP connection to the server, download the image, close the connection, and then move on to the next URL until all the images on the page have been downloaded. A much more efficient scheme would be to create separate threads, one for each server that the browser has identified on the Web page. Each thread would open a connection to its server that it is responsible for and download the images from that server one by one. The big difference here is that in a threaded implementation, the threads are executing in parallel, and should one (or more) thread block, because of some network condition, or perhaps because it must perform a disk write, the other threads will continue to execute unabated. The end result is that with the single-threaded, serial paradigm, any delays encountered will increase the overall time it takes for the Web page to completely load by the amount of the delay. Delays that are encountered by a multithreaded solution are likely to have little or no effect on the total amount of time it takes for the Web page to completely load.

Another place threads can be of help is in user interface programs. A common mistake is to execute some time-consuming task, such as a sort, on the same thread the user interface is executing on. Because the user interface is not given an opportunity to breathe during the execution of the task, it cannot be responsive to input from the system (for example, requests to repaint a window) or from the user of the application, who may be clicking buttons, or trying to change focus or otherwise interface with the application in some way. To the user, it usually appears as though the process (or their computer) has hung, and this may lead the user to kill the application, or to perhaps even reboot the system, depending on how severe the freeze appears to be.

To avoid situations such as this, applications should execute any time- or processor-intensive tasks on a thread that is separate from the thread executing the user interface code.

You need to know three basic things to use threads effectively:

- How to create, initialize, and start a thread
- How to coordinate access to shared resources among multiple threads
- How to deal with thread termination

In our browser example, these steps might equate to the following actions:

- Starting a thread for each HTTP server containing images referenced by the Web page
- Coordinating access to the Web browser's image cache
- Waiting for each thread to complete, and notifying the browser so that it can give feedback to the user that the page has been loaded, or stopping the threads if the user clicks the browser stop button during the load

Native Thread Implementations

Let's now take a look at how threads are implemented on the Win32, Linux, and Mac OS X platforms, focusing on the three basic areas of functionality mentioned previously. As it turns out, we only have to consider two sets of interfaces because the native APIs are the same on Linux and Mac OS X.

Win32 Threads

Under Win32, thread creation is performed by calling the `CreateThread()` function:

```
HANDLE CreateThread(
  LPSECURITY_ATTRIBUTES lpThreadAttributes,  // if \
    NULL, default security
  SIZE_T dwStackSize,  // if 0, default size for \
    executable
  LPTHREAD_START_ROUTINE lpStartAddress, // address \
    of thread proc
```

```
LPVOID lpParameter,    // address of application \
  context data
DWORD dwCreationFlags,  // if 0, thread starts \
  immediately
LPDWORD lpThreadId // if non-NULL, thread handle \
  returned through this argument
);
```

This function creates and, optionally, starts thread execution. The arguments to CreateThread() are as follows:

- **LPSECURITY_ATTRIBUTES lpThreadAttributes**—A pointer to a SECURITY_ATTRIBUTES struct. Passing NULL causes default security attributes to be applied to the thread, and makes the threat noninheritable for any child processes that the process creating the thread spawns. Most applications will set this argument to NULL.
- **SIZE_T dwStackSize**—The stack for the thread. Windows will round this value so that it is divisible by the system page size. If 0, the default size for the parent executable is used.
- **LPTHREAD_START_ROUTINE lpStartAddress**—A pointer to an application-defined function that represents the body of execution for the thread being created. The prototype for this function must be as follows:

```
DWORD WINAPI ThreadProc(LPVOID lpParameter);
```

- **LPVOID lpParameter**—This is a pointer to application specific context that will be passed to the ThreadProc specified by lpStartAddress upon start of the thread.
- **DWORD dwCreationFlags**—To cause the thread to start immediately upon invocation of CreateThread(), set this value to 0. Otherwise, setting it to CREATE_SUSPENDED will require the application to use ResumeThread() to start execution of the thread.
- **LPDWORD lpThreadId**—If non-NULL, CreateThread() will store the thread ID of the newly created thread in the DWORD variable pointed to by this argument.

The following example illustrates how you might go about using CreateThread():

```
typedef struct message_
{
     int count;
     char msg[128];
} Message;

DWORD WINAPI
MyThreadFunc( LPVOID lpParameter)
{
     Message *pMsg = (Message *) lpParameter;
     int i;

     for (i=0; i< pMsg->count; i++) {
         printf("%s\n", msg);

     ExitThread(0);
}

int
main( int argc, char *argv[])
{
     Message msg;
     DWORD dwThreadId;
     HANDLE hThread;

     msg.count = 16;
     strncpy(msg.msg, sizeof(msg.msg) - 1,
         "Hello World!");

     hThread = CreateThread(
         NULL, // default security attributes
         1024, // set the stack size to 1K
         MyThreadFunc, // thread function
         &msg, // argument to thread function
         0, // use default creation flags
         &dwThreadId); // returns thread identifier

     // Check the return value for success.

     if (hThread == NULL) {
         printf( "Failed to create thread\n");
     }
     else {
         while (WaitForSingleObject(hThread, 1000)
             == WAIT_TIMEOUT);
     }
  }
}
```

The `main()` function listed here calls `CreateThread()` to create a new thread, which starts its life executing in the function `MyThreadFunc()`. `MyThreadFunc()` is passed a pointer to a struct of type `Message`, which is initialized just prior to the call to `CreateThread()`. `MyThreadFunc()` then prints the contents of the `msg` field in a loop, using the `count` field to determine how many times the loop should iterate. If the call to `CreateThread()` is successful, `main()` goes into a loop waiting for the thread to exit, putting the main thread to sleep for periods of a second waiting for the child thread to complete. When the thread is done, `MyThreadFunc()` sets its return value with a call to `ExitThread()`, causing the main thread to exit.

Linux and Mac OS X Threads

Enough for Win32. Now it is time to look at how it is done on Linux and Mac OS X. To create a thread on these platforms, we turn to the POSIX `pthread` library. In reality, there are two ways threads can be created on Mac OS, by using `pthreads`, or with Cocoa, which supports threading in the AppKit via Objective-C interfaces. POSIX, which is described in Item 16, provides the more portable solution, so I focus on it. (You can read more about Cocoa threads by searching for NSThread online at http://developer.apple.com if you are interested.)

To create a POSIX thread, call `pthread_create()`, which has the following prototype:

```
#include <pthread.h>

int pthread_create(
  pthread_t *thread,  // on success, a thread handle \
     returned through this argument
  const pthread_attr_t *attr,  // if NULL, use default \
     thread attributes
  void *(*start_routine)(void*), // address of thread \
     proc
  void *arg  // address of application context data
);
```

The arguments to `pthread_create()` are as follows:

- **pthread_t** *thread—This argument is analogous to the `lpThreadId` argument of Win32's `CreateThread()` function and is used to return a handle to the newly created thread.

- **const pthread_attr *attr**—This argument, if non-NULL, specifies attributes of the thread that will be created. Passing NULL causes default attributes to be applied. I illustrate below how to use this argument to specify the stack size for the thread.
- **void *(*start_routine)(void *)**—This argument is a pointer to the function that will be executed when the thread starts. The function prototype, as you may be able to guess, is as follows:

```
void *
ThreadProc(void *arg);
```

- **void *arg**—This is a pointer to application context data that is passed to the thread proc as its only argument.

The following code implements the sample code provided earlier for Win32 threads, but uses POSIX **pthreads** calls:

```
#include <stdio.h>
#include <pthread.h>

typedef struct message_
{
    int count;
    char msg[128];
} Message;

void *
MyThreadFunc(void   *pParameter)
{
    Message *pMsg = (Message *) pParameter;
    int i;

    for (i=0; i< pMsg->count; i++)
        printf("%s\n", pMsg->msg);

    pthread_exit((void *)0);
}

int
main(int argc, char *argv[])
{
    Message msg;
    pthread_t threadId;
    pthread_attr_t attr;
```

```
    int ret;

    msg.count = 16;
    strncpy(msg.msg, "Hello World!",
        sizeof(msg.msg) - 1);

    // set the stack size attribute

    ret = pthread_attr_init(&attr);
    if (ret == 0)
        ret = pthread_attr_setstacksize(&attr,
            (1024 >= PTHREAD_STACK_MIN ?
            1024 : PTHREAD_STACK_MIN));

    if (ret == 0)
        ret = pthread_create(
            &threadId, // on return, the thread ID
            &attr, // set the stack size to 1K
            MyThreadFunc, // thread function
            (void *) &msg); // argument to thread \
                function

    // Check the return value for success.

    if (ret) {
        printf( "Failed to create thread\n");
    }
    else {
        pthread_join(threadId, (void *) &ret);
        printf("Back from join\n");
        pthread_attr_destroy(&attr);
    }
}
```

Perhaps the only code in the preceding listing that requires explanation
is the code that is used to set the stack size of the thread to 1K, the call to
pthread_exit() in MyThreadFunc(), and the call to pthread_join() near
the end of main(). First, let's deal with setting the stack size. The second
argument to pthread_create() can either be NULL or the address of a
variable of type pthread_attr_t. The pthread_attr_t type is an opaque
type used to store attributes that control the operation of the thread created
by pthread_create(). If you decide to specify attributes, you must declare
and initialize a pthread_attr_t variable by calling pthread_attr_init()

and passing a pointer to the variable as an argument, as illustrated in the previous listing. On successful return from `pthread_attr_init()`, the `pthread_attr_t` variable will contain default settings. You can modify these default settings by making calls to the `pthread_attr_*()` family of functions. Here, I call `pthread_attr_setstacksize()` to set the stack size of the thread to 1024; this corresponds to the stack size that was set in the Win32 example I presented earlier.

Now let's turn our attention to `pthread_join()` and `pthread_exit()`. The call to `pthread_join()` performs the same function as the `while` loop that was coded in the Win32 version, which is reproduced here for convenience:

```
while (WaitForSingleObject(hThread, 1000) == \
    WAIT_TIMEOUT);
```

The call to `pthread_join()` blocks until the thread identified by its first argument exits. The second argument to `pthread_join()` can either be set to `NULL`, which I do in the preceding example, or it can point to a variable that, on return, will contain the return value set by the thread function, which I set to 0 in this example by calling `pthread_exit()`. I could have also simply executed a `return()` statement from `MyThreadFunc()`, passing 0 as an argument, to return a simple value like 0; but using `pthread_exit()` allows more complex values to be returned by the thread. In any event, calling `pthread_exit()` (or simply returning from the thread function) will cause the main thread to unblock and return from the call that it had made to `pthread_join()`.

NSPR Threads

As you can see, there are major syntactic differences between the POSIX and Win32 versions of threads. However, there are also some major similarities. Both versions of the sample program

- Invoke a thread proc that accepts a pointer to context data
- Return a status value from the thread `proc`
- Create and execute the thread by making a single function call
- Specify the stack size of the thread
- Block for completion of the thread

NSPR capitalizes on these commonalities in the implementation of its threading API, which I describe now.

NSPR Thread Creation

To create a thread in NSPR, you call PR_CreateThread():

```
#include <prthread.h>

PRThread* PR_CreateThread(
    PRThreadType type, // the thread type
    void (*start)(void *arg), // the thread func
    void *arg, // context data passed to the thread proc
    PRThreadPriority priority, // thread priority
    PRThreadScope scope, // see description, below
    PRThreadState state, // specifies if thread is \
        joinable or not
    PRUint32 stackSize // stack size for the thread
);
```

The arguments to PR_CreateThread(), as described on the mozilla.org site, are as follows:

- **type**—Specifies that the thread is either a user thread (PR_USER_THREAD) or a system thread (PR_SYSTEM_THREAD). Clients can synchronize on the termination of user threads, but not system threads.
- **start**—A pointer to the thread proc. The prototype for the thread proc is the same as used by POSIX threads.
- **arg**—A pointer context data passed to the thread by the caller of PR_CreateThread().
- **priority**—The initial priority of the newly created thread. The following defines can be used to specify the thread priority, from lowest to highest: PR_PRIORITY_LOW, PR_PRIORITY_NORMAL, PR_PRIORITY_HIGH, and PR_PRIORITY_URGENT. In most cases, you should set this argument to PR_PRIORITY_NORMAL.
- **scope**—The scope of an NSPR thread can be specified as local (PR_LOCAL_THREAD), global (PR_GLOBAL_THREAD) or global bound (PR_GLOBAL_BOUND_THREAD). Global threads are scheduled by the host operating system and compete with all other threads on the host operating system for resources. Local threads are scheduled by NSPR within the process. In most cases, according to the NSPR documentation, the use of local threads can lead to a significant performance benefit. However, if a thread is likely to do a lot of I/O, making it a global thread is a better choice. Finally, a global bound thread is a kernel thread, and is, like a global thread, scheduled by the host operating system.

- **state**—Specifies whether the thread is joinable (PR_JOINABLE_THREAD) or unjoinable (PR_UNJOINABLE_THREAD). You should specify PR_ JOINABLE_THREAD() if the process needs to await termination of the thread.
- **stackSize**—Specifies your preference for the size of the stack, in bytes, associated with the newly created thread. If you pass 0 in this parameter, PR_CreateThread() chooses the most favorable machine-specific stack size.

PRCreateThread() returns an opaque handle of type PRThread * on success or the value NULL on failure. The handle can be used as an argument to NSPR functions that require a PRThread * argument.

Let's now take a look at the NSPR version of our thread sample. The code below is portable to Mac OS X, Windows, and Linux when the application using it is linked to the NSPR library; later in this item I will provide a Makefile that will illustrate how to link to NSPR. For now, here is the code:

```
#include <stdio.h>
#include <prtypes.h>
#include <prthread.h>

typedef struct message_
{
    PRUint16 count;
    char msg[128];
} Message;

void
MyThreadFunc(void *pParameter)
{
    Message *pMsg = (Message *) pParameter;
    PRUint16 i;

    for (i=0; i< pMsg->count; i++)
        printf("%s\n", pMsg->msg);
}

int
main(int argc, char *argv[])
{
```

```
    Message msg;
    PRThread *threadId;
    PRIntn ret;
    PRStatus status;

    msg.count = 16;
    PL_strncpy(msg.msg, "Hello World!",
        sizeof(msg.msg) - 1);

    threadId = PR_CreateThread(
            PR_USER_THREAD,
            MyThreadFunc,
            (void *) &msg,
            PR_PRIORITY_NORMAL,
            PR_GLOBAL_THREAD,
            PR_JOINABLE_THREAD,
            0);

    // Check the return value for success.

    if (threadId == NULL) {
        printf( "Failed to create thread\n");
    }
    else {
        status = PR_JoinThread(threadId);
        printf("Back from join\n");
    }
}
```

Additional NSPR Functionality

In the NSPR thread sample code, I used PL_strncpy() to copy the "Hello
World!" string into the Message struct passed as an argument to the thread
root function. PL_strncpy() is just one example of functionality provided
by NSPR. This item ends with brief descriptions of a few of the major
categories of portable functionality provided by NSPR, followed by some
recommendations regarding the use of NSPR in your C++ code. You can
obtain further details about NSPR from the NSPR reference material
located at mozilla.org or by inspecting the source code.

Standard Library (libc) Functions

Portable, thread-friendly versions of standard library string functions are
provided by NSPR in this category. Functions are prefixed with PL_; for

example, PL_strncpy() replaces the standard library function strncpy().
Other examples include PL_CreateOptState() and PL_GetNextOpt(),
which are intended to replace getopt(), as well as PL_strdup(),
PL_strlen(), PL_strrstr(), and PL_strncasestr(), which are a few of
the many string-related functions for which NSPR provides implementations.

I/O
Portable functionality in this category includes the following:

- Support for opening, reading, creating, and removing directories
- File descriptor implementation (PRFileDesc), and support for opera-
  tions upon these descriptors such as open(), read(), write(), and
  seek(), among others
- Log file support
- Timers and alarms
- sprintf and sscanf
- Sockets

Linking
PRLibrary is a platform-independent opaque type that represents a handle
to an open library. PR_LoadLibrary() accepts a path; if the path points to a
loadable library, it opens the library and returns a non-NULL PRLibrary
handle:

```
PRLibrary *
PR_LoadLibrary(const char *path);
```

PR_LoadLibrary() corresponds to LoadLibrary() on Win32, and
dlopen() on Linux and Mac OS X systems. After a library has been opened
by PR_LoadLibrary(), it can be searched for symbols. The following
example illustrates how to open a DLL named mydll and locate and execute
an exported function named Init() contained within the library:

```
#include <stdio.h>
#include <prtypes.h>
#include <prlink.h>

int
main(int argc, char *argv[])
{
    PRLibrary *lib;
```

```
    PRStatus status;
    int (*symbol)();

    lib = PR_LoadLibrary("mydll");

    if (lib != (PRLibrary *) NULL) {
        symbol = PR_FindSymbol(lib, "Init");
        if (symbol) {
            status = symbol();
            printf("Init function returned %d\n",
                status);
        } else {
            printf("Unable to find Init symbol\n");
        }
        PR_UnloadLibrary(lib);
    } else {
        printf("Unable to load mydll\n");
    }
}
```

The library source is

```
#include <prtypes.h>
#include <stdio.h>

Init()
{
    printf( "Inside Init\n");
    return PR_SUCCESS;
}
```

A simple Makefile on Win32 and Linux that builds all the preceding source is

```
all: library mydll

library: library.o
    gcc -g -o library library.o -L/usr/local/nspr/lib \
        -lnspr4 -lplc4

library.o: library.c
    gcc -g -c library.c -I/usr/local/nspr/include

mydll: mydll.o
```

```
    gcc -dynamiclib -fPIC -o mydll mydll.o \
        -I/usr/local/nspr/include

mydll.o: mydll.c
    gcc -fPIC -c mydll.c -I/usr/local/nspr/include

clean:
    rm *.o
```

On Mac OS X, the `-shared` argument to GCC needs to be replaced with `-dynamiclib`.

When to Use NSPR

NSPR first came into existence in the middle 1990s, and its intent is to support a wide variety of operating systems and compilers, both new and legacy. Some of what NSPR provides, however, can (and should) be avoided in our code. This is because the premise of this book is working with a fixed set of modern operating systems (Linux, Mac OS X, and Windows) and a single, well-supported, compiler family. These facts allow us to rely on functionality provided elsewhere, such as STL.

Perhaps it is best to consider the tools we are provided as forming a hierarchy of choices:

- C/C++ core language
- ANSI C Standard Library, POSIX, and STL
- Boost and NSPR
- Custom solutions

We might then use the following as guidelines for making a choice among the various options:

- If it can be done portably and efficiently in the core language (ignoring libraries such as STL, POSIX, or the C Standard Library), do it in straight C or C++.
- Favor STL, the C Standard Library, and POSIX when the core C/C++ language does not provide a solution.
- If STL, POSIX, and the C Standard Library do not offer a solution, seek one out in Boost or NSPR.
- Avoid platform-specific APIs at all costs; if you do find yourself having to go there (GUI code, for example), however, always code to abstract interfaces, even if you have to construct and support these abstractions yourself.

The preceding guidelines are just that: guidelines. You will occasionally find yourself with multiple possible solutions to a problem. In cases such as these, consider the following issues, among others, when deciding on the solution that works best for you:

- Code readability
- Complexity of the solution
- The likelihood of the code being ported to legacy platforms or compilers, where support for the solution is perhaps missing or deficient

By looking at a concrete example, you will begin to understand the thought process that goes behind selecting the appropriate tools for the job.

The requirement for this example is to implement code that iterates a directory specified by the user, searches for files that match a specific mask (for example, *.txt), allows the user to select one of the files, and then opens the file and reads its contents into memory.

First, assume that some interface (not discussed here) is provided which allows the user to specify a directory to search, displays the list of files found in the directory, and allows the user to select one of the files to be read. The rest of the functionality—opening the directory, iterating its contents, and then opening and reading the contents of the selected file—is what we focus on here.

Let's start with deciding how to deal with opening a directory and reading its contents. On Mac OS X and Linux, POSIX provides opendir(), readdir(), and closedir(). On Windows, one must use FindFirstFile(), FindNextFile(), and FindClose(). (You can find out more about these functions and example code by searching for FindFirstFile at www.msdn.com.) Clearly then, our task is not supported by a portable API. We could create our own abstractions or use NSPR, which provides portable functions for performing these tasks:

```
PRDir *
PR_OpenDir(const char *name);

PRDirEntry *
PR_ReadDir(PRDir *dir, PRDirFlags flags);

PRStatus
PR_CloseDir(PRDir *dir);
```

Next, we need to implement a list to hold the results for `PR_ReadDir()`. There are several options:

- We could use core C/C++ and C Standard Library functionality such as `malloc()` to implement a linked list from scratch.
- We could use STL list containers.
- NSPR provides a circular list implementation (see prclist.h in the NSPR distribution for details) that could be adapted to our needs.

First, we discard NSPR as an option, because it is higher in the hierarchy than both the STL and the core C/C++ options. The NSPR solution would work if there were no other choice or if we didn't have STL.

STL, although it is higher in the hierarchy than a pure C/C++ solution, is actually a much better solution because a linked list implementation is not a part of the core C/C++ language and it requires effort on the part of the developer to implement a link list from scratch using only the features of the C Standard Library. It can be done, of course, and I am sure it can be done efficiently; but the fact is, STL hands you this code on a silver platter, it's already debugged, it's type safe, and it's guaranteed to be efficient. So, why would you even think of duplicating the effort?

If the choice came down to C/C++ and the C Standard Library versus NSPR, the same argument would apply. I would go with NSPR in this case, because you should always favor using code that has already been written and debugged in favor of developing and debugging your own solution.

The next step is to filter the file entries based on the mask provided by the user. To make it simple, we will assume that mask is one of the following: *.*, *.txt, or *.dat. Let's start from the bottom of the hierarchy this time. We know that the C/C++ core language does not provide any support for regular expressions. The C Standard Library provides a solution, at least in GCC, because it supports POSIX regular expressions via `regex(3)`. But support for this is missing in the Microsoft implementation. STL does not provide any regular expression support nor does NSPR. Boost, however, provides a regular expression library based on the C Standard Library `regex(3)` implementation that was previously mentioned.

So, the choice really comes down to Boost, unless you are using Cygwin on Windows, which provides a POSIX `regex` function.

Fortunately, there are two options for using Boost's regex library. The first option is to use the Boost regex++ C++ class on all platforms. Doing so requires us to link to the Boost regex library on all platforms. The other option, which I favor, is to use the POSIX regex API on Win32 which is identical to the API that is provided by the GNU C Standard Library implementation. By using the POSIX API, we get the functionality of regex for free on Mac OS X and Linux; and on Win32, for portability sake, we distribute the regex library along with our application. About the only work it requires on Win32 is building the Boost regex library and making sure that the regex.h include file in located in the standard search path.

Now that we have a list of files that match the user-defined pattern, let's assume that the user has selected an entry from the list and that it is time for our program to open the file and read its contents into memory. We'll assume it is a small file and that we are going to read it, in a single operation, into a buffer that is big enough to hold the result.

We have a few options here. The C language and the C Standard Library provide us with a few well-known choices, including low-level system I/O calls:

```
open(2), read(2), close(2)
```

and higher-level stream-based I/O:

```
fopen(3), fread(3), fclose(3)
```

NSPR provides portable versions of the low-level system I/O calls:

```
PRFileDesc *
PR_Open(const char *name, PRIntn flags, PRIntn mode)

PRInt32
PR_Read(PRFileDesc *fd, void *buf, PRInt32 amount)

PRStatus
PR_Close(PRFileDesc *fd)
```

The C++ language supports file open, read, and close operations at the same low level as both C and NSPR, through its `fstream` class.

Use of the C++ `fstream` class is preferred over the other options. It is low enough in the hierarchy, and it is also a bit simpler to use than either NSPR or the C-based APIs. Finally, the use of `fstream` is consistent with Scott Meyer's advice in Item 2 of *Effective C++* (Addison-Wesley, 2005), which says to favor C++ `iostream`-based classes over the `stdio`-based alternatives.

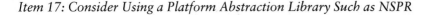

The following code brings this all together:

```
01 #include <sys/types.h>
02
03 #include <regex.h>
```

On line 3, we bring in the POSIX regex support, which comes for free on Linux and Mac OS X, and from either Cygwin or Boost on Windows.

```
04
05 #include <prtypes.h>
06 #include <prio.h>
07 #include <prprf.h>
```

Lines 5–7 bring in the needed NSPR headers, prio.h, for dealing with directory opens and reads, and prprf.h for PR_snprintf().

```
08
09 #include <list>
10 #include <string>
11 #include <fstream>
```

On lines 8–11, we call our C++ headers, supporting STL lists, file IO, and C++ strings.

```
12
13 using namespace std;
14
15 PRStatus GetMatchingFiles(char *dir, char *mask, \
      list <string *>& files);
16 PRStatus LoadFile(string* file, char **buf, \
      PRUint32 *size);
17
18 int
19 main(int argc, char *argv[])
20 {
21     list <string *> files;
22     list <string *>::iterator itr;
23     PRStatus ret;
24     char *buf = NULL;
25     PRUint32 size;
26
27     // user wants to open all files ending in .cpp
28
29     ret = GetMatchingFiles(".", "*.cpp", files);
```

```
30
31     if (ret == PR_SUCCESS && files.size() > 0) {
32
33         // user picks the first item in the list
34
35         ret = LoadFile(files.front(), &buf, &size);
36         if (ret == PR_SUCCESS) {
               // do something with the result here, \
      and free the buffer when done
38             if (buf)
39                 free(buf);
40         }
41     }
42     return 0;
43 }
```

The main() function illustrates how we call functions that

- Get the list of files that match the user-defined mask.
- Read the contents of a file selected by the user into a buffer.

```
44
45 PRStatus
46 GetMatchingFiles(char *dir, char *mask, \
       list <string *>& files)
47 {
48     regex_t regex;
49     PRDir *hdir;    // NSPR directory handle
50     char re[32];
51     int ret;
52
53     PR_snprintf(re, sizeof(re) - 1, \
           "[:print:,:space:]%s$", mask);
54     ret = regcomp(&regex, re, \
           REG_NOSUB | REG_ICASE);
```

On lines 53 and 54, I create the regular expression string that will be processed by regex. In this string, the substring [:print:,:space:] is used by regex to represent the set of printable and space characters. The mask variable, passed to GetMatchingFiles() as an argument, is appended to this string to create the final regular expression evaluated by regex. For example, if the user passes *.txt as the value of the mask argument, the resulting regular expression, [:print:,:space:]*.txt, would match any filename that consists of printable characters or spaces, followed by the string.`txt`, which is pretty much what a filename is.

The function `regcomp()` takes the regular expression string that was formed on line 53 and initializes and returns an opaque variable of type `regex_t`. This variable is passed to the regular expression parser, `regexec()`, which I describe later. The final argument passed to `regcomp()` tells `regexec()` to ignore case (`REG_ICASE`), and that we are not interested in learning the matching substring, just a pass or fail result (`REG_NOSUB`). There are many other flags accepted by `regcomp()`; see the `regex(3)` man page for more details.

```
55
56      if (ret == 0) {
57          hdir = PR_OpenDir(dir);
58          if (hdir != (PRDir *) NULL) {
59              PRDirEntry *dirEnt;
60
61              while (1) {
62                  dirEnt = PR_ReadDir(hdir,
63                      (PRDirFlags) (PR_SKIP_BOTH | \
                        PR_SKIP_HIDDEN));
```

On line 57, I call NSPR's `PR_OpenDir()` function to open a handle to the directory that was passed as an argument to `GetMatchingFiles()`. Then on line 61, I enter a loop that reads the contents of the directory, one by one, by calling `PR_ReadDir()`. The `PR_SKIP_BOTH` flag tells `PR_ReadDir()` to not read "." and "..", if present; and the `PR_SKIP_HIDDEN` flag causes hidden directories—for example, directories on Mac OS X and Linux that start with "."—to be ignored.

```
64                  if (dirEnt != NULL &&
65                      !regexec(&regex, dirEnt->name,
                        0, NULL, 0)) {
66                      string *str =
                            new string(dirEnt->name);
67                      files.push_back(str);
68                  } else if (dirEnt == NULL)
69                      break;
70              }
71              PR_CloseDir(hdir);
72          }
73          regfree(&regex);
```

```
74    }
75      return PR_SUCCESS;
76 }
```

On line 65, I pass the directory name as the second argument to regexec(),
which uses the compiled form of the regular expression, passed as the first
argument, to determine whether there is a match. If there is a match,
regexec() returns 0; and if this is the case, we allocate a C++ string to hold
the result and place it at the end of the list we are creating to hold the set of
filenames that match the pattern. On line 71, we close the directory because
it is no longer needed, and on line 73, we free the compiled form of the
regular expression.

```
77
78 PRStatus
79 LoadFile(string* file, char **buf, PRUint32 *size)
80 {
81      ifstream from(file->c_str());
82      PRStatus ret = PR_FAILURE;
83      char tbuf[32000];
84      streamsize nSize;
85      PRUint32 oldSize;
86
87      *size = 0;
88      if (from.is_open()) {
89          while (!from.eof()) {
90              from.read(tbuf, sizeof(tbuf));
91              nSize = from.gcount();
92              if (nSize) {
93                  oldSize = *size;
94                  *size += nSize;
95                  *buf = (char *) realloc(*buf,
                          *size);
96                  if (*buf)
97                      memcpy(*buf + oldSize, tbuf,
                              nSize);
98                  else
99                      break;
100             }
101         }
102         ret = PR_SUCCESS;
103     }
104     return ret;
105 }
```

The function `LoadFile()`, shown on lines 78 through 105, uses C++ Standard `iostream` functionality to open the file the user selected and read its contents into a buffer. `LoadFile()` uses `realloc(3)` to allocate a buffer. (The value of this buffer is initially set to `NULL` by the caller.) The caller is responsible to release the buffer when it is done with it. Note that it is perfectly legitimate in a C++ program to use `malloc()` and `free()`, as long as they are used as a pair; for example, it would be incorrect for the caller to release the memory returned by this function by calling `delete` on it. Also, notice that we are not dealing with a C++ object here, just a simple buffer that holds a sequence of bytes read from a file. There is, therefore, no constructor or destructor involved, and we do not need to allocate the buffer with `new`, or free it using `delete`, for the program to be correct.

6 Miscellaneous Portability Topics

In this chapter, several general tips related to portability are discussed. These concepts were not introduced by Netscape and Mozilla, and have been written about elsewhere, but are included for completeness.

Speaking of Mozilla, a document hosted at www.mozilla.org/hacking/ portable-cpp.html provides nearly 40 tips for writing portable C++ code. Some of the suggestions are worth considering, but many of them (such as "Don't use the namespace facility" and "Don't use Run-time Type Information") are outdated, referring back to a time when C++ was a relatively new language, and compilers were not uniform in their support of the language standard. Many of the rules are designed to deal with issues related to compilers many of you will never encounter (for example, rules that try to address issues seen with the C++ compiler on HP/UX). These rules are important to Mozilla because its software is widely ported. They might not be so important to you, however.

The whole list brings up a good (however implied it might be) point: As the C++ language (and its libraries) evolves, there will always be the real issue of compiler vendors having to play catch up to the latest and greatest definition of the language standards. Depending on the compilers you use, the gulf will be narrow, or it will be wide. The C programming language, being relatively simple to implement, does not suffer from this issue nearly as badly as does C++.

So, what is implied by the aforementioned document at mozilla.org is, in actuality, really good advice: Be careful when dealing with new language features. Otherwise, you might be surprised to find one implementation supporting some feature "foo" correctly, whereas another implementation does not support it, or supports it badly, thus introducing a definite portability issue in your code.

Item 18: Take Care When Using Floating Point

Consider the following code:

```
#include <stdio.h>

int
main(int argc, char *argv[])
{
    float x = 4.0/5.0;

    if (x == 4.0/5.0)
        printf("Same\n");
    else
        printf("Different\n");
}
```

When run, this program produces the following output:

```
% ./compare
Different
```

What is happening here? The answer becomes apparent if we modify the code to store the result of the first computation as a double instead of as a float:

```
#include <stdio.h>

int
main(int argc, char *argv[])
{
    double x = 4.0/5.0;

    if (x == 4.0/5.0)
        printf("Same\n");
    else
        printf("Different\n");
}
```

When we run this code, we get a more expected result:

```
% ./compare
Same
```

The reason for this apparent anomaly is that C mandates that floating-point expressions be evaluated using the greatest precision representation available. As a result, in either version of the program, both the right-hand side of the assignment to x, and the computation to the right of the == in the conditional statement, are performed as double precision. However, the variable x in the first version, being float, causes the result of the double-precision expression to be stored as a float, modifying its value as the higher-precision value is cast down to a lower-precision value. Which, of course, is disastrous when in comes to the correctness of the program. As it turns out, this code is portable, at least when tested with GCC on Linux (Intel), GCC on Mac OS X (G4), and with Visual C++ on Windows XP (Intel). But, it does highlight how problematic floating-point code can be.

Floating-point variables (float and double) in C and C++ are used to represent values that are continuous in nature (for example, 3.14159265354), versus discrete values, which are stored as integers (int and long). Adding, subtracting, multiplying, and dividing integers is very portable, assuming the size of an int or long (as the case may be) is identical on the platforms involved. Furthermore, all possible integer values, in the range supported by the hardware and compiler, are representable.

With floating point, the hardware, the compiler, and the way code is written can influence the accuracy of results obtained. Most hardware these days conforms to the IEEE-754 (IEC 60559) floating-point standard, which defines how floating-point values are represented, and how arithmetic involving floating-point values and rounding is performed. Following the IEEE standard means that an implementation will use specific algorithms, defined by the standard, to compute results. However, compilers are not required to conform to the standard. (C99 specifies several IEEE-754 defined requirements, but they are optional. One reason the standard is optional is that the standard is difficult to conform to on hardware that is not IEEE-754 compliant, and C, of course, is not restricted to being implemented on just IEEE-754-compliant hardware.) And, as of GCC 4.1, support for IEEE-754 is declared as broken (see http://gcc.gnu.org/gcc-4.1/c99status.html).

It is beyond the scope of this item to discuss the architecture of IEEE-754 or explore all the possible issues that might arise when writing floating-point code. Several resources on the Internet do a better job at this than I could ever hope to do. However, I can provide some basic advice to make your code more portable.

Don't Serialize Floating-Point Values as Binary

If you have to store floating-point values to files (which could be later loaded by your application running on a different platform), or send them across a network connection (again, to be used by your application on a different platform), you should convert these values into a non-floating-point representation beforehand (preferably ASCII). The same can be said for integers, too, because even within the same operating system family, there can be issues. For example, is Mac OS X 32-bit or 64-bit, and is it little endian (Intel) or big endian (PPC)? But it is worse for floating point; even if the sizes and endianess of the platforms are known to be the same, floating-point formats are not guaranteed to be the same. (Recall what I previously said about support for IEEE-754.)

In the following code, I illustrate how C code can serialize a double to a string and back, using `snprintf()` and `strtod()`:

```
double a, b;
char buf[128];

a = 17.1234567890;
snprintf(buf, sizeof(buf), "%.10f", a);
printf("a is %.10f buf is %s\n", a, buf);
b = strtod(buf, NULL);
printf("b is %.10f\n", b);
if (a == b)
    printf("same\n");
else
    printf("different\n");
```

When run, one gets the following output:

```
% ./floats
a is 17.1234567890 buf is 17.1234567890
b is 17.1234567890
same
```

Is there a better way to do this in C++ than with `snprintf()`? As Herb Sutter has written (www.gotw.ca/publications/mill19.htm), `snprintf()` had some nice attributes—code readability, length safety, and efficiency. It's also a good choice for those of you who are familiar with `printf()`, or have experience with the `sprintf()` family of functions (as is the case for me). I tend to value code readability, so two of his C++ suggestions, `std::stringstream` and `std::strstream`, are not appealing to me. The last option he poses, Boost.org's `lexical_cast`, seems to stack up favorably to `snprintf()`; it certainly is readable:

```
std::string s;

s = boost::lexical_cast<std::string>(a);
printf("a is %.10f buf is %s\n", a, s.c_str());
b = strtod(s.c_str(), NULL);
printf("b is %.10f\n", b);
if (a == b)
    printf("same\n");
else
    printf("different\n");
```

At a cost of efficiency (which probably doesn't matter; if you are serializing data to a disk or across the network, I/O is going to be the bottleneck, not the creation of an object or two), `lexical_cast` has the benefits of `snprintf()`, and it is less likely to be abused. (The format string of `snprintf()` can be a source of typos, and, of course, the size argument that is passed could be made incorrect with some sloppy programming.)

Equality

Sometimes you see code that defines equality between two floating-point numbers as their values are within some small value epsilon. For example:

```
if (fabs(a - b) < 0.00001)
    printf("same\n");
else
    printf("different\n");
```

The main problem associated with this, besides seeming kludgy, is that the value of epsilon you pick is arbitrary, often not rooted in the reality of the way the two values a and b were computed, or in how they are represented, on the affected platforms. The real problem to solve is ensuring that all platforms serialize the same results. That is, if platform A computes some value b given some input x, platform B and C should also compute the same result b given the same input x. If this can be done, we don't have to worry about epsilon. If it can't be done, how can one reliably pick an epsilon that will represent the differences that exist?

Truth is, none of this is easy. For one thing, it is important that everyone use the same representations. The size of a double needs to be the same for all players. But, all that C++ says is that `sizeof(float) <= sizeof(double)` `<= sizeof(long double)`, meaning that on one platform, you might encounter a 4-byte double, whereas on another, a double can be 8 bytes. And, even if the sizes are the same, there is the issue of whether all platforms/compilers support IEEE-754. You can test for this support as follows:

```
#include <limits>

main(int argc, char *argv[])
{

    bool is754 =
        std::numeric_limits<double>::is_iec559;

    printf("Compiler is%s IEEE-754\n",
        (is754?"":" not"));
...
}
```

Even if the platforms support IEEE-754, and you ensure that the floating-point sizes used are the same, extensive testing is critical. In applications where exact values are not critical, perhaps it is not worth sweating the small stuff. In other cases, strategies such as the use of fixed-point arithmetic may be a better option.

Item 19: Be Explicit Regarding the Sign of Char Types

C/C++ has traditionally been difficult in terms of the sign of char types. Is a char signed, or is it unsigned? Well, on some platforms, chars are signed; on others, they are unsigned—and it is up to compiler vendors to make the choice. This is true for C and C++, standards notwithstanding.

In most cases, the difference is not relevant. In code such as the following, where char is used to store ASCII data, the signedness of a char is of no relevance:

```
...

char *msg = {"Hello, World!" };

printf("%s\n", msg);

...
```

Where it does matter is in code that attempts to store numeric values in char variables. Consider the following C++ program:

```
#include <iostream>

using namespace std;

void SomeFuncInt(int value)
{
    if (value >= 128)
        cout << "SomeFuncInt value is >= 128\n";
    else
        cout << "SomeFuncInt value is < 128\n";
}

void SomeFuncUInt(unsigned int value)
{
    if (value >= 128)
        cout << "SomeFuncUInt value is >= 128\n";
    else
        cout << "SomeFuncUInt value is < 128\n";
}

int
main(int argc, char *argv[])
{
    char foo = 0xd7;

    SomeFuncInt(foo);
    SomeFuncUInt(foo);

    foo = -17;

    SomeFuncInt(foo);
    SomeFuncUInt(foo);
}
```

When char is signed, the output of the preceding code is as follows:

```
SomeFuncInt value is < 128
SomeFuncUInt value is >= 128
SomeFuncInt value is < 128
SomeFuncUInt value is >= 128
```

However, when char is unsigned, you get the following:

```
SomeFuncInt value is >= 128
SomeFuncUInt value is >= 128
SomeFuncInt value is >= 128
SomeFuncUInt value is >= 128
```

Thus, the code behaves differently depending on the signedness of a char. And therefore, it is nonportable. Here are my recommendations:

- Don't use char variables to hold integer values. Use int variables instead. If a value starts out stored as a char, assign it to a signed or an unsigned integer variable, depending on the intended usage.
- If you must use a char variable to store an integer, do not leave things to chance. g++ lets you set the type of char as being either signed or unsigned as a compiler argument: -fsigned-char tells g++ to treat characters as signed, whereas -funsigned-char causes all chars to be interpreted as unsigned. Use the interpretation that is available on all platforms and all compilers used, to ensure portability. If you are using g++ on all platforms, you can select whichever makes best sense for the application. If using Visual C++ on Windows, chars are signed by default, but the /J option to the Visual C++ compiler is equivalent to g++'s -funsigned-char, so make sure that whatever choice you make for g++ is consistent with that made for Visual C++.

Item 20: Avoid the Serialization of Binary Data

Data serialization (a fancy term for writing application data to persistent storage) requires extra consideration in cross-platform applications, primarily because of the requirement that data written by an application running on one platform (for example, Windows) should be readable by instances of the application running on all other platforms.

In some cases, the use of binary data is unavoidable. Multimedia data—audio files (for example, MP3) and image files (for example, PNG) in particular—are invariably stored on disk as binary, compressed data. The advantages of compression rule in this case; the large size of data involved is such that it would not be practical to store the image data as ASCII. A single band, grayscale image file stores pixels as values in the range of 0 to 255. As binary data, each pixel occupies a byte. As ASCII, each pixel would require a minimum of 2 bytes of storage (if stored in hex); for example, for the pixel value 0x74, you would need to write an 8-bit ASCII 7 and an 8-bit ASCII 4, twice the amount of storage required compared to binary.

But penalties are involved with reading and writing binary data in a cross-platform context. Here are some examples:

- **Endian issues.** On some platforms (PowerPC), data larger than a byte in size is stored in big endian order, and on some (Intel/AMD), it is stored in little endian order. Reading a short (2-byte) binary integer from a binary file created on a big endian system will require a little endian system to swap bytes. And vice versa.

- **Struct layout.** In addition to endian issues, binary data can also suffer from how the compiler chooses to layout structs in memory, which is entirely compiler dependent, and impacted by the architecture being targeted. Structs written in binary form (to memory or disk) by code generated by a compiler may be a completely different size, or be organized in memory in a completely different way, by another compiler, even on the same platform.

- **Size of intrinsic data types and enums.** No guarantees are made by standard C++ regarding the number of bytes used to represent intrinsic types (for example, bool, char, int, long, double, float, short)—other than a char, which must be 1 byte in size. What the standard does guarantee are the relationships among these types in terms of their sizes. For example, a short is no larger than an int, which is no larger than a long. The size of enumerated types (enums) is also implementation dependent; compilers are free to use any size as long as it is large enough to hold the values of the enumeration (although they are limited to the size of an int in doing so). How this is implemented is implementation dependent; g++, for example, defines the -fshort-enums command-line argument that tells g++ to use the smallest possible size. Item 17 says more about dealing with the size of intrinsic data types and how to specify them in a platform-independent way.

- **Differences in type definitions.** Some types are not implemented the same on all platforms. Take for example struct sockaddr_in (netinet/in.h), commonly encountered in networking applications. On FreeBSD and MacOS X, sockaddr_in is defined as follows:

```
struct sockaddr_in {
    u_char   sin_len;
    u_char   sin_family;
    u_short  sin_port;
```

```
    struct  in_addr sin_addr;
    char    sin_zero[8];
};

struct in_addr {
    in_addr_t s_addr;
};

typedef   u_int32_t       in_addr_t;
```

On Linux, it is defined as follows:

```
struct sockaddr_in
{
    __SOCKADDR_COMMON (sin_);
    in_port_t sin_port; /* Port number. */
    struct in_addr sin_addr; /* Internet address. */

    /* Pad to size of 'struct sockaddr'. */
    unsigned char sin_zero[sizeof (struct sockaddr) -
            __SOCKADDR_COMMON_SIZE -
            sizeof (in_port_t) -
            sizeof (struct in_addr)];
};
```

where `__SOCKADDR_COMMON` is defined as follows:

```
#define __SOCKADDR_COMMON(sa_prefix) \
  sa_family_t sa_prefix##family

typedef unsigned short int sa_family_t;
```

Although the size in bytes of these two types is the same (you can confirm this with a simple C program), we see that Linux version doesn't define `sin_len` as a field (POSIX makes this field optional, and Linux does not require it), and `sin_family` is an unsigned short (and an unsigned char under FreeBSD). So, if for some reason we were to save this to disk on, say, Linux, we would be expect to be unable to read the result on Mac OS X or FreeBSD.

The preceding points should convince you that writing binary data in a cross-platform manner is not just a matter of opening a stream and writing out the bits.

Binary multimedia files are clearly cross-platform, or they appear to be at least; after all, it would be odd to find a JPEG image or MP3 sound file that is not readable by applications running on any given platform, right? The reason for this portability is that multimedia files contain sequences of bytes, and those portions of the file that define metadata about the stored data are invariably stored according to convention; for example, they are explicitly little endian or big endian, they have a fixed and agreed-upon size in bytes, they occur at fixed and agreed-upon offsets within the file, and writers and readers of these files are required to perform swapping, should it be necessary. This represents one strategy for dealing with interchange of binary data in a portable manner: Define a convention for the storage of the data, and ensure that readers and writers conform to the defined conventions.

Let's see whether we can develop some code that can read and write a binary `sockaddr_in` variable in a portable manner. The following program, which compiles cleanly on both Mac OS X and Linux, accepts the following arguments on the command line:

- `-a addr`—IP address in dot notation (for example, 192.168.1.123)
- `-p port`—Port number
- `-o path`—Generate a `sockaddr_in struct` and write it as binary to the named file (requires –a and –o)
- `-i path`—Load and dump a `sockaddr_in struct` stored as binary in the named file

The application allows both -i and -o to be specified. -o will be processed first, followed by -i. That way, specifying the same path for both allows you to generate a binary `socakddr_in` file, and then read it back and display its contents. Here is the full source for the application:

```
#include <fstream>
#include <iostream>
#include <string>

#include <netinet/in.h>
#include <sys/types.h>
#include <sys/socket.h>
#include <arpa/inet.h>

#include <unistd.h>  // getopt

using namespace std;
```

```
void usage();

// display the content of a sockaddr_in to stdout

void
DumpAddr(struct sockaddr_in * saddr)
{
    cout << "-------------------------------------\n";
    cout << "saddr.sin_family is ";
    switch(saddr->sin_family) {
        case AF_INET:
            cout << "AF_INET\n";
            break;
        case AF_UNIX:
            cout << "AF_UNIX\n";
            break;
        default:
            cout << "Unknown: " << saddr->sin_family
                << "\n";
            break;
    }
    cout << "saddr.sin_port is " <<
        ntohs(saddr->sin_port) << "\n";
    char buf[128];
    inet_ntop(saddr->sin_family,
        reinterpret_cast<void *>(&saddr->sin_addr),
        buf, sizeof(buf) );
    cout << "saddr.sin_addr is " << buf << "\n";
}


// do a binary read of file containing a
// sockaddr_in struct

int
BinaryRead(struct sockaddr_in * saddr,
    const char *path)
{
    ifstream ifile(path, ios_base::binary |
        ios_base::in);
    unsigned int retval = 1;
    if (ifile.is_open()) {
        ifile.read(reinterpret_cast<char *>(saddr),
            sizeof(struct sockaddr_in));
        retval = !(ifile.gcount() ==
            sizeof(struct sockaddr_in));
        ifile.close();
```

```
        }
        return retval;
}


// binary write a sockaddr_in value to a file. The
// file will be truncated before the write is performed

int
BinaryWrite(struct sockaddr_in * saddr,
    const char *path)
{
    ofstream ofile(path, ios_base::binary |
        ios_base::out | ios_base::trunc);
    unsigned int retval = 1;
    if (ofile.is_open()) {
        ofile.write(reinterpret_cast<char *>(saddr),
            sizeof(struct sockaddr_in));
        retval = !ofile.good();
        ofile.close();
    }
    return retval;
}

main(int argc, char *argv[])
{
    struct sockaddr_in saddr;
    string ofile, ifile, addr;
    short int port;
    bool haveo(false), havei(false), havea(false),
        havep(false);

    int ch;

    while((ch = getopt(argc, argv, "oiap")) != -1) {
        switch(ch) {
            case 'o':
                if (optind < argc) {
                    ofile = argv[optind];
                    haveo = true;
                }
                optind++;
                break;
            case 'i':
                if (optind < argc) {
                    ifile = argv[optind];
                    havei = true;
```

```
                }
                optind++;
                break;
            case 'a':
                if (optind < argc) {
                    addr = argv[optind];
                    havea = true;
                }
                optind++;
                break;
            case 'p':
                if (optind < argc) {
                    port = atoi(argv[optind]);
                    havep = true;
                }
                optind++;
                break;
        }
    }
    argc -= optind;
    argv += optind;

    if (!havei && !haveo)
        usage();
    if (haveo && (!havep || !havea))
        usage();

    if (haveo) {
        bzero(&saddr, sizeof(saddr));
        saddr.sin_family = AF_INET;
        saddr.sin_port = htons(port);
        inet_pton(AF_INET, addr.c_str(),
            &saddr.sin_addr);
        DumpAddr(&saddr);
        if (BinaryWrite(&saddr, ofile.c_str()))
            cerr << "Problem writing " << ofile
                << "\n";
    }
    if (havei) {
        bzero(&saddr, sizeof(saddr));
        if (BinaryRead(&saddr, ifile.c_str()))
            cerr << "Problem reading " << ifile
                << "\n";
        DumpAddr(&saddr);
    }
    exit(0);
```

```
}

void
usage() {
    cerr << "usage: rwsockaddr [-o file | -i file] \
        -a addr -p port\n";
    exit(1);
}
```

Before I describe the source code, let's see what happens when we use the application to generate a binary file on Linux and Mac OS X.

On Linux:

```
$ ./rwsockaddr -a 192.168.1.123 -p 30 -o linuxbin.out
-------------------------------------
saddr.sin_family is AF_INET
saddr.sin_port is 30
saddr.sin_addr is 192.168.1.123
```

Looking at the result with od(1), we see the following. (The output is in hex, with two digits used to represent each character in the file.)

```
$ od -x linuxbin.out
0000 0200 001e c0a8 017b 0000 0000 0000 0000
0020
```

The first two characters, `0200`, are the `sin_family` field. The next two characters, `001e`, is the port number (30 decimal). This is followed by four characters (c0a8 017b), which denotes the IP address 192.168.1.123 in hex. The remaining eight characters in the file contains the value of the `sin_zero` field.

On Mac OS X, we get similar output from the command line, but the first two characters in the resulting binary file differ:

```
$ od -x macosbin.out
0000 0002 001e c0a8 017b 0000 0000 0000 0000
0020
```

The first character in the file is the `sin_len` field, which is not being set by the application, and the second character is the `sin_family`, which under FreeBSD is a character, not a short as it is under Linux.

Naturally, one would expect problems trying to read the Mac OS X version of the file on Linux, and similarly, reading the Linux file on Mac OS

X should be expected to fail. On Mac OS X, reading the Linux file, we get the following output:

```
$ ./rwsockaddr -i linuxbin.out
------------------------------------
saddr.sin_family is Unknown:
saddr.sin_port is 30
saddr.sin_addr is
```

And likewise, on Linux, reading the Mac OS X file gives the following result:

```
$ ./rwsockaddr -i macosxbin.out
------------------------------------
saddr.sin_family is Unknown:   512
saddr.sin_port is 30
saddr.sin_addr is
```

There are some things to note. First of all, the port number was read correctly by both platforms. However, you might wonder how that was possible, given that `sin_port` is a short int, and therefore subject to endian issues. Second, the IP address was stored the same by both platforms. Let's look at the source code that constructs the `sockaddr_in` struct prior to writing to see why this is the case:

```
bzero(&saddr, sizeof(saddr));
saddr.sin_family = AF_INET;
saddr.sin_port = htons(port);
inet_pton(AF_INET, addr.c_str(),
    &saddr.sin_addr);
DumpAddr(&saddr);
if (BinaryWrite(&saddr, ofile.c_str()))
    cerr << "Problem writing " <<
        ofile << "\n";
```

The reason that the `sin_port` field was read correctly is that it was converted to a network short (big endian) by passing the value to `htons(3)`. This is done in networking apps because by convention, the port value must be transmitted as a network short. On big endian systems such as PowerPC, `htons()` is a no-op, because short values are already stored big endian. On little endian systems, `htons()` swaps the 2 bytes of the short so that it is big endian. When reading the binary value from the file, we must convert the port value from a network short to a native byte ordering; this is done with a call to ntohs(3)—you can see this in the function DumpAddr():

```
cout << "saddr.sin_port is " << ntohs(saddr->sin_port)
    << "\n";
```

Just as htons() is a no-op on big endian systems, so is ntohs().

Next, we consider the IP address stored in sin_addr. The IP address value is, by convention, arranged in the sin_addr field as a sequence of bytes, ordered left to right. The function inet_pton(3) takes care of doing the conversion from a human-readable character string to a network-ordered sequence of bytes, and upon reading, we can use inet_ntop(3) to obtain from the sin_addr field a printable string that can be printed to the console.

The preceding treatment of the port and IP address fields implies a general strategy for making binary data resilient to cross-platform differences:

- Agree on the number of bytes used to store values.
- Agree on a byte-ordering convention (that is, little endian versus big endian), and ensure that writers convert to that convention before writing, and readers convert, too, before using the result as a value.

Obviously, the treatment of the port and address, although correct, is not enough to solve our problem. The reason for this is clear; the first two bytes of the file store the sin_family field as a short, whereas on Mac OS X, the first two bytes are used to store a sin_len value, followed by a 1-byte long sin_family field. So, on Linux, reading the Mac OS X file places the value 0x0020 in the sin_family field, with is 512 and not recognized as a legitimate value by the DumpAddr() function. Likewise, inet_ntop() fails to convert the sin_addr() field because the first argument passed to it is not a legitimate value either. A similar problem is seen when reading the Linux-generated file on Mac OS X; this time, the first character 0x02, is loaded into the sin_len field, and the value 0 is loaded into the sin_family, and similar results are generated by DumpAddr().

There are two ways to deal with this problem:

- Come up with a platform-neutral way of writing the sin_family field.
- Write metadata that tells readers what the format of the data is.

The second of these two options can be handled by requiring the writer to output at the beginning of the file a token that can be used to identify the format of the data in the file. Image file formats often do this as a way to help readers identify the format of the file being read; PNG files, for example, always start with an 8-byte sequence of characters that identifies the file as holding PNG image data. We would then read the value into a struct with the appropriate layout, and then copy fields from that struct to the native `sockaddr_in` struct. In short

- Writers output a sequence of 1 or more bytes (with an agreed-upon length and value) to the beginning of the file, to identify the format, followed by native data.
- Readers read the identifying bytes from the start of the file, and based on these bytes, read data from the file into a structure that corresponds to the format identified, and then copy each field from the result to the native structure.

The first of these two options, generating a platform-neutral format, is nearly identical, but it is simpler to implement because it has the advantage that there is no need to generate identifying bytes at the start of the file, and that readers are not required to be aware of all possible formats that might need to be supported. All that is required is for writers to copy from the native representation to the agreed-upon platform-neutral format, and for readers to copy from the platform-neutral format to the native representation before using the data.

The following functions, `XPBinaryRead()` and `XPBinaryWrite()`, implement the changes required to support a cross-platform version of `sockaddr_in`. It turns out that the BSD version of `sockaddr_in` is suitable; we need to preserve the `sin_len` field because it is supported by BSD, and there is no need for the `sin_family` field to be a short as it is in Linux—a char is plenty big enough to hold the possible values that would be assigned. Here is the definition of the cross-platform struct:

```
// cross platform sockaddr_in

struct xpsockaddr_in {
    u_char  sin_len;            // BSD only
    u_char  sin_family;         // only 1 byte is needed
    u_short sin_port;           // same on BSD and Linux
    struct  in_addr sin_addr;   // ditto
    char    sin_zero[8];        // ditto
};
```

XPBinaryRead()reads the xpsockaddr_in data stored in the specified file, and copies it to a native sockaddr_in struct:

```
int
XPBinaryRead(struct sockaddr_in * saddr,
    const char *path)
{
    xpsockaddr_in xpsaddr;
    bzero(&xpsaddr, sizeof(xpsaddr));

    ifstream ifile(path, ios_base::binary |
        ios_base::in);
    unsigned int retval = 1;
    if (ifile.is_open()) {
        ifile.read(reinterpret_cast<char *>(&xpsaddr),
            sizeof(struct xpsockaddr_in));
        retval = !(ifile.gcount() ==
            sizeof(struct xpsockaddr_in));
        if (!retval) {
#if !defined(linux)
            saddr->sin_len = xpsaddr.sin_len;
#endif
            saddr->sin_family = xpsaddr.sin_family;
            saddr->sin_port = xpsaddr.sin_port;
            memcpy(&saddr->sin_addr, &xpsaddr.sin_addr,
                sizeof(saddr->sin_addr));
            memcpy(&saddr->sin_zero, &xpsaddr.sin_zero,
                sizeof(xpsaddr.sin_zero));
        }
        ifile.close();
    }
    return retval;
}
```

Likewise, XPBinaryWrite() copies the fields from the passed-in native sockaddr_in struct to an xpsockaddr_in struct, and writes the result to a file:

```
int
XPBinaryWrite(struct sockaddr_in * saddr,
    const char *path)
{
```

```
    xpsockaddr_in xpsaddr;
    bzero(&xpsaddr, sizeof(xpsaddr));

    // copy saddr to xpsaddr

#if !defined(linux)
    xpsaddr.sin_len = saddr->sin_len;
#endif
    xpsaddr.sin_family = saddr->sin_family;
    xpsaddr.sin_port = saddr->sin_port;
    memcpy(&xpsaddr.sin_addr, &saddr->sin_addr, sizeof(xpsaddr.sin_addr));
    memcpy(&xpsaddr.sin_zero, &saddr->sin_zero, sizeof(xpsaddr.sin_zero));

    ofstream ofile(path, ios_base::binary |
        ios_base::out | ios_base::trunc);
    unsigned int retval = 1;
    if (ofile.is_open()) {
        ofile.write(reinterpret_cast<char *>(&xpsaddr),
            sizeof(struct xpsockaddr_in));
        retval = !ofile.good();
        ofile.close();
    }
    return retval;
}
```

Notice that both of these functions have an `#if !defined(linux)` around code that copies to or from the `sin_len` field because this field is not present in the Linux implementation of `sockaddr_in`. Ideally, we wouldn't use `#ifdefs` in our code; see Item 2 for strategies for eliminating them.

Finally, you should be aware of compiler options that affect the sizes used to represent data in a program, or how data is arranged in structures. Several options supported by g++ fall into this category, including the following:

- **-fshort-enums**—Only use as many bytes as required to represent the values associated with an enum (up to an int).
- **-fshort-double**—Doubles are given the same size as a float.
- **-fpack-struct**—Pack structure members in memory so that there are no holes, instead of aligning them on boundaries that might otherwise be optimal for the platform.

These and other options that affect the layout of variables will cause problems if an effort is not made to ensure that the same options are enabled consistently across all platforms and by all compilers used by your project. There is nothing wrong with using them, but some testing (using programs similar to the one developed here) should be performed to verify that no compatibility issues are introduced by their use.

Item 21: Avoid Problems Related to the Size and Organization of Types

In practice, the areas I am about to discuss in this item are not ones that have typically caused me much grief. Perhaps it is because the type of applications I have written over the years have not led me to situations where trouble of this kind was lurking around the corner. I don't recall these issues ever specifically coming up during my time at Netscape, either, perhaps for the same reasons.

Still, I think it would be remiss for me not to at least mention a few things that should be on the radar of every C and C++ programmer, because at least indirectly, these items can all have an effect on the portability of your code. (Some of what follows has been mentioned in lesser detail in other contexts throughout this book.)

Size of Integer Types

In some cases, portability errors can be introduced by making bad assumptions about the size of int, and related types short and long (and the unsigned variants of each). The integer types are very much CPU and compiler dependent.

You can usually bet that the number of bits used to represent an int coincides with the word size of the CPU for which the compiler is generating code. For example, on a 32-bit CPU, an int is going to be 32 bits (or 4 bytes) in size. The same can be said for unsigned int. On a 64-bit CPU, you can expect both int and unsigned into to be 64 bits in size. However, what is less certain are the sizes of short, long, long long, and their unsigned variants. Many of you have come to expect short, for example, to be 16 bits in size. However, this is not guaranteed by the language, even though it makes certain sense on a 32-bit system to have short be half of what int is. (After all, short implies it is smaller.)

The language guarantees a short to be at least 16 bits in size. This is useful because, on a two's-complement machine, it allows us to feel safe knowing that a short variable will hold a value that falls within a specific range. How do we find out how big a short actually is? One candidate way is to compute the number of bits in a short:

```
int shortSizeInBits = sizeof(short) * 8;
printf("size of short in bits is %d\n", shortSizeInBits);
```

which will print, when compiled by GCC and run on my G4-based Mac OS X system, as follows:

```
size of short in bits is 16
```

Using this result, we might deduce that the two's complement range of a short is, on this system, exactly [-32768, 32767]. However, this isn't guaranteed. Why? Here, we rely on the `sizeof` operator returning the size of the type in terms of characters, which we assume are 8 bits in size. The use of `sizeof` was a good idea, but the assumption, like many, was a dangerous one to make, because 8 bits is a minimum size guarantee for char, not an absolute requirement. Meaning, it could be that our char is 16 bits, 32 bits, or even 7,649 bits in size, for that matter. To determine the actual range of an integer type, we need something a bit more reliable, and for that, we need to look elsewhere.

The header `limits.h` (or `climits` in C++) is that elsewhere. This file contains macros that enumerate the minimum and maximum values that short, int, long, and long long (and their unsigned counterparts) integer types can take on. The macros defined are all the form T_MAX and T_MIN, where T is one of CHAR, SHRT, INT, LONG, and LLONG. Unsigned versions of T_MAX are also provided, by prefixing the above with a U; for example, UCHAR and USHRT. (There is no need for T_MIN for unsigned types, because T_MIN is always 0.)

Here, then, is the bread and butter of limits.h for Darwin/Mac OS X:

```
#define SCHAR_MAX   127     /* min value for a signed char */
#define SCHAR_MIN   (-128)    /* max value for a signed char */

#define UCHAR_MAX   255     /* max value for an unsigned char */
#define CHAR_MAX    127     /* max value for a char */
#define CHAR_MIN    (-128)    /* min value for a char */

#define USHRT_MAX   65535      /* max value for an unsigned short */
#define SHRT_MAX    32767     /* max value for a short */
#define SHRT_MIN    (-32768)    /* min value for a short */
```

```
#define UINT_MAX    0xffffffff   /* max value for an unsigned int */
#define INT_MAX     2147483647   /* max value for an int */
#define INT_MIN     (-2147483647-1) /* min value for an int */


#ifdef __LP64__
#define ULONG_MAX   0xffffffffffffffffUL    /* max unsigned long */
#define LONG_MAX    0x7fffffffffffffffL  /* max signed long */
#define LONG_MIN    (-0x7fffffffffffffffL-1) /* min signed long */
#else /* !__LP64__ */
#define ULONG_MAX   0xffffffffL  /* max value for an unsigned long */
#define LONG_MAX    2147483647L  /* max value for a long */
#define LONG_MIN    (-2147483647L-1) /* min value for a long */
#endif /* __LP64__ */


#define ULLONG_MAX  0xffffffffffffffffULL    /* max unsigned long long */
#define LLONG_MAX   0x7fffffffffffffffLL     /* max signed long long */
#define LLONG_MIN   (-0x7fffffffffffffffLL-1) /* min signed long long */
```

We can see from this that on Mac OS X, word size only affects the range of long, which is 32 bits (the same as int) on 32-bit systems, but 64 bits (different than int) on 64-bit systems. And, notice that shorts are the same size, 16 bits, on both 32-bit and 64-bit systems.

One interesting thing to note here is the use of the U and L suffixes on unsigned and long constants, respectively. The U suffix tells the compiler that the constant is unsigned, whereas the L suffix tells the compiler the constant is long. They can be applied to any of the integer types, and they can also be combined to denote an unsigned long constant.

Appending these suffixes is, in my experience, always a good idea. Doing so at least documents intent in your code, and it may, in some cases, lead to the compiler doing the right conversion or promotion (see "Integer Conversions" section), or even make it easier for the compiler to find an inconsistency that would lead to a warning, which in turn should require you to put a bit more thought on the line of code in question (as advocated in Item 6.)

Of course, when the code we are talking about is C++, you should favor using the numeric_limits template, which is found in the header <limits>. Here is a portion of the specialization for short supplied with GCC on Mac OS X, where we can see how, for short, the numeric_limits interfaces min() and max() are implemented:

```
/// numeric_limits<short> specialization.
template<>
  struct numeric_limits<short>
```

```
{
  static const bool is_specialized = true;

  static short min() throw()
  { return -__SHRT_MAX__ - 1; }
  static short max() throw()
  { return __SHRT_MAX__; }

  ...
```

Similar specializations exist for bool, int, unsigned int, char, unsigned char, and so on.

The following example checks that a variable contains a value that is less than or equal to the maximum possible value of a signed short:

```
#include <limits>

...

if (val <= std::numeric_limits<short>::max())
    ...
```

NSPR and Types

The Netscape Portable Runtime Library (NSPR) provides another way to tackle the issue by providing its own types, which, through their naming convention, convey the bit sizes of each type without any sort of ambiguity at all. By way of example, you can ensure a 16-bit integer is declared (when supported by the platform) by using the following code:

```
#include <prtypes.h>

...

PRInt16 val;    // a 16-bit integer

...
```

If the preceding type does not exist on the platform, a compiler error will be generated. The definition of types is done via **typedefs** and

conditional compilation. The implementation of PRInt16 (and PRUint16) is
as follows:

```
/*********************************************************************
** TYPES:        PRUint16
**               PRInt16
** DESCRIPTION:
**   The int16 types are known to be 16 bits each.
*********************************************************************/
#if PR_BYTES_PER_SHORT == 2
typedef unsigned short PRUint16;
typedef short PRInt16;
#else
#error No suitable type for PRInt16/PRUint16
#endif


/*********************************************************************
* MACROS:        PR_INT16_MAX
*                PR_INT16_MIN
*                PR_UINT16_MAX
* DESCRIPTION:
*   The maximum and minimum values of a PRInt16 or PRUint16.
*********************************************************************/

#define PR_INT16_MAX 32767
#define PR_INT16_MIN (-32768)
#define PR_UINT16_MAX 65535U
```

See Item 17 for more details on NSPR types and their use.

Sizes and Efficiency

C++ has the following to say about things: A short is no bigger than an int,
which is in turn no bigger than a long, and a long is no bigger than a long
long—and the same for the unsigned versions of each. Also, signed and
unsigned versions of a given type (for example, int, signed int, and unsigned
int) all use the same number of bits to represent them. And, short int will be
represented by at least 16 bits, and int and long will be represented by at
least 32 bits. So, what does this all mean? First, you should favor using the
type corresponding to the word size of the hardware when nothing else
matters. These days that means 32 bits, and increasingly, 64 bits, which
yields ranges that are often more than adequate. A for loop variable, for

example, is often best declared as an int. Why not use a short int in the following code?

```
int i;

for (i = 0; i < 10000, i++) {
    ....
}
```

After all, 16 bits is clearly sufficient to handle the range of the for loop variable in the preceding code.

The problem is not so much related to portability as it is to efficiency. Often, the use of a short or long will lead to less-efficient code, either in terms of size, speed, or both, because the CPU has to do extra work to deal with something that is not its natural word size. Will that result in a noticeable penalty in your particular application? Perhaps not. But all things equal, using int versus short or long, whenever possible, is to be preferred.

Integer Conversions

Besides ensuring that we select a type that is big enough to hold the values that we expect a variable to hold during the lifetime of the program, some thought should be spent, as we write code, on type promotions and conversions performed by the compiler, based on explicit rules of the language. For example, what happens when an unsigned constant is assigned to a short variable? In looking for potential gothas of this type, what we hope for is help from the compiler, for example when we mismatch the types of the lhs and rhs of an assignment or expression, as in the following examples:

```
unsigned int foo_u;
int foo;

foo_u = -1;     // possible logical error, -1 is not unsigned
foo = foo_u;    // possible logical error as well

if (foo == foo_u) ... // are we testing, for example, for foo_u to be -1?
```

Let's see what happens when we try compiling with g++:

```
$ g++ -o foo2 foo2.cpp  -Wall -pedantic
foo2.cpp: In function 'int main(int, char**)':
foo2.cpp:13: warning: comparison between signed and unsigned integer expressions
```

There is a little less complaining by the compiler here than I would want. Truth is, although it is legal to assign -1 to an unsigned type (the language states what happens in this case), or to go the other way, and assign an unsigned value to a signed type (they are the same size, after all), signed and unsigned mean different things from at least a logical, if not an implementation, standpoint.

Let's follow the advice of Item 3 and try a different compiler (this time Visual C++ on Windows), and see what it says with the warnings turned all the way up to level 4:

```
Compiling...

warnings.cpp

c:\foo2.cpp(10) : warning C4245: '=' : conversion from 'int' to 'unsigned int',
signed/unsigned mismatch
c:\foo2.cpp(13) : warning C4389: '==' : signed/unsigned mismatch
```

Although it still didn't catch the assignment of a signed constant to an unsigned variable, it did warn about the assignment of an unsigned variable to a signed variable. The right thing to do now would be to fix the compiler warnings, and while doing so, question the thought process that led to the issue in the first place. Was it just a typo (leaving unsigned off of a declaration) or something deeper in the design that led me to the issue? Better to figure that out now, while the warning is being dealt with, than later, when some seemingly random bug manifests itself.

For the rules behind promotions and conversions in C++, I strongly suggest you carefully read Appendix C (specifically, section C.6) of Bjarne Stroustrup's *The C++ Programming Language* (Addison-Wesley, 2000).

Struct Alignment and Ordering

I'm going to make this short and sweet. Don't rely on the size of structs, or for that matter, the offset of fields in a struct. Compilers are allowed to align fields on word boundaries, and introduce "holes" in a struct via padding to achieve alignment. And, they can also rearrange the ordering of fields in a struct to achieve the same.

As an illustration, consider the following code:

```
#include <stdio.h>

main(int argc, char *argv[])
```

```
{
    typedef struct _foo {
        char a;
        int b;
        char c;
        int d;
    } Foo;

    typedef struct _fee {
        char a;
        char c;
        int b;
        int d;
    } Fee;

    printf("sizeof(Foo) %d sizeof(Fee) %d\n",
        sizeof(Foo), sizeof(Fee));
}
```

When compiled with GCC on Mac OS X (with the size of an int equal to four bytes, and the size of a char equal to one byte), and then run the resulting executable, we get the following output:

```
$ ./structs
sizeof(Foo) 16 sizeof(Fee) 12
```

If you were to compute the size manually, you probably would have come up with ten bytes (assuming a 32-bit word size), as I did, and you probably did not expect the sizes of the structs to be different.

In the gdb debugger, we can see how these two structs are allocated by modifying the code to allocate a couple of variables of type Foo and Fee, respectively:

```
(gdb) x/10x &foo
0xbffff928:     0x61000000      0xdeadbeef      0x62000000      0xaabbccdd
0xbffff938:     0x61620000      0xdeadbeef      0xaabbccdd      0x00000001
0xbffff948:     0xbffffa88      0xbffffa38
(gdb) x/10x &fee
0xbffff938:     0x61620000      0xdeadbeef      0xaabbccdd      0x00000001
0xbffff948:     0xbffffa88      0xbffffa38      0xbffffa30      0x00002dbc
0xbffff958:     0x00000003      0x00000003
(gdb) print sizeof(foo)
$6 = 16
(gdb) print sizeof(fee)
$7 = 12
```

We can see then that three bytes of padding were added to Foo after both fields a and b, and two bytes of padding were added after fields a and b in Fee. How and why this was done was dependent both upon the architecture and the compiler.

Recompiling the code and then executing the same debugging steps an Intel-based system, also using GCC, this time under Fedora Core 3, yields the following:

```
(gdb) x/10x &foo
0xbfa00ad0:     0x00000061      0xdeadbeef      0x00000062      0xaabbccdd
0xbfa00ae0:     0x0034aca0      0x080483d8      0xbfa00b48      0x00125de6
0xbfa00af0:     0x00000001      0xbfa00b74
(gdb) x/10x &fee
0xbfa00ac4:     0x00006261      0xdeadbeef      0xaabbccdd      0x00000061
0xbfa00ad4:     0xdeadbeef      0x00000062      0xaabbccdd      0x0034aca0
0xbfa00ae4:     0x080483d8      0xbfa00b48
(gdb) print sizeof(foo)
$3 = 16
(gdb) print sizeof(fee)
$4 = 12
(gdb)
```

You can see the sizes are the same, and the general strategy for padding is the same, but the layout of memory is not the same as it was for Mac OS X. On Windows, dumping memory for foo and fee, respectively, gives us yet a third result:

```
0x0012FEC8 61 cc cc cc ef be ad de 62 cc cc cc dd cc bb aa
0x0012FEB4 61 62 cc cc ef be ad de dd cc bb aa
```

Although the sizes are the same, clearly, binary compatibility is not achieved here. So, tread carefully: Don't assume the layout, or size, of a struct as computed by one platform/toolchain combination is going to be the same for some other combination.

7

User Interfaces

Earlier I covered abstraction application programming interfaces (APIs) such as Portable Operating System Interface (POSIX, Item 16) and the Netscape Portable Runtime Library (NSPR, Item 17). The use of APIs like these go a long way to making applications portable. What these APIs do not address is the important area of the user interface (UI). Nor are there any standards for user interface, or the toolkits used to create them, making the UI a thorny issue when it comes to portability. It is easy to explain why there is no standard user interface; the user interface has always been a major mechanism by which platforms differentiate themselves from one other. Since the early 1980s, operating system vendors (Apple and Microsoft, in particular) have churned out toolkit after toolkit, forcing developers to rewrite applications along the way, so that even portability within the confines of a platform, over some period of time, can be an elusive goal. (Microsoft has, as of this writing, yet to release a native Cocoa UI for its Office suite of products on Macintosh, years after the Cocoa API was introduced.) The degree to which graphical user interface (GUI) toolkit architectures and APIs differ is perhaps, more than anything else, the main reason why some software can be found on only one operating system and absent on the rest.

As different as the platform UIs, and the toolkits that support them are, they fortunately share some significant commonalities. Some of these are obvious—all platforms use windows to display content, have menus, radio buttons, and scrollbars, for example. Some of the commonalities are less obvious, yet will be familiar to a programmer who has had some experience writing GUI applications (especially if the experience encompasses a variety of toolkits). An example is the way that toolkits communicate events to applications; for example, when a button is pressed by the user. In some cases, the communication is done via a message sent to an event queue, and in others, programmer-written callback functions, of one sort or another, are invoked. Regardless of the mechanism employed, the basic concept behind the communication is generally the same.

We can take advantage of these toolkit commonalities and abstract them in ways that enable us to converge toward a single, unified GUI toolkit model, one that can support the needs of the application that we are trying to build. This is exactly what Netscape and Mozilla did with their toolkit named XML User Interface Language (XUL), and what I have done with my GUI toolkit named Trixul, both of which are described later in this book. It is also what has been done by other cross-platform GUI toolkits, in particular Qt and wxWidgets. (wxWidgets is also covered later in this book.)

Much of the rest of this book focuses on how to approach the development of cross-platform user interfaces. In this chapter, I present a couple of items that will lay important foundations. In Chapter 8, "wxWidgets," I go on to provide a detailed overview and tutorial of a cross-platform GUI toolkit named wxWidgets, which was used by AOL to create a product (which competed directly with Netscape) named AOL Communicator. Then, in Chapter 9, "Developing a Cross-Platform GUI Toolkit in C++," I describe XUL and Trixul, and their implementations, in great detail.

Item 22: Separate the User Interface from the Model

One of the more difficult aspects of cross-platform software development comes into play when creating applications that have a GUI. The appearance, behavior, and tools used to create the UI itself all vary greatly across platforms.

The look and feel associated with a given environment is generically known as a theme, and each theme, in turn, is associated with a GUI toolkit that programmers use to create applications that conform to it. The Macintosh theme is named Aqua, and the toolkit used to develop Aqua UIs is named Cocoa. On Linux systems, there are seemingly countless themes, but the two most popular are those associated with the KDE and GNOME desktop environments, which are based on the Qt and Gtk+ toolkits, respectively. Windows GUI applications are developed using Win32, MFC, and, more recently, .NET Forms APIs. As is the case with Mac OS X, there is only one look and feel standard associated with the Windows platform.

In general, it is best to code your UI so that it conforms as closely as possible to the default theme, and use the platform UI toolkit to create it. By doing so, you give your application the best chance possible to integrate well, both functionally and aesthetically, with other applications, and with the desktop environment.

However, the problem with using native toolkits such as Cocoa, Gtk+, and .NET Forms is that they are all extremely nonportable. In fact, each of the three toolkits just mentioned are based on completely different programming languages—Cocoa is Objective-C based, Gtk+ is based on C, and .NET Forms is based on Microsoft's managed C++ (CLR) language.

This lack of portability means that a special approach is required when it comes to creating a portable UI for an application that wants to base its UI on native toolkits. The keys to the approach that will be described in this Item are as follows:

- A well-defined separation of the code that maintains the data in an application from the code that displays this same data to the user
- A platform-agnostic interface by which these two bodies of code can communicate

Separating the User Interface and Application Logic with Model/View

Every GUI application consists of two major components:

- The logic (code) and data that forms the basis of the application
- The UI, which allows the user to manipulate and view the data managed by the application

The model/view paradigm is a common way of separating these two components. In an application that lists the processes currently being managed by the system (see Item 2), a Standard Template Library (STL) vector holding the names and processes IDs of the processes scanned by the program, and the code that obtains the process information from the operating system and stores it in the list would be the model. The view in such a program would be console output listing the process names and IDs, or in a graphical application, a table with two columns, one displaying the name of the process, and the other displaying the ID. Or the view would be the very same data serialized to a text file. The key advantage of the model/view paradigm, when implemented correctly, is that both model and view are cleanly separated from each other. That is, you can change the way that the program goes about retrieving the process information from the operating system (as Item 2 illustrates, the methods for obtaining process information is very platform-specific), or you can modify the method by which this information is displayed to the user, but neither change to the model or to the view should affect the other. Of course, if the model changes (for example, we decide to extend the model to represent the ID of the parent process, or the state of the process), the view needs to be given some mechanism by which this information can be obtained so that the view can represent it, too.

The model/view paradigm can be effectively implemented in a number of ways. As stated in Erich Gamma's *Design Patterns* (Addison-Wesley, 1995), the Observer (also known as publish and subscribe) design pattern is a useful tool in the implementation of a model/view architecture, but it is certainly not required that one use this design pattern to build a model/view-based application architecture. All that is required of model/view is a clean separation of application data from how it is displayed, and this can be achieved in a variety of ways. I cover the use of the Observer design pattern in implementing model/view architectures later in this item.

The View

First, let's take a look at strategies for implementing the view, and then after we have that covered, return to a discussion on how to thread both the model and the view together using the Observer pattern. To keep things simple, the view will consist of a window that contains a single scrolled list. The scrolled list will display the name and process ID (PID) of the processes running at the time the application was launched. Figure 7-1 illustrates the UI we are going after.

Following the advice that was given in Item 2, the view itself will be segmented into platform-specific and platform-neutral code using the factory design pattern. (If you haven't yet read Item 2, now would be a good time to do so, because the remainder of this item builds upon it.) To implement the view, we rely on the native toolkits (Cocoa, Gtk+, and .NET Forms) for implementing the actual UI, writing code in whatever languages these toolkits require.

We can isolate all of this nonportable code behind a factory, too. In fact, the very same factory can be used—all that we need to do is add an API to support the abstractions needed to support a UI. The following code should make this clearer. The first class to look at is `ProcessesFactory`, which was first introduced in Item 2. Code specifically added for the GUI is highlighted in bold here:

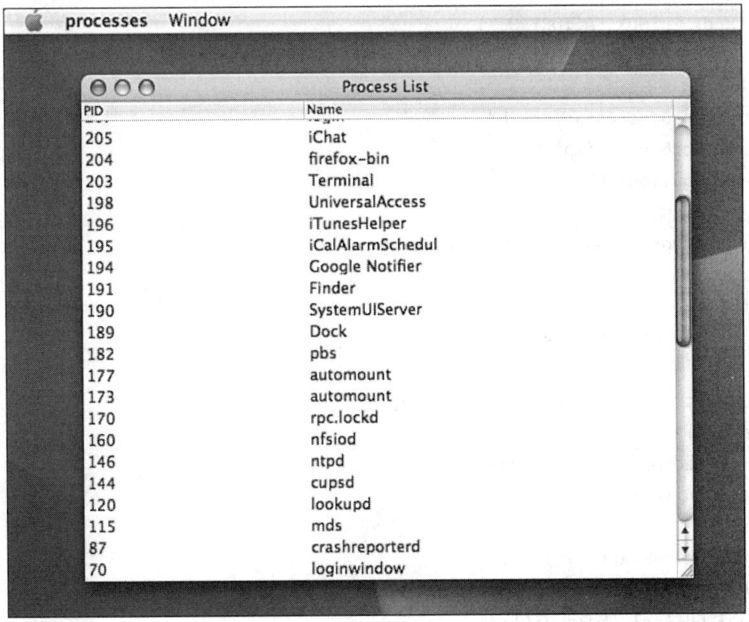

Figure 7-1 Process list on MacOS X

```
#if !defined(__PROCESSES_FACTORY_H__)
#define __PROCESSES_FACTORY_H__

#include "processesimpl.h"
#include "guiimpl.h"

class ProcessesFactory
{
public:
    virtual ~ProcessesFactory() {};
    virtual ProcessesImpl* MakeProcesses() = 0;
    virtual GUIImpl* MakeGUI() = 0;
    static ProcessesFactory *GetProcessesFactory();
};

#endif
```

The function MakeGUI(), because it is pure virtual, must be implemented by each platform. Linux, for example, compiles the following class, which inherits from ProcessesFactory:

```
#if !defined(__LINUX_FACTORY_H__)
#define __LINUX_FACTORY_H__

#include "../processesfactory.h"
#include "../processesimpl.h"
#include "../guiimpl.h"

class LinuxFactory : public ProcessesFactory
{
public:
    static LinuxFactory *GetFactoryInstance()
    {
        static LinuxFactory *factory = 0;
        if (!factory)
            factory = new LinuxFactory;
        return factory;
    }
    virtual ~LinuxFactory() {};
    virtual ProcessesImpl *MakeProcesses();
    virtual GUIImpl *MakeGUI();
private:
    LinuxFactory() {};
};

#endif
```

The function `LinuxFactory::MakeGUI()` simply instantiates `LinuxGUIImpl`, which inherits the interfaces that are defined by `GUIImpl()`, and returns a pointer to it:

```
#include "linuxfactory.h"
#include "linuxprocessesimpl.h"
#include "linuxguiimpl.h"

ProcessesImpl *LinuxFactory::MakeProcesses()
{
    return new LinuxProcessesImpl;
}

GUIImpl *LinuxFactory::MakeGUI()
{
    return new LinuxGUIImpl;
}
```

That's it for the factory class. Similar steps are used for both Windows and Mac OS X. While we are at it, if you need to provide abstractions to some other platform-specific functionality that does not fit into the category of process handling or GUI (for example, threads support), the preceding steps can be repeated:

1. Define a base implementation class, similar to `ProcessImpl` or `GUIImpl` (for example, `ThreadsImpl`).
2. Declare in the factory class a pure virtual function that can be called to create an instance of the base implementation class (for example, `ProcessesFactory::MakeThreads()`).
3. Implement the preceding function in the platform-specific factory class (for example, `LinuxFactory::MakeThreads()`).

Abstracting the GUI Application Main Loop
We now need to turn our attention to the abstract class that the application will use to create and manage the UI. The abstraction is based upon the fact that most modern GUI toolkits are similar in design:

- They often implement some sort of function that must be called to initialize the toolkit.
- They require the application to create, and show, a basic UI, usually consisting of a main window, and a menu. The UI is created, generally, by creating instances of objects (widgets) that represent items that are visible in the UI. For example, in Gtk+, one creates a push button by calling a function named `gtk_button_new()`.
- They require the application, after the user interface has been created and shown, to enter into an **event** loop. This loop processes events (such as keyboard and mouse I/O), dispatching events to code that goes on to create and show even more user interface. In all modern toolkits, this is done by calling a single function. For example, in Gtk+, one calls `gtk_main()` to enter this loop.

An additional function in the toolkit allows the application to break the GUI toolkit out of its `main` loop, causing the application to exit. Such a function is usually called in response to the user selecting the Exit or Quit menu of the application.

In Gtk+, a simplified "Hello World" application illustrates this basic structure, which is inherent in all GUI applications:

```
int
main( int argc, char *argv[] )
{
```

```
GtkWidget *window, *label;

gtk_init(&argc, &argv);

window = gtk_window_new(GTK_WINDOW_TOPLEVEL);

vbox = gtk_vbox_new(FALSE, 0);
gtk_container_add(GTK_CONTAINER (window), vbox);

label = gtk_label_new("Hello World!");
gtk_box_pack_start(GTK_BOX(vbox), label, FALSE,
    FALSE, 0);

gtk_widget_show_all(window);

gtk_main();
return(0);
}
```

The call to gtk_init() initializes the toolkit. Following this, a window is created, and into this window is placed a label widget that displays the string "Hello World!". Next, gtk_main() is called, which enters the application main loop, processing events. As mentioned previously, a similar application structure is used in both Cocoa and .NET Forms applications, and to support it, a platform-agnostic class that I have named GUI can be defined that contains interfaces that correspond to the initialization of the toolkit, the creation of the UI, the entering of the application main loop, and finally main loop termination (the corresponding functions shown in bold here, respectively):

```
#if !defined(__GUI_H__)
#define __GUI_H__

class GUIImpl;
class ProcessList;

#include "processlistener.h"

class GUI : public ProcessListener
{
public:
    static GUI *GetInstance() {
        static GUI *gui = 0;
        if (!gui)
```

```
            gui = new GUI();
        return gui;
    };
    int Init(int argc, char *argv[],
        ProcessList *processes);
    int CreateUI();
    int MainLoop();
    int Shutdown();
    int AddProcess(const char *name, const int pid);
    int ClearList();
    void OnNewProcess(const char *name, const int pid);
private:
    GUI();
    GUI(const GUI &gui);
    GUIImpl *m_guiImpl;
};
#endif
```

The functions not shown in bold (specifically AddProcess() and OnNewProcess()) relate to functionality that I cover later in this item.

The member m_guiImpl is a pointer to the base class of the platform-specific GUI implementation class that is obtained in the GUI constructor using the factory that we discussed earlier:

```
#include "gui.h"
#include "processes.h"
#include "processesfactory.h"

GUI::GUI(): m_guiImpl(NULL)
{
    ProcessesFactory *factory = ProcessesFactory::GetProcessesFactory();

    if (factory)
        m_guiImpl = factory->MakeGUI();
}
```

As you can see, the constructor obtains the singleton instance of ProcessesFactory, and then calls its MakeGUI() function, which in turn instantiates the platform-specific GUI class that derives from GUIImpl. We'll look at the Linux implementation of GUIImpl shortly but first, let's look at the Init(), CreateUI(), MainLoop(), and Shutdown() functions. If you have read Item 2, how these functions work should be no surprise: all they do is forward the request made via the abstract API to the platform-specific

implementation, which in most cases just means invoking a function of the
same name. Here is the code for the `Init()`, `CreateUI()`, `MainLoop()`, and
`Shutdown()` functions, illustrating how the implementation class is used:

```
int
GUI::Init(int argc, char *argv[],
        ProcessList *processes)
{
        // ignoring the processes argument for now

        if (m_guiImpl)
                return m_guiImpl->Init(argc, argv);
        return -1;
}

int
GUI::CreateUI()
{
        int ret = -1;
        if (m_guiImpl) {
                if (!(ret =
                        m_guiImpl->CreateProcessListWindow()))
                        return m_guiImpl->CreateMenus();
        }
        return -1;
}

int
GUI::MainLoop()
{
        if (m_guiImpl)
                return m_guiImpl->MainLoop();
        return -1;
}

int
GUI::Shutdown()
{
        if (m_guiImpl)
                return m_guiImpl->Shutdown();
        return -1;
}
```

Notice the structure of `Create()`, which differs from the other
functions in that it makes calls to two platform-specific functions, one that

creates the main window displaying the scrolled list, and the other that
creates the application's menu bar and menus. The choice to do this was
somewhat arbitrary—I could have performed the segmentation further
down in the implementation class, simplifying things at this level. However,
doing so here illustrates that you have some flexibility in terms of how code
is implemented at this level. All that matters is that the API to the application be abstract. What needs to be called in the implementation class to
provide the needed functionality is largely irrelevant.

Before we go on to discuss the implementation class GUIImpl, it is
worth taking a look at how the GUI class is used in the application. The
following listing (with the relevant code in bold) provides the details:

```
#include <stdio.h>
#include "processes.h"
#include "gui.h"

int
main(int argc, char *argv[])
{
    ProcessList processList;
    GUI *gui;

    gui = GUI::GetInstance();
    if (gui) {
        gui->Init(argc, argv, &processList);
        gui->CreateUI();

        processList.Scan();
        gui->MainLoop();
    }
}
```

In the preceding code, Scan() is called to grab the process list and feed it
to the GUI prior to entering the GUI main loop. Typically, application
actions are performed as the result of user interactions, such as the clicking
of buttons or the selection of menu items. However, in this simple example,
it is sufficient to place the call within main(), as long as this is done after the
GUI has been created, and before the main loop is entered. You'll see later
what happens inside the Scan() function to tie the ProcessList class and
the GUI class together.

GUI Implementation Classes

But first, let's look at the implementation classes for each of the platforms. First up is the class GUIImpl, which defines interfaces that are called upon from the abstract class GUI (as was illustrated earlier), and from which each of the platform-specific implementation classes inherits:

```
#if !defined(__GUI_IMPL_H__)
#define __GUI_IMPL_H__

class GUIImpl
{
public:
    GUIImpl() {};
    virtual ~GUIImpl() {};
    virtual int Init(int argc, char *argv[]) = 0;
    virtual int MainLoop() = 0;
    virtual int CreateMenus() = 0;
    virtual int CreateProcessListWindow() = 0;
    virtual int Shutdown() = 0;
    virtual int AddProcess(const char *name,
        const int pid) = 0;
    virtual int ClearList() = 0;
};

#endif
```

There should be no surprises here; the implementation class is abstract, and defines each of the interfaces that the GUI class will invoke via the GUIImpl pointer that the factory provided. Three classes, one for each supported platform, instantiate GUIImpl-derived classes. The following listings illustrate these classes for Cocoa, .NET Forms, and Gtk+, respectively. The thing to notice is that each class implements the same public interface, but has a very different private implementation, consisting of functions and member variables that are specific to the platform GUI toolkit supported by the class. As long as the public interfaces are consistent, the class can, and usually must, implement private code needed to implement against the platform GUI toolkit. As you can see in the following listings, Cocoa has the most complex private implementation, whereas Gtk+ has the simplest of the three.

Cocoa/MacOS X

```
#if !defined(__COCOAGUIIMPL_H__)
#define __COCOAGUIIMPL_H__

#include "../guiimpl.h"
#import <Cocoa/Cocoa.h>
#import "gridlistdatasource.h"

class CocoaGUIImpl : public GUIImpl
{
public:
    CocoaGUIImpl();
    virtual ~CocoaGUIImpl();
    virtual int Init(int argc, char *argv[]);
    virtual int MainLoop();
    virtual int CreateMenus();
    virtual int CreateProcessListWindow();
    virtual int Shutdown();
    virtual int AddProcess(const char *name,
        const int pid);
    virtual int ClearList();
private:
    int CreateMenusInternal();
    int AddToMenubar(NSMenu *menu);
    int AddToMenubar(NSMenu *menu, int index);
    void SetQuitMenuItem(NSMenuItem *menuItem)
        {m_quitMenuItem = menuItem;};
    void SetPreferencesMenuItem(NSMenuItem *menuItem)
        {m_preferencesMenuItem = menuItem;};
    int CreateAppleMenu();
    int CreateWindowMenu();
    int CreateScrolledList(NSRect &graphicsRect);

    NSAutoreleasePool *m_pool;
    NSMenu *m_menubar;
    NSView *m_view;
    NSWindow *m_window;
    NSTableView *m_gridlist;
    NSScrollView *m_scrolledWindow;
    GridListDataSource *m_dataSource;
    NSMenuItem *m_preferencesMenuItem;
    NSMenuItem *m_quitMenuItem;
    NSTableColumn *m_pidColumn;
    NSTableColumn *m_nameColumn;
};
#endif
```

.NET Forms/Windows

```cpp
#if !defined(__WINDOWSGUIIMPL_H__)
#define __WINDOWSGUIIMPL_H__

#include "../guiimpl.h"

#include <gcroot.h>

#using <mscorlib.dll>
#using <System.dll>
#using <System.Drawing.dll>
#using <System.Windows.Forms.dll>

using namespace System;
using namespace System::Data;
using namespace System::ComponentModel;
using namespace System::Drawing;
using namespace System::Windows::Forms;

class WindowsGUIImpl : public GUIImpl
{
public:
    WindowsGUIImpl();
    virtual ~WindowsGUIImpl();
    virtual int Init(int argc, char *argv[]);
    virtual int MainLoop();
    virtual int CreateMenus();
    virtual int CreateProcessListWindow();
    virtual int Shutdown();
    virtual int AddProcess(const char *name,
        const int pid);
    virtual int ClearList();
    int HandleCommand();
private:
    gcroot <DataGrid *> m_gridlist;
    gcroot <Form *> m_form;
    gcroot <Panel *> m_panel;
    gcroot <DataTable *> m_processTable;
};
#endif
```

Gtk+/Linux

```
#if !defined(__LINUXGUIIMPL_H__)
#define __LINUXGUIIMPL_H__

#include "../guiimpl.h"
#include <gtk/gtk.h>

class LinuxGUIImpl : public GUIImpl

public:
    LinuxGUIImpl();
    virtual ~LinuxGUIImpl();
    virtual int Init(int argc, char *argv[]);
    virtual int MainLoop();
    virtual int CreateMenus();
    virtual int CreateProcessListWindow();
    virtual int Shutdown();
    virtual int AddProcess(const char *name,
        const int pid);
    virtual int ClearList();
private:
    GtkWidget *m_window;
    GtkWidget *m_main_vbox;
    GtkWidget *m_clist;
};
#endif
```

The details behind the implementation of each of these platform-specific classes are not terribly relevant. Suffice to say that each class is free to implement the interface as best fits the corresponding platform GUI toolkit. As mentioned earlier, the interfaces I designed for the GUI class were defined with much prior knowledge of GUI toolkits and their APIs in mind, so the implementation of these classes was straightforward for me.

To further illustrate the platform-specific nature of the code at this level, the following listing shows the implementation of CreateMenus() for Gtk+. The Cocoa implementation (not shown) is written in Objective-C++, and is much more complicated. The .NET Forms implementation (also not shown) is written in Managed C++:

```
int LinuxGUIImpl::CreateMenus()
{
    static GtkItemFactoryEntry menu_items[] = {
        { "/_File",      0,  0, 0, "<Branch>" },
        { "/File/sep1", 0,  0, 0, "<Separator>" },
        { "/File/Quit", "<control>Q",
            gtk_main_quit, 0, 0 }
    };

    GtkAccelGroup *accel_group;
    gint nmenu_items = sizeof(menu_items) /
        sizeof(menu_items[0]);
    GtkItemFactory *item_factory;

    accel_group = gtk_accel_group_new();
    item_factory = gtk_item_factory_new(
        GTK_TYPE_MENU_BAR, "<main>", accel_group );

    gtk_item_factory_create_items(item_factory,
        nmenu_items, menu_items, (void *)"foo");

    gtk_accel_group_attach(accel_group,
        GTK_OBJECT(m_window));

    GtkWidget *menubar;

    menubar = gtk_item_factory_get_widget(
        item_factory, "<main>");

    gtk_box_pack_start(GTK_BOX(m_main_vbox), menubar,
        FALSE, FALSE, 0);
    gtk_widget_show(menubar);

    return 0;
}
```

Using Publish/Subscribe to Communicate between the View and the Model

Now that the basic structure supporting the GUI is understood, there is one final detail to discuss. That detail is how the ProcessList class communicates the process list to the GUI class. In a nutshell, we want the model (ProcessList) to tell the view (GUI) about each of the processes that it has found. When told about a process by the model, the view will add the process, including its name and PID, to the scrolled list for display.

Implementing the communication between the model and view can be done using the Observer (or publish/subscribe) design pattern. The Observer design pattern is based on a "don't call us, we'll call you" paradigm. In this paradigm, an *observer* (in this case, the GUI object that implements the view) registers itself with a *subject* (the ProcessList object, which implements the model). The contract between the observer and subject is an interface defined by the subject—to participate, the observer must instantiate an object that inherits that interface, and pass a pointer to this object to the subject when registering itself. The subject places this pointer into a list; and when the time comes for it to communicate with the observers currently on the list, it iterates the list, calling each object on it. In our application, only one function is defined by the subject interface, OnNewProcess(). This function is called once for each process that is read by the model when it queries the operating system for the list of current processes. The following code defines the interface that must be implemented by the observer object:

```
#if !defined(__PROCESSLISTENER_H__)
#define __PROCESSLISTENER_H__

class ProcessListener
{
public:
    virtual ~ProcessListener() {};
    virtual void OnNewProcess(const char *name,
        const int pid) = 0;
};

#endif
```

Notice that OnNewProcess() is pure virtual, requiring an implementation from classes inheriting ProcessListener. Two arguments are passed by the model to the view using this interface for each process in the list: the name of the process, and its PID. We might choose to extend this class to contain a function that is called when a process is removed from the list, but to keep things simple, let's just worry about the one function here.

To allow observers to register (and unregister) themselves with the subject, the subject needs to inherit or implement interfaces for this purpose.

In the following code, the functions for doing so are `RegisterListener()` and `UnregisterListener()`, respectively:

```
#if !defined(__PROCESSPUBLISHER_H__)
#define __PROCESSPUBLISHER_H__

class ProcessListener;

#include "process.h"

#include <list>

class ProcessPublisher
{
public:
    virtual ~ProcessPublisher() {};
    void RegisterListener(ProcessListener *listener);
    void UnregisterListener(ProcessListener *listener);
    void SendNotification(Process &proc);
private:
    std::list <ProcessListener *> m_listeners;
};


#endif
```

Both of these functions take, as an argument, a pointer to an object that inherits from `ProcessListener`, previously defined. Below is the implementation of `ProcessPublisher`. The functions `RegisterListener()` and `UnregisterListener()` are trivial, used to add and remove the observer from an STL list, respectively. `SendNotification()` is called by the model to perform the notification to all observers that a process has been detected. Its argument is a simple class that manages the PID and name of a single process:

```
#include "processpublisher.h"
#include "processlistener.h"

void ProcessPublisher::RegisterListener(
    ProcessListener *listener)
{
    if (listener)
        m_listeners.push_back(listener);
}
```

```
void ProcessPublisher::UnregisterListener(
    ProcessListener *listener)
{
    if (listener)
        m_listeners.remove(listener);
}


void ProcessPublisher::SendNotification(Process &proc)
{
    std::list <ProcessListener *>::iterator iter;

    for (iter = m_listeners.begin();
        iter != m_listeners.end(); ++iter)
    {
        (*iter)->OnNewProcess(proc.GetName(),
            proc.GetPID());
    }
}
```

The implementation of OnNewProcess() is, of course, platform neutral, implemented by the GUI object, which simply calls a function in the GUI implementation class that knows how to take the name and PID and add them to a scrolled list:

```
void
GUI::OnNewProcess(const char *name, const int pid)
{
    if (m_guiImpl)
        m_guiImpl->AddProcess(name, pid);
}
```

Finally, the implementation of AddProcess() for Mac OS X is written in Objective-C++. Once again, code at this level is very platform and GUI-toolkit specific. Regardless, its job is simple—ensure that the process data passed in is added to the scrolled list. Here is the implementation:

```
int CocoaGUIImpl::AddProcess(const char *name, const int pid)
{
    int ret = -1;
    if (name) {
        char buf[16];
        snprintf(buf, sizeof(buf) - 1, "%d", pid);
        NSString *namestr =
            [NSString stringWithCString: name];
```

```
        NSString *idstr =
            [NSString stringWithCString: buf];
    if (namestr && idstr && m_gridlist &&
        m_dataSource) {
        [m_dataSource addObjectForColumn:
            m_pidColumn id: idstr nameTableColumn:
            m_nameColumn name: namestr];
        [m_gridlist reloadData];
        [m_gridlist sizeToFit];
        ret = 0;
    }
    }
    return ret;
}
```

Summary

This item presented a lot of information, and so it is a good idea to summarize what has been discussed:

- The best GUIs adhere to the standard theme provided by the desktop or operating environment (for example Aqua on Mac OS X), and are built using native toolkits (such as Cocoa). However, using native toolkits is inherently nonportable.
- Model/view is a paradigm that is commonly used to separate the logic and data of an application (the *model*) from the UI that represents it to the user (the *view*). A clean separation of the model and view greatly enhances portability.
- Native GUI toolkit APIs are highly nonportable. However, they do share some major things in common, allowing an abstract API to be designed for use by an application to initialize the toolkit, create a UI, and manage the GUI toolkit's main loop. A factory can be used to obtain a class that provides this abstract API.
- The Observer design pattern (also known as Publish/Subscribe) can be used to implement an effective form of communication between the model and view portions of the application. The view (an *observer*) registers itself with the model (a *subject*) by calling a function publicly defined by the model, `RegisterListener()`, passing a pointer to an object (possibly itself). This view object inherits from a class (defined by the model) that defines interfaces that will be called by the model when state changes occur. Multiple objects can be registered with the model;

the model iterates a list of view objects when state changes, invoking the appropriate methods on each of the objects found in the list.

Item 23: Develop a Cross-Platform User Interface Strategy

A few issues complicate the successful implementation of cross-platform GUI applications. These are described in the next few sections. Following this, options for selecting a GUI toolkit are presented.

Issues Affecting Portable Cross-Platform GUI Development

Look and Feel Standards

Each platform has its own native look and feel standard. This look and feel standard is, depending on the platform, defined by a document (sometimes referred to as a style guide). Or it is not defined at all. Some platforms, such as Linux, have multiple native look and feel standards. These standards, as you might guess, vary greatly from each other.

For Mac OS X, the look and feel standard is named Aqua, and is described by the Apple Human Interface Guidelines (see http://developer. apple.com/documentation/UserExperience/Conceptual/OSXHIGuidelines/X HIGPartIII/chapter_10_section_1.html).

On Windows, the situation is similar, but it is a harder to identify a style guide, or give a name to the Windows UI look and feel. The book *Microsoft Windows User Experience* (Microsoft Press, 1999) is perhaps the closest to an official style guide for the platform that I have seen.

On Linux (and other UNIX-like systems), UI standardization is a bit harder to pin down.

In the late 1980s, the SunOS operating system was shipped with its proprietary Open Look user environment. Eventually, vendors (notably IBM, Hewlett-Packard, DEC, and later, Sun) adopted a UI standard known as the Common Desktop Environment (CDE), which was the GUI portion of an initiative known as the Common Software Environment (COSE). CDE was based on the X Window System.

Although CDE is still shipped by one or two vendors (it was included in Solaris 10), the open source community ignored CDE because it was never open sourced, and because Motif, the toolkit that it was based on, did not go open source until after the community came up with replacement toolkits (more on these toolkits in the following sections). These new open source toolkits led to the adoption of two new user environments, both of which are available under Linux. The first, GNOME, is based on a toolkit named Gtk+. The second environment, KDE, is based on a toolkit named Qt. KDE and GNOME are very different in terms of their look and feel, and the existence of two "standards" on Linux makes it difficult for developers to choose which to develop for. Often, that choice comes down to a personal preference on the part of the developer, based on familiarity of the toolkit itself, the language that it is based on (Qt is based on C++, whereas Gtk+ is C based); or, the issue revolves around acceptance of the licensing terms associated with the toolkit. Gtk+ is open source (Lesser General Public License [LGPL]), while Qt also has an open source version, but requires vendors to pay a license fee to Trolltech for its use in commercial products.

GUI Toolkits

The second hurdle facing the development of cross-platform GUI applications is the fact that each platform that we consider in this book offers multiple options when it comes to a GUI toolkit. On Macintosh, two toolkits can be used to implement an Aqua UI. The primary toolkit is named Cocoa, and it requires the developers to use Objective-C to program against its API. Carbon, which was introduced by Apple to aid in the porting of legacy Mac OS applications to Mac OS X, is a C-based API that also supports Aqua. All new GUI development is done in Objective-C using the Cocoa API.

On Windows (from most recent to least recent in terms of date of first introduction), .NET Forms, the Microsoft Foundation Classes (MFC), and Win32 all support the Windows look and feel. .NET Forms is to be preferred over Win32 and MFC, not only because it has a well-designed widget hierarchy and API, but also because it will scale forward into Microsoft's next-generation operating system, Vista. .NET Forms is used by Trixul (Chapter 9) for these reasons.

On Linux, things are a bit more complicated. As mentioned earlier, X11 does not define UI policy, but instead allows the toolkits that are built above X11 to make the look and feel decisions. This has led to a wide variety of toolkits on UNIX-like systems, with Motif (the basis for CDE), Gtk+ (the basis for GNOME), and Qt (the basis for KDE) being the most popular. Gtk+ is described in great detail in my book *Gtk+ Programming in C* (Prentice Hall, 2001). Qt is a cross-platform toolkit created and maintained by a company named Trolltech, and is described in C++ *GUI Programming with Qt 4* (Prentice Hall, 2006). The user environments (CDE, GNOME, and KDE) all have their own philosophy regarding what constitutes a proper UI and each toolkit (Motif, Gtk+, and Qt, respectively) implements its own set of widgets.

Choosing a GUI Strategy

In the preceding section, we saw that:

- Each platform has its own UI look and feel, and UNIX-like platforms have more than one look and feel.
- Multiple options are available to developers when it comes to choosing a toolkit with which to implement the GUI of an application.

As a developer, what must you do to level the playing field, so to speak, and come up with a UI for your application that looks and behaves the same on each of the platforms that you want to support?

The answer isn't always easy. In this section, let's take a look at some of the options, and discuss the benefits and trade-offs of each.

Use Native GUI Toolkits

The first option is to code directly to the API of one of the available native GUI toolkits on each of the platforms that you want to support. For example, use .NET Forms on Windows, Gtk+ or Qt on Linux, and Cocoa on Mac OS X. The obvious drawback in doing so is that the code that you write for one platform to implement a UI will not port to the other platforms (the exception being Qt). However, by carefully separating the code that implements the UI from the code that implements the application, you can isolate the code that is platform specific such that the impact is minimal. Item 22 discusses this strategy in more detail.

You must be careful when coding cross-platform applications to ensure that all platforms move forward at the same pace. (See Item 1 for more details on this issue.) I think, in general, coding to a native platform GUI toolkit is, among the three options presented here, the least likely to enforce adoption of this guideline. Discipline on the part of developers will therefore be needed to ensure that no platform is left behind.

Another disadvantage to coding to native GUI toolkits is that it requires knowledge of each toolkit, which often means hiring developers for each of the supported platforms. (There are developers out there that are fluent in multiple platforms and GUI toolkit APIs, but specialization is more the norm.) Cross-platform toolkits, mentioned later, minimize this need for specialized knowledge, because only one API is required for all supported platforms.

Obviously, the first place that new platform functionality is going to show itself is via the native toolkits. So, a big advantage associated with the use of native GUI toolkits is that the applications you write will not be compromised in terms of platform-specific functionality. Of course, this is a dual-edged sword of sorts, because often this functionality will not be portable to the other platforms. Care must be taken to ensure that adopting functionality that is specific to a platform enhances the product in a way that does not compromise the overall goal of equality in terms of platform support. In other words, it is okay for platforms to diverge, but it is not okay for such divergence to go unchecked. I have no specific guidelines to offer in terms of what is too much divergence; it is up to you to try and balance the extremes in a way that is most beneficial to the product and its users.

Once again, refer to Item 22 for details on how to structure code to allow for the use of native GUI toolkits.

Use a Cross-Platform GUI Toolkit

A few cross-platform GUI toolkits are available for use in developing professional-quality applications for Windows, Mac OS X, and Linux. Qt, mentioned previously, is one of them. Chapter 8 introduces wxWidgets, a popular cross-platform GUI toolkit that also supports each of the three platforms covered by this book.

The main advantages in using a cross-platform GUI toolkit is that the code used to implement the GUI is shared across all platforms, and developers only have to know one API to build the UI. A related advantage is that the use of a single toolkit encourages concurrent development and release of the product on all supported platforms.

The disadvantages, depending on the GUI toolkit, include the following:

- The GUI may look foreign compared with applications based on native GUI toolkits. Mac OS X users are notorious for demanding that an application's look and feel is in accordance with Apple Human Interface Guidelines, and it is very possible, in the desire to be portable, for a cross-platform GUI toolkit to make compromises that are in conflict with the recommended look and feel standards.
- The GUI might not be able to take advantage of any special enhancements that would otherwise be available only via the native GUI toolkits.

Write Your Own GUI Toolkit (or Modify an Open Source One)

For the past 20+ years, with few exceptions, GUIs have been either designed and implemented in nonportable integrated development environments (IDEs) such as Visual Studio or Xcode, or have been coded by hand in a programming language (usually C or C++) against a native GUI toolkit API. Or, some combination of the two approaches has been used. However, the explosion of the Web (and the development of XUL, which I witnessed firsthand as an employee of Netscape) has me convinced that UIs are best described in Extensible Markup Language (XML).

In Chapter 9, I describe Trixul, which is my attempt at developing an XML-based, open source cross-platform GUI toolkit. I designed Trixul primarily to aid me in describing, in this book, some of the principles behind the design and implementation of such a toolkit. I am hoping that it will get enough open source contributors hacking on it to make it a viable toolkit choice for future desktop application development.

Netscape designed one of the first XML-based GUI toolkits, XUL, because they needed a highly portable GUI toolkit that meshed well with the Netscape/Mozilla browser. But they are not alone in having built such a toolkit. America Online developed an internal, XML GUI toolkit, a follow on to yet another internal GUI toolkit (FDO) that was used by AOL in the late 1980s and most of the 1990s as the basis of the AOL client UI. All of these toolkits were developed because they satisfied needs that no other toolkit was able to satisfy, and both AOL and Netscape had enough time, money, and people to do the job. (Well, there is never enough time, or money, but that's another story.)

I don't expect many of you will want to go as far as designing your own cross-platform GUI toolkit. Toolkit design takes a lot of time, and effort, and for most of us, the process of implementing a new toolkit would only delay getting applications into the hands of users. But sometimes, you need something other than what is currently available. If you do have needs that are not serviced elsewhere, perhaps the best way to get to where you need to go is base your work on an existing open source GUI toolkit, make whatever changes to the toolkit are needed, and contribute them back to the codebase so that others will benefit.

8 wxWidgets

Now that we have covered how a graphical user interface (GUI) fits into a cross-platform project, it is time to take a look at the first cross-platform GUI toolkit covered in this book, wxWidgets. wxWidgets (at one time, known as wxWindows but forced to change its name because of pressure from a rather large software company in the state of Washington) is one of two very popular desktop GUI toolkits, the other being Trolltech's Qt.

wxWidgets first came to my attention while I was a developer at Netscape, and in fact played a role in the history of Netscape (and, one might argue, it helped to hastened the demise of the Netscape division that was responsible for Netscape versions 6.x and 7.x). Let me tell you a story.

Prior to the development of versions 6.x and 7.x of Netscape, Netscape 4.x enjoyed significant success in corporate America, because of its integrated e-mail and Web browsing capabilities. In fact, my first job at Netscape took me to Wall Street, where I spent a month supporting the UNIX version of Netscape 4.x on the trading floor of Morgan Stanley. (Never had I seen, nor have I since seen, so many Sun workstations under one roof.) The popularity of Netscape 4.x in this enterprise role resulted in significant support revenue for Netscape, which helped the company to offset the unfortunate fact (for Netscape) that by the late 1990s, the majority of the Netscape 4.x user base was getting the browser suite for free via download. (The other major source of revenue by this time was advertising associated with the Netscape Web portal, which generated millions of looks when users flocked to the site to download the latest update to Netscape, which was still wildly popular.)

Netscape 6.x (and 7.x) were both based on the same layout engine (Gecko) and user interface toolkit (XML User Interface Language [XUL]). Both Gecko and XUL are complicated pieces of software, and share many interdependencies. Thus, development was difficult, and very time-consuming. Before the release of the first Netscape browser based on these technologies, Netscape was acquired by AOL. Pressures from management at AOL caused Netscape 6.0 to be shipped before it was really ready. (My estimate would place the release date about a year before it was actually of the quality required for public release.) The significant public expectations behind Netscape 6.0, due in no small part to the partnership it had with the open source community through Mozilla, magnified the low quality that this first release of Netscape, post 4.x, was perceived as having. As a result, Netscape 6 was considered somewhat of a disaster.

Based on the poor reception of Netscape 6, those within Netscape and AOL who were banking on further enterprise revenue decided to create a Netscape-like browser suite of their own. Instead of waiting for XUL to mature, this group decided to go with wxWidgets as their GUI toolkit of choice. The effort, largely supported by AOL management, but frowned upon by Netscape management, eventually turned out a fairly decent application suite named AOL Communicator, which supported Web browsing, e-mail, and instant messaging, and like Netscape 6.x, was cross-platform (supporting Mac and Windows only; Linux was left from the mix for reasons unknown). Politically, this was more bad news for the Netscape campus in Mountain View, and as a result, it only helped to hasten its eventual demise with the layoff, or reassignment within AOL, of most of its engineers.

After the Netscape campus was shut down, I was one of the engineers who stayed on, to be reassigned on projects within AOL. My first task was as a member of the team tasked with developing a peer-to-peer video application based on Session Initiation Protocol (SIP) and Real-time Transport Protocol (RTP) for the AOL 9.0 client Instant Messenger. It was after this project that I got my first experience with wxWidgets, by porting the video work I did on the AOL client over to the AOL Communicator codebase (although the result was never released, because AOL Communicator got shelved before the product could be shipped). After AOL, I eventually I went on to use the wxWidgets to develop some cross-platform freeware applications on my own time.

The material in this chapter presents a very detailed overview of wxWidgets. Both wxWidgets, and Qt, which I do not cover in this book but I encourage you to look at, are good candidates for any cross-platform project that has a GUI and must run on Windows, Mac OS X, and/or Linux. One major difference between the Qt and wxWidgets GUI toolkits is the licensing terms employed by each; Qt is free for noncommercial use, with a General Public License (GPL) and its associated requirements, whereas wxWidgets has a license that is more Berkeley Software Distribution (BSD)-like, allowing you to modify it without contributing your changes back to the wxWidgets project (although, it is encouraged that you do so). Qt can also be used for commercial development, but requires developers to purchase a license from a company called Trolltech if it is to be used in this way. wxWidgets does not impose licensing fees for commercial use.

Prentice Hall publishes books that cover GUI programming for both Qt (Jasmine Blanchette and Mark Summerfield's *C++ GUI Programming with Qt 3* [2004]) and wxWidgets (Julian Smart *et al.*'s *Cross-Platform GUI Programming with wxWidgets* [2006]) that you should consider reading if you decide to use either of these GUI toolkits. However, the material presented in this section should go a long ways toward getting you up and running with wxWidgets.

wxWidgets

wxWidgets is a cross-platform GUI toolkit. The wxWidgets project began in the early 1990s at the Artificial Intelligence Applications Institute, University of Edinburgh, where a developer named Julian Smart was tasked with developing an application that needed to run on Windows as well as X-based UNIX workstations. Because commercial cross-platform toolkits were out of the financial reach of Julian's group, they were forced to develop a toolkit of their own. The wxWidgets toolkit was originally implemented as a layer above an X Window System toolkit named XView (which was itself derived from Sun's native GUI toolkit of the time, OpenLook), and above the Microsoft Foundation Classes (MFC) toolkit on the Windows platform. Although neither of these toolkits is used by wxWidgets in its current form, much of the legacy of MFC is evident in the design of both the wxWidgets application programming interface (API) and its event system, which makes learning to use wxWidgets somewhat easier for programmers that have prior experience with MFC.

wxWidgets is distributed in source and binary form. Downloading the source gives you access to sample code that you might find useful as you develop wxWidgets code. The home page for wxWidgets, www.wxwidgets. org, contains download links for the source, as well as links to online documentation. Perhaps the most useful documentation available at that site is the Alphabetical Class Reference, which can be found by searching for the same on the wxWidgets Web site. The contents of this chapter, combined with the Alphabetical Class Reference and sample code from the source distribution should be all you need to develop serious wxWidgets applications.

wxWidgets is similar in scope to both Trixul, described earlier in this book, and another open source toolkit named Qt, which is not described in this book, but is covered in detail in C++ *GUI Programming with Qt 4* (Prentice Hall, 2004). Each of these toolkits provides an abstract API that has implementations for the Mac OS X, Linux, and Windows desktop environments.

Licensing

The license for the version of wxWidgets current at the time this was written is titled wxWindows Library License, Version 3.1. The license basically states that wxWidgets is GPL, with one exception: The copyright owners of the software allow any to use, copy, link, modify, and distribute, under the user's own terms, binary object code versions of works based on the wxWidgets library, and that this exception does not apply to code that is derived from files that are derived in whole or in part from GPL sources different from those distributed as a part of wxWidgets. See the license files distributed along with the wxWidgets sources for the exact details of the wxWidgets licensing terms.

Installing wxWidgets

In this section, I describe how to install wxWidgets on Mac OS X, Windows, and Linux. The instructions are based on the 2.8 stable version of wxWidgets. Your best bet for problem-free development is to always base your work on a stable version of wxWidgets. By the time you read this, the stable version of wxWidgets may be greater than 2.8; if this is the case, download the latest stable version and make the appropriate adjustments. Whatever version of wxWidgets you choose, make sure to use the same version on all three platforms; by mixing versions of wxWidgets, you are likely to encounter portability problems at some point.

See the end of this section for details on integrating wxWidgets into a development tree, and hints on how to distribute wxWidgets with your application.

Mac OS X

First, try running the following command from a terminal:

```
$ wx-config -libs
```

If you get output, wxWidgets is already installed. If not, you need to download sources, build, and install wxWidgets yourself, which I will assume was the case in the remainder of this section. The source is packaged in a tar.gz file. Using a Web browser, visit www.wxwidgets.org, click the Download link, locate the file named wxMac-2.8.0.tar.gz, and download it to a suitable location (for example, your home directory). Next, launch terminal, cd to the directory you just downloaded the tar.gz file to, and enter the following:

```
% tar -zxvf wxMac-2.8.0.tar.gz
% cd wxMac-2.8.0
% ./configure
% make
% sudo make install
```

The preceding steps build and install shared libraries in /usr/local/lib. In /usr/local/include, a directory of include files named wx is installed.

In addition, a utility application named wx-config is installed in /usr/local/bin. This utility can be used from the command line or within a Makefile to generate compiler and linker flags appropriate for the wxWidgets installation. For example, running wx-config with a -libs argument generates the following output suitable for use when linking your application:

```
% wx-config -libs
-L/usr/local/lib -framework QuickTime -framework IOKit\
-framework Carbon -framework Cocoa -framework System \
-lwx_mac_aui-2.8 -lwx_mac_xrc-2.8 -lwx_mac_qa-2.8 \
-lwx_mac_html-2.8 -lwx_mac_adv-2.8 -lwx_mac_core-2.8 \
-lwx_base_carbon_xml-2.8 -lwx_base_carbon_net-2.8 \
-lwx_base_carbon-2.8
```

Similarly, the -cppflags argument generates flags suitable for use in compilation of C++ sources:

```
% wx-config --cppflags
-I/usr/local/lib/wx/include/mac-ansi-release-2.8 \
-I/usr/local/include/wx-2.8 -D_FILE_OFFSET_BITS=64 \
-D_LARGE_FILES -D__WXMAC__
```

Linux

Installation on Linux is similar to Mac OS X. Likely, it will be already available on your system. If not, use your platform's update mechanism (for example, yum `install wxGTK-devel` under Fedora Core) to obtain a developer package, or grab sources from the wxWidgets Web site, and build them as described earlier for Mac OS X, making sure instead to grab the wxGTK sources.

Windows

To install wxWidgets on a Windows system, you need to download the source code and build wxWidgets libraries and dynamic link libraries (DLLs). The following instructions assume use of Visual Studio .NET to build the wxWidgets libraries:

1. Download wxMSW-2.8.0-setup.zip from wxWidgets.org to a temporary directory on your PC, and unpack it using WinZIP or a similar program.
2. Run setup.exe, installing in the default location (c:\wxWidgets-2.8.0).
3. Using Windows Explorer, change to c:\wxWindows-2.8.0\ build\msw.
4. Double-click the file named wx.dsw. You may be asked whether you want to convert the project files to .NET. Click the Yes to All button to convert this file and all others to .NET.
5. Select the Build, Configuration Manager menu item in Visual Studio.
6. Select Debug DLL from the Active Solution Configuration combo box.
7. Click the Close button to dismiss the dialog.
8. Select Build, Build Solution to build the wxWidgets debug DLLs.
9. Select the Build, Configuration Manager menu item in Visual Studio.
10. Select Release DLL from the Active Solution Configuration combo box.

11. Click the Close button to dismiss the dialog.

12. Select Build, Build Solution to build the wxWidgets release DLLs.

See the install.txt in c:\wxWidgets-2.8.0\docs\msw for more information.

A Simple Example: Hello wxWidgets

A simple "Hello World" program illustrates the portability of wxWidgets, and provides some insight into the mechanics behind building and linking wxWidgets applications on Linux, Mac OS X, and Windows.

The application is, by design, a simple one. It does little more than display a resizable window with the text "Hello World!" at its center. If the window is resized by the user, the text is redrawn so that "Hello World!" always remains centered in the window.

wxWidgets is organized as a set of classes that, when combined, can be used to create and manage a user interface (UI). Most of these classes implement what is referred to as a *widget,* a term which goes back to the early days of X11's Xt toolkit; Gtk+, Qt, MFC, and many other GUI toolkits embody the same term. In the abstract, a widget is something that is displayed in the UI, but not all widgets are necessarily visible to a user. Windows, buttons, icons, scrollbars, and static text are all examples of widgets. (Often, classes implementing such objects derive from a class named Widget or something similar.)

The "Hello World" application uses several widgets to make up its UI. These widgets fall into one of two generic categories found in most widget sets: container and control. Control widgets represent objects in the UI that are visible and can be interacted with (for the most part) by the user— buttons, menu items, scrollbars, and labels are all examples of control widgets. Container widgets organize control widgets in some way, and affect how they are laid out. For example, a grid or table widget manages controls as a set of cells in a table with some number of rows and columns. A tab widget, to cite another example, organizes groups of related widgets into tabs that can be selected and traversed by a user. A menu is a container that manages a set of menu items (and a menu bar is a container that manages a set of menus). Container widgets can manage other container widgets, too, which allows a UI designer to create complicated layouts that are otherwise not directly supported by the container widgets supplied by the toolkit. The nesting of containers can occur to an arbitrary depth.

"Hello World" Control Widgets

The only control widget class used directly in the "Hello World" application is wxStaticText. The wxStaticText widget class does one thing only: display a text string. The content of the string displayed by wxStaticText and the placement of the control in its parent container can both be specified as arguments to the wxStaticText constructor. wxStaticText member functions allow you to retrieve, as a wxString object, the value of the text displayed by a wxStaticText widget, and set its value. (The value can be changed dynamically during the lifetime of the widget.)

The wxStaticText class, as you might imagine, inherits from other classes in the wxWidgets class hierarchy. The inheritance hierarchy for wxStaticText (in increasing order of abstraction, or, if you prefer, decreasing order of specialization) is as follows: wxControl, wxWindow, wxEvtHandler, and finally, wxObject. These classes are ubiquitous, and seen in the inheritance hierarchies of a great many wxWidgets control classes. We saw that member functions in wxStaticText allow us to manipulate the label displayed by instances. wxControl provides an interface by which code can send commands to a widget for it to process. wxWindow is the largest class in the hierarchy, which reflects the fact that most widgets are, in fact, windows. wxWindow is responsible, by and large, for managing window attributes such as size, position, visibility, and state. Because of the importance of wxWindow, I cover it in detail later in this chapter. wxEvtHandler implements the grander scheme of event and command processing, which is central to the client architecture of a wxWidgets application, and which, once again, I will go into in greater detail later in this chapter. Finally, wxObject implements extremely abstract functionality needed by all widgets in the wxWidgets class hierarchy, functionality that can be largely ignored by programmers.

"Hello World" Container Widgets

Far more interesting, at least in the context of the "Hello World" application, are the container widgets that it uses. The two wxWidgets container classes instantiated in "Hello World" are wxFrame and wxBoxSizer. A wxFrame widget simply creates a window with a given size, which is positioned on the screen at a given location, and supports a title bar and menus. A wxBoxSizer widget (or sizer, for short), the more conceptually difficult of the two widgets used, is responsible for maintaining the layout of the content displayed in the wxFrame widget. The position (or layout) of the static text widget, which is placed inside of a sizer, is dependent on attributes defined by the sizer. Among these attributes are the orientation of the widgets parented by the sizer (either horizontal or vertical), and the spacing that exists between them. Two sizer widgets are used in the "Hello World" application to implement the requirement that the static text label be centered vertically and horizontally within the application's top-level window. Sizers are active during the lifetime of the application; as the window is resized by the user, the sizers compute the layout of their children. Thus, even after a resize, "Hello World!" will remain centered in the top-level window. (I have more to say about sizers later in this chapter.)

Creating the Application User Interface

Abstractly speaking, the UI for the application is created as follows. First, an instance of wxFrame is created with a specified width, height, and screen location. Next, a horizontal sizer widget is created and made a child of the top-level window. Next, a vertical sizer widget is created and made a child of the horizontal sizer. Finally, an instance of wxStaticText is created and made a child of the vertical sizer.

Before we look at source code that implements the concepts just described, there is one more, very important class that needs to be described: wxApp.

wxApp

wxApp is, roughly speaking, the wxWidgets analogue of the main() function in a C or C++ program. All wxWidgets applications must instantiate wxApp, which provides event loop management, and overall application context. There is a well-defined pattern for the use of wxApp. Perhaps the best way to go about communicating this pattern is to look at the related code snippets from the "Hello World" application.

First, your application must declares a class that inherits from wxApp:

```
class MyApp : public wxApp
{
public:
    virtual bool OnInit();
};
```

The wxApp base class contains a variety of virtual functions, but only one, OnInit(), must be overridden by applications:

```
bool MyApp::OnInit()
{
    // code to create main UI goes here,
    // as described in the text
    return TRUE;
}
```

OnInit() is where your application creates its main window, as discussed in more detail in the next section. On success, OnInit() should return TRUE; returning FALSE will cause your application to exit.

The final step is to use the macro IMPLEMENT_APP to, in essence, register your wxApp-derived class with wxWidgets:

```
IMPLEMENT_APP(MyApp)
```

The IMPLEMENT_APP macro also defines your application's main() function.

The Application Main Window

Now let's take a closer look at OnInit(). Once again, this required function is where you implement your application's main window. Here is the complete version of OnInit() from the "Hello World" application:

```
bool MyApp::OnInit()
{
    MyFrame *frame = new MyFrame(_T("Hello World"),
        wxPoint(50, 50), wxSize(600, 340));

    if (frame) {
        frame->Show(TRUE);
        return TRUE;
    } else
        return FALSE;
}
```

MyFrame is a class, defined by the application, that inherits from wxFrame. The MyFrame constructor takes three arguments: the title of the window, the initial position of the window on the screen, and the initial size of the window. After the main window has been constructed, the Show() method is called to display it, and TRUE is returned to let wxWidgets know that everything went as planned. As mentioned earlier, returning FALSE causes wxWidgets to exit the application. Here is the declaration of the class MyFrame:

```
class MyFrame : public wxFrame
{
public:
    MyFrame(const wxString& title, const wxPoint& pos,
        const wxSize& size);
};
```

Once again, the constructor accepts as arguments a window title, the x and y position of the window, and its size. The constructor is defined as follows:

```
MyFrame::MyFrame(const wxString& title,
    const wxPoint& pos, const wxSize& size)
    : wxFrame((wxFrame *)NULL, -1, title, pos, size)
{
    wxBoxSizer *topsizer =
        new wxBoxSizer(wxHORIZONTAL);
    wxBoxSizer *vertsizer =
        new wxBoxSizer(wxVERTICAL);
    wxStaticText *text = new wxStaticText(this, -1,
        _T("Hello World!"));
    topsizer->Add(vertsizer, 1,
        wxALIGN_CENTER | wxALL, 10);
    vertsizer->Add(text, 1,
        wxALIGN_CENTER | wxALL, 10);
    SetSizer(topsizer);
}
```

This is where all the complexity of the "Hello World" application is implemented. Notice the initialization of wxFrame. Its constructor is defined as follows:

```
wxFrame(wxWindow* parent,
    wxWindowID id,
    const wxString& title,
    const wxPoint& pos = wxDefaultPosition,
    const wxSize& size = wxDefaultSize,
    long style = wxDEFAULT_FRAME_STYLE,
    const wxString& name = "frame");
```

Notice that only the first three arguments to the constructor are actually required, because the remaining have default initializations. The constructor arguments reflect a design decision to allow my application to override the position and size of the window; that the parent, although not supported by a default initializer, is always NULL; and that the application has no concern with the style of the frame, nor does it care what internal ID or name it is assigned.

The bulk of MyFrame's constructor responsibility is to define the content and layout of the frame. As previously mentioned, the content is a text string with the value "Hello World!" and the layout is managed by two sizers, one vertical and one horizontal, to achieve the desired effect of centering "Hello World!" in the frame. Let's build out the implementation of this function step by step, starting with the creation of the static text, and then moving on to the layout of the frame itself.

Static text is implemented, naturally enough, by the wxStaticText class. Its constructor is nearly the same as wxFrame:

```
wxStaticText(wxWindow* parent, wxWindowID id,
    const wxString& label, const wxPoint& pos,
    const wxSize& size = wxDefaultSize, long style = 0,
    const wxString& name = "staticText");
```

To create the static text widget, allocate an instance of wxStaticText on the heap, as follows:

```
wxStaticText *text = new wxStaticText(this, -1,
    _T("Hello World!"));
```

So far, we have this:

```
MyFrame::MyFrame(const wxString& title,
    const wxPoint& pos, const wxSize& size)
    : wxFrame((wxFrame *)NULL, -1, title, pos, size)
{

    wxStaticText *text = new wxStaticText(this, -1,
        _T("Hello World!"));
}
```

After compiling and running this program, we get the result shown in Figure 8-1.

Figure 8-1 wxWidgets "Hello World!"

Note a few things here. First, because the static text widget is managed by the frame widget's sizer, it is automatically displayed along with the content of the frame when Show() is called by MyApp::OnInit(). Therefore, there is no need to call Show() explicitly for the static text widget. Second, wxWidgets ensures that destruction of the static text widget occurs when the containing frame is destroyed; there is no need, therefore, to retain a copy of the wxStaticText instance pointer to perform the destruction explicitly. (You might want to retain the pointer for other reasons, such as changing the text it displays, but that is not a requirement in this application.)

Before I go on to describe the use of the sizers, imagine for a moment how you might go about implementing the layout of the window in a toolkit that does not provide explicit layout support. (MFC is an example of such a toolkit.) The only rational approach would be to explicitly compute the position of the static text widget whenever the user resizes the window. Without going into great detail here, wxWidgets enables you to handle window size events, and within this handler, you can query for the width and height of the containing window, and, along with the length of the string being displayed and font metrics such as width and height, compute a new x, y position for the string and, finally, change the position of the text string in the window by calling the SetSize() function that wxStaticText inherits from wxWindow. However, it's much easier to let a pair of sizers do the work for you. Let's add a horizontal sizer to the frame, discuss the mechanics behind the change, and see what effect it has on the layout of the window:

```
MyFrame::MyFrame(const wxString& title,
    const wxPoint& pos, const wxSize& size)
    : wxFrame((wxFrame *)NULL, -1, title, pos, size)
{
    wxBoxSizer *topsizer =
        new wxBoxSizer(wxHORIZONTAL);
    wxStaticText *text =
        new wxStaticText(this, -1, _T("Hello World!"));
    topsizer->Add(text, 1, wxALIGN_CENTER | wxALL, 10);
    SetSizer(topsizer);
}
```

The sizer, as was the case with the static text widget, is allocated on the heap. The function prototype for the wxBoxSizer constructor is simple:

```
wxBoxSizer(int orientation);
```

where *orientation* is either wxHORIZONTAL or wxVERTICAL. A vertical sizer organizes its children from top to bottom, whereas a horizontal sizer organizes children left to right. The wxStaticText widget, after creation, is made a child of the horizontal sizer with a call to its Add() member function:

```
topsizer->Add(text, 1, wxALIGN_CENTER | wxALL, 10);
```

The Add() member function accepts as arguments a child widget, which in this case is the static text widget instance, and, optionally, a proportion, a set of flags, and a border width. The proportion argument is used to control how much of the available window real estate is consumed by the widget being added to the sizer, in relation to other children that the sizer manages. Generally speaking, proportion should be set to either 0 or 1. If set to 0, the widget yields window real estate to other children of the sizer, consuming only that which its intrinsic size demands. If set to 1, however, the child will consume all the available space that is not already being consumed by the other children of the sizer. (How much space is available is based on the proportions that each of the other children have requested.) Some progressive examples illustrate the point. If three widgets are added to a sizer and each specifies a proportion of 0, each will be allocated only the space they need to display their content. If one of the widgets specifies a proportion of 1, the remaining two widgets will obtain only the space they need, while the widget claiming a proportion of 1 claims all the remaining space. If one widget specifies a proportion of 0, and the other two widgets specify a proportion of 1, the first widget will be given only the space needed to display itself, and the other two widgets will split the remaining space among themselves. Finally, if all three widgets specify a proportion of 1, the available space is split into three equally sized chunks to be allocated to each of the widgets sharing the overall space of the containing widget.

The flags argument (wxALIGN_CENTER | wxALL in this example) controls two aspects of the widget's layout within the sizer. wxALIGN_CENTER tells the sizer how to align the child in its major orientation, but to understand the effect, it is better to think of what happens in terms of the opposite orientation. In this example, the major orientation is horizontal, because we passed wxHORIZONTAL as an argument to the wxBoxSizer constructor, so you'll want to think of placements relative to the top, center, and bottom of the space occupied by the sizer. The effect of specifying wxALIGN_CENTER, for example, is that the text is placed halfway from the top and bottom of the sizer (see Figure 8-2). To align the static text to the top of the sizer, specify wxALIGN_TOP; likewise, wxALIGN_BOTTOM causes the text to be placed at the bottom of the sizer.

Figure 8-2 wxALIGN_CENTER applied to a horizontal sizer

When applied to a vertical sizer (that is, wxVERTICAL is passed as an argument to the wxBoxSizer constructor), the flags wxALIGN_CENTER, wxALIGN_RIGHT, and wxALIGN_LEFT apply in analogous ways. Figure 8-3 illustrates the result for wxALIGN_CENTER.

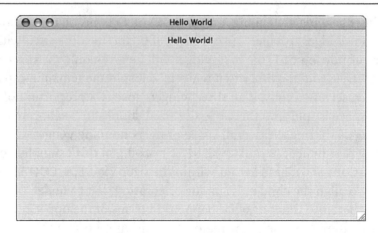

Figure 8-3 wxALIGN_CENTER applied to a vertical sizer

The other option specified in the call to Add(), wxALL, is one of several flags that are used to control how spacing is placed around the child widget. wxALL tells the sizer to add space to the left and right of the widget, as well as above and below, and is equivalent to specifying wxTOP | wxBOTTOM | wxLEFT | wxRIGHT. The size of the border comes from the fourth argument to Add(), which in the sample code presented above, is equal to 10 pixels.

So far, we have a window that displays static text aligned to the left edge of the window, halfway between the window top and bottom. Although the vertical placement is correct, we need to find a way to nudge the text so that it is centered horizontally between the left and right edges of the window. To do this, we introduce another box sizer, this time a vertical one. Here is the final code:

```
MyFrame::MyFrame(const wxString& title,
    const wxPoint& pos, const wxSize& size)
    : wxFrame((wxFrame *)NULL, -1, title, pos, size)
{
    wxBoxSizer *topsizer =
        new wxBoxSizer(wxHORIZONTAL);
    wxBoxSizer *vertsizer =
        new wxBoxSizer(wxVERTICAL);
    wxStaticText *text =
        new wxStaticText(this, -1, _T("Hello World!"));
    topsizer->Add(vertsizer, 1,
        wxALIGN_CENTER | wxALL, 10);
    vertsizer->Add(text, 1,
        wxALIGN_CENTER | wxALL, 10);
    SetSizer(topsizer);
}
```

The major change here involves replacing the child of the horizontal sizer, previously a static text widget, with a vertical sizer. The vertical sizer is aligned in the center of the horizontal sizer, halfway between the top and bottom of the window, just as was the case for the static text widget. The static text widget is then made a child of the vertical sizer, and because wxALIGN_CENTER is specified when adding the text widget to the vertical sizer, it is placed halfway between the left and right edges of the window. The net effect is that the static text widget is centered in the window, as desired (see Figure 8-4).

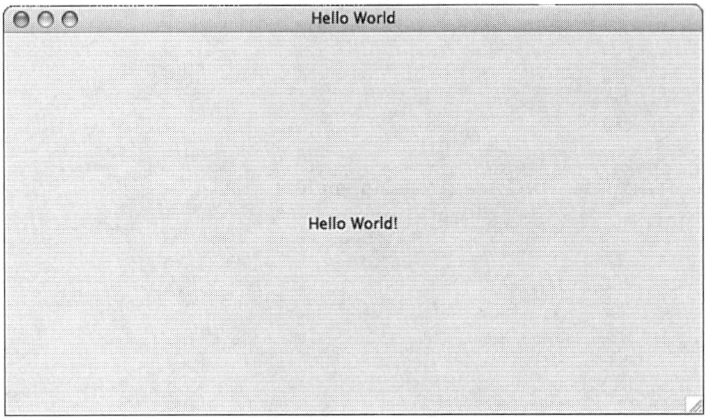

Figure 8-4 Combining vertical and horizontal sizers to center text in a window

The sizer will automatically recompute the layout of the window whenever the user sizes the window, ensuring that the text is vertically and horizontally centered.

Building wxWidgets Applications

So, now that we have taken a look at the design and implementation of the "Hello World" application, it's time to investigate what is required to build and run it on Linux, Mac OS X, and Windows.

Here is the complete source code for "Hello World." Type it into a text file named hello.cpp, or download hello.cpp from the book's Web site before continuing. If you haven't yet installed wxWidgets on your system(s) using the steps described earlier in this chapter, do so now.

```
#include "wx/wx.h"

class MyApp : public wxApp
{
public:
    virtual bool OnInit();
};

class MyFrame : public wxFrame
{
public:
    MyFrame(const wxString& title,
        const wxPoint& pos, const wxSize& size);
};

bool MyApp::OnInit()
{
    MyFrame *frame = new MyFrame(_T("Hello World"),
        wxPoint(50, 50), wxSize(600, 340));

    frame->Show(TRUE);

    return TRUE;
}

IMPLEMENT_APP(MyApp)

MyFrame::MyFrame(const wxString& title,
    const wxPoint& pos, const wxSize& size)
    : wxFrame((wxFrame *)NULL, -1, title, pos, size)
{
    wxBoxSizer *topsizer =
        new wxBoxSizer(wxHORIZONTAL);
    wxBoxSizer *vertsizer =
        new wxBoxSizer(wxVERTICAL);
    wxStaticText *text =
        new wxStaticText(this, -1, _T("Hello World!"));
    topsizer->Add(vertsizer, 1,
        wxALIGN_CENTER | wxALL, 10);
    vertsizer->Add(text, 1,
        wxALIGN_CENTER | wxALL, 10);
    SetSizer(topsizer);
}
```

Linux

We begin with Linux because it is the easiest of the three platforms. I'm not going to get fancy with Makefiles; I'll keep it simple so we can focus on issues specific to wxWidgets. In your home directory (~/ or $HOME), create a directory called `hello`, and then copy the hello.cpp file to this directory. Next, create the following Makefile in the same directory, being mindful of the correct location of tabs. If you prefer, you can download Hello.Makefile.Linux from this book's Web site and rename it to Makefile.

```
CXX = g++
PROGRAM = hello
OBJECTS = $(PROGRAM).o
.cpp.o :
    $(CXX) -c `wx-config --cxxflags` -o $@ $<
$(PROGRAM): $(OBJECTS)
    $(CXX) -o $(PROGRAM) $(OBJECTS) `wx-config --libs`
clean:
    rm -f *.o $(PROGRAM)
```

There are two aspects of this Makefile worth describing; the rest is boiler-plate that anyone familiar with make should immediately recognize. The first involves the lines used to create hello.o from hello.cpp:

```
.cpp.o :
$(CXX) -c `wx-config --cxxflags` -o $@ $<
```

The shell command `wx-config -cxxflags` generates output that sets appropriate compiler flags, defines, and header paths (as described earlier in this chapter). Similarly, `wx-config` with a `-libs` argument is used to generate linker arguments, and is used here in the Makefile:

```
$(PROGRAM): $(OBJECTS)
$(CXX) -o $(PROGRAM) $(OBJECTS) `wx-config --libs`
```

To build the "Hello World" application, make sure `wx-config` is in your search path, and then type `make` at the shell prompt:

```
$ make
g++  -c `wx-config --cxxflags`
-o hello.o hello.cpp
g++  -o hello hello.o `wx-config --libs`
```

To run the application, just type `./hello` at the prompt:

```
$ ./hello
```

Try resizing the window, both vertically and horizontally. You will see that the "Hello World!" text remains centered. The automatic handling of resize events is one of the advantages of using sizers in a dialog or window.

Mac OS X

Building the "Hello World" application on Mac OS X is nearly identical to building it on Linux, with one exception: You must place the resulting binary in an app bundle (see Item 15). To do so, create the following folder hierarchy:

```
hello.app/Contents/MacOS
```

and copy hello, after it is built, into the Mac OS directory. It is important that the .app suffix be used. You can use something other than hello; it does not matter, but it is important that the name used matches the name of the application. (For example, if the application is named foo, the folder must be named foo.app.) Then, from the finder, navigate to the parent directory, and click the icon named hello to launch the application.

One difference that you will notice when running "Hello World" on Mac OS X is that the menu bar on Mac OS X will be blank whenever "Hello World" has application focus. (There is no menu bar specified in the source, which explains this behavior; "Hello World" is a toy application that doesn't have a menu bar.) Menus are discussed later in this chapter.

Windows

The steps required to build on Windows are different from those of both Linux and Mac OS X, mostly because of the use of the MS-DOS command window, `nmake`, and the command-line compiler provided with Visual Studio .NET, all of which are patently dissimilar to the tools one encounters on Mac OS X and Linux.

Notice that wxWidgets on Windows does not provide a utility like `wx-config`. Because of this, the compiler and linker flags need to be determined externally, and supplied explicitly in the text of the Makefile. Numerous Makefile examples are provided by wxWidgets that you can use as a starting point for creating your own Makefiles. For example, look at c:\wxWidgets-2.8.0\samples\dialogs\makefile.vc for a Makefile compatible with Microsoft Visual C++.

Controls and Events

Controls are the items in a window or a dialog that users interact with; buttons, labels, lists, check boxes, radio buttons, and scrollbars are among the controls one finds in nearly every desktop application. Each control class in wxWidgets inherits from a few fundamental wxWidgets base classes. Because a control is a window, it inherits from wxWindow, the wxWidgets class that provides support for all classes that manage a window of their own. Because a control needs to process events, and needs to provide a mechanism through which application code can be notified of events, it inherits also from wxEvtHandler. Finally, all controls inherit from a simple class named wxControl.

Using a control is a matter of creating an instance of the desired control class, adding it to the UI, and arranging for it to communicate with the application as the design of the application dictates. One then, optionally, uses interfaces from wxWindow to manage aspects of the control as, once again, the needs of the application dictate.

The following listing illustrates the basics involved in using controls—in this case, menus and buttons—in a wxWidgets application. The application creates a window that has a button labeled "Click Me!" When this button is clicked, the application prints "I've been clicked!" to the console. The application also illustrates the creation of a File menu with a Quit menu item which, when selected, causes the application to exit.

This application exhibits an architecture similar to the one presented earlier in this chapter by the "Hello World" application. The class MyApp remains the same as in the "Hello World" application. However, as the following code shows, two functions, OnQuit() and OnClickMe(), and one new member variable, m_clickButton, have been added to the definition of MyFrame. The new functions are callback functions. The function OnQuit() is invoked when the user selects the Quit menu item in the File menu. The function OnClickMe() is called when the user clicks the Click Me! push button. The member variable m_clickButton stores a pointer to the Click Me! push button, which is an instance of wxButton. Storing this pointer in the class isn't required at this point (it could be declared on the stack, and often this is exactly what applications do), but storing a pointer to the button in the MyFrame object will come in handy later in this section when we make modifications to the application. Here is the code discussed so far:

```
#include "wx/wx.h"

class MyApp: public wxApp
{
    virtual bool OnInit();
};

class MyFrame: public wxFrame
{
public:
    MyFrame(const wxString& title, const wxPoint& pos,
        const wxSize& size);
    void OnQuit(wxCommandEvent& event);
    void OnClickMe(wxCommandEvent& event);
private:
    wxButton *m_clickButton;

    DECLARE_EVENT_TABLE()
};
```

An important modification to the MyFrame class is the introduction of a
wxWidgets macro named DECLARE_EVENT_TABLE. The event table is the
basis by which events are dispatched to objects in your application. The
event table supports both low-level events one would expect to receive from
the underlying native toolkit, such as window resizing and mouse movement, and more abstract events such as menu item selections and push
button presses. Declaring an event table in a class with the DECLARE_EVENT_
TABLE macro is the first step toward making a class a sink for either type of
event. The following code is the definition of the DECLARE_EVENT_TABLE
macro as of wxWidgets 2.4.2:

```
#define DECLARE_EVENT_TABLE() \
    private: \
        static const \
            wxEventTableEntry sm_eventTableEntries[]; \
    protected: \
        static const wxEventTable sm_eventTable; \
        virtual const wxEventTable* \
            GetEventTable() const;
```

Let's look at this macro in detail. The event table (sm_eventTable) is
little more than a struct that contains two fields. One field points to the event
table of the base class (which, in this case, is wxFrame). Notice that the event

table is static; later we will see where the event table is actually declared. The other field points to the `sm_eventTableEntries` member variable that is declared immediately above it as a private member variable. When an event comes in (for example, left mouse button down), wxWidgets obtains a pointer to the event table of the class, using the `GetEventTable()` function implementation that is provided by the class. (Notice that `GetEventTable()` is declared virtual; the expectation of wxWidgets is that `MyFrame` will provide an implementation, and I show how this is done later.) With this table in hand, wxWidgets then iterates the `sm_eventTableEntries` vector, searching for an element in the table that implements a handler for the event that is being processed. If a match is found in this table, wxWidgets simply invokes the handler function that is stored in that entry of the table. If no match is found in this table, wxWidgets then continues its search for a handler by looking in the event table of the base class (using the base class pointer stored in the event table of the object). If the base class does not supply a handler, the search continues up through the inheritance hierarchy.

If no handler is found in the inheritance hierarchy, and the event is a `wxCommandEvent`-derived event (`wxCommandEvent` is defined later), then the window containment hierarchy is searched. The window containment hierarchy represents the nesting of wxWidgets class instances in other wxWidgets class instances by the application. For example, an instance of `wxButton` might be the child of an instance of `wxFrame` in the window containment hierarchy of an application. If an instance of `wxButton` (and its parent classes) does not implement an event handler for a button press, wxWidgets will then query the instance of `wxFrame`, and if it handles that event, its event handler function will be invoked. The code described later in this section illustrates exactly the containment hierarchy just described. By handling `wxButton` events in `MyFrame` (which derives from `wxFrame`), my code avoids needing to implement a class derived from `wxButton`, which would be needed to implement button press events at the level of wxButton. It also makes more sense implementing the event handler in `MyFrame` because `MyFrame` is much better suited to perform the logic associated with the button press.

Before we continue, I need to describe `wxCommandEvent` events. A `wxCommandEvent` event is an abstract event that corresponds to an action involving a control, such as the push of a button or the selection of a menu item. Events that do not derive from `wxCommandEvent` correspond to system-level events, such as mouse movement, keyboard pressing, window resizing, to mention just a few. Most applications are not concerned with lower-level

events, and focus most of their effort on the handling of wxCommandEvent-
derived events. It makes sense that event propagation in the containment
hierarchy is only performed for wxCommandEvent-derived events. Only
the widget that implements the window that pertains to the non-
wxCommandEvent event needs to know about the event. The fact that a
window has been resized, or a low-level mouse move event has occurred, is
only of interest to the widget that created the window. It needs to decide
how to handle the event on its own; and if communication with other
widgets in the inheritance or class hierarchy is required as a part of that
processing, it is up to the widget handling the event to ensure that whatever
communication needed is performed.

The second step in wiring up event handlers is to add entries in the event
table so that each of the events you want an instance of a class instance to
handle will be dispatched correctly by wxWidgets as they occur. This is done
by defining, at file scope, the event table that was declared by the DECLARE_
EVENT_TABLE macro inside the class (recall that the event table was declared
static, so it needs a definition outside the class), and adding entries to the
table for each event you want the class instance to handle. To define the
event table, wxWidgets provides the BEGIN_EVENT_TABLE and END_EVENT_
TABLE macros:

```
#define BEGIN_EVENT_TABLE(theClass, baseClass) \
    const wxEventTable \
        *theClass::GetEventTable() const \
        { return &theClass::sm_eventTable; } \
    const wxEventTable theClass::sm_eventTable = \
        { &baseClass::sm_eventTable, \
        &theClass::sm_eventTableEntries[0] }; \
    const wxEventTableEntry \
        theClass::sm_eventTableEntries[] = { \

#define END_EVENT_TABLE() DECLARE_EVENT_TABLE_ENTRY( \
    wxEVT_NULL, 0, 0, 0, 0 ) };
```

The following code illustrates these macros in use:

```
BEGIN_EVENT_TABLE(MyFrame, wxFrame)
    EVT_MENU(ID_Quit, MyFrame::OnQuit)
    EVT_BUTTON(ID_CLICK_ME, MyFrame::OnClickMe)
END_EVENT_TABLE()
```

The first argument to the BEGIN_EVENT_TABLE macro is the name of the concrete class (MyFrame) that will be handling the events enumerated in the event table, and the second argument is the name of the base class (wxFrame), which will be searched if the search in the event table for the concrete class comes up empty. The END_EVENT_TABLE macro terminates the event table definition by adding an end marker; iteration of entries in the event table stops when this end marker is reached.

Between the BEGIN_EVENT_TABLE and END_EVENT_TABLE macros are macros that map specific events to handler functions implemented by the MyFrame class. The preceding code illustrates two of these macros. The first, EVT_MENU, is used to map menu item selection events, and the second, EVT_BUTTON, is used to map clicks of wxButton widget instances. The first argument to each of these macros is the window ID of the widget for which the mapping is being specified, and the second argument is a reference to the class member function that will be invoked when the event occurs. The window ID is specified by the application as an argument to the function that instantiates the widget, as I illustrate later. The window ID usually comes from an enumeration provided by the programmer in the same source file, before the event table declaration is made, or in a header file:

```
enum
{
    ID_Quit,
    ID_CLICK_ME,
};
```

The values used are not important, other than they must be unique (and because controls do not contain other controls, uniqueness is not a problem in practice).

There are well over one hundred EVT_ macros defined by wxWidgets. I describe many of them later when I discuss the widget classes that they support.

Now all that remains is to provide implementations for the handler functions OnClickMe() and OnQuit(). First, we need to work through some more of the source code. The following lines should be familiar from the "Hello World" application described earlier in this chapter:

```
IMPLEMENT_APP(MyApp)

bool MyApp::OnInit()
{
```

```
MyFrame *frame = new MyFrame( "Click Me Demo",
    wxPoint(50,50), wxSize(450,340) );
frame->Show(TRUE);
SetTopWindow(frame);
return TRUE;
}
```

Creating the User Interface

It is within the constructor of the MyFrame class that we create the UI. One of the UI items that we must create is a File menu with a single menu item labeled Exit. The following code illustrates the creation of the menu, which involves creating the File menu (an instance of wxMenu), appending an Exit menu item to the File menu, creating a menu bar, and finally, appending the File menu to the menu bar. The last step is making the menu bar active for the window associated with the MyFrame instance with a call to SetMenuBar():

```
MyFrame::MyFrame(const wxString& title,
    const wxPoint& pos, const wxSize& size)
    : wxFrame((wxFrame *)NULL, -1, title, pos, size),
    m_enabled(true)
{
    wxMenu *menu = new wxMenu;

    menu->Append(ID_Quit, "E&xit");

    wxMenuBar *menuBar = new wxMenuBar;
    menuBar->Append(menu, "&File");

    SetMenuBar(menuBar);
```

The only remaining task in creating the UI is to instantiate the push button widget and make it a child of the frame. Creating the button is easy; we just invoke the wxButton constructor, passing it a pointer to its parent widget, its ID (ID_CLICK_ME), and the text that it should display as a label:

```
m_clickButton = new wxButton(this, ID_CLICK_ME,
    "Click Me!");
```

To manage the layout of the button in the frame, we next make use of the wxBoxSizer class. In general, each dialog, window, or frame that you create in an application that manages one or more controls should use an instance of wxSizer or one of its derived classes to manage the layout of its child widgets. (See "A Simple Example: Hello wxWidgets" presented earlier in this chapter for an example of the use of sizers to center a text widget in a window.) Most likely, you will be using a wxBoxSizer widget for this task. Below, I instantiate a horizontal wxBoxSizer widget. Horizontal box sizers lay out their children, horizontally, left to right, as children are added. First, we instantiate the sizer:

```
wxBoxSizer *topSizer =
    new wxBoxSizer(wxHORIZONTAL);
```

and then we add the push button widget as its child:

```
topSizer->Add(m_clickButton, 0,
    wxTOP | wxALL, 5);
```

Later, I illustrate how to add a second button, also managed by the horizontal sizer.

The final step is to make the topSizer instance the sizer for the frame; this is done by calling SetSizer() as follows:

```
SetSizer(topSizer);
}
```

Event Handler Function Implementations

Now on to the event handler functions. First up is MyFrame::OnQuit():

```
void MyFrame::OnQuit(wxCommandEvent& WXUNUSED(event))
{
    Close(TRUE);
}
```

The OnQuit() function is invoked when the Quit menu item in the File menu is selected by the user. It calls Close() (which is implemented by wxWindow, a class inherited by wxFrame) to cause the application to exit. The TRUE argument to Close() sets a flag that indicates the close should not be vetoed by a close handler. I talk more about this flag and vetoing (or event skipping) later.

The other handler function, OnClickMe(), simply prints "I've been clicked!" to stdout. To see this output, run the sample from a command window. Here is the code for OnClickMe():

```
void MyFrame::OnClickMe(
    wxCommandEvent& WXUNUSED(event))
{
    printf("I've been clicked!\n");
    fflush(stdout);
}
```

Adding a Second Button

You have now learned the basics for creating controls and wiring them up to event handlers. To see some of the other things you might do with a control, let's add a second button to our UI. This button will initially display the label "Disable." When it is clicked, it will disable the Click Me! button and change its label to "Enable." Clicking it again will enable the Click Me! button, and change its label back to "Disable." Here is the complete listing for this application (with new code shown in bold):

```
#include "wx/wx.h"

class MyApp: public wxApp
{
    virtual bool OnInit();
};

class MyFrame: public wxFrame
{
public:

    MyFrame(const wxString& title, const wxPoint& pos,
        const wxSize& size);

    void OnQuit(wxCommandEvent& event);
    void OnClickMe(wxCommandEvent& event);
    void OnDisableEnable(wxCommandEvent& event);
private:
    bool m_enabled;
    wxButton *m_enableButton;
    wxButton *m_clickButton;

    DECLARE_EVENT_TABLE()
};

enum
{
```

```
      ID_Quit,
      ID_CLICK_ME,
      ID_DISABLE_ENABLE
};


BEGIN_EVENT_TABLE(MyFrame, wxFrame)
    EVT_MENU(ID_Quit, MyFrame::OnQuit)
    EVT_BUTTON(ID_CLICK_ME, MyFrame::OnClickMe)
    EVT_BUTTON(ID_DISABLE_ENABLE,
        MyFrame::OnDisableEnable)
END_EVENT_TABLE()


IMPLEMENT_APP(MyApp)


bool MyApp::OnInit()
{
    MyFrame *frame = new MyFrame( "Click Me Demo",
        wxPoint(50,50), wxSize(450,340) );
    frame->Show(TRUE);
    SetTopWindow(frame);
    return TRUE;
}


MyFrame::MyFrame(const wxString& title,
    const wxPoint& pos, const wxSize& size)
    : wxFrame((wxFrame *)NULL, -1, title, pos, size),
    m_enabled(true)
{
    wxMenu *menu = new wxMenu;

    menu->Append(ID_Quit, "E&xit");

    wxMenuBar *menuBar = new wxMenuBar;
    menuBar->Append(menu, "&File");

    SetMenuBar(menuBar);

    wxBoxSizer *topSizer =
        new wxBoxSizer(wxHORIZONTAL);
    m_clickButton =
        new wxButton(this, ID_CLICK_ME, "Click Me!");
    topSizer->Add(m_clickButton, 0, wxTOP | wxALL, 5);
    m_enableButton =
        new wxButton(this,
            ID_DISABLE_ENABLE, "Disable");
```

```
    topSizer->Add(m_enableButton, 0, wxTOP | wxALL, 5);
    SetSizer(topSizer);
}

void
MyFrame::OnQuit(wxCommandEvent& WXUNUSED(event))
{
    Close(TRUE);
}

void
MyFrame::OnClickMe(wxCommandEvent& WXUNUSED(event))
{
    printf("I've been clicked!\n");
    fflush(stdout);
}

void
MyFrame::OnDisableEnable(
    wxCommandEvent& WXUNUSED(event))
{
    m_enabled = (m_enabled == true ? false : true);
    m_clickButton->Enable(m_enabled);
    if (m_enabled) {
        m_enableButton->SetLabel("Disable");
    } else {
        m_enableButton->SetLabel("Enable");
    }
}
```

Let's start with the event handler function for the Disable/Enable button, and work our way to the other code changes from there. The handler makes use of a member variable, m_enabled, that maintains the state of the Click Me! button. In the constructor for MyFrame, the m_enabled variable, which is a bool, is initialized to false. Its value is toggled in the event handler, and its new value is passed to the wxWindow function Enable() to enable or disable the Click Me! button; if the value passed is true, the button can be clicked by the user. Otherwise, the button redraws itself so that it appears dim, and any button presses received by the button are discarded by the widget from this point on. (I discuss this in more detail in the next section.) Finally, the callback changes the label of the Disable/Enable button based on the value of the m_enabled variable. If the Click Me! button is disabled, we want the Disable/Enable button to display "Enable" to reflect the operation that will be performed when it is clicked; otherwise, it should display "Disable."

In the MyFrame constructor, the following lines create the Disable/Enable button and add it to the horizontal box sizer:

```
m_enableButton =
    new wxButton(this, ID_DISABLE_ENABLE, "Disable");
topSizer->Add(m_enableButton, 0, wxTOP | wxALL, 5);
```

The resulting button widget pointer is saved in the m_enableButton member variable so that the OnDisableEnable() callback function can gain access to it to change the value of its label. Because it is added to the horizontal box control after the Click Me! button, it will appear to the right of the Click Me! button.

The rest of the code changes should be familiar by now. We create an ID for the new button by adding an entry in the enum at the top of the file, add a declaration in MyFrame for the OnDisableEnable() function, and finally add an entry to the MyFrame event table to map button click events occurring in the Disable/Enable button to the OnDisableEnable() callback function.

Skipping Events

Earlier I mentioned that event handlers can veto events. One normally would not veto events like those that we have been using so far; these events (menu item selections and push button presses) are application-level command events that only classes in our application are intended to process, and given the current requirements of the application, there is little need to do additional processing. After all, if the user selects the Quit menu item, we want the application to exit; so, calling Close() from MyFrame::OnQuit() is a proper and sufficient response to the menu item selection.

However, if you were to compile the application with a –g flag, and set a breakpoint on MyFrame::OnQuit() in gdb, and then, when the application is running, click the close control of the window, what you would observe is the application would exit, without control passing through MyFrame::OnQuit(). This should not be a surprise, because there is no relationship between the OnQuit() function and the window's close control. But what if the requirements were modified so that closing the application were only allowed when the Click Me! button is enabled, regardless of how it is closed (Quit menu item, or close control on the window)? How might we go about implementing this strategy? One way is to disable the Quit

menu item in the File menu whenever the Click Me! button is disabled, and
that is easily done by adding code to `MyFrame::OnDisableEnable()`.
However, this isn't a complete solution because it still leaves us with the
problem of the user closing the application by clicking the window's close
control. There is, however, a simple solution to the problem. As mentioned
earlier, calling `Close()` on a window generates an EVT_CLOSE event. We can
arrange to capture that event, and in its handler we can check the state of
the Click Me! button. Only if the Click Me! button is enabled will we allow
the close operation to be performed; otherwise, we will arrange for the
handler to swallow the event, thereby preventing the close operation from
being performed.

Here is a patch file that shows the modifications needed to the application source to add this functionality (see Item 14 for a discussion of patch):

```
--- test1.cpp   Mon Aug 16 22:46:20 2004
+++ test.cpp    Mon Aug 16 23:04:16 2004
@@ -13,6 +13,7 @@

    void OnQuit(wxCommandEvent& event);
    void OnClickMe(wxCommandEvent& event);
+    void OnClose(wxCloseEvent& event);
    void OnDisableEnable(wxCommandEvent& event);
 private:
    bool m_enabled;
@@ -31,6 +32,7 @@

 BEGIN_EVENT_TABLE(MyFrame, wxFrame)
    EVT_MENU(ID_Quit, MyFrame::OnQuit)
+    EVT_CLOSE(MyFrame::OnClose)
    EVT_BUTTON(ID_CLICK_ME, MyFrame::OnClickMe)
    EVT_BUTTON(ID_DISABLE_ENABLE, \
        MyFrame::OnDisableEnable)
 END_EVENT_TABLE()
@@ -89,3 +91,12 @@
        }
    }

+void MyFrame::OnClose(wxCloseEvent& event)
+{
+    if (m_enabled == true)
+        event.Skip();
+    else {
+        wxMessageDialog msg(this, "You must enable \
```

```
           the Click Me! button before exiting!", \
           "Message Dialog", \
           wxICON_INFORMATION | wxOK);
+          msg.ShowModal();
+    }
+}
```

The lines prefixed with + identify those lines that were added to the source file. (Although not seen here, a - identifies a line that was removed.) Three separate additions are evident in the patch. First, a declaration of the OnClose() member function in the MyFrame class declaration was added. Notice that a reference to a wxCloseEvent object is passed to the callback by wxWidgets. The signature of this callback function is determined by the event that triggers its being called. The event, in turn, is defined by the entry in the event table, which in this case is made by invoking the EVT_CLOSE() macro. Notice that only one argument, the name of the callback function, is passed to EVT_CLOSE(). Close events do not need a window ID because the window receiving the event is the window that is being closed. The EVT_CLOSE event, as I mentioned, dictates the signature of the callback function. To determine the signature, I grepped for EVT_CLOSE in the wx/event.h header file:

```
% grep EVT_CLOSE event.h
    DECLARE_EVENT_TYPE(wxEVT_CLOSE_WINDOW, 402)
wxEVT_CLOSE_WINDOW,
#define EVT_CLOSE(func)  DECLARE_EVENT_TABLE_ENTRY( \
    wxEVT_CLOSE_WINDOW, wxID_ANY, wxID_ANY, \
    (wxObjectEventFunction) (wxEventFunction) \
    (wxCloseEventFunction) & func, (wxObject *) NULL),
```

Notice the fourth argument to the DECLARE_EVENT_TABLE_ENTRY macro is a pointer to a function which has the following C-style cast applied to it:

```
(wxObjectEventFunction) (wxEventFunction) \
    (wxCloseEventFunction)
```

Further grepping results in the following (only the relevant line is shown):

```
% grep wxCloseEventFunction event.h
typedef void (wxEvtHandler::*wxCloseEventFunction)\
    (wxCloseEvent&);
```

The preceding `typedef` indicates that the callback function takes as its only argument a reference to an object of type `wxCloseEvent`, and returns void.

However, because of the casts used in the `EVT_CLOSE()` macro, I could have declared the `MyFrame::OnClose()` function to also be the following:

```
void OnClose(wxEvent& event);
```

Although there are three casts, it turns out that `wxObjectEventFunction` and `wxEventFunction` map to essentially the same function signature.

Let's look a bit more closely at what is being done inside the callback function. Here is the source code again:

```
void MyFrame::OnClose(wxCloseEvent& event)
{
    if (m_enabled == true)
        event.Skip();
    else {
        wxMessageDialog msg(this,
            "You must enable the Click Me! button \
            before exiting!",
            "Message Dialog",
            wxICON_INFORMATION | wxOK);
        msg.ShowModal();
    }
}
```

As I described earlier, the `OnClose()` function is called whenever the `MyFrame` window is about to close. The application requirements state that we must only allow the close to occur if the Click Me! button is enabled. The code, as you can see, checks to see whether the `m_enabled` member variable is set to `true`. If it is, the button is enabled, and we want to allow the close to occur. If it is `false`, we post a `wxMessageDialog` that informs the user that he or she must enable the Click Me! button before the application can exit.

By adding an event handler for the close event, we have effectively told wxWidgets that we want an opportunity to handle the event before any other handler in the event handler chain has a chance to handle the event. If we want the event to continue on to the next handler in the event chain, we just call the event object's `Skip()` member function. If we return without calling `Skip()`, wxWidgets will assume that we have handled the event, and no additional event handlers are invoked. Therefore, to allow the close to

complete, and the application to exit, we call the event object's Skip()
member function if the m_enabled member variable is set to true. Otherwise, we display the warning message to the user and then return from the
event handler; by not calling Skip(), the close operation is effectively
canceled.

Before we leave the subject of vetoing, recall that the Close() call in
MyFrame::OnQuit() passes a force flag of TRUE. The documentation at
wxWidgets.org indicates that close handlers such as OnQuit() should call
the wxCloseEvent CanVeto() method to determine the value of this flag,
and act accordingly. If TRUE is returned, the application can return without
calling Skip(); otherwise, if FALSE is returned, the close handler should call
Skip(). Functions that call Close() in an application should, in most cases,
always pass TRUE and use additional logic to determine whether the close
should be allowed.

Container Widgets

In wxWidgets, there are two types of container widget. A frame is a top-
level window that contains a title bar, system controls (close, minimize/
maximize, and hide), and optionally, a menu bar. Usually, top-level windows
are resizable, and can be moved on the desktop as needed by the user. A
frame is invariably the parent for other widgets, usually controls. Frames
are used to display the main content of your application. An editor would
use a frame to display a document, an image-viewing application would use
a frame to display an image, and a Web browser would use a frame to
display the content of a Web page to the user. In wxWidgets, frames are
implemented by the wxFrame widget class. Each of the sample applications
that I have presented in this chapter have made use of wxFrame as a base
class for implementing an application-specific top-level window class.

The other container widget supported by wxWidgets is the dialog. A
dialog is a window used by an application to obtain information from the
user, or display status information to the user. A dialog is similar to a frame
in several ways; both widgets parent other widgets, and both display a title
bar. Unlike a frame, a dialog does not support menus, nor does it display
window controls that allow the user to resize, minimize, hide, or close the
window. Classes that your application implements for the purpose of
displaying dialog-like windows should always inherit from wxDialog.

The layout of a dialog usually consists of two logically distinct areas.
One area displays controls or a message to the user, and the other area
consists of one or more push buttons that the user can click to dismiss or

close the dialog. The push buttons displayed in this area depend on the intended use of the dialog.

Dialogs can either be modal or modeless. (Frames, on the other hand, are always modeless.) A modal dialog forces the user to interact with the dialog when it is displayed; any attempts to interact with other windows in the application are not allowed until the modal dialog has been successfully closed by the user. The display of modal dialogs makes sense when the program cannot continue until the user has viewed the information being displayed by the dialog, or makes some choice that the modal dialog is requesting the user to make.

wxFrame

As mentioned previously, wxFrame is the class that implements frames (or top-level windows) in wxWidgets applications. For each type of top-level window your application creates, it will implement at least one class that inherits from wxFrame. In this section, I present the general pattern that one follows to create and use wxFrame-derived classes.

To illustrate the concepts, let's create a simple application that displays a 640x480 top-level window. To accomplish this, create two source files, toplevel.h and toplevel.cpp, and enter the code that follows.

First, toplevel.h:

```
#ifndef __TOPLEVEL_H
#define __TOPLEVEL_H

#include "wx/wx.h"

class Toplevel: public wxFrame
{
public:

    Toplevel(const wxString& title, const wxPoint& pos,
        const wxSize& size);
};

#endif
```

Here, we simply define a class named Toplevel that inherits from wxFrame, and define its constructor. The constructor is defined with the wxFrame constructor in mind, which is as follows:

```
wcFrame::wxFrame(
    wxWindow *parent,
    wxWindowID id,
    const wxString& title,
    const wxPoint& pos = wxDefaultPosition,
    const wxSize& size = wxDefaultSize,
    long style = wxDEFAULT_FRAME_STYLE,
    const wxString& name = wxFrameNameStr
)
```

The first three arguments to the constructor are mandatory:

- parent is the parent widget of the frame. For top-level windows, it can be set to NULL.
- id is an application-specified integer, which is usually set to –1.
- title is a wxString object that defines the label displayed in the title bar of the window.

The remaining constructor arguments are all optional:

- pos is a wxPoint object that defines the position of the upper-left corner of the frame window when it is first displayed.
- size is a wxSize object that defines the width and height of the window associated with the window
- style is a bitmask specifying attributes of the frame. The value of this bitmask is formed by or'ing together constants, among them are the following:
  - **wxSTAY_ON_TOP**—Frame stays on top of all other windows (MS Windows only).
  - **wxCAPTION**—Display a caption in the frame title bar.
  - **wxCLIP_CHILDREN**—Do not repaint frame background for regions occupied by child windows (Microsoft Windows only).
  - **wxICONIZE**—Display the frame iconified (Microsoft Windows only).
  - **wxMINIMIZE**—Synonym for wxICONIZE.
  - **wxMAXIMIZE**—Display the frame maximized (Microsoft Windows only).
  - **wxSYSTEM_MENU**—Display a system menu (if supported by the desktop environment).
  - **wxMINIMIZE_BOX**—Display a minimize box (if supported by the desktop environment).
  - **wxMAXIMIZE_BOX**—Display a maximize box (if supported by the desktop environment).

- **wxRESIZE_BORDER**—Provide controls which allow the window to be resized by the user.
- **wxFRAME_NO_TASKBAR**—Frame does not appear in taskbar (Microsoft Windows only).
- **wxFRAME_TOOL_WINDOW**—Frame with a small title bar, does not appear in Microsoft Windows taskbar.
- **wxFRAME_FLOAT_ON_PARENT**—Frame always floats on top of its parent. Requires the application to specify a non-NULL parent.
- **wxFRAME_SHAPED**—If supported by the client, frames with this attribute support nonrectangular shaped windows. (The shape is specified with a call to the wxFrame::SetShape() method.)

The default value, wxDEFAULT_FRAME_STYLE, is defined as follows:

```
#define wxDEFAULT_FRAME_STYLE \
  (wxSYSTEM_MENU | wxRESIZE_BORDER | \
  wxMINIMIZE_BOX | wxMAXIMIZE_BOX | \
  wxCAPTION | wxCLIP_CHILDREN)
```

Now that we have defined the Toplevel class, let's see how it is used by taking a look at the source for toplevel.cpp:

```
#include "wx/wx.h"
#include "toplevel.h"


Toplevel::Toplevel(const wxString& title,
    const wxPoint& pos, const wxSize& size)
    : wxFrame((wxFrame *)NULL, -1, title, pos, size)
{
}
```

All that we need to do in the Toplevel constructor is invoke the wxFrame constructor from the C++ member initialization list. The arguments passed to the wxFrame constructor were defined previously.

To round out the source code, main.cpp defines and declares the object MyApp, which, as you can see, inherits from wxApp. As described earlier in this chapter, wxApp provides a wxWidgets application with its main() implementation from where it initializes the wxWidgets environment and invokes the application main loop. (This functionality is encapsulated within the IMPLEMENT_APP macro.) In MyApp::OnInit(), we create the UI of the application by instantiating the Toplevel class. The wxWindow method

Show() (wxFrame inherits from wxWindow, where Show() is defined) causes the frame to be displayed. SetTopWindow() is a wxApp method that tells wxApp which window is the main window of the application. This is a completely optional step; wxApp will use the top window as a parent for certain dialogs that are not created with a parent. If you don't specify a top window, wxApp simply chooses a window for these purposes from a window list that it maintains. Finally, we return TRUE to tell wxApp that everything was successful; returning FALSE causes the application to exit. Here is the source for main.cpp:

```cpp
#include "wx/wx.h"
#include "toplevel.h"

class MyApp: public wxApp
{
    virtual bool OnInit();
};

IMPLEMENT_APP(MyApp)

bool MyApp::OnInit()
{
    Toplevel *frame = new Toplevel( "Toplevel",
        wxPoint(50,50), wxSize(640,480) );
    frame->Show(TRUE);
    SetTopWindow(frame);
    return TRUE;
}
```

Building the source code and running the application results in the display of a resizable 640x480 window on the desktop. You should be able to resize the window and close it by clicking the close box displayed by the desktop. The source code for this application can be later reused as a template for your own wxWidgets applications, because most wxWidgets applications that you create can be based, fundamentally, on the structure exemplified by the source code that we have developed so far.

Adding a Menu

Let's continue our look at wxWidgets by defining some new requirements for our application. By implementing this new functionality, several additional wxWidgets patterns will emerge. The new requirements for the application are as follows:

- The main frame should display a menu with menu items that allow the user to exit the application and to display an about box.
- The main frame should display a filled circle that redraws each time the user resizes the window.

By implementing these requirements, we will fully develop patterns for adding menus to a frame and for responding to menu item selections that were introduced earlier. We will also discuss patterns for managing application-drawn content, and drawing 2D graphics in a window.

Menus

Let's start with menus. A menu consists of one or more menu items. Menu items, when selected, perform some action, and the name or title of the menu item is used to communicate what action will be performed when the menu item is selected. Common application menus include the File and Edit menus. Typical menu items in an Edit menu are Cut, Copy, Paste, and Undo. The set of application menus are displayed as a group at the top of a window using a menu bar. On Mac OS X, only one menu bar is displayed at a time on the desktop, corresponding to the currently active window. wxFrame supports menus intrinsically. To add a menu to a wxFrame, you must do the following:

1. For each menu, create a wxMenu object.
2. Append menu items to the wxMenu objects.
3. Create a wxMenuBar object.
4. Append each wxMenu object to the wxMenuBar object.
5. Make the wxMenuBar object the active menu bar for the wxFrame object.

Let's run through each of these steps. Creating a wxMenu object is done with code similar to the following:

```
wxMenu *menuFile = new wxMenu;
```

The wxMenu constructor takes two arguments, a title and a style, but neither is required, and so here we simply allow the default constructor to be invoked. As can be inferred by the name of the variable that holds the pointer to the wxMenu object, menuFile, the menu we are creating is the application's File menu. Your code must create an instance of wxMenu for each menu in the frame's menu bar.

Appending menu items to a menu is simply a matter of invoking the wxMenu::Append() method for each menu item in the menu, passing to it arguments that specify the ID of the menu item and its label. The following code adds an About menu item to the File menu:

```
menuFile->Append( ID_About, _T("&About...") );
```

Notice the & character that prefixes the label. The character immediately following the & character identifies the menu key equivalent for the menu item.

The first argument to Append() is the ID of the menu item, which only needs to be unique for the frame that contains the menu item, and its children.

Next, we create a menu bar. This is done by executing code like the following:

```
wxMenuBar *menuBar = new wxMenuBar;
```

With the menu bar object in hand, we can add the menu to it by calling its Append() member function:

```
menuBar->Append(menuFile, _T("&File"));
```

Finally, we make the menu bar active for the frame by calling wxFrame's SetMenuBar() method:

```
SetMenuBar(menuBar);
```

Seeing the preceding steps in code should make everything clearer if you are confused at this point. Here is the code so far:

```
enum
{
    ID_Quit = 1,
    ID_About,
};


Toplevel::Toplevel(const wxString& title,
    const wxPoint& pos, const wxSize& size)
    : wxFrame((wxFrame *)NULL, -1, title, pos, size)
{
    wxMenu *menuFile = new wxMenu;
```

```
    menuFile->Append( ID_About, _T("&About...") );

    wxMenuBar *menuBar = new wxMenuBar;
    menuBar->Append( menuFile, _T("&File") );

    SetMenuBar( menuBar );
}
```

The About menu item, when selected, does nothing. Before I describe
how to wire menu item selections to the application, let's add a separator
and a Quit menu item to the File menu (with changes shown in bold in the
following listing):

```
enum
{
    ID_Quit = 1,
    ID_About,
};

Toplevel::Toplevel(const wxString& title,
        const wxPoint& pos, const wxSize& size)
        : wxFrame((wxFrame *)NULL, -1, title, pos, size)
{

    wxMenu *menuFile = new wxMenu;

    menuFile->Append(ID_About, _T("&About..."));
    menuFile->AppendSeparator();
    menuFile->Append(ID_Quit, _T("&Quit"));

    wxMenuBar *menuBar = new wxMenuBar;
    menuBar->Append(menuFile, _T("&File"));

    SetMenuBar(menuBar);
}
```

Wiring Menu Item Selections to Class Member Functions

Now that we have the UI for the menu added to the application, we need to
associate menu item selections with code in the application. The strategy is
similar to the one used to wire member functions to clicks of wxButton
widgets earlier in this chapter. The steps involved include the following:

In the header file toplevel.h

1. Add `DECLARE_EVENT_TABLE()` to the definition of the class that is going to handle the menu selections.
2. Add public member functions to the class definition that will handle the menu selection events. Add one member function for each menu item. The prototype for these member functions is as follows:

```
void FunctionName(wxCommandEvent& event);
```

In the source (toplevel.cpp) file

1. Declare an event table and add entries for each function added in the previous step.
2. Implement the member functions.

Here are the changes (in bold) made to toplevel.h:

```
#ifndef __TOPLEVEL_H
#define __TOPLEVEL_H

#include "wx/wx.h"

class Toplevel: public wxFrame
{
public:

    Toplevel(const wxString& title, const wxPoint& pos,
        const wxSize& size);

    void OnQuit(wxCommandEvent& event);
    void OnAbout(wxCommandEvent& event);

    DECLARE_EVENT_TABLE()
};

#endif
```

The following listing shows the changes made to toplevel.cpp:

```
#include "wx/wx.h"
#include "toplevel.h"
```

```
enum
{
    ID_Quit = 1,
    ID_About,
};

BEGIN_EVENT_TABLE(Toplevel, wxFrame)
    EVT_MENU(ID_Quit, Toplevel::OnQuit)
    EVT_MENU(ID_About, Toplevel::OnAbout)
END_EVENT_TABLE()

Toplevel::Toplevel(const wxString& title,
    const wxPoint& pos, const wxSize& size)
    : wxFrame((wxFrame *)NULL, -1, title, pos, size)
{
    wxMenu *menuFile = new wxMenu;

    menuFile->Append( ID_About, _T("&About...") );
    menuFile->AppendSeparator();
    menuFile->Append( ID_Quit, _T("&Quit") );

    wxMenuBar *menuBar = new wxMenuBar;
    menuBar->Append( menuFile, _T("&File") );

    SetMenuBar( menuBar );
}

void Toplevel::OnQuit(wxCommandEvent& WXUNUSED(event))
{
    Close(TRUE);
}

void Toplevel::OnAbout(wxCommandEvent& WXUNUSED(event))
{
    wxMessageBox(_T("Toplevel wxWidgets Sample"),
        _T("About Toplevel"),
        wxOK | wxICON_INFORMATION, this);
}
```

As you can see, `Toplevel::OnQuit()` invokes the `wxWindow` function `Close()` to cause the application to exit. (`Close()` was described earlier.) To implement the About functionality, `Toplevel::OnAbout()` creates an instance of `wxMessageBox()` to display a short message about the program to the user. I describe `wxMesssageBox()` in more detail later when I describe dialogs in wxWidgets.

Drawing Content in a Frame

Clearly, the Toplevel application as it stands is rather uninteresting and unrealistic. Frames in actual applications display graphical data, controls, or some combination of the two. In this section, I modify the application so that the top-level frame will display a filled, blue circle. As the user resizes the frame, the application will redraw the circle so that it fits the width of the frame.

Widgets inheriting from wxWindow, including wxFrame, receive wxPaint events whenever wxWidgets identifies a need for the window managed by the widget to be redrawn. wxPaint events are sent when a window is first made visible, whenever it becomes unobscured (part of its window becomes visible, usually because it is raised above some other window), and whenever it is resized (by the user or the application). For those of you familiar with Win32, a wxPaint event is closely related to Win32's WM_PAINT message, and is sent under the same circumstances for the most part.

Like any event, two steps are involved in arranging for your class to handle a wxPaint message:

1. Add an entry to the event table of the class that will be handling the wxPaint event.
2. Code the wxPaint event handler.

To add an entry to the event table, you must use the EVT_PAINT() macro. This macro takes one argument: the name of the function that handles the wxPaint messages. The name of the function is, by informal convention, usually OnPaint(). The function prototype for the handler is as follows:

```
void OnPaint(wxPaint& event)
```

Coding the event handler for a wxPaint message involves the following steps:

1. Allocate a wxPaintDC object on the stack.
2. Draw the graphics.

The wxPaintDC object encapsulates the platform-specific graphic device context described previously (for example, Win32's DC or X11's GC). Methods implemented by the wxPaintDC object are called from within the wxPaint event handler by the application to set attributes of the drawing (for example, the foreground or fill color), and perform graphics operations (for example, drawing a circle).

Here is the basic template for an OnPaint handler:

```
void OnPaint(wxPaintEvent& event)
{
    wxPaintDC myDC(this);

    // set attributes of the drawing

    // perform the graphics operation
}
```

In our case, the attribute that we need to set is the foreground color (blue), and the graphics operation will be to draw a circle that fits the width of the frame's window. The following implementation of Toplevel::OnPaint() achieves these goals. Here's the listing:

```
void Toplevel::OnPaint(wxPaintEvent& event)
{
    int width, height;
    wxBrush brush(wxColour(0,0,255), wxSOLID);

    wxPaintDC myDC(this);
    myDC.SetBrush(brush);

    GetClientSize(&width, &height);

    myDC.DrawCircle(width >> 1, height >> 1,
        width >> 1);
}
```

A wxBrush object creates, as you might expect, a brush that defines the fill color and style that is used when drawing rectangles, circles, and other closed polygonal 2D graphics in wxWidgets. A brush can be solid, transparent, hashed, or stippled. (A stipple bitmask can be supplied as an argument to one of the wxBrush constructors.) The constructor I use here accepts a reference to a wxColour object, which is initialized here to the RGB triplet red=0, green=0, blue=255, and a style argument, which is set here to wxSOLID. The wxDC SetBrush() method is then used to associate this brush with the device context, so that when we draw our circle (by calling wxDC::DrawCircle()), it will be filled with a solid blue. The arguments to wxDC::DrawCircle() are the x and y coordinates of the center of the circle, and the radius of the circle. We use wxWindow's `GetClientSize()` method (recall that wxFrame inherits wxWindow) to determine the width and height of the client area of the window managed by wxFrame, the values are used, as you can see, to compute the x, y, and radius arguments to `wxDC::DrawCircle()`. `GetClientSize()` returns the dimensions of the client area, which is the area of the window that does not include the menu bar at the top or the status bar at the bottom of the frame, when present.

All that remains is adding `OnPaint()` to the `Toplevel` event table. This can be done by adding the following line between the `BEGIN_EVENT_TABLE()` and `END_EVENT_TABLE()` macros:

```
EVT_PAINT(Toplevel::OnPaint)
```

Improving the Quality of the OnPaint Handler

To an experienced graphics programmer, drawing graphics directly to a window as is done in `OnPaint()` above is not considered ideal, especially in cases when the graphics are complicated or time-consuming to draw. This is because drawing to the window, in this way, can cause noticeable flicker.

A strategy that is often used to overcome flicker involves restructuring a function like `OnPaint()` so that it draws its graphics to an offscreen buffer instead of directly to the window. When the drawing is completed, `OnPaint()` copies the content of the offscreen memory directly to the window, where it is displayed. Because the time it takes to copy offscreen memory to a window is extremely fast, changes made to the window appear instantly to the user, without flicker or any of the other artifacts one might otherwise see.

To draw offscreen in wxWidgets involves the following easy steps:

1. Create an offscreen, memory DC.
2. Draw the graphics using the memory DC.
3. `blit` the contents of the memory DC to the window.

Creating a memory DC is trivial, and can be done by instantiating the wxMemoryDC class, using code such as the following:

```
wxMemoryDC dc;
```

Because wxMemoryDC inherits from wxDC, as does wxPaintDC, the same methods that can be invoked against wxPaintDC, for example `SetBrush()` and `DrawRectangle()`, can be invoked against a memory DC. After the graphics have been drawn to the memory DC using these methods, transferring content from the memory DC to the window is done by invoking the wxPaintDC's Blit() method. The function prototype for Blit() is as follows:

```
bool Blit(
    wxCoord xdest, // destination x coordinate
    wxCoord ydest, // destination y coordinate
    wxCoord width, // width of region to be copied
    wxCoord height,// height of region to be copied
    wxDC* source,  // DC containing the memory to
                   // be copied
    wxCoord xsrc,  // source x coordinate
    wxCoord ysrc,  // source y coordinate
    int logicalFunc = wxCOPY, // logical operation
                   // applied to bits (see below)
    bool useMask = FALSE, // if TRUE, use the bitmap
                       // selected into source
                       // as a mask for the copy
    wxCoord xsrcMask = -1, // x origin for mask if
                       // useMask is TRUE
    wxCoord ysrcMask = -1  // y origin for mask if
                       // useMask is TRUE
)
```

The argument logicalFunc controls how bits are transferred from the source DC to the destination DC. There are 16 standard possible values for this argument, listed in Table 8-1.

Table 8-1 logicalFunc Argument Values

Value	Operation
wxAND	src AND dst
wxAND_INVERT	(NOT src) AND dst
wxAND_REVERSE	src AND (NOT dst)
wxCLEAR	0
wxCOPY	src
wxEQUIV	(NOT src) XOR dst
wxINVERT	NOT dst
wxNAND	(NOT src) OR (NOT dst)
wxNOR	(NOT src) AND (NOT dst)

Value	Operation
wxNO_OP	dst
wxOR	src OR dst
wxOR_INVERT	(NOT src) OR dst
wxOR_REVERE	src OR (NOT dst)
wxSET	1
wxSRC_INVERT	NOT src
wxXOR	src XOR dst

For our purposes, we just want to copy all the bits from the source memory DC to the destination window DC, so we pass wxCopy. Here is our call to Blit():

```
myDC.Blit(0, 0, width, height, &memdc, 0, 0, wxCopy);
```

The first four arguments passed to Blit() in the preceding code specify the region in the source DC to be copied, the fifth argument identifies the source DC, the sixth and seventh arguments specify the origin of the copy in the destination DC, and the final argument tells Blit() to copy the pixels from the source directly to the destination, unmodified.

Here is the complete source code for the OnPaint() function after changes have been made to use a memory DC to manage flicker:

```
void Toplevel::OnPaint(wxPaintEvent& event)
{
    int width, height;
    wxBrush bgBrush(wxColour(255,255,255), wxSOLID);
    wxMemoryDC memdc;

    GetClientSize(&width, &height);

    wxBitmap bmp(width, height);
    memdc.SelectObject(bmp);

    memdc.SetBrush(bgBrush);
    memdc.DrawRectangle(0, 0, width, height);

    wxBrush fgBrush(wxColour(0,0,255), wxSOLID);
    memdc.SetBrush(fgBrush);
    memdc.DrawCircle(width >> 1, height >> 1,
        width >> 1);
```

```
wxPaintDC myDC(this);
myDC.Blit(0, 0, width, height, &memdc, 0,
    0, wxCOPY);
}
```

Sizers

Rarely is a top-level window designed as illustrated previously, as a single frame containing no controls. Even windows designed to display a document, graphic, or image are likely to be augmented with a status area, a toolbar, or a set of controls. Anytime a window in a wxWidgets application contains more than just a frame, you will make use of one or more of wxWidget's sizer widgets to organize the content. The job of a sizer is to impose a layout policy on the content in some portion of a window. There are four basic sizers in wxWidgets:

- **wxBoxSizer**—A sizer that organizes regions of a window into boxes within which other sizers and controls are packed
- **wxStaticBoxSizer**—A box sizer that displays a frame and a label around the region it manages, to organize a small group of related controls in a window
- **wxGridSizer**—Organizes its children in rows and columns, similar to a <table> in HTML
- **wxNotebookSizer**—Organizes a single region as a set of tabbed pages in a notebook

Due to its flexibility, the most commonly used sizer, by far, is wxBoxSizer. Just about any layout imaginable can be achieved by combining and nesting box sizers in a window. The next most popular sizer widget is wxGridSizer, the use of which simplifies the layout of controls and sizers as cells in a row- and column-oriented table. (You can achieve a grid-like layout using boxes, but the application code needed to do this is much greater than what is required when using wxGridSizer.)

Anytime a window (be it a top-level window or a dialog) contains multiple children, a sizer is needed to organize the layout of the children in the window. After the sizer has been created, children can be instantiated and added to the sizer. Even if there is only one child in a window, it makes sense to use a sizer, because doing so simplifies development should the need to add additional children to the window arise at a later time.

Factoring `OnPaint()`

In the example program presented in the previous section, the content of the top-level frame was drawn by `Toplevel`'s `OnPaint()` handler. What we want, instead, is for the drawing to occur in a region, or subset, of the top-level window. If the entire content of the frame consisted of graphics drawn by our application, we could retain the current architecture, and just manage the various regions of the frame in the `OnPaint()` handler. To do this, we would compute our own layout based on the size of the frame, and draw the content accordingly. However, when other widgets are children of the frame, we must use a sizer to manage the layout, we must make all children of the frame widgets so that they can be managed by the sizer, and the frame that acts as the parent of the sizer and its children should no longer draw content from its own `OnPaint()` handler.

The first step for us in preparing the top-level window to use a sizer is to create a new widget that behaves like the frame from the previous sample: When it needs to be redrawn, its `OnPaint()` handler is invoked, and it draws a circle. To create this new widget, we just factor the code that handled the drawing from the `Toplevel` class and place it in a new class that we will call `DrawingArea`.

Before we implement `DrawingArea`, let's look at what needs to be removed from `Toplevel`. In the following listings, code shown in bold is removed from toplevel.h and toplevel.cpp. First, let's look at toplevel.h:

```
#ifndef __TOPLEVEL_H
#define __TOPLEVEL_H

#include "wx/wx.h"

class Toplevel: public wxFrame
{
public:

    Toplevel(const wxString& title,
        const wxPoint& pos, const wxSize& size);

    void OnQuit(wxCommandEvent& event);
    void OnAbout(wxCommandEvent& event);
    void OnPaint(wxPaintEvent& event);

    DECLARE_EVENT_TABLE()
};

#endif
```

Next, toplevel.cpp:

```cpp
#include "wx/wx.h"
#include "toplevel.h"

enum
{
    ID_Quit = 1,
    ID_About,
};

BEGIN_EVENT_TABLE(Toplevel, wxFrame)
    EVT_MENU(ID_Quit, Toplevel::OnQuit)
    EVT_MENU(ID_About, Toplevel::OnAbout)
    EVT_PAINT(Toplevel::OnPaint)
END_EVENT_TABLE()

Toplevel::Toplevel(const wxString& title,
    const wxPoint& pos, const wxSize& size)
    : wxFrame((wxFrame *)NULL, -1, title, pos, size)
{
    wxMenu *menuFile = new wxMenu;

    menuFile->Append( ID_About, _T("&About...") );
    menuFile->AppendSeparator();
    menuFile->Append( ID_Quit, _T("&Quit") );

    wxMenuBar *menuBar = new wxMenuBar;
    menuBar->Append( menuFile, _T("&File") );

    SetMenuBar( menuBar );
}

void
Toplevel::OnQuit(wxCommandEvent& WXUNUSED(event))
{
    Close(TRUE);
}

void
Toplevel::OnAbout(wxCommandEvent& WXUNUSED(event))
{
    wxMessageBox(_T("Toplevel wxWidget Sample"),
        _T("About Toplevel"),
        wxOK | wxICON_INFORMATION, this);
}
```

```
void Toplevel::OnPaint(wxPaintEvent& event)
{
    int width, height;
    wxBrush bgBrush(wxColour(255,255,255), wxSOLID);
    wxMemoryDC memdc;

    GetClientSize(&width, &height);

    wxBitmap bmp(width, height);
    memdc.SelectObject(bmp);

    memdc.SetBrush(bgBrush);
    memdc.DrawRectangle(0, 0, width, height);

    wxBrush fgBrush(wxColour(0,0,255), wxSOLID);
    memdc.SetBrush(fgBrush);
    memdc.DrawCircle(width >> 1, height >> 1,
        width >> 1);

    wxPaintDC myDC(this);
    myDC.Blit(0, 0, width, height, &memdc, 0,
        0, wxCOPY);
}
```

Now, let's look at the definition of DrawingArea. To create DrawingArea, we simply take what was removed from Toplevel, and wrap it in a new class that inherits from wxWindow. Because we are, in effect, creating a new widget, we place the definition of DrawingArea in its own include file so that it can be used in contexts other than the one illustrated here. Below is the listing for drawing.h, with the code factored from toplevel.h shown in bold:

```
#ifndef __DRAWING_H
#define __DRAWING_H

#include "wx/wx.h"

class DrawingArea: public wxWindow
{
public:

    DrawingArea(wxWindow *parent,
        const wxPoint& pos = wxDefaultPosition,
        const wxSize& size = wxDefaultSize);
```

```
    void OnPaint(wxPaintEvent& event);

    DECLARE_EVENT_TABLE()
};

#endif
```

DrawingArea inherits from wxWindow, not only because classes that
inherit from wxFrame cannot have other classes inheriting from wxFrame as
children, but because wxWindow really provides all we need to manage a
region of a top-level window. The only difference between DrawingArea and
Toplevel, besides the inheritance chain, are the arguments passed to the
constructor, and the removal of callback functions for the menu items. Our
application only needs to supply the first argument of the constructor, as the
size and position of the DrawingArea widget will be controlled by the sizer.
Therefore, the design of DrawingArea provides default values for both pos
and size.

Let's now take a close look at the implementation details of
DrawingArea, the source code of which is found in drawing.cpp. The code
that was factored from toplevel.cpp is shown in bold:

```
#include "wx/wx.h"
#include "drawing.h"

BEGIN_EVENT_TABLE(DrawingArea, wxWindow)
    EVT_PAINT(DrawingArea::OnPaint)
END_EVENT_TABLE()

DrawingArea::DrawingArea(wxWindow *parent,
    const wxPoint& pos, const wxSize& size)
    : wxWindow(parent, -1, pos, size)
{
}

void DrawingArea::OnPaint(wxPaintEvent& event)
{
    int width, height;
    wxBrush bgBrush(wxColour(255,255,255), wxSOLID);
    wxMemoryDC memdc;

    GetClientSize(&width, &height);

    wxBitmap bmp(width, height);
    memdc.SelectObject(bmp);
```

```
    memdc.SetBrush(bgBrush);
    memdc.DrawRectangle(0, 0, width, height);

    wxBrush fgBrush(wxColour(0,0,255), wxSOLID);
    memdc.SetBrush(fgBrush);
    memdc.DrawCircle(width >> 1, height >> 1,
        width >> 1);

    wxPaintDC myDC(this);
    myDC.Blit(0, 0, width, height, &memdc, 0,
        0, wxCOPY);
}
```

The function OnPaint() is unmodified from the code we lifted from toplevel.cpp, other than the namespace change. The same is true for the event table entry; it is identical to the one in toplevel.cpp, except for the namespace change, and the omission of the menu item handler entries.

We can now use this class to create a functional equivalent to the original Toplevel class by rewriting the Toplevel constructor to use a box sizer that manages an instance of DrawingArea. Here is the source code of the new Toplevel constructor. Lines shown in bold reflect additions to the constructor to make use of the DrawingArea class:

```
#include "drawing.h"

...


Toplevel::Toplevel(const wxString& title, const wxPoint& pos, const wxSize& size)
: wxFrame((wxFrame *)NULL, -1, title, pos, size)
{
    wxBoxSizer *topSizer =
        new wxBoxSizer(wxHORIZONTAL);

    wxMenu *menuFile = new wxMenu;

    menuFile->Append( ID_About, _T("&About...") );
    menuFile->AppendSeparator();
    menuFile->Append( ID_Quit, _T("&Quit") );

    wxMenuBar *menuBar = new wxMenuBar;
    menuBar->Append( menuFile, _T("&File") );

    SetMenuBar( menuBar );
```

```
    DrawingArea *drawing = new DrawingArea(this);

    topSizer->Add(drawing, 1, wxEXPAND | wxALL, 0);

    SetSizer(topSizer);
}
```

The following line

```
wxBoxSizer *topSizer =
        new wxBoxSizer(wxHORIZONTAL);
```

creates an instance of wxBoxSizer. By passing wxHORIZONTAL as an argument to the constructor, we are telling the box sizer to layout its children left to right in a horizontal fashion as they are added to the sizer. We could have, instead, passed wxVERTICAL; because there is only one child being added to the sizer, the orientation of the sizer is not relevant. When the sizer is created, we instantiate an instance of DrawingArea and add it to the sizer:

```
DrawingArea *drawing = new DrawingArea(this);
topSizer->Add(drawing, 1, wxEXPAND | wxALL, 0);
```

The arguments to Add() were described earlier, but let's take another look and see how they are used here. Notice that we pass as the second argument the value 1; this tells the sizer that drawing should dominate the region or area managed by the sizer. The third argument to Add(), flags, is set to the bitmask wxEXPAND | wxALL. wxALL simply tells the sizer to place a border around all edges of the region. The size of the border is specified as the final argument to Add(), which we set to 0 here. Because the border is set to 0, wxALL is effectively a no-op, but I specify it anyway because if I later want to add a border, all I need to do is specify a nonzero size argument (which is not as simple an arrangement as would be achieved using a style system such as Cascading Style Sheets [CSS], of course, but it is the best that we can do). Because the sizer is horizontal, the DrawingArea widget will fill the region maintained by the sizer in the horizontal direction (that is, until a second widget is added as a child of the sizer, at which point the DrawingArea widget will share the region with the second widget). However, in the vertical dimension, the DrawingArea will take on a default height (or the height that we pass to the DrawingArea constructor, if one is supplied), unless wxEXPAND is specified as a flag. For the drawing area to completely fill the vertical area managed by the sizer, we need to specify wxEXPAND as a flag.

The final change is to associate the sizer with the `Toplevel` widget. This is done by calling `wxWindow::SetSizer()` as follows:

```
SetSizer(topSizer);
```

At this point, adding new children to the sizer is a simple matter of instantiating the child widget and then calling `Add()` as was done before.

Adding Controls to Toplevel

Now let's implement new requirements for the Toplevel application. To see the UI changes imposed by these new requirements, look at Figure 8-5, which illustrates the desired layout of the frame. To the right of the `DrawingArea` are several controls that can be used to change characteristics of the drawing. A slider widget is used to control the radius of the circle as a percentage of the width of the `DrawingArea` widget. Below that, three check box widgets are used to select the color of the circle. Checking an individual color adds that color to the background at full intensity. For example, a green circle will be drawn if Green is checked with Red and Blue unchecked. Checking multiple colors will mix them to create the resulting fill color. (For example, selecting Red and Blue will result in a purple circle.)

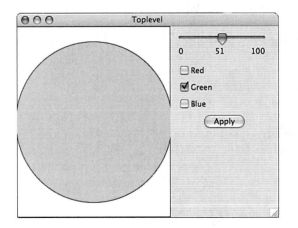

Figure 8-5 Colored circles application layout

The radius slider takes effect in real time as the control is manipulated by the user. A push button labeled "Apply," located below the color check boxes, must be clicked for the color changes to be applied to the drawing.

An additional requirement for the application is that the controls to the right of the drawing must retain their size and position as the user resizes the window. The `DrawingArea` widget will be resized to fill the remaining width and height of the window.

Adding the code in bold to the `Toplevel` constructor, as shown in the following listing, gives the desired results:

```
enum
{
    ID_Quit = 1,
    ID_About,
    ID_RADIUS_SLIDER,
    ID_RED_CHECKBOX,
    ID_GREEN_CHECKBOX,
    ID_BLUE_CHECKBOX,
    ID_COLOR_APPLY
};


...


Toplevel::Toplevel(const wxString& title,
    const wxPoint& pos, const wxSize& size)
    : wxFrame((wxFrame *)NULL, -1, title, pos, size)
{
    wxBoxSizer *topSizer =
        new wxBoxSizer(wxHORIZONTAL);

    wxMenu *menuFile = new wxMenu;

    menuFile->Append(ID_About, _T("&About..."));
    menuFile->AppendSeparator();
    menuFile->Append(ID_Quit, _T("&Quit"));

    wxMenuBar *menuBar = new wxMenuBar;
    menuBar->Append(menuFile, _T("&File"));

    SetMenuBar(menuBar);

    DrawingArea *drawing = new DrawingArea(this);

    topSizer->Add(drawing, 1, wxEXPAND | wxALL, 0);

    wxBoxSizer *controlSizer =
        new wxBoxSizer(wxVERTICAL);

    topSizer->Add(controlSizer, 0,
        wxEXPAND | wxALL, 5);
```

```
wxSize ssize(200,100);
wxSlider *slider = new wxSlider(this,
    ID_RADIUS_SLIDER, 50, 0, 100,
    wxDefaultPosition, ssize, wxSL_LABELS);

controlSizer->Add(slider, 0, wxALL, 5);

wxBoxSizer *colorSizer =
    new wxBoxSizer(wxVERTICAL);

controlSizer->Add(colorSizer, 0,
    wxEXPAND | wxALL, 5);

wxCheckBox *redCheckBox =
    new wxCheckBox(this, ID_RED_CHECKBOX, "Red");
wxCheckBox *greenCheckBox =
    new wxCheckBox(this, -ID_GREEN_CHECKBOX,
        "Green");
wxCheckBox *blueCheckBox =
    new wxCheckBox(this, ID_BLUE_CHECKBOX, "Blue");

colorSizer->Add(redCheckBox, 0, wxALL, 5);
colorSizer->Add(greenCheckBox, 0, wxALL, 5);
colorSizer->Add(blueCheckBox, 0, wxALL, 5);

wxButton *applyButton =
    new wxButton(this, ID_COLOR_APPLY, "Apply");

colorSizer->Add(applyButton, 0,
    wxALIGN_CENTER | wxALL, 5);

SetSizer(topSizer);
}
```

The result of the preceding changes is, in principle, no different from
what was achieved earlier when a second DrawingArea widget was added to
Toplevel's horizontal sizer. All we did above was replace the second
DrawingArea widget with a vertical sizer (named controlSizer). To the
containing top-level sizer, all it knows is that it has a second child to
manage. The content of the child is irrelevant to the sizer, other than the
sizer needs to know the size requirements of its children so that it can
correctly compute a layout.

(You might be wondering why I specified a size for the wxSlider
instance. It appears there is a bug in the Gtk+ version of wxWidgets that
results in a size reported to the sizer by the wxSlider instance that is smaller

than actual, which results in the sizer allocating less horizontal space than is required to display the slider without clipping. Adding an explicit size fixed this problem.)

The bulk of the remaining new code in the above listing simply creates and adds children to this vertical sizer: an instance of wxSlider; a second vertical sizer, colorSizer, which manages three check boxes labeled "red," "green," and "blue"; and a button labeled "Apply."

Wiring Controls to User Code

Now that the layout for the top-level window has been established, let's turn our attention to adding callback functions that respond to user input. Let's begin with the slider. As the user moves the slider from left to right, the radius of the circle should change in real time based on the reported value of the slider. We will use the EVT_COMMAND_SCROLL(id, func) macro to attach a callback to slider events. In this callback, when it is invoked, we need to tell the DrawingArea widget the radius percentage, and then force it to redraw itself.

To do this, we add the following line to the Toplevel event table:

```
BEGIN_EVENT_TABLE(Toplevel, wxFrame)
...
    EVT_COMMAND_SCROLL(ID_RADIUS_SLIDER, \
Toplevel::OnSliderChange)
...
END_EVENT_TABLE()
```

The implementation of OnSliderChange() retrieves the current slider position by calling the GetPosition() member function of the passed in wxScrollEvent object, and then invokes the DrawingArea's SetRadiusPercent() member function:

```
void Toplevel::OnSliderChange(wxScrollEvent& event)
{
    m_drawing->SetRadiusPercent(event.GetPosition());
}
```

In the Toplevel class constructor, we need to store the pointer to the instantiated DrawingArea widget as a new Toplevel member, m_drawing, so that we can access it later.

Here are the implementations of the SetRadiusPercent() and GetRadiusPercent() member functions. GetRadiusPercent() is called from `DrawingArea::OnPaint()` to retrieve the radius percentage, as you will see below:

```
class DrawingArea: public wxWindow
{
public:
...
    void SetRadiusPercent(int percent)
        { m_percent = percent; Refresh(); };
    int GetRadiusPercent() { return m_percent; };
private:
    int m_percent;
...
};
```

The red, green, blue check boxes are wired to callbacks using `EVT_CHECKBOX(id, func)` macros. In these callbacks, a call is made to tell the `DrawingArea` object the value of the corresponding color; if checked, the color value is set to 255, and if unchecked, the color is set to 0. Several code changes are required to support this. First, we must add member variables to `DrawingArea` to store the values of the check boxes as they change, and we also need to define setter and getter functions to set and read, respectively, their values:

```
class DrawingArea: public wxWindow
{
public:
...
    void SetRed(int value) { m_red = value; };
    void SetGreen(int value) { m_green = value; };
    void SetBlue(int value) { m_blue = value; };

    int GetRed() { return m_red; };
    int GetGreen() { return m_green; };
    int GetBlue() { return m_blue; };
private:
    int m_red;
    int m_green;
    int m_blue;
...
};
```

Next, the event table needs entries that map the events to member functions in Toplevel that handle them:

```
BEGIN_EVENT_TABLE(Toplevel, wxFrame)
...
    EVT_CHECKBOX(ID_RED_CHECKBOX, Toplevel::OnRed)
    EVT_CHECKBOX(ID_GREEN_CHECKBOX, Toplevel::OnGreen)
    EVT_CHECKBOX(ID_BLUE_CHECKBOX, Toplevel::OnBlue)
...
END_EVENT_TABLE()
```

The implementation of these functions is straightforward. The
IsChecked() function is used to determine whether the check box corresponding to the event is checked. A call is made to the setter function for the
corresponding color; if the check box is checked, the value of the color will
be set to full intensity (255); otherwise, it will be set to 0:

```
void Toplevel::OnRed(wxCommandEvent& event)
{
    m_drawing->SetRed(event.IsChecked() ? 255 : 0);
}

void Toplevel::OnGreen(wxCommandEvent& event)
{
    m_drawing->SetGreen(event.IsChecked() ? 255 : 0);
}

void Toplevel::OnBlue(wxCommandEvent& event)
{
    m_drawing->SetBlue(event.IsChecked() ? 255 : 0);
}
```

Finally, the Apply button is wired to its callback with a EVT_BUTTON(id,
func) macro; and in this callback, we simply call wxWindow::Refresh() to
cause the DrawingArea's OnPaint() function to be invoked:

```
void Toplevel::OnApply(wxCommandEvent& event)
{
    m_drawing->Refresh();
}
```

The only code we need to look at now is in the constructor of
DrawingArea. The only change required in the OnPaint() function is that
needed to retrieve the radius and color values for use in drawing the circle.
We also need to change the DrawingArea constructor to provide initialization

for the radius percent (m_percent) and color member variables. The changes to DrawingArea are shown in bold in the following listing:

```
#include "wx/wx.h"
#include "drawing.h"

BEGIN_EVENT_TABLE(DrawingArea, wxWindow)
    EVT_PAINT(DrawingArea::OnPaint)
END_EVENT_TABLE()

DrawingArea::DrawingArea(wxWindow *parent,
    const wxPoint& pos, const wxSize& size) :
    wxWindow(parent, -1, pos, size), m_percent(50),
    m_red(0), m_green(0), m_blue(0)
{
}

void DrawingArea::OnPaint(wxPaintEvent& event)
{
    int width, height;
    wxBrush bgBrush(wxColour(255,255,255), wxSOLID);
    wxMemoryDC memdc;

    GetClientSize(&width, &height);

    wxBitmap bmp(width, height);
    memdc.SelectObject(bmp);

    memdc.SetBrush(bgBrush);
    memdc.DrawRectangle(0, 0, width, height);

    int red = GetRed();
    int green = GetGreen();
    int blue = GetBlue();
    wxBrush fgBrush(wxColour(red,green,blue),
        wxSOLID);
    memdc.SetBrush(fgBrush);
    memdc.DrawCircle(width >> 1, height >> 1,
        (int)(width *
            (GetRadiusPercent() / 100.0)));

    wxPaintDC myDC(this);
    myDC.Blit(0, 0, width, height, &memdc, 0, 0,
        wxCOPY);
}
```

Dialogs

A dialog is similar to a top-level window. Like a top-level window, a dialog is a window that contains a title bar and manages child content consisting of controls or other widgets (for example, an instance of the DrawingArea class we created earlier). Usually, a dialog is used to prompt a user for information that is needed by the application for it to continue execution, or to display an error or warning message of some sort.

There are two types of dialog. A *modal dialog* grabs application focus, meaning that only the dialog will respond to mouse or keyboard input from the user while the modal dialog is being displayed, forcing the user to interact with the dialog before continuing. Generally speaking, modal dialogs are used for situations where information must be displayed or retrieved at a specific point in the execution of a program for the program to continue. If the user has selected Open from the File menu, for example, a modal dialog will be used to retrieve the pathname of the file to be opened. Here the dialog is modal because the application cannot proceed with the file open operation until the user specifies the name of the file to open. Another typical use of a modal dialog is to prompt a user for a username and password when signing on to a service of some kind. Once again, the application cannot go forward until the user responds. Finally, modal dialogs are often appropriate for displaying errors and warning message to users, because messages of these types usually make sense only at a particular point in time or in a specific context.

The other type of dialog is the *modeless dialog*. Modeless dialogs are similar to modal dialogs in terms of the content they manage, However, displaying a modeless dialog does not result in application focus being restricted to only that dialog while the dialog is visible. One might use a modeless dialog to display controls that affect the content of a main application window. A word processor such as Microsoft Word or an image-editing application such as GIMP or Photoshop might display formatting tools within a modeless dialog, for example. (See Figure 8-7.) Later, we will modify the Toplevel example to make use of modeless dialogs.

Modal Dialogs

The simplest (and perhaps most common) use of a modal dialog is to display a message of some kind to the user. Toplevel has, in fact, used a modal dialog from the beginning to display an About box to the user when the About menu item is selected from the File menu:

```
void Toplevel::OnAbout(wxCommandEvent& WXUNUSED(event))
{
    wxMessageBox("Toplevel wxWidgets Sample",
        "About Toplevel",
        wxOK | wxICON_INFORMATION, this);
}
```

`wxMessageBox()` creates a modal dialog, and waits for the user to dismiss the dialog before returning to the caller. The first argument to the constructor is the text displayed by the dialog, and the second argument is the text displayed in the title bar of the modal dialog window. The next argument specifies flags that define the appearance of the dialog and the buttons that it displays. The flags that define which buttons are displayed include those shown in Table 8-2.

Table 8-2 wxMessageBox Button Flags

Flag	Result
wxOK	Show an OK button.
wxCANCEL	Show a Cancel button.
wxYES_NO	Show Yes and No buttons.
wxYES_DEFAULT	Used with wxYES_NO, makes Yes button the default.
wxNO_DEFAULT	Used with wxYES_NO, makes No button the default.

`wxOK` can only be used alone—if specified with any of the other flags, the OK button will not be displayed. Similarly, `wxCANCEL` cannot be used alone, but only in combination with `wxYES_NO`. The flags that define the icon displayed by the dialog include those shown in Table 8-3.

Table 8-3 wxMessageBox Icon Flags

Flag	Result
wxICON_EXCLAMATION	Shows an exclamation mark icon.
wxICON_HAND	Shows an error icon.
wxICON_ERROR	Shows an error icon - the same as wxICON_HAND.
wxICON_QUESTION	Shows a question mark icon.
wxICON_INFORMATION	Shows an information (i) icon.

If we are displaying multiple buttons (for example, ones labeled Yes and No) and want to learn which of the buttons was pressed by the user in response to the dialog, we must use other methods to create and display the modal dialog than were illustrated previously. Specifically, wxMessageDialog is similar to wxMessageBox, but allows us to control its display and determine which button was pressed by the user. Here is a version of OnAbout() that illustrates its use:

```
void
Toplevel::OnAbout(wxCommandEvent& WXUNUSED(event))
{
    wxMessageDialog mydlg(this,
        "Toplevel wxWidgets Sample",
        "About Toplevel", wxOK | wxICON_INFORMATION);
    if (mydlg.ShowModal() == wxID_OK) {
        // user clicked OK button
    }
}
```

Of course, because the dialog is only displaying an OK button to begin with, there is really no reason to check the return value. More likely, we would reconfigure the dialog so that it is displaying both Yes and No buttons as in the following code which asks the user a Yes/No question:

```
wxMessageDialog mydlg(this,
    "Are you sure you want to save?",
    "Confirm Save",
    wxYES_NO | wxNO_DEFAULT | wxICON_QUESTION);
if (mydlg.ShowModal() == wxID_YES) {
    // user wants to save
} else {
    // user does not want to save
}
```

wxWidgets provides several classes in addition to wxMessageDialog that are designed to be displayed in a modal fashion. Some of these classes will be discussed in the "Composite Widgets" section later in this chapter.

Designing a Custom Modal Dialog

On rare occasion, you might find the need to implement a custom modal dialog. The pattern that one uses to accomplish this is similar to the pattern that we have been following in this chapter when defining new classes, and

involves inheriting from the wxWidgets class that the new class extends.
(So far, we have created classes that inherit from wxFrame, wxApp, and
wxWindow.) In this case, the class we need to inherit from is wxDialog,
because it implements the ShowModal() method that we will want to make
use of.

In this section, I demonstrate the steps necessary to create and display
your own custom modal dialog by implementing a password entry dialog.
There is a class in wxWidgets named wxTextEntryDialog that supports the
display of a modal dialog that accepts from the user a single line of text.
However, our dialog must support three separate text entry fields for the
following data: a username, a password, and (optionally) a reentry of the
password for the purpose of confirmation.

The constructor for the wxTextEntryDialog class gives us a good
starting point for the design of our class:

```
wxTextEntryDialog(
    wxWindow* parent,
    const wxString& message,
    const wxString& caption = "Please enter text",
    const wxString& defaultValue = "",
    long style = wxOK | wxCANCEL | wxCENTRE,
        const wxPoint& pos = wxDefaultPosition
)
```

The following minor changes get us closer to what we need:

- Removal of the message and defaultValue arguments
- A change to the default value for caption
- The addition of a Boolean argument, showConfirm, used to show or hide
  the password verification field
- Removal of the wxCENTER flag

The result is the constructor for our new class, PasswordEntryDialog:

```
PasswordEntryDialog(
    wxWindow* parent,
    bool showConfirm = false,
    const wxString& caption = "Enter username and password",
    long style = wxOK | wxCANCEL,
        const wxPoint& pos = wxDefaultPosition
)
```

The following code illustrates how you might use
PasswordEntryDialog in an application (see Figure 8-6). The function
OnPassword(), shown below, is a callback function implemented by the
application using the PasswordEntryDialog class, that might be invoked,
for example, when the user selects a menu item labeled "Set Password."

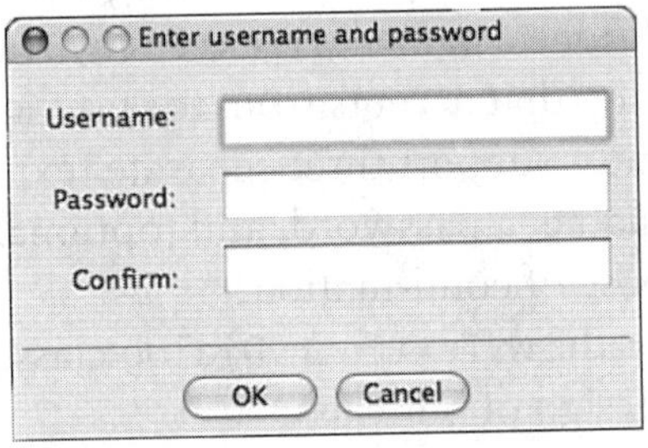

Figure 8-6 Password entry dialog

```
void Toplevel::OnPassword(wxCommandEvent& WXUNUSED(event))
{
    bool confirm = true;

    PasswordEntryDialog dialog(this, confirm);
    if (dialog.ShowModal() == wxID_OK) {
        wxString userStr = dialog.GetUsername();
        wxString passStr = dialog.GetPassword();
        wxString confirmStr = dialog.GetConfirm();
        ValidateAndSave(userStr, passStr,
            confirmStr, confirm);
    }
}
```

The lines in bold are typical when using modal dialogs: First, you create
an instance of the wxDialog object, and then you invoke its ShowModal()
method to display the dialog and retrieve the ID of the button clicked by the
user. Support for ShowModal() is inherited from wxDialog, but we do need
to do a bit of extra work in our class to properly dismiss the modal dialog
when the user clicks OK or Cancel, and ensure that the value returned by
ShowModal() correctly identifies the button that was used to dismiss the
dialog.

The other thing we must do is provide a method by which the data entered into the dialog can be retrieved. For example, to get the username, we need to provide a method named `GetUsername()`:

```
wxString userStr = dialog.GetUsername();
```

Here is the code from password.h that defines `PasswordEntryDialog`:

```
#ifndef __PASSWORD_ENTRY_DIALOG_H
#define __PASSWORD_ENTRY_DIALOG_H

#include "wx/wx.h"

class PasswordEntryDialog: public wxDialog
{
public:
    PasswordEntryDialog(wxWindow *parent,
        bool showConfirm = false,
        const wxString& caption =
            "Enter username and password",
        long style = wxOK | wxCANCEL | wxCENTRE,
        const wxPoint& pos = wxDefaultPosition);
    wxString GetUsername();
    wxString GetPassword();
    wxString GetConfirm();
private:
    void OnOK(wxCommandEvent& event);
    void OnCancel(wxCommandEvent& event);

    wxTextCtrl *m_userNameEntry;
    wxTextCtrl *m_passwordEntry;
    wxTextCtrl *m_confirmEntry;
    bool m_showConfirm;

    DECLARE_EVENT_TABLE()
};

#endif
```

The important points to extract from the preceding listing are the inheritance from wxDialog, and the inclusion of a DECLARE_EVENT_TABLE() macro, which is needed so that we can map the OK and Cancel buttons in the UI to the callback functions OnOK() and OnCancel().

Let's take a look at the implementation of these callbacks, because it is within these callbacks that we must implement the desired modal dialog behaviors:

```
void
PasswordEntryDialog::OnOK(wxCommandEvent& event)
{
    if (IsModal() == true)
        EndModal(wxID_OK);
}

void
PasswordEntryDialog::OnCancel(wxCommandEvent& event)
{
    if (IsModal() == true)
        EndModal(wxID_CANCEL);
}
```

EndModal() is a wxDialog method that dismisses a modal dialog, causing ShowModal() to return. The argument to EndModal() specifies the return value of ShowModal(); it can be any int value, but is typically the ID of a button displayed by the modal dialog. I chose to return wxID_OK and wxID_CANCEL rather than class-specific values because these values are typically what programs expect to be mapped to OK and Cancel buttons. However, I used ID values defined in an enum declared in the PasswordEntryDialog source so that I could be sure the values I used were unique and did not conflict with the values of wxID_OK and wxID_CANCEL, which should be treated as opaque by applications.

That's pretty much it for modal dialogs. To summarize, remember the following points:

- Modal dialogs must always inherit from wxDialog.
- Invoke EndModal() from an OnOK() or OnCancel() callback to dismiss the modal dialog, passing it an int that can be used by the caller of ShowModal() to determine the user action.
- Application programmers will expect wxID_OK and wxID_CANCEL as return values from ShowModal()(if the dialog you design has OK or Cancel buttons), so it is a good idea to arrange for ShowModal() to return these values, but be careful not to use these IDs to define items in your dialog, because the use of these constants may lead to logic errors.

Modeless Dialogs

Now that we have modal dialogs out of the way, let's turn our attention to modeless dialogs. Just like there are times when a modal dialog makes sense, there are times when the use of a modal dialog can restrict the usability of an application. Consider the GIMP layers dialog shown in Figure 8-7. The GIMP layers dialog provides the user with a set of controls that can be used to manipulate the layers of an image. The GIMP layers dialog is most effective when it persists on the desktop—it would significantly decrease the usability of the application if the user were required to click a button or select a menu item each and every time the layers dialog were needed. It would be equally unusable if the layers dialog, while being displayed, grabbed input focus and did not allow the user to interact with any of the top-level image windows. Because of this, the only choice from a usability standpoint is to make the layers dialog modeless.

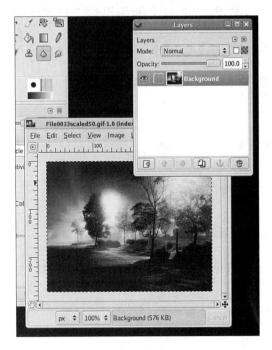

Figure 8-7 Modeless dialog in GIMP

Using Modeless Dialogs

As a simple example of the creation and use of modeless dialogs, let's modify the Toplevel application (presented earlier) by moving the check

boxes used to set the fill color of the circle drawn by the `DrawingArea` into a
separate, modeless dialog (see Figure 8-8).

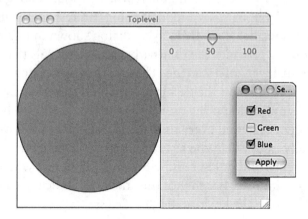

Figure 8-8 wxWidgets modeless dialog

A new class, `ColorDialog`, which inherits from `wxDialog` is needed:

```
#ifndef __COLOR_DIALOG_H
#define __COLOR_DIALOG_H

#include "wx/wx.h"

class DrawingArea;

class ColorDialog: public wxDialog
{
public:
    ColorDialog(wxWindow *parent,
        const wxString& title, const wxPoint& pos,
        const wxSize& size, DrawingArea *drawing);
    void OnRed(wxCommandEvent& event);
    void OnGreen(wxCommandEvent& event);
    void OnBlue(wxCommandEvent& event);
    void OnApply(wxCommandEvent& event);
private:
    DrawingArea *m_drawing;
    int m_red;
    int m_green;
    int m_blue;
    DECLARE_EVENT_TABLE()
};

#endif
```

The bulk of this new class consists of callbacks that are invoked as the user interacts with the controls displayed in the dialog. OnRed(), OnGreen(), and OnBlue() are called as the user clicks the Red, Green, and Blue check boxes, respectively, and the current state of each check box is stored as a color value in a ColorDialog member variable:

```
void ColorDialog::OnRed(wxCommandEvent& event)
{
    m_red = (event.IsChecked() ? 255 : 0);
}


void ColorDialog::OnGreen(wxCommandEvent& event)
{
    m_green = (event.IsChecked() ? 255 : 0);
}


void ColorDialog::OnBlue(wxCommandEvent& event)
{
    m_blue = (event.IsChecked() ? 255 : 0);
}
```

When the user clicks the Apply button, methods on the DrawingArea widget are invoked to set the new colors, and the DrawingArea's Refresh() method is called to cause the circle to be redrawn with the new fill color:

```
void ColorDialog::OnApply(wxCommandEvent& event)
{
    m_drawing->SetRed(m_red);
    m_drawing->SetGreen(m_green);
    m_drawing->SetBlue(m_blue);
    m_drawing->Refresh();
}
```

The above is reminiscent of a pattern that is often encountered when working with dialogs, be they modal or modeless. The class that creates and manages the dialog (in this case, ColorDialog) maintains any and all changes made by the user, but does not act upon these changes until the user "accepts" the dialog by clicking an OK button (or its equivalent). In the OnApply() callback, we push the changes to the DrawingArea widget via a pointer to the DrawingArea instance that is maintained in ColorDialog. A similar strategy was used in the implementation of PasswordEntryDialog (see the "Modal Dialogs" section, earlier in this chapter). However, the drawback to the `ColorDialog` design used here is that we really should not be coupling the `DrawingArea` class to the `ColorDialog` class in this way; after all, some class other than `DrawingArea` may want to make use of the service that `ColorDialog` provides. A more general design would supply a scheme by which classes (such as `Toplevel`) could register a listener that would notify them when the user has accepted the changes made in the `ColorDialog` dialog, and perhaps a set of getter functions provided by `ColorDialog` that can be used by the listening object to retrieve the color value changes once the listening object has been notified that the user has accepted the dialog. Or, perhaps more simply, the notification scheme would pass the red, green, and blue values to the listening object directly when it sends the notification. In either case, `Toplevel`, as the listening class and creator of both the `ColorDialog` and `DrawingArea` instances, would act as a bridge between these two classes.

Creating and displaying the modeless dialog is simply a matter of creating an instance of `ColorDialog` and invoking its `Show()` method from within the `Toplevel` constructor:

```
Toplevel::Toplevel(const wxString& title,
    const wxPoint& pos, const wxSize& size) :
    wxFrame((wxFrame *)NULL, -1, title, pos, size)
{

    ...

    wxSize dsize(300, 200);
    m_colors = new ColorDialog(this, "Set Colors",
        wxDefaultPosition, dsize, m_drawing);

    m_colors->Show(TRUE);

    ...

}
```

Because `ColorDialog` is a child of `Toplevel` (parent is set to this in the above code), we don't need to do anything to close the modeless dialog when the user destroys the `Toplevel` instance, or exits the application; wxWidgets makes sure that all the widgets in the parent-child hierarchy will be destroyed properly, automatically. However, if we want to close the modeless dialog during execution of the application for some reason, we need to adopt one of two strategies. To illustrate the options, assume there is a menu item in the Toplevel application that displays two labels. The first label, "Show Color Dialog," is displayed when the ColorDialog instance is not visible. Selecting the Show Color Dialog menu item causes the Toplevel object to create an instance of ColorDialog and invoke its Show() method, using the same code illustrated previously. When the ColorDialog instance is visible, the label of the menu item is changed by Toplevel from "Show Color Dialog" to "Hide Color Dialog." Selecting the menu item when it is displaying the "Hide Color Dialog" label will result in the ColorDialog being dismissed.

To dismiss the dialog, we can destroy the ColorDialog instance with a call to Destroy():

```
m_colors->Destroy();
m_colors = NULL;
```

The code shown above (repeated here)

```
    wxSize dsize(300, 200);
    m_colors = new ColorDialog(this, "Set Colors",
        wxDefaultPosition, dsize, m_drawing);

    m_colors->Show(TRUE);
```

would then need to be executed once again to create and display the ColorDialog dialog whenever the user selects the Show Color Dialog menu item.

The other option is to hide the dialog by calling the wxWindow method Show():

```
m_colors->Show(FALSE);
```

To redisplay the ColorDialog dialog, all that is needed is another call to Show(), this time with the application passing TRUE as an argument:

```
m_colors->Show(TRUE);
```

Showing and hiding the dialog with wxWindow::Show() has two benefits:

- It is more efficient—the ColorDialog is only created once, and it is never destroyed.

- Because the `ColorDialog` object exists while hidden, it can maintain current state. (In this case, the currently selected colors are maintained in `ColorDialog` member variables.)

This strategy is illustrated in the next section.

Composite Widgets

wxWidgets provides a comprehensive set of composite widgets. Referred to as Common Dialogs in wxWidgets documentation, these widgets provide complete implementations of dialogs that are commonly needed by applications. By using these widgets, developers can provide users with a more consistent UI across applications, and reduce the amount of code that they must write and debug. Each of these dialog classes inherits from `wxDialog`, and supports modal operation. In the following subsections, I introduce the most useful of the composite widgets supported by wxWidgets: `wxFontDialog`, `wxFileDialog`, and `wxColourDialog`.

wxFontDialog

Figure 8-9 illustrates an instance of `wxFontDialog` as would be displayed by the Gtk+ implementation of wxWidgets running on Linux. A native font selection dialog is displayed by `wxFontDialog` on Windows, and on Mac OS X a custom (that is, wxWidgets-implemented) font dialog is provided (see Figure 8-10).

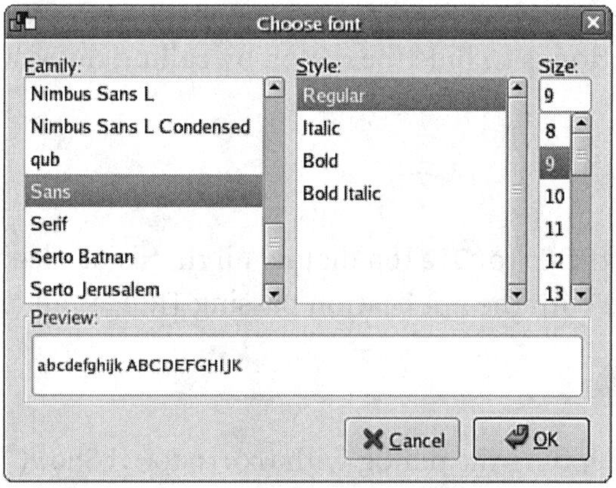

Figure 8-9 Gtk+ implementation of `wxFontDialog`

To create an instance of `wxFontDialog` (from, for example, a callback function), you must allocate a `wxFontData` object and either pass a reference to the object to the wxFontDialog constructor or invoke wxFontDialog::Create(), once again, passing a reference to your wxFontData object. The wxFontData object acts as a bidirectional communication channel between your application and the wxFontDialog object; before invoking the wxFontDialog constructor (or calling Create()), you initialize the wxFontData object to specify attributes of the fonts that the wxFontDialog object will display. When the user dismisses the font dialog, wxFontDialog will store the results in the wxFontData object; you then use getter methods provided by wxFontData to retrieve these results.

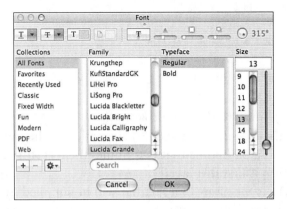

Figure 8-10 Mac OS X implementation of wxFontDialog

The following implementation of a menu handler for a Set Font menu item provides an illustration for the use of wxFontDialog:

```
void Toplevel::OnFont(wxCommandEvent& WXUNUSED(event))
{
    wxFontData data;
    static wxColour color(255, 0, 0);
    static wxFont font(12, wxROMAN, wxNORMAL, wxBOLD,
        FALSE, "Times");

    data.SetInitialFont(font);
    data.SetColour(color);
    wxFontDialog dialog(this, &data);
    if (dialog.ShowModal() == wxID_OK) {
        wxFontData retData = dialog.GetFontData();
        font = retData.GetChosenFont();
        color = retData.GetColour();
    }
}
```

wxFileDialog

`wxFileDialog` implements the file selection dialog typically displayed when users select Open and Save As menu items from the File menu of an application. The constructor for `wxFileDialog` is as follows:

```
wxFileDialog(
    wxWindow* parent,
    const wxString& message = "Choose a file",
    const wxString& defaultDir = "",
    const wxString& defaultFile = "",
    const wxString& wildcard = "*.*",
    long style = 0,
    const wxPoint& pos = wxDefaultPosition
);
```

where

- `parent` is a pointer to the parent window.
- `message` is the message displayed by the dialog to the user.
- `defaultDir` is a pathname that determines the directory displayed when `wxFileDialog` is first displayed.
- `defaultFile` is the name of a file that will be supplied (on some platforms) as the default selection.
- `wildcard` is a string that defines a series of masks that are applied to files in the `defaultDir`. Only files matching the mask will be displayed (or selectable). See below for more details.
- `style` is a bitmask consisting of one or more of the values in Table 8-4.

Table 8-4 `wxFileDialog` Styles

Flag	Dialog Type
wxOPEN	Create file Open dialog.
wxSAVE	Create a file Save As dialog.
wxHIDE_READONLY	If the Open dialog supports a "read-only" check box setting, don't show it.
wxOVERWRITE_PROMPT	If the user selects an existing file in a Save As dialog, prompt for a confirmation.
wxMULTIPLE	If the Open dialog supports it, allow multiple file selection.
wxCHANGE_DIR	Change the current working directory to the directory that contains the file selected by the user.

Displaying a file selection dialog is simply a matter of creating an instance of wxFileDialog, invoking its ShowModal() method, and if ShowModal() returns wxID_OK, retrieving the pathname of the file (or files in the case of multiple selection) that were selected by the user. The following is the implementation of a menu callback that demonstrates all you need to know to use wxFileDialog effectively. The file selection dialog displayed by this function allows the user to select either C++ source and header files, or all files. (The user can control which applies by selecting either file type from a combo box displayed by the file selection dialog.) The wildcard string in this example

```
"C++ Source Files (*.cpp,*.h)|*.cpp;*.h|All Files|*.*"
```

consists of two logical sections, one that defines the label and the mask for the C++ Source Files item in the combo box, and the other which supplies the label and mask for the All Files combo box item. The | character in the preceding wildcard string plays a dual role, separating not only the two logical wildcard components:

```
C++ Source Files (*.cpp,*.h)|*.cpp;*.h
```

and

```
All Files|*.*
```

but also separating, within each component, the label from the mask. The generic form of a wildcard string is, therefore, the following:

```
"label-1 | mask-1 | label-2 | mask-2 | label-3 | \
mask-3 | … | label-n | mask-n"
```

Although the dual use of the | character might be confusing at first glance, just remember the following:

- Each component of the wildcard string is separated by a | character.
- Each component consists of a label and mask that is also separated by a | character.

In the following listing, you can see that if ShowModal() returns wxID_OK, we know the user clicked the Open button in the file selection dialog. The check to see whether the style contained wxMULTIPLE is redundant, but protects us if we decide to later remove that flag from the style argument that is passed to the wxFileDialog constructor:

```
void Toplevel::OnFile(wxCommandEvent& WXUNUSED(event))
{
    char *cwd = ::getcwd(NULL, 0);
    wxFileDialog myFileDialog(this, "Choose a file",
        cwd, "toplevel.cpp",
        "C++ Source Files (*.cpp,*.h)|*.cpp;*.h|\
        All Files|*.*", wxOPEN | wxMULTIPLE);

    if (myFileDialog.ShowModal() == wxID_OK) {
        if (myFileDialog.GetStyle() | wxMULTIPLE) {
            wxArrayString paths;
            wxArrayString files;
            myFileDialog.GetPaths(paths);
            myFileDialog.GetFilenames(files);
            for (int i = 0; i < paths.GetCount(); i++)
                printf("%d %s %s\n", i,
                    paths[i].c_str(),
                    files[i].c_str());
        }
        else {
            wxString path = myFileDialog.GetPath();
            wxString file = myFileDialog.GetFilename();
            printf("%s %s\n", path.c_str(),
                file.c_str());
        }
    }
    free(cwd);
}
```

Two pairs of methods are supplied by wxFileDialog to retrieve the user
selection from the wxFileDialog widget. One pair is used if the style is single
selection: GetPath() returns the full pathname of the selected file, and
GetFilename() returns the filename portion of the path. Both return a
wxString reference, and wxString::c_str() can be used to get C-style
string versions. If style contains wxMULTPLE, the methods GetPaths() and
GetFilenames() should be used rather than GetPath() and GetFilename(),
respectively. Both of these return a reference to a wxArrayString object. The
preceding listing shows how to iterate a wxArrayString object and obtain
the pathnames and filenames. Experimentation shows that the *i*th entry of
the GetFilenames() wxArrayString object corresponds to the *i*th entry of
the wxArrayString object returned by GetPaths(). For example, if the
second entry of paths in the preceding listing is /home/syd/main.cpp, the
second entry of files will be set to main.cpp.

wxColourDialog

The final wxWidgets composite widget class discussed in this book is
wxColourDialog. wxColourDialog implements a platform-specific color
picker like the one displayed for Mac OS X in Figure 8-11.

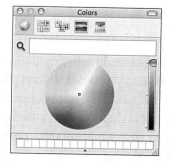

Figure 8-11 wxColourDialog

Use of wxColourDialog is similar in some respects to wxFontDialog; a
helper object (in this case wxColourData) is passed to the constructor to
initialize the color that is initially displayed by the color picker, and on
return from ShowModal(), the application queries for a wxColourData
object reference that, in turn, can be queried for the RGB components of the
color selected by the user. The following is the wxColourDialog constructor:

```
wxColourDialog(wxWindow* parent,
    wxColourData* data = NULL)
```

As we have been doing all along, a menu item callback illustrates the
creation and use of a wxColourDialog widget:

```
void Toplevel::OnColor(wxCommandEvent& WXUNUSED(event))
{
    wxColourData data;
    int red, green, blue;

    red = m_drawing->GetRed();
    green = m_drawing->GetGreen();
    blue = m_drawing->GetBlue();

    wxColour color(red, green, blue);
    data.SetColour(color);
    wxColourDialog myColorDialog(this, &data);

    if (myColorDialog.ShowModal() == wxID_OK) {
```

```
        data = myColorDialog.GetColourData();
        color = data.GetColour();
        m_drawing->SetRed(color.Red());
        m_drawing->SetGreen(color.Green());
        m_drawing->SetBlue(color.Blue());
        m_drawing->Refresh();
    }
}
```

The first few lines of the preceding listing extract the current fill color component values from the `DrawingArea` widget. (`DrawingArea` was introduced previously.) A `wxColour` object is constructed and initialized with these values; this object is then used to initialize the color component of the `wxColourData` object that we ultimately pass by reference to the `wxColourDialog` constructor.

Following the same pattern exhibited for `wxFontDialog` and `wxFileDialog`, we query the `wxColourDialog` object for the user selection, but only if `wxID_OK` is returned by `ShowModal()`. The `GetColourData()` method retrieves a reference to a `wxColorData` object that can be then queried for the red, green, and blue components of the color selected by the user. As you can see in the preceding listing, the retrieved colors are then passed directly to the `DrawingArea` object, and its `Refresh()` method is invoked, which causes the `DrawingArea::OnPaint()` function to repaint the window, using the assigned colors to define the fill color of the circle that it draws.

Internationalization and Localization

wxWidgets uses a catalog-based approach for internationalization (i18n) that is based on the gettext(1) package from GNU. The gettext tools are in fact required when developing i18n-based applications for wxWidgets, as you will see later.

In this section, I introduce a new type of source file—the PO file—which contains native translations of all literal strings used by the application; there is one PO file for each language supported by the application. The strings in a PO file cover all text displayed by the application, be it the content of a tooltip, the label of a button or a menu item, or the text displayed in an error message generated by the program during runtime. What is *not* represented in PO files are strings that come from external sources, such as error messages generated by libraries or the operating system, or application data that is read from external sources, such as files or databases.

You, as the developer, are responsible for creating the content of a baseline PO file, which contains strings that are translated to your native language. Translators are responsible for converting the baseline PO file to additional PO files, one such file for each language supported by your application.

So far, the examples in this chapter have not made use of wxWidget's internationalization support; all text in the source code presented so far has been literal, and in English, which is not recommended if you wish to support more than one language. In the following example:

```
void Toplevel::OnFile(wxCommandEvent& WXUNUSED(event))
{
    char *cwd = ::getcwd(NULL, 0);
    wxFileDialog myFileDialog(this, "Choose a file",
        cwd, "toplevel.cpp",
        "C++ Source Files (*.cpp,*.h)|*.cpp;*.h|\
        All Files|*.*", wxOPEN | wxMULTIPLE);
```

the message and wildcard arguments to the `wxFileDialog` constructor are in English and are subject to translation. The same is true for the following code used to create a menu:

```
wxMenu *menuFile = new wxMenu;

menuFile->Append(ID_About, "&About...");
menuFile->AppendSeparator();
menuFile->Append(ID_Quit, "&Quit");

wxMenuBar *menuBar = new wxMenuBar;
menuBar->Append(menuFile, "&File");

SetMenuBar(menuBar);
```

In the preceding code, the strings **"&About"**, **"&Quit"**, and **"&File"** all need to be replaced as a part of the task of internationalizing the application.

Using Gettext

The ideal time to adopt gettext is at the beginning of development, not at the end. The gettext suite of tools supports the creation of a baseline PO file from existing sources, as I show later, but I firmly believe using gettext from the beginning simplifies things over the long haul.

To use gettext, you need to do the following:

1. Replace all literal strings in the application with symbolic names; these names will be used to index translated literal strings located in the PO files.
2. Create the baseline PO file using the xgettext utility, which is a part of the gettext package.
3. Edit the PO file, supplying translated literal strings for each item in the file.
4. Compile the PO file into a binary MO file that can be shipped with the application.
5. For each language you support, clone the baseline PO file, and then repeat Steps 3 and 4.

Step 1 involves assigning symbolic names to literal strings in your application. You should choose symbolic names that make it easy for translators (and you) to locate strings in the PO file. The following is an example strategy that you can use or modify as you see fit. Each symbolic name is more or less of the form *class.object.attribute.value*, where

- *class* is the name of the class that makes use of the literal string.
- *object* informally identifies the object that makes use of the literal string.
- *attribute* is the attribute of the object that is assigned the literal string.
- *value* is the nontranslated (baseline) string that helps to identify the meaning of the translated literal string.

A few examples are definitely needed to make the above clear. Let's take a look at portions of the `Toplevel` class source, presented earlier in the chapter, that contain literal strings (lines with literal strings shown in bold):

```
Toplevel::Toplevel(const wxString& title,
    const wxPoint& pos, const wxSize& size) :
    wxFrame((wxFrame *)NULL, -1, title, pos, size)
{
    wxBoxSizer *topSizer =
        new wxBoxSizer(wxHORIZONTAL);

    wxMenu *menuFile = new wxMenu;

    menuFile->Append(ID_About, "&About...");
    menuFile->AppendSeparator();
    menuFile->Append(ID_Quit, "&Quit");
```

```
wxMenuBar *menuBar = new wxMenuBar;
menuBar->Append(menuFile, "&File");

...


wxSize dsize(300, 200);
m_colors = new ColorDialog(this, "Set Colors",
    wxDefaultPosition, dsize, m_drawing);

m_colors->Show(TRUE);

SetSizer(topSizer);
}


...


void
Toplevel::OnAbout(wxCommandEvent& WXUNUSED(event))
{
    wxMessageDialog mydlg(this,
        "Toplevel wxWidgets Sample",
        "About Toplevel",
        wxOK | wxICON_INFORMATION);
    mydlg.ShowModal();
}
```

As you can see in Table 8-5, six distinct literal strings are used in the Toplevel class:

Table 8-5 Literal Strings Used in the Toplevel Class

String	Purpose
&About...	File menu About menu item label
&Quit	File menu Quit menu item label
&File	File menu label
Set Colors	ColorDialog window title bar label
Toplevel wxWidgets Sample	Message displayed in About box
About Toplevel	About box window title bar label

Given these literal strings and their descriptions, one might come up with the following symbolic names:

```
Toplevel.MenuItem.About.Label
Toplevel.MenuItem.Quit.Label
Toplevel.Menu.File.Label
Toplevel.ColorDialog.TitleBar.Label
Toplevel.AboutBox.Message.Text
Toplevel.AboutBox.TitleBar.Label
```

Let's do the same thing for the `ColorDialog` class. In bold, here are portions of colors.cpp that contain literal text:

```
ColorDialog::ColorDialog(wxWindow *parent,
    const wxString& title, const wxPoint& pos,
    const wxSize& size, DrawingArea *drawing):
    wxDialog(parent, -1, title, pos, size),
        m_drawing(drawing)
{

...

    wxCheckBox *redCheckBox =
        new wxCheckBox(this, ID_RED_CHECKBOX, "Red");
    wxCheckBox *greenCheckBox =
        new wxCheckBox(this, ID_GREEN_CHECKBOX,
            "Green");
    wxCheckBox *blueCheckBox =
        new wxCheckBox(this, ID_BLUE_CHECKBOX, "Blue");

...

    wxButton *applyButton =
        new wxButton(this, ID_COLOR_APPLY, "Apply");

...

}
```

The following possible symbolic names can be derived from the preceding source:

```
ColorDialog.CheckBox.Red.Label
ColorDialog.CheckBox.Green.Label
ColorDialog.CheckBox.Blue.Label
ColorDialog.Button.Apply.Label
```

Remember, it's not critical that you follow my suggestions to the letter; all that is required by gettext is that the symbolic names you chose be unique. You are free to devise whatever strategy makes best sense for you and your application. But, it should be clear to you when looking at the symbolic names I have chosen not only what the symbolic names refer to, but also where you would find them when searching for them in the source code. Therefore, I hope you are convinced that a well-thought out policy for naming symbolic names is important, because it can lead to a dramatic improvement in the readability (and maintainability) of your PO files.

Continuing on with Step 1, let's modify the source to use these symbolic names. First, toplevel.cpp:

```
Toplevel::Toplevel(const wxString& title,
    const wxPoint& pos, const wxSize& size) :
    wxFrame((wxFrame *)NULL, -1, title, pos, size)
{
    wxBoxSizer *topSizer =
        new wxBoxSizer(wxHORIZONTAL);

    wxMenu *menuFile = new wxMenu;

    menuFile->Append(ID_About,
        _("Toplevel.MenuItem.About.Label"));
    menuFile->AppendSeparator();
    menuFile->Append(ID_Quit,
        _("Toplevel.MenuItem.Quit.Label"));

    wxMenuBar *menuBar = new wxMenuBar;
    menuBar->Append(menuFile,
        _("Toplevel.Menu.File.Label"));

    ...



    wxSize dsize(300, 200);
    m_colors = new ColorDialog(this,
        _("Toplevel.ColorDialog.TitleBar.Label"),
        wxDefaultPosition, dsize, m_drawing);

    m_colors->Show(TRUE);

    SetSizer(topSizer);
}
```

...

```
void
Toplevel::OnAbout(wxCommandEvent& WXUNUSED(event))
{
    wxMessageDialog mydlg(this,
        _("Toplevel.AboutBox.Message.Text"),
        _("Toplevel.AboutBox.TitleBar.Label"),
        wxOK | wxICON_INFORMATION);
    mydlg.ShowModal();
}
```

Next, colors.cpp:

```
ColorDialog::ColorDialog(wxWindow *parent,
    const wxString& title, const wxPoint& pos,
    const wxSize& size, DrawingArea *drawing) :
    wxDialog(parent, -1, title, pos, size),
    m_drawing(drawing)
{

...

    wxCheckBox *redCheckBox =
        new wxCheckBox(this, ID_RED_CHECKBOX,
            _("ColorDialog.CheckBox.Red.Label"));
    wxCheckBox *greenCheckBox =
        new wxCheckBox(this, ID_GREEN_CHECKBOX,
            _("ColorDialog.CheckBox.Green.Label"));
    wxCheckBox *blueCheckBox =
        new wxCheckBox(this, ID_BLUE_CHECKBOX,
            _("ColorDialog.CheckBox.Blue.Label"));

...

    wxButton *applyButton =
        new wxButton(this, ID_COLOR_APPLY,
            _("ColorDialog.Button.Apply.Label"));

...

}
```

The preceding source makes use of the wxWidgets _() macro, which is defined in wx/intl.h as follows:

```
#define   _(str)  wxGetTranslation(_T(str))
```

where the function wxGetTranslation() takes a symbolic name and looks it up in the binary version of the PO file at runtime, returning whatever string it finds. If no string is found, the symbolic name is returned. If we were to recompile the sources at this point, and run the application without a properly constructed binary PO file, we would get results where the labels are based on the symbolic names specified in the code.

This completes Step 1. The next step, Step 2, involves generating a PO file from the sources. To do this, we enlist the help of the xgettext(1) tool provided by the gettext package. If you are doing this work on Mac OS X (as I did during the preparation of the book) and you don't yet have gettext installed, you can get it by installing fink (see http://fink.sourceforge.net). On Windows, the tools you need are a part of Cygwin, which you should also have installed on your system (www.cygwin.com; see Item 9. Of course, on Linux, you need do nothing, because gettext is a intrinsic part of any Linux-based development system. After you install gettext, run the following command to generate a baseline PO file:

```
% xgettext -a --no-location  toplevel.cpp colors.cpp
```

This command generates a file named messages.po, which will look something like this:

```
# SOME DESCRIPTIVE TITLE.
# Copyright (C) YEAR Free Software Foundation, Inc.
# FIRST AUTHOR <EMAIL@ADDRESS>, YEAR.
#
#, fuzzy
msgid ""
msgstr ""
"Project-Id-Version: PACKAGE VERSION\n"
"POT-Creation-Date: 2004-09-11 01:38-0700\n"
"PO-Revision-Date: YEAR-MO-DA HO:MI+ZONE\n"
"Last-Translator: FULL NAME <EMAIL@ADDRESS>\n"
"Language-Team: LANGUAGE <LL@li.org>\n"
"MIME-Version: 1.0\n"
"Content-Type: text/plain; charset=iso-8859-1\n"
"Content-Transfer-Encoding: 8bit\n"

msgid "ColorDialog.CheckBox.Red.Label"
msgstr ""

msgid "ColorDialog.CheckBox.Green.Label"
msgstr ""
```

```
msgid "ColorDialog.CheckBox.Blue.Label"
msgstr ""

msgid "ColorDialog.Button.Apply.Label"
msgstr ""

msgid "Toplevel.MenuItem.About.Label"
msgstr ""

msgid "Toplevel.MenuItem.Quit.Label"
msgstr ""

msgid "Toplevel.Menu.File.Label"
msgstr ""

msgid "Toplevel.ColorDialog.TitleBar.Label"
msgstr ""

msgid "Toplevel.AboutBox.Message.Text"
msgstr ""

msgid "Toplevel.AboutBox.TitleBar.Label"
msgstr ""
```

As you can see, each of the symbolic names in the source file are represented by two lines of code in the PO file. For example:

```
msgid "Toplevel.Menu.File.Label"
msgstr ""
```

The first line, `msgid`, identifies the symbolic name, and the line below it, `msgstr`, contains the localized version of the string that should be displayed by the application in place of the symbolic name. The translator's job, given the preceding PO file, is to replace each `msgstr` value with a translated string appropriate for its corresponding `msgid`.

After adding the English language text for each item in the PO file (Step 3), and modifying the comments at the top of the file (optional), we get the final version of the baseline PO file:

```
# Toplevel baseline PO file, English language
# Copyright (C) YEAR Free Software Foundation, Inc.
# FIRST AUTHOR <EMAIL@ADDRESS>, YEAR.
#
#, fuzzy
```

```
msgid ""
msgstr ""
"Project-Id-Version: PACKAGE VERSION\n"
"POT-Creation-Date: 2004-09-11 01:38-0700\n"
"PO-Revision-Date: YEAR-MO-DA HO:MI+ZONE\n"
"Last-Translator: FULL NAME <EMAIL@ADDRESS>\n"
"Language-Team: LANGUAGE <LL@li.org>\n"
"MIME-Version: 1.0\n"
"Content-Type: text/plain; charset=CHARSET\n"
"Content-Transfer-Encoding: 8bit\n"

msgid "ColorDialog.CheckBox.Red.Label"
msgstr "Red"

msgid "ColorDialog.CheckBox.Green.Label"
msgstr "Green"

msgid "ColorDialog.CheckBox.Blue.Label"
msgstr "Blue"

msgid "ColorDialog.Button.Apply.Label"
msgstr "Apply"

msgid "Toplevel.MenuItem.About.Label"
msgstr "&About"

msgid "Toplevel.MenuItem.Quit.Label"
msgstr "&Quit"

msgid "Toplevel.Menu.File.Label"
msgstr "&File"

msgid "Toplevel.ColorDialog.TitleBar.Label"
msgstr "Set Colors"

msgid "Toplevel.AboutBox.Message.Text"
msgstr "Toplevel wxWidgets Sample"

msgid "Toplevel.AboutBox.TitleBar.Label"
msgstr "About Toplevel"
```

Step 4 involves converting the PO file into a binary MO file that can be shipped with the application. To do this, we use the `msgfmt` command provided by the gettext package:

```
$ msgfmt messages.po -o messages.mo
```

The first argument to `msgfmt` in the preceding command line is the pathname of the PO file that is to be converted. The –o argument specifies the name of the target MO file. You will typically execute `msgfmt` from a Makefile, with the MO file as the target, and the PO file as the dependency.

Locating PO and MO Files

To be effective, MO files for languages other than English (or the primary language of the developer, whatever that may be) need to be provided for an application to be truly internationalized (at least, in terms of the strings it displays). This brings us to the problem of how to organize the PO files in the source tree, and how to distribute MO files with the application.

Let's start with the location of PO files in the source tree. Because PO files are merely sources that are used to create MO files, there is considerable flexibility regarding where they can be located in the source tree. However, you usually find PO files located in a dedicated directory; typically, with the name *locale* or *language*. Within this directory (we'll assume that it is called *locale*), you can either create a subdirectory for each language, and store in each directory a translated copy of the PO file, as follows:

```
/locale
    /en
        messages.po
    /es
        messages.po
    /ru
        messages.po
    /fr
        messages.po
    /de
        messages.po
```

or the locale can be a flat directory that contains a uniquely named PO file for each language that is supported:

```
/locale
    messages.en.po
    messages.es.po
    messages.ru.po
    messages.fr.po
    messages.de.po
```

My personal preference is to store PO files in individual subdirectories. The reason for this is that as a developer, I am only going to maintain the PO file for my native language. Translators are going to take that native PO file and convert it to the remaining supported languages. Therefore, for me, it is simpler to cd into the en directory, for example, and work with a set of English language PO files, versus searching for the correct files in a flat directory among a sea of PO files intended for other languages. The same advantage applies to translators; the Spanish language translator assigned to the project needs to work only in the es directory, and is unconcerned with the other PO files (well, except for the PO file of the native language, which it must use as a source for translations). This might not seem like a big deal, but as the number of languages and PO files grows, such an organization can really help reduce complexity.

Distributing MO Files

Now on to the problem of distributing MO files with the application. Notice the names chosen for the subdirectories (for example, en, es, fr in the previous section). These are standard two-letter language codes that are defined by ISO 639. (You can search the Web for more information on ISO 639; several sites list the entire set of ISO 639 codes.) The language of the application (details on setting the language are given below) is mapped to its corresponding two-letter ISO 639 code, and this name is used to form a search path used by wxWidgets to find MO files at runtime. For example, if the application is installed in/usr/local/toplevel, and the language is French, wxWidgets will search for message files, by default, in /usr/local/toplevel/fr. This is another reason for using a directory layout which separates PO files in the source tree; it more directly maps to the directory layout that many applications would likely choose to implement in their installers.

Creating a Locale

So, how do you set the language for the application? To do this, an application creates an instance of wxLocale in the Init() function of wxApp:

```
#include "wx/wx.h"
#include "toplevel.h"

class MyApp: public wxApp
{
    virtual bool OnInit();
```

```
protected:
    wxLocale myLocale;  // declare the wxLocale object
};

IMPLEMENT_APP(MyApp)

bool MyApp::OnInit()
{
    myLocale.Init(wxLANGUAGE_DEFAULT);

...


    return TRUE;
}
```

The function wxLocale::Init() accepts a language identifier, which it stores internally. Before returning, Init() loads a standard message catalog named wxstd, which contains strings that were culled by xgettext from the wxWidgets sources and translated to several languages.

The set of language identifiers is defined in wx/intl.h in an enum named wxLanguage, and includes more than 200 languages and locales, including the following shown in Table 8-6.

Table 8-6 Core wxLanguage Enums

Language	Meaning
wxLANGUAGE_DEFAULT	Language defined by the operating system
wxLANGUAGE_UNKNOWN	Unknown language, set if lookup of default language fails
wxLANGUAGE_USER	Application-defined language

Examples of some of the many languages defined by the wxLanguage enum are wxLANGUAGE_ENGLISH, wxLANGUAGE_FRENCH, wxLANGUAGE_GERMAN, and wxLANGUAGE_SPANISH.

Often, variations of a given language are provided; for example, the following variations of the English language are all represented in the wxLanguage enum:

```
wxLANGUAGE_ENGLISH_UK
wxLANGUAGE_ENGLISH_US
wxLANGUAGE_ENGLISH_AUSTRALIA
wxLANGUAGE_ENGLISH_BELIZE
wxLANGUAGE_ENGLISH_BOTSWANA
wxLANGUAGE_ENGLISH_CANADA
wxLANGUAGE_ENGLISH_CARIBBEAN
wxLANGUAGE_ENGLISH_DENMARK
wxLANGUAGE_ENGLISH_EIRE
wxLANGUAGE_ENGLISH_JAMAICA
wxLANGUAGE_ENGLISH_NEW_ZEALAND
wxLANGUAGE_ENGLISH_PHILIPPINES
wxLANGUAGE_ENGLISH_SOUTH_AFRICA
wxLANGUAGE_ENGLISH_TRINIDAD
wxLANGUAGE_ENGLISH_ZIMBABWE
```

Let's look at these variations in more detail. Earlier, I described a strategy for how to locate MO files in a development tree and in a distribution, and how wxWidgets uses the ISO 639 language name for locating MO files at runtime. Obviously, "en" is not a sufficient means to differentiate among the various dialects of English listed here. What we are dealing with here is not strictly a language, but a *locale*. A locale is a community or a geographic region that shares a common language and a set of customs within a specific geographic region. Dissecting the wxLANGUAGE_ENGLISH CANADA enum gives us the language (ENGLISH) and the geographic region (CANADA); combined these form the locale represented by the wxLANGUAGE_ ENGLISH_CANADA enum. As it turns out, the two components ENGLISH and CANADA map to a single string much like ENGLISH in wxLANGUAGE_ENGLISH maps to the ISO 639 language name "en." As before, the ENGLISH portion of wxLANGUAGE_ENGLISH_CANADA maps to "en." For the country, wxWidgets makes use of two-letter codes based on another standard: ISO 3166. ISO 3166 maps the country Canada to the two-letter code CA. To construct the language name, you just concatenate the ISO 639 language name with the IS 3166 country code, placing an underscore character (_) between the two. Canadian English would therefore be en_CA. The names for the languages (locales) shown above are listed in Table 8-7.

Table 8-7 English Language wxLanguage Enums

wxLanguage Value	ISO 639/3166 Mapping
wxLANGUAGE_ENGLISH_UK	en_UK
wxLANGUAGE_ENGLISH_US	en_US
wxLANGUAGE_ENGLISH_AUSTRALIA	en_AU
wxLANGUAGE_ENGLISH_BELIZE	en_BZ
wxLANGUAGE_ENGLISH_BOTSWANA	en_BW
wxLANGUAGE_ENGLISH_CANADA	en_CA
wxLANGUAGE_ENGLISH_CARIBBEAN	en_CB (see below)
wxLANGUAGE_ENGLISH_DENMARK	en_DK
wxLANGUAGE_ENGLISH_EIRE	en_IE (see below)
wxLANGUAGE_ENGLISH_JAMAICA	en_JM
wxLANGUAGE_ENGLISH_NEW_ZEALAND	en_NZ
wxLANGUAGE_ENGLISH_PHILIPPINES	en_PH
wxLANGUAGE_ENGLISH_SOUTH_AFRICA	en_ZA
wxLANGUAGE_ENGLISH_TRINIDAD	en_TT
wxLANGUAGE_ENGLISH_ZIMBABWE	en_ZW

The country code CB (wxLANGUAGE_ENGLISH_CARIBBEAN) is not defined by ISO 3166, and IE (wxLANGUAGE_ENGLISH_EIRE) is defined by ISO 3166 to be Ireland, not Eire. Therefore, you need to be careful in choosing the appropriate language code for installing the MO file. To be sure what country code should be used, the wxWidgets source file src/common/ intl.cpp initializes a table that contains this information; I recommend that you grep intl.cpp for the wxLANGUAGE_ enum to determine the proper value, as follows:

```
$ grep wxLANGUAGE_ENGLISH_EIRE intl.cpp
   LNG(wxLANGUAGE_ENGLISH_EIRE,     \
       "en_IE", LANG_ENGLISH , SUBLANG_ENGLISH_EIRE \
           , "English (Eire)"
```

To add language support for Eire English, we would add an entry in our dev tree for en_IE, as follows:

```
/locale
    /en
        messages.po
    /en_IE
        messages.po
    /es
        messages.po
    /ru
        messages.po
    /fr
        messages.po
    /de
        messages.po
```

and modify the call to wxLocale::Init() to the following:

```
bool MyApp::OnInit()
{
    myLocale.Init(wxLANGUAGE_EN_EIRE);

    …

}
```

In general, it is best to use wxLANGUAGE_DEFAULT, and make sure that the MO files for the locale and language environments that your application must support are distributed properly.

Loading Message Files at Runtime

Now, all that remains is to ensure that the message file(s) that your application needs are loaded. As mentioned previously, wxWidgets will load an internal file named wxstd that contains error messages and labels that are defined in the source code for wxWidgets. But, it knows nothing of your application MO files. To load your own MO file(s), you must call the wxLocale method AddCatalog() as in the following example:

```
bool MyApp::OnInit()
{
    myLocale.Init(wxLANGUAGE_DEFAULT);

    if (myLocale.AddCatalog("messages") == FALSE) {
        printf("Unable to load catalog\n");
```

```
        exit(1);
    }

    Toplevel *frame = new Toplevel("Toplevel",
        wxPoint(50,50), wxSize(450,340));
    frame->Show(TRUE);
    SetTopWindow(frame);
    return TRUE;
}
```

AddCatalog() will tack on the .mo extension, and look for the specified file in the directory specified by the locale's language (which was set with wxLocale::Init(), as illustrated earlier). Suppose you are ultra-organized and decide to have several message files, one for menu items (menu.mo), one for error messages (errors.mo), and one for control labels (labels.mo). You would then load each with separate calls to AddCatalog() as follows:

```
bool MyApp::OnInit()
{
    myLocale.Init(wxLANGUAGE_DEFAULT);

    if (myLocale.AddCatalog("menu") == FALSE) {
        printf("Unable to load catalog\n");
        exit(1);
    }

    if (myLocale.AddCatalog("errors") == FALSE) {
        printf("Unable to load catalog\n");
        exit(1);
    }

    if (myLocale.AddCatalog("labels") == FALSE) {
        printf("Unable to load catalog\n");
        exit(1);
    }

    Toplevel *frame = new Toplevel("Toplevel",
        wxPoint(50,50), wxSize(450,340));
    frame->Show(TRUE);
    SetTopWindow(frame);
    return TRUE;
}
```

9

Developing a Cross-Platform GUI Toolkit in C++

Of the issues facing developers of cross-platform desktop software, perhaps none is greater than the user interface (UI), as the considerable amount of space I have devoted so far in this book to the subject attests. Netscape, at the time 4.x transitioned from being a flagship product into a sustaining one, and efforts turned toward the development of the Netscape 6/7 and Mozilla codebase, the following three platforms—UNIX, Windows (95/98 and NT), and Mac OS (System 8)—were identified as being "tier-1," meaning these platforms were highest in priority when it came to shipping product. In the new codebase, the way in which these three platform UIs were supported was to undergo a dramatic change. It was observed that in a very general way, the lingua franca of the Web (HTML+DOM+CSS+ JavaScript) provided much of what would be needed to support the development of more traditional desktop UIs. From this realization, the XML User Interface Language (XUL) emerged. XUL introduced an Extensible Markup Language (XML)-based language that could be used to describe the layout of a dialog or window, much like HTML is used to describe the layout of a Web page to a browser. The underlying architecture of the browser was designed to handle the rendering of both Hypertext Markup Language (HTML) and XUL, and exploited the similarities of both to do so efficiently. Cascading Style Sheets (CSS), Document Object Model (DOM), and JavaScript remained largely unchanged, meaning, for the most part, a developer who was able to create Web pages with these technologies stood a good chance of quickly learning the skills needed to write XUL applications for the Netscape and Mozilla platforms.

When I joined the Netscape 6 team, my job was to do the UI programming for Netscape 6's implementation of AOL Instant Messenger. By then, significant progress had been made on XUL, but it would be many more months before the toolkit was ready for prime time. Still, it was clear to me the power of this paradigm. After many years of constructing user interfaces procedurally (from code, as is done with wxWidgets), creating a UI statically in a language like XUL was both empowering and enlightening.

In this chapter, I describe the core components used to create a Netscape/Mozilla XUL UI: HTML, DOM, CSS, and JavaScript. I then go on to describe Trixul, a graphical user interface (GUI) toolkit inspired by XUL, which I created specifically to support this chapter of the book.

One of the goals in writing this book is to describe the internals of XUL. XUL's contribution to the cross-platform portability of the Netscape/Mozilla browser suite was so significant that the book would not be complete without describing it. There are some valuable lessons to be taught in terms of architecting a toolkit of this type that I believed would be lost in the complexity of the Mozilla architecture had I tried to describe them relative to XUL and the Netscape/Mozilla codebase, and so I felt by describing them in the context of a smaller, simpler toolkit and codebase, I might stand a better chance of communicating the material contained in this chapter.

Parenthetically, I should mention that Trixul is an open source GUI toolkit that perhaps someday might advance the state of the art in the area of cross-platform GUI development, much like wxWidgets and Qt has in their own ways. I believe that describing UIs in an XML-based language such as those supported by XUL and Trixul is the wave of the future. Whether Trixul succeeds in its goals will, of course, depend on the open source community. If you are interested in contributing, please visit www.trixul.org.

What is XUL?

In this chapter of the book, we turn our focus to the design and implementation of an open source cross-platform GUI toolkit that I designed named Trixul. Trixul was inspired by the Netscape/Mozilla cross-platform GUI toolkit named XUL, which is currently in use by all browser products derived from the Mozilla project, including Firefox and Netscape.

Before describing Trixul, I want to take a bit of a detour and discuss Mozilla's XUL, with the goal of giving you a good understanding of what it is, and how it influenced the Netscape and Mozilla browser projects. XUL has been around since the first versions of Mozilla (and it made its first appearance in Netscape in version 6, which was based on the Mozilla codebase). The previous versions of Netscape, up until 4.x, were all cross-platform, but the architecture had outlived its ability to move forward. The prospect of starting fresh with the development of a new Mozilla browser, and a next generation of Mozilla-based Netscape browsers, gave engineers an opportunity to revisit the problem of how to architect a cross-platform toolkit. Applying lessons that were learned from earlier efforts of designing and implementing cross-platform Web browsers, engineers came up with a relatively easy-to-use toolkit named XUL. The UI of all products like Mozilla are coded entirely in XUL. This includes the Web browser, programs such as Thunderbird (the Mozilla e-mail user agent), Netscape Composer (a WYSIWYG editor), Chatzilla (an Internet Relay Chat [IRC] client), and the product that I worked on, Netscape Instant Messenger (NIM).

Both Trixul and XUL are similar, at least from the point of view of the developer who is creating a UI with either toolkit. Both of these toolkits, it turns out, trace their origins to a common ancestor, Dynamic HTML (DHTML). DHTML, as many of you know, is the collection of Web standards and technologies used by developers to create content for the Web. In the next section, I introduce DHTML and its core technologies. I then describe XUL, attempting to make its relationship to DHTML clear. The remainder of the chapter describes Trixul, its architecture, and implementation.

DHTML

The design of XUL was influenced by the design and use of Dynamic HTML (DHTML). For those of you who do not know what DHTML is, it is a combination of the following:

- A markup language, such as HTML
- A Document Object Model (DOM)
- A scripting language, most typically JavaScript
- A style system (such as CSS)

Let's take a look at each of these Web technologies individually. If you already are familiar with DHTML, feel free to skip through the following subsections.

HTML

HTML is the language with which static content distributed by the Internet, and displayed in a Web browser, is expressed. An HTML document consists of a combination of elements and attributes. Elements describe the overall layout of the page, and attributes are used to refine the specification of the individual elements within an HTML document.

Perhaps the best way to describe HTML is to take a look at a progressive example, to see how it us used. Let's start with the obvious example, a Web page that displays the string "Hello World!" Here is the source:

```
<html>
    <head>
        <title> Hello World Page </title>
    </head>
    <body>
    Hello World!
    </body>
</html>
```

Saving the above HTML to a file and then opening the file in a Web browser gives the result shown in Figure 9-1.

Elements seen in HTML markup are of the following two forms:

```
<element_name attr1="value" attr2="value" ...>
...
</element_name>
```

or

```
<element_name attr1="value" attr2="value" .../>
```

Depending on the element type, additional elements can be nested within the first form, as you will see.

The name of the element gives a hint as to its purpose. In this document, the <html> element is used to indicate that the document contains HTML, and describes the layout of a Web page. The <head> element holds metadata about the Web page. In this simple example, the only metadata expressed for the document is the document's title, using the <title> element. The title ("Hello World Page") is defined by text that is contained within the <title> element, and as you can see, is displayed by Firefox (or other Web browser) in the title bar of the browser window.

Following the <head> element is the <body> element, which is used to specify the visible content of the Web page. This content typically consists of additional elements, but in this simple example, it consists only of a text string, "Hello World!".

Figure 9-1 HTML Hello World!

There are many elements defined by HTML. Let's use a few more to display an image and a bulleted list, giving us a layout like that shown in Figure 9-2.

To achieve this layout, we replace the "Hello World!" text with an `<image>` element, which displays the image, and below, with the `<ul>` element, which displays an ordered list. The `<ul>` element is a container that manages `<li>` elements, which define the bulleted items displayed in the list. Here is the source:

```
<html>
    <head>
        <title> Surf Report </title>
    </head>
    <body>
        <image src="surf.png"
            width="350" height="200"/>
        <ul>
            <li>Wave Height: 5 to 7 feet</li>
            <li>Water Temperature: 68 F (20 C)</li>
```

```
                <li>Rip Current Potential: High</li>
        </ul>
    </body>
</html>
```

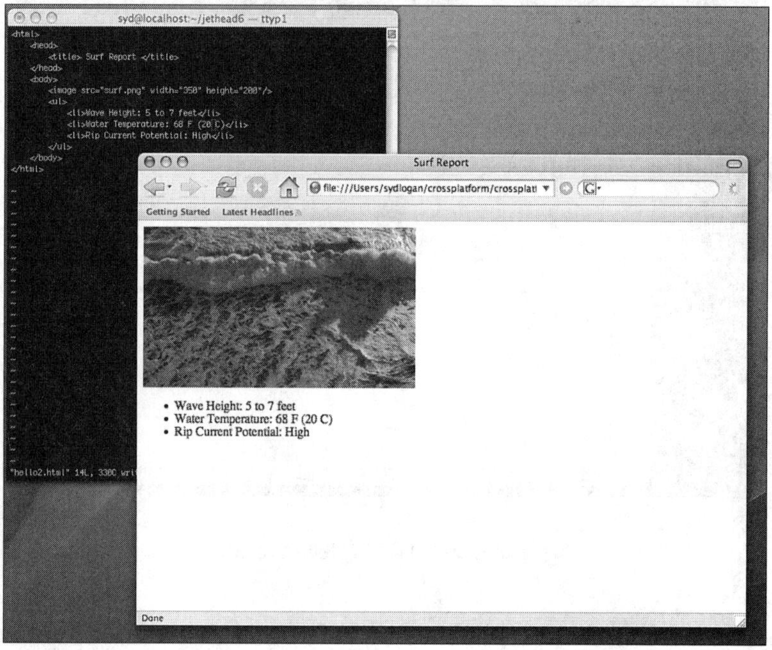

Figure 9-2 A more complicated HTML layout

The <image> element gives us our first look at an element that specifies attributes. An attribute is an expression of the following form:

```
lhs = rhs
```

where lhs is the name of the attribute, and rhs is the value of the attributes. In the <image> tag, we use three attributes. The src attribute specifies a URL defining the location of the image file, and the width and height attributes specify the width and height of the image, respectively, as it will be displayed by the browser in the Web page. If necessary, the Web browser will scale the image to fit the specified dimensions.

For more information about HTML, see www.w3.org/html.

Scripting Language

The next component of DHTML is the scripting language. The scripting language enables the Web site designer to attach code to specific HTML content, or to the overall Web page. Scripting languages can be either be embedded in Web pages or they can be defined in a separate file and included in the Web page.

To embed code, you use the <script> element. Code can also be added as attributes to specific elements. The most commonly used scripting language in DHTML applications is JavaScript, which was invented at Netscape. (The language, standardized by the European Computer Manufacturers Association [ECMA], is also known as ECMAScript.) Documentation for JavaScript can be found at http://developer.mozilla.org/en/docs/JavaScript.

The following HTML markup illustrates the structure of an embedded <script> element that declares three JavaScript functions:

```
<script language="javascript">
    function function1()
    {
    }

    function function2()
    {
    }

    function function3()
    {
    }
</script>
```

To bring in external script source, you remove the body of the <script> element and use the src attribute. The value of the src attribute is a URL that identifies the location of the source:

```
<script language="javascript" src="myscript.js"/>
```

A third way to embed script is to specify it as an attribute of an element. For example, the <image> element has an attribute, onmouseover, which allows the Web page developer to associate code with the event of a mouse being moved over the image by the user. We can either inline the script or refer to a function that was specified either elsewhere in the document, or externally. Here is an inline example that causes a JavaScript function named handleMouseOver() to be called whenever the mouse is moved over the image:

```
<image src="surf.png" width="350" height="200"
    onmouseover="handleMouseOver();"/
```

The Document Object Model

Closely associated with elements and attributes, as well as the scripting language, is the Document Object Model, or DOM (defined at www. w3.org/DOM). The DOM is a hierarchical data structure implemented by the Web browser that contains a representation of all the elements and attributes defined by the Web page, and an API that allows you to access this structure. As you will see, the DOM is used by scripting languages to locate and modify elements and their attributes.

When a Web page is parsed and rendered by a browser, a DOM is created to represent the page in the Web browser. The DOM, being a tree, contains nodes to represent each element, and the DOM also represents the parent and child relationships that exist among the elements that make up the Web page.

To be accessible to scripts, an element in the DOM needs to be uniquely identified. One way this can be achieved is by specifying a unique value for the id attribute of the element. For example, we can set the id attribute of the <image> element to "surfimage" using the following markup:

```
<image id="surfimage" src="surf.png" width="350"
    height="200"/>
```

The DOM provides an application programming interface (API) that can be called by a scripting language to locate elements within the DOM, and to read and write attributes of these elements. For example, to locate the preceding <image> tag in the DOM, we can call the DOM's getElementById() function from JavaScript, like this:

```
var imageElement = document.getElementById("surfimage");
```

The JavaScript variable imageElement will either be null, if an item with an id attribute equal to "surfimage" could not be found in the DOM, or it will be an object that represents the element in the DOM. Assuming we get back a non-null `imageElement` that represents our image element from earlier, we could change the `src` attribute of the element to something completely different using code like the following:

```
imageElement.src = "wave.png";
```

It is code like the above that makes content on a Web page dynamic, hence the name DHTML. Given an appropriate mix of DOM and JavaScript, any Web page can completely change its structure at runtime, not only by modifying its elements as in the above example, but also by inserting and removing elements, if needed.

The following simple application extends the HTML previously presented. The Web page displays three icons, one representing temperature, one representing wave height, and one representing riptide risk. (A riptide is current that flows from the shore back out to sea, which can pose a danger to swimmers not trained in how to deal with being caught in one.) Mousing over each image will cause the Web page to display information related to the image that is being moused over. Figure 9-3 shows the UI for the application.

Figure 9-3 DHTML example

The HTML markup and script for this page is shown in the following listing:

```html
<html>
    <head>
        <title> Surf Report </title>
    </head>
    <body>
        <script language="javascript">
            function RemoveSpan()
            {
                var span =
                    document.getElementById("message");
                if (span) {
                    span.parentNode.removeChild(span);
                }
            }
            function ShowHeight()
            {
                var message =
                    document.getElementById("message");
                if (message) {
                    message.innerHTML =
                        "Wave Height: 5 to 7 feet";
                }
            }
            function ShowTemp()
            {
                var message =
                    document.getElementById("message");
                if (message) {
                    message.innerHTML =
                        "Temperature: 68 F (20 C)";
                }
            }
            function ShowRip()
            {
                var message =
                    document.getElementById("message");
                if (message) {
                    message.innerHTML =
                        "Rip Current Potential: High";
                }
            }
        </script>
```

```
<center>
<image src="surf.png" width="350" height="200"/>
<br/><br/>
<span id="message">
Mouse over the icons below to get surf conditions
</span>
<br/><br/>
<table>
    <tr>
        <td>
            <image src="height.png"
                onmouseover="ShowHeight();"/>
        </td>
        <td>
            <image src="temp.png"
                onmouseover="ShowTemp();"/>
        </td>
        <td>
            <image src="rip.png"
                onmouseover="ShowRip();"/>
        </td>
    </tr>
</table>
</center>
</body>
</html>
```

As you can see, each <image> tag in the markup has embedded script associated with the onmouseover attribute. Each of the JavaScript functions called when a mouseover occurs has a similar task: use the DOM's getElementById() function to locate the span with the id equal to "message", and if found, set the HTML within that span to the appropriate text.

You can learn more about DOM by visiting www.w3.org/DOM.

Style Systems

The final component of DHTML, the style system, is implemented by Cascading Style Sheets (CSS). CSS enables Web developers to decouple certain aspects of the look and feel of a page from the HTML markup. Such attributes might include the font and color used for text, the background color of a page, or the margin spacing used by the Web browser when rendering cells in an HTML table. CSS is defined and documented at www.w3.org/Style/CSS.

To use CSS in a Web page, the developer must specify the style sheet. Style sheets are typically external files, brought in using the `<link>` element. The following brings in a style sheet named surfreport.css:

```
<link rel="stylesheet" href="surfreport.css"
    type="text/css" />
```

A style sheet is made up of a set of rules. A rule has two main parts: the *selector* and the *declaration*. The selector defines the context by which the declaration is applicable. In the simple case, a selector is the name of a class. The declaration is a list of property/value pairs, each separated by a colon.

Two commonly used selectors are the element name and the class. The element name is just that, the name of an element. For example, to style the `<span>` element in a document, we can specify the string "span" as the selector, as in this example:

```
span {declaration}
```

To use the class, you just specify a class attribute on the element. Here, we set the class attribute of the span to `"messageclass"`:

```
<span id="message" class="messageclass">
    Mouse over the icons below to get surf conditions
</span>
```

The corresponding selector is then

```
messageclass {declaration}
```

On to the declaration—the declaration, as mentioned before, is a series of attribute/value pairs; each pair is terminated with a semicolon, and the attribute and value within each pair are separated by a colon. For example, the following declaration sets the color attribute to red, and the font size to 12pt:

```
{font-size: 12pt;  color: red;}
```

XUL

In XUL, markup is defined using XML. Elements in XUL correspond closely to widgets found in native GUI toolkits such as Gtk+, Cocoa, or .NET

Forms. The following sections classify the basic XUL elements in terms of their functionality. (The following is not intended to be exhaustive. However, for those of you who are familiar with GUI toolkits, it will give you an idea of the functionality provided by XUL.) You can find more detail about XUL by visiting www.mozilla.org, and using their search tool to locate references to online XUL documentation.

Windows and Dialogs

XUL is used mainly to describe the content of windows and dialogs. In a way analogous to the `<html>` tag in an HTML document, the `<window>` tag is used to wrap content for display in a window, and the `<dialog>` tag is used to wrap content displayed in a dialog.

Boxes

The box elements (`<hbox>`, `<vbox>`) are the primary widgets with which XUL programmers specify the layout of content within a window or a dialog. (Their purpose is similar to that of sizers in wxWidgets, which are described fully in Chapter 8, "wxWidgets.") An `<hbox>` element arranges its children from left to right, whereas the `<vbox>` widget organizes children from top to bottom. Both the `<vbox>` and `<hbox>` elements can be arbitrarily nested, allowing for the specification of complex layouts. The `<spacer>` element can be used to create empty space between children managed by a `<vbox>` or `<hbox>` element, allowing for even more flexibility in how a window is laid out and how the widgets within the window are placed when the size of the window changes. The following example illustrates the XUL used to specify the layout of a window that displays text edit fields and buttons (see Figure 9-4). The dialog uses the `<vbox>`, `<hbox>`, and `<spacer>` elements to arrange the layout of the widgets within the dialog. Here is the XUL markup:

```
<?xml version="1.0"?>
<?xml-stylesheet href="chrome://global/skin/"
    type="text/css"?>

<window
    xmlns="http://www.mozilla.org/keymaster/gatekeeper\
    /there.is.only.xul">
    <hbox flex="1">
        <spacer flex="1"/>
        <vbox>
```

```
                <spacer flex="1"/>
                <textbox value="Message 1"/>
                <spacer flex="1"/>
                <textbox value="Message 2"/>
                <spacer flex="1"/>
            </vbox>
            <vbox>
                <spacer flex="1"/>
                <button label="Button 1"/>
                <spacer flex="1"/>
                <button label="Button 2"/>
                <spacer flex="1"/>
            </vbox>
            <spacer flex="1"/>
        </hbox>
    </window>
```

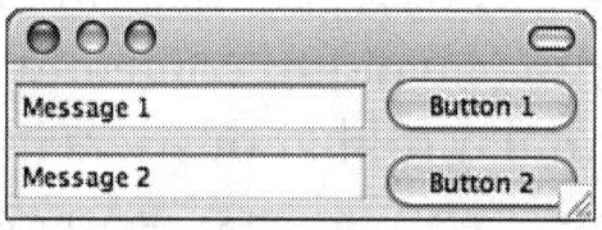

Figure 9-4 XUL box layout

The <spacer> elements are used to define how empty space in the
window is used as the window is resized. The placement of <spacer>
elements in this window is used to keep each <textbox> and its associated
<button> together horizontally, and to split up any remaining horizontal
and vertical space in the window equally between and around the
<textbox> and <button> pairs. Figure 9-5 illustrates a resized window to
show how the remaining space is distributed among the <spacer> widgets
in the window.

Toolbars

Toolbar elements can be used to organize groups of buttons within a region
of a window (usually the top of a window or dialog). The <toolbar> widget
organizes a set of <toolbarbutton> widgets horizontally. Separators can be
added to physically group a set of <toolbarbutton> widgets within the
<toolbar>.

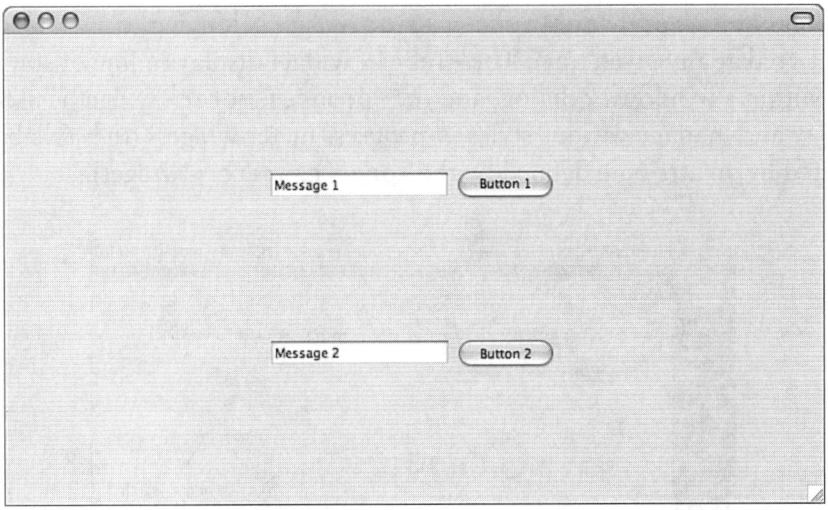

Figure 9-5 XUL box layout after resize

Menus

Menus are an essential part of any application. The following widgets all support the use of menus within an application:

```
<menubar>
<menu>
<menupopup>
<menuitem>
```

The engine supporting XUL is aware of, and supports, the differences in how menus are used by the various platforms. (Mac OS X requires the use of certain menus and specific menu item placements. It also does not display menu bars within windows. Rather, the menu bar of the currently raised application is displayed on the desktop—see Figure 9-6.) Later, we discuss how cross-platform menu support is provided by Trixul.

Controls

XUL supports several core controls. Two of them, `<button>` and `<textbox>`, we have already seen. The `<checkbox>` widget displays a checkbox that can be checked or unchecked by the user. The `<radio>` widget is used to implement the radio button paradigm, which is similar to check boxes except that only one <radio> widget belonging to a group can be selected at any given time. The <label> widget displays a line of static text within a window or dialog, and the <progressmeter> widget is used to display and manage various styles of progress meter widgets (the style being selected by an attribute defined by the <progressmeter> widget).

Figure 9-6 Mac OS X menu bar

Other Widgets

In addition, XUL supports widgets used to display trees of items, list boxes, and composite widgets like embedded HTML editors and HTML browsers, file choosers, and color pickers. As evidenced by the fact the Firefox and Thunderbird clients are completely implemented in XUL, the XUL widget set is complete and sufficient for implementing sophisticated, modern GUI desktop applications.

Programming with XUL

XUL's similarity to DHTML is very apparent, as you will see in this section. Many XUL elements can be linked to code that is written in JavaScript, in a manner that is very similar to the ways by which elements in HTML are linked to JavaScript code in DHTML. As is the case with parsing an HTML document, parsing a XUL document results in a DOM. Finally, CSS can be used to specify style in both XUL and DHTML.

Adding Logic to the UI with JavaScript

Let's take a look at how DOM and JavaScript might be used to provide functionality to the XUL window we presented earlier. When the button to the right of the top text edit field is clicked, a JavaScript function is called. In this function, we retrieve the current value of the text field, reverse it, and then set the value of the text edit field to the result. When the other button is clicked, we call a different function that, in a similar fashion, converts the value of the corresponding text edit field to uppercase.

The first steps occur in the XUL markup. First, we assign each `<textbox>` element its own ID, so that we can use the DOM function `getElementById()` to retrieve it as an object from within the callback. We then add oncommand handlers in JavaScript to each of the `<button>` elements; these handlers are nothing more than inline JavaScript code that call functions that implement the desired functionality. A `<script>` element is used to specify the JavaScript source containing the implementations of `ReverseValue()` and `UppercaseValue()`, the two functions that perform the actual work. Here is the XUL source after adding these changes (changes shown in bold):

```
<?xml version="1.0"?>
<?xml-stylesheet href="chrome://global/skin/"
    type="text/css"?>

<window
    xmlns="http://www.mozilla.org/keymaster/gatekeeper/\
    there.is.only.xul">
    <script src="chrome://sample/content/ \
        myfunctions.js"/>
    <hbox flex="1">
        <spacer flex="1"/>
        <vbox>
            <spacer flex="1"/>
            <textbox id="textbox1" value="Message 1"/>
            <spacer flex="1"/>
            <textbox id="textbox2" value="Message 2"/>
            <spacer flex="1"/>
        </vbox>
        <vbox>
            <spacer flex="1"/>
            <button label="Reverse"
```

```
                     oncommand="ReverseValue();"/>
            <spacer flex="1"/>
            <button label="Uppercase"
                     oncommand="UppercaseValue();"/>
            <spacer flex="1"/>
        </vbox>
        <spacer flex="1"/>
    </hbox>
</window>
```

The supporting JavaScript code that implements the oncommand
handlers should be very familiar to those who understand DHTML:

```
function ReverseValue()
{
    var element = document.getElementById("textbox1");
    if (element) {
        var src = element.value;
        var dest = "";

        if (src.length > 1) {
            for (j = 0, i = src.length-1;
                i>=0; i--, j++) {
                dest += src.charAt(i);
            }
        }
        element.value = dest;
    }
}


function UppercaseValue()
{
    var element = document.getElementById("textbox2");
    if (element)
        element.value = element.value.toUpperCase();
}
```

To a client-side JavaScript programmer, there is nothing fancy about the
preceding code—it consists of nothing but calls to the DOM and basic
JavaScript string object manipulation.

Interfacing JavaScript and C/C++ Code with XPCOM and XPConnect

So far, we have seen the power of XUL in terms of its ability to express UIs
in platform-agnostic XML, and we have learned how to tie a XUL UI and

code together with JavaScript and DOM (which are also platform agnostic). What we have seen so far, although interesting and powerful in its own right, is limiting to those of us who are used to developing applications in C++. Desktop-class applications will invariably need to interface to the outside world via libraries that have been written in C or C++. Fortunately, Mozilla-based projects support the integration of JavaScript and C++ code via a pair of Mozilla technologies: one named XPCOM, and the other named XPConnect.

XPCOM stands for Cross-Platform COM, which is based on Microsoft's COM technology that allows applications to locate and call functions in a dynamic link library (DLL; shared library). XPCOM enables component software development, a paradigm that is heavily leveraged in the Mozilla product line. DLLs that implement the required external functions and classes defined for this purpose by XPCOM can be registered as components with a Mozilla-based project, and applications can then use XPCOM to query these components for classes and interfaces, and then make calls against the interfaces to obtain the services provided by the component.

XPConnect is a technology that allows for the calling of code in an XPCOM component from JavaScript and other languages. (In practice, only JavaScript and C/C++ make calls to XPCOM components.) Interfaces exposed by classes in a component are defined using XPCOM's own flavor of interactive data language (IDL); this IDL is then processed to generate include files that can be used to implement the classes, and type information files that are used by XPConnect to facilitate calls into the component, and the return of results to the caller.

The following code from the Mozilla project gets an instance of the `printsettings-service` class (in XPCOM, a service is a singleton component, of which only one instance is created), and queries it for an interface (`nsIPrintSettingsService`). This interface, if found, is returned as an object. The JavaScript code then calls that object's `availablePrinters()` function to obtain an enumerator with which a list of the available printers can be inspected. Presumably, this list will then be displayed to the user so that the user can select which printer he or she want to print to. Here is the code:

```
printService = Components.classes["@mozilla.org/gfx/ \
    printsettings-service;1"];
if (printService) {
    printService = printService.getService();
```

```
    if (printService) {
        printService = printService.QueryInterface(
            Components.interfaces.\
            nsIPrintSettingsService);
        printOptions = printService.QueryInterface(
            Components.interfaces.\
            nsIPrintOptions);
    }
}
var printerEnumerator =
    printOptions.availablePrinters();
```

...

The key things to notice here are as follows:

- XPCOM provides a JavaScript object, `Components`, that allows code to determine whether a class is available among the components that have been registered with XPCOM.
- `QueryInterface()` is used to obtain the contract (a contract is defined in IDL by the component) for a named set of functions and properties exposed by the component. In the above, `nsIPrintOptions` and `nsIPrintSettingsService` are examples of contracts.
- If successful, calls can be made to the functions defined by a contract. (In the above, the call to `availablePrinters()` is an example of this.)

In my opinion, writing Mozilla components for XPCOM is not for the faint of heart. The subject deserves a book of its own to describe fully. (You can find an online version of an unpublished book on the subject at www.mozilla.org/projects/xpcom/book/cxc if you are interested in the details.) One of the reasons I created Trixul was so that I could produce a less-complicated means by which JavaScript and C++ code could be interfaced—and as a result, something that is simpler to describe. Later in this chapter, I describe the Trixul component system in much detail.

Trixul

Trixul is, as of this writing, the beginnings of a cross-platform GUI toolkit that supports, but is not limited to, the Mac OS X, Windows, and Linux platforms. I designed and implemented Trixul primarily because I wanted to design a toolkit that is

- Lightweight (The source code for Trixul is only around 15,000 lines, whereas Mozilla's source code is in the millions.)
- Easy to understand and describe
- Specifically designed for stand-alone application development

None of these goals is met by Mozilla's XUL-based toolkit. Importantly, keeping things simple allows me to more easily (and hopefully, more clearly) describe its architecture. Learning about the design of Trixul is a jumpstart into understanding XUL's architecture, as well as the architecture of related toolkits.

Trixul supports the following features, many similar to what one finds in XUL and XPToolkit:

- An XML UI description language inspired by XUL.
- Integration of the cross-platform, Mozilla-based JavaScript engine for the C programming language (SpiderMonkey).
- Support for component-based development. C++ classes can be instantiated from JavaScript code, and functions and properties associated with these classes can be interacted with, again from JavaScript.
- Variant types are used to support communication of data between components and JavaScript.
- Extensible support for native GUI toolkits. Trixul supports Windows .NET Forms on Windows XP (and presumably on Windows Vista), Gtk+ on Linux, and Cocoa on Mac OS X. Other toolkits and platforms are relatively easy to add, as you will see.
- Support for localizable strings via XML DTD files.

In the following sections, I introduce the features of Trixul and describe its architecture and implementation.

Widget Support in Trixul

The following widgets are currently supported by Trixul:

- `Button`—A standard push button widget.
- `GridList`—A list widget that manages a single list of selectable items.
- `MenuBar`—A menu bar widget that manages a set of menus.
- `Menu`—A menu widget that manages a set of menu items.
- `MenuItem`—A menu item widget. `MenuItem` supports both separators and accelerators.
- `OpenPicker`—A dialog used to select an existing file in the native file system.

- **SaveAsPicker**—Similar to `OpenPicker`, but used to select or create a file.
- **CheckBox**—A button that can show two states: checked and unchecked.
- **RadioButton**—A radio button widget, similar to a check box but allowing only one item in a group of radio buttons to be selected.
- **StaticText**—A widget that displays a single line of uneditable text, usually used for labels.
- **Text**—Similar to `StaticText`, except the text is editable.
- **Box**—A container widget that arranges its children vertically, top to bottom; or horizontally, left to right; based on the value of its `orient` attribute.
- **Window**—The outermost widget of a Trixul document. A `Window` widget can be used to create both modeless windows, and modal dialogs. The layout semantics of a `Window` are identical to those of a vertical `Box`.
- **ScrolledWindow/ScrolledView**—A widget that manages a group of children, displaying both vertical and horizontal scrollbars, as needed.
- **Spacer**—A widget that is used to define the semantics of whitespace that exists between widgets in a container like `HBox` and `VBox`.

Basic Operation of Trixul

Trixul is, for all intents and purposes, an interpreter. When executed, Trixul is provided the name of an XML file as a command-line argument. A Trixul document describes the layout of a window, and the initial document parsed by Trixul always defines the main window of the GUI application. Additional Trixul documents can be opened from JavaScript code (how this is done will be explained later), and they, too, consist of XML that will be parsed by Trixul.

For each document parsed by Trixul, a DOM is created. The DOM represents the elements that were parsed in the document, and the hierarchical relationships that exist among the elements in the document. For each element, the DOM maintains any attributes that were specified for the element in markup.

The following Trixul markup defines the initial UI for an application. The window specified by this markup will contain a push button, which, using `<box>` and `<spacer>` elements, will be centered in the window:

```
<!DOCTYPE window SYSTEM "dialog.dtd">

<window name="main" title="&dialog.title;"
    main="true" width="250" height="100">
```

```
<script type="text/javascript"
    src="resources/content/dialog.js"/>
<box orient="vertical">
    <spacer/>
    <box orient="horizontal">
        <spacer/>
        <button onclick="return Button1Click();"
            label="&button1.label;"/>
        <spacer/>
    </box>
    <spacer/>
</box>
</window>
```

To run this application, Trixul is invoked with the path to the above markup specified as an argument:

```
$ layout -r resources/content/simple.xul
```

Widgets

Let's say that Trixul is in the process of parsing the preceding document on Mac OS X, and the parser encounters the `<button>` element. To handle this situation, Trixul instantiates a `Button` object, using code similar to the following:

```
Widget *w;

if (!PL_strcasecmp(name, "button")) {
    w = new Button();
    w->SetType(TYPE_BUTTON);
}
```

In all platform GUI toolkits, UI objects, or widgets, must be created, positioned, and then shown to be included in the UI. In some cases, widgets can be hidden, too, but this is not a very common operation. To support this functionality, `Button` derives from a base class named `Widget`. The core interfaces of `Widget`—`Create()`, `SetGeometry()`, `Show()`, and `Hide()`, respectively—reflect this support:

```
class Widget : public Element, public BoxLayout
{
public:
    Widget();
```

```
    virtual ~Widget() {};
    virtual PRStatus SetGeometry(const int &x,
        const int &y,
        const int &width, const int &height,
        const char &mask) = 0;
    virtual PRStatus GetGeometry(int &x, int &y,
        int &width, int &height) = 0;
    virtual PRStatus Create() = 0;
    virtual PRStatus Show() = 0;
    virtual PRStatus Hide() = 0;
    virtual ElementType GetType() = 0;
    virtual WidgetImpl *GetImpl() = 0;
};
```

In addition, most GUI toolkits define two types of widget. The first type of widget, the control widget, represents items that users can interact with. Buttons, menus, and radio buttons are examples of control widgets, and there are many others. The other class of widget is the container widget, which is used to organize, or position, control widgets within a window or a dialog. Tables and boxes are examples of container widgets. Examples of both types of widgets in the wxWidgets toolkit were described in some detail in Chapter 8. Controls are by far the more prevalent of these two types of widget, although both are important in crafting a UI. In Trixul, the Control class is used to represent two attributes of a control that are commonly encountered in native GUI toolkit implementations:

- Controls can be enabled and disabled.
- Most controls can have a value that can be read or written by the application, and can be modified by the user.

Disabling a control makes it unreceptive to user input, by virtue of the fact that it is unable to obtain the input focus. Disabled controls are usually displayed dimmed, and often, labels associated with a disabled control are shown in a degraded or lighter font, compared to the font used to display enabled controls. The value of a control varies based on the intent and design of the control in question. For example, the value of a text widget is a string, and the value of a radio button is its state. Both setters and getters for the value of a control are a necessary part of a control widget's API: A setter allows the application to initialize the value of a control upon creation to reflect the data that it represents, and a getter allows the application to retrieve the current value of a control, should the user modify it.

The Trixul `Control` class, which inherits from `Widget`, represents each of these aspects of controls through the interfaces that it defines:

```
class Control : public Widget
{
public:
    Control() : m_isEnabled(true),
        m_contentType(ContentTypeNone) {}
    virtual ~Control() {};
    virtual PRStatus Disable() = 0;
    virtual PRStatus Enable() = 0;
    virtual PRStatus GetValue(XPVariant &v) = 0;
    virtual PRStatus SetValue(const XPVariant &v) = 0;
};
```

Now that we have introduced the base classes, we can define the class `Button`, which inherits from both `Control` and `Widget`. `Button` is an instantiable class and provides implementations for all the interfaces that are required of the classes that it inherits from. In addition, `Button` defines two interfaces of its own, `SetLabel()` and `GetLabel()`, which can be used to set and get the label displayed by the button, respectively. As Trixul evolves, `SetLabel()` and `GetLabel()` may find themselves needed by other control widgets, and if this becomes the case, these interfaces will be refactored up into `Control` or some other base class; but for now, only buttons have labels in Trixul, and so these interfaces are restricted to the `Button` class. Here is the definition of `Button`:

```
class Button : public Control,
    public ButtonPressObserver
{
public:
    Button();
    Button(string& label);
    ~Button();
    PRStatus SetLabel(string& label);
    string& GetLabel();
    PRStatus Create();
    PRStatus Show();
    PRStatus Hide();
    PRStatus Disable();
    PRStatus Enable();
    PRStatus GetValue(XPVariant &v);
```

```
    PRStatus SetValue(const XPVariant &v);
    PRStatus SetGeometry(const int &x, const int &y,
        const int &width, const int &height,
        const char &mask);
    PRStatus GetGeometry(int &x, int &y, int &width,
        int &height);
    ElementType GetType() {return TYPE_BUTTON;};
    WidgetImpl *GetImpl() {return m_button;};
private:
    ButtonImpl *m_button;
};
```

Notice that `Button` has a private member, `m_button`, of type
`ButtonImpl *`. The following section discusses `ButtonImpl`, and the base
class that it and other implementation classes derive from, `WidgetImpl`.

Implementation Classes

Widget classes such as `Button` implement an abstract, idealized interface for
Trixul to make use of, without it needing to worry about how a button
might actually be implemented in the native GUI toolkit. However, to
function properly, Trixul must go beyond the abstract, and execute
platform-specific code provided by the native GUI toolkit. Each creation of
a `Button` object, for example, must result in the creation of a native button.
In Gtk+, this means someone needs to make a call to `gtk_button_new()`.
Or in Cocoa, an `NSButton` object must be instantiated. Or, in .NET Forms,
`System::Windows::Forms::Button` must be instantiated.

We saw in the previous section that `Button` defines a private member
named `m_button`, of type `ButtonImpl *`. This member represents a path to
the concrete, platform-specific code that sits behind each of `Button`'s
abstract interfaces. In most cases, calls made to `Button`'s interfaces are
forwarded directly to `ButtonImpl` for handling. The relationship between
`Button` and `ButtonImpl` is exemplified best by the "Bridge" design pattern,
which is well documented in *Design Patterns* (Addison-Wesley, 1995).

Each platform-agnostic widget class, like `Button`, needs a corresponding
platform-specific implementation class like `ButtonImpl`. `ButtonImpl` is not
instantiable, but is a base class that is inherited by the platform-specific class
that implements its interfaces. A similar situation exists for each of the
widgets supported by Trixul. Trixul's `Menu` class, for example, corresponds
to a platform-specific class that inherits from `MenuImpl`.

Let's take a quick look at the implementation of a few of **Button**'s primary functions to see how **Button** and **ButtonImpl** interact:

```
PRStatus Button::Show()
{
    if (m_button)
        m_button->Show();
    return PR_SUCCESS;
}


PRStatus Button::Hide()
{
    if (m_button)
        m_button->Hide();
    return PR_SUCCESS;
}


PRStatus Button::Enable()
{
    if (m_button)
        m_button->Enable();
    SetEnabled(true);
    return PR_SUCCESS;
}


PRStatus Button::Disable()
{
    if (m_button)
        m_button->Disable();
    SetEnabled(false);
    return PR_SUCCESS;
}


PRStatus Button::SetLabel(string& label)
{
    AddAttribute(string("label"), label);

    if (m_button)
        m_button->SetLabel(label);
    return PR_SUCCESS;
}


string& Button::GetLabel()
{
```

```
    AnAttribute *attribute;
    static string failret("");

    attribute = GetAttributeByName(string("label"));
    if ( attribute )
        return attribute->GetValue();
    return failret;
}
```

As you can see, the steps taken by each function couldn't be more straightforward—ensure that the implementation class pointer is non-NULL, and if so, call the corresponding function in the implementation class. As you can see, in some cases, additional code is present (for example, Enable() and Disable(), which record the state of the widget locally in Button in addition to making calls to the implementation class). SetLabel() caches the label locally in addition to passing it down to the implementation class, and GetLabel() does not make use of the implementation class at all; it just returns the cached copy instead which is more efficient.

As you might expect, the relationship that exists between Button and ButtonImpl is general and it applies, in varying degrees, to the other widget classes implemented by Trixul. Because the Trixul widget classes derive from Control and Widget, you might expect that the ButtonImpl does, too. At first blush, you might be tempted to think that doing so would create too tight of a coupling between the interfaces defined by the platform-neutral classes (Button), and those defined by the platform-specific classes (ButtonImpl). We visit this notion momentarily.

Commonality exists among the platform-specific classes, suggesting that they, too, inherit from base classes. In the current incarnation of Trixul, these classes are (in the case of buttons), ButtonImpl, which we have mentioned already, and its base class, WidgetImpl, both which are shown here. Let's start with WidgetImpl:

```
class WidgetImpl
{
public:
    WidgetImpl() : m_parent(NULL), m_document(NULL) {};
    virtual ~WidgetImpl() {};
    virtual PRStatus Create() = 0;
    virtual PRStatus Show() = 0;
    virtual PRStatus Hide() = 0;
    virtual PRStatus Disable() = 0;
```

```
    virtual PRStatus Enable() = 0;
    virtual PRStatus SetGeometry(const int &x,
        const int &y, const int &width,
        const int &height, const char &mask) = 0;
    virtual PRStatus GetGeometry(int &x, int &y,
        int &width, int &height) = 0;
    virtual PRStatus SetParent(WidgetImpl *parent)
    {
        m_parent = parent;
        return PR_SUCCESS;
    };
    virtual WidgetImpl *GetParent() {return m_parent;};
    virtual WidgetImpl *GetRootWidget();
    void SetType(ElementType type) {m_type = type;};
    ElementType GetType() {return m_type;};
    void SetDocument(Document *document)
        {m_document = document;};
    Document *GetDocument() {return m_document;};
protected:
    WidgetImpl *m_parent;
    ElementType m_type;
    Document *m_document;
};
```

As you can see, `WidgetImpl` has much in common with `Widget` and `Control`, while adding several member functions and variables of its own. This leads us back to the issue raised above: should `WidgetImpl` and `Widget` be refactored such that both inherit interfaces such as `Show()`, `Hide()`, `Disable()`, `Enable()`, `SetGeometry()`, and `GetGeometry()` from a common base class, say, `WidgetCommon`? At this point in the life of Trixul, several widgets have yet to be implemented. So, it is hard to say. The advantage of factoring out those interfaces seems clear: Changes made to the factored interfaces would force both the platform-specific and platform-agnostic classes to change. However, doing so may impede the ability of `Widget` and `WidgetImpl` to vary independently, and to be resilient to the requirements that additional platform toolkits may impose in the future. Time will tell—the point is that such a choice exists, and it must be considered.

Let's now take a look at `ButtonImpl`:

```
class ButtonImpl : public WidgetImpl,
    public ButtonPressSubject
{
```

```
public:
    ButtonImpl() {};
    virtual ~ButtonImpl() {};
    virtual PRStatus SetLabel(const string& label) = 0;
};
```

ButtonImpl, like WidgetImpl from which it inherits, is a base class. It extends WidgetImpl with an additional interface, SetLabel(), which is currently only necessary for buttons. Like WidgetImpl and its relationship to Widget and Control, you might be tempted to factor the SetLabel() function out from both Button and ButtonImpl, and force both of these classes to inherit it from elsewhere. The same issues and conclusions made above regarding factoring WidgetImpl and the Widget and Control classes can be drawn. Here, it even seems a bit silly to consider factoring; the resulting class would only have a single function, and would not dramatically improve the maintainability of the source code, while adding another class and potentially making Button and ButtonImpl a bit harder to read. (The code reader would at least be forced to open a header file to see what the inherited class brought in.) I'm not even sure what I would call such a class—WidgetWithLabel? When the name of the class is hard to come up with, or sounds hokey, I have to think it is probably a bad idea. But like I said earlier, time will tell.

So far, none of the classes we have looked at (WidgetImpl or ButtonImpl) have platform-specific code in them. Which is fine, as they just define interfaces, imposing rules on the platform-specific classes that inherit from them. Let's turn our attention now to these platform-specific classes. Trixul provides three concrete implementations of ButtonImpl, one for each supported platform and toolkit—CocoaButtonImpl, GtkButtonImpl, and WindowsButtonImpl. The following listings define each of these classes.

Cocoa

```
#include "buttonimpl.h"
#import <Cocoa/Cocoa.h>

#include "cocoawidgetimpl.h"
#include "commandhandler.h"

class CocoaButtonImpl : public ButtonImpl,
    public CocoaWidgetImpl, public CommandHandler
{
public:
```

```
    CocoaButtonImpl();
    virtual ~CocoaButtonImpl();
    virtual PRStatus Create();
    virtual PRStatus Show();
    virtual PRStatus Hide();
    virtual PRStatus Enable();
    virtual PRStatus Disable();
    virtual PRStatus SetLabel(const string& label);
    virtual PRStatus HandleCommand();
    virtual PRStatus GetGeometry(int &x, int &y,
        int &width, int &height);
    virtual PRStatus SetGeometry(const int &x,
        const int &y, const int &width,
        const int &height, const char &mask);
private:
    NSButton *m_button;
};
```

Gtk+

```
#include "../buttonimpl.h"
#include <gtk/gtk.h>

#include "gtkwidgetimpl.h"

#include "commandhandler.h"
class GtkButtonImpl : public ButtonImpl,
    public GtkWidgetImpl, public CommandHandler
{
public:
    GtkButtonImpl();
    virtual ~GtkButtonImpl();
    virtual PRStatus Create();
    virtual PRStatus Show();
    virtual PRStatus Hide();
    virtual PRStatus Enable();
    virtual PRStatus Disable();
    virtual PRStatus SetLabel(const string& label);
    virtual PRStatus HandleCommand();
    virtual PRStatus SetGeometry(const int &x, const int &y,
        const int &width, const int &height,
        const char &mask) {
        return SetGeometryImpl(x, y, width, height,
        mask);
    };
};
```

```
    virtual PRStatus GetGeometry(int &x, int &y,
        int &width, int &height) {
        return GetGeometryRequestImpl(x, y, width,
            height);
    };
};
```

Windows

```cpp
#include "buttonimpl.h"

#include <gcroot.h>

#using <mscorlib.dll>
#using <System.dll>
#using <System.Drawing.dll>
#using <System.Windows.Forms.dll>

using namespace System;
using namespace System::ComponentModel;
using namespace System::Drawing;
using namespace System::Windows::Forms;

#include "windowswidgetimpl.h"
#include "commandhandler.h"
#include "buttoncallbackhelper.h"

class WindowsButtonImpl : public ButtonImpl,
    public WindowsWidgetImpl, public CommandHandler
{
public:
    WindowsButtonImpl();
    virtual ~WindowsButtonImpl();
    virtual PRStatus Create();
    virtual PRStatus Show();
    virtual PRStatus Hide();
    virtual PRStatus Enable();
    virtual PRStatus Disable();
    virtual PRStatus SetLabel(const string& label);
    virtual PRStatus HandleCommand();
    virtual PRStatus SetGeometry(const int &x,
        const int &y, const int &width,
        const int &height, const char &mask);
```

```
    virtual PRStatus GetGeometry(int &x, int &y,
        int &width, int &height);
private:
    gcroot<Button *> m_button;
    gcroot<ButtonCallbackHelper *> m_buttonHelper;
};
```

As you can see, these classes vary to some degree. This should come as no surprise, given that these classes implement platform-specific functionality. The first difference is that each implements a platform-specific base class (`WindowsWidgetImpl`, `GtkWidgetImpl`, and `CocoaWidgetImpl`). The intent of these classes is to aggregate functions and member variables that are needed by all the widget implementations on that platform only. `CocoaWidgetImpl`, for example, maintains a member variable, `m_view`, that is used by widget classes on Mac OS X to cache an `NSView` object, the use of which is beyond the scope of this section. It also defines interfaces to set and get the value of this member variable. Similarly, `GtkWidgetImpl` caches two pointers to Gtk+ variables, one that represents the native widget, and another that is needed to properly lay out widgets in a window.

Another difference is that each of the preceding classes brings in platform-specific headers, and maintains different member variables to hold pointers to the native widget instances. (In Gtk+, all widgets are instances of `GtkWidget`, so the member variable has been factored into `GtkWidgetImpl`.)

Before we move on, it is interesting to compare the code used by different platforms. The `Create()` function performs the following tasks:

- Instantiate a platform widget (`GtkButton` for Gtk+, `NSButton` for Cocoa, `Button` for .NET Forms).
- Register a callback function to be invoked when the button is clicked by the user. This allows us to then notify listeners (more on this later).
- Make the button a child of its parent view.

Creating Widget Implementation Objects

Below is the source code for the concrete implementations of `WidgetImpl::Create()` at the time this book was written. Each of the above tasks (creating the button, registering the callback, and parenting the button) is handled differently, due to differences in how these operations are carried out in the native GUI toolkit.

Cocoa

On Mac OS X, the first thing you will notice is the strange (at least to C++ programmers) syntax that is used. To create an instance of NSButton, you execute the following code:

```
m_button = [[NSButton alloc] initWithFrame:graphicsRect];
```

The preceding code is written in the Objective-C programming language, which is the only programming language (besides Java) that Cocoa interfaces are defined for by Apple in Mac OS X. Fortunately, GNU's GCC supports embedding Objective-C code in C or C++ sources. (The resulting language is called Objective-C++.) In Objective-C++, C++ classes can contain Objective-C members, and vice versa. Objective-C classes can also make calls to C++ functions. Without the support of Objective-C++, Trixul would have been a much more difficult toolkit to engineer.

```
PRStatus CocoaButtonImpl::Create()
{
    NSRect graphicsRect =
        NSMakeRect(1.0, 1.0, 1.0, 1.0);
    ButtonAction *action;

    action = [ButtonAction alloc];

    [action setHandler: this];

    m_button = [[NSButton alloc]
        initWithFrame:graphicsRect];

    if (m_button) {

        [m_button setBezelStyle: NSRoundedBezelStyle];
        [m_button setTarget:action];
        [m_button setAction:@selector(onClick:)];
        m_view = (NSView *) m_button;

        WidgetImpl *parentImpl = GetParent();

        if (parentImpl) {

            NSView *parentView =
                dynamic_cast<CocoaWidgetImpl *>
```

```
            (parentImpl)->GetView();

        if (parentView) {
            [parentView addSubview: m_view];
            return PR_SUCCESS;
        }
    }
}
return PR_FAILURE;
}
```

Gtk+

The Gtk+ implementation of `ButtonImpl` is, in my view, the least complicated of the three platform implementations. In the Gtk+ implementation of
Trixul, all controls, including buttons, are parented by an instance of
`GtkFixed`, which allows the layout code in Trixul to position controls based
on its own layout algorithm. (The box layout algorithm is discussed later.)

```
PRStatus GtkButtonImpl::Create()
{
    m_widget = gtk_button_new();
    if (m_widget) {

        if (!m_fixedParent) {
            WidgetImpl *top = GetRootWidget();
            if (top) {
                SetFixedParent(top);
            }
        }

        if (m_fixedParent) {
            gtk_fixed_put(GTK_FIXED(m_fixedParent),
                m_widget, 0, 0);
            gtk_signal_connect(GTK_OBJECT(m_widget),
                "clicked",
                GTK_SIGNAL_FUNC(HandleCommandThunk),
                this);
            return PR_SUCCESS;
        }
    }
    return PR_FAILURE;
}
```

Windows

The .NET Forms toolkit was used in Trixul for a couple of reasons:

- Win32 and MFC are things of the past.
- .NET Forms is the cleanest and best thought out GUI API that Microsoft has yet to design. The API is more intuitive than either Cocoa or Gtk+, although at times, it does have its annoyances.

Using .NET Forms requires the compilation of code for the CLR. The CLR is Microsoft's common execution environment. In effect, the CLR is an abstract platform, much like the Java virtual machine. Code written in Microsoft-supported languages (for example, Fortran, C, C++, C#, COBOL, or whatever) can be compiled to execute against the CLR using Microsoft tools. Such code is known as "managed" code. Trixul isolates the use of managed code to a single DLL that contains the concrete widget class implementation and supporting code. This code is compiled with Microsoft C++, as is all the code in Trixul. However, the compiler flags and link lines used to compile and link the concrete widget implementation on Windows are specific to building managed code, as required when coding against the .NET Forms API. For details, you can download the Trixul source code and look at the file Makefile.windows in layout/windows.

Here is the code for Windows:

```
PRStatus WindowsButtonImpl::Create()
{
    m_button = __gc new Button();
    if (m_button) {
        if (!m_formParent) {
            WidgetImpl *top = GetRootWidget();
            if (top) {
                SetWidgetParent(top);
            }
        }
    }

    bool added = false;
    if (m_formParent) {
        m_formParent->Controls->Add(m_button);
        added = true;
    } else if (m_svParent) {
        m_svParent->Controls->Add(m_button)
        added = true;
    }
    if (added) {
```

```
            ButtonCallbackHelper *pHelper;
            pHelper = m_buttonHelper =
                __gc new ButtonCallbackHelper(this);
            m_button->add_Click(
                new EventHandler(pHelper,
                &ButtonCallbackHelper::OnButtonClick));
            return PR_SUCCESS;
        }
    }
    return PR_FAILURE;
}
```

Widget Factories

Now that we have seen both the platform-neutral `Button` class (and the classes that it derives from, `Control` and `Widget`), and the platform-specific `Button`-derived classes `GtkButtonImpl`, `CocoaButtonImpl`, and `WindowsButtonImpl`, it remains to be seen how Trixul instantiates the correct platform-specific class. Somehow, we need to ensure that `GtkButtonImpl` is instantiated on Gtk+, for example, and not `WindowsButtonImpl`. To achieve this, we make use of the *Abstract Factory* design pattern, documented in *Design Patterns* (Addison-Wesley, 1995).

The `WidgetFactory` base class defines interfaces that can be used to create platform-specific instances of widgets:

```
class WidgetFactory {
public:
    virtual ~WidgetFactory() {};
    virtual AppImpl* MakeApp() = 0;
    virtual ButtonImpl* MakeButton() = 0;
    virtual GridListImpl* MakeGridList() = 0;
    virtual StaticTextImpl* MakeStaticText() = 0;
    virtual TextImpl* MakeText() = 0;
    virtual WindowImpl* MakeWindow() = 0;
    virtual BoxImpl* MakeBox() = 0;
    virtual SpacerImpl* MakeSpacer() = 0;
    virtual MenuImpl* MakeMenu() = 0;
    virtual MenubarImpl* MakeMenubar() = 0;
    virtual MenuItemImpl* MakeMenuItem() = 0;
    virtual OpenPickerImpl* MakeOpenPicker() = 0;
    virtual SaveAsPickerImpl* MakeSaveAsPicker() = 0;
    virtual ScrolledWindowImpl*
        MakeScrolledWindow() = 0;
```

```
    virtual ScrolledViewImpl* MakeScrolledView() = 0;
    virtual RadioButtonImpl* MakeRadioButton() = 0;
    virtual CheckBoxImpl* MakeCheckBox() = 0;
};
```

Each of the abstract UI elements supported by Trixul (for example, Button, CheckBox, Menu) is supported by a function in WidgetFactory that can be called to create a platform-specific instance of these elements as Trixul parses a document. (The App object, which is described later in this chapter, is created internally by Trixul and is not specified in markup.)

WidgetFactory is an abstract class. Platform-specific classes provide the implementation of WidgetFactory. There are three classes— WindowsFactory, CocoaFactory, and GtkFactory—that provide implementations of WidgetFactory for Windows, Mac OS X, and Linux, respectively. We obtain the appropriate object by calling GetWidgetFactory(). GetWidgetFactory() is a C function that is conditionally compiled (one of the very few places in Trixul that one encounters #ifdefs to isolate platform-specific code). Its job is to return an instance of a concrete object that implements the WidgetFactory interfaces. The code is linked, based on the platform detected by the build process, to the platform-specific shared library (or DLL) that provides the concrete implementations. Here is the implementation of GetWidgetFactory():

```
class WidgetFactory;

#if defined(HAVE_WIN32)
#include "windows\windowsfactory.h"
#endif
#if defined(HAVE_MACOS)
#include "cocoa/cocoafactory.h"
#endif
#if defined(HAVE_GTK)
#include "gtk/gtkfactory.h"
#endif

WidgetFactory *GetWidgetFactory()
{
    static WidgetFactory *widgetFactory = 0;

    if (!widgetFactory)
#if defined(HAVE_WIN32)
        widgetFactory =
            WindowsFactory::GetFactoryInstance();
```

```
#endif
#if defined(HAVE_MACOS)
        widgetFactory =
            CocoaFactory::GetFactoryInstance();
#endif
#if defined(HAVE_GTK)
        widgetFactory =
            GtkFactory::GetFactoryInstance();
#endif
    return widgetFactory;
}
```

To make things a bit clearer, each platform-specific factory class is given a unique name that identifies the platform (for example, `WindowsFactory`). Doing so is not strictly necessary; because conditional compilation and the implementation of these classes as separate, platform-specific shared libraries would allow for using a more generic name (for example, `PlatformFactory`). Let's now take a look at `CocoaFactory`, the Mac OS X implementation of `WidgetFactory`:

```
class CocoaFactory : public WidgetFactory
{
public:
    static CocoaFactory *GetFactoryInstance()
    {
        static CocoaFactory *factory = NULL;
        if (!factory)
            factory = new CocoaFactory;
        return factory;
    }
    virtual ~CocoaFactory();
    virtual TextImpl *MakeText();
    virtual StaticTextImpl *MakeStaticText();
    virtual ButtonImpl *MakeButton();
    virtual MenuImpl *MakeMenu();
    virtual MenubarImpl *MakeMenubar();
    virtual MenuItemImpl *MakeMenuItem();
    virtual BoxImpl *MakeBox();
    virtual SpacerImpl *MakeSpacer();
    virtual WindowImpl *MakeWindow();
    virtual OpenPickerImpl *MakeOpenPicker();
    virtual SaveAsPickerImpl *MakeSaveAsPicker();
    virtual ScrolledWindowImpl *MakeScrolledWindow();
    virtual ScrolledViewImpl *MakeScrolledView();
    virtual GridListImpl *MakeGridList();
```

```
    virtual RadioButtonImpl *MakeRadioButton();
    virtual CheckBoxImpl *MakeCheckBox();
    virtual AppImpl *MakeApp();
    AppImpl *GetAppImpl() {return m_appImpl;};
private:
    CocoaFactory();
    AppImpl *m_appImpl;
};
```

Button's constructor, shown in the following listing, obtains the platform-specific singleton instance of an object that implements the WidgetFactory interface by calling GetWidgetFactory(). It then calls a method of the factory object, MakeButton, to create a platform instance of a ButtonImpl object:

```
Button::Button()
{
    WidgetFactory *factory = GetWidgetFactory();

    if (factory)
        m_button = factory->MakeButton();
}
```

CocoaFactory implements GetFactoryInstance(), which is called by GetWidgetFactory(), above. The rest of the interfaces defined by the CocoaFactory class are implementations of the interfaces defined by WidgetFactory.

As you saw, GetWidgetFactory(), on Mac OS X, calls CocoaFactory::GetFactoryInstance() to get the platform instance of WidgetFactory. This ensures that when MakeButton() is called, the Cocoa implementation of MakeButton() will be invoked. CocoaFactory::MakeButton() is implemented as follows:

```
ButtonImpl *CocoaFactory::MakeButton()
{
    return new CocoaButtonImpl;
}
```

Application Main Loop

One of the first things that Trixul does is instantiate an App object. App is a singleton object that represents the main loop of the GUI application. App has the following definition:

```
#include "appimpl.h"

class App
{
public:
    static App *GetAppInstance() {
        static App *app = NULL;
        if (!app)
            app = new App();
        return app;
    };
    PRStatus Initialize(int *argc, char *argv[]);
    PRStatus Shutdown();
    PRStatus MainLoop();
private:
    App();
    AppImpl *m_app;
};
```

The three main interfaces of App—Initialize(), Shutdown(), and MainLoop()—provide abstractions of functionality that one typically finds in modern GUI toolkits. Qt, Gtk+, .NET Forms, Xt, and Cocoa all provide objects or APIs that can be mapped directly to those of Trixul's App object.

After App has been instantiated, Trixul calls the App object's Initialize() member. It then creates the UI (discussed below), and calls App's MainLoop() function. After App::MainLoop() has been called, the application enters its main loop, processing events. Once MainLoop() returns, Trixul exits.

As you can see, App contains a private member variable, m_app, of type AppImpl. AppImpl defines a simple interface that maps to those defined by App:

```
class AppImpl
{
public:
    AppImpl() {};
    virtual ~AppImpl() {};
    virtual PRStatus Initialize(int *argc,
        char *argv[]) = 0;
    virtual PRStatus Shutdown() = 0;
    virtual PRStatus MainLoop() = 0;
};
```

The `Initialize()`, `Shutdown()`, and `MainLoop()` functions in `App` all make use of `m_app` as a bridge to calling the platform implementations of these functions. The functions defined by `App` all follow a simple pattern— they check to see whether `m_app` is non-NULL, and if so, invoke the corresponding function in the implementation object, where the actual work is done:

```
PRStatus App::Initialize(int *argc, char *argv[])
{
    if (m_app)
        return m_app->Initialize(argc, argv);
    return PR_FAILURE;
}


PRStatus App::Shutdown()
{
    if (m_app)
        return m_app->Shutdown();
    return PR_FAILURE;
}


PRStatus App::MainLoop()
{
    if (m_app)
        return m_app->MainLoop();
    return PR_FAILURE;
}
```

In App's constructor, one finds the code that instantiates the `AppImpl` object:

```
App::App() : m_app(NULL)
{
    WidgetFactory *factory = GetWidgetFactory();

    if (factory)
        m_app = factory->MakeApp();
}
```

This code uses `WidgetFactory`, which was described in the previous section.

For completeness, here are the platform-specific implementations of `App`, all which derive from the base class, `AppImpl`, described earlier. The main differences are as follows:

- Cocoa uses Objective-C++ APIs, Gtk+ is C based, and .NET Forms is based on managed C++.
- Neither Cocoa nor .NET Forms makes use of the command-line arguments passed to them.
- .NET Forms `Initialize()` function does nothing. The .NET Forms implementation of the `AppImpl` interfaces is clearly the simplest of the three toolkits.

Cocoa

```
PRStatus CocoaAppImpl::Initialize(int *argc,
    char *argv[])
{
    m_pool = [[NSAutoreleasePool alloc]init];
    NSApp = [NSApplication sharedApplication];

    return PR_SUCCESS;
}


PRStatus CocoaAppImpl::Shutdown()
{
    [NSApp terminate:nil];
    return PR_SUCCESS;
}


PRStatus CocoaAppImpl::MainLoop()
{
    // in cocoa, we invoke the main loop this way

    [NSApp run];

    // application has left its main loop here

    [NSApp release];
    [m_pool release];
    return PR_SUCCESS;
}
```

Gtk+

```
#include "gtkappimpl.h"

PRStatus GtkAppImpl::Initialize(int *argc, char *argv[])
{
    gtk_set_locale();
    gtk_init(argc, &argv);
    return PR_SUCCESS;
}

PRStatus GtkAppImpl::Shutdown()
{
    gtk_main_quit();
    gtk_exit(0);
    return PR_SUCCESS;
}

PRStatus GtkAppImpl::MainLoop()
{
    gtk_main();
    return PR_SUCCESS;
}
```

Windows

```
#include "windowsappimpl.h"

#include "stdafx.h"

#using <mscorlib.dll>
#using <System.dll>
#using <System.Drawing.dll>
#using <System.Windows.Forms.dll>

using namespace System;
using namespace System::ComponentModel;
using namespace System::Drawing;
using namespace System::Windows::Forms;

PRStatus WindowsAppImpl::Initialize(int *argc,
    char *argv[])
{
    return PR_SUCCESS;
}

PRStatus WindowsAppImpl::Shutdown()
```

```
{
    Application::Exit();
    return PR_SUCCESS;
}

PRStatus WindowsAppImpl::MainLoop()
{
    Application::Run();
    return PR_SUCCESS;
}
```

Steps Taken by Trixul to Create a User Interface

A lot of detail was presented in the preceding sections. The following summarizes the material presented so far by listing the steps taken by Trixul to create and manage a UI:

- Trixul is launched, and it opens the document specified on the command line. This document represents the main window of the application.
- Trixul instantiates the abstract class App. App obtains an instance of WidgetFactory and then it instantiates the corresponding platform-specific class. Which platform implementation is used is decided at compile time; GetWidgetFactory() is conditionally compiled to return the appropriate platform-specific factory object.
- Each of the platform-specific, implementation classes inherits from a platform-neutral class that defines the API it must implement. In the case of App, this class is AppImpl. A pointer to the AppImpl-derived class (GtkAppImpl, CocoaAppImpl, or WindowsAppImpl) is obtained by calling MakeApp(). The return value from MakeApp() is stored as a member variable in the App object. Calls made to App APIs are passed to the platform GUI toolkit for handling using this pointer. In this way, the App object acts, more or less, as a bridge between Trixul and the platform toolkit APIs. The same strategy is not only used by App, but also by all widget classes in Trixul.
- Trixul opens, and begins to parse, the XML document that describes the UI of the application's main window, and its menus.
- During the parse of the XML document, Trixul encounters a `<button>` element.
- Trixul instantiates Button, which is the platform-neutral class that represents button objects. Button's constructor, just like App's constructor, gets an instance of WidgetFactory, and it then calls MakeButton()

to instantiate a platform specific implementation of `ButtonImpl`.
(This will be either `CocoaButtonImpl`, `GtkButtonImpl`, or
`WindowsButtonImpl`.) Calls made to `Button` APIs (for example,
`Create()`, `Show()`, and `Enable()`) are handled by forwarding the call
directly to the implementation class, just as `App` forwarded its calls via
its `AppImpl` pointer.

■ After the XML document that describes the UI of the main window has
been parsed, and the corresponding UI objects have been created, Trixul
invokes `App::MainLoop()`, which, in turn, causes `CocoaAppImpl::`
`MainLoop()`, `GtkAppImpl::MainLoop()`, or `WindowsAppImpl::`
`MainLoop()` to be invoked, depending on the platform. At this point,
the application main window will be shown, the controls in the window
will have been laid out by Trixul, and events are processed by the native
application toolkit.

■ When the application calls `App::Shutdown()` (typically, this will be
done in response to the user selecting a menu item; for example, Exit or
Quit), the platform `AppImpl` object will fall out of its `main` loop, causing
Trixul to exit.

Documents, Elements, and the DOM

As shown previously, Trixul is provided, at startup via a command-line
argument, the pathname of an XML document that describes the layout of
the application's main window. Parsing this document results in the creation
of a Trixul `Document` object. In addition to specifying the initial document
on the command line, JavaScript code can open additional documents by
calling a function, and specifying the document's path. Therefore, at any
given time during the lifetime of the application, multiple `Document` objects
can coexist within the layout engine.

The `Document` object maintains the following data:

■ A list of each element that is parsed by Trixul from the document
■ A pointer to the root element of the document (usually a `<window>`
element)
■ A list of JavaScript `<script>` elements associated with the document, in
parsed form
■ A JavaScript object that can be used to access the `Document` object's
attributes and functions from JavaScript

The Document object declares a function, GetElementById(), that can be used by C++ code to locate an element based on its id attribute. Similar to what was described earlier in this chapter for DHTML, an id attribute can be specified for each element (although, in some cases, it makes little sense to do so). For example, the following <button> widget has the id "OkButton":

```
<button id="OkButton">
```

The JavaScript object maintained by the Document object has a function of the same name that will invoke the Document's GetElementById() function internally when called by JavaScript. Using GetElementById(), JavaScript code can obtain a JavaScript object that maps to a specific Element within the document as in the following example:

```
Element *okButton = document.GetElementById("OkButton");
```

The ability to locate elements by ID is critical to integrating the UI described by Trixul markup with JavaScript code. How this integration is done will be discussed later, in the section "Integration with JavaScript."

Let's take a closer look now at the Element object. For each element parsed, a C++-based Element object will be instantiated and added to the list that is maintained in the C++ Document object. Just like the C++ Document object has a JavaScript object that maps to it, each C++ Element object has a JavaScript Element object that maps to it, allowing JavaScript code to access that element's attributes and functions.

The C++ Element object manages the following information:

- The type of the element
- A pointer to the Document object that the element belongs to
- A pointer to its parent (also of type Element)
- A list of the element's children
- A list of the element's attributes
- A JavaScript object that represents the element

The Element class also maintains a list of all attributes, such as the ID mentioned previously, that were specified for the element in markup. Attributes, important although not supported or recognized by all widgets, include the value of the widget, its geometry (x, y position, width, and

height), label, and callbacks. Attributes are specified in markup using
name="value" expressions. Here are some examples:

A radio button with the ID "Agree":

```
<radio id="Agree"/>
```

An editable text field with width of 100 pixels and initialized to the
string "Hello World!":

```
<text editable="true" width="100"
    string="Hello World!"/>
```

A 640x480 window positioned at 100, 100 on the desktop:

```
<window x="100" y="100" width="640" height="480">
```

JavaScript source embedded in an XUL document:

```
<script type="text/javascript"
    src="resources/content/simple.js"/>
```

A button labeled "Ok", which will call a JavaScript function named
OnOk() when clicked:

```
<button onclick="return OnOk();" label="Ok"/>
```

Support for adding, maintaining, and searching for an element's
attributes is provided by the AttributeList base class, which is inherited
by Element.

As mentioned earlier, parsing the elements in a document results in a
Document object that contains a list of Elements objects, one per element
that was parsed in the XML document. The following XML document:

```
<window name="main" title="&hello.title;"
    width="320" height="200"
    x="100" y="100">
    <script type="text/javascript"
        src="resources/content/simple.js"/>
    <box orient="vertical">
        <statictext string="&statictext.value;"
            width="100" height="40"/>
        <box orient="horizontal">
            <button onclick="return Button1Click();"
                label="&button1.label;"/>
```

```
            <button onclick="return Button2Click();"
                label="&button2.label;"/>
        </box>
    </box>
</window>
```

results in the construction of the data structure shown in Figure 9-7.

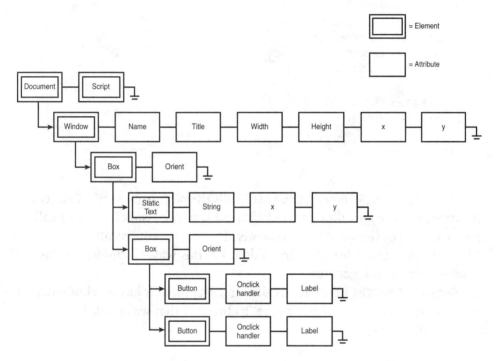

Figure 9-7 Document object example

Widget Creation

After the XML document describing the main window of the GUI has been parsed, Trixul queries the Document object for a Widget pointer to the main window of the document by calling GetMainWindow(). If found, Trixul calls its Create() function:

```
Widget *w;
w = reinterpret_cast<Widget *>(
    document->GetMainWindow(NULL));

if (w)
    w->Create();
```

The Create() function is pure virtual in Widget and implemented by derived classes (Window in this case). (The main window widget is an instance of Window, which derives from Widget.) Here is the code for Window::Create():

```
PRStatus Window::Create()
{
    PRStatus status;

    status = m_window->Create();
    if (status == PR_SUCCESS) {
        status = SetTitle(GetTitle());
    }
    if (status == PR_SUCCESS) {
        CreateChildren();
    }
    return status;
}
```

As you can see, Window::Create() calls the platform-specific Create() function, and then it calls CreateChildren(), which issues Create() calls for each child of the window. (Window is also an Element; recall that Elements maintain a list of their children.) In this way, all children of the Window element will get created.

Button's Create() function is similar, except that it has no children, and this does not make the call to CreateChildren() that was made by Window::Create():

```
PRStatus Button::Create()
{
    PRStatus status;

    status = m_button->Create();
    if (status == PR_SUCCESS) {
        status = SetLabel(GetLabel());
    }
    return status;
}
```

The platform-specific code, derived from ButtonImpl, was described earlier. Once again, here is the code for GtkButtonImpl::Create():

```
PRStatus GtkButtonImpl::Create()
{
    m_widget = gtk_button_new();
    if (m_widget) {

        if (!m_fixedParent) {
            WidgetImpl *top = GetRootWidget();
            if (top) {
                SetFixedParent(top);
            }
        }

        if (m_fixedParent) {
            gtk_fixed_put(GTK_FIXED(m_fixedParent),
                m_widget, 0, 0);
            gtk_signal_connect(GTK_OBJECT(m_widget),
                "clicked",
                GTK_SIGNAL_FUNC(HandleCommandThunk),
                this);
            return PR_SUCCESS;
        }
    }
    return PR_FAILURE;
}
```

In Trixul, the parent/child relationships that exist among the widgets found in a window are expressed by the nesting of elements in the XML markup. Two instance hierarchies are created in Trixul to represent these relationships, one consisting of Element-derived objects, which are stored in the DOM, and one consisting of WidgetImpl-derived objects. Both of these hierarchies are instantiated at the time the XML document that describes the window and its children is parsed. The hierarchical relationship among the widgets needs to be reflected natively in the platform toolkit, too. For example, in the Gtk+ implementation, the GtkButton widget needs a parent widget, and it must specify this widget as an argument to the Gtk+ function gtk_button_create().

Layout

After the widget instance hierarchy has been created both in the DOM and, natively, in the platform toolkit, the next step is to compute the layout of window or dialog.

In Mozilla's XUL, there are several layout widgets, but none is more fundamental and flexible than the box layout widget. There are two kinds of box widget: vertical boxes and horizontal boxes. A vertical box arranges its children vertically, top to bottom, in the order that the children are added to the box. Similarly, a horizontal box arranges its children from left to right once again in the order that children are added. Figure 9-8 illustrates a vertical box that contains three buttons labeled "Button 1," "Button 2," and "Button 3." Figure 9-9 illustrates the same widgets packed into a horizontal box. In both cases, Button 1 was added to the box first, and Button 2 was added second.

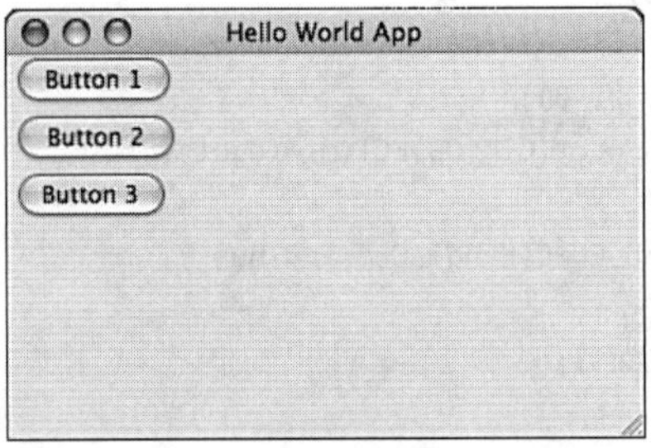

Figure 9-8 Buttons packed into a vertical box

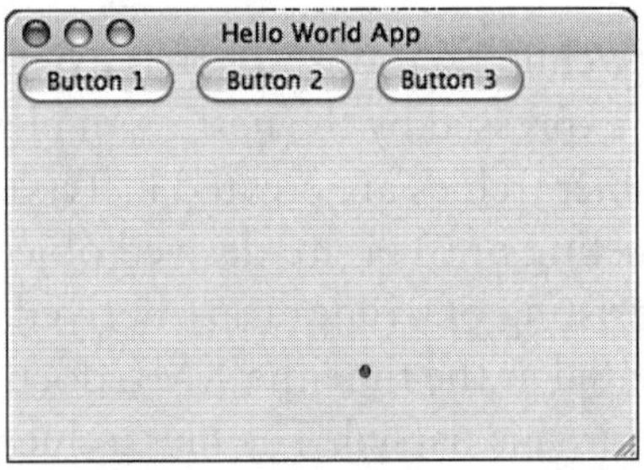

Figure 9-9 Buttons packed into a horizontal box

In Trixul, boxes are specified in markup with the <box> element, with the orientation of the box specified by the orient attribute. The markup for Figure 9-8 is, therefore, as follows:

```
<box orient="vertical">
    <button label="Button 1"/>
    <button label="Button 2"/>
    <button label="Button 3"/>
</box>
```

The markup for Figure 9-9 is the same except that the orient attribute of the <box> element has the value "horizontal".

Boxes can be nested, leading to interesting layouts. In Figure 9-10, a grid of buttons is created by nesting three horizontal boxes inside a vertical box. (The same layout could also be achieved by nesting three vertical boxes inside of a horizontal box.)

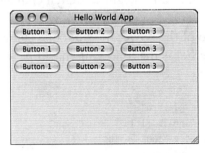

Figure 9-10 Grid of buttons created by nesting box elements

The following code was used to create the layout in Figure 9-10:

```
<!DOCTYPE window SYSTEM "simple.dtd">

<window name="main" title="&hello.title;" main="true"
    width="320" height="200" x="100" y="100">
    <box orient="vertical">
        <box orient="horizontal">
            <button label="Button 1"/>
            <button label="Button 2"/>
            <button label="Button 3"/>
        </box>
        <box orient="horizontal">
            <button label="Button 1"/>
            <button label="Button 2"/>
            <button label="Button 3"/>
        </box>
        <box orient="horizontal">
            <button label="Button 1"/>
            <button label="Button 2"/>
            <button label="Button 3"/>
        </box>
    </box>
</window>
```

Additional control over the placement of widgets is obtained by using <spacer> elements. A <spacer> element consumes space in a window or box that is not used by its other children. In Trixul, the free space in the box or window is divided evenly among the <spacer> elements. If there are, for example, two <spacer> elements in the box, each <spacer> element gets one half of the unused space. As a window or dialog is resized, the <spacer> elements adjust their width and height to match changes in the free space available.

A good illustration of the power of <spacer> elements and <box> elements working together is the following markup, which centers a button in a window:

```
<!DOCTYPE window SYSTEM "simple.dtd">
<window name="main" title="&hello.title;" main="true"
    width="320" height="200" x="100" y="100">
    <spacer/>
    <box orient="vertical">
        <spacer/>
        <box orient="horizontal">
            <spacer/>
            <button label="Button 1"/>
            <spacer/>
        </box>
        <spacer/>
    </box>
    <spacer/>
</window>
```

Figure 9-11 illustrates the window as it is first displayed, and Figure 9-12 shows the same window after resizing.

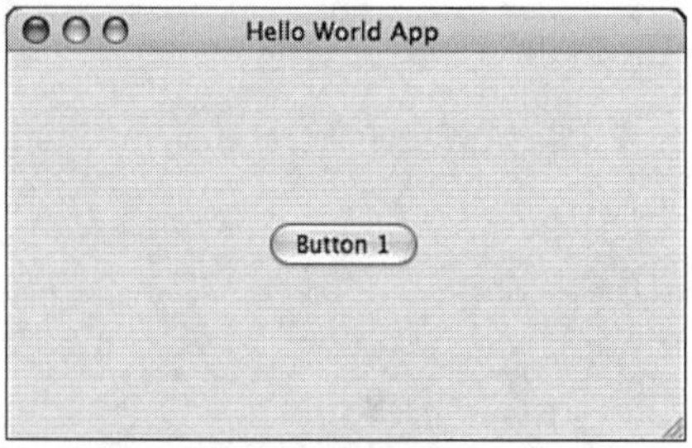

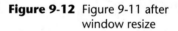

Figure 9-11 Spacers used to center widget in window

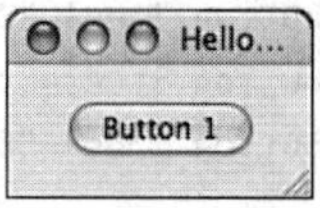

Figure 9-12 Figure 9-11 after window resize

Regardless of how the window is resized, the button will remain centered.

As a final illustration of spacer elements, we can add `<spacer>` elements around each element in the markup used to create Figure 9-10:

```
<!DOCTYPE window SYSTEM "simple.dtd">

<window name="main" title="&hello.title;" main="true"
    width="320" height="200" x="100" y="100">
    <spacer/>
    <box orient="vertical">
        <spacer/>
        <box orient="horizontal">
            <spacer/>
            <button label="Button 1"/>
            <spacer/>
            <button label="Button 2"/>
            <spacer/>
            <button label="Button 3"/>
            <spacer/>
        </box>
        <spacer/>
        <box orient="horizontal">
            <spacer/>
            <button label="Button 4"/>
            <spacer/>
            <button label="Button 5"/>
            <spacer/>
            <button label="Button 6"/>
            <spacer/>
        </box>
        <spacer/>
        <box orient="horizontal">
            <spacer/>
            <button label="Button 7"/>
            <spacer/>
            <button label="Button 8"/>
            <spacer/>
            <button label="Button 9"/>
            <spacer/>
        </box>
        <spacer/>
    </box>
    <spacer/>
</window>
```

Figures 9-13 through 9-15 illustrate the result after various resizings of the window:

Figure 9-13 Grid of buttons separated by spacers

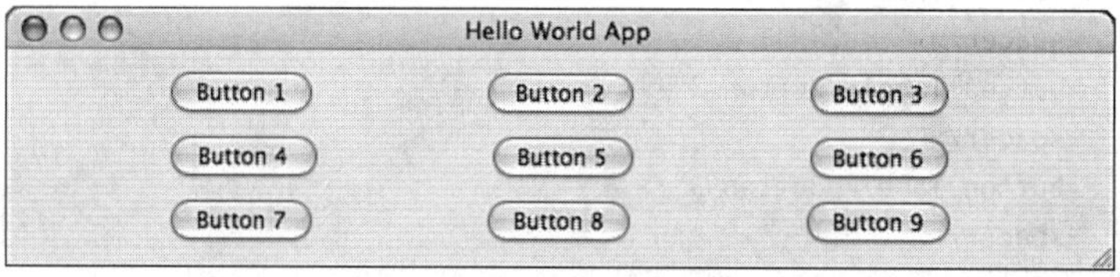

Figure 9-14 Figure 9-13 after window resized larger horizontally

Figure 9-15 Figure 9-14 after window resized smaller in both dimensions

Some GUI toolkits, such as Gtk+, natively support box layout widgets or semantics. Trixul does not use these, even when provided by the platform. There are a few reasons for this:

■ Support for box-like layouts is not universal among native GUI toolkits. By implementing its own support for box layout, Trixul ensures that a successful port to a given native GUI toolkit is not dependent on that toolkit providing support for box layouts.

- By supporting its own box layout algorithm, Trixul ensures the semantics of the box layout algorithm will be identical across all platforms.

Layout is computed after the window and its widgets have been instantiated (in Trixul's DOM, and in the native GUI toolkit). The layout algorithm operates basically as follows:

1. Recursively, the size requirements of each nonspacer widget is determined. If explicit geometry (for example, width and height) has been specified for an element as attributes in markup, these values are used. Otherwise, the native widget, which has been instantiated in the native GUI toolkit, is asked for its preferred size. The width and height of box widgets are set to the accumulated preferred width and height of their children, respectively.
2. The size of spacers in the window is computed. This is done recursively for each box in the window, too.
3. When the requested size of each widget and spacer is known, the layout code computes the position of each box, widget, and spacer in the window, and calls the platform GUI widgets to tell them what their position is. The native GUI toolkit, in turn, places each widget at its specified location.

Don't forget that the while Trixul computes the positions of each widget and passes these down to the native GUI toolkit, there is another layout algorithm in effect—that of the native GUI toolkit itself. Trixul forces the native toolkit to use an algorithm based on absolute positioning of the widgets in a window, canvas, or view. (The names vary among the various toolkits, but the purpose is the same.) When a window is created by Trixul, a listener or callback is registered with the native GUI toolkit that will be invoked whenever the window is resized (by the user or otherwise). Trixul, in turn, subscribes to this event with the native toolkit. When the event is published, the size of the window is passed to the listener callback, and Trixul uses this to recompute the layout of the window.

A few of the native widgets that are compatible with Trixul's layout algorithm are listed in Table 9-1.

Table 9-1 Some Toolkit Widgets that Are Compatible with Trixul

Toolkit	Widget
Gtk+	`GtkFixed`
.Net Forms	`Form`
Cocoa	`NSWindow/NSView`
wxWidgets	`wxFrame`
Qt	`QWidget` with a custom layout manager that subclasses `QLayout`
Xt/Motif	`XmBulletinBoard`

Scrolled Windows and Layout

Trixul supports two widgets, `<scrolledwindow>` and `<scrolledview>`, which effectively allow for the embedding of a window inside of a window. The `<scrolledwindow>` widget is a fixed-sized widget that parents a `<scrolledview>` widget. The dimensions of the `<scrolledview>` widget match, or more typically, exceed, those of the `<scrolledwindow>` widget that parents. (If the size of the view does not exceed that of the scrolled window, there is little need for scrollbars, and hence, these widgets.) When either dimension of the `<scrolledview>` widget exceeds that of the `<scrolledwindow>` widget, a scrollbar is shown for that dimension, allowing the user to scroll through the `<scrolledview>` widget's content. The code in the following listing illustrates the markup of a `<scrolledwindow>` and `<scrolledview>` widget embedded in a `<window>`. The geometry of the `<scrolledview>` widget is 500 by 500, and that of the `<scrolledwindow>` is 200 by 200. Thus, the `<scrolledwindow>` widget effectively provides a 200 by 200 window into the larger `<scrolledview>` child. The `<scrolledview>` widget, in turn, parents two `<button>` widgets, as well as some `<spacer>` widgets:

```
<!DOCTYPE window SYSTEM "simple.dtd">

<window name="main" title="&hello.title;" main="true"
    width="500" height="300" x="100" y="100">
    <scrolledwindow x="0" y="0"
        width="200" height="200"
        vertical="yes" horizontal="yes">
        <scrolledview x="0" y="0" width="500"
            height="500">
            <spacer/>
            <button label="ScrolledWindow Button 1"/>
```

```
          <spacer/>
          <button label="ScrolledWindow Button 2"/>
          <spacer/>
      </scrolledview>
   </scrolledwindow>
</window>
```

Figure 9-16 illustrates the window displayed by the above markup.

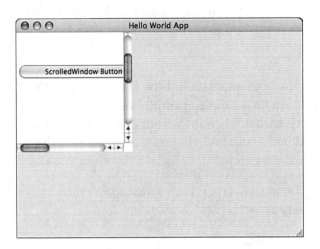

Figure 9-16 Trixul `ScrolledView` example

When the layout engine is in the process of computing the size requirements of a window, and it encounters a `<scrolledwindow>` widget, it uses the explicit size of the widget as its size, and then it recursively reenters the entire layout algorithm with the `<scrolledwindow>` widget as the root. Similar steps are taken when computing the size of `<spacer>` elements, and when calculating the position of widgets.

Integration with JavaScript

Now that we have covered how a UI is specified and how layouts work, we are left with a pretty window that, without some code behind it, is pretty much useless. Code is typically needed in GUI applications to handle basic tasks such as the following:

- Respond to button presses
- Respond to menu item selections
- Initialize controls (for example, place initial values in text fields)

■ Retrieve changes made to controls (for example, the value of a text field)
by users

To support these and other tasks, Trixul integrates SpiderMonkey, the
Mozilla JavaScript C embedding engine (www.mozilla.org/js/spidermonkey),
allowing Trixul programmers to implement code in JavaScript that interfaces
with widgets in a window. This section describes the integration of JavaScript
with Trixul in general detail, emphasizing the interface that exists between
JavaScript code and XML markup, as well as the role played by Trixul's
DOM.

An Example

Perhaps the best way to understand how JavaScript and the XML GUI
interact is to start with a simple example, and build upon it. The following
markup was seen earlier when the layout engine was described. It displays a
button centered in the window. (Figure 9-11 illustrates the window
displayed by this markup.)

```
<window name="main" title="&hello.title;" main="true"
    width="320" height="200" x="100" y="100">
    <spacer/>
    <box orient="vertical">
        <spacer/>
        <box orient="horizontal">
            <spacer/>
            <button label="Button 1"/>
            <spacer/>
        </box>
        <spacer/>
    </box>
    <spacer/>
</window>
```

When a user clicks the button labeled "Button 1," nothing happens
(except, of course, the native GUI toolkit will redraw the button to give
visual feedback during the state changes that occur when the button is
clicked). As a first step, let's add code that will respond to the button press
by breaking Trixul out of its main loop, exiting the application.

To associate code with the click of a button, we must add an onclick
attribute to the <button> element. The value of the onclick attribute is a

string that contains arbitrary JavaScript code, code that will be executed by Trixul's embedded JavaScript engine.

As it turns out, Trixul makes available two functions that can be invoked directly from JavaScript: `quit()` and `dump()`. The `dump()` function takes a string argument and simply displays it to the console. The `quit()` function takes no arguments and invokes the App object's `Shutdown()` method, which, as we want, will cause Trixul (and our application) to exit. The modified markup is trivial (changes in bold):

```
<!DOCTYPE window SYSTEM "simple.dtd">

<window name="main" title="&hello.title;" main="true"
    width="320" height="200" x="100" y="100">
    <spacer/>
    <box orient="vertical">
        <spacer/>
        <box orient="horizontal">
            <spacer/>
            <button onclick="quit();"
                label="Button 1"/>
            <spacer/>
        </box>
        <spacer/>
    </box>
    <spacer/>
</window>
```

Using External JavaScript Sources

Typically, the code that you invoke from the `onclick` handler will be a JavaScript function that you have written, which is located in a JavaScript source file. The `<script>` tag can be used to include external JavaScript source files and make their functions available to your `onclick` handler, just like in DHTML as described earlier in this chapter. You can specify as many `<script>` tags as you like. Instead of calling `quit()` directly, let's call a JavaScript function named `OnClickHandler()` that we will place in a JavaScript source file name clickhandler.js:

```
function OnClickHandler()
{
    quit();
}
```

We can then rewrite the XUL file as follows (again, differences in bold):

```
<!DOCTYPE window SYSTEM "simple.dtd">

<window name="main" title="&hello.title;" main="true"
    width="320" height="200" x="100" y="100">
    <script type="text/javascript"
        src="resources/content/clickhandler.js"/>
    <spacer/>
    <box orient="vertical">
        <spacer/>
        <box orient="horizontal">
            <spacer/>
            <button onclick="OnClickHandler();"
                label="Button 1"/>
            <spacer/>
        </box>
        <spacer/>
    </box>
    <spacer/>
</window>
```

As a part of processing of the preceding document, Trixul will pass any source files referenced by <script> elements (via the src attribute) to the JavaScript engine for interpretation. The code will be scoped to the document, meaning that another document that includes the same JavaScript source will have its own version of the functions, and global variables, as defined in the source file.

Interacting with Widgets from JavaScript Using the DOM

As mentioned earlier, one of the key reasons for supporting JavaScript is that it allows programmers to put code behind the UI. In particular, it allows code to initialize widgets and, when the time comes, read their state or values, and do something meaningful with the results. In this section, we modify the example we have been working with by adding two editable text fields to the UI. One text field will be initialized with a string that the user can modify, if he or she so desires. The second text field will contain a number, initially zero. The UI will also have two buttons. The first, named Quit, will simply call the internal quit() function. The second, Encrypt, will call a JavaScript function to encrypt the data in the first text field, using the number in the second text field as a key. The resulting cipher text will be displayed in a static text field immediately below the original plain text.

In terms of interaction with widgets in the document, we need to be able to do the following:

1. Read the plain text from the first text field.
2. Read the cipher key from the second text field.
3. After the encryption has been performed, set the value of the static text field with the result.

The preceding steps will require interaction with the DOM that was created by Trixul to represent the document, and the native toolkit.

Before we go any further, let me describe how the encryption will be performed. The encryption algorithm that I will be using is a very insecure, but nonetheless, historically interesting one: the Caesar Cipher. The Caesar Cipher is, as you might have guessed, attributed to Julius Caesar, who used it to protect important military messages during times of war. Here's how it works. Let's assume an alphabet consisting of the 26 uppercase letters A–Z, and number each of these A=1, B=2, ... Z=26. The key to the cipher is a value in the range [0, 25] that will be added to each plain-text letter to obtain the corresponding letter in the cipher text. (Subtracting this key from each letter of the cipher text will obtain the original plain-text message.) For example, if the key is 3, and the plain-text message is this:

```
HELLO WORLD
```

The resulting cipher text would be as follows:

```
KHOOR ZRUOG
```

If a letter, plus the key, goes past the letter Z (the value of which is 26), the value will wrap around. For example, adding 3 to 25 gives us 28, which is 2 past the end, so we assign the second letter of the alphabet as the cipher text—in this case, the letter B. To get the plain text from the cipher text, you just subtract the key (for example, 3) from each letter (and deal with the wrap around in the inverted sense).

As an aside, the Caesar Cipher is, like many substitution ciphers, fundamentally weak because it cannot stand up to an attack based on known frequencies of letters in the language of the plain text, or to a trivial brute-force attack, should it be known that the Caesar Cipher was used in the first place. (The brute-force attack is to simply try every key in the range [0, 25] until the resulting plain text makes sense to the attacker; the chance that more than one key will yield intelligible results is unlikely.) Don't ever use the Caesar Cipher in real applications. I use it here only because it is simple to describe.

The lack of security associated with the Caesar Cipher does not mean it isn't still used. I recently read a newspaper story online about a mafia leader in Italy who got caught by the police in 2006, in part because they were able to obtain incriminating information from a message that he had encrypted using a variation of the Caesar Cipher. (Try searching for the string "Italian mafia Caesar Cipher" in a search engine if you want to read more about it.)

Surely, the mafia has heard about GPG by now, right?

With the help of JavaScript's `String` object, the algorithm for encryption is simple enough to implement in JavaScript.

A function called `HandleEncrypt()` will be mapped to the Encrypt button's `onclick` handler. Its job is to retrieve the plain text and the key from the editable text fields, call `CaesarEncrypt()`, and then set the value of the static text field to the cipher text result. Here is the code for `CaesarEncrypt()` and `HandleEncrypt()`:

```
function CaesarEncrypt(key, plaintext)
{
    var result = "";
    var keyval= parseInt(key);
    plaintext = plaintext.toUpperCase();

    var length = plaintext.length;
    for (var i = 0; i < length; i++) {
      var val = plaintext.charCodeAt(i) - 65;
        if (val > 0)
            result += String.fromCharCode(
                ((val + keyval) % 26) + 65);
    }
    return result;
}

function HandleEncrypt()
{
    var key;
    var plaintext;

    // To be done: get the key
    // To be done: get the plaintext
```

```
    var ciphertext = CaesarEncrypt(key, plaintext);

    // To be done: set the value of the static text
    // field to ciphertext
}
```

Now that we have these functions out of the way, let's take a stab at completing the "To be done" items in the preceding code. We'll start by taking a look at the markup that describes the layout of the window:

```
<window name="main" title="Caesar" main="true"
    width="320" height="200" x="100" y="100">

    <!--UI to obtain the plaintext message to be
        encrypted -->

    <box orient="horizontal">
        <statictext string="Plaintext:" width="130"/>
        <text editable="true" selectable="true"
            id="plaintext" string="Enter message here"
            width="300"/>
    </box>

    <!--UI to get the key value from the user -->

    <box orient="horizontal">
        <statictext string="Key:" width="130"/>
        <text editable="true" selectable="true"
            id="key" string="1" width="50"/>
    </box>

    <!--UI to display the resulting ciphertext -->

    <box orient="horizontal">
        <statictext string="Ciphertext:" width="130"/>
        <statictext id="ciphertext" string=""
            width="100"/>
    </box>
    <spacer/>

    <!--button box -->

    <box orient="horizontal">
        <spacer/>
```

```
        <button onclick="HandleEncrypt();"
            label="Encrypt"/>
        <spacer/>
        <button onclick="quit();" label="Quit"/>
        <spacer/>
    </box>
</window>
```

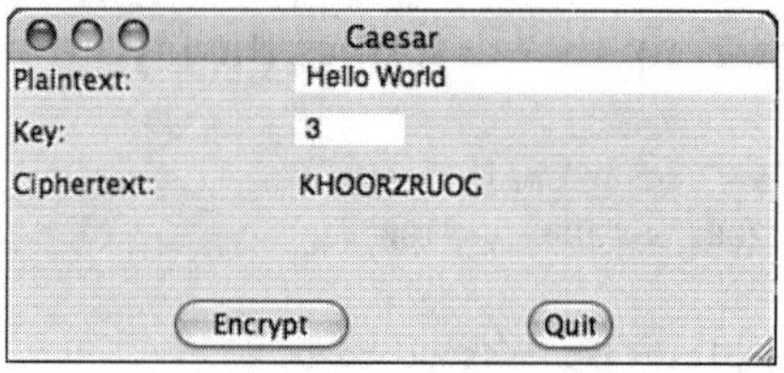

Figure 9-17 Caesar Cipher GUI

In the preceding markup (as well as in Figure 9-17), you can see that our
dialog contains three text fields, two of them editable (with IDs plaintext
and key) and one which is static and has the ID ciphertext. When the user
clicks the button labeled Encrypt, HandleEncrypt() needs to read the
values entered by the user in the plaintext and key text fields, compute the
ciphertext using these values, and then place the result in the ciphertext
static text field. In Trixul, the reading or writing of an element's value can be
achieved by 1) using the DOM function getElementById() to obtain a
JavaScript object that represents the element, and 2) by reading or writing
its value attribute. The following code illustrates:

```
function HandleEncrypt()
{
    var key;
    var plaintext;

    // read the plaintext

    plaintext =
        document.getElementById("plaintext").value;

    // read the key

    key = document.getElementById("key").value;

    // compute the ciphertext
```

```
var ciphertext = CaesarEncrypt(key, plaintext);

// display the result

document.getElementById("ciphertext").value =
    ciphertext;

}
```

The preceding use of `getElementById()` to obtain an object, and the subsequent reading and writing of its value attribute, is a pattern that is widely used in DHTML code and in XUL applications as well.

It is instructive to see how this functionality is implemented under the hood—much can be learned about how JavaScript integrates with the Trixul DOM by looking at how the expression

```
key = document.getElementById("key").value;
```

is handled by Trixul and the embedded JavaScript engine. To understand how it works, one needs to understand how DOM and JavaScript objects are related to each other.

Mapping DOM Document and Element Objects to JavaScript Objects

The story begins when the document's XML source is parsed. Recall that a DOM is created as a result of the parsing to represent the document, with each element in the XML document represented by a node in the DOM's hierarchical data structure. Attributes parsed from an element are stored along with the element in the DOM; this includes the `id` attribute of the element, if one was specified in markup. Given an ID, Trixul can search the DOM to find the corresponding DOM element.

After all the elements in the DOM document have been processed, the layout engine obtains an instance of a singleton Trixul object that provides a C++ interface to the embedded SpiderMonkey JavaScript engine. It then calls a function defined by this object to create a JavaScript object that will represent the DOM document. This JavaScript document object can then be referenced from any user-written JavaScript associated with that same document, as illustrated in the preceding code where it uses the document object to call `getElementById()`. Importantly, the JavaScript object that is returned by the SpiderMonkey engine to represent the DOM document is stored in a map along with a pointer to the DOM document object that it represents. Let's call this map *DocumentMap*.

Before I describe how *DocumentMap* is used, let's turn our attention to the implementation of the `getElementById()` function. The SpiderMonkey JavaScript engine allows Trixul, when it creates a JavaScript object, to define functions like `getElementById()` that can be invoked from user scripts on the object. Trixul can also create properties which can be referenced much like fields in a C language struct. The `.value` portion of `getElementById(id).value` is an example of how code might access a value property defined on an object. Below, I will describe how values references are implemented, but let's continue our discussion of the `getElementById()` function.

There is no restriction on the number of functions an object can define or on their names. These functions, however, must be mapped to C functions implemented by the code that is embedding the SpiderMonkey JavaScript engine. When the JavaScript document object is created, the SpiderMonkey engine is passed an array of C structs that map function names (for example, `getElementById()`) to their corresponding C functions implemented by the Trixul layout engine. For example, the JavaScript `getElementById()` function might be mapped to a Trixul function that is named `HandleGetElementById()`. (I will assume such a mapping in the text that follows.)

Assume we have created a document object in the JavaScript engine, and the function `getElementById()` has been defined on this object as described above. When the user script calls `document.getElementById("key")`, the SpiderMonkey JavaScript engine will invoke `HandleGetElementById()` and pass to it two arguments: 1) a copy of the JavaScript document object that the function was invoked from, and 2) the id argument (`key`) that was passed to `getElementById()` by the caller. With the JavaScript object in hand, Trixul can easily look up the corresponding DOM document object in *DocumentMap*. After the DOM document object has been retrieved from the map, Trixul can search the DOM for a child element that contains the specified ID. If the element is found, we then call a SpiderMonkey function to create yet another JavaScript object, this time to represent the DOM element that we found (see Figure 9-18).

When we create this new JavaScript object that represents the DOM element, we define no user callable functions on it, but we do create a property named "value". We also provide to the JavaScript engine pointers to two functions, one that will be called by SpiderMonkey when the value property is set in JavaScript code (a setter), and another that will be called when the value attribute is read by JavaScript code (a getter).

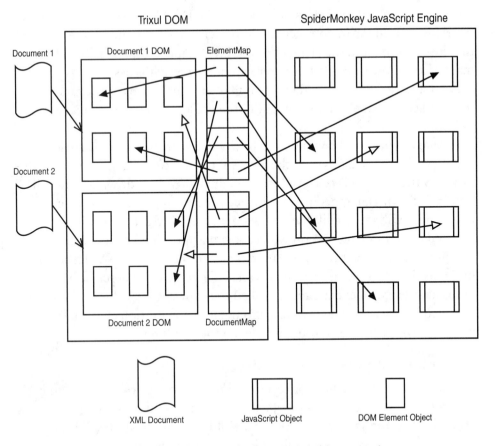

Figure 9-18 DOM object to JavaScript object mapping

Now that we have created the JavaScript object that represents the DOM element, we place it in yet another map, along with a pointer to the DOM element object it represents. Let's call this map *ElementMap*. We then return the JavaScript object just created to the SpiderMonkey engine, which will use it as the return value of the call to `document.getElementById("key")`.

Now that the JavaScript code has returned from its call to `getElementById()`, it makes reference to the value property (the `.value` portion of the expression is evaluated). This triggers the JavaScript engine to call the getter function Trixul specified when the value property was defined, because it needs Trixul's help to retrieve the value the user has typed into the text field. The JavaScript engine passes Trixul a pointer to the JavaScript object for which the value is being retrieved. Trixul looks this JavaScript object up in its *ElementMap*, and with the DOM element object that it retrieves, it can call interfaces provided by the DOM element object to read the element's value. To complete the transaction, Trixul returns the value that it retrieved from the element to the JavaScript engine, which will then make it available to the JavaScript user code, where it is assigned as the value of the variable named key. A similar sequence of events occurs when the user script makes an assignment to the value property of a JavaScript object.

Some of you may be wondering how a value property set by a user script ends up being passed down to the native GUI toolkit widget, or how a value property that is read is retrieved from a native GUI toolkit widget. Recall that an element is mapped to an abstract widget instance, in this case either a static text widget or editable text widget. This abstract widget in turn is mapped to an implementation widget that was provided by a widget factory. This was all described earlier in this chapter in the section, "Widgets" and in the section, "Implementation Classes." These sections describe how code in the abstract widget class that is called to set or get the value of the widget is routed by the abstract class down to the implementation class (a Trixul class that wraps platform toolkit widgets) for handling.

Integrating with C++ Components

Although JavaScript is fine for certain things, in no way can it match the power of a language like C++ or Java. Few meaningful desktop applications are possible using JavaScript alone. To build such applications, Trixul supports external component libraries. These libraries are written in the C++ language, and JavaScript code can create objects defined within them. This is a powerful concept: JavaScript code, ideally, is only used as a controller between the UI, designed in XML, and the guts of the application which is written in C++. No restrictions are placed on the C++ component objects, and thus, a Trixul application can be as powerful as any other desktop application. In fact, as you will see, it can effectively be linked to any library that is provided in the native environment.

Mozilla has a similar technology called XPConnect which, like Trixul, allows JavaScript to instantiate C++ objects in component libraries. XPConnect is based on XPCOM (Mozilla's portable COM implementation). Much of what you will learn here about Trixul applies to Mozilla's XPConnect, in the general sense. My feeling is Trixul's implementation is much easier to describe, owing to its simplicity both in terms of design and implementation. (The main reason for designing Trixul was to give me something I could easily describe, and give you something you could easily experiment with.) I also think Trixul is a bit easier on developers; writing components in Mozilla with XPCOM and XPConnect is much more complicated than I think it needs to be.

The goal of Trixul's component architecture is to provide the means by which JavaScript code can instantiate C++ objects, and once instantiated, call its member functions and interact with its member variables. The C++ objects are implemented in component libraries that Trixul discovers at runtime.

Using Components in Trixul

To develop and use a component in Trixul, a developer must follow a sequence of steps:

1. Describe the component, and the objects it implements, abstractly in a file using a special dialect of XML.
2. Use Trixul to create a C++ header file that defines each class specified in XML, as well as header and source files for code that can be used to interface each class to JavaScript.
3. Implement, in C++, the bodies of each C++ class defined in XML, conforming to the header file that was generated by Trixul.
4. Compile the sources and link them into a dynamic shared library.
5. Place the resulting shared library in a components directory that is created along with the application so that it can be discovered by Trixul at runtime.
6. Create JavaScript code that can be used to query for the existence of the component, and instantiate objects defined by the component. This step will result in JavaScript object(s) that contain functions and properties that map to the C++ objects in the shared library. When these JavaScript functions are called, Trixul will route them to the corresponding function in the C++ object for handling.

Let's look at each of the preceding steps in detail, and as we do, we will learn about the design and implementation of Trixul's component-based architecture. The component we will create will implement interfaces above the GNU cryptographic library `libgcrypt`. These interfaces will allow JavaScript to use the library to encrypt and decrypt strings using Advanced Encryption Standard (AES), a much more powerful cipher than the Caesar Cipher, which was introduced earlier in this chapter. Roughly the same XML/XUL UI will be used by this application to test the component as was used by the Caesar Cipher application, although some changes will be needed in the JavaScript code, as you will see. Figure 9-19 illustrates the UI for the AES encryption application.

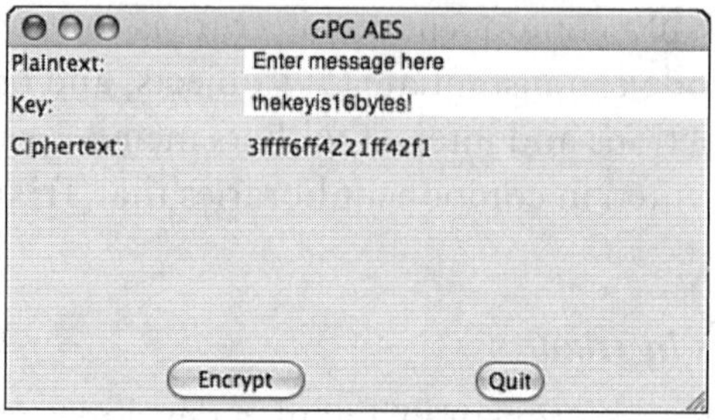

Figure 9-19 GPG AES example GUI

Describing the Component in XML

The very first step in creating a component in Trixul is to describe it. The description of a component is contained in a text file, written using a special dialect of XML named SIL. (SIL is a Trixul term which stands for Simple Interface Language.) Within the SIL file, the programmer assigns a name and a unique identifier to the component, and defines each of the objects that can be instantiated from JavaScript. (A component library can be used to represent any number of objects.) For each object, the public functions that can be called, and the properties of the object are also specified.

The component is defined using a <component> element, which contains two attributes:

- **name**—The name of the component
- **id**—A unique string that identifies the component

The name can be any text. The id is a universally unique identifier (UUID) that can be generated using uuidgen(1) on Linux or Mac OS X from the command line:

```
$ uuidgen
F4F99524-4035-41BC-A241-D48F1ED7A20B
$
```

Objects are defined with the <class> element. Like the <component> element, it has both name and id attributes. <class> elements are children of <component> elements. A <component> element can parent any number of <class> elements.

A `<class>` element can contain `<function>` elements or `<property>` elements. There can be any number of either embedded within a `<class>` element. The `<property>` function has two attributes, a name and a type. Think of a `<property>` element as defining a member variable in the class that has the specified name and type. Trixul will provide setters and getters that are callable from JavaScript for each property, as shown later. The `<function>` element has a single attribute, which is the name of the function. A `<function>` element represents what you might expect—a public interface defined by the class that can be called directly from JavaScript. Each `<function>` element can parent any number of `<arg>` elements, which are used to define an argument and its type to the function, and a single `<return>` element, which defines the return type of the function. If the `<function>` element does not embed a `<return>` element, the function is deemed void.

Let's now take a look at the XML that is used to define the AES encryption interface object and its enveloping component:

```
<component name="encrypt"
    id="79463AD7-02C3-42FD-A8F0-061525C45FF8">
    <class name="AESEncrypt"
        id="6F2AD801-85A4-4FF4-A0F3-42B013ED2C8E">
        <function name="SetKey">
            <arg name="Key" type="string"/>
            <return type="PRStatus"/>
        </function>
        <function name="Encrypt">
            <arg name="Plaintext" type="string"/>
            <return type="string"/>
        </function>
        <function name="Decrypt">
            <arg name="Ciphertext" type="string"/>
            <return type="string"/>
        </function>
        <property name="key" type="string"/>
    </class>
</component>
```

Here is what the XML above accomplishes:

- First, it defines a component named `encrypt` with the `id` 79463AD7-02C3-42FD-A8F0-061525C45FF8.
- It then defines a class named `AESEncrypt` with the `id` 6F2AD801-85A4-4FF4-A0F3-42B013ED2C8E. The class represents an object that can be

instantiated from the component, while the component represents the DLL or shared library that that class is implemented within.

- The class AESEncrypt defines three functions. The first, SetKey(), takes a single argument of type string and returns a pass/fail status of type PRStatus. The second, Encrypt(), encrypts the plain text passed in as its argument, and returns the cipher text as its return value. The final function, Decrypt(), inverts the argument and return value of Encrypt(), accepting cipher text as the argument, and returning plain text as the result.
- A string property named "key" is also defined. The value of this property can be set and read directly from JavaScript.

Accessing Components and Objects from JavaScript

The SpiderMonkey JavaScript engine allows for embedding software to instantiate objects in C++ that can then be accessed directly from JavaScript code. This capability is the basis for the JavaScript to C++ integration in Trixul, and is also used in Mozilla to provide similar functionality in conjunction with XPConnect and XPCOM.

At startup, Trixul searches for any SIL files and shared libraries that are located in a special directory named components, located in the same directory as the Trixul executable. A singleton ComponentManager object instantiated by Trixul performs this work. For each SIL file that ComponentManager finds and successfully parses, a C++ Component object is instantiated and stored in an STL map that the ComponentManager object maintains. The index of the component in this map is the UUID that was parsed from the <component> element in the SIL file.

A Component object maintains a Standard Template Library (STL) list of Object objects, one for each <class> element parsed. In turn, each Object object maintains a list of Function objects, one such object for each child <function> element of the <class> element. As you might be guessing by now, each Function object maintains a list of objects that represent the arguments passed to the function, as well as a member variable that specifies the function's return type. In addition to Function objects, an Object object also manages a list of Property objects, corresponding to <property> element children of the <class> element. The Property object represents the name and type of the property.

After the data structure hierarchy described previously is created for a Component, Trixul calls the Component object's CreateJSObject() member function to create a JavaScript object to represent the component. A global

JavaScript object named `componentmgr` is created by Trixul to allow JavaScript code to query for components by calling a function named `getComponent()`, passing as an argument the component's UUID to identify the desired component. If the UUID corresponds to a component discovered by Trixul, the `componentmgr` object will create and return a JavaScript object that represents the component.

Let's now take a look at the JavaScript object that is returned by the `componentmgr` object to represent a component. Each object exposes two important functions, `getObject()` and `releaseObject()`, which can be called directly from JavaScript to create and destroy, respectively, instances of any class that are defined by the component. To identify which class to create, the `getObject()` function takes as an argument a UUID, the same UUID that was specified as the `id` attribute of the corresponding `<class>` element in the SIL file. If such a class exists, yet another JavaScript object, this time representing an instance of the class identified by the UUID, is returned. With this object in hand, the JavaScript code finally has an object that it can use, calling any of the functions that it defines, and reading and writing any of its properties as needed. When done with the object, the JavaScript code simply calls the object's `releaseObject()` function to release the object.

To summarize:

1. The JavaScript code calls the JavaScript object's `getComponent()` function to get an object representing a specific component. `getComponent()` is passed the UUID of the component desired.
2. If an object is returned, the JavaScript code then calls that object's `getObject()` function to instantiate a JavaScript object representing an instance of a C++ class implemented in the component. `getObject()` is passed the UUID of the class desired.

The following example code should make the previous steps clear. The function `GPGAESEncrypt()` is analogous to the `CaesarEncrypt()` function presented earlier. Like `CaesarEncrypt()`, it takes two arguments: a key and the plain text to be enciphered, and it returns the resulting cipher text:

```
function GPGAESEncrypt(key, plaintext)
{
    var result = "";
    var component = componentmgr.getComponent(
        "79463AD7-02C3-42FD-A8F0-061525C45FF8");
    if (component) {
```

```
    var anobject = component.getObject(
        "6F2AD801-85A4-4FF4-A0F3-42B013ED2C8E");
    if (anobject) {
        try {
            dump("GPGAESEncrypt got an object\n");
            anobject.SetKey(key);
            result = anobject.Encrypt(plaintext);
        } catch (ex) {
            dump(ex);
        }
        component.releaseObject(anobject);
    }
}
return result;
}
```

One thing that I haven't yet mentioned, which might or might not be obvious, is that Trixul not only must instantiate a JavaScript object for each class it returns, but it must also instantiate the C++ object that corresponds to that class. After all, it is the C++ object that we are trying to interface to. The JavaScript object does not implement the functionality of the object; instead, it is used as a proxy of sorts between the JavaScript application and a C++ object that provides the object's functionality. In the next few sections, I describe how the C++ code for a component is created, how runtime instances of a components' classes are created, and finally, how the interfacing between these C++ objects and their corresponding JavaScript objects is achieved.

Coding the C++ Component

An SIL file, as you saw earlier, is used to describe the following:

- A component and its UUID
- The classes that are implemented by the component, also identified by UUIDs
- For each class in the component, the functions and properties that it implements
- For each function implemented by a class, its arguments and return type

A similar function is performed by IDL in Microsoft COM, Mozilla XPCOM, XML-RPC, SOAP, and OMG CORBA technologies. In Trixul, the ComponentManager object in the Trixul-based application uses SIL files to identify components at runtime by searching for SIL files in a directory named components at startup. For each one found, a Component object is created to represent the component and the classes it implements, and this object is maintained in an STL map by ComponentManager, indexed by its UUID. In addition, a JavaScript object that represents the component is created and attached to the Component object. When the JavaScript code calls the ComponentManager via the componentmgr object's getComponent() interface, the UUID is used to find the Component object in the map, and the JavaScript object is returned.

The creation of the JavaScript object corresponding to a component is performed lazily. That is, it is not created until some JavaScript code actually requests the component via the component manager. When this happens, the JavaScript object for the component is created, and then the ComponentManager attempts to load the shared library for that component. The pathname of the shared library directory is components, relative to the directory in which the Trixul application is executing. NSPR's cross-platform library support is used to perform this task. The resulting Netscape Portable Runtime Library (NSPR) library object is stored in the Component object.

Now that a JavaScript object corresponding to a component has been returned, the next step the JavaScript code will do is instantiate one of its classes. This is done by calling the Component object's getObject() interface, as you have seen. This call gets handled by the corresponding Component instance in Trixul which, also lazily, will create the C++ class instance in response. This class instance will be represented internally by an instance of Trixul's Object class which contains the following members, among others:

```
Component *m_component; // the parent component
JSObject *m_jsObj; // the corresponding JavaScript obj
```

As implied by this, a JavaScript object will be created for the class instance and stored in the Object instance. Importantly, a reference to the Component object is stored as well within the object, so that we can get to it when the JavaScript code calls methods on this object. We need to do this to reference the NSPR library object, which in turn will enable us to make function calls into the library (for example, to call the class constructor, destructor, and methods) in response to calls made from JavaScript on the corresponding object.

In a moment, I describe how the call chain from JavaScript is made into an instance of the C++ object representing the class, and how the C++ object itself is instantiated. First, however, let's summarize where we are because quite a bit of detail has been presented so far, and I want to make sure you understand the big picture:

When the JavaScript code calls `componentmgr.getComponent()`, Trixul creates a `Component` object to represent the component. The `Component` object contains an NSPR-based object that represents the shared library for the component and a JavaScript object that can be used to create class instances by the JavaScript application. The JavaScript object is returned to the caller. Trixul can use the `ComponentManager` to look up the `Component` object in a map indexed by the component's UUID.

JavaScript code can use the `Component` object returned above to call `getObject()` to create an instance of a class implement in the component. This will result in the creation of a Trixul `Object` instance, which maintains a reference to the corresponding component, and a JavaScript object that represents the class. This JavaScript object is returned to the caller. Like `Component` objects, `Object` instances can be located in a map indexed by the UUID of the class/object.

Now let's turn our attention to how JavaScript calls a method on a C++ class object or sets and gets one of its properties. JavaScript objects in the SpiderMonkey JavaScript engine are relatively simple to create. Just like Trixul classes, a JavaScript object implements functions and properties. Each Trixul `Object` object maintains a list of the functions and properties defined by the class, including, for each function, its return type and arguments. When it comes time to create the corresponding JavaScript object, Trixul uses this information to define functions on the JavaScript object. Here is the code that performs the JavaScript object creation:

```
PRStatus
Object::CreateJSObject()
{
    PRStatus ret = PR_SUCCESS;
    JSEngine *js = JSEngine::GetJSEngine();

    if (!js)
        return PR_FAILURE;

    Component *comp = GetComponent();
    if (!comp)
        return PR_FAILURE;

    Library *lib = comp->GetLibrary();
```

```
if (!lib)
    return PR_FAILURE;

JSContext *ctx = js->GetContext();
JSObject *obj = js->GetGlobalObject();

string name = GetAttributeByName(
    string("name"))->GetValue();

// create an instance of the proxy class

string creator, destroyer, lookup;

creator = "New" + name + "Proxy";
destroyer = "Delete" + name + "Proxy";

CreatorFn pCreator;

pCreator = (CreatorFn) lib->FindSymbol(creator);
m_pDestroyer = (DestroyerFn)
    lib->FindSymbol(destroyer);

if (!pCreator || !m_pDestroyer)
    return PR_FAILURE;

m_name = name;

JSClass objectClass = {
    m_name.c_str(), 0,
    JS_PropertyStub,    JS_PropertyStub,
    JS_PropertyStub,    JS_PropertyStub,
    JS_EnumerateStub,   JS_ResolveStub,
    JS_ConvertStub,     JS_FinalizeStub
};

m_jsClass = objectClass;

m_jsObj = JS_DefineObject(ctx, obj, name.c_str(),
    &m_jsClass, NULL, 0);
if (!m_jsObj)
    return PR_FAILURE;

ret = (*pCreator)(m_jsObj);
if (ret != PR_SUCCESS) {
    m_jsObj = NULL;
```

```
        return PR_FAILURE;
    }


    // iterate the functions defined by this object

    list <Function *> funcs = GetFunctionList();
    list <Function *>::iterator funciter;
    for (funciter = funcs.begin(); funciter !=
        funcs.end(); ++funciter) {

        Function *func = *funciter;
        AnAttribute *nameattr;

        nameattr = func->GetAttributeByName("name");
        string fnName = nameattr->GetValue();

        string name2 = name + "_" + fnName;

        list <Arg *> args = func->GetArgumentList();
        int size = args.size();

        // query component for proxy lib entry point

        JSNative fptr = (JSNative)
            lib->FindSymbol(name2);

        if (fptr) {
            JSFunction *func =
                JS_DefineFunction(ctx, m_jsObj,
                fnName.c_str(),
                fptr,  // JSNative
                size, 0);
            if (!func) {
                ret = PR_FAILURE;
                m_jsObj = NULL;
                break;
            }
        } else {
            ret = PR_FAILURE;
            m_jsObj = NULL;
            break;
        }
    }
}
```

The steps performed by the preceding code include the following:

1. Get the NSPR-based library object, and with it, resolve pointers to the C++ creator and destroyer functions.
2. Create the base JavaScript object.
3. Call the library's creator function which will instantiate the C++ class. The base JavaScript object is passed as an argument so that the C++ object can store a reference to it.
4. For each function defined for the class, resolve a reference to a C++ proxy function defined in the library, and then define a function on the JavaScript object that, when invoked, will call the proxy function.

Let's go through each of these steps, one by one.

Resolve Pointers to the Creator and Destroyer Functions in the Library

The `Component` object (a reference of which is stored in the `Object` object) contains a pointer to the NSPR library object. Using this library object, we must resolve function pointers to two functions. The first, the `Creator` function, is used to create instances of the class. The second, the `Destroyer` function, is used to delete these instances. Each C++ component library must provide these functions as exports. The names of the `Creator` and `Destroyer` functions are `NewClassProxy()` and `DeleteClassProxy()`, where *Class* is the name of the class.

Create the Base JavaScript Object

The SpiderMonkey JavaScript engine supports the creation of JavaScript objects with the `JS_DefineObject()` function. It is not within the scope of this book to describe the SpiderMonkey engine in detail, but I do want to cover in general detail how object creation is performed. Doing so will help to clarify the bridge between the JavaScript object and the C++ object instantiated from the component library.

Before calling `JS_DefineObject`, a `JSClass` struct must be allocated and initialized. Here, I simply provide the class name and use default stub values for the rest of the fields in the struct:

```
JSClass objectClass = {
    m_name.c_str(), 0,
    JS_PropertyStub,  JS_PropertyStub,
    JS_PropertyStub,  JS_PropertyStub,
    JS_EnumerateStub,  JS_ResolveStub,
```

```
    JS_ConvertStub,   JS_FinalizeStub
};


m_jsClass = objectClass;
```

Next, I call `JS_DefineObject()` to create the JavaScript object. Once created, a pointer to the object is stored as a member function. When the `ComponentManager`'s `getObject()` method is called from JavaScript, this object will be returned:

```
m_jsObj = JS_DefineObject(ctx, obj, name.c_str(),
    &m_jsClass, NULL, 0);
```

Instantiate the C++ Object

Now that we have the JavaScript object, we create an instance of the C++ class by invoking the aforementioned `Creator` function in the shared library. The `Creator` function will instantiate the class and add it to a static STL map, indexed by the JavaScript object. Later, we can easily look up the C++ object using the JavaScript object as an index into the map.

Define JavaScript Functions on the Base JavaScript Object

Each JavaScript function is defined by its name, and the address of a native C++ proxy function in the shared library that will be invoked when the JavaScript program calls the function. The proxy functions, generated by Trixul as you will see later, are the magic that bind JavaScript objects to C++ objects at runtime. For each function defined for a class in the SIL file, the source for a corresponding C language proxy function is *generated* by Trixul. For those of you familiar with Java's Java Native Interface (JNI), what Trixul does is similar, in a sense, except Trixul generates not just the headers but the implementations as well. These proxy functions must be linked to the shared library that contains the implementation of the corresponding class. The proxy functions have a predefined signature that is mandated by the JavaScript engine. Here is the proxy function for the C++ `AESEncrypt::Encrypt` function:

```
extern "C" EXPORT JSBool
AESEncrypt_Encrypt(JSContext *cx, JSObject *obj,
    uintN argc, jsval *argv, jsval *rval);
```

This function simply takes the passed in `obj` argument, looks up the C++ object instance in the map that was created previously using `obj` as an index, and then calls the Encrypt() function implemented by the C++ object. Here is the code for the proxy function:

```
extern "C" EXPORT JSBoolAESEncrypt_Encrypt(
    JSContext *cx, JSObject *obj, uintN argc,
    jsval *argv, jsval *rval)
{
    AESEncrypt *ptr = GetAESEncryptClass(obj);
    if (!ptr)
        return JS_FALSE;
    JSString *str_0 = JSVAL_TO_STRING(argv[0]);
    string arg_0(JS_GetStringBytes(str_0));
    string ret;
    ret = ptr->Encrypt(arg_0);
    JSString *str = ::JS_NewStringCopyN(cx,
        ret.c_str(), ret.size() + 1);
    *rval = STRING_TO_JSVAL(str);
    return JS_TRUE;
}
```

GetAESEncrypt() is a function generated by Trixul that gets an instance of AESEncrypt from the map, using the obj argument as an index, and invokes its Encrypt() member function. Prior to calling Encrypt(), arguments that were passed by the JavaScript program are converted from JavaScript types to C++ types. After the call to Encrypt(), the return value of Encrypt() is converted from a C++ type to a JavaScript type.

Generating Source Code for the Proxy and C++ Classes from an SIL File
As mentioned in the previous section, the proxy code in a component shared library that sits between a JavaScript object and an instance of a C++ class defined in the component shared library is generated by Trixul and must be linked to the component shared library. In this section, I describe the proxy code that is generated and talk about how the C++ component itself is defined.

Given an SIL file, Trixul can be invoked from the command line to generate the source and header files for the corresponding proxy code, as well as a header file that contains declarations for each class specified in the SIL file. Here are the arguments accepted by Trixul to perform these tasks:

- **-p path**—Path to the SIL file to be processed
- **-h path**—Path to the proxy header generated by Trixul
- **-s path**—Path to the proxy source generated by Trixul

- **-c path**—Path to the source code generated by Trixul that defines the classes specified in the SIL file

The following command line causes Trixul to process the SIL file components/encrypt.sil and generates the corresponding proxy and class headers and proxy source code to the specified files:

```
sydlogan% ./layout -p components/encrypt.sil -h \
components/encrypt_proxy.h \
-s components/encrypt_proxy.cpp -c components/encrypt.h
```

The following listings show the code generated by the preceding command line. First is the header file (components/encrypt_proxy.h) declaring the function prototypes for the C language proxy functions that will be invoked by the JavaScript engine when the corresponding functions are called from JavaScript:

```
/* This is generated source code. Do not edit */

#if !defined(__79463AD7_02C3_42FD_\
A8F0_061525C45FF8_PROXY_H__)
#define __79463AD7_02C3_42FD_\
A8F0_061525C45FF8_PROXY_H__

#if defined(WIN32)
#define EXPORT __declspec(dllexport)
#else
#define EXPORT
#endif

#include <prtypes.h>
#include "jsapi.h"

extern "C" EXPORT JSBool
AESEncrypt_Get_key(JSContext *cx, JSObject *obj,
    uintN argc, jsval *argv, jsval *rval);

extern "C" EXPORT JSBool
AESEncrypt_Set_key(JSContext *cx, JSObject *obj,
    uintN argc, jsval *argv, jsval *rval);

extern "C" EXPORT JSBool
AESEncrypt_SetKey(JSContext *cx, JSObject *obj,
    uintN argc, jsval *argv, jsval *rval);
```

```
extern "C" EXPORT JSBool
AESEncrypt_Encrypt(JSContext *cx, JSObject *obj,
    uintN argc, jsval *argv, jsval *rval);

extern "C" EXPORT JSBool
AESEncrypt_Decrypt(JSContext *cx, JSObject *obj,
    uintN argc, jsval *argv, jsval *rval);

extern "C" EXPORT PRStatus
    NewAESEncryptProxy(JSObject *obj);

extern "C" EXPORT PRStatus
    DeleteAESEncryptProxy(JSObject *obj);

#endif
```

The next listing is the header file (components/encrypt.h) that contains the declaration of the C++ class named AESEncrypt. The functions Get_key() and Set_key() are public functions that support AESEncrypt's key property. In Trixul, properties are scoped to the object and implemented as member variables in the corresponding class. The remaining functions, SetKey(), Encrypt(), and Decrypt(), correspond to the interfaces defined for the class in the SIL file:

```
/* This is generated source code. Do not edit */

#if !defined(__79463AD7_02C3_42FD_A8F0_\
    061525C45FF8_COMP_H__)
#define __79463AD7_02C3_42FD_A8F0_\
    061525C45FF8_COMP_H__

#include "prtypes.h"
#include <string>
using namespace std;
class AESEncrypt {
public:
    AESEncrypt();
    ~AESEncrypt();
    PRStatus Get_key(string& val) {val = m_key;
        return PR_SUCCESS;};
    PRStatus Set_key(string& val) {m_key = val;
        return PR_SUCCESS;};
    PRStatus SetKey(string& Key);
    string Encrypt(string& Plaintext);
```

```
    string Decrypt(string& Ciphertext);
private:
    string m_key;
};


#endif
```

Finally, the following file (components/encrypt_proxy.cpp) implements the STL map used to link JavaScript objects and instances of the
AESEncrypt() class together, and the functions that support adding, removing, and looking up C++ classes in the map (AddAESEncryptClass(),
RemoveAESEncryptClass(), and GetAESEncryptClass(), respectively). In
addition, Creator and Destroyer functions (NewAESEncryptProxy() and
DeleteAESEncryptProxy(), respectively), as well as the source code for
proxy functions, are also defined in the proxy source file generated by Trixul:

```
/* This is generated source code. Do not edit */

#include "encrypt_proxy.h"
#include "encrypt.h"
#include "prtypes.h"
#include "jsstr.h"
#include <map>

using namespace std;

static map<JSObject *, AESEncrypt*> objAESEncryptMap;

static AESEncrypt *
GetAESEncryptClass(JSObject *obj)
{
    return objAESEncryptMap[obj];
}

static void
AddAESEncryptClass(JSObject *obj, AESEncrypt *cPtr)
{
    objAESEncryptMap[obj] = cPtr;
}

static void
RemoveAESEncryptClass(JSObject *obj)
{
    objAESEncryptMap.erase(obj);
```

```
}

extern "C" EXPORT PRStatus
NewAESEncryptProxy(JSObject *obj)
{
    AESEncrypt *ptr = new AESEncrypt();
    if (!ptr)
        return PR_FAILURE;
    AddAESEncryptClass(obj, ptr);
    return PR_SUCCESS;
}

extern "C" EXPORT PRStatus
DeleteAESEncryptProxy(JSObject *obj)
{
    AESEncrypt *ptr;
    if (obj) {
        ptr = GetAESEncryptClass(obj);
        RemoveAESEncryptClass(obj);
        delete ptr;
    }
    return PR_SUCCESS;
}

extern "C" EXPORT JSBool
AESEncrypt_SetKey(JSContext *cx, JSObject *obj,
    uintN argc, jsval *argv, jsval *rval)
{
    AESEncrypt *ptr = GetAESEncryptClass(obj);
    if (!ptr)
        return JS_FALSE;
    JSString *str_0 = JSVAL_TO_STRING(argv[0]);
    string arg_0(JS_GetStringBytes(str_0));
    ptr->SetKey(arg_0);
    return JS_TRUE;
}

extern "C" EXPORT JSBool
AESEncrypt_Encrypt(JSContext *cx, JSObject *obj,
    uintN argc, jsval *argv, jsval *rval)
{
    AESEncrypt *ptr = GetAESEncryptClass(obj);
    if (!ptr)
        return JS_FALSE;
    JSString *str_0 = JSVAL_TO_STRING(argv[0]);
```

```cpp
    string arg_0(JS_GetStringBytes(str_0));
    string ret;
    ret = ptr->Encrypt(arg_0);
    JSString *str = ::JS_NewStringCopyN(cx,
        ret.c_str(), ret.size() + 1);
    *rval = STRING_TO_JSVAL(str);
    return JS_TRUE;
}


extern "C" EXPORT JSBool
AESEncrypt_Decrypt(JSContext *cx, JSObject *obj,
    uintN argc, jsval *argv, jsval *rval)
{
    AESEncrypt *ptr = GetAESEncryptClass(obj);
    if (!ptr)
        return JS_FALSE;
    JSString *str_0 = JSVAL_TO_STRING(argv[0]);
    string arg_0(JS_GetStringBytes(str_0));
    string ret;
    ret = ptr->Decrypt(arg_0);
    JSString *str = ::JS_NewStringCopyN(cx,
        ret.c_str(), ret.size() + 1);
    *rval = STRING_TO_JSVAL(str);
    return JS_TRUE;
}


extern "C" EXPORT JSBool
AESEncrypt_Get_key(JSContext *cx, JSObject *obj,
    uintN argc, jsval *argv, jsval *rval)
{
    string arg_0;
    AESEncrypt *ptr = GetAESEncryptClass(obj);
    if (!ptr || ptr->Get_key(arg_0) != PR_SUCCESS)
        return JS_FALSE;
    JSString *str = ::JS_NewStringCopyN(cx,
        arg_0.c_str(), arg_0.size() + 1);
    *rval = STRING_TO_JSVAL(str);
    return JS_TRUE;
}


extern "C" EXPORT JSBool
AESEncrypt_Set_key(JSContext *cx, JSObject *obj,
    uintN argc, jsval *argv, jsval *rval)
{
    JSString *str_0 = JSVAL_TO_STRING(argv[0]);
    string arg_0(JS_GetStringBytes(str_0));
```

```
    AESEncrypt *ptr = GetAESEncryptClass(obj);
    if (!ptr || ptr->Set_key(arg_0) != PR_SUCCESS)
        return JS_FALSE;
    return JS_TRUE;
}
```

Writing the C++ Code that Implements the Component

All that remains is the C++ code that implements the component. This code is supplied by the component developer and is not generated by Trixul. (Trixul could generate stubs for each function defined by the class, but I made the design decision to restrict Trixul to only generate a header file that declares the class and leaves the definition completely to the developer of the component.) Here is the code I wrote to implement AESEncrypt(). As you can see, it includes the header generated by Trixul (encrypt.h) and gcrypt.h, which contains declarations for interfaces to the GNU library (libgcrypt) that it makes use of to perform the encryption using the AES algorithm:

```
#include "encrypt.h"
#include <gcrypt.h>

AESEncrypt::AESEncrypt()
{
}

AESEncrypt::~AESEncrypt()
{
}

PRStatus
AESEncrypt::SetKey(string& Key)
{
    m_key = Key;
    return PR_SUCCESS;
}

string AESEncrypt::Encrypt(string& Plaintext)
{
    gcry_cipher_hd_t hd = 0;
    gcry_error_t err = 0;
    char *iv = "1234567812345678";
    char ctext[128] = "";
    char actext[256] = "";
```

```cpp
    err = gcry_cipher_open(&hd, GCRY_CIPHER_AES,
        GCRY_CIPHER_MODE_CFB, 0);
    if (!err) {
        err = gcry_cipher_setkey(hd, m_key.c_str(),
            m_key.length());
    }
    if (!err) {
        err = gcry_cipher_setiv(hd, iv, strlen(iv));
    }
    if(!err) {
        err = gcry_cipher_encrypt(hd, ctext,
            sizeof(ctext), Plaintext.c_str(),
            Plaintext.length());
    }
    if (!err) {
        int i;
        char ascbuf[3];

        for (i=0; i < strlen(ctext); i++) {
            snprintf(ascbuf, 2, "%02x", ctext[i]);
            strcat(actext, ascbuf);
        }
    }
    if (hd)
        gcry_cipher_close(hd);
    return actext;
}


string AESEncrypt::Decrypt(string& Ciphertext)
{
    gcry_cipher_hd_t hd = 0;
    gcry_error_t err = 0;
    char *iv = "1234567812345678";
    char ptext[128] = "";

    err = gcry_cipher_open(&hd, GCRY_CIPHER_AES,
        GCRY_CIPHER_MODE_CFB, 0);
    if (!err)
        err = gcry_cipher_setkey(hd, m_key.c_str(),
            m_key.length());
    if (!err)
        err = gcry_cipher_setiv(hd, iv, strlen(iv));
    if(!err)
        err = gcry_cipher_decrypt(hd, ptext,
            sizeof(ptext), Ciphertext.c_str(),
```

```
          Ciphertext.length());
   if (hd)
      gcry_cipher_close(hd);
   return ptext;
}
```

Linking and Distributing the Component

The proxy source generated by Trixul, along with the source file(s) implementing the C++ classes that make up a component, must be linked together to generate the component library. The result is placed in the components directory which is located in the same directory as the Trixul executable. The following commands perform these tasks for the Mac OS X version of the component:

```
g++ -g -I../dist/include -I../dist/include/expat \
    -I../dist/include/nspr - I../dist/include/jsengine \
    -Wall -c encrypt.cpp
g++ -g -I../dist/include -I../dist/include/expat \
    -I../dist/include/nspr - I../dist/include/jsengine \
    -Wall -c encrypt_proxy.cpp
g++ -g -dynamiclib -arch ppc -compatibility_version 1 \
    -current_version 1 -install_name  \
    @executable_path/libencrypt.dylib -fPIC -framework \
    Cocoa -o libencrypt.dylib encrypt.o \
    encrypt_proxy.o -L../dist/macosx/debug/layout.app/\
    Contents/MacOS -lmozjs -lnspr4 -lplc4 -lplds4 \
    -L/usr/local/lib/ -lgcrypt -lgpg-error
cp libencrypt.dylib ../dist/macosx/debug/layout.app/\
    Contents/MacOS/components
```

Index

A

abstraction, 10-15
  definition, 10
  in APIs, 14
  in assembly language,
    11-12
  in C language, 13-14
  GUI application main
    loops, 309-313
    CreateUI()
      function, 312
    gtk_init()
      function, 310
    gtk_main()
      function, 310
    GUI class, 310-313
    Init() function, 312
    MainLoop()
      function, 312
    m_guiImpl
      member, 311
    Shutdown()
      function, 312
  in IDL (interactive data
    language), 13
AC_MSG_CHECKING
  macro, 89
AC_MSG_RESULT
  macro, 89
AC_TRY_RUN macro, 89

accessibility, bug reporting
  and tracking systems, 133
Add() function,
  342-344, 384
AddAESEncryptClass()
  function, 512
AddCatalog() function,
  425-426
addDirectory() function, 169
addFile() function, 169
AddProcess() function,
  321-322
AESEncrypt() function, 515
AESEncrypt_Decrypt()
  function, 514
AESEncrypt_Encrypt()
  function, 513
AESEncrypt_Get_key()
  function, 514
AESEncrypt_SetKey()
  function, 513
AESEncrypt_Set_key()
  function, 514
Alexandrescu, Andrei, 31
alignment of structs,
  299-301
Alphabetical Class Reference
  (wxWidgets), 331
–ansi argument (gcc), 227

APIs (application
  programming interfaces),
  221-222. *See also* NSPR
  (Netscape Portable
  Runtime Library)
  advantages, 244
  abstraction, 14
  API differences, 243
  BSD (Berkeley Standard
    Distribution), 225
  choosing, 240-241
  GCC standards support
    compiler flags, 227
    Cygwin, 238-240
    headers, 227-228
    macros, 228-231
    MinGW, 234-237
  GNU C library, 226
  POSIX, 222-223
    Microsoft Runtime
      Library support
      for, 231-233
    The Single UNIX
      Specification,
      224-225
    System V Interface
      Description (SVID),
      223-224
  XPG (X/Open Portability
    Guide), 225

App object, 466-469
$APPDATA variable, 218
Append() function, 369
AppImpl class, 467
Apple Human Interface
  Guidelines, 323
application main
  loop (Trixul)
    App object, 466-469
    AppImpl class, 467
    in Cocoa, 469
    in Gtk+, 470
    in Windows, 470-471
application programming
  interfaces *See* APIs
applications
  adding to Start
    menu, 178-181
  Hello World, 335
    Add() function,
      342-344
    building on Linux,
      347-348
    building on Mac
      OS X, 348
    building on Windows,
      348-349
    container widgets,
      336-337
    control widgets, 336
    main window,
      338-345
    MyFrame class,
      338-339
    OnInit() function, 338
    portability, 1-3
    source code listing,
      345-346
    wxBoxSizer class,
      341-345
    wxFrame class, 339
    wxStaticText class,
      340-341
  Mac OS X application
    layout, 196-202

MIME types, setting, 181
  restricting for use with
    GNOME or KDE, 181
wxWidget. *See*
  wxWidgets
Aqua, 304, 323
arg element, 499
*The Art of UNIX
  Programming*, 158
assembly language, 11-12
atof() function, 227-228
autoconf utility, 87-90
automake utility, 87-90
availablePrinters()
  function, 445

B

Backprop, 181-182, 185
bar program
  bar.cpp file, 78, 113
  bar.h file, 77, 112
  building with Imake
    utility, 95-98
  building with make
    utility, 78-81
  main.cpp file, 77
base OS service routines
  (POSIX), 223
BEGIN_EVENT_TABLE
  macro, 352-353
Berkeley Standard
  Distribution (BSD),
  225-226
binary data, 280
  binary socakddr_in file,
    generating, 283-293
    command line
      arguments, 283
    compiler options,
      292-293
    cross-platform
      solutions, 288-293
    DumpAddr()
      function, 289
    htons() function, 288

ntohs() function, 289
  on Linux, 287
  on Mac OS X,
    287-288
  sin_family field, 287
  sin_len field, 287
  sin_port field, 288
  sockaddr_in
    struct, 290
  source code listing,
    283-287
  XPBinaryRead()
    function, 290-292
  XPBinaryWrite()
    function, 290-292
effect on software
  portability, 5
endian issues, 281
intrinsic types and
  enums, 281
NSPR operators, 248-249
serializing floating-point
  numbers as, 276-277
struct layout, 281
type definitions, 281-282
Blanchette, Jasmine, 331
Blit() function, 376-377
Bluecurve, 179
body element (HTML), 430
Boost, 6, 263-266
boxes
  Box class, 448
  box element, 478
  XUL, 439-441
BSD (Berkeley Standard
  Distribution), 225-226
_BSD_SOURCE macro, 230
bug reporting and tracking
  systems
    accessibility, 133
    Bugzilla, 133-140
      filing bug reports, 138
      installing, 134-135
      main screen, 135
      Platforms screen, 137

Products screen, 136
searching for bugs,
138-140
platform-specific bugs,
tracking, 133
Bugzilla, 133-140
filing bug reports, 138
installing, 134-135
main screen, 135
Platforms screen, 137
Products screen, 136
searching for bugs,
138-140
**build systems, effect on
software portability, 9**
build.sh script, 78-80
building code, 49-52, 76
autoconf/automake,
87-90
Imake
bar program example,
95-98
building debug, 130
building projects with
subdirectories,
108-130
darwin.cf file, 107
darwin.rules file, 107
eliminating #ifdefs in
code, 101-106
Hello World
example, 93-94
Imake.rules file, 107
Imake.tmpl file, 107
Imakefiles, 94-95, 108
installing on Mac
OS X, 91
installing on
Windows, 91-93
linux.cf file, 107
Makefiles, 108
overriding defaults
with site.def, 99-101
Site.def file, 108
Win32.cf file, 107

Win32.rules file, 107
make utility
bar program
example, 77-78
bar.cpp file, 78
bar.h file, 77
main.cpp file, 77
compared to build.sh
script, 78-80
Makefiles, 79-81
on Windows
conditional
compilation, 84-85
nmake utility, 81-84
separate source
files, 85-87
wxWidget
applications, 345
on Linux, 347-348
on Mac OS X, 348
on Windows, 348-349
**bundle icon files,
creating, 207-208**
Button class
implementation classes
ButtonImpl, 453-456
CocoaButtonImpl,
456-457
GtkButtonImpl,
457-458
WidgetImpl, 454-455
WindowsButtonImpl,
458-459
instantiating, 449-452
button element (XML), 440
ButtonImpl class, 453-456
buttons
Button class
implementation
classes, 453-459
instantiating, 449-452
button element
(XML), 440
ButtonImpl class,
453-456

Click Me button,
creating, 354-355
Enable/Disable button,
creating, 356-359

C

C language
abstraction, 13-14
portability, 3
**C++ integration with
Trixul, 496-497**
accessing components
from JavaScript,
500-502
coding C++ components,
502-507
creating base JavaScript
objects, 507-508
defining JavaScript
functions, 508-509
describing components in
XML, 498-500
generating source code
from SIL files, 509-515
instantiating C++
objects, 508
linking and distributing
components, 517
resolving points to
creator/destroyer
functions, 507
step-by-step sequence,
497-498
writing C++ code
to implement
components, 515-517
*C++ GUI Programming with
Qt 3*, **331**
*C++ GUI Programming with
Qt 4*, **324, 332**
*The C++ Programming
Language*, **299**
**CaesarEncrypt()
function, 490**

cancelInstall() function, 169
canonical data, 248
Cascading Style Sheets
    (CSS), 437-438
CDE (Common Desktop
    Environment), 323
CDEBUGFLAGS
    macro, 130
CFAppleHelpAnchor key
    (Mac OS X), 200
CFBundleDevelopment
    Region key (Mac
    OS X), 201
CFBundleDocumentTypes
    key (Mac OS X), 201
CFBundleExecutable key
    (Mac OS X), 201
CFBundleGetInfoString key
    (Mac OS X), 201
CFBundleIconFile key
    (Mac OS X), 201, 207
CFBundleIdentifier key
    (Mac OS X), 201
CFBundleInfoDictionary
    Version key (Mac
    OS X), 201
CFBundleName key
    (Mac OS X), 201
CFBundlePackageType key
    (Mac OS X), 201
CFBundleShortVersionString
    key (Mac OS X), 201
CFBundleSignature key
    (Mac OS X), 202
CFBundleURLTypes key
    (Mac OS X), 202
char types, signed versus
    unsigned, 278-280
CheckBox class, 448
checkbox element
    (XML), 441
checksetup command, 134
choosing
    compilers, 66-67
    standards, 240-241
chrome, 169

class element, 498
classes
    AppImpl, 467
    Box, 448
    Button
        implementation,
            453-459
        instantiating, 449-452
    ButtonImpl, 453-456
    CheckBox, 448
    CocoaButtonImpl,
        456-457
    CocoaFactory, 465-466
    CocoaGUIImpl, 315
    CocoaProcessesImpl,
        38-42
    ColorDialog, 400-404
    Control, 450-451
    DrawingArea,
        379-384, 391
    fstream, 266
    GridList, 447
    GtkButtonImpl, 457-458
    GUI, 310-313
    GUIImpl, 314
    LinuxFactory, 307-308
    LinuxGUIImpl, 308, 317
    LinuxProcessesImpl,
        35-38
    Menu, 447
    MenuBar, 447
    MenuItem, 447
    MFC (Microsoft
        Foundation
        Classes), 324
    MyFrame, 338-339
    OpenPicker, 447
    PasswordEntryDialog,
        395-398
    printsettings-service, 445
    ProcessesFactory, 28-29,
        306-307
    ProcessesImpl
        base class, 31
        CocoaProcessesImpl
            class, 38-42

    LinuxProcessesImpl
        class, 35-38
    WindowsProcesses-
        Impl class, 32-35
    ProcessList, 23-29, 42-45
    ProcessListener, 319
    RadioButton, 448
    SaveAsPicker, 448
    ScrolledView, 448
    ScrolledWindow, 448
    Spacer, 448
    StaticText, 448
    Text, 448
    TopLevel, 364
    WidgetFactory, 463-465
    WidgetImpl, 454-455
    Window, 448
    WindowsButtonImpl,
        458-459
    WindowsFactory, 29-31
    WindowsGUIImpl, 316
    WindowsProcessesImpl,
        32-35
    wxApp, 337-338
    wxBoxSizer, 336,
        341-345, 378, 384-388
    wxBrush, 374
    wxColour, 374
    wxColourDialog,
        409-410
    wxEvtHandler, 336
    wxFileDialog, 406-408
    wxFontDialog, 404-405
    wxFrame, 336, 339,
        364-366
        constructor, 364-365
        sample
            implementation,
            364-367
    wxGridSizer, 378
    wxLocale, 421-422
    wxMemoryDC, 375
    wxMenu, 368-369
    wxMenuBar, 369-370
    wxMessageBox, 393-394
    wxNotebookSizer, 378

wxPaint, 373
wxPaintDC, 373-375
wxSlider, 387
wxStaticBoxSizer, 378
wxStaticText, 336,
340-341
wxTextEntryDialog, 395
wxWindow, 336
Click Me button, creating,
354-355
Cocoa, 304, 324
CocoaButtonImpl class,
456-457
CocoaFactory class,
465-466
CocoaGUIImpl class, 315
Trixul application main
loops, 469
Trixul implementation
objects, 460-461
CocoaButtonImpl class,
456-457
CocoaFactory class, 465-466
CocoaGUIImpl class, 315
CocoaProcessesImpl
class, 38-42
CodeWarrior IDE, 67
ColorDialog class, 400-404
command-line utilities
autoconf, 87-90
automake, 87-90
checksetup, 134
cp, 75
CreateShortCut, 217
cvs
cvs add, 157
cvs checkout, 154
cvs commit, 155-157
cvs diff, 150-151
cvs init, 154
echo, 75
Imake
bar program
example, 95-98
building debug, 130

building projects
with subdirectories,
108-130
darwin.cf file, 107
darwin.rules file, 107
eliminating #ifdefs in
code, 101-106
Hello World
example, 93-94
Imake.rules file, 107
Imake.tmpl file, 107
Imakefiles, 94-95, 108
installing on Mac
OS X, 91
installing on
Windows, 91-93
linux.cf file, 107
Makefiles, 108
overriding defaults
with site.def, 99-101
Site.def file, 108
Win32.cf file, 107
Win32.rules file, 107
listdlls, 236
ls, 172
make
bar program example,
77-78
compared to build.sh
script, 78-80
Makefiles, 79-81
makensis, 214
man, 186-189
mingwtest, 235-236
mkdir, 75
msgfmt, 419
nmake, 81-84
nroff, 192
otool, 203
open, 185
sed, 75
uname, 50
UninstPage, 216
view, 185
wx-config, 333
xmkmf, 96-98

Common Desktop
Environment (CDE), 323
Common Software
Environment (COSE), 323
compatibility files, 105-106
compatibility libraries,
Imakefiles, 116-119
compilers
building source code
with multiple
compilers, 52-56
choosing, 66-67
compiler differences,
242-243
conditional compilation,
84-85
effect on software
portability, 3-4
g++, 280
GCC
compiler flags, 227
headers, 227-228
macros, 228-231
MinGW, 234-240
warnings, 61-62
GNU flags, 62-63
Microsoft Visual C++
flags, 63-64
compiling code. *See also*
building code
conditional compilation,
84-85
NSIS script, 214
ComplexProgramTarget
macro, 116
component element, 498
composite widgets
(wxWidget)
wxColourDialog class,
409-410
wxFileDialog class,
406-408
wxFontDialog class,
404-405
Concurrent Version System.
See **CVS**

conditional compilation,
84-85
configuration
　CVS (Concurrent Version
　　System), 152-156
　software configuration
　　management. *See* SCM
constants,
　XP_PUTENV, 102
container widgets
　(wxWidget), 363-364, 450
　responding to user input,
　　388-391
　　EVT_CHECKBOX
　　　macros, 389-390
　　EVT_COMMAND_S
　　　CROLL macro, 388
　　GetRadiusPercent()
　　　function, 388
　　IsChecked()
　　　function, 390
　　OnSliderChange()
　　　function, 388
　　SetRadiusPercent()
　　　function, 388
wxBoxSizer class,
　378, 384-388
wxBrush class, 374
wxColour class, 374
wxFrame class
　constructor, 364-365
　sample
　　implementation,
　　364-367
wxGridSizer class, 378
wxMemoryDC class, 375
wxMenu class, 368-369
wxMenuBar class,
　369-370
wxNotebookSizer
　class, 378
wxPaint class, 373
wxPaintDC class,
　373-375

wxSlider class, 387
wxStaticBoxSizer
　class, 378
Control class, 450-451
control widgets, 450
controls (XUL), 441
conversion operators
　(NSPR), 247
converting integers, 298-299
COSE (Common Software
　Environment), 323
cp command, 75
CppCmd macro, 93
–cppflags argument
　(wx-config), 333
CppFileTarget macro, 126
creat() function, 232
Create() function, 449,
　459, 475-476
CreateChildren()
　function, 476
CreateFile() function, 232
CreateJSObject() function,
　500, 504-506
CreateMenus() function,
　317-318
CreateProcess() function, 6
CreateShortCut
　command, 217
CreateThread() function,
　251-254
CreateUI() function, 312
*Cross-Platform GUI
　Programming with
　wxWidgets*, 331
cross-platform GUI toolkits,
　326, 427-428. *See also*
　Trixul; XUL (XML User
　Interface Language)
CSS (Cascading Style Sheets),
　437-438
custom GUI toolkits, 327.
　See also Trixul

CVS (Concurrent Version
　System), 10, 149-157
　commands
　　cvs add, 157
　　cvs checkout, 154
　　cvs commit, 155-157
　　cvs diff, 150-151
　　cvs init, 154
　organizing projects
　　in, 45-49
　running, 157
　setting up, 152-156
CVSROOT directory,
　154-156
Cygwin, 71-76
　downloading and
　　installing, 238-239
　Imake for GCC,
　　installing, 91-92
　testing, 239-240
cygwintest.cpp file, 239-240

D

darwin.cf file, 107
darwin.rules file, 107
data serialization, binary
　data, 280
　binary socakddr_in file,
　　generating, 283-293
　endian issues, 281
　intrinsic types and
　　enums, 281
　struct layout, 281
　type definitions, 281-282
data types
　char, 278-280
　DIR, 229-230
　integers, 298-299
　NSPR types, 245-246
　sizes
　　efficiency, 297-298
　　integer conversions,
　　　298-299
　　integer types, 293-296

Netscape Portable
Runtime Library
(NSPR), 296-297
struct alignment and
ordering, 299-301
debuggers
GNU debugger (gdb), 69
Xcode, 68
**DECLARE_EVENT_TABLE
_ENTRY macro, 361**
**DECLARE_EVENT_TABLE
macro, 350-351, 371**
Decrypt() function, 511, 516
defaults (Imake), overriding
with site.def, 99-101
DeleteAESEncryptProxy()
function, 513
Delete*Class*Proxy()
function, 507
**design, Observer
(publish/subscribe) design
pattern, 318-322**
desktops. *See*
GNOME; KDE
Destroy() function, 403
DHTML (Dynamic HTML)
CSS (Cascading Style
Sheets), 437-438
DOM (Document Object
Model), 434-437
HTML (Hypertext
Markup Language),
429-432
elements, 430-432
Hello World!
example, 430
scripting language,
433-434
dialog element (XML), 439
dialogs (wxWidget)
modal dialogs, 392-394
creating with
wxMessageBox,
393-394
custom dialogs,
394-398

definition of, 392
PasswordEntryDialog
class, 395-398
wxTextEntryDialog
class, 395
modeless dialogs,
392, 399-404
wxColourDialog class,
409-410
wxFileDialog class,
406-408
wxFontDialog class,
404-405
diff files, creating, 150-151
DIR type, 229-230
directories
CVSROOT, 154-156
dist, 74
inc, 47
lib, 46
main, 48
Resources (Mac
OS X), 204-205
/usr/local/man, 195
Disable() function, 453
**Disable/Enable button,
creating, 356-359**
disabling controls, 450
dist directory, 74
distributing
components, 517
man pages, 195-196
MO files, 421
NSIS installer, 214
dlopen() function, 261
Document object, 472-473
**Document Object Model
(DOM), 434-437**
interacting with Trixul
widgets from
JavaScript, 488-493
mapping DOM objects to
JavaScript, 493-496
XUL, 443-444
**documentation
(wxWidgets), 331**

documents (Trixul), 472-473
**DOM (Document Object
Model), 434-437**
interacting with Trixul
widgets from
JavaScript, 488-493
mapping DOM objects to
JavaScript, 493-496
XUL, 443-444
downloading
Cygwin, 238-239
MinGW, 234
wxWidgets, 331
**drag-and-drop installation
(Mac OS X), 208**
DrawCircle() function, 374
drawing content in frames
Blit() function, 376-377
DrawCircle()
function, 374
GetClientSize()
function, 375
OnPaint() function,
373-378
SetBrush() function, 374
wxPaint class, 373
wxPaintDC class, 373
**DrawingArea class,
379-384, 391**
dump() function, 487
DumpAddr() function, 289
DXP_PUTENV macro, 85
Dynamic HTML.
See DHTML

E

echo command, 75
ECMA (European
Computer Manufacturers
Association), 433
ECMAScript, 433
Effective C++, 63, 266
Element object, 473-475

elements, 430-432
arg, 499
body, 430
box, 478
checkbox, 441
class, 498
component, 498
Element object, 473-475
function, 499
head, 430
html, 430
image, 432
label, 442
li, 431
link, 438
progressmeter, 442
property, 499
radio, 441
return, 499
script, 433
scrolledview, 484-485
scrolledwindow, 484-485
spacer, 480
title, 430
ul, 431
window, 439
Enable() function, 358, 453
Enable/Disable button,
creating, 356-359
Encrypt() function,
508-511, 515
endian systems, binary data
issues, 281
EndModal() function, 398
END_EVENT_TABLE
macro, 352-353
enums
binary data issues, 281
wxLanguage, 422-424
environment variables,
LD_LIBRARY_PATH,
173-176
equality of floating-point
numbers, 277-278
/etc/gnome-vfs-mime-magic
file, 183

/etc/group file, 171
/etc/mime-magic file, 183
/etc/password file, 171
European Computer
Manufacturers Association
(ECMA), 433
event handler functions.
See functions
events (wxWidget), 349
BEGIN_EVENT_TABLE
macro, 352-353
Click Me button,
creating, 354-355
DECLARE_EVENT_TAB
LE macro, 350-351
Enable/Disable button,
creating, 356-359
END_EVENT_TABLE
macro, 352-353
event handler function
implementations, 355
EVT_BUTTON
macro, 353
EVT_MENU macro, 353
File menu, 354
skipping, 359-363
wxCommandEvent
events, 351
EVT_BUTTON macro, 353
EVT_CHECKBOX macros,
389-390
EVT_CLOSE macro, 361
EVT_COMMAND_SCROL
L macro, 388
EVT_MENU macro, 353
EVT_PAINT() macro, 373
execute (x) permissions, 172
expat shared library, 203

F

factories, 29, 463-466
CocoaFactory class,
465-466
GetWidgetFactory()
function, 464

ProcessesFactory class,
28-29
WidgetFactory class,
463-465
fields
sin_family, 287
sin_len, 287
sin_port, 288
File menus, creating, 354
files
associating with
icons, 183-186
bar program
bar.cpp, 78, 113
bar.h, 77, 112
main.cpp, 77
binary socakddr_in file,
generating, 283-293
command-line
arguments, 283
compiler options,
292-293
cross-platform
solutions, 288-293
DumpAddr()
function, 289
htons() function, 288
ntohs() function, 289
on Linux, 287
on Mac OS X,
287-288
sin_family field, 287
sin_len field, 287
sin_port field, 288
sockaddr_in
struct, 290
source code listing,
283-287
XPBinaryRead()
function, 290-292
XPBinaryWrite()
function, 290-292
bundle icon files, creating,
207-208
cygwintest.cpp, 239-240

determining file types, 182-183

diff files, creating, 150-151

/etc/gnome-vfs-mime-magic, 183

/etc/group, 171

/etc/mime-magic, 183

/etc/password, 171

gnumeric.keys, 184

Hello World program
  hello.cpp, 93
  hello.h, 93
  Imakefiles, 94

Imake
  building debug, 130
  darwin.cf, 107
  darwin.rules, 107
  Imake.rules, 107
  Imake.tmpl, 107
  Imakefiles, 108
  linux.cf, 107
  Makefiles, 108
  Site.def, 108
  Win32.cf, 107
  Win32.rules, 107

Info.plist, 199-200

install.js, 167-169

Localizable.strings, 205-206

Makefiles, 49-52, 79-81

message files, loading at runtime, 425-426

MO files
  distributing, 421
  generating, 419
  locating, 420-421

per-platform compatibility files, 105-106

permissions, 171-173

PkgInfo, 198

PO files
  generating, 417-419
  locating, 420-421

reject files (patch program), 162-163

SIL files, 509-515

version.plist, 197-198

XPI files, 167

filing bug reports (Bugzilla), 138

finding bugs (Bugzilla), 138-140

flags. *See specific flags*

floating-point numbers
  equality, 277-278
  serializing as binary, 276-277
  support for IEEE-754 standard, 274-275

folders, MacOS, 202-206

frames
  drawing content in, 373-378
    Blit() function, 376-377
    DrawCircle() function, 374
    GetClientSize() function, 375
    OnPaint() function, 373-378
    SetBrush() function, 374
    wxPaint class, 373
    wxPaintDC class, 373
  wxFrame class, 364

free() function, 271

fstream class, 266

function element, 499

FunctionName() function, 371

functions. *See also* **macros**
  Add(), 342-344, 384
  AddAESEncryptClass(), 512
  AddCatalog(), 425-426
  addDirectory(), 169
  addFile(), 169
  AddProcess(), 321-322
  AESEncrypt(), 515

AESEncrypt_Decrypt(), 514

AESEncrypt_Encrypt(), 513

AESEncrypt_Get_key(), 514

AESEncrypt_SetKey(), 513

AESEncrypt_Set_key(), 514

Append(), 369

associating with menu items, 370-372

atof(), 227-228

availablePrinters(), 445

Blit(), 376-377

CaesarEncrypt(), 490

cancelInstall(), 169

creat(), 232

Create(), 449, 459, 475-476

CreateChildren(), 476

CreateFile(), 232

CreateJSObject(), 500, 504-506

CreateMenus(), 317-318

CreateProcess(), 6

CreateThread(, 251

CreateThread(), 252-254

CreateUI(), 312

Decrypt(), 511, 516

defining, 508-509

DeleteAESEncrypt-Proxy(), 513

Delete*Class*Proxy(), 507

Destroy(), 403

Disable(), 453

dlopen(), 261

DrawCircle(), 374

dump(), 487

DumpAddr(), 289

Enable(), 358, 453

Encrypt(), 508-511, 515

EndModal(), 398

free(), 271

FunctionName(), 371
GetAESEncrypt(), 509
GetAESEncryptClass(),
    512
GetAlignment(), 150
GetAppInstance(), 467
GetClientSize(), 375
GetColourData(), 410
getComponent(), 501
GetCount(), 24
getElementById(), 434,
    437, 443, 473, 493-495
GetFactoryInstance(),
    29-31, 43, 466
GetFilename(), 408
GetFilenames(), 408
GetLabel(), 451-453
GetMatchingFiles(), 268
GetName(), 24
getObject(), 501-504
GetPaths(), 408
GetPID(), 24
GetProcessesFactory(),
    28, 43
GetRadiusPercent(), 388
GetUsername(), 397
GetWidgetFactory(),
    464-466
Get_key(), 511
GPGAESEncrypt(),
    501-502
gtk_button_new(), 452
gtk_init(), 310
gtk_main(), 310
HandleEncrypt(),
    490-492
Hide(), 449, 453
htons(), 288
Init(), 312, 421
Initialize(), 467-468
initInstall(), 169
IsChecked(), 390
JS_DefineObject(),
    507-508
LoadFile(), 270-271

LoadLibrary(), 261
MainLoop(), 312,
    467-468
MakeButton(), 466
MakeGUI(), 307
MakeProcesses(), 30
malloc(), 271
MyThreadFunc(), 254
NewAESEncryptProxy(),
    513
New*Class*Proxy(), 507
nice(), 27
NSPR standard library
    (libc) functions, 260
    I/O functions, 261
    linking functions,
        261-263
NtCreateFile(), 232
ntohs(), 289
OnApply(), 401
OnBlue(), 401
OnCancel(), 397
OnClickHandler(), 487
OnClickMe(), 355
OnClose(), 361-362
OnColor(), 409
OnDisableEnable(), 359
OnFile(), 408
OnFont(), 405
OnGreen(), 401
OnInit(), 337
OnNewProcess(),
    319-321
OnOK(), 397, 474
OnPaint(), 373-378
OnPassword(), 396
OnQuit(), 355, 359
OnRed(), 401
OnSliderChange(), 388
open(), 233
opendir(), 236
performInstall(), 169
PL_CreateOptState(), 261
PL_GetNextOpt(), 261
PL_strdup(), 261

PL_strlen(), 261
PL_strncasestr(), 261
PL_strncpy(, 261
PL_strrstr(), 261
PortableOpen(), 14
POSIX SVID (System V
    Interface Description)
    base OS service
        routines, 223
    general library
        functions, 224
    mathematical
        functions, 223
    networking
        functions, 224
    string functions, 224
PR_CreateThread(),
    258-259
PR_htonl(), 249
PR_htons(), 249
PR_LoadLibrary(),
    261-263
PR_ntohl(), 249
PR_ntohs(), 249
PR_OpenDir(), 269
PR_ReadDir(), 269
PrintProcessName
    AndID(), 33
pthread_attr_init(), 257
pthread_attr_setstack-
    size(), 257
pthread_create(), 254-256
pthread_exit(), 256-257
pthread_join(), 256-257
PutBar(), 78, 85, 100
putenv(), 84, 102-105
QueryInterface(), 446
quit(), 487
Refresh(), 401
regcomp(), 269
regex, 265-268
regexec(), 269-270
registerChrome(), 169
RegisterListener(), 320
releaseObject(), 501

RemoveAESEncrypt-
Class(), 512
rename(), 241
ReverseValue(), 443-444
Scan(), 23, 26-27, 31-33,
39, 43-45, 313
ScanProcesses(), 33-34
SendNotification(),
320-321
SetBar(), 78
SetBrush(), 374
setenv(), 84
SetGeometry(), 449
SetKey(), 511, 515
SetLabel(), 451-453
SetMenuBar(), 354, 369
SetPriority(), 27
SetPriorityClass(), 27
SetRadiusPercent(), 388
SetSizer(), 355, 385
SetTopWindow(), 367
Set_key(), 511
Show(), 367, 402-403,
449, 453
ShowModal(), 395-398,
407
Shutdown(), 312,
467-468
sizeof(), 294
Skip(), 362
snprintf(), 276
SomeFuncInt(), 279
SomeFuncUInt(), 279
strftime(), 88-89
strtod(), 276
sysctl(), 38
UnregisterListener(), 320
UppercaseValue(),
443-444
wxGetTranslation(), 417
XPBinaryRead(), 290-292
XPBinaryWrite(),
290-292

G

g++ compiler, 280
GCC
compiler flags, 227
Cygwin
downloading and
installing, 238-239
testing, 239-240
headers, 227-228
Imake for GCC,
installing, 91-92
macros, 228-231
MinGW
definition of, 234
downloading and
installing, 234
testing, 235-236
verifying libraries,
236-237
gdb (GNU debugger), 69
general library functions
(POSIX), 224
Get_key() function, 511
GetAESEncrypt()
function, 509
GetAESEncryptClass()
function, 512
GetAlignment()
function, 150
GetAppInstance()
function, 467
GetClientSize() function, 375
GetColourData()
function, 410
getComponent()
function, 501
GetCount() function, 24
getElementById() function,
434, 437, 443, 473,
493-495
GetFactoryInstance()
function, 29-31, 43, 466
GetFilename() function, 408

GetFilenames() function, 408
GetLabel() function, 451-453
GetMatchingFiles()
function, 268
GetName() function, 24
getObject() function,
501-504
GetPaths() function, 408
GetPID() function, 24
GetProcessesFactory()
function, 28, 43
GetRadiusPercent()
function, 388
gettext, 411-420
GetUsername() function, 397
GetWidgetFactory()
function, 464-466
GNOME
integrating with Linux
installer, 177-178
adding applications to
Start menu, 178-181
associating files with
icons, 183-186
determining file types,
182-183
restricting
applications for use
with GNOME or
KDE, 181
setting application
MIME types, 181
overview, 304, 324
GNU
C library, 226
compiler warnings, 62-63
debugger (gdb), 69
_GNU_SOURCE
macro, 231
gnumeric.keys file, 184
GPGAESEncrypt() function,
501-502
graphical user interfaces.
See GUIs

GridList class, 447

Gtk+
  GtkButtonImpl class,
    457-458
  LinuxGUIImpl class, 317
  Trixul application main
    loops, 470
  Trixul implementation
    objects, 461

*Gtk+ Programming in
  C*, 324

gtk_button_new()
  function, 452

gtk_init() function, 310

gtk_main() function, 310

GtkButtonImpl class,
  457-458

GUI class, 310-313

GUIImpl class, 314

GUIs (graphical user
  interfaces), 303-304
  effect on software
    portability, 8-9
  look and feel
    standards, 323
  model/view paradigm,
    305-306
    Observer (publish/
      subscribe) design
      pattern, 318-322
    view implementation,
      306, 309-318
  themes, 304-305
  toolkits, 324-325. *See
    also specific toolkits*
    cross-platform GUI
      toolkits, 326,
      427-428
    custom GUI
      toolkits, 327
    native GUI toolkits,
      325-326

H

HandleEncrypt() function,
  490-492

HasPutenv macro, 98

hbox element (XML),
  439-440

head element (HTML), 430

headers (GCC), 227-228

Hello World program
  (wxWidgets), 335
  Add() function, 342-344
  building on Linux,
    347-348
  building on Mac
    OS X, 348
  building on Windows,
    348-349
  building with Imake,
    93-94
  container widgets,
    336-337
  control widgets, 336
  main window, 338-345
  MyFrame class, 338-339
  OnInit() function, 338
  portability, 1, 3
  source code listing,
    345-346
  wxBoxSizer class,
    341-345
  wxFrame class, 339
  wxStaticText class,
    340-341

Hello World! Web page, 430

hello.cpp file, 93

hello.h file, 93

Hide() function, 449, 453

history of wxWidgets, 331

HTML (Hypertext Markup
  Language), 429-432. *See
  also* DHTML (Dynamic
  HTML)
  elements, 430-432
  Hello World!
    example, 430

html element (HTML), 430

htons() function, 288

Hypertext Markup
  Language. *See* HTML

I

I/O functions (NSPR), 261

icns files, creating, 207-208

icons, associating files
  with, 183-186

id argument (wxFrame), 365

IDEs
  Metrowerks CodeWarrior
    IDE, 67
  native IDEs, 67-71
  Xcode IDE, 68

IDL (interactive data
  language), 13

IEEE-754 standard, 274-275

#ifdefs, eliminating, 101
  per-platform
    compatibility files,
    105-106
  putenv function, 102-105

IHaveSubdirs macro, 114

image element (HTML), 432

Imake utility
  bar program
    example, 95-98
  building debug, 130
  building projects with
    subdirectories, 108-111
    compatibility library
      Imakefiles, 116-119
    Makefiles, 119-130
    Windows
      implementations,
      111-116
  darwin.cf file, 107
  darwin.rules file, 107
  eliminating #ifdefs in
    code, 101
  per-platform
    compatibility
    files, 105-106
  putenv() function,
    102-105

Hello World example,
93-94
hello.cpp file, 93
hello.h file, 93
Imakefiles, 94
Imake.rules file, 107
Imake.tmpl file, 107
Imakefiles, 94-95, 108
installing on Mac
OS X, 91
installing on Windows
Imake for GCC, 91-92
Imake for Visual
C++, 92-93
linux.cf file, 107
Makefiles, 108
overriding defaults with
site.def, 99-101
Site.def file, 108
Win32.cf file, 107
Win32.rules file, 107
Imake.rules file, 107
Imake.tmpl file, 107
Imakefiles, 94-95, 108
IMPLEMENT_APP
macro, 338
inc directory, 47
Info.plist file, 199-200
Init() function, 312, 421
Initialize() function, 467-468
initInstall() function, 169
input, responding to,
388-391
EVT_CHECKBOX
macros, 389-390
EVT_COMMAND_SCR
OLL macro, 388
GetRadiusPercent()
function, 388
IsChecked() function, 390
OnSliderChange()
function, 388
SetRadiusPercent()
function, 388
install.js file, 167-169

installation (software),
165-166
Cygwin, 76, 238-239
Linux platform installs,
170-173
/etc/group file, 171
/etc/password file, 171
executing as root,
176-177
execution environ-
ment, 173-177
file permissions,
171-173
integrating with
GNOME and KDE
desktops, 177-186
man pages, 186-196
Mac OS X platform
installs
application layout,
196-202
bundle icon files,
creating, 207-208
drag-and-drop
installation, 208
MacOS folder,
202-206
MinGW, 234
Windows XP NSIS
installer
application data,
217-218
compiling NSIS
script, 214
creating, 210
defining, 210-214
distributing, 214
documentation, 208
documents and
settings, 208-209
integrating into
Start menu and
desktop, 216-217
program
installation, 210
testing, 214
uninstallers, 215-216

Weather Manager
sample installer
script, 218-220
XPInstall, 166-170
wxWidgets, 332
on Linux, 334
on Mac OS X, 333
on Windows, 334-335
instance hierarchies,
creating, 42-45
instantiating C++
objects, 508
integers
conversions, 298-299
m_bar, 78
sizes, 293-296
interactive data language
(IDL), 13
internationalization
(wxWidgets), 410-411
gettext, 411-420
locales, creating, 421-425
message files, loading at
runtime, 425-426
PO/MO files, 417-421
wxLanguage
enums, 422-424
wxLocale class, 421-422
intrinsic types
binary data issues, 281
type definitions, 281-282
IsChecked() function, 390
ISO/IEC 9945-1. *See* POSIX
_ISOC99_SOURCE
macro, 230

J

JavaScript, 433
functions, defining,
508-509
integration with Trixul,
485-486
example, 486-487
including external
JavaScript sources,
487-488

interacting with
widgets from
JavaScript, 488-493
mapping DOM
objects to
JavaScript, 493-496
XUL, 443-444
JS_DefineObject()
function, 507-508
JSClass struct, 507

K

KDE
integrating with Linux
installer, 177-178
adding applications to
Start menu, 178-181
associating files with
icons, 183-186
determining file types,
182-183
restricting applications
for use with
GNOME or KDE,
181
setting application
MIME types, 181
overview, 304, 324

L

label element (XML), 442
language, effect on software
portability, 3
layouts (Trixul), 477,
480-483
LD_LIBRARY_PATH
environment variable,
173-176
lexical_cast, 277
li element (HTML), 431
lib directory, 46
libraries
effect on software
portability, 5-6
expat shared library, 203

GNU C library, 226
Microsoft Runtime
Library, 231-233
NSPR (Netscape Portable
Runtime Library)
advantages of,
242-244
binary data, 248-249
operators, 246-247
standard library (libc)
functions, 260
I/O functions, 261
linking functions,
261-263
threads. *See* threads
types, 245-246,
296-297
when to use, 263-271
STL (Standard Template
Library), 5-6
–libs argument
(wx-config), 333
licensing terms
Qt, 331
wxWidgets, 331-332
link element (HTML), 438
LINKFLAGS macro, 86
linking functions (NSPR),
261-263
Linux
binary socakddr_in file,
generating, 287
Bluecurve, 179
building wxWidget
applications on,
347-348
GNOME, 304, 324
GUI view implementation
LinuxFactory class,
307-308
LinuxGUIImpl
class, 308
ProcessesFactory
class, 306-307
installs. *See* Linux
installer

KDE, 304, 324
LinuxGUIImpl GUI
implementation
class, 317
LinuxProcessesImpl
class, 35-38
threads, 254-257
wxWidget
installation, 334
Linux installer, 170-173
/etc/group file, 171
/etc/password file, 171
executing as root,
176-177
execution environment,
173-177
file permissions, 171-173
integrating with GNOME
and KDE desktops,
177-178
adding applications to
Start menu, 178-181
associating files with
icons, 183-186
determining file types,
182-183
restricting applications
for use with
GNOME or
KDE, 181
setting application
MIME types, 181
man pages
benefits of, 186-189
creating, 189-195
distributing, 195-196
linux.cf file, 107
LinuxCompatibility.cpp
file, 106
LinuxFactory class, 307-308
LinuxGUIImpl class,
308, 317
LinuxProcessesImpl class,
35-38
listdlls command, 236
LL_EQ macro, 246

LL_L2I macro, 247
LL_MAXINT macro, 246
LL_NOT macro, 247
LL_OR macro, 247
LL_SHL macro, 247
LL_XOR macro, 247
LoadFile() function, 270-271
loading message files at runtime, 425-426
LoadLibrary() function, 261
locales, creating, 421-425
Localizable.strings file, 205-206
logical operators (NSPR), 247
logicalFunc argument (Blit() function), 376-377
look and feel standards (GUIs), 323
ls -l command, 172
LSHasLocalizedDisplay-Name key (Mac OS X), 202

M

m_bar integer, 78
m_enabled variable, 358
m_guiImpl member, 311
Mac OS X
    Aqua, 304, 323
    binary socakddr_in file, generating, 287-288
    building wxWidget applications on, 348
    Cocoa, 324
        CocoaButtonImpl class, 456-457
        CocoaFactory class, 465-466
        Trixul application main loops, 469
        Trixul implementation objects, 460-461

CocoaGUIImpl GUI implementation class, 315
CocoaProcessesImpl class, 38-42
Gtk+
    Trixul application main loops, 470
    Trixul implementation objects, 461
Imake installation, 91
software installation
    application layout, 196-202
    bundle icon files, creating, 207-208
    drag-and-drop installation, 208
    MacOS folder, 202-206
threads, 254-257
Windows
    Trixul application main loops, 470-471
    Trixul implementation objects, 462-463
wxWidget installation, 333
MacOS folder, 202-206
macros. *See also* functions
    AC_MSG_CHECKING, 89
    AC_MSG_RESULT, 89
    AC_TRY_RUN, 89
    BEGIN_EVENT_TABLE, 352-353
    _BSD_SOURCE, 230
    CDEBUGFLAGS, 130
    ComplexProgramTarget, 116
    CppCmd, 93
    CppFileTarget, 126
    DECARE_EVENT_TABLE_ENTRY, 361

DECLARE_EVENT_TABLE, 350-351, 371
DXP_PUTENV, 85
END_EVENT_TABLE, 352-353
EVT_BUTTON, 353
EVT_CHECKBOX, 389-390
EVT_CLOSE, 361
EVT_COMMAND_SCROLL, 388
EVT_MENU, 353
EVT_PAINT, 373
GCC, 228-231
_GNU_SOURCE, 231
HasPutenv, 98
IHaveSubdirs, 114
IMPLEMENT_APP, 338
_ISOC99_SOURCE, 230
LINKFLAGS, 86
LL_EQ, 246
LL_L2I, 247
LL_MAXINT, 246
LL_NOT, 247
LL_OR, 247
LL_SHL, 247
LL_XOR, 247
MkdirHierCmd, 93, 120
PassCDebugFlags, 130
_POSIX_C_SOURCE, 230
_POSIX_SOURCE, 228-230
PR_INT16_MAX, 245
PR_INT16_MIN, 245
.SH, 192
SharedLibraryTarget, 126
_SVID_SOURCE, 230
.TH, 192
_XOPEN_SOURCE, 230
main directory, 48
main.cpp file (bar program), 77
MainLoop() function, 312, 467-468

make systems, 76
   autoconf/automake,
      87-90
   building on Windows
      conditional
         compilation, 84-85
      nmake utility, 81-84
      separate source
         files, 85-87
   Imake
      bar program
         example, 95-98
      building debug, 130
      building projects
         with subdirectories,
         108-130
      darwin.cf file, 107
      darwin.rules file, 107
      eliminating #ifdefs in
         code, 101-106
      Hello World
         example, 93-94
      Imake.rules file, 107
      Imake.tmpl file, 107
      Imakefiles, 94-95, 108
      installing on Mac OS
         X, 91
      installing on
         Windows, 91-93
      linux.cf file, 107
      Makefiles, 108
      overriding defaults
         with site.def, 99-101
      Site.def file, 108
      Win32.cf file, 107
      Win32.rules file, 107
   make utility
      bar program
         example, 77-78
      compared to build.sh
         script, 78-80
      Makefiles, 79-81

make utility
   bar program example
      bar.cpp file, 78
      bar.h file, 77
      main.cpp file, 77
   compared to build.sh
      script, 78-80
   Makefiles, 79-81
MakeButton() function, 466
Makefiles, 49-52, 79-81, 108
   Imakefiles, 94-95, 108
MakeGUI() function, 307
makensis command, 214
MakeProcesses() function, 30
malloc() function, 271
man command, 186-189
man pages
   benefits of, 186-189
   creating, 189-195
   distributing, 195-196
management
   building source code
      on multiple platforms,
      56-60
   building source code
      with multiple
      compilers, 52-56
   organizing projects in
      CVS or SVN, 45-49,
      149-151
   overview, 17
   parity, 17-21
   responding to compiler
      warnings, 61-62
      GNU flags, 62-63
      Microsoft Visual C++
         flags, 63-64
   sharing code across all
      supported platforms
      abstraction layers, 22
      advantages, 22
      implementation
         classes, 31-32
      instance hierarchies,
         42-45

   Makefiles and building
      code, 49-52
   platform factory
      implementations,
      29-31
   platform-specific
      ProcessesImpl
      classes, 32-42
   ProcessList class
      example, 23-29
   software configuration
      management. *See* SCM
   testing builds on all
      supported platforms,
      60-61
mapping DOM objects to
   JavaScript, 493-496
mathematical functions
   (POSIX), 223
mathematical operators
   (NSPR), 247
memory DCs, creating,
   375-378
menu bars
   MenuBar class, 447
   wxMenuBar class,
      369-370
Menu class, 447
MenuBar class, 447
MenuItem class, 447
menus, 367
   associating with
      functions, 370-372
   creating with wxMenu
      class, 368-369
   menu bars, creating,
      369-370, 447
   XUL, 441-442
message files, loading at
   runtime, 425-426
Metrowerks CodeWarrior
   IDE, 67
Meyer, Scott, 266
MFC (Microsoft Foundation
   Classes), 324

Microsoft Runtime Library,
231-233, 240
Microsoft Visual C++, 63-64
*Microsoft Windows User
Experience*, 323
MIME types, 181
MinGW
definition of, 234
downloading and
installing, 234
testing, 235-236
verifying libraries,
236-237
mingwtest command,
235-236
mkdir command, 75
MkdirHierCmd macro, 93,
120
MO files
distributing, 421
generating, 419
locating, 420-421
modal dialogs, 392-394
creating with
wxMessageBox,
393-394
custom dialogs, 394-398
definition of, 392
PasswordEntryDialog
class, 395-398
wxTextEntryDialog
class, 395
model/view paradigm
(GUIs), 305-306
Observer (publish/
subscribe) design
pattern, 318-322
view implementation
abstracting GUI main
loop, 309-313
CocoaGUIImpl
class, 315
CreateMenus()
function, 317-318
GUIImpl class, 314

illustration of UI
implementation, 306
LinuxFactory class,
307-308
LinuxGUIImpl class,
308, 317
ProcessesFactory class,
306-307
WindowsGUIImpl
class, 316
modeless dialogs, 392,
399-404
*Modern C++ Design:
Generic Programming
and Design Patterns
Applied*, 31
Motif, 324
Mozilla
chrome, 169
Mozilla LXR, 167
XPCOM, 444-446
XPConnect, 444-446
XPInstall, 166-170
XUL (XML User Interface
Language). *See* XUL
msgfmt command, 419
MyApp, 216
Myers, Scott, 63
MyFrame class, 338-339
MyThreadFunc()
function, 254

N

native GUI toolkits,
325-326. *See also
specific toolkits*
native IDEs, 67-71
.NET Forms, 304, 316, 324
Netscape versions, 329
Netscape Portable Runtime
Library. *See* NSPR
networking functions
(POSIX), 224

NewAESEncryptProxy()
function, 513
New*Class*Proxy()
function, 507
nice() function, 27
nmake utility, 81-84
nroff command, 192
NSHumanReadable
Copyright key (Mac
OS X), 202
NSIS installer
application data, 217-218
compiling NSIS
script, 214
creating, 210
defining, 210-214
distributing, 214
documentation, 208
documents and
settings, 208-209
integrating into
Start menu and
desktop, 216-217
program installation, 210
testing, 214
uninstallers, 215-216
Weather Manager sample
installer script, 218-220
NSPR (Netscape Portable
Runtime Library)
advantages of, 242-244
binary data, 248-249
operators, 246-247
standard library (libc)
functions, 260
I/O functions, 261
linking functions,
261-263
threads, 249
advantages of,
250-251
creating, 258-260
definition of, 250
Linux threads,
254-257

Mac OS X threads, 254-257
Win32 threads, 251-254
types, 245-246, 296-297
when to use, 263-271
NtCreateFile() function, 232
ntohs() function, 289
numbers, floating-point numbers
equality, 277-278
serializing as binary, 276-277
support for IEEE-754 standard, 274-275
numeric_limits template, 295

O

O_APPEND flag (open() function), 233
O_CREAT flag (open() function), 233
O_EXCL flag (open() function), 233
O_EXLOCK flag (open() function), 233
O_NONBLOCK flag (open() function), 233
O_RDONLY flag (open() function), 233
O_RDWR flag (open() function), 233
O_SHLOCK flag (open() function), 233
O_TRUNC flag (open() function), 233
O_WRONLY flag (open() function), 233
objects
App, 466-469
Document, 472-473

DOM (Document Object Model), 434-437
interacting with Trixul widgets from JavaScript, 488-493
mapping DOM objects to JavaScript, 493-496
XUL, 443-444
Element, 473-475
Observer (publish/subscribe) design pattern, 318-322
observers, 319
OnApply() function, 401
OnBlue() function, 401
OnCancel() function, 397
OnClickHandler() function, 487
OnClickMe() function, 355
OnClose() function, 361-362
OnColor() function, 409
OnDisableEnable() function, 359
OnFile() function, 408
OnFont() function, 405
OnGreen() function, 401
OnInit() function, 337
OnNewProcess() function, 319-321
OnOK() function, 397, 474
OnPaint() function, 373-378
OnPassword() function, 396
OnQuit() function, 355, 359
OnRed() function, 401
OnSliderChange() function, 388
Open Look, 323
open command, 185
Open Group Base Specifications Issue 6, IEEE Std 1003.1, 2003 Edition, 224-225
open() function, 233
opendir() function, 236
OpenLook, 331

OpenPicker class, 447
operating systems. *See* platforms
operators (NSPR), 246-247
ordering structs, 299-301
organizing projects
CVS, 45-49, 149-157
running, 157
setting up, 152-156
SVN, 45-49, 149-151
OSXCompatibility.cpp file, 106
otool utility, 203
overriding defaults with site.def (Imake), 99-101

P

–p argumen (path program), 161-162
parent argument (wxFrame), 365
parity, 17-21
PassCDebugFlags macro, 130
PasswordEntryDialog class, 395-398
patch program, 157
cross-platform development, 163-164
example, 158-160
options, 161-162
reject files, 162-163
–pedantic-errors compiler warning (GNU), 63
–pendantic argument (gcc), 227
per-platform compatibility files, 105-106
performInstall() function, 169
permissions (Linux), 171-173
PFloat, 247
PkgInfo file, 198

PL_CreateOptState()
  function, 261
PL_GetNextOpt()
  function, 261
PL_strdup() function, 261
PL_strlen() function, 261
PL_strncasestr()
  function, 261
PL_strncpy() function, 261
PL_strrstr() function, 261
platform installs
  Linux, 170-173
    /etc/group file, 171
    /etc/password file, 171
    executing as root,
      176-177
    execution environ-
      ment, 173-177
    file permissions,
      171-173
    integrating with
      GNOME and KDE
      desktops, 177-186
    man pages, 186-196
  Mac OS X
    application layout,
      196-202
    bundle icon files,
      creating, 207-208
    drag-and-drop
      installation, 208
    MacOS folder,
      202-206
  Windows XP NSIS
    installer
    application data,
      217-218
    compiling NSIS
      script, 214
    creating, 210
    defining, 210-214
    distributing, 214
    documentation, 208
    documents and
      settings, 208-209

integrating into
  Start menu and
  desktop, 216-217
program
  installation, 210
testing, 214
uninstallers, 215-216
Weather Manager
  sample installer
  script, 218-220
platform-specific bugs,
  tracking, 133
platforms. *See also*
  platform installs
  building source code
    on multiple platforms,
    56-60
  effect on software
    portability, 6-8
  parity, 17-21
  platform-specific bugs,
    tracking, 133
  prioritizing, 17-21
  sharing code across all
    supported platforms
    abstraction layers, 22
    advantages, 22
    implementation
      classes, 31-32
    instance hierarchies,
      42-45
    Makefiles and building
      code, 49-52
    platform factory
      implementations,
      29-31
    platform-specific
      ProcessesImpl
      classes, 32-42
    ProcessList class
      example, 23-29
  testing builds on
    all supported
    platforms, 60-61
  tier-1 platforms, 18, 427

Platforms screen
  (Bugzilla), 137
PO files
  generating, 417-419
  locating, 420-421
pointers, resolving, 507
policy
  building source code
    on multiple platforms,
    56-60
  building source code
    with multiple
    compilers, 52-56
  organizing projects in
    CVS or SVN, 45-49,
    149-151
  overview, 17
  parity, 17-21
  responding to compiler
    warnings, 61-62
    GNU flags, 62-63
    Microsoft Visual C++
      flags, 63-64
  sharing code across all
    supported platforms
    abstraction layers, 22
    advantages, 22
    implementation
      classes, 31-32
    instance hierarchies,
      42-45
    Makefiles and building
      code, 49-52
    platform factory
      implementations,
      29-31
    platform-specific
      ProcessesImpl
      classes, 32-42
    ProcessList class
      example, 23-29
  testing builds on all
    supported platforms,
    60-61

portability, 273
  binary data, 5, 280
    binary socakddr_in
      file, generating,
      283-293
    endian issues, 281
    intrinsic types and
      enums, 281
    struct layout, 281
    type definitions,
      281-282
  build systems, 9
  char types, 278-280
  compilers, 3-4
  configuration
    management, 9-10
  definition, 1-3
  floating-point numbers
    equality, 277-278
    serializing as binary,
      276-277
    support for IEEE-754
      standard, 274-275
  language, 3
  operating system
    interfaces, 6-8
  standard libraries, 5-6
  type sizes
    efficiency, 297-298
    integer conversions,
      298-299
    integer types, 293-296
    Netscape Portable
      Runtime Library
      (NSPR), 296-297
    struct alignment and
      ordering, 299-301
  user interfaces, 8-9
Portable Operating System
  Interface for Computer
  Environments *See* POSIX
PortableOpen() function, 14
pos argument
  (wxFrame), 365

POSIX, 222-223
  GNU C library
    support, 226
  Microsoft Runtime
    Library support for,
    231-233
  The Single UNIX
    Specification, 224-225
  System V Interface
    Description
    (SVID), 223
    base OS service
      routines, 223
    general library
      functions, 224
    GNU C library
      support, 226
    mathematical
      functions, 223
    networking
      functions, 224
    string and character
      handling, 224
_POSIX_C_SOURCE
  macro, 230
_POSIX_SOURCE
  macro, 228-230
PR_CreateThread() function,
  258-259
PR_htonl() function, 249
PR_htons() function, 249
PR_INT16_MAX
  macro, 245
PR_INT16_MIN macro, 245
PR_LoadLibrary()
  function, 261-263
PR_ntohl() function, 249
PR_ntohs() function, 249
PR_OpenDir() function, 269
PR_ReadDir() function, 269
PRDir, 264
PRDirEntry, 264
PRDirFlags, 264
PRFileDesc, 266
PRInt16, 245

PRInt16 type, 297
PRInt32, 245, 266
PRInt64, 245
PRInt8, 245
PrintProcessNameAndID()
  function, 33
printsettings-service
  class, 445
prioritizing platforms, 17-21
PRLibrary, 261
processes, creating, 6-7
ProcessesFactory class,
  28-29, 306-307
ProcessesImpl class
  base class, 31
  CocoaProcessesImpl
    class, 38-42
  LinuxProcessesImpl
    class, 35-38
  WindowsProcessesImpl
    class, 32-35
ProcessList class, 42-45
ProcessListener class, 319
Products screen
  (Bugzilla), 136
ProessList class, 23-29
programs. *See specific*
  programs
progressmeter element
  (XML), 442
projects, organizing in CVS
  or SVN, 45-49, 149-151
property element, 499
PRStatus, 266-270
PRThread, 258
PRThreadPriority, 258
PRThreadScope, 258
PRThreadState, 258
PRThreadType, 258
PRUint8, 245
PRUint16, 245, 297
PRUint32, 245
PRUint64, 245
pthread_attr_init()
  function, 257

pthread_attr_setstacksize() function, 257
pthread_create() function, 254-256
pthread_exit() function, 256-257
pthread_join() function, 256-257
pthreads, 254
publish/subscribe design pattern, 318-322
PutBar(function, 85
PutBar() function, 78, 100
putenv function, 102-105
putenv() function, 84

Q

Qt, 324, 331-332
QueryInterface() function, 446
quit() function, 487

R

r (read) permissions, 172
radio element (XML), 441
RadioButton class, 448
Raymond, Eric, 157
read (r) permissions, 172
Refresh() function, 401
regcomp() function, 269
regex function, 265-268
regexec() function, 269-270
registerChrome() function, 169
registering with subjects, 319
RegisterListener() function, 320
reject files (patch program), 162-163
relational operators (NSPR), 246
releaseObject() function, 501

RemoveAESEncryptClass() function, 512
rename() function, 241
repositories
  CVS (Concurrent Version System), 149-157
    organizing projects in, 45-49
    running, 157
    setting up, 152-156
  SVN (Subversion), 45-49, 149-151
resolving pointers, 507
Resources directory (Mac OS X), 204-205
responding to user input, 388-391
  EVT_CHECKBOX macros, 389-390
  EVT_COMMAND_SCR OLL macro, 388
  GetRadiusPercent() function, 388
  IsChecked() function, 390
  OnSliderChange() function, 388
  SetRadiusPercent() function, 388
restricting applications for use with GNOME or KDE, 181
return element, 499
ReverseValue() function, 443-444
root, executing Linux installer as, 176-177
RTL (Microsoft), 240

S

SaveAsPicker class, 448
Scan() function, 23, 26-27, 31-33, 39, 43-45, 313
ScanProcesses() function, 33-34

SCM (software configuration management), 131-132
  bug reporting and tracking systems accessibility, 133
  Bugzilla, 133-140
    platform-specific bugs, tracking, 133
  CVS (Concurrent Version System), 149-157
    running, 157
    setting up, 152-156
  effect on software portability, 9-10
  importance of, 147-149
  patch program, 157
    cross-platform development, 163-164
    example, 158-160
    options, 161-162
    reject files, 162-163
  SVN (Subversion), 149-151
  Tinderbox, 140-147
    brief log output, 143
    capabilities, 140, 145-147
    L1 link output, 143
    lists of check-ins, 144-145
    versions, 140
script element (HTML), 433
scripting language (DHTML), 433-434
scripts
  build.sh, 78-80
  install.js, 167-169
  /usr/bin/mozilla, 174
scrolled windows (Trixul), 484-485
ScrolledView class, 448
scrolledview element, 484-485
ScrolledWindow class, 448

scrolledwindow element, 484-485

searching for bugs (Bugzilla), 138-140

sed command, 75

SendNotification() function, 320-321

separate source files for cross-platform development, 85-87

serialization of binary data, 280
  binary socaddr_in file, generating, 283-293
  endian issues, 281
  floating-point numbers, 276-277
  intrinsic types and enums, 281
  struct layout, 281
  type definitions, 281-282

SetBar() function, 78

SetBrush() function, 374

setenv() function, 84

SetGeometry() function, 449

SetKey() function, 511, 515

SetLabel() function, 451-453

SetMenuBar() function, 354, 369

SetPriority() function, 27

SetPriorityClass() function, 27

SetRadiusPercent() function, 388

SetSizer() function, 355, 385

SetTopWindow() function, 367

Set_key() function, 511

.SH macro, 192

SharedLibraryTarget macro, 126

sharing code across all supported platforms, 22
  abstraction layers, 22
  advantages, 22

implementation classes, 31-32

instance hierarchies, 42-45

Makefiles and building code, 49-52

platform factory implementations, 29-31

platform-specific ProcessesImpl classes, 32-42

ProcessList class example, 23-29

Show() function, 367, 402-403, 449, 453

ShowModal() function, 395-398, 407

Shutdown() function, 312, 467-468

signed char types, 278-280

SIL files, 509-515

sin_family field, 287

sin_len field, 287

sin_port field, 288

The Single UNIX Specification, 224-225

Site.def file, 108

size argument (wxFrame), 365

sizeof() function, 294

sizers (wxWidgets)
  associating, 385
  DrawingArea class, 379-384
  wxBoxSizer class, 378, 384-388
  wxGridSizer class, 378
  wxNotebookSizer class, 378
  wxSlider class, 387
  wxStaticBoxSizer class, 378

sizes (type)
  efficiency, 297-298
  integer types, 293-296
  Netscape Portable Runtime Library (NSPR), 296-297

Skip() function, 362

skipping events, 359-363

Smart, Julian, 331

$SMPROGRAMS variable, 216

snprintf() function, 276

socaddr_in file, generating, 283-293
  command-line arguments, 283
  compiler options, 292-293
  cross-platform solutions, 288-293
  DumpAddr() function, 289
  htons() function, 288
  ntohs() function, 289
  on Linux, 287
  on Mac OS X, 287-288
  sin_family field, 287
  sin_len field, 287
  sin_port field, 288
  sockaddr_in struct, 290
  source code listing, 283-287
  XPBinaryRead() function, 290-292
  XPBinaryWrite() function, 290-292

sockaddr_in struct, 290

software configuration management. *See* SCM

software installation, 165-166
  Linux platform installs, 170-173
    /etc/group file, 171
    /etc/password file, 171

executing as root, 176-177
execution environment, 173-177
file permissions, 171-173
integrating with GNOME and KDE desktops, 177-186
man pages, 186-196
Mac OS X platform installs
application layout, 196-202
bundle icon files, creating, 207-208
drag-and-drop installation, 208
MacOS folder, 202-206
Windows XP NSIS installer
application data, 217-218
compiling NSIS script, 214
creating, 210
defining, 210-214
distributing, 214
documentation, 208
documents and settings, 208-209
integrating into Start menu and desktop, 216-217
program installation, 210
testing, 214
uninstallers, 215-216
Weather Manager sample installer script, 218-220
XPInstall, 166-170
SomeFuncInt() function, 279

SomeFuncUInt() function, 279
source files for cross-platform development, 85-87
source trees, building with Imake, 108-111
compatibility library Imakefiles, 116-119
Makefiles, 119-130
Windows implementations, 111-116
SourceVersion key (Mac OX S), 198
Spacer class, 448
spacer element, 440, 480
SpiderMonkey JavaScript engine, 494
standard libraries
effect on software portability, 5-6
STL (Standard Template Library), 5-6
standards-based APIs
BSD (Berkeley Standard Distribution), 225
choosing, 240-241
GCC standards support compiler flags, 227
Cygwin, 238-240
headers, 227-228
macros, 228-231
MinGW, 234-237
GNU C library, 226
POSIX, 222-223
Microsoft Runtime Library support for, 231-233
System V Interface Description (SVID), 223-224
The Single UNIX Specification, 224-225

XPG (X/Open Portability Guide), 225
Start menu, adding applications to, 178-181
StaticText class, 448
-std=c++98 compiler warning (GNU), 63
STL (Standard Template Library), 5-6
strftime() function, 88-89
string functions (POSIX), 224
Stroustrup, Bjarne, 299
strtod() function, 276
structs
alignment and ordering, 299-301
binary data issues, 281
JSClass, 507
numeric_limits, 295
sockaddr_in, 290
xpsockaddr_in, 290
style argument (wxFrame), 365
styles, CSS (Cascading Style Sheets), 437-438
subdirectories (project), building with Imake, 108-111
compatibility library Imakefiles, 116-119
Makefiles, 119-130
Windows implementations, 111-116
subjects, 319
subscribe. *See* publish/ subscribe design pattern
Subversion (SVN), 10, 45-49, 149
Summerfield, Mark, 331
SunOS Open Look, 323
Sutter, Herb, 276

SVID (System V
  Interface Description)
  base OS service
    routines, 223
  general library
    functions, 224
  GNU C library
    support, 226
  mathematical
    functions, 223
  networking
    functions, 224
  string and character
    handling, 224
_SVID_SOURCE macro, 230
SVN (Subversion), 10,
  45-49, 149
sysctl() function, 38
system calls, effect on
  software portability, 6-8
System V Interface
  Description. *See* SVID

T

templates
  numeric_limits, 295
  STL (Standard Template
    Library), 5-6
Terminal, 196-197
testing
  building source code with
    multiple compilers, 53
  Cygwin, 239-240
  MinGW, 235-236
  NSIS installer, 214
  on all supported
    platforms, 60-61
Text class, 448
textbox element (XML), 440
.TH macro, 192
themes (GUIs), 304-305
threads, 249
  advantages of, 250-251
  definition of, 250
  Linux threads, 254-257

Mac OS X threads,
  254-257
NSPR threads, 257-260
Win32 threads, 251-254
tier-1 platforms, 18, 427
Tinderbox, 21, 140-147
  brief log output, 143
  capabilities, 140, 145-147
  L1 link output, 143
  lists of check-ins, 144-145
  versions, 140
**title argument
  (wxFrame), 365**
title element (HTML), 430
toolbar element (XML), 440
**toolbarbutton element
  (XML), 440**
toolbars (XUL), 440
toolchains
  autoconf/automake,
    87-90
  compilers, 66-67
  Cygwin, 71-76
  definition of, 65-66
  Imake
    bar program
      example, 95-98
    building debug, 130
    building projects
      with subdirectories,
      108-130
    darwin.cf file, 107
    darwin.rules file, 107
    eliminating #ifdefs in
      code, 101-106
    Hello World
      example, 93-94
    Imake.rules file, 107
    Imake.tmpl file, 107
    Imakefiles, 94-95, 108
    installing on Mac
      OS X, 91
    installing on
      Windows, 91-93
    linux.cf file, 107

Makefiles, 108
  overriding defaults
    with site.def, 99-101
  Site.def file, 108
  Win32.cf file, 107
  Win32.rules file, 107
make utility
  bar program
    example, 77-78
  compared to build.sh
    script, 78-80
  Makefiles, 79-81
native IDEs, 67-71
nmake utility, 81-84
toolkits (GUIs), 324-325.
  See also specific toolkits
  cross-platform GUI
    toolkits, 326
  custom GUI toolkits, 327
  native GUI toolkits,
    325-326
TopLevel class, 364
Trixul, 327
  application main
    loop, 466-469
    App object, 466-469
    AppImpl class, 467
    in Cocoa, 469
    in Gtk+, 470
    in Windows, 470-471
  basic operation, 448-449
  capabilities, 447
  documents, 472-473
  elements, 473-475
  goals, 446-447
  implementation
    classes, 452
    ButtonImpl, 453-456
    CocoaButtonImpl,
      456-457
    GtkButtonImpl,
      457-458
    WidgetImpl, 454-455
    WindowsButtonImpl,
      458-459

implementation
objects, 459
in Cocoa, 460-461
in Gtk+, 461
in Windows, 462-463
integration with C++
components, 496-497
accessing components
from JavaScript,
500-502
coding C++
components,
502-507
creating base
JavaScript objects,
507-508
defining JavaScript
functions, 508-509
describing components
in XML, 498-500
generating source
code from SIL files,
509-515
instantiating C++
objects, 508
linking and
distributing
components, 517
resolving points to
creator/destroyer
functions, 507
step-by-step sequence,
497-498
writing C++ code
to implement
components,
515-517
integration with
JavaScript, 485-486
example, 486-487
including external
JavaScript sources,
487-488

interacting with
widgets from
JavaScript, 488-493
mapping DOM objects
to JavaScript,
493-496
layouts, 477, 480-483
scrolled windows,
484-485
UI creation, 471-472
widget creation, 475-477
widget definitions,
449-452
widget factories, 463-466
CocoaFactory class,
465-466
GetWidgetFactory()
function, 464
WidgetFactory class,
463-465
widget support, 447-448
Trolltech, 324
troubleshooting
bug reporting and
tracking systems, 133
accessibility, 133
Bugzilla, 133-140
platform-specific bugs,
tracking, 133
compiler warnings, 61-62
GNU flags, 62-63
Microsoft Visual C++
flags, 63-64
types
DIR, 229-230
NSPR types, 245-246
sizes, 293-298

U

UIs (user interfaces). *See*
GUIs (graphical user
interfaces)
ul element (HTML), 431
Umbrello, 42
uname command, 50

uninstallers (NSIS), 215-216
UninstPage command, 216
unregistering from
subjects, 319
UnregisterListener()
function, 320
unsigned char types, 278-280
UppercaseValue()
function, 443-444
user interfaces. *See* GUIs
(graphical user interfaces)
/usr/bin/mozilla script, 174
/usr/local/man
directory, 195
utilities. *See*
command-line utilities

V

variables
$APPDATA, 218
$SMPROGRAMS, 216
m_enabled, 358
vbox element (XML),
439-440
verifying MinGW libraries,
236-237
version.plist file, 197-198
view command, 185
views (GUIs), 306
abstracting GUI main
loop, 309-313
CreateUI()
function, 312
gtk_init()
function, 310
gtk_main()
function, 310
GUI class, 310-313
Init() function, 312
MainLoop()
function, 312
m_guiImpl
member, 311
Shutdown()
function, 312

CocoaGUIImpl class, 315
CreateMenus()
    function, 317-318
GUIImpl class, 314
illustration of UI
    implementation, 306
LinuxFactory class,
    307-308
LinuxGUIImpl class,
    308, 317
ProcessesFactory
    class, 306-307
WindowsGUIImpl
    class, 316
Visual C++
    compiler warnings, 63-64
    Imake for Visual C++,
        installing, 92-93

W

w (write) permissions, 172
–Wall argument (gcc), 227
–Wall compiler warning
    (GNU), 63
/Wall flag (Visual C++), 64
warnings (compilers), 61-62
    GNU flags, 62-63
    Microsoft Visual C++
        flags, 63-64
Weather Manager sample
    installer script, 218-220
-Weffc++ flag, 63
–Werror compiler warning
    (GNU), 63
WidgetFactory class,
    463-465
WidgetImpl class, 454-455
widgets, Trixul
    Button, 449-452
    container widgets, 450
    control widgets, 450
    creating, 475-477
    defining, 449-452

factories, 463-466
    CocoaFactory class,
        465-466
    GetWidgetFactory()
        function, 464
    WidgetFactory class,
        463-465
implementation
    classes, 452
    ButtonImpl, 453-456
    CocoaButtonImpl,
        456-457
    GtkButtonImpl,
        457-458
    WidgetImpl, 454-455
    WindowsButtonImpl,
        458-459
implementation
    objects, 459
    in Cocoa, 460-461
    in Gtk+, 461
    in Windows, 462-463
layouts, 477, 480-483
scrolled windows,
    484-485
support for, 447-448
XUL, 442
widgets, wxWidgets. *See*
    wxWidgets
Win32, 251-254, 304, 324
Win32.cf file, 107
Win32.rules file, 107
Window class, 448
window element (XML), 439
Windows
    building source code on
        conditional
            compilation, 84-85
        nmake utility, 81-84
        separate source files,
            85-87
    building wxWidget
        applications on,
            348-349

Cygwin, 71-76, 238
    downloading and
        installing, 238-239
    testing, 239-240
Imake installation
    Imake for GCC, 91-92
    Imake for Visual C++,
        92-93
MFC (Microsoft
    Foundation
    Classes), 324
MinGW
    definition of, 234
    downloading and
        installing, 234
    testing, 235-236
    verifying libraries,
        236-237
.NET Forms, 324
project source trees,
    building, 111-116
Trixul application main
    loops, 470-471
Trixul implementation
    objects, 462-463
Win32, 251-254,
    304, 324
Windows XP NSIS
    installer
    application data,
        217-218
    compiling NSIS
        script, 214
    creating, 210
    defining, 210-214
    distributing, 214
    documentation, 208
    documents and
        settings, 208-209
    integrating into Start
        menu and desktop,
            216-217
    program
        installation, 210

testing, 214
uninstallers, 215-216
Weather Manager
    sample installer
    script, 218-220
WindowsButtonImpl
    class, 458-459
WindowsFactory
    class, 29-31
WindowsGUIImpl
    GUI implementation
    class, 316
WindowsProcessesImpl
    class, 32-35
wxWidget installation,
    334-335
windows (XUL), 439
Windows XP NSIS installer
application data, 217-218
compiling NSIS
    script, 214
creating, 210
defining, 210-214
distributing, 214
documentation, 208
documents and
    settings, 208-209
integrating into
    Start menu and
    desktop, 216-217
program installation, 210
testing, 214
uninstallers, 215-216
Weather Manager sample
    installer script, 218-220
WindowsButtonImpl
    class, 458-459
WindowsFactory
    class, 29-31
WindowsGUIImpl class, 316
WindowsProcessesImpl
    class, 32-35
/Wn flag (Visual C++), 64
write (w) permissions, 172
wx-config command, 333

/WX flag (Visual C++), 64
wxALIGN_CENTER
    argument (Add()
    function), 343
wxAND_INVERT value
    (logicalFun argument), 376
wxAND_REVERSE value
    (logicalFun argument), 376
wxAND value (logicalFun
    argument), 376
wxApp class, 337-338
wxBoxSizer class, 336,
    341-345, 378, 384-388
wxBrush class, 374
wxCAPTION argument
    (wxFrame), 365
wxCHANGE_DIR style
    (wxFileDialog), 406
wxCLEAR value (logicalFun
    argument), 376
wxCLIP_CHILDREN
    argument (wxFrame), 365
wxColour class, 374
wxColourDialog
    class, 409-410
wxCommandEvent
    events, 351
wxCOPY value (logicalFun
    argument), 376
wxEUIV value (logicalFun
    argument), 376
wxEvtHandler class, 336
wxFileDialog class, 406-408
wxFontDialog class,
    404-405
wxFrame class, 336, 339,
    364-366
    constructor, 364-365
    sample implementation,
    364-367
wxFRAME_FLOAT_ON_
    PARENT argument
    (wxFrame), 366
wxFRAME_NO_TASKBAR
    argument (wxFrame), 366

wxFRAME_SHAPED
    argument (wxFrame), 366
wxFRAME_TOOL_
    WINDOW argument
    (wxFrame), 366
wxGetTranslation()
    function, 417
wxGridSizer class, 378
wxHIDE_READONLY style
    (wxFileDialog), 406
wxICONIZE argument
    (wxFrame), 365
wxINVERT value
    (logicalFun argument), 376
wxLanguage enums,
    422-424
wxLANGUAGE_* values
    (wxLanguage enum),
    422-424
wxLocale class, 421-422
wxMAXIMIZE argument
    (wxFrame), 365
wxMAXIMIZE_BOX
    argument (wxFrame), 365
wxMemoryDC class, 375
wxMenu class, 368-369
wxMenuBar class, 369-370
wxMessageBox class,
    393-394
wxMINIMIZE argument
    (wxFrame), 365
wxMINIMIZE_BOX
    argument (wxFrame), 365
wxMULTIPLE style
    (wxFileDialog), 406
wxNAND value (logicalFun
    argument), 376
wxNOR value (logicalFun
    argument), 376
wxNotebookSizer class, 378
wxNO_OP value (logicalFun
    argument), 377
wxOPEN style
    (wxFileDialog), 406

wxOR_INVERT value
(logicalFun argument), 377
wxOR_REVERSE value
(logicalFun argument), 377
wxOR value (logicalFun
argument), 377
wxOVERWRITE_PROMPT
style (wxFileDialog), 406
wxPaint class, 373
wxPaintDC class, 373-375
wxRESIZE_BORDER
argument (wxFrame), 366
wxSAVE style
(wxFileDialog), 406
wxSET value (logicalFun
argument), 377
wxSlider class, 387
wxSRC_INVERT value
(logicalFun argument), 377
wxStaticBoxSizer class, 378
wxStaticText class, 336,
340-341
wxSTAY_ON_TOP
argument (wxFrame), 365
wxSYSTEM_MENU
argument (wxFrame), 365
wxTextEntryDialog
class, 395
wxWidgets, 329-331
building applications, 345
on Linux, 347-348
on Mac OS X, 348
on Windows, 348-349
container widgets,
363-364
definition of, 331
dialogs
ColorDialog
class, 400-404
modal dialogs,
392-398
modeless dialogs,
399-404
PasswordEntryDialog
class, 395-398

wxTextEntryDialog
class, 395
downloading, 331
DrawingArea class,
379-383, 391
events, 349
BEGIN_EVENT_TAB
LE macro, 352-353
Click Me button,
creating, 354-355
DECLARE_EVENT_
TABLE macro,
350-351
Enable/Disable button,
creating, 356-359
END_EVENT_TABLE
macro, 352-353
event handler function
implementations,
355
EVT_BUTTON
macro, 353
EVT_MENU
macro, 353
File menu, 354
skipping, 359-363
wxCommandEvent
events, 351
frames
drawing content
in, 373-378
wxFrame class,
364-367
Hello World program,
335
Add() function,
342-344
building on Linux,
347-348
building on Mac OS
X, 348
building on Windows,
348-349
container widgets,
336-337
control widgets, 336

main window,
338-345
MyFrame class,
338-339
OnInit() function, 338
source code listing,
345-346
wxBoxSizer class,
341-345
wxFrame class, 339
wxStaticText class,
340-341
history and
development, 331
IMPLEMENT_APP
macro, 338
installing, 332
on Linux, 334
on Mac OS X, 333
on Windows, 334-335
internationalization,
410-411
gettext, 411-420
locales, creating,
421-425
message files, loading
at runtime, 425-426
PO/MO files, 417-421
wxLanguage enums,
422-424
wxLocale class,
421-422
licensing terms, 331-332
menus, 367
associating with
functions, 370-372
creating with wxMenu
class, 368-369
menu bars, 369-370
online
documentation, 331
responding to user
input, 388-391
EVT_CHECKBOX
macros, 389-390

EVT_COMMAND_ SCROLL macro, 388
GetRadiusPercent() function, 388
IsChecked() function, 390
OnSliderChange() function, 388
SetRadiusPercent() function, 388
wxApp class, 337-338
wxBoxSizer class, 336, 341-345, 378, 384-388
wxBrush class, 374
wxColour class, 374
wxColourDialog class, 409-410
wxEvtHandler class, 336
wxFileDialog class, 406-408
wxFontDialog class, 404-405
wxFrame class, 336, 339, 364-366
constructor, 364-365
sample implementation, 364-367
wxGridSizer class, 378
wxLocale class, 421-422
wxMemoryDC class, 375
wxMenu class, 368-369
wxMenuBar class, 369-370
wxMessageBox class, 393-394
wxNotebookSizer class, 378
wxPaint class, 373
wxPaintDC class, 373-375
wxSlider class, 387
wxStaticBoxSizer class, 378

wxStaticText class, 336, 340-341
wxWindow class, 336
wxXOR value (logicalFun argument), 377

X-Y-Z

x (execute) permissions, 172
X/Open Portability Guide (XPG), 224-226
X11, 324
X11R6, 111
XBD, 225
Xcode IDE, 68
xmkmf command, 96-98
XML elements. *See* elements
XML User Interface Language. *See* XUL
_XOPEN_SOURCE macro, 230
XP_PUTENV, 102
XP_WIN, 85
XPBinaryRead() function, 290-292
XPBinaryWrite() function, 290-292
XPCOM, 444-446
XPConnect, 444-446
XPG (X/Open Portability Guide), 224-226
XPI files, 167
XPInstall, 166-170
xpsockaddr_in struct, 290
XSH, 225
XUL (XML User Interface Language), 428-429
boxes, 439-441
controls, 441
DHTML (Dynamic HTML)
CSS (Cascading Style Sheets), 437-438
DOM (Document Object Model), 434-437

HTML (Hypertext Markup Language), 429-432
scripting language, 433-434
dialogs, 439
DOM (Document Object Model), 443-444
JavaScript, 443-444
menus, 441-442
programming with, 442
toolbars, 440
toolkit, 327
widgets, 442
windows, 439
XPCOM, 444-446
XPConnect, 444-446
XView, 331

/Za flag (Visual C++), 64